Herbert de Losinga

Life, letters, and sermons, of Bishop Herbert de Losinga

Herbert de Losinga

Life, letters, and sermons, of Bishop Herbert de Losinga

ISBN/EAN: 9783744746397

Printed in Europe, USA, Canada, Australia, Japan

Cover: Foto ©Lupo / pixelio.de

More available books at **www.hansebooks.com**

THE

LIFE, LETTERS, AND SERMONS

OF

BISHOP HERBERT DE LOSINGA

(*b. circ.* A.D. 1050, *d.* 1119):

The LETTERS (as translated by the Editors) being incorporated with the LIFE, and the SERMONS being now first edited from a MS. in the possession of the University of Cambridge, and accompanied with an English Translation and Notes.

BY

EDWARD MEYRICK GOULBURN, D.D.
DEAN OF NORWICH,

AND

HENRY SYMONDS, M.A.
RECTOR OF TIVETSHALL,
AND LATE PRECENTOR OF NORWICH CATHEDRAL.

VOL. I.
THE LIFE AND LETTERS.

Oxford and London:
JAMES PARKER AND CO.
1878.

TO

THE HONOURABLE AND RIGHT REVEREND

JOHN THOMAS,

𝕷𝖔𝖗𝖉 𝕭𝖎𝖘𝖍𝖔𝖕 𝖔𝖋 𝕹𝖔𝖗𝖜𝖎𝖈𝖍,

WHO BY "SIMPLICITY AND GODLY SINCERITY,"

FERVENT PIETY,

AND LABOURS, UNOSTENTATIOUS AND UNWEARIED,

IN THE OVERSIGHT OF HIS LARGE DIOCESE,

HAS ILLUSTRATED THE SEE WHICH

HERBERT DE LOSINGA

FOUNDED,

THESE LITERARY REMAINS OF HIS PREDECESSOR

ARE, BY HIS KIND PERMISSION, INSCRIBED,

WITH SENTIMENTS OF VENERATION FOR HIS OFFICE,

AND ESTEEM AND AFFECTION FOR HIS PERSON.

ERRATUM.

P. 78, footnote 5, last line, *for* "Appendix B" *read* "Appendix F."

PREFACE.

THE occasion of this work was an accident, which befel one of the Editors in the winter of the year 1867, and confined him to a couch for many months. Thus precluded from active work, he turned his thoughts to the question whether something might not be done in the line of literature, to throw light upon the origin of the institution with which he had recently become connected. And what so obvious as the story of the Founder, illustrated by his Letters, several of which had never been translated (though all of them had been published in the original Latin), and by his Sermons, which had never yet appeared in print at all? If he is asked to shew any motive for turning his studies in this particular direction, beyond the fact of his connexion with the cathedral which Herbert founded, he can only plead a desire to do such honour as might be done (consistently with the truth of history) to the name and memory of one, to whose pious munificence in times of old he and others at the present day are much indebted. The light esteem of founders and benefactors, which has led to the reckless and undutiful alienation of their endowments, not only from the special purposes for which they made them, but from all objects which bear in a changed state of society a similar character, seems to him and his fellow-labourer to be as heartless and ungrateful, as it undoubtedly is contrary to the spirit of the Fifth Commandment. And the study of the works, which Herbert has left behind, convincing both of them that his memory had been recklessly disparaged and blackened, they have thought it all the more incumbent upon them to exhibit him truthfully, and to allow him to speak for himself. That he had his faults, both of character and conduct, no one who looks into his history will be disposed to doubt; but that they were more than counterbalanced by his great amiability, by a warmth and geniality of disposition, which was sometimes extravagant in its expressions, and thus was mistaken for falseness and insincerity, and by a sincere piety (cast in the mould which piety in that age naturally and necessarily took), the Editors have convinced themselves, and trust they may have done something to convince others. And, independently of all local and personal considerations, they have been stimulated in their work by the desire to make some contribution, however humble and quite in a corner of the field, to the knowledge of mediæval literature. The treasures of this literature are at present open to none but scholars. It is thought that the translation and annotation of the remains of a Bishop of the twelfth century, may serve to give a glimpse of these treasures to a wider class of readers.

The work has been executed *aux plusieurs reprises*, amid engagements and pursuits, which had a prior claim upon the time of the Editors; and has been sometimes, by stress of circumstances, dropped for two or three months together, and then resumed,—which is the only apology they can offer for what they fear may prove a more than usual number of mistakes and inconsistencies. It has given full occupation to the *horæ subsecivæ* of ten long years, and in that considerable tract of time has become linked in their associations with many happy hours of quiet study and research. They lay it down at length, thankful that it has been permitted them to bring it to a close, and thankful also for what they have gained from it (more, doubtless, than the public will gain); but at the same time sorrowfully conscious that they are laying down an interest which has relieved, refreshed, and brightened their lives, and to which they have always turned with pleasure amid the petty vexations and disquietudes which are incidental to affairs of every kind.

In conclusion, they desire to make a cordial acknowledgment of the large help which they have received from many friends interested in their work, specially from those whose literary contributions appear in the Appendices and elsewhere; Mr. James Parker, their publisher; Mr. Henry Bradshaw, Librarian of the University of Cambridge; Mr. R. L. Bensly; Mr. E. A. Bond, of the British Museum; the late Venerable Archdeacon Hopper; Mr. Edward Beloe, of Lynn; the late Mr. John Lestrange, and the Rev. John Gunn, of Norwich. Their thanks are also due for much valuable information to Dr. Bensly, who has always been at hand as a referee, and has spared no pains or time in assisting their researches; to the Bishops of Lincoln and Truro, who have favoured them with many conjectural emendations of the text of Herbert's Letters; to the Venerable Archdeacon Groome, who has given them a clue to the meaning of one or more obscure passages; to the Rev. Dr. Jessopp, who has always taken a warm interest in their work, and helped it forward as much as his engagements would permit; to Sir Thomas Duffus Hardy, who has most kindly assisted them in their search among the public records; and last, not least, to Miss Frederica Franks and Miss Blanche Daniell, who have given invaluable aid in the work of transcribing and indexing.

E. M. G.
H. S.

Brighton, May 4, 1878.

P.S. The Letters of Herbert de Losinga, in the original Latin, having appeared in print thirty-two years ago (*Epistolæ Herberti de Losinga, primi Episcopi Norwicensis, nunc primum editæ à Roberto Anstruther* [Bruxellis: A. Vandale; Londinii: D. Nutt, 1846]), and being now easily accessible to all who desire to consult them, the Editors have not thought it necessary to do more than present the reader with an English translation, and with the results of a careful collation of the printed text with the only known manuscript, which is found in the library of the Dukes of Burgundy at Brussels. A full description of this manuscript, and of the variations from it which the printed text exhibits, will be found in Appendix H.

The noble manuscript of the Sermons, once in the possession of the cathedral church of Norwich, but alienated, with other MS. treasures of the church, in evil times, is described in the Introduction to the Sermons; and a facsimile of its first page is exhibited in the frontispiece.

CONTENTS.

	PAGE
DISCREPANCIES about the Bishop's Christian name . .	1
The surname "Losinga"	2
Reason for questioning the received interpretation . .	ib.
Probability of "Losinga" being a clan name . . .	3
Controversy respecting Herbert's birthplace . . .	4
Herbert born *circ.* A.D. 1050	6
The disputes about Investiture, which characterized his times	ib.
Bishop Herbert's family	7
Letter to his only Brother	ib.
Herbert's education	8
Evidence of his literary tastes	10
Letter to a cultivated layman	ib.
The layman's reply	13
Unworthy insinuations of Mr. Spurdens against Herbert rebutted	18
Herbert reproves the boys, Otto and Willelm, for lingering in the rudiments	19
A sharp reproof of the two boys for indolence and sluggishness	21
The two boys are urged to versification, which Herbert promises to criticise	22
Herbert excuses himself for not replying to the boys in verse, and reproves their backwardness	ib.
Herbert reproves Oto for the trifling nature of his studies, while his preceptor is in such danger and conflict ; and severely criticises some verses of his . . .	24
An apology for not answering the boys in verse, drawn from the style of the Scriptural writers and early Fathers .	29
A letter, the address of which is lost, in the same strain as the preceding	31
Willelm is exhorted to the study of Philosophy and the liberal arts. Oto's superficiality and sloth are glanced at with disapproval	35
Otto and Willelm are exhorted to avoid the moral snares of youth, and to take Christ as their pilot in the perilous voyage of life	37
Herbert describes a vision, in which he is warned against the study of heathen literature, and made to recall what had been said by Jerome and Boëthius to the same effect ; and concludes by announcing to his pupils his resolution to speak to them in future only of Christ . . .	43

CONTENTS.

	PAGE
Samson and Roger are lectured upon expensiveness and love of games, and warned that they will be strictly examined in their studies, when they return to Herbert	52
W. G. and W. are exhorted to self-denial in the pursuit of their studies, and particularly of logic	53
Herbert made Prior of Fécamp	54
The foundation of the Abbey of Fécamp by Richard the Fearless	55
Possible effect of early associations upon Herbert	56
Legend of "the Precious Blood," and how it came to Fécamp	ib.
Supposed etymology of the name Fécamp	57
Mass of "the Precious Blood," and devotions in connection with it	58, 59
Abbot John of Fécamp, his *soubriquet*, his humility, and his devotional writings	60, 61
Herbert probably educated under Abbot John	61
How Herbert may have been brought before the Conqueror and his sons	ib.
William de Ros, Abbot of Fécamp, 1082	62
The daily dole at Fécamp	ib.
Herbert made Abbot of Ramsey, 1088	63
His affection for Fécamp in after life	ib.
Roger d'Argences, fourth Abbot of Fécamp, 1107	ib.
Herbert professes his love and reverence for Fécamp, and begs to have a copy made of Suetonius	64
Herbert commends Brother Stannard to the Abbot of Fécamp, and professes his devotion to the Abbey, and his desire to frame the usages of his own Convent on that model	65
Similarity of the ground-plans of Fécamp Abbey and Norwich Cathedral	66
Objects of interest in Fécamp Abbey	67
The wheel of fortune	ib.
The Organ	68
Mediæval objections to Organs	ib.
Herbert sent for to England, and made Abbot of Ramsey	69
No allusion in his Letters to his Abbacy, and why	70
Eminence and opulence of the Abbots of Ramsey	71
Herbert's other sources of income	72
Death of Lanfranc, and vacancy of the Primatial See	73
William of Beaufeu, Herbert's immediate predecessor	ib.
Herfast, his penultimate predecessor, turned into ridicule by Lanfranc	74
William resents the insult; but his wrath is turned aside	74, 75
The prognostic at Herfast's consecration	75

	PAGE
Ralph Flambard negotiates with Herbert in the king's interests	76
Herbert's appointment as bishop indicated by his previous position	ib.
Enfeoffment customarily purchased by Ecclesiastics	77
The indignation aroused by Herbert's simoniacal practices finds vent in verse	79
Bartholomew Cotton's apology for Herbert	80
Probable uneasiness of Herbert as the day of consecration approaches	ib.
Herbert's reproachful prognostic	81
Consecration of Anselm to Canterbury by Thomas of York, Herbert assisting	82
Proof of Herbert's penitence	83
Herbert excuses himself to Norman, on the ground of the sinfulness of his past life, for making no collection of his letters	83, 84
Herbert determines to lay aside his episcopal office, and decides upon resigning it to the Pope	88, 89
Bishops not allowed to leave the kingdom without the King's permission	90
Two claimants of the papacy	ib.
Herbert's choice between the rival popes	ib.
The Red King assists at the dedication of St. Martin's Abbey	91
The Red King surprises Herbert when on the point of escaping from the kingdom, and deprives him of the insignia of the episcopal office	ib.
Herbert contrives to effect his escape	92
How the Red King's attention may have been distracted from Herbert's proceedings	ib.
Herbert's interview with Pope Urban II.	94
Encroachments of the Papal upon the Regal power	ib.
The Pope re-instates Herbert, and gives his assent to the removal of the See from Thetford to Norwich	94, 95
Herbert's return, and his doing of the penance prescribed him	96
Bale's coarse language on the subject of the removal of the See	97
The fanaticism enlisted in the great religious movement of the first Crusade	98
The Crusade never alluded to in Herbert's extant writings	99
Possible reasons for his silence	ib.
Herbert reproves and threatens a British monk for his fickleness in repudiating his profession; and in doing so, gives a sketch of British character	100, 101
Thurstan is warned by Herbert to eschew luxury, and carnal	

xiv   CONTENTS.

                                                                PAGE
pleasures, and to return to the monastery, where he is
  to anticipate an examination in the proficiency he has
  made in his studies. 101, 102
Godfrey is reprimanded for dissipation and violations of dis-
  cipline, and reminded of the kindness shewn to his
  family, and of his broken vow   .   .   . 105, 106
Date of the foundation of Norwich Cathedral .   .   . 110
Previous removals of the East Anglian See   .   .   . *ib.*
The Cowholm chosen as the site of the Cathedral   .   . 111
Boundaries of the Cowholm   .   .   .   .   . *ib.*
Foundation-stone of the Cathedral   114
Its inscription   .   .   .   . *ib.*
Its site   115
Probable error of Blomefield on the site of the foundation-
  stone   116
How much of the present Cathedral is due to Herbert   . 117
Original Norman roofs of the choir and transept destroyed . 120
Herbert's Lady-chapel destroyed by fire   .   .   . *ib.*
The second Lady-chapel, and its fate 121
Architectural taste of the age .   .   .   .   . *ib.*
Transference of Sees in that age   122
Reasons for it   123
Herbert's motive in transferring his See need not have been
  purely ambitious   .   .   .   .   .   . *ib.*
Synodical decision, A.D. 1075, on the transference of Sees   . 125
Herbert assists at the consecration of Gerard and Samson . *ib.*
How the difference between Anselm and the King about the
  pallium was adjusted   126
Fresh quarrel between Anselm and the King, on account
  of the former's neglect of feudal duty: which leads to
  a final parting 126, 127
Death of Herbert's father   127
Herbert commends the great hospitality which Rodbert had
  shown him; and announces his intention of keeping
  a palfrey which his correspondent had lent him . 127, 128
Death of Urban II., and accession of Paschal II.   .   . 130
Capture of Jerusalem by the Crusaders   .   .   . *ib.*
Slow progress of Norwich Cathedral .   .   .   . *ib.*
Herbert reproves his monks for indolence in building their
  church, and stirs them up to collect funds, and exert
  themselves actively in the work   131
Herbert, about to start for the court, commends to the Prior
  the work going on in the Cathedral   .   .   . 135
Herbert excuses himself for writing so often to the commu-
  nity, and expresses the hope that, on his return to them,

he shall find them in a good state of devotion, discipline,
and diligence 135, 136
Herbert directs that Alexander be retained in the community,
and makes some observations respecting the local cha-
racter of monastic vows 138
William, the custodian of Thorpe wood, is required to be true
to his trust 141
Death and burial of the Red King 142
Death of Thomas I. of York, Herbert's consecrator . . *ib.*
The crown seized by Henry I. . . . . . *ib.*
Archbishop Anselm recalled 143
Morals of the court reformed . . . . . *ib.*
Coronation of Queen Matilda, Nov. 11, 1100 . . . *ib.*
The investiture controversy breaks out afresh . . . 144
Change of Anselm's views on the subject of investitures . *ib.*
William of Warelwast sent to Rome, to obtain some settle-
ment of the investiture question 145
Good service done by Anselm to the King in A.D. 1101 . *ib.*
Consecration of Norwich Cathedral . . . . *ib.*
The Charter of the foundation of the Cathedral . . 146
Herbert excuses himself for the severity of his discipline, by
the enormity of the crimes which he sought to repress
thereby 155
Herbert refuses to sanction the marriage of William's sister,
while her husband is alive 161
Herbert declines to consecrate the *atrium* of the new
church at Thetford without a previous reference to the
king 168
Herbert fixes a day with the Prior for the consecration of the
atrium, and desires notice to be given of it . . 169
Herbert excommunicates with awful anathemas those who
had killed a deer in his park at Homersfield . . 170
Herbert confirms Dean Bond's possession of, and authority
over, the schools at Thetford 173
Herbert warns Athselinus, the provost (or mayor) of Thetford,
not to throw off his clerical character, or be ashamed of
his orders, not to vex the Church at Thetford with suits
and summonses, and to maintain peace with the dean 174, 175
Robert Courthose, the King's elder brother, allies himself with
the Earl of Shrewsbury, but is defeated under the walls
of Tinchebray, taken prisoner with Edgar Atheling,
blinded, and thrown into captivity . . 178, 179
To a youth who had sent him fruit Herbert gives a playful
hint that he might have sent him more; and then dismisses him on his voyage across the channel with his

absolution, and instructions to plead Herbert's cause
with the King 180, 181
Herbert warmly thanks the King for conferring upon him
some great favour at a time when Henry's thoughts
were engrossed by war and affairs of state, and promises to requite it with his prayers . . . 182
Short summary of the Benedictine rule . . . 186
Extract from the fourth chapter of the Benedictine rule, showing its moral and spiritual character . . 188, 189
The twelve grades of humility as given by St. Bernard out of
the Benedictine rule 190
The grades of humility compared by Bernard to the steps of
Jacob's ladder 191
Herbert excuses himself for slackness in his correspondence
with Felix, because only the self-indulgent monks need
his letters; but Felix is a model of humility and every
other grace, and is felicitated on the prospect of the glorious end of his conversation 192
Herbert reproves Felix for a falling off in the character of his
studies, and for becoming copyist general for the house . 196
Herbert, thinking that monks have no business with money,
pays F. for his psalter in tablets and ink . . . 198
In connexion with thefts which had frequently occurred in
their house, Herbert reproves the Prior and other officers
for slackness of discipline 200, 201
Herbert, going to court, expresses his anxiety for the spiritual wellbeing of the convent in his absence, and his
apprehension lest some root of bitterness should spring
up among them. He exhorts them to walk worthy of
their vocation 203
Herbert defends his discipline as not being inconsiderate or
excessive, but insists upon conventual silence, except at
stated times and in stated places 207
Herbert defends himself against the charge, brought against
him by a young student, of having kept him back in his
studies, and justifies his own motives in the good which
he had done 210
Abbot Richard of Ely, after deposition by the King, and
re-instatement by the Pope, determines to translate
the body of St. Etheldreda from the old into the new
church 211, 212
Anselm invited to the ceremony 213
Herbert attends . . . . . . *ib.*
Herbert's sermon at the translation of St. Etheldreda, and
its effects 215

CONTENTS. xvii

PAGE

Herbert inspects the body of St. Withburga, and addresses the people on the prodigy, of which he had been an eye-witness 220
Abbot Richard of Ely possibly the same man as the 'Ricardus Abbas' of Herbert's letters . . . 223
Herbert assists in consecrating five bishops at Canterbury . *ib.*
Roger of Sarum; the circumstance to which he owed his first rise in life; he is made Chancellor, Bp. of Salisbury, Chief Justiciary 224
His political tergiversation . . . . . *ib.*
His quarrel with King Stephen, and death . . . 225
His character and influence with princes . . . *ib.*
Herbert vindicates himself from a calumny against him, which had reached Roger's ears, and which he promises to explain further when they meet. He also entreats Richard to send back Walter the Archdeacon, whom he finds indispensable for his coming synod. He himself is unable to move from a complaint of the leg 226, 227
Herbert, being in weak health, and in great trouble about certain exactions and assessments, implores Roger to maintain the exemptions of the manor of Thorpe from all fiscal burdens, which had been granted by Royal Charter 229
Death of Roger Bigot 233
Dispute of Herbert with the Prior of Thetford with reference to Roger's burial . . . . *ib.*
Part of the Cathedral in which the burial took place unknown 234
Failure of Warelwast's embassy to the papal court . . *ib.*
Herbert with other ecclesiastics appointed to represent the King on the second embassy 235
The course taken by the Pope still evasive . . . 236
Dean Church's account of the proceedings on the return of the envoys 237
Private ends which Herbert had to serve at Rome . . 239
Jurisdiction over St. Edmund's Abbey eagerly coveted by the East Anglian bishops 240
Probable reasons for Herbert's attempt upon the liberties of St. Edmund's Abbey 241
He falls into the hands of Count Guido, and is imprisoned; but released on paying down, as the ransom of his retainers, the sum which he had brought from England, wherewith to purchase the jurisdiction over St. Edmund's 242
Anselm holds a council, at which the independence of St. Edmund's is finally decreed . . . 242, 243
Herbert's frantic expression of disappointment . . 243

CONTENTS.

	PAGE
Herbert, in an hysterical fit of anguish over some disaster which he describes figuratively as a shipwreck, admits at length that he was himself in fault, and turns his grief into repentance	243
Herbert remonstrates with Abbot Richard for having turned his back on him in adversity, and begs to be recognised as a friend once more, now that brighter days shine on him	248
Thomas II. appointed to the Archiepiscopal See of York	252
While only Archbishop-designate he joins Anselm in holding a synod	ib.
Anselm requires from Thomas a profession of obedience to the See of Canterbury, which Thomas, by the King's advice, declines	253
Herbert's qualifications for negotiating between the parties .	254
Anselm, on his terms of accommodation being rejected, interdicts Thomas from the exercise of the priesthood, and forbids any other English bishop to give him consecration	254, 255
Death of Anselm	256
Difference of opinion between the regulars and the bishops as to the necessary qualifications of an Archbishop of Canterbury	260
Ralph de l'Escures translated from Rochester to Canterbury	ib.
Abbot Richard complains to Herbert of the canons who, under the instigation of the devil, disparaged the monks and their way of life, and exhorts him to write a short treatise in vindication of monasticism . .	261, 262
Herbert replies to Richard that monks and clergy are on a level as to dignity, and equally to be respected, if their lives are equally good	266
Herbert consecrates churches and ordains out of his own diocese	269
Plague at Norwich	270
The last bishops whom Herbert joins in consecrating	271
Herbert begs Ralph to fulfil his promise of visiting him at Norwich	272
Thurstan declines to take the oath of canonical obedience to Ralph	274
The reasons of Herbert's last visit to Rome . .	ib.
The legate not allowed to land without an invitation from the King	275
Deputation to the Pope on the subject of the independence of the English Church	276

CONTENTS. xix

	PAGE
Herbert compelled by illness to return from Placentia without going on to Rome	277
Return of the deputation	*ib.*
Herbert congratulates Wido on his way of life, warns him against the snares of it, and asks his prayers	279
Herbert remonstrates with Turbo for communicating to him the secrets of his conscience through a third person	282
Herbert, hearing of Turbo's penitence, absolves him, and gives to him and one of his fellow-students a rule for mastering difficult study	282, 283
Herbert remonstrates with Robert upon his fickleness to an old and attached friend, and promises to requite his friendship, if he will be more steady for the future	284
Herbert, admitting that Bp. Richard has reason to complain of Hunfrid's conduct, urges many passages of Scripture, and finally Richard's own comfort, as reasons why he should be forgiven	286
Herbert assures Godwin and William that their father, who has been recently reconciled with their uncle, has good reasons for staying away from home, and has all he wants where he is	287
Herbert implores Odo not to draw back from the monastic life, but to take up the cross, that he may win the crown, resisting by a strong will all temptations to softness	288, 289
A short affectionate letter, asking for ink and parchment	296
Herbert expresses his ardent desire to see the Queen, compares her to the Queen of Sheba, eulogises her devotion to the Virgin Mary, and deprecates misrepresentations which had been made of him to Roger of Salisbury	298, 299
Death of Bishop Herbert	314
Bartholomew Cotton's lamentation, in looking back at the event	*ib.*
The monkish epitaph and its translation	315, 316
Its probable erasure by the Puritans	317
Weever's probable authority for the epitaph	318
De Turbe conjectured to be its author	319, 320
Origin of Leonine verses	*ibid.*
Sir Thomas Browne's notice of Herbert's tomb	321
Letters of Prebendary Prideaux to John Ellis	322, 323
Question whether Herbert was ever Chancellor investigated and discussed	323—328
Monument to the Founder erected by the Dean and Chapter	329
Prebendary Prideaux's epitaph on Herbert	330
How the Chapter was composed at that time	331, 332
Taking down of the tomb by Dean Pellew	332

	PAGE
Lost works of Herbert, and works perhaps ascribed to him by mistake	333
Translation of Herbert's Anniversary Service in the Norwich *Ordinale*	334—345
Fruitless efforts of the Norwich monks to procure the canonisation of Herbert	345
Concluding summary of his character . . .	346, 347

APPENDIX A.
Letters from the late Archdeacon Hopper on the name LOSINGA 349

APPENDIX B.
Original of Herbert's Anniversary Service in the Norwich *Ordinale* 352

APPENDIX C.
A Translation of the Royal Charter confirming to Abingdon Monastery the grant of the church of Edwardston . 355

APPENDIX D.
Sources of the History of Herbert de Losinga, Arranged in Chronological Order 357

APPENDIX E.
Mr. E. M. Beloe on Herbert's Birthplace . . . 409

APPENDIX F.
Reasons for inferring that the charges of simony and deceitfulness were preferred against Herbert on account of the enmity which he excited by assisting Archbishop Anselm in the reformation of clerical abuses (Rev. J. Gunn) 412

APPENDIX G.
A Charter of Herbert, confirming the grant of Cressingham, held by Godwin of the fee of the Bishop, to the Benedictine Priory of Norwich 414

APPENDIX H.
Results of the Collation of the MS. of Herbert's Letters with Mr. Anstruther's Printed Text . . . 416

THE LIFE AND LETTERS OF HERBERT DE LOSINGA,

FIRST BISHOP OF NORWICH, AND FOUNDER OF NORWICH CATHEDRAL.

THE questions which have been raised about the Founder of Norwich Cathedral begin with his name. Herbert, Hervey, Robert, Henry, William,—he goes under each of these[a] names

Discrepancies about the Bishop's Christian name.

---

[a] He is generally called Herbert (or Herebert [*]), but one † monastic writer (by a slip of the pen possibly) calls him *Hervey*. Eadmer, his contemporary, secretary of Abp. Anselm, once calls him (probably by a slip of the pen) Robert. (Hist. Nov., p. 45, Lut. Par. 1721.) Polydore Vergil, an Italian who held many English preferments, and composed a history of England at the request of Henry VII., writes the name in one place *Henry* (Henricus), and is followed by the Centuriators of Magdeburg, who however give *Herebertus* as an *alias*. Be the true name Herbert, or Hervey, or Henry, one is inclined to regard it as a Christian name. But Alexander Neville (Secretary of Abps. Parker and Grindal), the author of the first printed account of Norwich, calls our author William Herbert, as if Herbert had been his family name. And this view of the matter is adopted by the Rev. W. T. Spurdens, an antiquary of our own times, who, in a learned paper read before the Norfolk Archæological Association, speaks of the Bishop as *William* Herbert, and of the Abbot his father as *Robert* Herbert. Godwin, too, in his "Catalogue of the Bishops of England," (a work which Queen Elizabeth rewarded with the Bishopric of Llandaff) calls him *William, surnamed Galfagus*, in one sentence, and *Herbert* in another. Upon the whole, we are disposed to demur to the conclusion arrived at by Mr. Spurdens, and to believe that the attributing to our Founder the name of William arose from a confusion between him and his immediate predecessor, William Belfagus, or Galfagus, of whom

[*] *Herebertus* is the form of the name as given by William of Malmesbury, who flourished in the year 1130.
† Thomas Stubbs. It will be seen that Stubbs himself in another excerpt calls our prelate *Herbertus*. And as in the excerpt where he calls him *Hervey*, he mentions another Bishop, whose name was really Hervey (*Hervè le Breton*, consecrated to Bangor), it is probable that he might have written *Herveus* by mistake for *Herbertus*.

B

in one or other chronicle, the discrepancy being probably due in some cases to a confusion between him and some contemporary, in others to mere carelessness, or a slip of the pen.

The surname "Losinga." The surname " Losinga," popularly attributed to the Bishop, raises also, no less than his name, several questions which it is difficult to answer [b]. It is often connected with our word "glozing" (compare the phrase a "glozing tongue"); and Malmesbury (a writer contemporary with Herbert) says that it was given to him for his skill in adulation. Harpsfeld, in his English Ecclesiastical History, makes the most of this hint, and represents the influence which Herbert exercised on men in power, by means of his flattering and fulsome speeches, as something extraordinary, adding that, where he failed by these arts to carry his point, he brought his money to bear. How far the good Bishop's letters supply internal evidence of his having flattered the great, we shall see further on. Mean-

Reason for questioning the received interpretation. while we observe that, according to Malmesbury's own testimony, *his father bore this surname as well as himself,* (indeed Alexander Neville seems to ascribe the surname *exclusively* to the father),

little or nothing is known. It does not seem likely that Bartholomew Cotton, a monk of the Cathedral monastery at Norwich, who was born not much more than a century after Herbert's death, should have placed (as he does) a William Belfagus among the Bishops of East Anglia, if no such prelate ever existed. But we shall have to revert to this subject, and go into it more fully, at a later period of our Memoir.

[b] We observe that there was a contemporary Bishop of Hereford who had also this surname, one Robert *de Losing,* consecrated at Canterbury by Lanfranc, Dec. 29, 1079. (Stubbs's "Registrum Sacrum Anglicanum," p. 22.) Would this furnish any clue to the meaning of the name?

which throws much doubt upon the assertion that the designation denoted a moral quality of the son. For ourselves, we have been led to form quite another view of the origin of the name Losinga. "The syllable ING," Mr. Isaac Taylor tells us, "was the usual Saxon patronymic. The Saxon immigration was an immigration of clans. The head of the family built or bought a ship, embarked in it with his children, his freedmen, and his neighbours, and established a family colony on any shore to which the winds might carry him." And, accordingly, "in the Saxon districts of the island we find the names, not of individuals, but of clans. It is these family settlements which are denoted by the syllable ING." (Thus we have Read*ing*, Wok*ing*, Bas*ing*, Hast*ings*.) Now in East Suffolk, the county in which Herbert certainly possessed property, there is a Hundred of *Loes*, and also a Hundred of Lothingland, which would seem to point to a settlement of Saxons there, deriving their parentage from some Saxon forefather of the name of Loid or Loth. Thus the surname Losinga, malevolently interpreted perhaps by monks whom Herbert's simoniacal practices had shocked, or his reforming tendencies had offended, might really mean nothing more than that he was a descendant of this Loid or Loth, and came from a part of the country where that family was settled. His father would of course bear the surname as well as himself, and Robert de Losing, Bishop of Hereford, might be another offset of the same stock.

[margin: Probability of "Losinga" being a clan name.]

This view of the name Losinga is more fully discussed in two letters from Archdeacon Hopper, the substance of which, by his kind permission, we have printed in the Appendix[c]. So much for the name and surname of our author, whom we shall call henceforth, with the majority of writers, HERBERT.

Controversy respecting Herbert's birthplace.
Next to the questions respecting his name come those respecting his birthplace. Deeply as we revere our Herbert's memory, we do not make him out to be quite as great a man as Homer. But yet he is claimed by different countries, as Homer was. Bartholomew Cotton, (the earliest writer who assigns him a birthplace,) says that he was born "in pago Oxymensi." This is supposed to be Exmes in Normandy; certainly the structure of Cotton's sentence seems as if it were some place *out of England.* Bale (himself a Suffolk man), and after him Pits, make him out to have been a native of Suffolk, "ex *pago* Oxunensi (whatever part of Suffolk that may mean). Godwin, in the *text* of the "De Præsulibus," says that he was born "Oxoniæ" (at Oxford); while in his *notes* he follows Cotton in ascribing to him a Norman extraction, and refers to Giraldus Cambrensis for one of the names of the place in Normandy. Weever, wishing possibly to maintain at the same time a Suffolk extraction, and a sound like that of Oxford, hazards the conjecture "*Orford* in Suffolk." While good old Fuller in his "Worthies of England," finding this discrepancy of testimony

[c] See Appendix A.

on the subject of Herbert's birthplace, gives a notice of him under each of the two counties, Oxfordshire and Suffolk, professing however that he cannot understand Bale's words, "hamlet of Oxun in Suffolk," for "on the perusing of all the lists of towns in the county of Suffolk, no *Oxun* appeareth therein, or name neighbouring thereon in sound and syllables." We have no doubt that Mr. Spurdens has hit upon the part of Suffolk which Bale alluded to, and rightly decided the controversy. Aspirates, as they are often not pronounced, so they are liable sometimes to be left out in writing. Thus the "pagus Oxunensis" of Bale turns out to be the town, (or perhaps the hundred,) of Hoxne (pronounced Hoxon) in Suffolk. And Godwin, animated by a laudable ambition to connect a great man with a great seat of learning, thought he would ignore Bale's assertion of a˙ Suffolk extraction, and read " Pagus Oxunensis," (the hundred of Hoxne), as if it were " Civitas Oxoniensis," or " Oxonia," the city of Oxford. We conclude, then, with Mr. Spurdens, that Herbert was a Suffolk man, born either at Hoxne, or in the hundred of that name. His father held manors there, (as Mr. Spurdens goes on to show,) and in other parts of the eastern counties.

The exact date of his birth is nowhere given to us. But we know that he died either in A.D. 1119 or 1120, probably in the earlier of these two years. And in the Letter, which stands first in the Collection of his Epistles (not on account of its being the earliest of them in date, but because it records his own unwillingness to make and publish any such collection) he speaks of himself as having lost all the vigour of youth, and having become a prey (both mentally and physically) to the infirmities of age, *at sixty*. We cannot suppose, therefore, that he outlived the "threescore years and ten" assigned by the Psalmist as the limit of human life; and, allotting to him that span, his birth would fall about A.D. 1050, exactly in the middle of the eleventh century; so that he would be a youth of fifteen or sixteen at the time of the Norman Conquest. It was just about the period of his birth (in the year A.D. 1049) that Leo IX., having been appointed by the Emperor Henry III. to the Papal chair, and intending to pass into Italy, in virtue of this appointment, in his Pontifical vestments, fell in with the monk Hildebrand (who, as Gregory VII., was to succeed him in A.D. 1073) at Clugny, and was persuaded by him to enter Rome in the guise of a pilgrim, and to receive the dignity, which no layman had a right to confer, from the clergy and people of the City. Thus Herbert first saw the light at a period when the struggle between the Church and the Sovereigns of Europe for the right of investiture to Ecclesiastical Offices was beginning to assume its most determined form. He lived in the very tug of that struggle, as it was carried on in this country between Anselm on the one side, and William the Red and Henry I. on the other.

Herbert born circ. A.D. 1050.

The disputes about Investiture, which characterized his times.

Of the Bishop's family we know next to nothing. Bale calls him "a monk begotten of a monk," intimating that the father was a monk at the time of Herbert's birth; but it is clear that this assertion rests on no evidence, and is made merely to give the foul-mouthed Bale an opportunity, (of which he is not slow to avail himself,) of declaiming against the incontinency of the monks and clergy, though they professed celibacy. Herbert's father, we know, became Abbot of Winchester ultimately; but there is no reason whatever to think that he had taken a monastic vow before the birth of his children. I speak of his *children*, because we find from the Epistles that he had one other son. And to this brother Herbert, after he became a Bishop, addressed the following letter. It is on a very trifling matter; but it gives a glimpse both of Herbert's scholastic tastes, and of the scarcity of writing materials in those days :— [Bishop Herbert's family.]

LETTER LIV.
To G., his only Brother.

[Letter to his only Brother.]

"Herbert the Bishop to G., his only Brother, greeting.

"I implore you with many entreaties that with your usual liberality you would lend me the box-wood tablets, which your friend Richard the Archdeacon gave you. He it was who informed me that you have these tablets, remembering that he handed over *your* tablets to a certain Eric for his school, and gave you in compensation for them those of which I speak. Do not fear my keeping them; for I do not care to owe any man any thing save love only, and the kind actions which are its fruit." [See Rom. xiii. 8.]

The tablets in question were no doubt the

tabulæ dictales (see Ducange, *sub voce*) on which young[d] scholars composed their exercises for the inspection of their masters—the *slates* of our schools. As to the concluding sentence of the Letter, the reader will be amused to find further on that our Herbert did once shew a tenacity for what was only lent him, keeping for his own a palfrey which a worthy Abbot had supplied him with as a temporary accommodation. But we must not forestall.

<small>Herbert's education.</small> Like many other Saxon youths of the period, Herbert was sent into Normandy to receive his education. The light of letters in those days shone brightly in France, and more especially in Normandy. This was due partly to the efforts which King Robert of France (son of Hugh Capet) had made in the first quarter of the eleventh century for the revival of learning, and partly to the migration into Normandy of certain learned Italians (like Lanfranc), who came to seek the patronage which was more readily accorded to learning in France than in their own

---

[d] See Orderic's account (given by Mr. Church) of Abbot Osbern of St. Evroul, who must have been a contemporary of our Herbert's:

"He was from his childhood," says Orderic, . . . "exceedingly ingenious in all kinds of handicraft, such as carving, building, writing, and the like. . . . He himself with his own hands made the writing tablets for the children and the unlearned, and prepared frames covered with wax, and required from them daily the due portion of work appointed for each. Thus driving away idleness, he laid on their minds wholesome burdens." (St. Anselm, by R. W. Church, chap. v. p. 99.)

The letters of Herbert to the boys Otto and Willelm, soon to be introduced (p. 19, &c.), show him, too, "requiring from the young the due portion of work appointed for each," and "laying on their minds wholesome burdens." For some of his letters to these boys no more appropriate heading could be desired.

country. It is to be remembered also that Edward the Confessor, who in Herbert's childhood sat on the throne of England, had himself received his education at the Norman Court, and being (as he was) thoroughly Normanized, and surrounded even in England by Norman courtiers, would no doubt favour any design on the part of his wealthier subjects to educate their sons in a realm, which would seem to him, in comparison of England, one of high culture and civilization. Then, too, the Conqueror, into whose hands the realm of England fell when Herbert was a stripling, was himself a great Mæcenas, and made it one of his first studies to promote learning in his new dominions. Many influences, therefore, might induce Herbert's father, the wealthy squire of Suffolk, to send his son to a Norman Convent, to receive the best education the times afforded,—the high road this to what he probably coveted for him—ecclesiastical preferment. And the youth (being, if we may judge from his letters, of a quiet, sensitive, timid disposition, naturally averse to war, which was the only secular pursuit of the higher classes in those times) took kindly to his books, and became a proficient in learning. Judged by the standard of his age, he was a highly-educated man, "imbued," says Cotton, "with the knowledge of all profane as well as of all sacred literature." This knowledge is sometimes gained for ulterior ends, and where it is not fully appreciated; but we have proof in Herbert's letters that the literary training which he had received in his youth had formed in him

Evidence of his literary tastes.

literary tastes. We shall have the opportunity of observing that in several of his letters he solicits a loan of books from his friends. Here also is a letter of his to a literary friend, with the answer to it, which shews how deeply our author was imbued with a taste for the learning and philosophy of his day. John appears to have been a character very rare in those times,— a highly educated layman of independent resources, who cultivated both Philosophy and Religion without any kind of professional call to do so. Without denying that a vein of adulation runs through Herbert's letter to him, we can quite see that in those days of semi-barbarism and wild turbulence such a layman must have been regarded by the more enlightened of the clergy as a very precious treasure.

LETTER XLV.

To John.

Letter to a cultivated Layman.

"Herbert to John.

"John's own Herbert to Herbert's own John, greeting. In your letter, John, you give me many thanks, as if I had done you a great favour; but my favours and my munificence fall as much below the panegyric you pronounce upon them, as that panegyric, both in the originality of its topics and the beauty of its style, excels the orators of our day. Your writings would remind me of the periods of Seneca and the clauses of Tully, except that yours (to my judgment) appear all the more choice, as being imbued both with the wine of the Law and the milk ᵉ of the Gospel. Believe me

---

ᵉ "The wine of the Law and the milk of the Gospel." Wine, from its acrid taste, may be considered as symbolical of the Law; while milk re-

I speak the truth, without any design of fawning upon the rich; your genius is a perfect marvel to me, finding repose as you do in philosophy, though outside Philosophy's studio, and delighting yourself in spiritual exercises while outside [f] the Spirit's domicile. Do therefore what now you do; labour as now you labour; cultivate composition [as heretofore], devote yourself to reading. He who endowed you with these abilities foreknew before the foundation of the world what He meant to do with them; wait His time patiently; He who has bestowed upon you such excellent tools is preparing for you the material on which you are to work with them. I might say greater things than these; but let my good wishes supply what is wanting to the argument [of your praise]. I pledge you in a loving cup [g];

presents the mild and gentle precepts of the Gospel. It is extremely probable that some of the mediæval interpreters may have actually annexed this significance to the "wine and milk" of Isaiah lv. 1, "Yea, come, buy wine and milk without money and without price."

[f] By this Herbert probably means that John cultivated Philosophy and Religion as an amateur, and had never made a profession in a monastery.

[g] "Propino tibi; cum bibis de cuppâ meâ, duplum pro simplo promittis." An allusion to the mode of drinking healths among the ancients. The loving cup (ἡ φιλοτησία κύλιξ) after a libation poured from it in honour of the gods, was just sipped by the person who pledged the other, and then handed to the person pledged, who drained it. Thus at Dido's feast (Æn. i. 728 sq.) the queen after filling a golden jewelled goblet, which was an heirloom of the dynasty founded by Belus, invokes Jupiter, Juno, and Bacchus, and then,

"Dixit, et in mensam laticum libavit honorem,
Primaque libato, summo tenus attigit ore.
Tum Bitiæ dedit increpitans. Ille impiger hausit
Spumantem pateram, et pleno se proluit auro."

Herbert speaks figuratively of his letter as a loving cup, which he despatches rapidly, and passes on, with many kind wishes, to his friend. And he bids his friend remember, in drinking it, that he must send him two cups for his one, that is, write a letter in answer twice as long as that which he receives.

The *cupa* (for the true orthography is with a single *p*) originally signified an earthenware cask, coated with pitch, and half sunk in the earth, in which the wine was placed to ferment. "Cupâ potare magistrâ" in Horace, (if the reading be correct,) must mean "to drink with no other law than the capacity of the vat," i.e. to drink till the vat be exhausted.

remember, in drinking of it, that you promise me two cups for my one. For indeed in my necessities your lips prove the most acceptable offering I can receive, since words which come from the heart thrill to the heart, and intellect has an insight into the utterances of intellect. You magnify what is of little moment, you overpraise very slight service, imitating herein the fondness of parents, who are wont to call the blemishes of their children beauties. You promise me love; but with all your love you cannot equal the reciprocal affection which I bear to you; for after Henry the King nothing in this world is more precious to me than your love. Be you therefore another self to me; and let me be to you another self; let yours be mine, and mine yours; not as in the Amphitryon[h] Mercury personated Sosia,

It does not appear that in *classical* Latin, *Cupa* ever meant the small vessel from which the wine is *drunk*.

[h] "Not as in the Amphitryon Mercury personates Sosia."
The allusion is to the well-known comedy of Plautus, "the Amphitryo," in which Jupiter, in order to get access to Alcmena, disguises himself as Amphitryon her husband, and enjoins Mercury, in order further to facilitate his designs, to assume the garb and countenance of Sosia, Amphitryon's slave. Great part of the humour of the Comedy lies in the meeting of the real with the sham Sosia, and in the way in which Mercury attempts to reason the slave, by appeals to the *argumentum baculinum*, out of his conviction of his own personality. So in Molière's adaptation of the Latin play to the French stage;

"MERCURE.
Es-tu Sosie encore? dis, traître !
SOSIE.
Hélas ! je suis ce que tu veux.
Dispose de mon sort tout au gré de tes vœux ;
Ton bras t' en a fait le maître.
MERCURE.
Ton nom etait Sosie, à ce que tu disois?
SOSIE.
Il est vrai, jusqu' ici j' ai cru la chose claire ;
Mais ton bâton, sur cette affaire,
M'a fait voir que je m'abusois.
MERCURE.
C'est moi qui suis Sosie, et tout Thèbes l'avoue ;
Amphitryon jamais n'en eut d' autre que moi."

One evidence of the popularity of this play of Plautus's among the

but as in Christ's Gospel John represents Elijah, and Elijah, John. The only exception which I would make to this closeness of intimacy between us is that you shall always take precedence over me and dictate to my humility, and that I in my humility shall always obey your dictation. Do not shrink from my poverty, since Christ calls the poor kings of the kingdom of Heaven, and he whose mind is filled with love of the Truth abounds in all wealth."—*Collated*.[1]

See St. Matt. v. 3, and St. Luke vi. 20.

LETTER LVIII.
JOHN TO HERBERT.

"John to Herbert the Bishop.

"To his lord and father, Herbert the Bishop, his own John sendeth all greeting and obedience. I received your letter, my father, at a seasonable juncture, though somewhat late. For I had no sooner returned from Rome, and was rejoicing with my companions thereon, as one who had been welcomed back into his country, than the recent and unexpected death of my mother was suddenly announced to me, which, as was not to be wondered at, affected me more poignantly, from its being

John's reply.

---

moderns, is that the argument of it has been reproduced both by Molière and Dryden. (Alas! that we must add that it has gained little in humour, but much in impurity and indecency from the English poet; and certainly has lost nothing of the latter in the hands of the French—a melancholy consideration, when we reflect that both these "professed and called themselves" Christians!) It seems to have been equally popular with mediæval scholars.

We cannot but think Herbert's allusion to it exceedingly apposite, and his meaning very well expressed. He is John's, and John is his, "other self;" yet not because of an external disguise such as Mercury assumed, when he presented himself as Sosia's other self; but because of a harmony of character, sentiment, and aims, which made one the counterpart of the other. "John came *in the spirit and power* of Elias," and on that account "*was* Elias, which was for to come."

[1] *Collated*—"Contuli." This word appears again in the Brussels MS. at the end of Letters XII., XVII., XXX., XLIX., and LVIII. We can only suppose it to mean that the copyist, who made that MS., collated what he had written with the original, and after such collation certified it as a true copy.

signified to me in so sad a manner. In fact the circumstance of her death was communicated to me before I heard of her illness; and I was made aware of her decease before I knew its cause. The sudden grief disconcerted my joy, and following hard upon it, so changed into mourning all the happy smiles which had preceded, that the bystanders could not but wonder at the rivers of tears which burst forth almost at the same moment that my laughter had broken on their ear. I betook myself without delay to my chamber, that I might with the greater freedom indulge, and resign myself to, my grief. After three days your affectionate letter was put into my hands, from the expressive utterances of which such sweetness distilled into my mind, that your language seemed to assuage my grief, and, had not God preserved in me the grace of humility, might have lifted me up with pride on receiving so warm an encomium. I was charmed throughout with the charms of your diction, and, having for some time abstained from bodily food, I was greatly strengthened by the nourishment derived from your words. What moved my admiration in your letters was, that they display every species and every style of composition. In them the exuberant richness of your conceptions springs forth in flowers, and a brief line denotes a wide compass of meaning. Thanks be therefore to God, and thanks to you, by whose favour, to which none of my merits entitled me, the dignity of an everlasting name has been conferred upon me. In the catalogue of your great deeds my name is enrolled as it were in the annals of the Romans [k]; the panegyric which with such applause you have pronounced upon me, antiquity and the lapse of years will not be able entirely to efface; thanks to your works, the memorial of me has been perpetuated through the

---

[k] "Inscriptus sum factis tuis tanquam annalibus Romanorum."
The reference is to that record of events, which the Chief Pontiff of ancient Rome was obliged to keep, and to exhibit publicly on a white board suspended in his house, called an *album*. These records were called "the great Annals."

ages, so that by your gift of grace I, who cannot shew any title to renown, am privileged to receive high praise. He whose praises *you* shall choose to rehearse can never be obscure. In your language there is an echo of the first principles of philosophy, and the school of both Testaments[1] is thrown open to the learner. For you have been bred up in the court of Christ, and nourished at the breasts of His Gospel, and have also been fed with the bread of Heaven unto all holiness both of life and belief. If, then, I do not preserve the affection which you have pledged to me, I am not worthy of another communication or encomium from you. I do not doubt that the same friendly altercation, which took place between Orestes[m] and Pylades as to whether

[1] "Utraque duum schola canonis aperitur."
We offer the above translation of these difficult words with some hesitation. St. Jerome calls the Old Testament "Canon Hebraicæ veritatis" (Ep. 28). Probably the text is corrupt.

[m] "Quæ tam inter Orestem et Piladem habita est de morte contentio."
The story is told by Ovid, in his Letters from Pontus (Lib. iii. Ep. ii.). In the days when Thoas reigned over the Tauri (that is, in the Crimea, or Tauric Chersonese), Iphigenia, the virgin daughter of Agamemnon, who had been wafted to those shores by the agency of the goddess, was priestess of Diana. Savage and bloody, in unison with the manners of that savage race, were the rites which, in her character of virgin-priestess, she had to perform. Every stranger, whose unhappy lot threw him on the inhospitable coast, was to be slain by the priestess on the altar of Diana :

"Sacrifici genus est (sic instituere priores)
Advena virgineo cæsus ut ense cadat."

At last arrived two young and noble strangers, Pylades and Orestes, who, in accordance with the usual custom, were seized, bound, and conducted to the altar. Iphigenia excuses herself for the barbarity of the rites, of which she was the unwilling minister, and, before proceeding with the sacrifice, asks the extraction and destination of the strangers. Finding they were from her own city, she proposes that one only shall fall a victim to the goddess, the other being allowed to return home with the melancholy tidings. Then ensues the "de morte contentio," to which Herbert's correspondent refers. Pylades bids Orestes return, while he offers his own life at the shrine of the goddess. Orestes refuses, and a generous contest as to which of them should die ensues between the friends.

"Ire jubet Pylades carum moriturus Oresten.
Hic negat : *inque vicem pugnat uterque mori.*"

While the contest is proceeding, the priestess writes a line to her brother

of the two should die, will take place also between you
and me on the question of precedence, unless indeed
you quickly settle it by awarding the precedence at
once to rank and age; for you are clearly before me in
wisdom, in age, in rank, and in favour with God and
men. Farewell, you who are so able to fare well! Be
mindful of my late mother, my lord and father, and
request our brethren to intercede with God for her.
The hymn of Ambrose's [n], which you also subjoin to
your letters, I do not omit."—*Collated.* [o]

Orestes, and, giving it to Orestes, bids him convey it home. Then comes the *dénouement*. Iphigenia and Orestes recognising one another, the three, abandoning the design of the sacrifice, agree to steal away together, carrying with them across the sea the image of Diana, the pedestal of which was thenceforth unoccupied—a standing evidence to future generations of the sign and the wonder there wrought;

"Fama refert illic signum cœleste fuisse.
Quoque minùs dubites, stat basis orba Deâ.

Ovid, pining in banishment at Tomis, the capital of Scythia Minor, at the mouth of the Danube (a place which contrasted strangely and painfully with the civilization of Rome), introduces the story in a letter to Cotta, one of those "friends indeed" who had been "a friend in need." He praises the genuineness of Cotta's friendship, and says the praise of it will endure beyond the grave; for Ovid will embalm it in his writings. Even the rude Getæ and Sauromatæ, among whom the poet's lot is now cast, appreciate true friendship and hold it in esteem. He was recently mentioning Cotta's faithfulness in their company, and an old man said—"Yes, we too have heard of instances of warm and true friendship," and then retailed to Ovid the story above given.

John probably got the story from Ovid. Ovid himself borrowed it from Euripides (Iphigenia in Tauris, l. 674 et seq.). Another "de morte contentio" between Pylades and Orestes on a different occasion, appears in the Orestes of Euripides, l. 1069 et seq.

Herodotus says there was a tradition among the Tauri that Iphigenia was (not the *priestess*, but) the *goddess* of the people of those parts. (Her., iv. 119.)

[n] "The hymn of Ambrose's," &c.
"Ambrosianum illud, quod tu etiam tuis subjungis litteris, non omitto."
The hymns of St. Ambrose were held in the highest possible esteem, and circulated widely in the Western Church. In the Benedictine Rule, these Hymns are designated, as here, without a substantive—("an Ambrosian" meant an Ambrosian Hymn), and the recitation of one of them at each of the hours is prescribed.

"The hymns which go under the name of Ambrosian are very numerous, yet do not all appertain to Ambrose; the name having been freely given

And in this connexion we may give our reader a little relief from the dry details hitherto enu-

to as many as were formed after the model and pattern of those which he composed, and among these to not a few which were in every way unworthy of him. The Benedictine Editors do not admit more than twelve, as with any certainty of his composition; and even these, some in later times have affirmed to be ascribed to him upon doubtful authority, although no evidence can well be stronger than that which in regard of some of them we possess.", (Trench's Sacred Latin Poetry, p. 80.) The "Ambrosians" lack rhyme, and the usual metre adopted in them is the Iambic Dimeter. The hymn of Ambrose's which Abp. Trench embodies in his work is that grand Advent one, which begins "Veni, Redemptor Gentium," and contains the magnificent stanza descriptive of Christ, the Sun of Righteousness, making the circuit of creation, as the natural Sun does;

> " Egressus ejus e Patre,
> Regressus ejus ad Patrem,
> Excursus usque ad inferos,
> Recursus ad sedem Dei;"

Translated thus, with equal vigour and felicity;

> " From God the Father He proceeds;
> To God the Father back He speeds:
> Proceeds—as far as very hell;—
> Speeds back—to Light ineffable."

Herbert probably, being a devout Benedictine, had formed the habit of appending to his more important letters (as a species of consecration of them) some "Ambrosian," which happened to be a special favourite with him. The copyist does not copy it out, any more than we should think it necessary to publish a text of Scripture, which a pious man of these days might append to his letters. John tells Herbert, in the passage before us, that he imitates him, by appending the same Hymn to his own letter. One would like to know which of the Hymns it was. Possibly it may have been this little gem, which is quite of a general character;

> " O Lux beata Trinitas,
> Et principalis Unitas,
> Jam sol recedit igneus,
> Infunde lumen cordibus.
> 　Te mane laudum carmine,
> Te deprecamur vespere,
> Te nostra supplex gloria
> Per cuncta laudet sæcula."

> " O Blessed Trinity, true Light,
> O Unity, of sovereign might,
> Now that the fiery sun departs,
> Illume with heavenly light our hearts.

merated, by introducing Herbert's letters to Otto and Willelm,—two boys,—possibly choristers or acolytes, in whose education he takes an interest, which Mr. Spurdens calls "suspiciously paternal." We think the insinuation unworthy and groundless. It is true, indeed, that not until a quite late period of the eleventh century was marriage considered a stigma to the secular clergy. Speaking of the earlier part of it, Mr. Church says; "Marriage was common, even among bishops; it may not always have been marriage, but there plainly was a connexion which was not yet looked upon, as it came to be at the end of this century, as concubinage; and even a writer like Orderic, who of course condemns it unreservedly in the general, speaks of it incidentally in men whom he respects, and without being much shocked." (St. Anselm, ch. ii. p. 20). But Herbert seems to have been a monk from his early youth, having made his profession in the monastery of Fécamp, where he was educated; and a monk could in no way escape the vow of celibacy. His writings give no ground whatever for supposing that he would break that vow; nor do his temptations appear to have lain in the line of appetite, so much as in that of ambition. There was a tenderness in his

Unworthy insinuations of Mr. Spurdens against Herbert

rebutted.

<blockquote>
To Thee we sing at break of day,
To Thee at eventide we pray,
Thee may our prostrate souls adore
For ever and for evermore."
</blockquote>

The "nostra gloria," in the last line but one of this Hymn, means our soul,—that part of us which praises God. The phrase is taken from Psalm lvii. 8 [lvi. 11], "Awake up, *my glory;* awake, psaltery and harp: I myself will awake early." The immortal spirit of man, in which stands his capacity of holding communion with God, *is* his "glory." ° See p. 13, note i.

nature, which would attach him easily to any ingenuous youths placed under his care, and give him a fatherly interest in them. The letters which we here introduce shew him to us training two such youths, as he had himself been trained, in the rudiments of classical lore; reproving, encouraging, stimulating, with the zeal of a pedagogue, while the last of them exhibits him in the higher character of a spiritual father, turning the minds of the young to those studies, which alone have a permanent interest, as connecting themselves with our eternal future :—

LETTER IX.

To Otto and Willelm.

"Herbert to Otto and Willelm.

"I am sick of your delays, and pout very much, I assure you, as I reprove your indolent and sluggish want of exertion. How long do you mean to skulk in your Sedulius [p]? Great, no doubt, are the mysteries of Sedulius; but Matthew and Mark, Luke and John, methinks, relate those mysteries in a more excellent style. The Gospel story and doctrine are strong meat, to be retained [and digested] only by those whose minds have reached maturity. A tenderer age is nourished with a diet of milk; and amidst playful little pieces of fiction the tender minds of boys gradually but surely

Herbert reproves the boys Otto and Willelm for lingering in the rudiments.

[p] Sedulius was a Christian poet (a Presbyter or Bishop) who flourished about A.D. 450. He wrote what he calls a "Paschal Poem" in Hexameter verse, descriptive of the miracles of the Old and New Testaments; a Hymn which contained a collection of texts from the two Testaments, arranged in such a manner as to enable readers to compare the two Dispensations; and an account of the Life of Christ, from the Incarnation to the Ascension, in ninety-six Iambic Dimeters. His works were used as school-books in the middle ages, partly from the technical helps which they afforded to the memory.

imbibe polished diction and the method of tasteful composition. Rouse up; break off, as I have arranged for you, what you are reading at present; you are to expatiate by and bye with joyful briskness in the flowery meadows of the poets. There is something, however, which has to be done by you first; and I must by no means allow it to escape you. You are first to repeat to me your Donatus[q] by heart, with all the declensions conjugations and voices, and also your 'Compendium of Servius[r],' with the feet, and all the rules of grammar, wherein I instructed you all that year, sitting on the low form at your elbows. This, therefore, I prescribe to you, to get up your answers well for your examination, in which I shall take count of your stock of knowledge."

LETTER XXIV.

To Otho and Willelm.

" Herbert to Otho and Willelm.

"It is by the toil of the oxen that the earth is cultivated; and the usefulness of oxen is manifestly much

---

[q] Ælius Donatus was "a celebrated grammarian and rhetorician, who taught at Rome in the middle of the fourth century, and was the preceptor of St. Jerome. His most famous work is a system of Latin Grammar, which has formed the groundwork of most elementary treatises upon the same subject, from the period when he flourished down to our own times. ... It was the common school book of the Middle Ages, insomuch that in the English of Longlande and Chaucer a *donat* or *donet* is equivalent to a lesson of any kind, and hence came to mean an introduction in general. Thus among the works of Bishop Pecock are enumerated 'The *Donat* into Christian Religion,' and 'The Folower to the *Donat*;' while Cotgrave quotes an old French Proverb, 'Les diables étaient encores à leur *Donat*,' i.e. 'The Devils were but yet in their grammar.'" Smith's Dict. of Greek and Roman Biography, *Art.* DONATUS.

[r] "Serviolum" = "the little Servius;" in all probability an abridgement of some greater work which went under the name of Servius. The greater work may possibly have been the "In secundam Donati Editionem Interpretatio" of the celebrated Grammarian, Servius Maurus Honoratus, (contemporary with Macrobius and introduced in his Saturnalia), or the tractate on Grammar which bears the name of Servius, but whose author is unknown.

increased by the goad. The master is served by the compliance of his slaves; and the compliance of his slaves cannot be secured without the lash. So you also in like manner write nothing unless you are goaded to do so; say nothing, unless questions extract something from you. Once, at all events, [if it were only once] you might break forth of your own accord, might disturb my equanimity, might rid yourselves of the din I make [in your ears], and might move me, when I disguise [the interest I have in you], to lend a father's ear to your answers. Most indolent and sluggish of all youths, how long will you disgrace yourselves with these infantile dribblings? how long will you continue to throw up nothing but the refuse and sediment of your boyhood? Why spend ye not the livelong day in fasting, and the livelong night in watching? Ye eat, ye drink, ye sleep, and cherish all other pleasures on which your mind is bent. This, however, is not the way of arriving at that wisdom which you proposed to yourselves to follow. It is from the farthest and remotest quarters of the world that jewels are brought; it is from the bowels of the earth that gold and silver are extracted; so also, not without effort of the will and purity of the mind can wisdom be attained. [Rouse up!] Climb up mount Helicon[1]. Quaff intoxicating draughts from the fountain of the Muses. Write to me indefatigably and endlessly, even until I write back to you in these terms; 'Youths; your muse is getting wearisome to me. Give me a pause.'"

<small>A sharp reproof of the two boys for indolence and sluggishness.</small>

[1] "climb up mount Helicon"—*Conscendite Heliconem.*
It may be well for the sake of non-classical readers (and we hope to have some such, who will take an interest in Herbert), to say that Helicon is a mountain in the ancient Bœotia, the fabled resort of the Muses, and (with its fountains of Aganippe and Hippocrene) a great seat of the worship of those goddesses. The fable perhaps arose from the circumstance of Hesiod (one of the fathers of Greek Poetry) having resided at Ascra, a city at the foot of Helicon.

In the next sentence Herbert calls the Muses Pierides,—a name derived from another seat of their worship, Pieria, a district in the country of the Thracians, where Orpheus is said to have been buried, near the foot of Mount Olympus.

LETTER XLVII.

To Oto[1] and Willelm.

The two boys are urged to versification, which Herbert promises to criticise.

"Herbert to Oto and Willelm.

"There are certain species of wild beasts which leave off breeding as soon as their young begin to conceive; for, were it otherwise, the tame animals would not be able to hold out against the attacks of the wild. So I, too, my well-beloved sons, gave up my poetry, when you became poets, thinking it beneath me to employ myself in those studies, in which nevertheless I enjoin you to exercise your talents as boys. Write to me therefore in poetry, frame verses, compose odes, sing in metre, and rejoice the heart of your aged friend by cultivating the muses in every form. Henceforth I will sit as judge of your compositions, and criticising your poems will prepare a palm for the conqueror, a punishment for the careless. I am coming home shortly, and expect to receive from the other brethren the necessary [accounts and reports], but from you particularly poems."

LETTER XXXIX.

To Willelm and Oto.

Herbert excuses himself for not replying to the boys in verse, and reproves their backwardness.

"Herbert the Bishop to Willelm and Oto.

"In the last copy of verses I had from you, you charged me to reply to you in metre, and either to commend or censure your lines in a style similar to your own. But it is not consistent with a priest's course of life, whose meat is tears, and whose conversation is in heaven, to compose trifles and copy a poet's flights of fancy. The lips of the priest should be as honey in the comb, dropping down with words of grace and heavenly mysteries. Gold and precious stones, to which their own

---

[1] "Oto." We may take this opportunity of observing the great fluctuation in the spelling of names at the time Herbert wrote, and indeed for long afterwards. In the three Letters here presented to the reader consecutively, the same boy is called Otto, Otho, and Oto.

beauty sufficeth, need no exterior adornment. Ye seek [metrical] feet in my criticisms ᵘ ; but surely the polish of their eloquence and the weight of their sentiments is enough [without further decoration]. Lay aside your drivelling; and then ye shall find in your verses nothing more than an ass covered with a lion's skin. I am weary of your nerveless verses, which, like flowers, are fair only on the outside, and are not distinguished by any weight or solidity of sentiment. A new season in Nature ever succeeds to a decaying one; but your studies seem to continue stunted in their proportions as ever, [and are not improved by time]. What ye were when babies that ye were as boys; what ye were as boys, ye are as youths; most childishly ye stick still to your elisions ᵛ and barbarisms. To talk about Ovid is of very little value, unless you learn from Ovid how to talk. It is one thing to talk about skill in speech, quite another to speak skilfully. If henceforth, then, you mean to be guided by my judgment, adopt the style of Ovid, since I do not approve of your verses. If the sentiment lacks point and force, what effect is produced by it save the beating of the air, and a flourish in the figure of speech ; whereas the soul of the wise man derives nourishment from the bread of solid sentiments, and gratification from the word of God. The fear in which you stood of me seems to have vanished; you were wont

---

ᵘ We can only conjecture the sense of this passage, which stands thus in the Brussels MS. ; "Meis Indictaminibus pedes quæritis."

ᵛ Here again we give a conjectural sense for what (as it stands in the MS.) we cannot comprehend. The words are ;
"eisdem vestris sinalimphis et barbarissimis infantiliter inhæretis."
We read, "synalæphis et barbarismis." "Synalæpha" (συναλοιφὴ, from ἀλείφω, to erase, efface) is a grammatical term, expressing the coalition of two syllables into one. It may be done by the coalition of two vowels into a diphthong formed of themselves (συναίρεσις), or by their coalition into a long vowel, or a diphthong different from themselves (κρᾶσις), or by simply eliding a vowel (θλῖψις). Grammatical tricks of this kind are very acceptable to boys who have to make verses. One of their words is perversely too long to be got in to the line except by such manipulation. And their preceptors are well aware that the result of the elision (as boys practise it) is often most truly *barbarismus.*

to supply me with four or five hundred lines once in every two or three days; whereas now, at the expiration of two or three months, there come twenty or thirty verses, as inferior in polish as in number to the quota just now mentioned. Pray have a care of yourselves; you are writing not to a stock, but to a most acute and far-sighted man, who, when he has heard only one word, gains from it an insight into, and takes a survey of, your whole mind.

LETTER XXX.
To Oto.

"Herbert to Oto.

Herbert reproves Oto for the trifling nature of his studies, while his preceptor is in such danger and conflict; and severely criticises some verses of his.

"In taking up my pen to reply to a communication from a certain steady and worthy young gentleman, I call upon [the Lord] Jesus to give me His aid, that I may hit upon a criticism worthy of the productions of so subtle an intellect, and having hit upon such a criticism, may be enabled to embellish it judiciously and in adequate language. Be present with me, [Blessed] Jesus, and give power to my faltering tongue, that my mind may conceive things worthy of utterance, and that my slender powers of eloquence may be able to set it off, when it is conceived.

"Here am I then, that old and practised warrior, whose wrestling is not only with the powers of the air, and with spiritual wickedness in high places (as the Apostle boasts that his contention was), but against flesh and blood, against viscounts*, against county magis-

---

* These viscounts (Vice-comites) were not what we understand by the term at the present day. The Viscount was an officer annually appointed to the government of a county, whose business it was to see to the execution of the King's writs and decrees, and who occasionally sat (much like a Chairman of Quarter Sessions) to try subordinate causes. Three knights or esquires were annually nominated by the Privy Council out of each county, of whom the King selected one as his Viscount for that county. The Viscount acted under Letters Patent, after taking an oath to be faithful, and to receive no money from any one but the king. The name of the office is traced up to Alfred, who is said to have separated the func-

trates[x], against informers and apparitors[y], of whom there is such a multitude, who live in our immediate[z] neighbourhood, and against whom we watch by night, we exert ourselves to fight by day; nor is any time allowed to us, in which we are not forced to resist their wiles, their frauds, or their violence. Their very friendship is a two-edged[a] sword; and if at any time they remit

tions of the English Provincial Governors (called hitherto Vice-lords) into the judicial and the executive. The holders of the judicial functions he called Justiciaries, those of the executive functions, Viscounts. We are told that under this arrangement such extraordinary security of property prevailed, that if you dropped your purse on the road, you might pick it up again untouched a month after! The above particulars are drawn from Ducange, *sub voce*. Ingulf, Prior of Croyland, is responsible for the assertion about the purse.

[x] "adversus præpositos."

The *Præpositus* (or Provost) was a judge in the rural districts who tried minor causes, and was subordinate to the *Ballivus* or Bailiff.

[y] *adversus Bedellos*—"against apparitors."

The *Bedellus* (Bedell or Beadle) was an inferior officer who served citations on persons to appear before a court, and put in execution (often harshly and oppressively) the decrees and sentences which issued. The mediæval Bedell had a very bad name. "Drest in a little brief authority," he was formidable to all manner of folks, but especially to the poor. An edict of St. Louis, A.D. 1254, bids all seneschals and bailiffs rest content with as few bedells as possible; and Orderic says of bedells, "Bad officials are worse than robbers. The petty thieves, who haunt the rural districts, men may avoid by running away or turning aside, but in no wise can they give the slip to the crafty bedells" (versipelles bedellos) "without rueing it." One source of the odium which attached to the bedells was, that they occasionally levied fines and taxes, and probably (like the publicans among the Jews) enriched themselves by so doing.

The etymology of this curious word is doubtful. Some derive it from the Latin "pedum," *a shepherd's crook* ("At tu sume pedum .... Formosum paribus nodis atque ære, Menalca;" Virg. Eclog., lib. V. v. 88), because the Bedells carried a staff as the emblem of their office; others (with more probability) from the Saxon *beodan*, to *command, order*, with which our verb *bid* is connected.

[z] Here again we can make nothing of the text as it stands;
"quorum tanta est copia quo vicini nostri." Bp. Wordsworth suggests to us, "qui vicini nostri;" Rev. Dr. Benson, "provinciâ nostrâ."

[a] "Eorum amicitiæ spatæ sunt."
"Spătha" means a broad two-edged sword ("gladius major." Tacitus defines it, Ann. xii. 35), so called from its resembling a surgical instrument of that name, the "spatula," with which doctors spread their plaisters. The Italian *spada*, and the French *épée*, meaning a sword, are

something of their harsh claims, they make that indulgence a plea for devouring our substance with more than usual rapacity; their hands are full of blood, and they regard nothing but a bribe; as hell is never satisfied with its prey, so no amount of money can satisfy their thirst for gain. We are seized, we are tied hand and foot, we are scourged, we are imprisoned, and at periods, continually recurring through the day and night, we bewail our protracted miseries. Surely poetry is out of season in the house of mourning, and the strains of the Muses are far removed from a mind which laments its woe. Brother, he who can barely make shift to live, must not play. The wild ass, who is at large in the field [not at home in the stall], becomes the prey of the lion [b]. Even so the Church of God becomes meat for unclean dogs. I pass over much that I should otherwise say, as I am fearful of the effect of my own words. To-day the thoughts of men's hearts are revealed, and by the cunning of the informers the whole world lieth in wickedness. As for you, you have your cloister, and in the cloister peace; but remember that you enjoy this advantage at my expense, whose toils and labours have won it for you. The slanders and calumnies of the malignant storm around your quiet habitation, but my constant solicitude opposes them as a palisade, and secures you in the enjoyment of your repose, so that a thousand fall beside thee and ten thousand at thy right hand, but it shall not come nigh thee. You are wantonly trifling, Oto, when you provoke a soul full charged with bitterness to con over your verse exercises. Mind your own craft, [my good youth,] and understand distinctly that the toys of metre and the tears of mourning do not coalesce naturally in one and the same soul. You rally me for my sluggishness, you rally me for my drowsiness, you rally me

See 1 John v. 19.

Ps. xc. 7.

---

derived hence. This yields a sort of sense; but very possibly the place is corrupt.

[b] "Venatio leonis, onager in agro."
The rendering in the text was suggested to us by Bp. Wordsworth.

for my greediness; but the fact is that these vices are
the accompaniments and features of your own indolence,
and have long taken leave of my abode. 'In the day See Gen.
the drought consumeth me, and the frost by night,' and xxxi. 40.
sojourning, as I do, in rough and foul haunts, I sigh
exceedingly for the help which cometh of God, crying
with the Prophet; 'Wo is me, that my sojourning is Ps. cxix.
prolonged! I have dwelt with the inhabitants of Cedar: [cxx.] 5.
my soul hath been long a sojourner.'

"But now turn we to these noble compositions,—to
your verses, which I regard as so much mere trash and
sing-song. Thirty and six verses have you sent me,
not considering beforehand in your heedlessness that
thirty signifies the pleasure of the flesh and the number
six[e] the labours of this world. For you, who have renounced all worldly things, and have followed Christ,
ought to have indicated by the very number of your
verses that you were still devoted to your accustomed
chastity, that you were still estranged [in the spirit of
your mind] from the toils of secular affairs. You have
erred then in point of number, through not perceiving
the significance of the number [you send]. In the first
line you make a silly beginning, unwisely reproving at
the very outset the person [you address], whose good
graces you should have rather laid yourself out to win.
There is another fault moreover in the same line; you
apply the verb 'admire' to that which is bad, whereas
it is not commonly used but of that which is good. In
the 3rd line you make me angry, by asserting a falsehood and sheltering yourself under a foolish rule. Also
in line 7, you make a similar mistake. Also in line 9,

---

[e] Perhaps because the world's history was divided by mediæval writers
into six ages, the seventh period being that of the eternal Sabbath. [See
the Sermons, p. 63, note z.] Or because the world was created in six
days. As for the number "30 signifying the pleasure of the flesh," it
shews how utterly uncertain was the mediæval application of sacred numbers, that Bede, one of Herbert's favourite authors and models, speaking
of the age at which Our Lord commenced His ministry, says that "in
countless passages of Holy Scripture the number thirty is aptly used to
express the mysteries of Christ and His Church." (Bede in S. Luc. iii. 23.)

you use a wrong word, 'warn,' whereas what you really do is to reprove me. Also in line 10, 'base words' is a wrong expression, since baseness is an attribute of the mind only. Also in line 11, take note that I have never called you a youth, because you are still under age. Also in line 16, observe that a good matter is brought forth out of a good heart. Also in line 22, your rhyme has no reason. Also in the 33rd line, you ungrammatically place the word 'namque' [which should stand at the beginning] after two clauses of the sentence.

See St. Luke vi. 45.

"You see I have written back in answer to your writings, and I do earnestly hope that by the playfulness of my reply I shall have applied a remedy to your tiresome love of questioning[d]. Do then what you are doing; go on with what you have in hand, read your poets, make your centos out of the poets, since even in a dunghill that cock of Æsop's[e] picked up a pearl. Meanwhile I who am old and a priest advanced in years will speak to you of nought but Christ, and His eternal and delightsome promises.

[d] The MS. here has; "Rescripsi, ut vides, tuis scriptis, meorumque verborum ludo me sanativum fieri tuæ interrogationis desiderio, Respondit'⸺. Age igitur quod agis," &c. We can make no sense, except by substituting *spero* for *Respondit*.

[e] "even in a dunghill that cock of Æsop's picked up a pearl." The reference is to the 12th Fable of the IIIrd Book of Phædrus, of which we offer a translation.

That the best things are often held cheap.
THE PEARL ON THE DUNGHILL.

A cock, once strutting on the dunghill's mound,
In quest of grains for food, a jewel found.
"Unworthy place for pearl to hold," he cried;
"Oh! had some human eye thy worth espied,
Thou wouldst long since, at costliest price appraised,
To dignity and splendour have been raised.
I, who prefer by far a grain of food,
Can nought to thee, nor thou to me, do good."
Reader, my story hast thou understood?

Phædrus was a Thracian slave, brought to Rome, and, in acknowledgment of his literary skill, manumitted by Augustus. He professes to have taken Æsop's matter and turned it into Latin iambic senarii. Sometimes however he moralised on events of his own times. See III. 10.

"How is it that your colleague William has not added a line to your packet, and, as if he were out of charity with me, has not condescended to write me a word? The friendship, which only tells the truth, and which takes measures against and applies a remedy to an impending disease, surely does not merit anger. If he is hurt, let William open his heart [and tell me how]; and as hitherto he has been to me another self in my affairs, so now let him permit me to be to him another self in his. Let him write to me, if he wishes to get an answer from me."—*Collated*[f].

LETTER XXXII.

To Oto and Willelm.

"Herbert to Oto and Willelm.

"Ye work hard, my well-beloved sons, and endeavour to supplant my resolution by frequently coaxing me to write to you in verse; but it is impious and profane to offer resistance to divine oracles and sacred revelations. Much indeed should I wish to condescend to your request, and to reply to your compositions in a similar style; but the sternness of my [now] awakened resolve forbids me to do so, and makes me fearful of joining you in your literary sports, whatever grave sentences of authority might be pleaded for my doing so. To you, young as you are, it is permitted to amuse yourselves, while to my hoar hairs it is enjoined to meditate upon and search into the secret things of the Scriptures and the hidden [g] mysteries [of the Gospel]. Accordingly I have renounced the poets, and the dramas of the poets, and take no more delight in their buffooneries. It is not the part of a bishop to sit in the playhouse, but to preach in the church; he is not to occupy himself with the obscenities of the theatre, or the cruelties of the circus, but with the law of God and the words of the holy Gospel. We, too, have authors who indited

An apology for not answering the boys in verse, drawn from the style of the Scriptural writers and early Fathers.

---
[f] See p. 13, note i.
[g] "mistica Sacramenta." See note x, on Sermon I. p. 21.

the truth which we acknowledge, and who far excel your authors, inasmuch as they are proved to be lovers of God alone. Moses, that offspring of the Nile, to whom God first appeared in the bush, and who ten times scourged the obduracy of the Egyptians with so many strokes,—so sublime a prophet that he drowned the chariots of Pharaoh and his army in the Red Sea, and led forth the people of God dry shod through the same sea in safety;—Moses, who fed God's people with manna in the wilderness, reared up the tabernacle, promulgated the Law,—Moses who set forth in writing the early history of the world down to the entrance of the people upon the inheritance which God had covenanted to give them,—Moses did not cramp his inspired sentences into metrical feet, but threw his prophetic narrative into the form of prose. So did also Isaiah and the other prophets, who lingered fondly enough on weighty sentiments, not beneath that foliage of style which obscures while it embellishes. So, too, the Evangelists and Apostles served up to the world the sweet viand of the Incarnate Word (honey, as it were, in a comb[h] of frail wax), heeding little the graces of style, but having their whole minds absorbed in the greatness of the miracle. Look ye also to the modern Fathers, Jerome, Augustine, Ambrose, Gregory, or any other defenders of our holy religion; and ye shall find that they enlightened the holy Church, not by poetical strains but by the understanding of the truth. For which reasons, my well beloved sons, let it be clear to you that, your importunity notwithstanding, I have resolved that ye shall no more see any verses of mine, but that in my

---

[h] "velut mel in fragilis ceræ *fano*, Verbi incarnati dulcedinem mundo *propinaverunt.*" If Mr. Anstruther has represented the MS. correctly in printing *fano*[*], the translation of course must be, "in a *shrine* of pure wax." But we conjecture "favo," "in a comb of pure wax."

"Propino" generally means to drink to the health of a person; but it has also the meaning of giving him to drink, setting before him, administering (of medicine). Thus Pliny advises to administer water (aquam propinare) in epileptic seizures. Plin. 28. 1, 2.

[*] We have only collated Mr. Anstruther's Edition with the MS., where we had reason to suspect a mistake in the Edition.

replies to you ye will have to quaff draughts of divine truth out of earthen vessels. For we bear about the treasures of Christian wisdom not in the pride[1] of lofty eloquence, but in purity of conscience, in devotion of life, and in sanctification of the flesh."

See 2 Cor. iv. 7.

LETTER XL.[k]

"Be up and doing; apply to your studies; let there be no delay in meeting the expectations he has formed of you; for bound by his own decision he will return to you at latest before the Festival[1] of St. Peter's bonds.

A letter, the address of which is lost, in the same strain as the preceding.

[1] "in *tipo* sublimis eloquentiæ." See Sermon IV., p. 96 (note d).

[k] This Letter has no address. It begins with a sentence of which we can make nothing. We present it to the reader as we find it in the Brussels MS.

"Vester Zacheus decurio factus est, nostrosque curules vestro præfuit" (præfecit?) "eliconi."

The *c* of decurio is very unlike the usual *c* made by the scribe of the Brussels MS., and over the *u* is a perpendicular wavy line. The word decurio signifies etymologically the head of a body of ten. A member of the senate in a Roman colony was so called; and at the Imperial court the high Chamberlain.—"Curule magistrates," as is well known, were the consuls, prætors, and curule ædiles of ancient Rome, who were privileged to use the curule chair.

The reader with these helps must make for himself of this obscure sentence, what he can.

We give the Letter in this connexion, because its contents seem to be in the same strain with those addressed to Oto and Willelm.

[1] "citra Principis Apostolorum vincula."

The festival of St. Peter's Chains in the Roman Church (and it was the same in the use of Sarum) commemorates the imprisonment of St. Peter as recorded in Acts xii.

It is kept on the 1st of August, which requires to be accounted for, as it was during "the days of unleavened bread" (in the spring, that is,) that Herod took Peter (Acts xii. 3). The account is thus given by Wheatly on the Common Prayer, p. 67.

"Eudoxia, the wife of Theodosius the Emperor, having made a journey to Jerusalem, was there presented with the fetters which St. Peter was loaded with in prison; which she presented to the Pope, who afterwards laid them up in a church built by Theodosius in honour of St. Peter. Eudoxia, in the meantime, having observed that the 1st of Aug. was celebrated in memory of Augustus Cæsar, (who had on that day been saluted *Augustus*, and had upon that account given occasion to the changing of the name of the month from Sextilis to August,) she thought it not

The great number of your holidays gives me a pang and makes me anxious, and you who ought even to come down upon your Christmas [m] for the purpose of work, are solemnizing every day idle contemplations, and paying an empty homage [n] to the spirits of our departed forefathers, while ye relax the rigour of your studies. It was the custom of the naked [o] sages of

reasonable that a holy day should be kept in memory of a heathen prince, which would better become that of a godly martyr; and therefore obtained a decree of the emperor, that this day for the future should be kept holy in remembrance of St. Peter's bonds."
The 1st of August is called in our own Calendar Lammas Day, two derivations of which word have been given. 1st. a foolish conceit that St. Peter was the patron of the *lambs*, from our Saviour's saying to him, "Feed my lambs." 2. From a Saxon word, meaning "Loaf-mass," it having been the custom of the Saxons to offer on Aug. 1 an oblation of loaves made of new wheat, as the first-fruits of their wheat harvest." Hook's Church Dictionary, *sub voce*.

[m] "qui nec ipsis parcere debueratis *Saturnalibus*."
We have given a free translation of the word *Saturnalia*. The Saturnalia of ancient Rome was the festival of Saturnus, which fell towards the end of December, and was "viewed by all classes of the community as a period of absolute relaxation and unrestrained merriment. During its continuance no public business could be transacted, the law courts were closed, the schools kept holiday, ... all ranks devoted themselves to feasting and mirth, presents were interchanged among friends, ... many of the peculiar customs exhibited a remarkable resemblance to the sports of our own Christmas and of the Italian Carnival." [Dict. of Rom. and Greek Antiq, *sub voce*, p. 840 b, 841 a.]

[n] "vanis *pacentantes* manibus."
Such is Mr. Anstruther's text; but he alters the word in his "Errata" to "parentantes," which yields a good sense. "Parento" means to offer a solemn sacrifice in honour of deceased parents or relatives. Herbert's reference is probably to the numerous anniversaries and obits in the mediæval Church, celebrated on the day of decease of the person commemorated. They had grown very numerous; and no doubt gave boys a good excuse for asking and obtaining holidays, and so favoured their indolence. Even the few Saints Days of the Reformed Church of England, kept (formerly) as "whole holidays" at Eton and (perhaps) elsewhere, acted prejudicially upon the industry of the boys.
If our rendering of the words preceding these, "quotidianas celebratis expectationes" is objected to, we can only invite the reader himself to suggest one which may better meet the requirements of the word "expectationes."

[o] "Indorum gygnosophistarum" (*gymnosophistarum* must be meant) "fuit consuetudo."
Pliny (vii. 2) mentions two other austerities of the Gymnosophists (the

India to carry on their study of philosophy naked in the open air, and barely to sustain rather than to nourish life on black [p] bread and common [q] hyssop. So also those whom the Egyptians affirm to have been the earliest of the human race, maintained that long fasting acted as an aliment to their philosophy. The students [r] in our own seats of learning, too, were in the habit of taking their meals standing, just tasting their food rather than loading their bellies [s] with a

predecessors of the Fakirs) that they persisted in gazing on the sun with fixed eyes from his rising to his setting, and that they stood whole days with bare feet on the sand when it glowed fiercely with the sun's heat.

[p] "Cibario pane."

Cibarius (cibus), is an adjective which denotes any thing in the way of nourishment which is cheap, common, and coarse. It is used in this sense not only of bread, but of wine and oil, and even of a flavour generally—"a coarse homely taste."

[q] *vili isopo*—"common hyssop."

The hyssop of Scripture is spoken of as a humble and common plant. Solomon "spake of trees, from the cedar tree that is in Lebanon even unto the hyssop that springeth out of the wall." 1 Kings iv. 33.

Hyssop (whatever be the plant referred to) was used in sprinkling the blood of the Paschal Lamb (Ex. xii. 22) in the ceremony of cleansing the leper (Lev. xiv. 4) and in making the water of separation used for ceremonial cleansings (Num. xix. 6). In allusion to which rites the Psalmist prays; "Purge me with hyssop, and I shall be clean" (Ps. li. 7).—Hence in the mediæval Latin, *Hysopus* is often used for the *aspergillum*, or brush with which the priest sprinkled the holy water.

As to the use of hyssop for food, see Smith's Dictionary of the Bible (vol. i. p. 846, *sub voce*), where one of the five species of hyssop is thus mentioned as an article of sustenance;

"According to Porphyry (De Abstin. iv. 7), the Egyptian priests on certain occasions ate their bread mixed with hyssop; and the *yaatar*, or wild marjoram, with which it has been identified, is often an ingredient in a mixture called *dukkah*, which is to this day used as food by the poorer classes in Egypt."

The Greek form of the word is ὕσσωπος, (ἡ). In Latin it has two forms, hyssopus, i. *fem.*; and hyssopum, i. *neut.*

[r] "The students in our own seats of learning, too"—*Nostri quoque Academici*. It is possible, however, that by *nostri Academici* Herbert might mean the disciples of some particular philosophy, corresponding to the Academics of old, his view of whom would probably be drawn from Cicero's two Books of Academics.

[s] "loading their bellies"—*aqualiculos onerantes*.

Aquălĭcŭlus signifies, according to its etymology, a small vessel for holding water. Hence it is applied to the stomach, and especially, it is said, to

multitude of viands, fearing lest the keen bright edge of an intellect bent on philosophy should be clouded or dulled, when the belly was overcharged with surfeiting. The synagogue, too, had an Elijah, it had a John, it had sons of the Prophets, whose number did not [t] fall off, although no one was added to their company by natural generation. That fruitful olive-tree, the Church, the Saviour's bride, is adorned with its companies [both of men and women], who live in chastity,—a practice which has spread most widely where the name of Christ is invoked [u]. Let our house, too, have its celibate naked sages, our young pair of colts to wit, to whom I gave birth in my heart, and whom I nourished with the milk of my mind, and with more than maternal tenderness. Let them with their brethren be a shining light, an example of frugality, sobriety and chastity, of humility and patience, of purity and obedience; so that, provoked by the celibacy of our youths, the elders of our Church may be confirmed in the true religion. I send you a present [v]—nay, not a present but an earnest of a present, meaning to send my present when I see what yours will be."

See Rom. xi. 17.

the receptacle into which the food swallowed by swine passes. It seems to have been a coarse term—"paunch, belly."

[t] "whose number did not fall off"—"quorum numerus non minorabatur." A non-classical word, but one used by Tertullian.

[u] This is merely a conjectural translation of the text, which we suppose to be corrupt. It runs thus;

"Oliva fructifera, ecclesia videlicet, sponsa Salvatoris, suorum continentium decoratur agminibus, eo latissime dilatata, ubi nomen Christi fuerit invocatum."

[v] This last sentence falls into two Hexameters,
Mitto munus, non munus, sed muneris arram,
Missurus munus, conspecto munere vestro.
This may possibly be a quotation from some Anthology or Epigrammatist. Possibly, however, the metrical run of the words is no more designed than that of
Hŏw ărt thŏu fāllĕn frŏm hēavĕn, Ŏ Lūcĭfĕr, sŏn ŏf thĕ mōrnĭng!
Hŏw ărt thŏu cūt dōwn tŏ thĕ groūnd, whĭch dĭdst wēakĕn thĕ nātĭons!

LETTER XLIX.

To Willelm.

"Herbert to Willelm.

"If you have any regard for yourself, and wish to feel happy in my affection, strive to finish the different kinds of Topics, and take up diligently the Categories [w] of Aristotle before I come home. Do not heed the desultory ways of your colleague, who is quite content with knowing the names [only] of the books which he reads, and with being able to tell how many pages he has read; but do you rise before daybreak, join night to day and day to night in listening to instructions in logic, and training your mind by means of that study. I de-

[Side note: Willelm is exhorted to the study of Philosophy and the liberal arts. Oto's superficiality and sloth are glanced at with disapproval.]

---

[w] "Topics, Categories."
A reference to the Aristotelian Logic, comprised in six treatises, which are called collectively Aristotle's Organon (or "Instrument" of Science). One of these treatises is called the "Topics," and gives general heads of argument, in matters where scientific certainty cannot be had, and probability must be acquiesced in.

The Categories are a more scientific and advanced work. They exhibit ten heads, under which all our ideas must fall—essence, quantity, quality, relation, place, time, situation, possession, action, and suffering.—One can quite understand how a youth would find this sort of metaphysical reasoning a step in advance after the Topics, which would qualify him only to conduct an argument on general subjects, with an appearance of having reason on his side.

It was just about the time of Herbert's birth (1050) that, according to Mosheim, "the face of philosophy began to change, and the science of Logic assumed a new aspect. This revolution began in France, where several of the books of Aristotle had been brought from the schools of the Saracens in Spain, and it was effected by a set of men highly renowned for their abilities and genius, such as Berenger, Roscellinus, Hildebert, and after them by Gilbert de la Porre, the famous Abelard, and others. These eminent logicians, though they followed the Stagirite as their guide, took, nevertheless, the liberty to illustrate and model anew his philosophy, and to extend it far beyond its ancient limits."

Archbishop "Lanfranc was so deeply versed in the science of Dialectic that he was commonly called the Dialectician; and he employed with great dexterity the subtleties of Logic in the controversy which was carried on between him and the learned Berenger, against whom he maintained the Real Presence of Christ's Body and Blood in the Holy Sacrament." (Mosheim, Eccl. Hist., vol. ii. pp. 465, 466.)

sire that you should mould yourself after my example, and with all the eager interest and hope of a father, I am most anxious that your mind should receive the very impress of my own. May an ardent love of study be kindled in you; and may you hasten to the banquet of philosophy with the greater zest, because, out of the materials which it furnishes, you are to do service not to men but to God. Let but the great secret of that eternal life, which you propose to yourself [as your end], be revealed to your heart; and you will discover how little worthy is your present labour to be compared with the future rest which is prepared as the reward of your expectation. I have set thee as a lamp in the house of God; glow, then, with the light of wisdom, and shine with the brightness of the sciences. Lay up inexhaustible treasures of learning, that you may have a storehouse whence you may bring forth to your hearers things new and old. I commend to your ardent pursuit the study of the trivium and the quadrivium, that is, of the seven liberal[1] arts, since he who lacks instruction in these in vain professes himself a philosopher. Greet your young pupils [from me], that is, on the understanding that they shew up to me the sum of verses which I have enjoined them. As for Felix, I wish him

---

[1] "the trivium and quadrivium, that is, the seven liberal arts."

The passage shews how great a value scholars of that age attached to these seven liberal arts as instruments of Education. The *trivium* embraced Grammar, Logic, and Rhetoric; the *quadrivium* Music, Arithmetic, Geometry, and Astronomy; the subjects of which are enumerated in those two old mnemonic hexameters;

"GRAMM. loquitur; DIA. vera docet; RHET. verba colorat;

"MUS. canit; AR. numerat; GEO. ponderat; AST. colit astra."

Hallam says of these sciences (Literature of Europe, vol. i. ch. i. p. 3, note †), that, whatever may have been professed, "most of them were hardly taught at all. The arithmetic, for instance, is nothing but a few definitions mingled with superstitious absurdities about the virtues of certain numbers and figures. The arithmetic of Cassiodorus occupies little more than two folio pages, and does not contain one word of the common rules. The geometry is much the same; in two pages we have some definitions and axioms, but nothing further. His logic is longer and better, extending to sixteen folio pages. The grammar is very short and trifling, the rhetoric the same."

to keep up a plentiful supply of vegetables and other dainties."—*Collated*[y].

LETTER XXII.
TO OTTO AND WILLELM.

"Herbert to Otto and Willelm.

"After sailing down the impetuous streams of infancy and boyhood, ye are now fairly launched upon the open sea of youth, the navigation of which sea is fraught with great dangers, unless Christ be present at the helm. Youth is indeed afloat in the midst of divers dangers, unlimited in number, and the report of which may well inspire terror. On one side gluttony and drunkenness weigh down the soul, lust and incontinence disgrace the body, according to that [word] of the Apostle's; 'He that committeth fornication sinneth against his own body.' [In another quarter] covetousness and anger eat into the mind; melancholy and ennui[z]

Otto and Willelm are exhorted to avoid the moral snares of youth, and to take Christ as their pilot in the perilous voyage of life.
1 Cor. vi. 18.

[y] See above, p. 13, note i.
[z] *Tristitia et acidia suffocant intentionem* — "melancholy and *ennui* strangle good intention."

It is difficult—perhaps impossible—to find one English word which is a sufficient rendering of *acidia*. As it expresses a vice frequently censured in mediæval Divinity, we take this occasion of saying something upon it.

The word is of Greek origin (ἀκηδία, ἀκήδεια), and has found its way into the mediæval Latin under the forms *Acedia, Acidia, Accidia.* According to its etymology * (ἀ-κῆδος) it means simply *indifference, carelessness, unconcern.* *Accidia* was a great besetting sin of the monastic life. Many inmates of Convents had entirely mistaken their vocation in becoming inmates. They had too great sprightliness of mind,—lived naturally too much out of themselves, had too much enterprise and love of novelty in their character, to adjust themselves to one unwearied round of labour and devotion day by day. One can easily understand how the monotony and unvarying regularity of the life of the Convent told unfavourably upon such minds,—how they would be apt to lapse into a melancholy listlessness, which would take all interest out of life,—a compound of apathy, low spirits, ennui, and indolence. This was *accidia*, or *acidia*. A glimpse into its nature, and an indication of the suitable remedy, is given us by S. Ber-

* For we can hardly accept the etymology of the word quoted by Ducange from Cæsarius (Bishop of Arles in the sixth century):
Acedia, quasi Acida, eo quòd opera spiritualia nobis *acida* reddat et insipida."

strangle good intention; vainglory and pride empty out the treasures of a mind which is not on its guard

nard when he says (Epistle 78); "*Variety* in holy observances puts to flight weariness and ennui" (tædium et acediam). Monotony and overmuch solitude brought it on; change of employment and dissipation of the thoughts tended to disperse it. We have the following delineation of its features from one John of the Ladder, a Greek monastic writer of the sixth century, so called from his having written a treatise entitled "The Ladder of Paradise;"

"Accidy is a weariness of the soul, an unstringing of the mind, a want of courage in spiritual exercises, a strong disinclination to [the pursuit of] perfection. It calls men who lead a secular life blessed; it disparages God, as if He were cruel, and lacked kindness and fatherly affection. In reciting psalms it becometh dazed; it is feeble in prayer, though strong as iron when superfluous works of the hands are proposed to it; very naughty and spiritless when obedience is demanded from it." (Joannes Climacus, apud Politianum, quoted by Rev. W. Denton in his Commentary on the Epistles. Rom. xii. 11.)

But we gather from the circumstance of Accidy and its remedies forming one division of the "Persone's" Sermon in Chaucer's "Canterbury Tales," that it was a sin not confined exclusively to monastic life, but found al so among the lay-people, who formed the "Persone's" flock. That modern times know comparatively little of it, may be due perhaps to their restlessness and stir, their facilities of travel, increased means of observation, and rapid movement of thought. *Accidy* was induced by monotony and regularity of life; the feverish excitements and continual mental fermentation of modern days leave little room for it, although it cannot be doubted that these features of our times produce morbid habits of mind of a different and equally deplorable description. We think a few extracts from Chaucer's description of the sin of Accidy may not be unwelcome to the reader, while they will throw further light on the subject;

"Accidie is the anguish of a trouble herte." . . . "Certes this is a damnable sinne, for it doth wrong to Jesu Crist, in as moche as it benimeth [taketh away] the service that men shulde do to Crist with alle diligence, as sayth Salomon: but accidie doth non swiche diligence. He doth all thing with annoye, and with wrawness, [peevishness], slaknesse, and excusation, with idelnesse and unlust. Accidie is enemy to herying [praising] and adoring of God . . . to labour in praying to God for amendement of sinnes . . . to workes of penitence, for he loveth no besinesse at all. Now certes, this foule sinne of accidie is eke a ful gret enemie to the livelode of the body; for it ne hath no purveaunce ayenst temporel necessitee; for it forsleutheth [i.e. putteth off], forsluggeth [neglecteth] and destroieth all goodes temporel by recchelesnesse."

. . . .

"Of accidie cometh that a man is annoied and accombred to do any goodnesse, and that maketh that God hath abhomination of swiche accidie, as sayth Seint John. . . . . ."

[against their encroachments]. Worst of all, the fickleness of youth is such that it varies with every change of circumstance. Such are the perils of youth, deafer than the stones, more rugged than the rocks, more fell than Scylla and Charybdis, more calamitous than [the promontory] Palinurus[a], more cruel than quicksands and

> "Now cometh slouthe that wol not suffre no hardnesse ne no penaunce. ... Than cometh drede for to begin any good werkes. ... Now cometh wanhope, that is, despeir of the mercy of God. ... Than cometh somnolence, that is, sluggy slumbring, which maketh a man hevy, and dull in body and in soule. ... Than cometh negligence or recchelesnesse that recketh of nothing. ... Negligence ne doth no force whan he shal do a thing, whether he do it wel or badly. ... Than cometh idelnesse, that is the yate of all harmes. ... Than cometh the sinne that men clepen *tarditas*, as whan a man is latered [delayed], or taryed or he wol tourne to God. ... And this vice cometh of false hope, that thinketh that he shal live long, but that hope failleth ful oft. ... Than cometh lachesse, that is, he that whan he beginneth any good werk, anon he will forlete it [give it over]. ... Than cometh a maner coldnesse, that freseth all the hirt of man. Than cometh undevotion, thurgh which a man is so blont, as sayth Seint Bernard, and hath swiche languor in his soule, that he may neyther rede ne sing in holy chirche, ne here ne think of no devotion, ne travaile with his hondes in no good werk, that it n' is to him unsavory and all apalled. Than wexeth he sluggish and slombry, and sone wol he be wroth, and sone is enclined to hate and to envie. Than cometh the sinne of worldly sorwe as is cleped *tristitia*, that sleth [slayeth] a man, as sayth Seint Poule. For certes swiche sorwe werketh to the deth of the soule and of the body also, for therof cometh, that a man is annoied of his owen life. Wherefore swiche sorwe shorteth the life of many a man, or that his time is come by way of kinde [in the order of nature]."

In Dan Michel's Ayenbite of Inwyt (Remorse of Conscience), a treatise in the Kentish Dialect of the date A.D. 1340, *Accidy* figures as one of the seven heads of the Beast in the Revelation, those heads being 1. Pride. 2. Envy. 3. Anger. 4. Sloth, which is called among the Clergy *accidy*. 5. Covetousness. 6. Gluttony. 7. Lechery.

Part of the furniture of a monastic infirmary was a stone where the dying sick were washed and received the last Sacraments; and on this stone monks suffering from *Accidy* were directed to sit and meditate,—a remedy piously intended, no doubt, but hardly likely, one would think, to be effectual. (See Fosbrooke's British Monachism, vol. ii. p. 151.)

[a] For the sake of readers ignorant of the Classics, who may be interested in Bp. Herbert's letters, we may just say that Scylla and Charybdis were the names of two rocks between Italy and Sicily, very perilous to navigators, on the first of which there dwelt (according to the fable) a six-headed monster which barked like a dog, on the second a nymph who thrice every day swallowed in the waters of the sea and threw them up

pirates, winds and waves. Truly youth is a vast sea, and stretcheth[b] wide its arms; in it are creeping things which cannot be numbered. Songs of sirens, and infernal sand-reefs[c] beguile those who are not warned of them; and poor youths, deluded by that which has the

Ps. ciii. 25 (Vulg.)

again. Ships which passed between them running the risk of either being dashed against Scylla or swallowed by Charybdis, the two names passed into a proverb for opposite dangers;

> He who minded is to steer
> Of Charybdis' whirlpool clear,
> Soon he runs with fatal shock
> On to Scylla's ruthless rock.
> So the man who illness shuns
> Straight upon the doctor runs;
> Is not swallowed by disease,—
> No;—but eaten up by fees.

Palinurus was a promontory of Lucania, deserving the name of *tristis* (calamitous) on mythical and historical grounds. Palinurus, the pilot of Æneas, having been thrown into a deep slumber by the god of sleep, fell from the helm and was cast ashore at this promontory and murdered by the natives. The headland was vexed by violent and sudden storms which proved on more than one occasion fatal to the Roman fleets.

[b] This is a quotation from the Vulgate Version of the Psalms, which may not be immediately recognised. We give it after the Version of the English Bible, the Vulgate, and the Douay.

E. V.	VULG.	DOUAY.
Ps. civ. 25.	Ps. ciii. 25.	Ps. ciii. 25.
So is this great and wide sea, wherein *are* things creeping innumerable, both small and great beasts.	Hoc mare magnum, et spatiosum manibus; illic reptilia, quorum non est numerus.	So is this great sea, which stretcheth wide its arms: there are creeping things without number.

[c] "Infernal sand reefs"—*Tartarea bitalassa*. (Other forms of the word are *Bitalassus, bithalassium, bithalassus*.) *Bithalassum* means a place where two seas meet,—in Greek διθάλασσος, i.e. that which is washed on both sides by the sea, in which sense Corinth is spoken of by Horace as bimaris. In the Vulgate, Act. App. xxvii. 41, the form *bithalassum* ("in locum bithalassum") is used in some editions, in others *dithalassum*. In the Epistle of St. Clement to James, the brother of the Lord, the word is thus used; "Places *between two seas*, which are beaten by the fawning swell of a deceitful wave, may be compared to men wavering in mind, and vacillating concerning the truth of promises." Fulbertus in one of his Epistles gives this warning; "Beware of admitting into thy heart the bithalassus of doubt." (Ducange, *sub voce.*)

semblance of an anchorage, are dashed on foreign strands, to become the prey of unclean spirits. And who is sufficient for these things? Whose soul shall offer a firm resistance to dangers so many and so great? A raft is plainly requisite, but [it must be one] so strong, and so compacted of planks which cannot be sundered, that it shall not shrink from the encounter with such horrible dangers. This, therefore, is the raft on which, in the midst of this world's sea, our Saviour climbed up, and whereon he was transported from a state of suffering to a state exempt from suffering, from corruption to incorruption, from mortality to immortality, from death to life, from earth to heaven. Mount ye this raft, my sons, with speed and alacrity; by its safe conveyance surmount the shipwreck of this world's unbelief; come ye to Christ's ship, and quietly allow Christ to be your pilot, and ye shall find rest unto your [d] souls; for Christ's yoke is easy, and His burden is light. Why are ye in such a state of trepidation? Why dread ye the perils of the deep? Your Pilot laid His command upon the winds; your Pilot walked across the waves with feet which [e] sank not in. There is no handiwork which can resist the craftsman; unto Him who created all things out of nothing no circumstances can present an impossibility. The will of God is the alone cause of the existence of things. Ye are risen with Christ; seek those things which are above, not those which are upon the earth; sow ye to the Spirit, and not to the flesh; for he that soweth to the flesh shall of the flesh reap corruption, but he that soweth to the Spirit shall of the Spirit reap life everlasting. You allege youth as an excuse [for your excesses]; yet not all youths [in age] are youths [in

2 Cor. ii. 16.

St. Matt. xi. 29, 30.

St. Matt. xiv. 25, 26.

Col. iii. 1, 2.

Gal. vi. 7, 8.

[d] "unto your souls"—"*animabus* vestris." The Brussels MS. has the quotation quite correctly; but Mr. Anstruther's Edition has the strange misprint "*in malis* vestris," which moreover is not corrected in his *Errata*.

[e] *plantis non sidentibus*—"with feet which sank not in." On the curious coincidence of this expression with another in the Easter Sermon of Herbert, see the Sermons, pp. 154, 155, note c.

character]; whence comes that saying of Holy Scripture; 'Rejoice, O young man, in thy youth;' and in another place; 'The understanding of a man is gray hairs; and an unspotted life is old age.' Samuel, when a child, pronounced the deposition of Eli; and Daniel, while he was a young boy, convicted and condemned the elders in Babylon. Awake [to righteousness], and flee the unstable Euripus¹ of lust. Let your [only] brotherhood be one of chastity; and there fasten the anchor of your hope. Crucify your members with your vices and lusts; rear the mast of faith, and hoist upon it the sails of virtues. Catch in these the gales of the Holy Spirit. Make sail for your country and your city, having Christ for your Pilot; and so with prosperous course shall ye enter into the harbour of the heavenly shore. There shall ye find God your Father; ye shall find, too, your holy mother, to wit the Church. You shall find there your brethren and fellow-citizens, the saints, the angels, and all the elect of God; yea and the intimacy of every tender tie, whereby your enjoyment shall be continually renewed, and your eternity made delightful, and your bliss made eternal. Ye shall be enriched with treasures and delights which eye hath not seen, nor ear heard, neither hath it entered into the heart of man to conceive, which your Pilot hath prepared as a recompence for the labours of your trafficking. Wherever I am, I am mindful of the perils of your situation, and so have written this letter to remind you of them, as you probably disguise them from yourselves. See that ye write me an answer in a similar strain."

Margin references: Eccles. xi. 9. Wisdom iv. 8, 9. 1 Sam. iii. 12, 13, 18. Susanna 45, 55, 59, 61, 64, &c. Gal. v. 24. Gal. iv. 26. See Eph. ii. 19. 1 Cor. ii. 9.

¹ *fugite euripum libidinis*—"flee the unstable Euripus of lust."
The expression is very forcible. Euripus means any narrow channel of the sea, in which the tide is violent; but was particularly applied to the strait separating the island of Eubœa (Negropont) from the adjacent continent of Bœotia, in which the sea was said to ebb and flow seven times a-day. Hence the term *euripus* became a proverb for instability, and is used by Aristotle in his Ethics to denote a wavering fickle man. It is here well applied to the instability of lust, its *sudden changes*, and *its impetuosity*. "Unstable as water thou shalt not excel," said Jacob of lustful Reuben. See 2 Sam. xiii. 15.

LETTER XXVIII.

To Oto and Willelm.

"Herbert to Oto and Willelm.

"As not long ago I was musing in the silence of the night on your studies and what you are now learning, and was humming to myself some elegiac lines, sleep crept over me, the depth of which was due to the intentness of mind with which I was bent upon your profit. The images of what had previously passed [in my waking experience] haunted me; and my soul being liberated for the moment from the impressions of sense, vain phantoms surprised my spirit, which was labouring with real interests and cares. How wretched is the condition of mortals, that, when men are withdrawn from present things, and have laid them down to rest, false impressions are apt to torment them more cruelly than any waking and substantial anxiety. My soul was labouring, and endeavoured by the fixed gaze of the mind (yet was frustrated as fast as it endeavoured) to expel the throng of spectres, but settling down again into its own cares and interests, confessed itself unequal by any effort to chase away these harassing and confused phantoms. A figure then presented itself of awful majesty, formidable aspect, at whose entrance all that throng of spectres broke away from me, and disappearing in a manner for which I was quite unprepared forsook my spirit which they had been harassing. This figure, pausing for some time, and seeming to be lost in deep reflection on various subjects, at length with great solemnity thus began; 'Hearken, friend,' said she, 'with what dignity dost thou profess to have been invested?' To whom I made answer, 'I am a Christian, and the servant of your holiness.' But she rejoined, 'I enquire not concerning thy religion, but concerning thy dignity; for the dignity, in virtue of which thou excellest others, is one thing; the religion whereby thou art bound to thy God, is another.' Then I began to

Herbert describes a vision, in which he is warned against the study of heathen literature, and made to recall what had been said by Jerome and Boëthius to the same effect; and concludes by announcing to his pupils his resolution to speak to them in future only of Christ.

perceive, that it was respecting my episcopal office that she made inquiry; but I was ashamed nevertheless to avow myself a bishop, lest by making such a profession I should incur a censure for my arrogance. But she, persisting in her enquiries, demanded more than once that the dignity I had attained to should be disclosed to her. Then at length, perceiving that my efforts to suppress the truth could by no means escape her, I replied, 'Venerable Lady, I bear the name of a bishop, though all unworthy to do so.' Whereupon she rejoined; 'I was aware that from thy youth even to the hoar hairs of old age, which are now upon thee, thou hast taken upon thee the warfare of priestly functions; but [this being so [g]] how is it that thy hands are still busy with the fictions of Ovid and the fabrications of Virgil [h]? Unseemly it is that Christ should be preached

---

[g] It is singular that in the letters of Lanfranc, a contemporary of our Author in his youth, we find a similar statement of the impropriety of a Bishop cultivating profane literature. At the end of a letter to "Domnaldus, the venerable bishop of Ireland" (Letter 36, pp. 54—56, ed. Giles), which treats of the salvability of baptized infants even if they have not received the Eucharist, Lanfranc writes thus;

"You have sent us for solution certain questions of profane literature; but it is unsuitable to a bishop's calling to be occupied in such studies. Formerly, it is true, I wasted the period of my youth in such things; but when I undertook the pastoral charge, I determined that I ought to renounce them."

[h] Mr. Morison, in his most interesting Life of St. Bernard (p. 21, note 1), in commenting upon the statement that "to him" (St. Bernard) "the great past civilization of Greece and Rome was little more than a blank, across which moved the shadows of great names," says (a little too strongly; for our Herbert is a proof that the Roman Classics at all events were well known to the learned of the Middle Ages);

"The study of any writings not of Christian authorship had up to this period been neither practised nor recommended. The following anecdote of St. Odo of Cluny (who died 942) well illustrates the prevalent feeling:—

"'When he was minded to read the poems of Virgil, there was shewn to him in a vision a certain vessel, shewing beautiful outwardly, but within full of serpents, by whom he beheld himself all of a sudden to be compassed round about; and thereupon waking up he came to understand that the serpents were the lessons inculcated by the poets, the vessel, Virgil.'" [*Vita S. Odonis*, 'Annales Ord. St. Bened.,' Sæc. V.]

"John Foster, the essayist, would doubtless not have felt himself flattered at any resemblance he might bear to a middle-age saint. Yet

and Ovid recited by the same mouth, nor can that
heart set forth the truth of the Gospel aright, which
makes search into the shameful impurities of the poets:
he cannot be pure from the pollution of sin, who delights himself in a song which celebrates sins. Remember thine office, and rouse thy mind to consider what it
is thou offerest, and to whom thou offerest it; for thou
offerest not a corruptible animal, but the eternal Lamb[1],
which taketh away the sins of the world, and restoreth
life unto the world,—a most noble Victim, and needful
for thy sins, if thou offerest it worthily, if thou handlest
it with worthy hands; otherwise the office which thou
presumest to take upon thyself is turned into a judgment on the presumptuous, and worketh death to the

his essay on the 'Aversion of Men of Taste to Evangelical Religion,' contains passages which St. Odo might have cordially praised. Homer he thinks a most injurious author. 'Who can tell how much that passion for war may have been reinforced by the enthusiastic admiration with which young men read Homer? As to the far greater number of readers, it were vain to wish that pure Christian sentiment might be sufficiently recollected and loved, to accompany the study, and constantly to prevent the injurious impression, of the works of Pagan genius. A few maxims of Christianity will but feebly oppose the influence. The spirit of Homer will vanquish as irresistibly as Achilles vanquished.' St. Odo was even more moderate than this in his disapproval of the 'lessons inculcated by the poets.'"

Whoever wishes to gain a further insight into the "Dark Age View of Profane Learning," will do well to read Mr. Maitland's interesting Section on that subject in his "Dark Ages." (Sec. xi. pp. 171—187.) He shews that much as the Fathers and monastic writers dreaded the moral influence of the Classical authors, they found plenty of excuses for becoming acquainted with them. While Christians might not go down to Egypt for help, they might spoil the Egyptians; while they might not contract heathen alliances in a regular way, they might capture a heathen woman in war and wed her, after she had shaven her head and pared her nails;—they might taste Cicero, not as solid nourishment, but as a man takes dessert after dinner, and trifles with a few sweetmeats, &c. &c.

[1] The reader will not fail to notice these expressions, thrown out so recently after the doctrine of Transubstantiation had taken shape. Our author here seems to assert very definitely the doctrine repudiated in the Thirty-first Article of our Church, that in "the sacrifices of Masses the Priest offers Christ for the quick and the dead, to have remission of pain or guilt." See further for Herbert's Eucharistic opinions his Easter Sermon, p. 181 to the end, with the notes.

unworthy aspirant.' When the interview had gone no further than this, I was thrown into trouble and confusion of mind by reproofs administered with such dignity of manner, and began to ponder what I should say, and what apology I should offer in extenuation of the levity which had been brought home to me. But she, with angry countenance and altered tone, rebuked me with still sterner speech, and said, 'Thou canst not deceive God, nor allege unto Him as an excuse anything but what is really found in thy deeds and in thy conscience. Thou shouldest not have forgotten from what a dunghill God lifted thee up, and to what steps of dignity He hath advanced thee, having attained as thou hast by His grace a nobility of extraction, a security for thy person, an abundance of resources, a loftiness of rank, and an acquaintance and intimacy with men of the highest station, which thou hadst[j] not by nature. These, however, are but small matters, if you look at them in reference to more internal endowments; from God is derived into thy heart the piety whereby thou acknowledgest Him, the love with which thou lovest Him, the prudence wherewith thou orderest thine actions, the temperance by which thou restrainest thy passions when they provoke thee to sin, the fortitude by the strength of which thou calmest the waves of this troublesome world, the justice whereby thou renderest unto God the things that be His, and to thyself the things that be thine, and to every one of thy fellow-citizens what belongeth to him, with such regard to his rights as is

---

[j] We do not understand how *nobility of extraction* can be regarded as otherwise than an endowment of nature. Perhaps Herbert, having mixed up several endowments together, most of which came from God's special favour, forgot that he had mentioned nobility of extraction among them. The words of the original run thus;

"Debueras retinere quibus te ex stercoribus erexit Deus, et ad quos celsitudinum erexit gradus, quam non habueras ex naturâ, ex gratiâ Dei consecutus, et *generis claritatem*, corporis incolumitatem, divitiarum abundantiam, dignitatum celsitudinem, summorum virorum notitiam et familiaritatem."

The reader will not fail to observe the incidental testimony here borne to the high birth of our author.

meet. It remaineth to mention the hope which consoleth thee for the delay of thy reward, until thou comest unto that enjoyment of the truth, which thou art waiting for. There are also in thy mind rich stores of knowledge, which no plunderer can rob thee of, nor can thief carry them away, nor have moth and rust the power to destroy them. All these endowments come to thee from and by and in one God, from whom thou derivedst not only thine existence, but thine intellectual and rational existence, when thou, the image and likeness of God, wast stamped after the model of Him who created thee. Seest thou how many blessings thou hast received from thy Creator, and with what adornment of circumstance and of grace the author of thy being hath decked and ennobled thy mean and obscure estate? Most ungrateful of men, weigh well the argument which I have set before thee, and having poised the truth in thy own mind, pronounce a true sentence on the wantonness of thy conduct.' Then I 'calling to mind those scourges[k] of the presbyter Jerome, and with an

---

[k] The passage of Jerome alluded to is that on which Herbert's own vision seems to have been framed. Not that we would imply that the vision was an intentional fiction, but only that in his dream he fell unconsciously into a similar train of thought. We give the passage *in extenso*:—

"When several years ago I had renounced, for the kingdom of heaven's sake, home, parents, sister, relations, and (which is a still more difficult act of renunciation) the habit of taking dainty meals, and was setting out to fight my way to [the heavenly] Jerusalem, I found myself unable to do without the library, which with great care and labour I had collected for myself at Rome. And so, wretch that I was, I would fast as a preliminary to reading Tully; and after frequent nightly watchings, after the tears which the remembrance of my past sins drew forth from the very depths of my heart, I would take my Plautus in hand. If at any time I came to myself, and began to read the Prophets, their diction offended me by its ruggedness and want of elegance. I saw not the light, because my eyes were blind; yet I deemed not the fault to be in mine eyes, but in the sun. While the old serpent palmed off on me this deceit, about Midlent a fever poured into my vitals, and attacked my already weakened body, and so unremittingly preyed upon my wretched frame that (which perhaps may seem incredible) my bones would scarce cleave to my flesh. Meanwhile preparations were made for my interment; for the rest of my frame becoming cold, the vital heat only just fluttered in the breast, which was the

earnest effort of the memory thinking over Boethius's[1] work, the Consolation of Philosophy, I confessed my sole part of me that retained any warmth; when suddenly I was caught away in spirit, and dragged before the tribunal of the Judge, where such was the light, and such the glory which streamed from the brightness of those who stood around, that falling to the earth I dared not lift up mine eyes. When interrogated on my condition, I made answer that I was a Christian. To which He who presided made this retort; 'Thou liest,' said He, 'thou art a Ciceronian, not a Christian; *for where thy treasure is, there will thy heart be also.*' Thereupon I became dumb, and amidst the scourges which I received (for He had ordered me to be beaten) I was still more tortured by the [internal] fires of conscience, while I repeated to myself that versicle; '*Who will give thee thanks in the pit?*' Then began I to cry out, and in wailing accents to say; 'Have mercy on me, O Lord, have mercy on me.' And these cries made themselves heard even amid the sound of the stripes. At length those who stood by, throwing themselves down before the Judge's knees, implored Him to pardon the indiscretion of my youth, and give me an opportunity of repenting of my error, on the understanding that hereafter I should be made to pay the uttermost farthing, if I at any time read the books of Pagan Literature. I who, from being in so dire a strait, was quite willing to promise even greater things than these, began to abjure profane studies, and, calling His Holy Name to witness, said; 'Lord, if ever I shall possess profane books, if ever I shall read them, I will allow that I have denied thee.' After duly making oath to this effect, I was discharged, and returned to the land of the living. To the surprise of every one I opened my eyes, which were bathed in such showers of tears, as conciliated belief to my story even among the incredulous, from the grief which I manifested. Nor had my state been that of sleep, or of idle dreams, by which oftentimes we are deluded. The tribunal, before which I lay prostrate, attests the reality [of what I went through]; the solemn sentence, which I so much dreaded, attests it. May it never be my lot again to incur such torture, to have shoulder-blades livid with stripes, to feel blows after falling asleep, and in consequence to read things sacred thenceforth with a zeal which I had never shewn before for studies profane!" (Hieron. Opp., tom. iv. pars ii. col. 42, 43. Epistola xviii. ad Eustochium de Custodia Virginitatis.)

Alcuin (born 735), who, when a boy of eleven, was much attached to Classical lore, got off, we are told, with a frightening, the impression of which never forsook him in after life. He had been sent by his schoolmaster to keep company with an old monk, who was afraid of being left alone at night. The monk not rising to matins, his bed was surrounded by reproachful demons, who inflicted upon him a severe drubbing. The boy lay trembling under his coverlet, while this castigation was proceeding, his heart smiting him for his love of the Classics; and he vowed, "O Lord Jesus, if thou wilt deliver me from their bloody hands, and afterwards I am negligent of the vigils of thy Church and of the service of lauds, *and continue to love Virgil more than the melody of the Psalms*, then may I undergo such correction; only I earnestly pray that thou wouldst now

ignorance, and exposed the disgracefulness of my folly, which had now become by long use inveterate. 'True,

deliver me." But his fright had not yet proceeded to its extremity. The demons descried him huddled up in his bedclothes, and were preparing to give him a castigation similar to that which they had inflicted on his senior. But somewhat mollified by his screaming and tears, they agreed to let him off after operating upon his corns (risum teneatis, amici?) as a reminder of his vow. The bedclothes at the foot of the bed were turned up for the purpose; but Alcuin jumping out of bed, crossed himself, and sung stoutly the 12th Psalm, "Help me, Lord, for there is not one godly man left,"—whereupon, dismayed by the sight and sound of so much youthful piety, the infernal chiropodists vanished. The story is told very humorously by Mr. Maitland from Mabillon, pp. 181, 182 (*Dark Ages*). Alcuin was so much impressed by this juvenile experience, adds Mr. Maitland, that he specially warned his own pupils against polluting themselves with the impure eloquence of Virgil's language; and having (by the gift of discerning spirits) detected a father, who had ordered his sons to read Virgil with him under the rose, exposed and rebuked him as a *Virgilian*,—a term framed, no doubt, upon the model of that which the Eternal Judge applied to Jerome, "a Ciceronian."

[1] "With an earnest effort of the memory thinking over Boethius's work, the Consolation of Philosophy."

The reference is specially to the opening chapter of Boethius's work, in which Philosophy presents herself to him as "a woman of almost reverend countenance," who combined an appearance of great antiquity with vigour and a keen penetrating glance,—a person evidently full of years, like Moses, but like Moses, her eye not dim, nor her natural force abated. She was clad in a garment of finest texture, on the lower hem of which was embroidered a P, while the upper hem was decorated with a TH, and lower and upper were connected by a design of steps. (This emblematized the Practical and Theoretical Philosophy, and the gradual ascent from the latter to the former.) What follows shall be given in the writer's own words; "As soon as she saw the Muses, who are Patronesses of Poetry, standing by my bed, and dictating to me the language in which I should vent my griefs, 'Who,' cried she, 'hath allowed these wretched harlots of the stage to have access to this poor sick man? So far are they from relieving his pain by any remedies, that they actually foster his complaint by the sweet poisons they instil! These are they who kill the crop of reason, naturally so fertile in fruits, with the barren thorns of the passions, and who only inure men to the endurance of disease instead of liberating them from it. Had your caresses, ye Muses, only debauched from his fidelity to me a profane and ignorant person (as is mostly your way), I could have endured it with greater equanimity. But ye have actually laid your polluting hands on him whom I have nourished up in the studies of the Porch and the Academy. Begone then, ye Sirens, who beguile men to their destruction, and leave this patient to be treated and healed by my Muses.' Rebuked in these terms, the tuneful choir cast their eyes down to the

O Lady,' said I, 'are the things which you recount, nor can they be refuted by any resistance which I might think to oppose to the truth. I have sinned, I confess, and that not only in the reading of heathen authors, but

ground, and with countenances the blushes of which betrayed their shame, left the room." Thereupon Philosophy seated herself on the end of Boethius's bed, and began to remonstrate with him on his infidelity to her, and afterwards to instil her consolations.

It is quite clear that both this passage of Boethius, and that above quoted from Jerome, had sunk so deeply into Herbert's mind that his vision took its complexion and configuration from what he had read in them.

The "De Consolatione Philosophiæ" was the work of a period when consolation was sorely needed by the author. His protection of the provincials from rapine, and his setting his face against the oppression of the Ostrogoth officials, at the court of Theodoric, brought down upon Boethius a charge of attempting to deliver Rome from the barbarians, and a sentence of confiscation and death. He was imprisoned in the Baptistery of the Church at Ticinum (where he wrote the "Consolatio"), and afterwards beheaded, or, as some say, put to death by torture. It was a great fall for a man who had been *princeps Senatûs*, a high officer at the Ostrogoth court, and the father of two consuls,—and it must have needed every moral support, which Boethius had within his reach, to hold him up under such crushing calamities. Hence a very deep interest attaches to the treatise. Christianity is never referred to in it, which seems conclusive against the author's being a Christian, although he was considered in the Mediæval Church as a saint and martyr. "In the total ignorance of Greek writers" (says Dean Stanley, in his most interesting notice of Boethius in Smith's Dictionary of Roman and Greek Antiquities, vol. i. p. 497) "which prevailed from the sixth to the fourteenth century, he was looked upon as the head and type of all philosophers, as Augustine was of all theology, and Virgil of all literature; and hence the tendency throughout the Middle Ages to invest him with a distinctly Christian and almost miraculous character.... The first author who quotes his works is Hincmar, A.D. 850; and in the subsequent literature of the Middle Ages the 'Consolatio' gave birth to imitations, translations, and commentaries innumerable. ... Alfred the Great's translation into Anglo-Saxon is doubly interesting, (1) as one of the earliest specimens of Anglo-Saxon Literature; (2) as the chief literary relic of Alfred himself, whose own mind appears not only in the freedom of the translation, but also in large original insertions relative to the kingly office, or to Christian history, which last fact strikingly illustrates the total absence of any such in Boethius's own work."

But justice cannot be done by extracts. The whole of Dean Stanley's Article (it is not long) should be read by those who desire to be informed on the subject of Boethius. He was born about the last quarter of the fifth century, of one of the most illustrious houses in Rome.

also in the imitation of the base conduct and actions of the same. It remains that thou shouldest prescribe what thou wilt, and I will labour to carry into effect what thou shalt prescribe. I seek not impunity, but [on the other hand] I would implore thee to inflict such correction as is meet; the more severely thy hand shall lash the sides of my negligent soul, so much the more abundant will be the fruits of thy correction which I shall exhibit. Come,' said I, ' most passionless Judge' (for by the apostolic form which the figure wore it now seemed to me to be a judge); 'exact from me a worthy revenge; punish my levity; chastise my wantonness; and restore unto the truth him who hitherto has opposed himself to discipline.' To which it replied; 'Enough that thou art scourged by thine own penitence. By the sincerity with which thou hast acknowledged and confessed thy faults thou shalt win a perfect absolution from them.' With these words it disappeared, and by its disappearance it restored me, after my long abstraction, to present things. Whereupon, my well-beloved sons, I took counsel thenceforward to toil over the Sacred Books, to search into the sage maxims of the holy fathers, to alter the misshapen proportions of my studies, and to bring back my way of life and my actions to the impress and character of the Truth. Henceforth I will speak to you of Christ [only], I will write to you of Christ, by my words and by my letters will I imprint Christ on your minds, doing this one thing specially, and for the sake of that doctrine refraining from propounding to you any other."

Here is one more letter, in a similar strain, to two other Boys who were "his clerics," that is, engaged under him, as acolytes or otherwise, in the Services of his Church :—

LETTER XX.

To Samson and Roger, his Clerks [m].

Samson and Roger are lectured upon expensiveness and love of games, and warned that they will be strictly examined in their studies, when they return to Herbert.

"Herbert to Samson and Roger his Clerks.

"See that ye waste not your days, and waste not also the money of your parents, by laying it out upon vanities and useless articles of self-indulgence. I sent you [to school] to learn, not to play; bear in mind your vocation. I say to you moreover, take heed that, on your return, you do not prove a laughing-stock to your companions, and a disgrace to your friends. We have among us those who will be well able to test your proficiency in your studies, nor will the labour you have bestowed and the advancement you have made easily escape my penetration; wherefore fast, watch, toil; be slow in pursuing games, constant in your studies. I would have you first read the authors [n], next get up the trivium, thirdly the quadrivium. Until you have

---

[m] The word *Clerk* is only an abbreviation of the Latin *Clericus*, meaning a *Clergyman*. All [Clergymen, even of the higher orders, are, strictly speaking, *clerks*. (Thus the Clerk of the Royal Closet is with ourselves one of the Bishops.) But the word soon became appropriated to the inferior orders of the mediæval Hierarchy, subdeacons, acolytes, exorcists, door-keepers, and so forth. As these minor orders gradually dropped off, laymen took their places as assistants in the conduct of Divine Worship, and hence in our Cathedrals we have bodies of lay-clerks. The Prayer-book contemplates *Clerks* in every Parish. Thus in the Daily Service, "The Minister, Clerks, and people, shall say the Lord's Prayer;" in the Marriage Service, "The Minister or Clerks, going to the Lord's Table, shall say or sing this Psalm;" in the Burial Service, "The Priest and Clerks, meeting the Corpse at the entrance of the Churchyard, shall say, or sing;" and in the Commination Service, "The Priest and Clerks, kneeling (in the place where they are accustomed to say the Litany) shall say this Psalm."

But soon the *Clerks* dwindled down to one, the Parish Clerk of our present Parishes. A single clerk is only spoken of once in the Prayer-book, where the man is directed to lay the Ring upon the book with the accustomed duty to the Priest and Clerk. (Dr. Jebb, quoted in Hook's Church Dictionary.)

[n] By the "authors" he means probably Sedulius, Donatus, Juvencus, Pompeius Trogus, and so forth. For *trivium* and *quadrivium*, see above, p. 36, note x.

mastered these, do not presume on any consideration to return to me. Send me some of your compositions both in verse and prose; I shall soon understand from them how you are getting on."

And here another, addressed to an elder youth, and to two juniors, who were his pupils. It shews the high appreciation of Logic at that time entertained by the learned :—

LETTER LIII.

To W. G. and W., a Circular°.

"Herbert to W. G. and W., a Circular.

"I write the same letter to you all, although the relation in which you stand to one another, and which binds each of you to the rest, is different; for the preceptor is to be admonished in one manner, the pupils in another. The instruction to be given to the preceptor is, that he should studiously govern his pupils by example, rather than teach by means of words. On the pupils it is equally enjoined that they give all diligence to rise to the same level with their master, since then will the disciple be perfect when he is as his master. A philosopher contemns sumptuous banquets and copious cups; and taking delight as he does in prolonging his abstinences and his vigils, he is incapable of be-

[margin note: W. G. and W. are exhorted to self-denial in the pursuit of their studies, and particularly of logic.]

° "Ad W. G. et W. apares.
  Herbertus W. G. et W. aparibus.'
  The word *appar* the writers of lower Latin use to denote a general letter addressed, *mutatis mutandis*, to different persons. In the superscription of this letter, "Herbertus W. G. et W. aparibus," the adjective "aparibus" does not agree with W. G. et W., but with *epistolis* understood; and the full translation would be "Herbert to W. G. and W. in a circular letter." Ducange gives an instance of the use of the word, drawn from the letter which Cœur de Lion, when setting out on his Crusade, addressed to the nobles who were to govern the kingdom in his absence; "Richardus rex Angl. Willelmo Cancellario, G. Filio-Petri, W. Marescalle, et H. Bard. et W. Briwer, Apparibus." The word seems to be commonly, though not always, used in the ablative plural.

coming the slave of pleasure. He who is bent upon pursuing the liberal arts must free himself from the trammels of his vices; for they are not called liberal from their own nature, but specially on this account, that they have a tendency to raise and liberalize the minds of those who study them. Work hard to finish your course of logic, since, when once the door of the interior of a house is thrown open, the innermost chambers are reached with little trouble. Give heed to what I say; for no secrets are hid from him whom logic enlightens; but acuteness in logic is not acquired except by a studious and earnest mind, a spare and mortified body, and wakeful eyes. And on the other hand, the yearly unceasing round of the fables of Ovid is growing very wearisome to me. Have done with these follies, that ye may be known in the Lord's community for some branch of reading which is at least useful. Away with your entreaties to the contrary; no more let me speak to you in the accents of a father's fondness; henceforth look ye only for the strict severity of a master and judge, who will shew you no indulgence."

It was probably at the monastery of Fécamp that Herbert received his education, where he afterwards became a professed monk, and rose, we are told, to fill the office of Prior [p]. The abbey of Fécamp had been founded by the Norman Duke, Richard the Fearless, in the latter part of

Herbert made Prior of Fécamp.

---

[p] "to fill the office of Prior."

So William of Malmesbury; "Herebertus, ... ex Priori Fiscanii, et ex Abbate Rameseiæ factus episcopus;" and Bartholomew Cotton, who mentions that he discharged with vigour the duties of the Prior's Office; "Hic Herbertus, ... Fiscanni monachus, post ejusdem loci prioratum strenue administratum, translatus in Angliam," &c. (See the Authorities at the end of the Volume.)

We have looked through M. le Roux de Lincy's "Essai sur l'Abbaye de Fécamp," without finding anything about Herbert's Priorate; but this may well be, as the Essay does not profess to be a history.

the tenth century. Mr. Church gives, in his "Life of Anselm," (p. 17,) this account of its foundation, from Sir Francis Palgrave :—

"At Fécamp, where he had a palace, Richard the Fearless built or rebuilt an abbey and minster in prospect of the sea, from which his fathers had come; minster and palace, as at Westminster, Holyrood, and the Escurial, were in close neighbourhood. The church, one of the first of which we have any details, was costly and magnificent for the time; an architect was carefully sought out for it, and it was 'constructed of "well-squared masonry by a Gothic hand,"—the Goth being unquestionably a master mason from Lombardy or the Exarchate.' 'It was adorned by lofty towers, beautifully finished without and richly ornamented within.' 'There was one object, however, which excited much speculation. It was a large block of stone placed right across the path which led to the transept doorway, so close to the portal as to be beneath the drip of the eaves..... Fashioned and located by Duke Richard's order, the stone was hollowed out so as to form a huge strong chest, which might be used as a coffin or a sarcophagus. Its present employment, however, was for the living and not for the dead. On the eve of every Lord's-day the chest, or whatever it might be called, was filled to the brim with the finest wheat-corn—then a cate, or luxury, as it is now considered in many parts of France. To this receptacle the poor resorted, and each filled his measure of grain.' They also received a dole of money, and an almoner carried the gift to the sick. When Richard died, then the purpose of the chest was made clear. 'His last instructions were, that the chest should contain his corpse, lying where the foot should tread, and the dew descend, and the waters of heaven should fall.' He—

> "'Marked for his own,
> Close to those cloistered steps, a burial-place,
> That every foot might fall with heavier tread,
> Trampling his vileness.'"

The period which elapsed between the burial of Duke Richard and Herbert's being sent to the conventual school of the Abbey of Fécamp (probably not much exceeding half a century) was not long enough to obliterate the founder's memory, nor the associations which gathered round his gravestone. Such associations were the mould, into which Herbert's juvenile piety was thrown. And the type it preserved in after years seems to have been that given it by the mould. An acute sense of the sins of his past life, and profound humiliation for them, was one great feature of his spiritual character. In the early dawn of life, when his soul was yet tender and plastic, he had learnt the lesson of humiliation, as his feet pressed the grave of Richard the Fearless, and as his eye saw the raindrops on that grave twinkling with the sunbeam, — a beautiful emblem of the way in which the smile of Heaven irradiates the tears of true penitence.

Possible effect of early associations upon Herbert.

The great glory of the Abbey of Fécamp was the relic of the Saviour's Precious Blood. According to the legend (formally drawn up, in all probability, at the end of the eleventh century, but doubtless floating about from mouth to mouth in the Abbey ever since its foundation), Joseph of Arimathæa, who had scraped this Blood from around "the print of the nails" in the Lord's hands and feet, and had carefully preserved it, bequeathed it on his death to his nephew Isaac. Isaac stole away to Sidon with the sacred treasure, and secreted it (together with the knife that

Legend of "the Precious Blood," and how it came to Fécamp.

had been used in collecting it) in the hollowed trunk of a fig-tree which grew on the border of the sea, the bark of which closed up again miraculously as soon as the relics were enclosed in it. The sea seeming to woo the fig-tree by lovingly washing its roots, Isaac cut down the trunk, and committed it to the waves. It sank into the waters and disappeared; but in the course of ages was washed into a bay of France, where the waters withdrew from it, and left it stranded amid sand and seaweed. Here it put forth branches, and the fig-tree being unknown in those parts, it drew attention, and was removed on a waggon drawn by oxen. At a certain spot the trunk became so heavy that the waggon broke underneath it. It fell to the earth, and resisted all attempts to move it further. Thus was indicated the place where the great Abbey Church of Fécamp (a name meaning the "Plain of the Fig-tree," *Fici Campus* [q]) should be founded.

<small>Supposed etymology of the name Fécamp.</small>

---

[q] Another etymology, however, is given in p. 4. of M. Leroux de Lincy's work, where we are told that according to some antiquaries, Fécamp was the seat of the Roman prefect of the Province of Brittany, who there collected the tribute (quasi *Fisci campus*). What different associations are awakened by the term "Exchequer Plain," from those to which the graceful legend about the holy fig-tree of Fécamp gives rise!

The reader will be pleased, we think, with the following description of the natural beauty and fertility of the plain of Fécamp. It is drawn from Archbp. Baudry's encomium of Fécamp, as quoted by M. Leroux de Lincy (Essay, pp. 36, 37).

"This place resembles the terrestrial Paradise. It is situated in a fair valley between two hills; on one side are lands in cultivation, on the other a delicious forest. These divide the country so equally between them that one might think them to have been made by the hand of men, and at the same period of time. The shade formed by the branches of the trees is so dense as to be a delightful refreshment to the eye and a protection of the soil; it intercepts the burning rays of the sun, and is a shelter from the rain.

Duke Richard, minded to restore (or rather reconstruct) the Church, which had fallen into decay, and having found the above history in the archives of the former Abbey, made search for and discovered the miraculous trunk, and having drawn forth the sacred relic, placed it beneath a pillar of the new edifice, near the altar of Saint Saviour. Here it soon received a miraculous accession. For in a village church, about a league from the Abbey, the bread and wine with which the parish priest was celebrating the Eucharist at St. Maclou's altar were changed into actual Flesh and Blood. Duke Richard, having ascertained the truth of the miracle, added the Flesh and Blood to the former relic; and both together became the great centre round which all the worship of the Abbey revolved. The Mass of the Precious Blood was said there, the passage of St. Peter about our not being redeemed with corruptible things, as silver and

<small>Mass of "the Precious Blood,"</small>

> The trees shoot up straight into the air, but not sufficiently close together to hinder one's walking among them. The sea is quite near to Fécamp, indeed not a mile distant. It abounds in fish. Its ebb and flow fertilise this coast, which furnishes a secure harbour. A gentle and limpid stream waters the valley. Springs are found there, and fertile gardens filled with apple-trees. The little river which flows through the fortress loses itself in graceful bends, which protect the ramparts and the fortifications. From the river Seine to Fécamp there are about fifteen miles, and the fishery, which is abundant in these parts, is the means of support for the inhabitants. The monastery, girt by great walls, is almost entirely covered with lead. They compare it to the Heavenly Jerusalem; they call it the gate of Heaven, the palace of the Lord. Gold and silver blaze in every part of it; one sees there silk and ornaments, and very many relics under the invocation of the Holy Trinity; and there is preserved the precious Blood of Jesus Christ, who was buried by Nicodemus, as St. John tells us. Pilgrims come in crowds from all countries to this monastery, which is dedicated to the Holy Trinity."

gold, but with the Precious Blood of Christ, as of a lamb without blemish and without spot, forming the Epistle; while the Gospel was the account of the Agony and Bloody Sweat, as recorded by St. Luke. At the end of the Litanies of the Precious Blood, and other forms of devotion having reference to the great Relic, is given us the following touching

Act of Contrition, to be said daily.

" O good Jesus, gentle Saviour of my soul, from the very depth of my heart I ask pardon of Thee for all the sins I have committed against Thy Divine Majesty. Alas, my God, Thou didst so love me that Thou hast shed Thy Precious Blood for so detestable a creature. Ah, my Lord, let me not lose the fruit of that which is so precious. Let me rather die a thousand deaths, my God, than commit wilfully one single deadly sin against Thy so great goodness. And whatever death may befall me, O good Jesus, suffer not Thy poor servant, redeemed by Thy Precious Blood, to incur everlasting damnation. *and devotions in connection with it.*

Lord's Prayer. Hail Mary. Creed."

Such were some of the devotions which Herbert's early monastic life must have imprinted on his mind,—such the devotional associations in the midst of which he was reared.

If the dates of Herbert's life are given us with any approach to correctness, his monastic career at Fécamp must have been passed under two Abbots, both men of eminence,—the first, John Dalie, who ruled the Abbey from A.D. 1031 to

A.D. 1082; and the second, William de Ros, who, on the death of John, was translated by the Conqueror from the Abbey of St. Stephen's at Caen to that of Fécamp. If we are right in conjecturing the date of Herbert's birth to have fallen about 1050, he had probably taken the full monastic vow at Fécamp in the year 1075, when the Conqueror kept there the Easter festival (after the custom of his ancestors), and there consecrated to God his daughter Cecilia, who afterwards became Abbess of the Holy Trinity at Caen. This Royal taking of the veil would be one of the reminiscences of Herbert's early manhood. Abbot John was a superior under whom we like to think of him as receiving his education, and taking his vows—a man every way suited to inspire his congregation of monks with the love of virtue and devotion. John was a native of Ravenna, celebrated for learning, devotion, and knowledge of medicine; whose great gifts were enhanced, says the contemporary chronicler, by contrast with the smallness of his stature, which smallness procured for him the title of *Johannelinus*, or "Little John." A most interesting prayer by this "Little John," on the occasion of his entering on the office of Abbot, ("I know and am assured that Thou canst produce good and great increase of Thy flock by me, little and weak as I am; for I am but a child, and a little man of no strength, having none of the qualities which should be required, or which are worthy of such an office," &c., &c.), as also the Preface of a devotional work which he wrote for the Empress Agnes, (consort of Henry III. of Germany, who died in 1056, and mother of Henry IV.; mother-in-law, therefore, of our Princess Maud, daughter of Henry I. of England), are given by Mr. Maitland in his "Dark Ages," (pp. 315—321,) from whose notice of the Abbot these particulars are borrowed. "May God be with you," (he writes in this Preface,) "and may His hand strengthen you, that, becoming like the living creature with wings and eyes, you may every day make progress *in both modes of life,— now with Martha actively serving Christ in His members, now with Mary sitting in contemplation at the feet of the Lord, and intently listening to the words of His mouth,*—so that, *by well-doing and pure contemplation*, you may arrive at that beatific vision in which the Son speaketh openly of the Father;"—a great testimony from the pen of a regular priest to the importance of blending the active with the contemplative life.

and his devotional writings.

Most interesting it is to think of Herbert's having received his education (as is likely) under the auspices of such an Abbot, and having derived from a mind so pious and so pure his early religious impressions. A correspondence is extant between this "Little John" and William the Conqueror, which shews at all events that the attention of the new Royal Family of England had been directed to the Abbey of Fécamp. It may have been from John that the Conqueror and his sons first heard of Herbert, as a youth

Herbert probably educated under Abbot John.

How Herbert may have been brought before the Conqueror and his sons.

of great intellectual promise, and attainments beyond his age. It was probably under John that Herbert became Prior of Fécamp, in which capacity his vigorous administration may have recommended him more strongly to the notice of the Royal Family of England, and pointed him out as a candidate for higher preferment. But that preferment was not to come in John's days or in the Conqueror's days.

<small>William de Ros, Abbot of Fécamp, 1082.</small>

Abbot John died in 1082; and William de Ros, as we have said, was summoned from Caen to succeed him. From his modesty, purity, and graciousness this Abbot was named "the Maiden," and won all hearts. Great as previous Abbots had been, he outshone them all as the sun outshines the stars, and attracted to his monastery many persons of eminence both in the Church and in the world, just as Solomon by the fame of his wisdom drew the Queen of Sheba to his court. He only lived for works of piety and charity, visiting the hospitals, consoling the sick and afflicted by his instructions, and kissing the hands of the poor. He it was who instituted

<small>The daily dole at Fécamp.</small>

the daily dole which, down to the time of the revolution of 1789, was given to all the poor who presented themselves at the Abbey gates of Fécamp. This dole (suspended only during the month of August) consisted of half a pound of bread to each applicant; and we are told that in times when corn was dear, as many as twelve or fifteen hundred applicants would present themselves daily. By such doles as these many of these much-abused monasteries did, in a rough way no doubt, and without organization, the work which is now done by the Poor Law. After being five or six years under Abbot William's rule, Herbert was preferred to the mitred Abbey of Ramsey, in Huntingdonshire. *Herbert made Abbot of Ramsey, 1088.*

The two following letters shew the deep affection which he retained in after life for the house of Fécamp, an affection quite confirmatory of the statement that his boyhood had been passed there, and that he had there imbibed the first rudiments of learning and piety. These letters are not addressed either to "Little John" or William de Ros, but to their successor, Roger of Argences, who was ordained priest with the famous chronicler Ordericus Vitalis on the feast of St. Thomas, in the year 1107, and the next day received benediction as Abbot of Fécamp. It was in his days that Baudry, Archbishop of Dol, in Brittany, one of the principal movers of the Holy War, made a pilgrimage to Fécamp, and contracted an intimacy with its Abbot. To him Roger expressed himself as overwhelmed with the responsibility and dignity of his office, and as feeling himself utterly unworthy of a charge in which William de Ros had preceded him. Baudry was charmed by all he heard and saw, and frequently repeated his visits to Fécamp, and improved his acquaintance with the inmates. *His affection for Fécamp in after life. Roger d'Argences, fourth Abbot of Fécamp, 1107.*

To this Roger d'Argences, then, Herbert wrote as follows. The reader will understand that the letters, which belong to a date later than

1107, are only introduced here by anticipation, because both of them refer to the period which Herbert spent at Fécamp.

LETTER V.

To Roger the Abbot of Fécamp.

<small>Herbert professes his love and reverence for Fécamp, and begs to have a copy made of Suetonius.</small>

"Herbert to Roger the Abbot of Fécamp sendeth greeting.

"Being sprung from the womb of the Church at Fécamp, I have no need to commend to you my obedience, seeing that one of us is the father, the other the son, of the same Church. I beseech you that you will love me as a father, and instruct me as an Abbot, since I for my part desire to return your love as a son, and to obey you as a monk. Pray get Suetonius transcribed for me (I cannot find him in England;) and when he is transcribed, send the book to me by Dancard, the Presbyter, or by any other whom you may be minded to send on your errands [r]."

LETTER XXXIV.

To R., the Abbot of Fecamp.

"Herbert the Bishop of Norwich to R., the Abbot of Fécamp greeting.

"Let your fatherly goodness consider brother Stannard [s], whom I send as bearer of my message to the

---

[r] The literal rendering of these words would be, "Dancard, the Presbyter, or any other serving brother of your house whom you may be minded to send." The word Presbyter, however, is only another designation of Priest,—a member of the second order of the Christian ministry;—and it denotes not the age of the person holding the office, but the dignity of his order. It is hardly likely that a Presbyter would be employed merely as a servant. Ducange gives an instance in which the word Presbyter is used merely as the equivalent of "monk." Possibly that may be the case here. Or the meaning may be; "or by any other—one of your serving brothers."

[s] "brother Stannard." There are several families of the name of Stannard resident in Norwich and its neighbourhood at the present day.

King, commended to you by your remembrance of the ancient intimacy and affection subsisting between yourself and him (in case any necessity of his should demand your help). When he seeks for counsel or assistance, let him find a substitute for my presence in yours. Know ye that the uses and customs of the Church of Fécamp are observed by our brethren at Norwich, so far as we have been able to draw them out by questioning from the Lord Baldwin[u], or so far as I myself can collect them from memory: but, as you know from your own experience, the mind, when distracted by temporal wants, becomes unequal to retain ecclesiastical usages of this sort; for which reason I have often purposed to send one or two brethren to Fécamp, who might learn by personal inspection the practices which they might think meet to be transferred to our own brethren. This, however, I thought should only be done under your eye and by your permission. It is entirely left therefore to your discretion what answer you will make to our humble[v] petition in this matter. I send you one serving brother, to tarry some little time in your kitchen; keep him with you, and give orders that he be instructed in the secrets of that craft.

Herbert commends Brother Stannard to the Abbot of Fécamp, and professes his devotion to the Abbey, and his desire to frame the usages of his own Convent on that model.

[u] One would like to find this "Lord Baldwin" to be the same with Archbishop Baudry of Dol, whose admiration of Fécamp we have touched on above. The orthography of names in those days fluctuated much; and possibly it may be so.

[v] The very humble way in which Herbert, though at the time a Bishop, speaks to the Abbot of Fécamp, seems to shew the veneration in which Abbots were held. The tendency in the mediæval Church, which developed itself more and more as time went on, was to elevate the regular above the secular Clergy. The Abbots were ever encroaching, and their efforts after aggrandizement (favoured by the Popes, who always shewed themselves jealous of the Bishops, and prone to foster rival powers, more dependent on themselves) were crowned with success. But the independence of Abbots upon Bishops was not in accordance with the principles of the Primitive Church. "According to the ancient laws of Christendom, confirmed by general Councils, all heads of monasteries, whether abbots or priors, owed canonical obedience to their diocesan. And the same law subsisted till the Reformation, wherever special exemptions had not been granted, which however were numerous." (Hook's Church Dictionary, Art. ABBOT.)

Finally, be well assured that the profession which I made at the altar of Fécamp, and the benediction[1] which I received from the same altar, cannot be obliterated from my heart by any lapse of time, by any accession of worldly wealth; but, on the other hand, the more I advance in years, the more devoted and the more fervent am I in my obedience, and in complying with your commands, my venerable Father."

The last letter shews how desirous Herbert was of framing the "uses" of his Church at Norwich on those of the Abbey Church at Fécamp, with which he had been familiar in early life. Perhaps another indication of his desire to connect the two churches is to be found in the circumstance that Norwich Cathedral, as well as Fécamp Abbey, was dedicated to the Holy Trinity. And a third may be, that the arms of the Diocese of Norwich are the same three mitres which formed the arms of the Abbey of Fécamp, and which were adopted by the Abbot to indicate the three Suffragan Abbeys which owned his supremacy.—We think it will interest our readers to see the ground-plan of that part of the present structure which Herbert could have seen. Abbot William de Ros's church, which could not (according to the chronology adopted by us, see above, p. 62, *marg.*) have been begun before 1082, *may have been looked* upon by Her-

---

[1] "the profession ... and the benediction."
The benediction referred to is that which novices received when, after completing their novitiate, they took the vows, and became professed monks. Ducange gives instances in which *Benedictio* is used as exactly equivalent to *Professio*, e.g. "Novitii semper ad Missam benedicentur, et Abbas eam cantet." (Novices shall always make their profession at Mass; and let the Abbot sing the Mass on that occasion.)

Benediction was also the term used for the admission of an Abbot to his office by the Bishop.—Bishops themselves were made by Consecration; Abbots by Benediction.

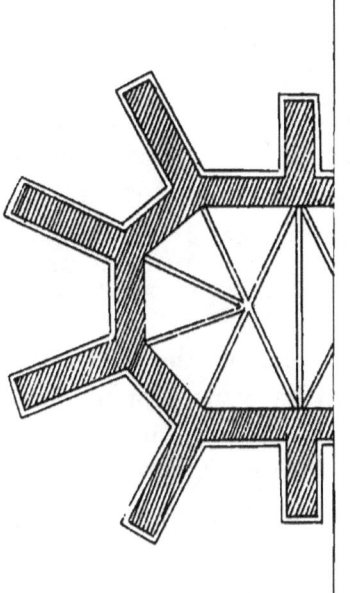

EAST END OF FÉCAMP ABBEY CHURCH.

bert. But of this nothing now remains, save the parts marked black in the accompanying plan, indicative of two northern apsidal chapels (the one semicircular, and the other rectangular) situated at the point where the apse narrows in towards the Lady Chapel. These remains are too slight to enable us to say for certain whether or not William de Ros's Church supplied a model for Herbert's. Yet M. Bouet, to whose kind assistance we are indebted for this plan, says in a letter which accompanies it;—

"Je pense que les constructions de Guillaume de Ros ont eu une grande influence sur les constructions de ses successeurs qui ont altéré les formes tout en conservant le plan en grande partie."

And the ground-plan of the present Abbey Church of Fécamp is very similar to that of Norwich Cathedral.—Before we bid adieu to the subject of Fécamp Abbey, we may just mention two objects in the interior of it, which excited the admiration of Archbishop Baldric (or Baudry) of Dol, before referred to. The one was a wheel which, by an ingenious mechanism, not only turned continually on its axis, but sometimes mounted high into the air, sometimes sank. It was designed to teach the brethren of Fécamp a moral lesson through the eye—the restless movement of a world which passeth away, and the instability of fortune which raises a man to-day on a pinnacle, to-morrow drops him into a dungeon. The wheel, as it sank after rising, seemed to be vocal with the words of Wolsey; *[margin: Objects of interest in Fécamp Abbey.] [margin: The wheel of fortune.]*

"I have touched the highest point of all my greatness;
And, from that full meridian of my glory,
I haste now to my setting."

Our Prelate had his ups and downs in life, over which he bemoans himself bitterly in his twelfth Letter; and perhaps at those moments he was reminded of the wheel of fortune in Fécamp Church. — The other was "a certain instrument of music which, by means of large iron tubes, emitted all sorts of sounds, sometimes deep, sometimes shrill, and resembled a chorus in which children, young men, and old men should unite their voices. They call it an organ," says Baudry, "and play upon it on different occasions." "I know there are some priests who, having no organ in their church, grievously censure the use of such music" (Wesleys of the twelfth century, who might have said with Wesley that they entertained "no objection to an organ in a church so long as it was neither seen nor heard;" but the views of these priests were to be followed neither in the Abbey Church of Fécamp, nor in the Cathedral Church of Norwich, and we leave them to be disposed of by Archbishop Baudry and Dr. Buck), "but they seem to have forgotten that it was by the melodies of his harp that David soothed and chased away Saul's access of madness," &c., &c.

The Organ.

Mediæval objections to Organs.

But we must hasten on with the fortunes of our Prelate. We have seen how easily he may have become acquainted with the Conqueror's family; and possibly there may have been something in his pliant (too pliant) humour and courtly manners, which attracted towards him the violent and domineering William Rufus, at all times so impatient of control. At all events in

Herbert de Losinga.

the winter of A.D. 1087[1], the year of the death of the Conqueror and the accession of his younger son, Herbert was sent for to England, and received an appointment as Abbot of Ramsey, a Benedictine Abbey in Huntingdonshire[a]. Edward the

A.D. 1087, Herbert sent for to England, and made Abbot of Ramsey.

---

[1] Bartholomew Cotton gives only three years for his Abbacy. This, as he was appointed Bishop in 1091, would fix his appointment as Abbot to the year 1088. (See *Authorities.*) But Leland makes his Abbacy to have lasted *four* years (*Authorities*). And the Register of Ramsey Abbey preserved in the Royal Exchequer (probably the best authority on the subject) also makes his Abbacy of *four* years' duration. It is a singular fact that in a MS. of the early part of the fourteenth century, preserved in the British Museum, which gives a list of the Abbots of Ramsey, with a brief notice of each, all mention of Herbert is omitted. The notices of the Abbots immediately preceding and succeeding are as follows;

"Eylsinus, abbas. Iste constituit celebrare conceptionem B. V. M. (This seems to shew how late was the general recognition of the Festival of the Conception of the Blessed Virgin Mary (Dec. 8). Blunt ("Annotated Book of Common Prayer") says; "Its observation began in the East in early times, but did not become general in the West till the fifteenth century. Its introduction into Britain has been ascribed, on doubtful grounds, to S. Anselm, long after whose time the observance of it was optional." Anselm was consecrated Dec. 4, 1093. The year in which Eylsinus instituted the observance of the Festival at Ramsey must have been at least ten years previously. See the Sermons, p. 3, note c, and p. 86, note o.) [Here comes in Herbert's abbacy according to Dugdale.] "Eldwynus, abbas. Iste fecit assissam domus Ramsey et degratus [degradatus?] fuit injuste a Lanfranco archiepiscopo, et postea recuperavit abbatiam suam." Vespasian, A. 18. Lanfranc died in 1089, and according to the chronology we are following, Herbert was made abbot in the end of 1087. The account of the omission of his name from the list of abbots may possibly be that he succeeded to the abbacy on the degradation of Eldwyn; but Eldwyn being subsequently restored, the chronicler thought Herbert's abbacy parenthetical and unworthy of being recorded. There is however considerable doubt as to the dates. Dugdale, on the authority of the Register preserved in the Exchequer, represents Eldwyn as having been deposed by *Anselm*, not by Lanfranc. He speaks of Bernard (1102—1107), not of Herbert, as the Abbot interpolated between Eldwyn's two periods of office.

[a] "Abbey in Huntingdonshire." The following derivation of the name is given in *Magna Britannia*, a Gazetteer of the date 1738;

"*Ramsey*, that is, *the Ram's Isle*, on the West Side (for all round it besides there are nothing else but impassable Fens for a great way together) is separated from the firm Ground almost two Bows-shot by rough

Confessor had given to the monks of this Abbey the privilege of choosing their own Abbot; but it is not likely that the Norman princes would respect this privilege. If they allowed the community to go through the form of electing its own chief, it would be only as a Chapter is now allowed to elect its own Bishop;—the nominee of the Crown must be accepted anyhow, whether reluctantly or willingly. We can trace no allusion whatever in Herbert's letters to the period when he ruled the Abbey of Ramsey and its affiliated houses and cells. It is quite conceivable that he may have been anxious to forget this epoch of his life, as that with which the

No allusion in his Letters to his Abbacy, and why.

Quagmires, which place formerly, up a shallow River, used to receive Vessels into the midst of it by gentle Gales of Wind. But now with great Pains and Cost these clay Quagmires are stopped with large Quantities of Wood, Gravel, and Stone, and Footmen may pass upon a firm Causey, almost two Miles long, but less in Breadth, surrounded with Alders, which with fresh green Reeds, intermixed with Bulrushes, make a beautiful Show."

The above etymology of the name is drawn from the *Historia Ramesiensis*, contained in Gale's *Scriptores Quindecim*, a collection of monkish chronicles, British, Saxon, and Anglo-Danish. It is added that in primitive times a solitary ram was found in the island, entangled by his horns in the boggy ground, and unable to extricate himself. Other wonderfully fantastic derivations are suggested; as for example; Ramsey *a ramis*, because of the abundant woods. "By divine Providence," the chronicler thinks, "this name was ordered, which from the beginning of the world foresaw that the spot would be inhabited by holy and religious men, who having cut themselves off from the *wild olive-tree* of worldly conversation, would become branches of the *good olive-tree*; and by virtue of their grafting into the fatness of the good olive, would bring forth the divers fruits of virtue and good works as blooming leaves."

Another derivation is suggested from Rameses in Egypt, which, at the beginning of the Exodus, gave their first resting-place to the people of God. Again, "*Rameses* means 'Commotion or Thunder.' Rightly then was this place so called, because the holy men dwelling here cease from evil through the terror inspired by the thunder (as it were) of psalms and the reading of divine words," &c., &c.

deterioration of his character commenced. Perhaps the secular affairs which devolved upon an Abbot, and which Malmesbury tells us he administered with consummate skill, deadened his spirituality of mind. Perhaps the opulence and the luxurious ease of the position in which he found himself operated to make him covetous, and to stir in him an unholy craving for a position still more dignified and lucrative. The Abbots of Ramsey were great feudal lords, one of whom, in the pride of his heart, adopted as his seal the device of a ram swimming across the sea (according to the ordinary passion for the *rebus* in those days), with the legend; "Cujus signa gero dux gregis est ut ego" ("Whose effigy I carry, he Is leader of the flock, like me"). Bale says that "the famous Abbey of Ramsey received a surname from its wealth,"—that is, it was proverbially called "Ramsey the rich[b]." And it is clear from the long lists of gifts to it, which are enumerated by Dugdale, that it *was* wealthy. Its timber was abundant; its soil fruitful[c]; and the marshes

A.D. 1087.

Eminence and opulence of the Abbots of Ramsey.

---

[b] "After the Abbey was destroyed, the town instead of Ramsey the rich, as it was proverbially called in this county before usually, it might have been truly called Ramsey the poor; for the Market was lost for many years, but has since recovered it again about sixty years since;" (*Magna Britannia* was published in 1738); "and seeing it lies so convenient for the sale of fat and lean Cattle, which are much brought thither since the dreining of the Fens, it is probable it may in time recover its reputation for riches by the greatness of the Market for Cattle, as well as Waterfowl, for which it is reckoned one of the best in England for plenty and cheapness." (*Magna Britannia*, vol. ii. p. 1053.)

[c] "its soil fruitful," &c. See Dugdale's *Monasticon Anglicanum* (London, 1718), vol. i. p. 34, b.

Here is another picturesque passage from *Magna Britannia;*

"Long before it was inhabited, Ramsey was covered over with several sorts of trees, but with wild Ashes in the greatest abundance; but now of

which lay around it were well stocked with fish
and waterfowl. Meanwhile Herbert, it must be
remembered, had other sources of income besides
his Abbey. He was *sewer*[d] to William Rufus,
a post which probably was endowed with certain
fees and perquisites; and "obtained," Godwin
tells us, "divers great preferments," leading us
to suppose that the Abbey and the sewership
were not the only proofs of royal favour which
Herbert received. Nor is he the only man whose
ambitious propensities have shot up, under the

Herbert's other sources of income.

late, since these Woods are partly cut down, the Land is found to be arable, and of a fat Mould, plentiful in Fruit, delightful in Corn, planted with Gardens, and rich in Pastures, which in the Spring time ravish the Eyes of Spectators with infinite Pleasures; for the whole Isle consisting chiefly of Meadow, seems embroidered, as it were, with Variety of Flowers.

"Besides all this, here are Meers full of Eels, Pools full of all sorts of Fish and Waterfowl, of which Ramsey Meer is one, so called from the Name of the Isle, far excelling all the adjoining Waters both in Fairness and Plenty. Out of its deep Holes the Inhabitants, who are much advantaged by fishing in it, draw out Pikes of a wonderful Bigness, which they call *Hakeds*, either with several Sorts of Nets, baited Hooks, or other fishing Instruments; and though it be perpetually haunted by Fowlers, Fishers, and Poachers, who take an Abundance of their several sorts of Game, yet there is still great Plenty left behind, which shews an inexhaustible Store of them all." (*Magna Britannia*, vol. ii. pp. 1052, 1053.)

[d] "Sewer to William Rufus."

A *Sewer* is described by Johnson as *an Officer who serves up a feast;* and the derivation given is from the French *asseoire,* 'to set down;' "because these officers set the dishes on the table."

The Latin equivalent of the word is *Dapifer* or *Seneschallus*.

Milton seems to distinguish between a *Sewer* and a *Seneschal*, though there does not seem to be much difference;

"Marshall'd feast,
Serv'd up in hall with sewers and seneschals,
The skill of artifice or office mean."

The Seneschal would perhaps be the superior of the Sewer, presiding over the whole Banquet Department in a great household.

See a Latin distich in Ducange (s. v. *Seneschallus*);

"Præsentat Dapifer epulas, Coquus excoquit illas,
Estque Seneschallus cujus fit sub Duce jussus."

sunshine of that favour, into a baleful luxuriance.
William Rufus was a needy prince, and his needs
made him a greedy one. Archbishop Lanfranc a.d. 1089.
had died in 1089 (the second year after Herbert Death of Lanfranc,
had taken possession of the Abbey of Ramsey); and vacancy of
and the king delayed for nearly four years the the Primatial See.
appointment of a successor, in order that he
might enjoy during the vacancy the revenues of
the see of Canterbury. When driven at length,
partly by the complaints of those interested in the
Church's welfare, partly by scruples of conscience
upon a bed of sickness[e], to nominate Anselm to
the archbishopric, he took in dudgeon, we are a.d. 1093.
told, the offering of five hundred[f] pounds of
silver, which Anselm made to the Crown on
taking possession of his see. The king thought
the offering ought to have been at least double
the amount, and returned it. We can well understand
that a prince who acted in this manner
would turn to as good an account as he could
every preferment which he had to bestow. In the
year 1091 died William de Beaufeu, Bishop of the a.d. 1091.
East Angles, whose seat was at Thetford. His William of
episcopate was short, lasting only five years[g], and Herbert's
seems to have been so obscure that it is over- immediate predecessor.
looked altogether by William of Malmesbury[h],

[e] Hook's Lives of the Archbishops of Canterbury, vol. ii. p. 190, et sequent.

[f] Ibid., vol. ii. p. 196.

[g] Stubbs's *Registrum Sacrum Anglican.*, p. 23.

[h] Mr. Spurdens (as we have already said, p. 1, note a) identifies William of Beaufeu with Herbert, and calls our Prelate "William Herbert," as if his Christian name were William. While we admit that Malmesbury's omission of William's Episcopate is difficult to account for, and also that the point

who makes Herfast to be the immediate predecessor of Herbert in the see of Thetford. Of Herfast something is known. He was the Conqueror's chaplain. When Lanfranc was Prior of Bec, and his learning was beginning to win for him a great reputation, Duke William had sent Herfast with a train of courtiers to visit and conciliate the Prior. The object was to bring Lanfranc round to a more favourable view of a matter[1], on which he had expressed himself warmly—the duke's marriage with Matilda of Flanders, which was within the prohibited degrees of consanguinity. The mission was an eminent failure. Lanfranc was one of the most learned men of his day; Herfast, though a duke's chaplain, was an ignoramus. Lanfranc, who was angry with the duke for neglecting him when he was a comparatively obscure teacher at Avranches[k], and who was of too proud and independent a spirit to be won over by flattering overtures, which came too late, turned his emissary into ridicule. He placed in Herfast's hand a spelling-book, and invited him to read it before the tittering scholars of the house. Herfast returned to his patron, boiling over with indignation. The duke was seized with one of his paroxysms of rage, and ordered Lanfranc to quit his dominions. Thus laid under a sentence of exile, Lanfranc went

Herfast, his penultimate predecessor,

turned into ridicule by Lanfranc.

William resents the insult;

of the story about the Prognostic is somewhat weakened by the insertion of a Bishop between Herfast and Herbert, we think (as we have said in the note above referred to) Bartholomew Cotton's testimony on such a point to be conclusive. And we are glad to see that Professor Stubbs agrees with us.

[1] Hook's Abps. of Cant., vol. ii. p. 92.
[k] Ibid., p. 78.

to the Court at Rouen to ask for a formal licence to leave the country. The duke, apprised of his approach, went out to meet him, expecting to find him accompanied with something like a retinue. But when Lanfranc alone appeared, mounted on a very sorry and stumbling jade, and asked the duke for a better horse, that he might leave his dominions the faster, the duke underwent one of those sudden revulsions of feeling so common with men of impulse. He laughed, and had a friendly interview with the Prior, and came to a perfect understanding with him. Herfast, however, did not lose his place in William's favour. In the same year in which Lanfranc was appointed to Canterbury (1070), Herfast received the king's nomination to Elmham, which was then the seat of the East Anglian bishop; indeed Herfast, who was consecrated earlier in the year, himself took part¹ in consecrating Lanfranc. At Herfast's own consecration, there was a dismal presage as to the character of one who should succeed him. Part of the rite of consecration consisted in opening the book of the Gospels at haphazard, and holding it open over the head of the bishop elect. The passage found at the top of the page was supposed in those days to give a presage of the character and conduct of the bishop, and was called his "Prognostic." When the page was inspected at Herfast's consecration, these words glared upon the eyes of the consecrating bishops; "Non hunc, sed Barabbam," *but his wrath is turned aside.*

The prognostic at Herfast's consecration.

A.D. 1070.

---

¹ Stubbs's *Registrum Sacrum*, p. 21.

"Not this man, but Barabbas." It seemed to augur ill for one who should come after, and a memorandum was made of it.—Sixteen years elapsed [m], and William de Beaufeu succeeded Herfast; but his career presented nothing for superstition or ill-nature to take hold of. In five years he too passed away, and made room for a successor. The Abbot of Ramsey coveted the vacant post, and let the king know that he did so. In all probability Ralph Flambard (or the firebrand), "the thorough-going and unscrupulous minister of a policy of fiscal wrong and oppression such as was never in England; ... the prompter and instrument of a system of barefaced and daring venality which set everything in Church and State to sale [n]," under whose administration the Red King held at the time of his death the revenues of the sees of Winchester and Sarum and of eleven abbeys, as well as those of the arch-diocese of Canterbury, was his medium of communication with the Crown. Ralph, bent upon pandering (by whatever means) to the ambition and lusts of his master, would have his ears open to any rumours of wealth accumulated, and preferments sought, by ecclesiastics, and would immediately institute a correspondence with them. As to Herbert's appointment to the vacant see, it was so natural and reasonable that it would pass without much outcry, and justify itself to the public. The Abbey of Ramsey had lands in

[m] Stubbs's *Registrum Sacrum*, pp. 21, 23.

[n] See the powerful sketch of his character in the Rev. R. W. Church's "Life of Anselm," p. 160, &c.

the diocese of the East Angles°, so that the Abbot might be accounted an East Anglian dignitary. To place him on the Episcopal throne would be only to bid him go up one step higher. Then, again, Herbert was a man eminent for learning at a time when, even among the Clergy, learning was scarce. And then—last, but not least —Herbert with his "divers great preferments," and perhaps some supplies from the worthy country gentleman, his father, who held estates in Suffolk, had amassed a little hoard of money, and could afford to make a handsome acknowledgment for any preferments bestowed upon him. It is quite unnecessary to suppose that he entered into any formal bargain with the Red King. Such open and undisguised simony would have shocked his conscience too much; nor is this the way in which corrupt practices, which shun the light, are at first adopted by the will. It was customary,—and, in view of the custom, we may say it was proper,—for ecclesiastics, who held property under the Crown, to purchase enfeoffment ᵖ by a sum of money. This sum corresponded to, and was supposed to be the equivalent of, the horse and armour of the deceased, which lay successors to an estate in those days tendered to the king. Anselm himself, as we have

Enfeoffment customarily purchased by Ecclesiastics.

A.D. 1091.

A.D. 1091.'

° In Norfolk the Abbey had these Hidages; *Brauncestre*, 10 Hides; *Brunham*, 2 Hides with *Depedale*; *Ryngstede*, 7 Hides with *Holm*; *Wynbodesham*; *Dounham* with the Soc, 4 Hides; *Helyngeye* with *Snore*, 6 Hides; *Walsokne*, 6 Hides; *Well*.

In Suffolk the Abbey had *Lansill*, 10 Hides.

[Dugdale's *Monasticon*, with two additional Vols. by John Stevens. (London, 1723), vol. iii. p. 410, a.]

ᵖ Hook's Abps. of Cant., vol. ii. p. 196.

seen, was obliged to make a money payment to the king on his presentation to the see of Canterbury,—though, in fear of the charge of simony, he pared it down to the lowest possible figure. Herbert did exactly the reverse. He let the king understand that if he were appointed [q] to the See of Thetford, and his father [r] (now a widower) to the Abbey of Winchester, the offering made in acknowledgment of these favours would be a handsome one. The king made the appointments desired; and Herbert, for himself and his father, paid [s] into the royal treasury £1,900 [t]—a large sum for those times.

[q] "Stringent regulations had been made against Simony" in the councils held by Lanfranc (from 1072 to 1086) at Winchester, London, and Gloucester. "It was one of those offences which, like bribery at elections in our own time, was universally condemned, but unblushingly practised." At the Synod held in Westminster Abbey by Anselm in 1102, "no fewer than six Abbots were deposed on account of Simony." (Hook's Abps. of Cant., vol. ii. pp. 146, 251.)

[r] There is considerable uncertainty as to how long Abbot Robert Losinga held the Abbacy of Hyde, at Winchester. Dugdale is at issue with himself on this point. He says; "During the whole of this unprincipled reign [W. Rufus] the New Minster [Hyde] was in the hands of the king's agent, Ralph Passflebere, who either sacrilegiously received the rents of it, for his master's use, or simoniacally sold them to the highest bidder. *For the space of seven years* the oppressed monks were forced to yield obedience to the unworthy Robert de Losinga, in quality of their Abbot, his son Herbert, Bishop of Norwich, having purchased this dignity of the corrupt minister, by way of provision for his father."

Yet afterwards he gives these dates;

"Robert de Losinga, appointed Abbot 1091, died 1093."

We can give no other explanation of the discrepancy than that 1093 may be a misprint for 1098.

[s] We have followed the ordinary accounts in ascribing Simoniacal practices to Herbert. But the Rev. John Gunn (whose reputation as an antiquarian stands very high in the Eastern counties) is of opinion that the charge of Simony was trumped up against Herbert by the spite of the secular clergy. It may have been so; but the regulars (like Malmesbury and Knighton) seem to have adopted it. However, Mr. Gunn having kindly favoured us with his views in writing, we give them *in extenso* in Appendix B.

Great seems to have been the indignation of the monks throughout England at these preferments. The public opinion of the ecclesiastical world was all against them. Some monkish versifier (to whom Malmesbury gives the name of a poet) celebrated the corrupt transaction in these lines. The allusion in them is to the legendary history of St. Peter and Simon Magus; according to which the latter, having challenged the former to a disputation and a display of miraculous powers, proceeded to fly in the air; but St. Peter by his prayers broke the magical spell, and brought him to the ground.

A.D. 1091. The indignation aroused by Herbert's simoniacal practices finds vent in verse.

> "Surgit in Ecclesiâ monstrum, genitore Losingâ,
> Simonidum secta, canonum virtute resectâ.
> Petre, nimis tardas, nam Simon ad ardua tentat:
> Si præsens esses, non Simon ad alta volaret.
> Proh dolor! Ecclesiæ nummis venduntur et ære;
> Filius est præsul, Pater abbas, Simon uterque!
> Quid non speremus, si nummos possideamus?
> Omnia nummus habet, quod vult facit, addit et aufert.
> Res nimis injusta, nummis fit præsul et abba."

Of which lines our accomplished publisher, Mr. Parker, has favoured us with the following faithful translation:

> "In the Church arises a scandal;
>   Losinga is first the cause;
> A sect is named from Simon,
>   And they scorn the Church's laws.
> O Peter! why come so slowly?—
>   To reach heaven Simon tries,
> Should'st thou but only be present,
>   Not from earth could Simon rise.
> O shame! that the Church should be bartered
>   For money—for sordid pelf!
> Son and Father, Bishop and Abbot—
>   Each a very Simon himself.

¹ This is Alexander Nevylle's statement, and Bishop Godwin's, and Fuller's. But Simeon of Durham and Roger of Hoveden, and after them Harpsfeld, represent the sum as only a thousand pounds. (See *Authorities*.)

A.D. 1091.

> What indeed may we not expect,
> If money we're able to pay?
> Money holds *all* in its grasp;
> It wishes, and has its way:
> It confers, and it also deprives;
> Nay—the thing is too base to be told—
> Both a Bishop and Abbot are made
> By the terrible power of gold!"

Bartholomew Cotton's apology for Herbert.

Bartholomew Cotton, a monk of Herbert's own monastery at Norwich, is of course bound to defend his (and our) Founder; but despite good Bartholomew's apology for him, which is to the effect that he was justified by the Apostle's advice to "redeem the time, because the days are evil," and by the Decretal[u], which allows a clerk to purchase jurisdiction in the Church from a layman, *in case it may not otherwise be had*,— we can well understand that what Herbert had done "wounded his conscience a little," and that he did not look forward to his consecration with

Probable uneasiness of Herbert as the day of consecration approaches.

that unmixed satisfaction, with which a good man, who feels that his own corrupt will has had no share in bringing about his call to government in the Church, hails the day that is to qualify him for the most arduous and responsible of duties. To Herbert this day was to bring a fresh opening of the wounds of his conscience. In the vacancy of the see of Canterbury, Thomas Archbishop of York consecrated the Bishops of the Southern Province. The service proceeded

---

[u] The letters of the Popes, written in answer to some Bishop or ecclesiastical judge who consulted them on Church questions, are called "Decretals." They profess to contain the judgments on various points of thirty Popes, who governed the Church during the three first centuries; but they did not see the light before the ninth century, and are now admitted to be forgeries.

to the point where the consecrators opened the book of the Gospels, and held it over the head of the new Bishop. They observe the top of the page, to gather his prognostic; and we may suppose that the heart of our Herbert (a man not above the superstitions of his age) beats quickly, as the omen is taken. The words were; "𝔄mice, a𝔡 qui𝔡 𝔟enisti?" "Friend, wherefore hast thou come?" What a dreadful rebuke to one who had thrust himself into this highest of all ministries by the aid of his money! It would seem to him to come from the mouth of the Chief Shepherd, who presided invisibly at the solemn function; it would seem to brand him as a traitor, and as a smooth-tongued traitor, "the words of whose mouth were softer than butter, while he had war in his heart,"—and the question "Ad quid venisti?" "For what hast thou come?" would seem to him to imply—"Was it to feed My sheep, or to aggrandize thyself; to be an ensample to the flock, or to lord it over God's heritage?" And then, as if to rivet the impressions made upon his mind, occurs to him the prognostic of one, who had preceded him in the office he was assuming. The omen, which had been taken at *Herfast's* consecration, indicated that he was to be removed, and a Barabbas to come in his stead. Had not this omen also come true? Was not Herbert in some sense a Barabbas? Had he not robbed God's poor of the wealth which he had amassed, with a view to enrich and aggrandize himself by a politic expenditure of it? This thought quite overwhelms him. One prognostic falling out true might have been after all accidental; but two could hardly conspire to indicate his guilt without having been traced by the finger of God. The service of Consecration is finished, while these scruples are still haunting and discomposing his mind. He leaves the Cathedral a bishop duly authorized by the Church, but stigmatised (as he supposes) by the Church's great Head.

These uncomfortable impressions, however, soon vanished when he reached his diocese and addressed himself to his work. David's repentance, between which and his sin there must have been an interval of at least nine months, shews us how long the spark of right feeling may smoulder at the bottom of the heart, overlaid with cares and riches and pleasures of this life, yet not altogether extinguished. Thus it was with our Herbert. His new duties may have diverted him from the dismal presage given at his consecration. In the December of 1093 we find him taking part in the consecration of Archbishop Anselm, whom at last (after four years vacancy of the Metropolitical see) the king had appointed to Canterbury. Thomas of York, who two years before had consecrated Herbert, officiated in chief on this great occasion, and he was "assisted by all the bishops except two, whose attendance was prevented by illness." No other act of Herbert as Bishop of Thetford is on record. One can conceive that, as the novelty of his duties wore off, they served less to distract him from the scruples which had been engendered at his consecration. Subsiding at last into the routine of his office, he became thoroughly miserable in the survey of the past. The following letter, written several years after, will serve to show the genuineness of his penitence for his sins, and how it abode with him till "grey hairs were here and there upon him." *Proof of Herbert's penitence.*

LETTER I.

To Norman the Ostiary[1].

"Herbert to Norman the Ostiary.

"You endeavour by your assidulty in writing, my esteemed brother Norman, to correct the negligence of *Herbert excuses himself to Norman, on*

---

[1] An "Ostiary" or "Door-keeper" (compare, "I had rather be a door-keeper in the house of my God," &c. Ps. lxxxiv. 10) was a member of the last or lowest Order of the inferior Clergy. These inferior Orders, according to the Roman Church, are five; Subdeacons, Acolytes, Exorcists, Readers, and Door-keepers. The office of the Door-keeper was to keep the doors of the Church in Divine Service, to open and shut them under the direction of higher authorities, and to give notice of the hours of public worship. The ordination to this office was by the Bishop's delivering the keys of the church into the hand of the Candidate with this charge;—"See thou behave thyself as one that must give an account to God of the things which be kept locked under these keys." [See Bingham's Antiquities of the Christian Church, Book III. ch. I. and VI.]

The five inferior Orders with the two superior make up the mystical number seven, Bishops and Priests not being reckoned by the Roman Church as distinct Orders, but rather distinct grades of the same Order.

It is however probable that by the *Ostiarius* here is meant, not a member of the so-called ecclesiastical Order, but the Porter of Herbert's Benedictine Monastery, who had the charge of the gates. *Portarius* was the usual name of this officer; but he is called in the Benedictine Rule *Ostiarius*, and in St. Isidore's Rule *Janitor*. The office was held in high esteem, men of ripe years and great integrity being chiefly appointed to it; and it appears from the Chronicle of Fountain's Abbey that there were instances of Porters preferred to be Abbots. This may explain Herbert's intimacy with Norman the Ostiary,—a fact which on the supposition that Norman was a serving brother or domestic, or even an ecclesiastic very

the ground which I have been guilty in not keeping the letters, which from time to time I have addressed to my friends, and making a collection of them in one small volume after the manner of a register ^y. I confess that I deserve the fearless reproofs with which, in your simple-hearted love, you chide me for my indolence in this matter; but hitherto, perturbed as I am with the distractions of temporal affairs, I have been quite unable to pay any attention to your censure. And indeed my thoughts

marginal note: the ground of the sinfulness of his past life, for making no collection of his letters.

---

low down in the scale of the Hierarchy, might occasion some surprise. (See Ducange, *sub voce* Portarius.)

The chapter of the Benedictine Rule treating of the office of *Ostiarius* is as follows;

"Let there be set at the door of the Monastery a wise old man, who may know how to receive a message and give an answer, whose ripeness of age may not allow of his wandering abroad. Which porter ought to have a cell near the gate, so that all comers may find him ever at his post, and may get an answer from him; and when any one hath knocked, or a poor man hath cried out, let him answer forthwith, Thanks be to God, or Bless the Lord. And with all the meekness of the fear of God let him speedily give an answer, with fervent charity. Which porter if he should want any solace, let him take to himself a younger brother," &c., &c. (Hospinian. de Monachis, Regula Sti. Benedicti, cap. 66.)

Fosbrooke (vol. i. p. 183) says;

"The Benedictine Porter... always lay at night at the gate, and had a horse, that, as often as the superior, or cellarer, wished, he might attend their summons, and ride with them. He had always a boy, who lay at the gate with the sub-porter, and took the key, after curfew, to the cellarer's bed, which he fetched again in the morning, sooner or later, as necessary."

All this goes to shew that the Porter's office was one of trust and importance, and more or less of dignity.

^y "after the manner of a register,"—*registri formâ*.

The original form of this word is *Regestum* (from *regero*), which means earth thrown up, or thrown back, in making a foss or trench. Hence it comes to signify any memorandum book in which, during the progress of a literary work, entries are made, a catalogue, list, index, &c. Ducange, quoting from Iso Magister, says, "A book is called a register, which contains notices of other books (*memorias aliorum librorum*) and *epistles collected into one volume;* and it is called *re*-gestum as being something produced again (*dicitur Regestum quasi iterum gestum*)."

It is possible that Norman the Ostiary may, despite Herbert's protests, have done for him as far as he could what he was unwilling to do for himself; and that to his friendly labours we owe the *Registrum*, or Collection of Letters, which is found in the Burgundian library at Brussels in a late MS., and which Mr. Anstruther was the first to exhibit in print.

on the subject often run in this direction, that I, who have lost the vigour of youth, *ought* not to note down for the criticisms of my successors the drivelling sentiments of advancing age; for as to the things which I have *hitherto* written, I have allowed them all to slip out of my hands, and have buried them in eternal silence. Why, therefore, do you persist in exacting from an old man, what you condemn him for neglecting as a young one? When the body is worn out, the mind flags; and he who is bent down with decaying age dotes, and has not the liveliness or subtilty of mind to penetrate into the secrets of philosophy. The spirits of youth are gone; and a wearisome torpor besets my aged limbs. Advanced as I am to my sixtieth year, I cannot think that the moments of my past life, which alas! is darkened by many foul sins, should be recorded for the hearing of my successors; for it is absurd for a man to desire to make himself known by his words, who has gained no reputation from the course of his past deeds. The repartee of the Roman buffoon [1]

---

[1] "The repartee of the Roman buffoon."
The benevolent reader would pity us if he could only know the trouble we have had in endeavouring to ascertain who "the Roman buffoon" (*Romanus mimus*) may have been. Scholars of great eminence have we consulted,—one, of whom we were assured that "if he does'nt know who the *Romanus mimus* is, nobody in England does," but in vain.—For ourselves, we incline to agree with the Rev. Dr. Jessopp, who regards Herbert as making a jumble in his mind on the subject, which men quoting from memory are apt to do. "The real source of the story," he writes, "is to be found, I believe, in Valerius Maximus," (Liber viii. 14, §§ 3, 4, 5. *De cupiditate Gloriæ*. In the first of these sections Valerius speaks of men, "qui dum æternam memoriam adsequerentur, etiam sceleribus *innotescere* non dubitarunt." Observe that the word *innotesco* is put by Herbert in the mouth of the *Romanus mimus;* "Quia bonis *innotescere* non poteram, *innotesco* vel malis." The succeeding sections give as instances the answer of the Sophist Hermocrates to the Macedonian youth Pausanias, that the shortest road to fame was to kill a man of high renown, whereon Pausanias assassinated King Philip; and the well-known burning of Diana's temple at Ephesus by Erostratus, to make himself a name.) "For a story of this kind I should always go to him, for there was no author more popular or more widely read in the Middle Ages (and very much after the Middle Ages too). I strongly suspect Herbert had the above passage in his mind (read perhaps many years before), and that he faintly

is worthy only of a laugh, who, when he was asked why he had set fire to the city, replied boldly, 'Because I was not able to make myself known by good deeds, I make myself known even by bad.' This, brother, is by no means my sentiment, who have thought it better to deplore the blackness of my sins in the privacy [of my closet], than publicly to rehearse fine speeches[a]; since it is not the brilliancy of our eloquence, but penitence of the heart, and a pure confession of the lips, which reconcile us unto God. And hence, dear brother, it is my wish so to pass through the present life, that I may not remain as an object of derision to posterity; I prefer to speak in such a manner, as to be burdensome to none; for our Saviour chose not the eloquent or wise of this world, but unlearned and simple folk; whence He saith, 'I came not to call the just, but sinners to repentance;' and, in another place, 'If any man will come after Me, let him deny himself, and take up his cross, and follow Me.' Observe then narrowly what I say, brother, and employ your assiduous persuasions in admonishing your friend rather to bewail his past sins, to amend his present life, and to labour on in works of holiness, than to inflate himself with empty words, which are 'to no profit, but to the subverting of the hearers.'

St. Luke v. 32.
St. Matt. xvi. 24.

See 2 Tim. ii. 14.

"'I know this;' you exclaim, and meet my modest excuses with gay and ready mien, as assured of an easy triumph over them. You allege that the Canonical

---

recollected the 'etiam sceleribus innotescere non dubitarunt,' and the two illustrative instances that follow; that he mixed up the burning of the temple of Diana with the burning of Rome by Nero, who might have been called a Roman buffoon, and that the result is the strange story of the *mimus.*"

[a] "fine speeches,"—*faleratas orationes.*

Phaleræ means a decoration of any sort. (1.) A military order of merit; (2.) the ornament of a lady's dress; (3.) trappings for horses, frontal and pectoral. Hence it passes into the meaning of *rhetorical ornament.* Thus in the Phormio of Terence, iii. 2. 14, "Adeon' te esse incogitantem atque impudentem, ut *phaleratis* dictis ducas me?" "Can you be so thoughtless and brazenfaced as to attempt to lead me by high-sounding pompous expressions?"

Scriptures, and the treatises of renowned men [in illustration of them] are indispensably necessary to Holy Church. Most true. These be those lights, which God hath set in the firmament, 'the greater light to enlighten the day, and the lesser light to enlighten the night.' These be those stars which God hath 'set in the firmament,' and appointed them 'to give light upon the earth.' But these, brother, are the writings of Saints, of men in whom the Holy Ghost spake, of men whose 'conversation was in heaven,' with whom God 'spake face to face,' and on whose breasts He reclined at supper, when about to meet His death. With such writings ours have neither part nor lot,—we, who are defiled with the mire of our lusts, in whom the spiritual life is strangled by the allurements of deadly passions, or haunted and harassed by anxious thoughts? 'Upon whom,' saith God, 'does My Spirit rest, save on him that is quiet and lowly-minded, and that trembleth at My word?' 'The Holy Spirit flieth from hypocrisy, and departeth from thoughts which are without understanding.'

See Gen. i. 16, 17.

See Phil. iii. 20, and Exod. xxxiii. 11, and 2 John 12, and St. John xiii. 23.

See 1 Pet. iv. 14, and Isaiah lxvi. 2.

Wisdom i. 5.

"Wherefore, brother, prythee leave off provoking your veteran friend to write or to publish his papers, whom you ought rather, as I said before, to instruct in the doing of good works, and continually to recall to repentance for the evils of his past life. You cannot institute any just comparison between saints and sinners; for as the doctrine of the saints derives a colour from their holy characters; so on the other hand the empty talk of sinners has discredit reflected on it by the impurity of their lives. Rightly does a divine oracle pronounce; 'It is of necessity that his doctrine should be despised, whose life is despised [b].'"

---

[b] This passage is not found either in Holy Scripture or in the Apocryphal Books. It may perhaps be a good moral apophthegm from one of the Fathers, or even from some heathen writer, which Herbert, by a slip of memory, supposed was to be found in the Sacred Books, and therefore calls it "divinum oraculum." Thus there is a story on record of an English Divine, who planned a Sermon on the words, "In the midst of life

At length he makes a resolve which seems to reinvigorate his will, and give a fresh spring of hope to his mind. "I entered on mine office disgracefully," cries he; "but, by the help of God's grace, I shall pass out of it with credit [c]—that credit which attaches to every act of sincere penitence." He is determined to lay down his ill-earned dignity, and to retire once more to the comparative privacy of monastic life. But how shall he do this most effectually, most satisfactorily to his conscience? He had received from the king the ring and the pastoral staff, the symbols of episcopal dignity and episcopal charge. Should he place them again in the hands from which he received them, with a meek acknowledgment that he had procured them wrongfully? But the king had been his accomplice in the unhallowed traffic; and if the purchaser was guilty, equally or more guilty was the seller. And what reception could he expect from this rough Esau,—like Esau, red, and like Esau, one who hesitated not to sell a sacred dignity for money? England's royal Esau was not ungenerous, nor wanting in a certain magnanimity; but, like his father, he was an utter stranger to self-control, and stormed and stamped, when his royal will was thwarted. He would laugh to scorn the scruples of a tender conscience; he would boil over with anger at the insinuation that he had made himself partner to an unholy bargain;

Herbert determines to lay aside his episcopal office,

we are in death," under the impression that they were to be found in the Bible.
  [c] See *Authorities.*

he would drive the bishop from his presence with sneers and sarcasms; he would address this remorseful Judas who had cast down his money into the royal treasury, and now came to cry "Peccavi," in the language of the hard Scribes and Pharisees; "What is that to us? see thou to that." No; Herbert, for his own comfort, as well as to give his penance a greater publicity, would resort to a spiritual, not to a political, shepherd of the people. The Pope could not, would not, receive him amiss. The Pope was the supreme Pastor, and bound by his office to say a word of consolation to every penitent. The Pope could not but be flattered by Herbert's resignation *to him* of the ring and the staff, because his right of investiture to all ecclesiastical dignities was the one point which he wished to establish against all sovereigns, and against the Sovereign of England in particular. And if the Pope should feel bound, in so flagrant a case of simony, to exercise discipline by way of making an example,—not only (perhaps) accepting the son's resignation of the bishopric, but also enforcing the father's resignation of the abbey,—it was only what the conscience of Herbert craved for as a means of gaining peace. A truly penitent soul wishes only to make such amends as it can, and takes to itself willingly the shame of exposure and the smart of punishment. And the soul of our Herbert was really penitent. His conscience had been overlaid for a time by the riches and pleasures of this life; but it had not lost its vitality; it

and decides upon resigning it to the Pope.

was only asleep; it was to shake off its deadly stupor, and assert once more its supremacy over the whole man. So Herbert resolved that he would without further delay make a journey to Rome, and place in the hands of the Pope, as the ecclesiastical head of Christendom, the office into which he had so discreditably thrust himself. In forming this project, he naturally thought but little of the king. His relations to the secular power were lost sight of in his spiritual trouble. Bishops in those days were not allowed to leave the kingdom without the king's permission,—a very necessary restriction upon the liberty of episcopal action, as the too free communication of the bishops with Rome might have seriously compromised the independence of the national Church. And there was another difficulty in the way of going to the Pope. For at this period there were two claimants to the papacy, Urban and Clement, and it was not for a bishop, in the absence of any authoritative decision by his sovereign, to settle which of the two was the lawful claimant. However, Herbert's mind was not in a state to give any heed to points, which he would regard as matters of etiquette rather than of conscience. He chose Urban for his pope, as Anselm did afterwards. And to Urban he determined to go, either overlooking the necessity of asking the royal permission, or fearing that, if he asked it, it would not be granted. He came to the coast, carrying with him his pastoral staff and ring, and intending to cross the water. This was at the Candlemas of the year 1094. Unfortunately the king was just then at Hastings. He was *en route* for Normandy, whither the threatening and defiant message received from his brother Robert [d] had made it expedient for him to go. He was waiting at Hastings for a favourable wind; and thought he would turn this enforced delay to account by solemnizing the dedication of the great Church of St. Martin at Battle. This Church, with the monastery annexed, had been commenced by William the Conqueror, who had offered up there the sword and royal robe [e] which he had worn on the day of his coronation. The high altar of the Abbey Church was situated on the spot where Harold and the royal standard had fallen; and the object of the foundation was twofold,—to keep up a continual praise of God for the victory gained at Hastings, and a continual intercession for the souls of those who had fallen in the battle.

<small>Feb., A.D. 1094.</small>

<small>The Red King assists at the dedication of St. Martin's Abbey.</small>

While the king was thus occupied, he heard of the bishop's approach, and was informed whither he was bound. In one of his impulsive fits of anger he summoned him, and deprived him of his pastoral staff. Most of the bishops (Anselm among them) had been sent for to the coast [f], to hallow with their blessing the expedi-

<small>The Red King surprises Herbert when on the point of escaping from the kingdom, and deprives him of the insignia of the episcopal office.</small>

---

[d] See *Authorities*.

[e] Dugdale's *Monasticon*, by Stevens (London, 1722), vol. iii. p. 511, a, b.

[f] Hook's Abps. of Cant., vol. ii. pp. 198, 199. From the charter given in Dugdale, iii. p. 246, it appears that the Bishops present at the consecration were Walkeline of Winchester, Ralph of Chichester, Osmund of

tion into Normandy. Perhaps Herbert was formally impeached before his peers, and the staff solemnly plucked out of his hand by the king in token of his removal from office. The censure would act, it might be thought, as a wholesome warning to Anselm.—How Herbert contrived under these circumstances to effect his journey, we are not told. If the dates are given us correctly, he can hardly have waited till the king's back was turned, for it was not till the middle of Lent, says the Saxon Chronicle[g], that the king passed over into Normandy. Probably (after resuming his staff, the withdrawal of which had been only a symbolical action), he removed to another place on the coast, and there disguising himself, bestowed some of his wealth in bribing the owner of a small craft to put him across the water. At all events, the king was so busy with other matters as to forget him. His mind was engrossed with his preparations for war. And moreover he had Archbishop Anselm on his hands, who was threatening with Church censures the young Norman courtiers of the expedition, if they did not clip their hair[h] and

Herbert contrives to effect his escape.

How the Red King's attention may have been distracted from Herbert's proceedings.

Salisbury, John of Bath, William of Durham, Roger of Coutance, and Gundulf of Rochester; and that they all joined in excommunicating any one who should take away any of the property granted by the King to the Abbey on the auspicious occasion. Anselm is not mentioned. Perhaps he did not arrive till the dedication was over.

[g] *Anglo-Saxon Chron.*, p. 255. A°. 1094.

[h] Nothing is new under the sun. The affectation of women's attire by men, of which we have heard so much lately, traces up in this country to the time of the Conquest and the early Norman Princes. Witness the following passages;

"As well in this King's dayes, as in the time of his brother William Rufus, men forgetting their own sexe and state, transformed themselves

shave their beards, and was equally severe upon the king, descanting on the frightful immorality which the Normans had introduced into the country, and warning him that he could not expect a blessing upon his expedition, if he did not take immediate steps to convoke a synod for the reformation of religion. He urged upon him also the filling up of the vacant abbacies, which William was keeping open that he might enjoy their revenues. All this exasperated the habitually irritable king; and it ended by his saying that he hated Anselm, and entirely refused[1] to receive his benediction. We can well understand how, amidst these cares and jars and

into the habite and fourme of women, by suffering their heares to growe at length, the which they curled and trimmed verie curiously, after the maner of Damosels and yong Gentlewomen: and suche account they made of their long bushing perukes, that those which woulde be taken for Courtiers, strove with women who shoulde have the longest tresses, and such as wanted, sought to amende it with arte and by knitting wreathes aboute their heades of those their long and side lockes for a brauerie. Yet we read that King Henrie gave commaundement to all his people to cut their heares, about the 28 yere of his reigne. Preachers in deed inueyed agaynst such unseemely maners in men, as a thing more agreeable for women, than for their estate." (Holinshed's Chronicles, vol. ii. p. 364.)

"Anselm, Archbishop of Canterbury, refused his benediction on Ash-Wednesday to those who would not cut their hair. Councils were held on this important matter. The razor and scissors were not only recommended *ex cathedra*, but positively produced sometimes at the end of a sermon against the sinfulness of long locks and curling mustaches. Serlo d'Abon, Bishop of Seez, on Easter Day, 1105, after preaching against beards before Henry I., cropped not only that of the King but those of the whole congregation with a pair of scissors he had provided for the occasion. But nothing could long repress these fashions, which in the time of Stephen again raged to such an extent that the fops of the day suffered their hair to grow till they looked more like women than men; and those whose ringlets were not sufficiently luxurious added false hair to equal or surpass in appearance their more favoured brethren." (Pictorial History of England, vol. i. p. 637.)

[1] This account of the King's dealings with Anselm is drawn from Hook's Abps. of Cant., 1862, vol. ii. pp. 199—204.

broils, the poor meek Bishop of Thetford was lost sight of. But, be this as it may, he contrived to reach Rome, and obtain an interview with Urban, in the course of which he laid down at the Pope's feet the insignia of his episcopal dignity, the pastoral staff and the ring, and confessing the unworthy practices by which he had obtained them, craved absolution from the successor of St. Peter. Had his proffered resignation been nothing more than an expression of penitence, no Pope of ordinary character could have been harsh or stern to him. But in the present case the resignation implied a tribute to papal claims, which no Pope could resist. It was now nearly twenty years since a synod held at Rome[k] had forbidden ecclesiastics to receive investiture from laymen. Ever since that time the papal power had been in almost all the European countries making more and more encroachments upon the regal. The resignation of an English bishopric to the Pope would be an emphatic mode of indicating that English bishoprics were held of him, not of the Crown. Urban, we may be sure, would want no other inducement to be very gracious. He would give the absolution demanded of him with soothing and comfortable words; and then lifting up the ring and staff which had been deposited at his feet, he would exercise the authority, which Herbert had so fully recognised, by placing the one on his finger and the other in his hand, and

Herbert's interview with Pope Urban II.

Encroachments of the papal upon the regal power.

The Pope re-instates Herbert,

[k] Hook, vol. ii. p. 243.

commanding the bishop to resume his sacred functions. Then raising and seating his guest, he would converse with him affably on the ecclesiastical affairs of England, and Herbert would take the opportunity of bringing before him the growth in population and importance of the town of Norwich, and the consequent desirableness of removing the see from Thetford to a place which was fast becoming a great commercial centre. An English synod[1] had already decreed the removal of sees under these circumstances, which was quite in accordance with the policy of the Conqueror, and the Pope would find little difficulty in giving his assent to an arrangement so wise in point of ecclesiastical policy, and so obviously consistent with common sense. Reinstated then in his epis- *and gives his assent to the removal of the See from Thetford to Norwich.*

[1] Held at London by Lanfranc, A.D. 1075. "Bishop Herfast, or Arfast, the Conqueror's Chaplain, who was made Bishop in the year 1070, removed the" (East Anglian) "See from *Elmham* to *Thetford* in 1075, according to the order of the council held by Lanfranc, Archbishop of Canterbury, which appointed that all Bishops' sees, which were settled in villages, should be removed to the most eminent cities in their dioceses,—Thetford being far superior to Elmham in populousness and wealth." Malmesbury accuses Herbert of being influenced in the removal of the see by "greater ambition than ought to have influenced a man of such eminence." (*Authorities.*) Bartholomew Cotton seems to say (*Authorities*) that he regarded a wandering see as a kind of indignity, and desired a fixed centre for his diocese. He adds that the see had once been "in a village called Elmham, where the church was a wooden structure; since that, in the small town of Thetford, in *a church which was in the possession of others*, or in any other places according to the fancy of individual Bishops." (*Authorities.*) Doubtless there may have been several motives (of a mixed character) inducing Herbert to remove the see.—But in *whose* possession was the old Cathedral at Thetford? Probably in that of the Abbey of Bury. We find in Martin's History of Thetford that three of the five Thetford churches (All Saints, St. George, and St. Bennet) belonged to Bury Abbey. (Martin's Thetford.) The Abbots of Bury always claimed exemption from episcopal jurisdiction, which was a constant source of dispute between them and the East Anglian Bishops. A church "in their possession" would naturally be unacceptable as a Cathedral to Herbert.

copal office, and charged also with a commission of great importance in connexion with his diocese, Herbert retraced his steps to this country. It is said, and we can well believe it, that the Pope had enjoined him as a penance for his simony to build, on his return, sundry churches and religious houses. Such a penance would be quite in accordance both with the views entertained at that time, and with the feelings of the bishop. A sincere penitent is not satisfied without some honest endeavour to make reparation for his fault. Herbert had sinned by an unhallowed use of wealth. He now resolved that the use of what remained to him should be hallowed and consecrated to the service of God. Norwich Cathedral, and the parish church of Great Yarmouth (in size and structure equal to some of our Cathedrals) are fruits of his penitence which remain to this day.

Herbert's return,

and his doing of the penance prescribed him.

He had left England soon after the Candlemas of 1094. We must suppose that he staid at Rome not much longer than would suffice for his interview with the Pope. For on his return he removed the see (together with the body [m] of his predecessor, William de Beaufeu) from Thetford to Norwich. And this removal took place, according to Cotton [n], on the 9th day of April, 1094. If therefore these dates be correct, we cannot allow more than two months for his journey to Rome and back—a short period in those days of

April 9, A.D. 1094.

---

[m] This is Harpsfeld's assertion. (*Authorities.*) We have not met with it in any earlier writer.

[n] *Authorities.*

slow travelling. But he went there on no other errand than an interview with the Pope; and we can well suppose that he was anxious to return as soon as might be, and to re-commence his episcopal duties under happier auspices. Bale, in the abusive language which is so natural to him, tells us that the removal of the see was an act "done without the king's° privity (for Herbert's king was Abaddon), on the sole authority of his Antichrist" (the Roman Pontiff). We must suppose that his journey to Rome was surreptitious, and never came to William's knowledge (for how could the Red King overlook such a flagrant defiance of his authority as the bishop had been guilty of?) and that under the pressure of his brother's threats and the troubles in Normandy, his anger with the bishop at Hastings had escaped his memory. Perhaps, as passionate men are wont to do, he thought his own vehemence had been excessive, and was not unwilling that it *should* escape. Herbert's see, too, remote from the metropolis and altogether provincial (even in these days), must have been very remote indeed, in times when the shortest journey was an operation. But at all events the king did not return from Normandy till the 29th of December; so that Herbert, reaching England before April 9 of that year, must have had time to make many moves "without the king's privity." At all events, the translation of the see to Norwich was effected during the king's absence from the country.

Bale's coarse language on the subject of the removal of the See.

Dec. 29, A.D. 1094.

° *Authorities.*

The fanaticism enlisted in the great religious movement of the first Crusade.

But when we speak of Herbert's proceedings as escaping notice in high places, we must not forget that just at this time there arose a mania in Europe, which absorbed into itself every other interest, and that under cover of this mania many a movement might be made, without attracting general attention. Men's minds were all aflame with curiosity, restlessness, the love of licence, thirst for war, emulation, and ambition; and when to these impulses was added that of religious fanaticism, the result was a wild frenzy, which seized all classes of society, beginning with the very lowest, and spreading like wildfire to the very highest. The preaching of the first Crusade supplied this spark of fanaticism; the Turkman was maltreating the pilgrims to the Holy Places; and it would be a noble enterprise, worthy of the sacrifice of property and life, to avenge those wrongs, and rescue the sepulchre of Christ from the intolerable dominion of the Infidel. Peter the Hermit, who recounted to large audiences, whose minds were like touchpaper, the barbarities he had himself seen inflicted on the pilgrims in Palestine, kindled the spirit of the Pope; and Urban II., emulous in all things of Gregory VII. (who twenty years ago had addressed an encyclical letter to the faithful on the subject), con-

A.D. 1095.

vened in 1095 the council of Clermont, where, in answer to the exhortations of the preachers, there rose from the heart and lips of the assembly the tumultuous cry; "It is the will of God!" Robert Courthose, Duke of Normandy, caught the infection, and in that same year raised ten thousand marks P by mortgaging his duchy to his brother the king of England for five years, and having thus provided resources for his expedition, received the cross from the Pope's own hands, and set forth for Palestine. It may appear surprising that nowhere in Herbert's Letters or Sermons is a single trace found of the interest excited by the Crusades. As far as we can see, Herbert makes not the faintest allusion to the great religious movement of his day. The Crusades were analogous in those days to a missionary enterprise of great calibre, which should take hold of the mind of all classes of a nation (as alas! no modern missionary enterprise really does),—an enterprise in the interest of which monster meetings should be called, to listen to recitals of the conversion of a whole country, and which meetings should succeed in enlisting not merely the purses, but the personal services, of high and low.—But Herbert had home-work of great importance on his hands, —the founding of Churches and monastic houses; and perhaps it is impossible that those whose interests are centred in grand religious works,

The Crusade never alluded to in Herbert's extant writings.

Possible reasons for his silence.

P "ten thousand marks."

The English mark (a sum of money, not a coin) is said to have been of the value of 13s. 4d. But we find that in Henry the First's reign (and therefore probably during Herbert's life) the mark was only 6s. 1d. In France there were four marks current, of different values, that of Troyes (= 14s. 2d.); that of Limoges (= 13s. 3d.); that of Tours (= 12s. 11d.); and that of La Rochelle, which was the same as the English mark (= 13s. 4d.) It will be observed that between the highest and lowest of these marks there was a difference of only 1s. 3d.; whereas the difference between the later English mark and that of Henry I. is 7s. 3d., Henry's mark being not one half of what the English mark ultimately became. These particulars are taken from Ducange, *sub voc.* MARCA, *Marca Anglicana.*

undertaken in and for their own country, can spare much thought for missionary enterprise, however popular and attractive. Moreover the monks, for and to whom Herbert wrote, would probably require an abstinence from such exciting topics. There were eager spirits in the monasteries, full of life and the love of adventure, disliking the restraints to which monastic discipline subjected them, and longing only for some reasonable pretext to break the chains which bound them to the convent. When Herbert wrote or preached to these, he would have to foster in them a love of home duties, not to give them an impulse for roaming.

That he had indeed such spirits to deal with among his monks, men who found the convent irksome, and were glad of a pretext to escape from it, may be seen from the following letters.

LETTER LV.
To G.

"Herbert to G.

See Jer. xiii. 23. Herbert reproves and threatens a British monk for his fickleness in repudiating his

"It is an awful condition, that of inability to be changed. What has become of you? The Ethiopian, though washed, is an Ethiopian still; nor can he, whose skin is dusky by nature, become white by Baptism. You Britons talk much; but none of you fulfils the promises he makes. The British, methinks, are as fickle ¶ in flying as they are ardent in making an

¶ These, and the other features mentioned in this letter, were always characteristic of the Keltic race, whether Britons or Gauls. Here are two descriptions of the latter people, one from an ancient, another from a modern pen, strongly resembling the attributes of the British Brother G.

"Cæsar, infirmitatem Gallorum veritus, quod sunt in consiliis capiendis mobiles, et novis plerumque rebus student, nihil his committendum existimavit." (De B. G., iv. 5.)

assault. [You fall on one or other horn of this di- profession;
lemma.] Either, if you are in health, you should have and in doing so,
followed up the labour which you set about with us, gives a sketch of
or if ill, you should have joined your supplications for British
your recovery with ours; by doing neither the one character.
nor the other, you have utterly broken your promises.
We have sent away the master whom we had for you;
and you, intoxicated with the good yield of your oats,
apply yourself to copious potations, quite unmindful of
all the philosophy which you proposed to yourself [to
master]. But as you became a fellow-citizen of ours,
and a monk of our cloister, why do you live in the
country? With us is God to be found, and a continual
communion with the holy angels. Having been made
to drink of heaven's own nectar, we dread to defile ourselves with the dregs of carnal affairs. Ficklest and most
deceitful of all the Britons, either come home with all
speed, or prepare yourself to receive the anathema
which is being got ready for you."

LETTER XXIX.

To Thurstan the Monk.

"Herbert to Thurstan the Monk.

"You shrink in aversion from your own inheritance, Thurstan
brother Thurstan, and delight yourself in a wealth which is warned by Herbert
you alienated from you [when you professed Religion]. to eschew
Disdaining our thatched huts^r, you dwell in marble luxury, and carnal

---

"Les traits saillans de la famille gauloise, ceux qui la différencient le plus, à mon avis, des autres familles humaines, peuvent se résumer ainsi : une bravoure personelle que rien n'égale chez les peuples anciens ; un esprit franc, impétueux, ouvert à toutes les impressions, éminemment intelligent ; mais, à côté de cela, une *mobilité extrême, point de constance,* une répugnance marquée aux idées de discipline et d'ordre" [no doubt Brother G. manifested a marked repugnance to monastic discipline] "si puissantes chez les races Germaniques, beaucoup d'ostentation. Enfin une désunion perpétuelle, fruit de l'excessive vanité." (Thierry, Hist. des Gaulois, Introd. iv. 5.)

^r "thatched huts"—*tuguria.*

Probably the conventual buildings were not finished when Herbert wrote

pleasures, and to return to the monastery, where he is to anticipate an examination in the proficiency he has made in his studies.

palaces,—a piece of good taste and prudence, which we all must applaud, if only amidst the abundance of your luxuries you are mindful of our poverty. We are your brethren; and however often you have to revisit your father's house and the home of your affections, we seek not to disinherit you. [Only] have some regard to yourself, and to what we expect from you; for [I tell you fairly that] we expect some of the wages* of your service as a soldier, or some of

thus. From a large ruin which remained in the Close up to the beginning of this century, these buildings must have been splendid; so that after rearing them, Herbert must have experienced an emotion kindred to that of Æneas, when surveying Carthage;

"Miratur molem Æneas, magalia quondam." (Æn. I. 421.)

* "We expect some of the wages of your service as a soldier, or some of the profits of your commerce"—*tu* [*tuæ?*] *militiæ solidos, tuæve negotiationis merces expectamus.*

The word *solidus* is of no small interest, if it were only that it is represented by an English and a French word of the very commonest occurrence.

(1.) The *solidus* (*numus*) was the standard gold coin of the Roman Empire, and would be roughly represented by the English guinea or sovereign, its value according to the present worth of gold being £1 1s. 1½d. (and a fraction); but according to its worth in those days 17s. 8½d. It was originally called *aureus;* but in the time of Constantine the term *solidus*, which had been for some time previously coming in, seems to have established itself. There are *aurei* of Augustus, which carry the Emperor's head on the obverse, and on the reverse an effigy of the Emperor seated in the curule chair, with two men holding palm-branches before him. *Solidus* of course is an adjective, meaning *complete* and *entire*, and its neuter, *solidum*, is used of a complete full sum, with no deficiency. Even in the classical writers we find this neuter used of a *soldier's* pay or wages. Thus in Livy, v. 4, "An tu æquum censes militiâ semestri solidum te stipendium accipere?" ("Think you it fair that for serving six months only you should receive your full annual pay?")

(2.) But in the mediæval Latin, the word seems to have clung very closely (not exclusively) to army payments and wages of *soldiers*. *Solidus, soldus, soldum*, are all words denoting soldier's wages*; *solidata* is a stipend of one *solidus* which is given to a soldier; *solido* is to pay a soldier's wages, subsidize him; while *solidarius, soldarius, soldatus*, is a soldier who serves for pay, and differs but little in sound and spelling from its English and French representatives, *soldier, soldat.*

The Greek word for soldiers' wages, notable as used twice in the New Testament in that sense ("Be content with your *wages*," St. Luke iii. 14;

* Called in the earlier period of the language *sal-arium* (soldiers' salt-money), and earlier still, *stip-endium* (payment of *stips*, small cash).

the profits of your commerce. Thou spiritual merchant-man, see that by careful and industrious barter thou lay in a stock of precious things, to be placed to the credit of thy house. We ask not gold, or silver, or Persian gems, or Indian garments. No other odours or cosmetics have any charm for us save those of the Church, with the fragrance of which the whole world is filled. We expect some evidence of your faith, we shall be as much gratified as you by the devout strictness of your life, we shall rejoice with you in your good works. Your prudence and temperance, your fortitude and justice, will elevate our affections; and we shall feast upon your humility, patience, sobriety, diligence in searching the Scriptures, and prompt obedience [to rule], with a keener appetite than on the most delicate viands.— My son, see to it that thou maintain thy chastity[t], without which it is impossible to please

See St. John xii. 3.

"Who goeth a warfare any time at his *own charges?*" (τίς στρατεύεται ἰδίοις ὀψωνίοις ποτέ), 1 Cor. ix. 7; and twice more generally, "The *wages* of sin is death," Rom. vi. 23; and "I robbed other Churches, taking *wages* of them, to do you service," 2 Cor. xi. 8) is ὀψώνια.

Ducange tells us, referring, as his authority, to a Law of William the Conqueror, that the *English* "solidus" contained 40 denarii.

Mr. Edward Hawkins, in his learned numismatic work on the Silver Coins of England, gives a plate of a coin of Cunobeline (Cymbeline) the British King, whose dominions stretched from Norfolk and Suffolk to the Severn, on the reverse of which is the word *soldo*. It is not known, Mr. Hawkins tells us, what this word means. May the Roman word *solidus* have been adopted by Cunobeline after his acquaintance with the Romans?

Sou is hardly a less common word in French than *soldat*. And it too is an abbreviation of *solidus*, the ancient form of it having been *sol*.

[t] "thy chastity"—*Fili, conserva sanctimoniam.*

Even in the classical writers the word *sanctimonia* (the general meaning of which is *sacredness, holiness*) had a specific meaning of chastity. It is used by Tacitus of the chastity both of unmarried and of married women; "Torquata *priscæ sanctimoniæ* virgo," ("Torquata, a maiden of a virtue now somewhat out of vogue"); "Deligi oportet feminam nobilitate, puerperiis, *sanctimoniâ* insignem," ("A matron must be chosen noble in blood, happy in her offspring, and virtuous in her conduct"). The writers of the Middle Ages had little or no meed of recognition for *conjugal* chastity; and hence with them the terms "Sanctimonia," "Sanctimonialis habitus," were equivalent to the monastic profession with its vow of virginity. *Sanctimoniales Virgines* were nuns,—maidens who had taken the vows. (See Ducange, *sub voce*). The word *sanctimonia* appears only twice in the

God. A virgin was Christ, a virgin was Mary the mother of Christ, a virgin was John the herald of Christ, a virgin was John the beloved of Christ; attend, and thou shalt find that everywhere in the mystery of our redemption virginity hath had the utmost efficacy. They who are redeemed from the earth, and not defiled Rev. xiv. 4. by carnal ᵘ intercourse, are they who follow the Lamb

---

Vulgate; once in Psalm xcv. (xcvi.) 6, where it is the equivalent of the Greek ἁγιωσύνη (LXX.); and again in Heb. xii. 14, "Sequimini sanctimoniam," where it is the equivalent of ἁγιασμός.

This last word ἁγιασμός has, at least in one place of the New Testament, the meaning of *chastity*. "For this is the will of God, even your sanctification," (ὁ ἁγιασμὸς ὑμῶν) "that ye should abstain from fornication: That every one of you should know how to possess his vessel in sanctification and honour (ἐν ἁγιασμῷ καὶ τιμῇ); Not in the lust of concupiscence, even as the Gentiles which know not God." (1 Thess. iv. 3—5.)

As to the etymology of the word *Sanctimonia* the same termination is seen in *Parsimonia, Acrimonia, Ceremonia, Alimonia, Castimonia*. The *o* in these terminations is long. According to Dr. Donaldson (Varronianus, London and Cambridge, 1852, p. 406), this termination has two pronominal elements,—the first and third,—M and N. He thinks that the first pronominal element "expresses that the thing proceeds from, or immediately belongs to, the *subject*; ... the third that it is a mere *object*, or something removed from the proximity of the subject;" ... and that "by subjoining any one of the pronominal elements to any other of them, we denote a motion or continuation from the position signified by the first element towards that indicated by the second." (p. 206.) He then applies this observation by stating that the words in *monia* express a quality or abstraction inferred from an act done—*alimonia*, for example, "the process of nourishing," *ceremonia*, the process of—what? Dr. Donaldson does not tell us. If the root of this famous word is, as Bopp supposes, the Sanskrit *kri*, meaning *facere* (ῥέζειν), *ceremonia* will be the process of performing a religious rite, the process of sacrifice.

ᵘ The passage referred to is of course Rev. xiv. 1—4. But whether the 144,000 redeemed ones, "which were not defiled with women, for they are virgins," are to be understood literally, or figuratively (as representing those who are undefiled by the spiritual fornication of idolatry and superstition), must always remain a question.

Bishop Wordsworth thinks they represent the whole body of the Apostolic or Primitive Church, and that the "women" stands for the woman who sits upon the scarlet-coloured beast (ch. xvii. 3), the plural being put for the singular, as in Acts xvii. 28 ("as certain also of your own poets have said," quoting only one of them), and in St. Matt. ii. 20 ("they that sought the young child's life," meaning only Herod).

It may be said, however, that our Church gives more or less sanction to the literal interpretation, by appointing this passage as the Epistle for the

whithersoever He goeth. Truly it is a blessed fellow-ship to dwell with Christ, and to sing the song which none but virgins sing. My son; let me counsel you to walk warily. When you return to our house, you will find many qualified to judge of your advancement, nor have I myself so little sagacity, that the proficiency you have made in the philosophers of your own choice, and the care with which you have studied them, will escape me." Rev. xiv. 3.

LETTER XVI.
To Godfrey the Monk.

" Herbert to Godfrey the Monk.

" I have been given to understand by many, who have informed me of it from a sense [v] of duty, that you are repeating your violations of discipline, and have returned again to your old habit of indolence: you are, they say, seldom seen in the cloister, often in the parlours [w]; slow

Godfrey is reprimanded for dissipation and violations of discipline, and

---

Day of the Feast of the Holy Innocents. It would be interesting to know when the idea of applying the passage to the innocent massacred babes of "Bethlehem and all the coasts thereof" was first broached.

Of course Herbert's application of the text to literal virginity, and the chastity professed in monastic vows, was the one more usually accepted in the Middle Ages. Yet Tichonius (quoted by Mr. Isaac Williams, Apocalypse with Notes and Reflections, p. 257), says very beautifully;

"Not virgins in body only do we understand in this place, but the whole Church which holds a pure faith. . . . For through Baptism, or through repentance, we are capable of being made in the inner man virgins and without guile."

[v] "Multorum religione cognovi te tuis redditum negligentiis, ad antiquum remeâsse torporem."

The word *religione* is found in the MS. (as we ascertained when we had an opportunity of consulting it); and it is our business to present the reader with a translation of that, wherever a translation is practicable. Adopting then this reading, we think the Latin words will bear the rendering given them in the text. But we cannot help seeing that Prebendary Benson's conjecture of *relatione* yields a much easier and more natural sense; "I hear from many," "I know by their telling it me." The Brussels MS. is a late and very indifferent one; and it is quite possible that the scribe wrote in a hurry *religione* for *relatione*.

[w] "often in the parlours"—continuus in *auditoriis*.

Auditorium in the old Latin had a twofold meaning. It meant a place for hearing the declamations of orators or the recitations of poets (a lecture-

reminded of the kindness shewn to his family, and of his broken vow.

in resorting to the church, swift in resorting to the grange[x], and the public roads which skirt it; you are

room, like the "school of one Tyrannus," in the Acts), and also a place where causes were tried, and the accused heard, a court, audience-chamber, justice-room. (From the place, it came to signify the persons who sat there, the judges' assessors, a consistory, &c.) The word in this sense, rendered into Greek, is ἀκροατήριον, which is used by St. Luke of the audience-chamber in Festus's palace at Cæsarea, called in our translation, the "place of hearing." (Acts xxv. 23.)

In the lower Latin the word has both an ecclesiastical and a conventual meaning. It was used to denote the lower end of a Christian Church, where such Catechumens or penitents as were called *audientes* stood to hear the Psalms, Lessons, and Sermon (being dismissed at the Prayers); and also (as here) the room in a monastery or nunnery used for the reception of strangers, and where the inmates of the convent were allowed to converse with their friends—a room called in Anglo-Saxon "Spræch-haus." (Thus, the decree of a council for the regulation of nunneries as given by Ducange, is; "Cum nullo masculo" [Sanctimonialibus] "colloquium habere liceat, nisi in Auditorio, et ibi coram testibus,"—"Let it never be lawful for the nuns to hold conversation with persons of the other sex, save in the parlour, and there only in the presence of witnesses.")

We are further informed by Ducange that in Cluniac and Cistercian convents, the Lecture-rooms or Schools, where the teaching went on, were also called "auditoria." Such however were certainly not the *auditoria* in which "Godfrey the Monk" found himself so much at home. His turn was for talking rooms rather than teaching rooms, for the chatter-house rather than the chapter-house.

The *locutorium* of a monastery seems to have been the room in which the monks were allowed to carry on general conversation *among themselves*. This would not suit Godfrey as well as communication with the world outside, which went on in the *auditorium*.

[x] *tardus ad ecclesiam, velox in curiâ*—"slow in resorting to the church, swift in resorting to the *grange*."

We give this translation of *curia* with some diffidence; but we think it most likely to be the correct one. *Curia* has the meaning of a piece of land in the country (often with a house on it),—an estate,—also sometimes called *mansus* (whence the word *manse*, so familiar in the Kirk of Scotland). No doubt the Cathedral Monastery at Norwich had farms and granges belonging to it in the neighbourhood; and Brother Godfrey's delight was to go down to one of these—(under some such pretext as that of the two "poure Scoleres" of Soler Hall, Cambridge, in Chaucer's "Reve's Tale," who—

> "to the wardein besily did crie,
> To yeve hem leve but a litel stound, (*time, while*)
> To gon to mille, and seen hir corn yground:
> And hardily they dorsten lay hir necke,
> The miller should not stele hem half a pecke
> Of corn by sleighte, ne by force hem reve" (*take away*,)—

constantly getting leave to have your blood let [y], con-

and there gossip, and do a little bit of business, and hear a little bit of news, while devouter brethren were attending to their duties in the Cathedral.

Curia is one of those many words which has wandered so far away from its earliest application, that in many of the derived significations not a feature of the parent signification survives.

Curia. (1.) A subdivision of the Roman citizens, who were divided into three tribes, and each tribe into ten curiæ.

(2.) The hall in which such a subdivision of the citizens met.

(3.) The senate-house—i.e. hall in which the representatives of *all* the *curiæ* met.

(4.) The Senate itself.

(5.) The Senate of a colony (a provincial Senate) as distinct from that of Rome.

The above are the classical meanings of the word. In the lower Latin it may be represented generally by our word *court*, which has forensic, political, and domestic meanings innumerable,—Court of justice; King's Court; High Court of Parliament; Court of Governors; Court-yard, &c.

With the latter meaning probably that of a *grange* connects itself,—outlying piece of land, *moated* perhaps (as in Shakspere), and with granaries (grange from *granum*) and farm-buildings on it. This we take to have been the sort of grange in which Brother Godfrey was so nimble (*velox*).

[y] "you are constantly getting leave to have your blood let"—*frequenter minueris*.

The tricks of monks resembled the tricks of boys at public schools. Blood-letting (called in the Mediæval Latin *Minutio*) was a practice in those days considered sanitary. In most monasteries there was a general bleeding of the whole community (with the exception of those who were required to provide for the spiritual and temporal necessities of the Brotherhood, and who were obliged to postpone their *minution* till the others had gone through it) five times a-year, in September, before Advent, before Lent, after Easter, and after Pentecost. The barber was the operator; a room was assigned for the operation; and it was done with prayer.

Thus much may easily be understood. But it does surprise us to find that the operation should be attractive. One could have thought of it as a penance which might have an effect upon a high-spirited and masterful monk like that of depriving a horse of his beans; but when we read that the monks had such a *penchant* for it as made it necessary to enact that blood-letting should never take place at other than the prescribed times, except in cases of serious illness; when we read that though "a canon of the Council of Aix had ordained that no fixed time should be observed, but that blood-letting should be allowed to any one according to his necessity," "the Cistercians" and other Orders "abridged the prescribed liberty," and that even the Cluniacs, who professed to give the same liberty as the Council of Aix, yet allowed no one to have his blood-let in Lent, we are curious to know the reason which made blood-letting so acceptable an operation to the flesh, that there was something in it that matched ill with

stantly getting leave to have a bath[z]. You are indulging [a] your body, you are ruining your soul, and not only yours,

a season of humiliation and fasting. And the reason was, that special exemptions and indulgences were granted at the period of blood-letting—"special consolation" (*specialis consolatio*) under the trial of a reduced and weakened physique. Those who had submitted to the operation were not expected to attend Church. Their presence in Chapter was dispensed with. Penal discipline, if any had to be inflicted, was remitted till they were strong again. They had *mixtum* (shall we call it negus?) for two days, or more if they required it. They might eat meat, and did eat it with great gusto. They were allowed a fire in the infirmary (how great an indulgence let poor Orderic's touching conclusion of his fourth book attest; "Many disasters are impending over mankind, which, if they should all be written, would fill huge volumes. Now, *stiffened with the winter cold*, I shall employ myself with other occupations, and, very weary, I propose to finish this present book. But when the fine weather of the calm spring returns, I will take up again what I have imperfectly related." [Ordericus Vitalis, as quoted in Dean Church's St. Anselm, pp. 48, 49.]) And the consequence of these exemptions and indulgences was, that the less spiritual members of the community, who gave trouble to their superiors, often "shammed ill," and got leave under false pretences to "stay out." They drew their cowls over their heads, and went hobbling about with a stick, until at length the Abbot's or Prior's heart relented, and they were consigned to the infirmary and to the operation of the barber. One of the Cottonian MSS. (Tib. B. 13) quoted by Fosbrooke, vol. ii. p. 154, says, "When, in compliance with the strictness of the monastic rule, meat cannot be eaten in the refectory or in public, it is taken in private *all the more greedily, and voraciously, and immoderately*, and for this purpose the Monks pretend frequent illnesses, and affect very frequent blood-letting to get this privilege." Herbert knew that Brother Godfrey was not above these tricks.

Those who are curious to see the authorities for these statements may consult Archdeacon Hale's Registrum Prioratus B. M. Wigorniensis, Notes, pp. cvii., cviii. ; Fosbrooke's British Monachism, vol. ii. pp. 152—154 ; and Ducange, *sub voce* MINUO.

[z] "constantly getting leave to have a bath."

In Mr. Anstruther's edition of the Letters, the words are "frequenter *bannearis.*" We did not, when consulting the Brussels MS., collate the word *bannearis;* but we strongly suspect that the right reading is that suggested to us by the present Bishop of Lincoln, "frequenter balnearis." The bath was just one of those indulgences which was allowed to sick or infirm monks, and which they affected infirmity to obtain. The Rev. D. J. Stewart, in his valuable "Architectural History of Ely Cathedral" (Van Voorst, 1868), says, p. 273 ;

"In early times many diseases were treated with baths, and accordingly in Benedictine convents a bath was provided for the sick, and kept almost entirely for their use. The young and old monks were alike forbidden to indulge in what was then considered to be luxury without a special permission."

but perchance also some of those souls, which I had entrusted to your guidance. Is this the recompense which you pledged yourself to make for the love shown you, in receiving and sheltering in God's house your aged father, and your son of seven years old? You err grievously, and by your heedlessness of my instructions, you have broken, in a spirit of sluggish indolence, the engagement you made with me to be zealous. Brace yourself for a new effort, and roused to a better mind, amend those faults [which I have in-

---

In a roll deposited in the Treasury of Norwich Cathedral of the date of 1341, containing the Cellarer's account, we find the following items;
"In balneatione fratrum, octo denarii."
"Item barbitonsori, quatuor denarii."
(For the bathing of the Fraternity, 8 Pence.
Item to the barber (for bleeding perhaps, as well as shaving), 4 Pence.)
And in one of the rolls of the *Camerarius* of Ely, of the date of Henry VI., which is given us by Mr. Stewart, p. 236, we find;
"In stipendiis unius balneatoris et eciam barbitonsoris, per annum xx*s*."
(Spent on the wages of one bathing man and also a barber, twenty shillings for the year.)
Fosbrooke (History of British Monachism, vol. i. p. 191) tells us that the bathing was usually under the superintendence of the *Camerarius* or *Chamberlain.*
"Three times in a year, at Easter, Christmas, and the Nativity of the Blessed Virgin Mary, the Chamberlain was to provide the use of baths for the refreshment of the bodies of the monks. . . . He was to hire a servant for the service of the baths" (the *balneator* probably of the Ely roll), "besides the one devoted to the bathed. . . . He had a tailor and two bathers in his service. . . . The monks were to go to the baths under the sub-chamberlain's direction; and, in the absence of the chamberlain, he could grant the use of them with the Prior's consent. He was to accompany the servant of the bathed in bringing and carrying back the clothes of the bathed into the dormitory; and that servant, in his presence, was to count the clothes, both in bringing them and returning them."

ᵃ *Curas cutem, perdis animam.*
Curare cutem is an Horatian phrase, which perhaps Herbert affected as being Horatian (see Hor., Ep. i. 4. 15); and which the great satirist varies in Sat. ii. 5. 37, where we read,

"... ire domum atque
Pelliculam curare jube."

Cutis is the serious and proper word, being the skin of the *living* being. *Pellicula* would be a slang expression, used *in chaff* ("Take care of your precious *little hide*"); *pellis* being the skin in severance from the body, the dried skin.

dicated], keep yourself in the cloister, be much in the church, if you wish to retain my esteem, and to abide faithfully by the promise you made me."

A.D. 1096. Date of the foundation of Norwich Cathedral. Previous removals of the East Anglian See. The year 1096 is memorable in the life of Herbert, and in the Annals of Norwich, as that in which the first stone of the Cathedral was laid. The see of the East Angles had been hitherto migratory. Dunwich on the coast, whose buildings, civil and ecclesiastical, have been merged by the encroachment of the waters, had been the centre of diocesan administration chosen by St. Felix. Nearly half a century after the time of St. Felix, in the year A.D. 673, the see had been bisected, and a bishop located at North Elmham as well as at Dunwich. Nearly two centuries more elapsed; and then, the second bishop being found superfluous, a succeeding generation (as so often happens) undid the work of its predecessor (A.D. 870), and Elmham alone enjoyed the honour of being the Cathedral city of the East Angles. Again two centuries rolled away; and then (A.D. 1075), Elmham having decayed in importance, the see was transferred by Bishop Herfast, the Conqueror's chaplain, to Thetford. But Thetford had a very brief career as an episcopal city. The second bishop from Herfast was once again to remove the see. Herbert, we are told, designed to make Norwich, which had now superseded Thetford in importance, a permanent diocesan centre, and to indicate this by building there a church of unusual architectural pretensions. The first step was to procure a site;

and one offered itself, suitable for his purpose, called the Cowholm. This word, according to its etymology, denotes a "green plot of ground environed by water, and just rising[b] above it," used for the pasture of kine. We are told that this plot of pasture-ground belonged to the manor of Thorpe, and, like Thorpe itself, to the hundred of Blofield; that its inhabitants were dependent upon Thorpe for the offices of the Church, and claimed the right of sepulture there; that the street bounding it on the north was called Holm Street; and that it contained a church built long before the Conquest, and called St. Mary-in-the-Marsh. The exact limits of the Cowholm are a moot-point, which it is not very easy to settle. Mr. Harrod ("Castles and Convents of Norfolk," p. 234) doubts whether it was conterminous with the modern Close. He says that "the name implies a pasture surrounded with water, which never could have been applicable to the whole of the present precinct." But might not the word "Holm" be used loosely (as indeed it is now-a-days) to indicate a tract of meadow-ground lying close upon the margin of a river, and seeming to rise out of it, without being exactly insulated? The best guide to the solution of the questions about the limits of the Cowholm will probably be the ancient registers preserved in the treasury of the Cathedral. Among these is found an elaborate treatise on the liberties and privileges of the

The Cowholm chosen as the site of the Cathedral.

Boundaries of the Cowholm.

---

[b] This is the meaning of the word "holm" given in Bosworth's Anglo-Saxon Dictionary.

Church of Norwich, compiled probably in the sixteenth century, with reference to the disputes between the Convent and the City. Here it is stated that Herbert built his monastery and palace in a marsh then called "the Cowholme;" and the charters are retailed which secured to him certain tracts of land for the purpose. The first is a charter of William II., granting him ("to make his church, his houses, and those of his monks upon") "lands at Norwich Castle," which are described as bounded on the East by the river Wensum from the Bishop's Bridge to Lovelly's Stathe (Lovelly's Stathe[e] or wharf was rather more than a third of the way from the present "Ferry" at the bottom of the Close to the Foundry Bridge), on the South by a line drawn from the river to the south-west angle of the monastery wall (passing by the Friars Minors and St. Cuthbert's Church on the west), on the West by the present frontage of the Close (from its south-west angle in Vinegar Yard to its north-west angle in St. Martin's Street), and finally on the North, by the line of St. Martin's Street, St. Martin's Plain, Tabernacle Street, Palace Street, and Bishopsgate Street (formerly Holm Street). All within these limits is coloured red in the Plan here submitted to the reader.—A second charter follows, in which the same king, at the request of Roger Bigod, grants to Herbert and

---

[e] We do not seem to know this word; but we believe it means wharf. A *staith* in modern engineering is, we believe, a line of rails abutting on a river, for the purpose of discharging coals or other articles into the holds of vessels.

36 Parochial Churches now in use
27 Churches demolished
16 Distinct Chapels, within the Walls
36 Cells, Hermitages, Anchorages &c } most of them having
 1 College .... } Chapels belonging to them,
22 Religious Houses, & Hospitals .... } which are not included
───
138 Within the Walls of the City

 8 Religious Houses & Chapels } — . . — —

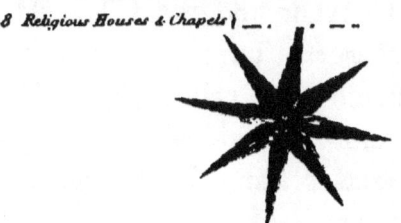

N.B. The Sites or Precincts of Religious }
    Houses are distinguished thus .... }
    The Sites of the present .... }
    Church Yards thus .... }

his Church the land of St. Michael, and the land of Taverham,—the former being a rectangular strip, which formed a south-west corner to the plot of ground granted by the previous charter. Upon this strip (somewhere near the line of houses which runs from Queen's Street to the Ethelbert Gate) Earl Roger's palace had formerly stood; and Herbert gave the earl in exchange for it some of his patrimonial property in Suffolk, —a carucate of land in Syleham, and another in Wykes. The strip is coloured blue in our plan. A charter of Henry I. follows, by which the manor of Eaton and a part of the king's borough of Norwich are assigned to the Convent. This would comprehend the present Hospital premises, and, in short, all the ground lying between the river on the north and the Close on the south, the western boundary being Whitefriars Street, St. Martin's Plain, and St. Martin's Street. This space is coloured green in the plan.—Such are the three assignments of territory made to Herbert. We venture to think, notwithstanding grave opinions to the contrary, that the earliest of these assignments was the Cowholm. It seems to have been in the possession partly of the king, partly of the citizens, from whom Herbert purchased it. In the succeeding reign, it would appear, the king granted the whole manor of Thorpe (of which the Cowholm was a part) to Herbert, in requital doubtless of the good service which he had done to the Church; and the Bishop made it over by charter to his Monastery.

A.D. 1096.
Foundation-stone of the Cathedral.

The site having been secured, Herbert laid the foundation-stone, we are told, with his own hands, and, in memory of the transaction, caused to be engraven thereon, in capitals, this brief inscription [d];

Its inscription.

"THIS, THE FIRST STONE OF THIS TEMPLE, THE LORD HERBERT LAID, IN THE NAME OF THE FATHER AND OF THE SON AND OF THE HOLY GHOST. AMEN."

Hubert de Rye, a certain baron of the realm, who was then under a vow to the Holy Land, laid the second stone. In acknowledgment of his father's services [e], he had been made Castellan

[d] Neville (*Authorities*), followed by Godwin accurately, and by Weever inaccurately. Neville's words are; "Cujus fundamenti lapidem primum ipse suis jecisse manibus dicitur, paucisque *majusculis* litteris lapide incisis, ejus rei memoriam posteris sempiternam tradidisse." *Majusculus* (the diminutive of the comparative form of *magnus*) has here doubtless its technical sense of capital characters, also called *uncials*. Its ordinary meaning is *somewhat greater*, just as the ordinary meaning of *minusculus* (applied technically to small characters) is *somewhat less*.

Old Fuller calls the inscription in question "this elogium." An "elogium" in Latin has several meanings,—a maxim or apothegm, an epitaph, an inscription on a statue, or on a votive tablet, a clause in a will, an indictment or specification of an offence. (Thus the τίτλος, *titulus*, or title written over our Saviour's Cross by Pilate might have been called an *elogium*.) The French derivative *éloge*, like our eulogy, is never used except in a good sense. Both these words connect themselves rather with the Greek εὐλογία, praise, panegyric, blessing, than with the Latin *elogium*.

[e] His father, the first Hubert de Rye, some twenty years before the Conquest, had saved the life of William the Bastard by putting on a wrong scent five powerful Norman Barons, who were pursuing, and intended to assassinate him. The insurrection of these Barons being quelled, Hubert naturally stood high in Duke William's favour, and was sent by him in great state on an embassy to Edward the Confessor, from which he returned "bearing the tokens by which William was declared heir to Edward, viz. a two-handled sword with a hilt, in which were enclosed the relics of certain saints, a hunter's horn of gold, and a great stag's head."

of Norwich Castle by the Conqueror in 1074, and in this capacity doubtless assisted at the laying of the first stone of Norwich Cathedral. But he had another tie to the diocese of the East Angles, which made his appearance on this occasion appropriate. He had married Agnes de Beaufeu, the widow of Herbert's immediate predecessor in the see; and he and she so richly endowed the Cathedral, that they deserve to be called part founders of it. Her son by Bishop William de Beaufeu was a member of the Cathedral Monastery, and became Archdeacon of Norwich[f] in 1107. He doubtless is the "Ricardus Archidiaconus" of Herbert's Letters (see Letter LIV.)

It would be most interesting to know under what part of the present building this first stone is located. We are indebted to Mr. J. L'Estrange, a learned antiquary of Norwich, for the following observations on this point. It will be seen that he does not accept the ordinary view, which, placing the foundation-stone somewhere beneath the present screen, between the Nave and the Choir, supposes Herbert to have built eastward. *Its site.*

"Blomefield tells us, vol. iv. p. 1, that Bp. Herbert laid the foundation-stone in 1096 in the place where afterwards was made the chapel of the Blessed Virgin of Pity. He afterwards (at p. 29, vol. iv.) identifies this chapel with the '*Antechoir.*'

"Now in the first Register of the Prior and Convent of Norwich there is an account of the foundation and

---

[f] These particulars are taken from a most interesting paper put forth by Mr. Walter Rye, giving an account of his family, and especially of the branch settled in Norfolk. This valuable paper appeared first in the Herald and Genealogist, vol. vi.

endowment of the Church (which I believe to have been written by Bartholomew Cotton, or to have been compiled by him), which Blomefield apparently quotes. There we are told that the Bishop[g] began the church in the place where now is the chapel of Blessed Mary, almost in the middle of the same chapel, where he made an altar in honour of St. Saviour. A line or two before, the writer tells us that Herbert completed the church *as far* as the altar of the Holy Cross, which is now called St. William's altar. The site of St. William's altar is well known to have been on the north of the Choir door. Blomefield did not know that Bishop Herbert had built a Lady-chapel: hence he corrupted his author by inserting 'of Pity.'

Probable error of Blomefield on the site of the foundation-stone.

"There can be no doubt, I think, that Bishop Herbert laid the foundation-stone at the extreme east end. When a much longer Lady-chapel was built by Bishop Suffield, the spot would be 'almost in the middle of the same chapel,' as may be seen on Mr. Harrod's plan."

We may add, that in the course of excavations recently made with the view of laying bare the foundations of the two Lady-chapels (foundations of an astonishing solidity), search was made for this stone, but in vain. Were "first stones" in those days, laid (as now for the most part) above

---

[g] The passage from the Register is as follows;

"Reg^r. I. P. and Conv. of Norwich, p. 22.

"Idem vero Episcopus de quolibet mesuagio sue dyocesis ad constructionem operis Ecclesie Norwycensis instituit quoddam certum solui. Perfecit autem idem Herbertus Ecclesiam Norwycensem suo tempore, prout ex relatione antiquorum didici, non tamen scriptum inueni, vsque ad altare sancte Crucis, quod modo vocatur altare Sancti Willelmi. Idem eciam omnes domus episcopales excepta magna aula construxit. Incepit autem opus ecclesie sue in loco ubi nunc est capella beate marie fere in medio loco eiusdem capelle, et ibidem fecit quoddam altare in honore sancti Salvatoris et in opere suo primum lapidem primus apposuit in quo scriptum erat. In nomine patris et filij et spiritus sancti amen? Ego Herbertus Episcopus apposui istum lapidem. Deinde quidam Baro nomine Hubertus de Ry deo devotus secundum lapidem in prædicto opere apponens."

ground, the substructure having been in great part completed before the "laying" begins? We cannot say.

Another question of interest, less doubtful perhaps than that of the exact whereabouts of the foundation-stone, is how much of the present building should be attributed to Herbert. On this point the only existing evidence is the first Register of the Prior and Convent, quoted in the last note. It will be observed that the writer states that he has no documentary evidence for his assertion, but received it from oral tradition. The assertion is that Herbert completed the church "as far as the altar of the Holy Cross, which is now called the altar of St. William." Now this altar of St. William[h] stood on the left

How much of the present Cathedral is due to Herbert.

[h] St. William of Norwich was a boy martyr, who, some twenty years after Herbert's death, was crucified by the Jews, in derision of the Christian faith. His body was honoured with miracles, and in the year 1150 removed into the choir of the Cathedral, where an altar was erected to him. A chapel also was built in his honour on the spot where his body was found, the foundations of which may still be clearly traced on Mousehold Heath,—then the site of a forest. It was called the chapel of St. William in the Wood. Here is an account of St. William, extracted from an old translation of Capgrave's *Nova Legenda*. We modernise the spelling.

"St. William, the child and martyr, was born in England; and when his mother was with child of him, she saw in a vision a fish called a luce" (a full-grown pike) "and twelve red fins, like as it had been sparkled with blood; and when she had put the fish into her bosom, she thought it grew so much that her bosom could not hold it; and suddenly it flew above the clouds into heaven. And a priest that had great grace in expounding of visions said she should have a blessed child, who at the age of twelve years should go into heaven. And when he was a young child, it happened to him to touch the irons of a man that was fettered, and anon the irons fell off. And when he was but seven years old, he would fast three days in the week, and would be at the church in prayer. And afterwards at Norwich he was put to a skinner to inform him, when on an Easter Day he was taken privily by the

of the present screen, as one enters the choir from the west, where the *piscina* attached to it may be seen at the present day. Accepting this assertion, in default of anything more certain, it will appear that the parts of the present church due to Herbert are the presbytery (or eastern arm beyond the transept), the transept itself with the lowest stage of the tower, and those three bays of the nave, which in Norman churches were

Jews, and they in despite of our Lord mocked him, and cruelly martyred him. They thrust all the blood out of his head with cords, and then they did shave his head, and pricked it with thorns, and put him upon a cross, and thrust him into the left side grievously; and so by great martyrdom he went to our Lord, the seventh of the Kalends of May; and that done, they carried him towards a wood to hide him. And a Christian man came by them, and perceived that they carried the dead man. Wherefore they feared much, and privily hung him up in a tree in the wood with a cord, and went to the sheriff, and for a hundred marks the sheriff caused the man to be sworn, that he should never discover it while he lived. And five years after, when he should die, St. William appeared to him, and bade him that he should discover it, fearing nothing. And so he did; and then a light from heaven shined upon the place where he lay. And afterwards on an Easter evening his body was found by a nun in the wood, lying at the root of an oak in his coat, hosed and shod, and his head shaven; and there were by him two crows, that attempted to have torn him and eaten him. But they had no power thereto; and then he was taken up with all the people, and buried with great joy. A man that had been long sick was led in a vision by an angel into a goodly place, full of pleasant flowers; and there he saw our Lord sitting on a throne, and innumerable angels and saints about him, and on his right hand in great majesty was the seat of our Blessed Lady; and at the feet of our Lord he saw a child, about the age of twelve years, sitting in a seat of gold, and a crown of gold upon his head, his face shining bright as the sun, and angels did honour to him. Then he asked of the angel who he was; and the angel said, 'This is he that in derision and opprobrium of the passion of our Lord the Jews of Norwich did put to death,' and by him he said he should be made whole. And he vanished away; and when his spirit was come again to the body, he went to Norwich, and was made whole as the angel said. And many other miracles our Lord had showed for this blessed child. Four that were blind, five that were mute, two of the dropsy, three vexed with devils, and men of the falling sickness, some perishing in the sea, fettered and deformed, and of divers other sickness, were healed and delivered by this glorious martyr."

screened off to form the choir. The nave proper, that portion of the church which lay beyond the screen westward, he left it to a future generation[1] to add, according to the wise plan of the great builders of those days, who did not hesitate to entrust to the labour and piety of after ages the completion of grand architectural designs.

[1] But Mr. Harrod, a very great authority on such subjects, is of opinion that the present nave as well as the choir is due to Herbert. These are his words;

"On the 24th of September, 1101, the Cathedral Church was dedicated to the Holy Trinity, and Herbert signed the foundation-deed. This was five years from the commencement of the work, and yet, although Herbert lived eighteen years after, Blomefield asserts that the nave was built by Eborard, his successor, and the whole of the buildings not completed until nearly the end of the century.

"But in whatever direction we look, we find traces of early Norman, the work of Bishop Herbert's time. Blomefield assigns the choir and transepts to him, and the nave to Bishop Eborard. The only shadow of a foundation for this lies in the occurrence of the zigzag or chevron moulding round the arches of the triforium. This has been very positively asserted to be a mark of late Norman; but the time of its introduction is not at all clearly ascertained, and as it appears here it is of the simplest kind, and has the billet-moulding, a very early form, in the arches above and below it." (Castles and Convents of Norfolk, pp. 245, 246.)

Professor Willis (another great authority) is in favour of the nave being of later date, founding his opinion partly on the zigzag ornament round the arches, which, he says, "was not introduced into Norman work till a very late period," partly on certain variations in the bases of the nave columns.

Mr. Harrod does not consider the Professor's reasoning satisfactory. Among other arguments which he assigns for believing that Herbert built the nave, is the following;

"All writers concur in assigning the steeple to Herbert. Is it at all probable it would be commenced and completed, and the west side of it left entirely open and without support? I do not think any architects would have ventured to raise it many feet above the roof of the choir and transepts, until a considerable portion of the four flanking structures had been raised around it." (Castles and Convents, p. 261.)

But surely, if the assertion of the First Register be true, "a considerable portion of the four flanking structures *was* raised around" the steeple in Herbert's time; nor was "the west side of it left entirely open and without support." If he finished the church "as far as the altar of St. William," he built three bays westward of the transept, which would be quite sufficient for the support of the tower. Professor Willis, we submit, has the best of it.

Original Norman roofs of the choir and transept destroyed.

But there were two important points in which the choir and transept, as Herbert left them, differ from the choir and transept of the present day. First, like all Norman choirs and transepts [k], they had wooden roofs. The stone roof of the present presbytery, with bosses at the intersections of the groining, on which is sculptured a well with a golden parapet, alternating with a shield, was the work of Bishop Goldwell in the fifteenth century; that of the transept, the bosses of which represent our Lord's early life and miracles, is due to Bishop Nix in the sixteenth century; while that of the choir *proper* (or space between the transept and the screen) is part of Lyhart's great work, and represents on its bosses the earlier part of Old Testament History. In this respect, then, the present presbytery, transept, and choir, are richer and more decorated than as Herbert left them. But in another respect, his fair work has been sadly

Herbert's Lady-chapel destroyed by fire.

mutilated. The church originally ended in a trefoil of chapels projecting from, and opening into, the beautiful apse at the east end. The northern and southern chapels, called respectively

---

[k] There is a most interesting Norman roof still in existence at Peterborough Cathedral, the date of which is between A.D. 1177 and 1199. It is of wood, painted in panels in the shape of lozenges and half-lozenges, and contains many curious representations of flowers and grotesque figures, —a bust of Janus, a picture of the Harvest Dame holding the harvest moon in her hand, and of a monkey carrying an owl on his paw and riding a goat. The last is supposed to be a caricature of the degenerate nobility, who were given up to hawking (represented by the owl) and to lust (represented by the goat). The monkey sits with his face to the goat's tail. An accurate lithographic drawing of this roof, with descriptive letter-press, has been published by Mr. Strickland, of Peterborough. (Bell, 186, Fleet-street.)

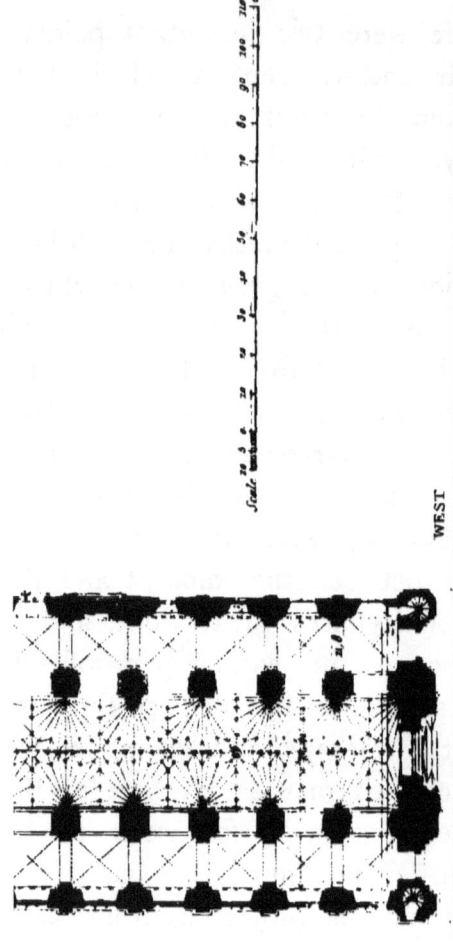

NORWICH CATHEDRAL CHURCH.
Ground-plan, to accompany the Life of Herbert de Losinga.

the Jesus Chapel and St. Luke's, still remain. But the eastern or central one, which was of a similar circular shape, and formed the Lady-chapel of the Cathedral, was accidentally destroyed by fire in 1171. A rectangular Lady-chapel was afterwards substituted for it by Bishop Walter Suffield (1245—1257); and this, judging from the entrance-arches to it, which still survive, and which are exquisite specimens of Early English architecture, must have been of singular beauty. It seems to have lingered, though in a state of great disrepair and dilapidation, till the reign of Elizabeth, when what still remained of it was taken down by Dean Gardiner and his Chapter, by way probably of evading the expense of restoration. Its foundations, with those of Herbert's Lady-chapel, may still be traced in the private garden at the east end of the church. *The second Lady-chapel, and its fate.*

In planning and rearing this noble structure, Herbert fell in with the taste of his age. There was a rage for magnificent edifices, by which he, in common with many of his contemporaries, seems to have been seized. The wealthier proprietors of those days either reared castles for purposes of state and security, or else sought to expiate the misdeeds of a life of violence and rapine, and to promote the interests of religion, by founding great monastic piles. Rochester, Chichester, and Durham Cathedrals, the crypt of Conrad's Choir at Canterbury, St. Alban's Abbey, parts of Norwich Castle, and the Church of Castle Rising in Norfolk, are all works of *Architectural taste of the age.*

Herbert's age. Conrad's Choir was commenced in the same year as our Cathedral. The Red King himself, who was then upon the throne, set the fashion of sumptuous architecture to his wealthier subjects. He threw a wall round the Tower, and a bridge over the Thames, and bequeathed to posterity, to attest the magnificence of his architectural designs, not only Westminster Hall[1], but the saying in regard to it,—that, "vast as it was, it was only the vestibule of the palace he intended to rear." Little thought he that a later generation would view his saying in the light of a suggestion, and convert that sumptuous hall into the vestibule of the Houses of Parliament, which go under the name of the National Palace of Westminster.

We must here say one more word respecting the removal of the see from Thetford to Norwich, which Bale attributes to this year (1096), and Rudborne to the year preceding, while Cotton (the most trustworthy of all the chroniclers, as having been himself a monk of the Benedictine monastery, which Herbert founded in connexion with his Cathedral) fixes it in 1094, two years before the laying of the foundation-stone of the Church. It was an age of transference of sees, as well as of sumptuous buildings; for Malmesbury tells us that "three sees were at this time transferred from their ancient situations; Wells

A.D. 1094.

Transference of sees in that age.

---

[1] Rufus's Westminster Hall exists no more. His hall had two rows of columns down the centre; these were removed by Richard II., and the whole rebuilt nearly from the foundations.

to Bath, by John; Chester to Coventry, by Robert; Thetford to Norwich, by Herbert, all through greater ambition than ought to have influenced men of such eminence." It is no infrequent experience in any country to find the centres of civilization and population moving. One or two generations suffice to draw off trade and factories from a particular spot, and fix them in another, where they thrive more vigorously. Fashion is still more capricious than trade, often throwing its votaries on comparatively unfrequented spots, for no better reason than some supposed superiority in the climate or the water, and gradually making out of a fishing hamlet or a remote country village an annual resort of persons of the higher classes, in quest of health or recreation. Thetford, the seat of the East Anglian see in Herbert's time, had begun to decline in commerce, in population, and consequently in importance. Herbert, in this respect like other prelates of his age, felt that the social and commercial centre of his see should be also its religious one. It may have been partly ambition, (as Malmesbury intimates), which led him to reason thus. Stationed in a city of waning importance, the bishop would no longer be felt as a power in his diocese. The Church could not have her headquarters in an obsolete decaying town, leading nowhere, and no longer drawing to it the wealthy classes, without imminent risk of being overlooked. But surely considerations of this kind need not have been purely am-

Reasons for it.

Herbert's motive in transferring his see need not have been purely ambitious.

bitious and interested. It would be a point of holy policy to make a rising thriving town, where there is movement of thought, collision of mind with mind, and progress by antagonism, into an ecclesiastical centre. It was on this principle that the Gospel was first propagated, our Blessed Lord choosing as the great scene of His ministry, not the sacred metropolis of Jerusalem, but the shore of the Galilæan Lake, the great highway of commerce between the East and West, and precisely that part of the promised land where thought would be most on the alert, and the agencies of civilization most at work. And it is a principle, which surely should be borne in mind and acted upon, in bringing the influences of religion to bear upon a country imperfectly civilized. Where the civilization has thoroughly penetrated the country, and risen to its highest point, the divorce of the religious and the political centres becomes naturally of far less moment. In these days of rapid locomotion, the Bishops of Chichester and Lichfield may acquiesce in the location of their respective sees at those cities, because a very short journey, attended neither with inconvenience nor fatigue, would bring the one to Brighton and the other to Wolverhampton; and yet even so, notwithstanding the venerable and precious associations which must always gather round the old Cathedral of a diocese, neither of these prelates might be sorry to be domesticated somewhat nearer to the centres of life and activity in their respective dioceses. And it should not be forgotten that, independently of the inclinations and preferences of particular bishops, there was on record a synodical decision of the English Church, which had ruled the removal of certain bishoprics from villages to cities. In compliance with this decision, which had been arrived at by a synod held at London under Lanfranc in 1075, Sherborn and Ramsbury had already been transferred to Old Sarum; Wells to Bath; Selsey to Chichester; Lichfield to Chester; Dorchester to Lincoln; and *Elmham to Thetford*. Herbert then was moving in a groove already cut for him by the Councils of his Church, when he determined to transfer his seat from Thetford, a city now on the wane, to Norwich, a town daily rising in importance.

Synodical decision, A.D. 1075, on the transference of sees.

We are not informed of the exact period of the year at which the foundation-stone of Norwich Cathedral was laid. But in the same year, either before or after it, Herbert was called up to London to assist in the consecration of Gerard to the see of Hereford, and of Samson[m] to the see of Worcester, which took place in St. Paul's Cathedral. Both these prelates had been ordained priests on the day previous to their consecration. Anselm himself was the chief consecrator. Thomas I. of York (who had consecrated Her-

Herbert assists at the consecration of Gerard and Samson.

---

[m] We are told by Eadmer (Hist. Nov., lib. ii. p. 45, D. Lut. Par. 1721) that these candidates for the Episcopate not yet having received all the minor Orders, Samson was ordained deacon and priest, and Gerard priest, *the day previously* by Anselm at Lambeth. Eadmer says the *Ordination* took place "in Sabbato jejunii quarti mensis." But Professor Stubbs's *Registrum Sacrum* would make it June 7, June 8 being the date there assigned to the *consecration*.

bert), Maurice of London, and Gundulf of Rochester, joined with the Archbishop of Canterbury and with our prelate, in raising the two novices to the Episcopal dignity. Anselm was now in full enjoyment of his powers as Metropolitan. In the June of the previous year (1095)[n] he had received the *pallium*, which was brought to him in great state by Walter, Bishop of Albano, the Pope's legate. Anselm had declined to receive it from the hands of the King. The King had equally made up his mind that he would have a voice in the conferring of it. The matter was at length arranged by a compromise. The King ordered the legate to place the *pallium* on the altar of the Cathedral of Canterbury. Thus he thought that he sufficiently maintained his claim to bestow it. Anselm took it from the altar, with the secret understanding that it was in this manner transmitted to him direct from St. Peter. He wore it doubtless on the occasion just referred to, when he consecrated Gerard and Samson, with the assistance of the Primate of York and his own three suffragans of Canterbury. But the understanding on the subject of the pall, which he had come to with the King, did not long serve to hold them together. In the course of the next year, a fresh quarrel arose on the subject of the contingent furnished by Anselm to the royal expedition into Wales. The King declared the Archbishop's retainers to be neither able-bodied nor sufficiently equipped, and pro-

[n] Hook, vol. ii. p. 215.

posed to fine him for his neglect of feudal duty. Anselm sought to evade the penalty, by asking permission to leave the kingdom, and go to the Pope for his advice. The King received his request with a menace that, if he went, he would confiscate the revenues of his see, and never receive him again in the character of Archbishop. Anselm persisted in his design of going, and, after a brief interview with the King, in which he offered and gave him his pastoral benediction, he set off (Oct., 1097°). His mind foreboded truly, when it told him that he should not again see William. He met him no more; and the suffragans of Canterbury were left for nearly three years without their head ᴾ.

A.D. 1097.

which leads to a final parting.

In the following year (1098) died Herbert's father, Abbot of Winchester. We insert a letter in which Herbert refers to this domestic loss, while writing to some bishop in whom he had found a second father. The reader will admire the humorous apology which Herbert makes at the close of the letter, for retaining as a gift a palfrey which he had received as a loan.

A.D. 1098. Death of Herbert's father.

LETTER XIX.

To Rodbert.

"To his host and potter ᑫ, Rodbert, Herbert, his guest and handiwork, sendeth greeting.

"By entertaining the angels, and bidding them courteously to his board, Abraham obtained for the

Herbert commends the great

° Hook, vol. ii. p. 224.

ᴾ Anselm returned to England Sept. 23, 1100.

ᑫ *Suo hospiti et figulo.* What Herbert means by calling Rodbert his

hospitality barren Sarah the gift of fruitfulness; and his nephew Lot, when shewing a similar hospitality, escaped the burning of Sodom. The two disciples going to Emmaus compelled the Saviour to enter into their lodging, and spread a table before Him, and finally recognised in the breaking of bread Him whom, in the interpretation of the Holy Scriptures, they had failed to discern. So you also, most hospitable bishop, compelled my lowly self to enter your house, lodged me in your own chamber, and sated me with an abundance of good things; so that, in short, the father, whom I buried some time ago at Winchester, I have recently found, come to life again, in London[r]. The very doors of your house sent forth a pleasant odour of charity, and its inner chambers oozed forth and distilled with an exuberant sweetness; in my welcome, in my stay, and particularly at my departure, whatever met my eye bespoke the father, and nothing wore a strange or foreign look. You loaded my pack-horses[s] with so many good things to eat and drink, that, on my return, there was a sufficiency not for me only, but for my household. Such were the favours which you bestowed on my necessities, not as the recompense of my merits, but of your own free will. And these favours, I say, since I cannot requite them to you, may our Lord and Saviour Christ requite them, who by His Spirit hath instilled this kindness into your heart, and hath comforted me in my necessity with the gifts which you have bestowed.—But as to your palfrey, I have long

marginalia: hospitality which Rodbert had shown him; and announces his intention of keeping a palfrey which his correspondent had lent him.

"potter," it is hard to say;—perhaps that he, as a younger and less experienced man, had taken a shape from this older and more venerable dignitary of the Church.

[r] All that appears from the Letter is that Rodbert was a bishop (*pontifex*) residing in London. The Bishops of London in Herbert's time were Maurice, consecrated by Lanfranc 1086, and Richard de Beames, consecrated by Anselm 1108.

[s] *Clitellarios meos. Clitellæ* are packsaddles or panniers; and *clitellarius* the animal carrying them. "Bovi clitellas imponere" is a Latin proverb for devolving an office on an unqualified person—"putting a square man into a round hole." (Cic. ad Att., lib. v. ep. 15).

thought what I should do with him, whether I should follow in regard to him the wish of your heart, or the bidding of your mouth? for in your heart you wished that I should keep the palfrey; with your mouth you bade me send him back. Pretending then not to hear the momentary bidding of your voice, I have discerned the secret intent of your heart, and have made up my mind to obey that. I have kept [t] your palfrey; but the most righteous Judge will restore him to thee [one day] in a flowery plain, at that last great jubilee [u], when unto all men all that has been theirs shall be restored."

Two events of great interest, one to the Church, A.D. 1099. and the other to the cause of civilization and pro-

---

[t] Robert Grosstête, Bishop of Lincoln (1235—1253), manifested rather a different spirit from our Herbert on this matter of palfreys. Witness the following anecdote, taken from Mr. Luard's Preface to his Letters;

"Soon after his promotion to Lincoln, when in great want of horses, his steward came, while he was sitting at his books, and told him that two white monks,—probably in hopes of future favours,—had brought him two very beautiful palfreys. He refused to receive either the monks or the horses, saying, 'Were I to take them, they would drag me down by their tails to hell.'" (Roberti Grossetete Episcopi quondam Lincolniensis Epistolæ, edited by H. R. Luard, Preface, p. lxxxix.)

[u] The reference is of course to the year of Jubilee prescribed in the Mosaic Law, in which land that had been alienated by sale returned to the families of those, to whom it had been allotted in the original distribution. "In the year of this jubilee ye shall return every man unto his possession." Lev. xxv. 13. But Herbert's view of the restoration of the *palfrey* in a better state of existence is very quaint. Was he a millenarian, and did he hold the Personal Reign of Christ on a regenerated earth? Many eminent divines have done so, and there is at all events nothing derogatory in such a doctrine to the ideas of blessedness and glory which we associate with the Second Advent. But too much homely detail is apt to make a picture grotesque (not to say vulgar); and the palfrey which Herbert had borrowed, grazing in a flowery mead belonging to his beatified owner, is certainly a detail of this kind. There are minds however (and subtle and powerful ones), which can see nothing incongruous or out of keeping in such a detail. We think we remember a very eminent Oxford Professor, who addressed a poem "To my pony in a better world," (we do not vouch for the exact words of the title, but such was the sentiment). If such addresses can be made with all gravity and reverence in an age, when Theology takes so demure a form, much more may they find a place in mediæval Theology, with its abundant quaintnesses, and exuberant frolicsome plays of the fancy.

gress, took place in the year 1099[1]. The one was the death of Pope Urban II., of France (to whom Herbert had resigned his pastoral staff and ring, and from whom he had received re-instatement in the Episcopal office), and the accession of Paschal II. (of Tuscany) to the Papal throne. The other was the capture of Jerusalem by the Crusaders (July 15, 1099), and the election of Godfrey de Bouillon as king of the Holy City, rather less than three years after he had assembled his army on the banks of the Moselle. During all this time Herbert was proceeding with the building of his Cathedral, the slow progress of which seems sometimes to have drawn down a censure upon his monks from their bishop. Thus he writes to them in somewhat angry terms. We observe that the servants of the King are spoken of as engaged, with those of the Bishop, on the building; and we may hence conclude with tolerable certainty that the King and he were now at one, and that William had overlooked (if indeed he ever heard of) Herbert's journey to Rome in defiance of his prohibition. With the policy of removing the see to the opulent commercial city of Norwich the Red King would no doubt gladly coincide. It was the policy of his father before him, who had seen the wisdom of planting the strongholds of the Church in the centres of social activity. And the propriety of signalizing the removal of the see by the erection there of a magnificent

[1] Hook, ii. p. 47.

Cathedral, would approve itself to a monarch, who had shewn in other instances a decided taste for sumptuous architecture.

LETTER XIV.
To Ingulf, William, and Stanus.

"Herbert to Ingulf, William, and Stanus—a circular.[y]

"I cannot forbear to express my anxieties, and my countenance indicates externally the fever which consumes me within; for I am not of that sort of men who speak in the heart and in the heart [only], but that which I conceive in my mind, my features and my speech at once give birth to [and bring to light]. This is the case more especially, when I see that the business which I have in hand was entered upon from a love of truth and justice. I am quite disposed to unbend [in due season], but not in the things pertaining to God, Whose eyes are everywhere, and Whose word is quick, discerning the very marrow of our intentions, and reaching unto the division of the soul and the spirit. The thought of this moves me to fear;—would that my fear were lively enough to rouse me out of my physical and mental indolence, and to make me as

[Marginal notes: Herbert reproves his monks for indolence in building their church, and stirs them up to collect funds, and exert themselves actively in the work. Heb. iv. 12.]

---

[y] "A circular." The original is "Herbertus Ingulfo Willelmo et Stano, Apparibus." In the lower (or mediæval) Latin, *apares epistolæ* were circular letters or general epistles addressed to several persons in common. (The singular, *appar*, sometimes means a copy or duplicate.) Letters of this kind were sometimes called also *uniformes*. *Apparibus* here is not to be taken as a dative, agreeing with "Ingulfo, Willelmo, et Stano." It is rather an ablative with an adverbial character, and, when subjoined in the address of a letter to the names of several specified individuals, means "of the same tenour," "in the same terms," &c. Salmasius thinks it should be written *à paribus*, and that its Greek equivalent would be ἀπὸ τοῦ ἴσου, ἀπὸ τοῦ ἰσοτύπου. Radulphus de Diceto gives us another example of the word in the address of the letter which Richard I. issued to the nobles of England, to whom he committed the charge of his kingdom, while he was on the crusade; *Richardus Rex Angl. Willelm Cancellario, G. Filio-petri, W. Mareschalle, et II. Bard., et W. Briwer, Apparibus.* See Ducange, *sub voce* APPARES.

<small>Ps. cx. 10, V.</small> wakeful as I need to be in the works of God. The fear of the Lord is the beginning of wisdom, saith [the <small>Ps. cxi. 1, V.</small> Divine] Wisdom; and blessed is the man that feareth the Lord, and hath a strong* desire in the way of His commandments. God loves not those who are lukewarm in His service, for by the infallible teaching of His beloved disciple He thus threatens a certain indolent and <small>From Rev. iii. 15, 16.</small> careless one; Would that thou wert hot or cold; but because thou art lukewarm, I will begin to vomit thee out of my mouth. Do ye mark what fervour and what carefulness the Almighty and most strict Judge requireth from His servants? That servant in the Gos- <small>See St. Matt. xxv. 27.</small> pels is condemned, not because he had lost his lord's money, but because he had not put it out to usury. Observe, brethren, and lay it up in your memory with the utmost care, that God does not readily suffer Himself to be defrauded in the things which belong to Him, seeing that with so severe a sentence He punishes a servant for not having usury to show. I love you, and I am striving to deliver you, slow and indolent as you are, out of the hands of the Divine severity. Often have I stirred you up in person, by reminding you both privately and publicly of your duty in this respect, to apply yourselves fervently and diligently to the work of your Church, and to show carefulness in that work, as done under the inspection of God's own eyes. I was wont to entreat, and to persuade you; and would that I had succeeded in convincing your minds how great is the sincerity with which God must be served! But alas! the work drags on; and in providing materials you show no enthusiasm. Behold, the servants of the king and my own are really earnest in the works allotted to them, gather stones, carry them to the spot, when gathered, and fill with them the fields and ways,

---

* We translate these words as we find them in the Brussels MS., which has "et in mandatis ejus *cupit* nimis." The words in the Vulgate are "in mandatis ejus volet nimis" ("he shall delight exceedingly in His commandments," *Douay*); and it is evident that the scribe of the Brussels MS. had written *volet* first, and then erased it.

the houses and courts; and you meanwhile are asleep with folded hands, numbed, as it were, and frost-bitten by a winter of negligence, shuffling and failing in your duty through a paltry love of ease.

"Pluck up heart once more; lift up the hands that hang down and strengthen the feeble knees; ye are striving for the mastery in a conflict; labour ye for the palm. The sufferings of this present time are not worthy to be compared with the glory to come, that shall be revealed in us. ^{From Heb. xii. 12.} ^{From Rom. viii. 18.}

"Ye came unto God that ye might serve God; not that ye might maintain the sons and daughters, whom for God's^a sake ye have abandoned. Gather monies and lay up for yourselves treasures in heaven, and with God, where thief approacheth not, nor moth or rust corrupteth; for they who, as the Apostle saith, lay up in store for themselves their own things, lay up in store for themselves wrath against the day of wrath, and of the righteous judgment of God, who rendereth to every man according to his works. Let us bear in mind the sudden destruction of Ananias and Sapphira, whom the Apostle Peter doomed to death, not because they had fraudulently possessed themselves of other men's goods, but because they kept back for their private use property which was common, thus upbraiding them with severe rebuke; 'Ye have lied,' saith he, 'to the Holy Ghost.' Mark, my brethren, the severity of God: Ananias is condemned for the way in which he dealt with money which was his own; while we dream that it is possible to escape Heaven's vengeance, if we have dealt fraudulently with the property of Holy Church. Naaman the Syrian, having dipped himself seven times in Jordan, was for his faith cleansed from his leprosy; ^{See St. Mark x. 29.} ^{From St. Matt. vi. 20.} ^{From Rom. ii. 2, 5, 6, said of the impenitent.} ^{See Acts v. 3 and 4.} ^{See 2 Kings ii. 5.}

---

^a They had forsaken them for God's sake, when they entered the monastery and took the vows. No doubt they applied to such an act the language of our blessed Lord in St. Matt. xix. 29 and St. Mark x. 29. If they were priests when they entered the monastery, the act of forsaking sons and daughters would seem even more meritorious, as being a mode of asserting clerical celibacy.

and Gehazi was overspread with the same leprosy for his covetousness and unbelief. Naked were we when we entered into the schools of our Saviour; let us not clothe ourselves, while there, with spoils stripped from man by theft, or from God by robbing His temple[b]—we, who in coming to such a Master have renounced all temporal pleasures for the hope of everlasting happiness. Wherefore, my well-beloved sons, take heart again; persist untiringly in your work; let not your hand or your foot rest; shiver in winter's cold, swelter under summer's sun; toil by day; watch by night. Gird yourselves [for your work], and bear in mind those Israelites who, in repairing the walls of Jerusalem, fought with one hand and built with another. Persevere bravely [in what you have undertaken], labour faithfully, let the work go on fervently, and let your labours have a sweet savour unto the saints who [as

See Neh. iv. 17.

[b] "non ibi induamur alienis exuviis furti et anathematis." The "anathema" here represents the Greek ἀνάθημα (not ἀνάθεμα), which was a votive offering set up, or hung up, in a temple, and dedicated to the deity, in gratitude for some deliverance. The Jewish Temple boasted many such votive offerings (specially Herod's golden vine, which was twined over the gates of the Temple, and had branches of an extraordinary size, Joseph. Ant. xv. 11, 3): and our Lord's attention was called to them by some who "spake of the temple, how it was adorned with goodly stones and *gifts*" (ὅτι λίθοις καλοῖς καὶ ἀναθήμασι κεκόσμηται). St. Luke xxi. 5. Ducange, s. v., gives an instance of a silver vessel dedicated thus at the sepulchre of St. Mary Magdalene of Pazzi, in honour of that saint.

The word *anathēma* is used by Prudentius of the spoils which Achan took from Jericho;—

"Cædibus insignis, murali et strage superbus,
    Succubuit capto victis ex hostibus auro,
    Dum vetitis insigne legens *anathema* favillis,
    Mæsta ruinarum spolia insatiabilis haurit."
                    (Prudentii Psychomachia);

a quotation which gives the quantity of the word. Here it means little more than "treasure," "spoil,"—"culling from the forbidden ashes a choice booty." The booty, or some part of it, was often dedicated in the temple of the god, to whom the victory was ascribed. Hence the application of the word to the spoil taken at Jericho is by no means inappropriate.

We are to understand then that some of Herbert's monks were in the habit of pilfering the offerings which were made at the shrines of the saints, and appropriating them to their own use.

a great cloud of witnesses] compass you about, until the Lord shall come, Who both will bring to light the hidden things of the heart, and unlock the secret intents, and then shall every righteous man have praise of God. For this is what the true Rewarder [of His people] holds forth; Well done, good and faithful servant, thou hast been faithful in a little; I will set thee over many things: enter into the joy of thy Lord." *See Heb. xii. 1. From 1 Cor. iv. 5. St. Matt. xxv. 21, V.; and St. Luke xix. 17, V.*

We subjoin three other letters to the Prior, in all of which some allusion is made to "the work of the Church," by which we understand the building of the Cathedral.

LETTER XV.

To Ingulf[c] the Prior.

"Herbert to Ingulf the Prior.

"I am going to court, almost without horses and without money, but God will go with me in my journey. To you I commend the Church of Norwich, and the work of the Church, and my own work, and unto God I commend you. If anything be wanting to you, get it on loan, and when I return, I will restore all to those of whom you have borrowed. Peace be with thee, and with all the brethren, who with thee in humility and truth maintain in our house the devout observance of our rule." *Herbert, about to start for the court, commends to the Prior the work going on in the Cathedral.*

LETTER XVII.

To Ingulf the Prior and all his Brethren.

"Herbert to Ingulf the Prior and to all his Brethren.

"There is a common proverb[d] [to this effect]; 'The *Herbert excuses himself for*

---

[c] Ingulf was the first Prior of Herbert's Benedictine monastery at Norwich. Blomefield tells us he was alive in 1121. He therefore outlived Herbert, by whom probably he was appointed. He "died on the 16th of January, on which day his anniversary was always kept." (Blomefield's Hist. of Norwich, Part I. p. 600. London, 1806.)

[d] "There is a common proverb"—*vulgare proverbium*. Very possibly some scholar, whose eye this page may meet, may know where this "vul-

writing so often to the community, and expresses the hope that, on his return to them, he shall find them in a good state of devotion, discipline, and diligence.

man who has a large stock of honey puts honey even in his porridge.' And so ye will say that, because I am a very literary man, I worry your brotherhood with frequent letters. To which I answer that [my pertinacity as a letter writer] does not proceed from pride in my literary powers, but from my unfailing and ardent love for you. My object is that partly by your reading [e] my letters, partly by my frequent visits to you, the innermost recesses of my mind may be opened, and all my heart's most secret intentions revealed. It is true that I have very many designs laid up in the treasure-house of my mind; but those are the most urgent, which have reference to God and to the work of the Church. Wherefore I beseech you to show yourselves conspicuously mindful of all my love and all my teasing, and to persevere without flagging in the work which ye have begun. I am haunted in my sleep by certain troublesome phantoms and visions, which I would fain hope may be confined to sleep and fancies, and not actually realised in fact. I desire on my return to find matter of rejoicing in the fervent homage which ye do to God in his holy Church, in the diligent attendance which ye give in the cloister [f], in the care and the in-

---

gare proverbium" is to be found. We have sought in vain for it elsewhere. It is very expressive. Horace has a proverbial phrase of the same import; "quo more pyris vesci Calaber jubet hospes," (in the same manner as a Calabrian insists upon your eating pears). This fruit is so abundant in Calabria, that it is chiefly used for feeding hogs. The application is therefore to those who officiously force upon you that which is of little value, and for which you have no liking.

[e] Being unable to make any good sense of what we find in the MS., we have substituted *lectione* for *dilectione*.

[f] *de assiduitate claustri*—"the diligent attendance which ye give in the cloister."

"The cloister," says Dean Church in his chapter on the Discipline of a Norman Monastery (S. Anselm, pp. 47, 48), "was the place of business, instruction, reading, and conversation, the common study, workshop, and parlour of all the inmates of the house—the professed brethren; the young men whom they were teaching or preparing for life, either as monks or in the world; the children (*infantes*) who formed the school attached to the house, many of whom had been dedicated to this kind of service. In

struction which ye bestow upon the boys[g], and especially in the works going on in the Church, the care of which

> this cloister, open apparently to the weather[*] but under shelter, all sat, when they were not at service in church, or assembled in the chapter, or at their meals in the refectory, or resting in the dormitory for their mid-day sleep; or teaching, reading, writing, copying, or any handicraft in which a monk might employ himself, went on here. Here the children learned their letters, or read aloud, or practised their singing under their masters; and here, when the regular and fixed arrangements of the day allowed it, conversation was carried on. A cloister of this kind was the lecture-room where Lanfranc taught 'grammar,' gave to Norman pupils elementary notions of what an Italian of that age saw in Virgil and S. Augustine, and perhaps expounded S. Paul's Epistles: where Anselm, among other pupils, caught from him the enthusiasm of literature: where, when Lanfranc was gone, his pupil carried on his master's work as a teacher, and where he discussed with sympathising and inquisitive minds the great problems which had begun to open on his mind. . . . Here went on the literary work of the time; here, with infinite and patient toil, the remains of classical and patristic learning were copied, corrected, sometimes corrupted, ornamented; here, and here almost alone, were the chronicles and records kept year by year, so scanty, often so imperfect and untrustworthy, yet on the whole so precious, by which we know the men and their doings, who turned and governed the course of English and European history; here too, when the true chronicles did not speak as people wished, or did not tell enough, were false ones invented and forged."

[g] The discipline for the boys in Norman convents was exceedingly strict, as may be seen in Lanfranc's Regulations for the Benedictine Order (cap. xxi.) While reading aloud in school, they were to sit so far apart that neither their hands nor their clothes could touch; they might not beckon or make signs to one another; none might move from his place without the master's command or express permission. When they walked any where, a master was to walk between each two of them. No one, but the Abbot, Prior, and Precentor might make any sign to them, or smile at them. They might confess to no one but the Abbot or Prior, or some brother specially authorised by the Abbot in Chapter to hear their confessions. While one confessed, another was to be sitting on the footstool of the confessional; and the schoolmaster himself was to be sitting outside the Chapter-house close by. No one might enter their school, or speak to them in any place, without the express permission of the Abbot

---

[*] "Open apparently to the weather." We find however in the Sacrists' Rolls of Norwich Cathedral a charge made in the year 1307 for glass windows for the cloister, which would seem to shew that at that time it was not open to the weather: and much must the monks have needed these glass windows under the severities of a Norwich winter, the blasts of which sweeping through the cloister prevent, even at the present day, any plant or shrub from thriving in the interior. We can well understand poor Orderic leaving off his literary work when stiffened with the winter cold (as exhibited in the extract which Dean Church, p. 49, gives from his work). This, however, was at St. Evroul. How would Orderic's fingers have been numbed at Norwich! We find also charges for mats in the cloister, which would seem as if it was fitted up for daily residence.

I commended to you, and solemnly charged you in the sight of God to be industrious therein, all the elect and blessed spirits being witnesses of the charge."

LETTER LI.
To Ingulf the Prior.

"Herbert to Ingulf the Prior.

Herbert directs that Alexander be retained in the community, and makes some observations respecting the local character of monastic vows.

"I had intended to exclude Alexander from our Society, and from all intercourse with us; but the persistency with which he importuned me to let him remain, softened my intention. I alleged against him his frequent gyrations[h], and the wandering habits engendered or Prior. Their beds were to be placed at the foot of their masters' beds; and if obliged to rise in the night for some necessity of nature, they were obliged to call their masters, who accompanied them with a lighted torch. No one might sit in the chamber appropriated to them but the Abbot, Prior, or one of their masters, nor communicate any thing to them by word or otherwise, except by special permission of the Abbot or Prior; and, when that permission was given, the communication might not be made except when a master was sitting between the parties. One youth might not speak to another, except while a master was listening and attending to what passed. (*D. Lanfranci pro Ordine S. Benedicti Regulæ*, cap. xxi. *De Disciplinâ Puerorum*.)

No one who has been conversant with boys can fail to see and respect the reasons, which dictated this minute and (one would think) irritating supervision. Moral contamination is readily spread by a few light words bandied about, when a master's back is turned; and who shall say how deeply it may eat, like a gangrene, into the nature of a susceptible lad? He who utters such words is like "the madman who scattereth firebrands, arrows, and death." Therefore let the eyes and ears of superiors be constantly upon the boys.

But of course there is another side to the question. Can independence of character be formed under such a system? Temptation excluded is not temptation resisted; and there is great risk lest the too vigilant attempt to exclude it may emasculate the character, and render it weak when temptation does come.

Perhaps the true solution is, that, while the age of childhood and *early* boyhood continues, the supervision should be very strict; but that, as the boy grows into the youth, there should be a corresponding relaxation. Lanfranc does not seem to have been wise in ordering (in the Chapter cited above) that the *juvenes* (youths) should be treated very much as the *infantes* (children).

[h] "his frequent gyrations, and the wandering habits engendered by his tours about the country"—*girationes et suæ vagationis circuitus.*

Probably Alexander belonged to that kind of monks called Gyrovagues.

dered by his tours about the country, but he ascribed
the odium of this accusation to the indolence of those
set over him. I brought up against him the payments[1]
which he had exacted for his labours in copying; but
this he simply denied; and assured me that he would
live henceforth within our cloister, and would be con-
tented with only food and raiment. Wherefore, I pray
you, receive this brother once more into fellowship with
you, and into obedience to your rule, for as the hard-
ened folly of an old offender drives him naturally to
despair, so on the other hand we may surely look for
amendment from lenity shown to a youth. Let Alex-

The first chapter of St. Benedict's rule says; "It is well known there are four kinds of monks. The first are the Cœnobites, or those who live in monasteries, or convents, and are subject to a rule and an abbot. The second are the Anchorites, or Hermits, that is to say, those who had exchanged the cloister for the desert . . . after having been long tried in a monastery. . . . The third sort are the Sarabites, a most wicked class" (they are said in a passage quoted by Ducange to find their prototypes in Ananias and Sapphira), "who make a public declaration of infidelity to their sacred engagements, by wearing the tonsure. Shutting themselves up, two or three together, and sometimes, even alone, without a shepherd —not in the sheepfolds of the Lord, but in those of their own choosing, they observe no other law than the gratifications of the vicious appetites. . . . . The fourth sort are the Gyrovagues, as they are called, who wander about all their lives from province to province, staying three or four days, now in one monastery, and then in another; they never confine themselves to a fixed abode; but are ever rambling—slaves to self-love and to all those disorders of which gluttony is the parent, and even worse in every respect than the Sarabites. So very wretched is the manner of life pursued by both one and the other, that we deem it more prudent to be silent than to dwell on it at greater length."

[1] "payments"—*solidos quos expostulaverat.*
For the word *solidus*, see pp. 102, 3, note s.

All property was strictly forbidden to monks by the xxxiiird chapter of St. Benedict's rule : "The abbot will take especial care to root the sin of proprietorship out of the monastery. Hence it shall be unlawful for any of the brethren to give, take, or appropriate anything whatever, either a book, a tablet, a pen, or anything at all, without the sanction of the abbot. For by their profession they have renounced all right even to their own bodies and their own wills." And again in ch. lviii. ; "If a novice have any property, he shall, before making his profession, either distribute it among the poor, or make it over to the monastery as a gift, in legal form, reserving nothing whatever for himself; for let him remember that from that day forward, it shall be unlawful for him to use even his own bodily faculties independently of the will of his superior."

ander live, then, and serve God in our house, and be obedient to our injunctions, since everywhere, as blessed Benedict maintains[k], citing for it the New Testament Scripture, we serve one Lord and go a warfare under one King. We make our monastic profession, it is true, both to the place and to God, but only to the place for God's sake; and if it should happen that the place chosen lies out of the way, so as to compel you to long absences from the Lord, you must then change your place, and hold fast by the one God, according to that true word of the prophet; 'It is good for me to hold me fast by God, to put my hope in the Lord God.' Attack forthwith the foundations of the [Cathedral] towers with all alacrity, as ye hope to repose with true devotion on Christ, Who is our tower of strength. Peace be to you and to all our brethren."

Ps. lxxii. 28, V.

We gather from a letter to Roger, Bishop of Salisbury, which we prefer to give in another connexion, that the King had made a grant of the manor of Thorpe to Herbert, to meet the expenses of building the Cathedral. In that which we now insert, we see Herbert acting as lord of the manor, and giving instructions about Thorpe wood.

---

[k] We suppose the reference to be to the Second Chapter of St. Benedict's rule, which treats of the qualities required in the abbot. He is to shew no favouritism or preference for one brother over another: "Because, whether slaves or freemen, we are all one in Christ; and serve alike one and the same Master, for *there is no respect of persons with God.*" The scriptural reference may be Eph. vi. 9, or possibly Acts x. 34, 5. The argument of St. Benedict's chapter would make the former more suitable, because he is speaking of the abbot's duty to shew no favour to social position. But the reference to the Acts would be more suitable to Herbert's argument, who is maintaining the indifference of place in the service of God. "Evangelicâ astipulatione," we render by "citing for it the New Testament," because "the Gospel" might seem to imply that the passage referred to was to be found in what are called "the Gospels." Possibly Herbert, quoting St. Benedict from memory, may have thought that the passage he quoted came from the Gospels.

LETTER VIII.
To William the Monk.

"Herbert to William the Monk.

"As to making a present of Thorpe wood[1] to the sick, or any one else, I gave you no orders, nor do I give nor will I give any; for I appointed you the custodian of the wood, not the rooter up of it. To the sick, when I come to Norwich, I will give as I did last year, not logs of wood, but pence[m]. Let this be your answer to them,—not a word besides. As for you, do you guard the wood of the Holy Trinity, as you wish to be guarded by the Holy Trinity, and to continue in my favour."

William, the custodian of Thorpe wood, is required to be true to his trust.

The new century (1100) opened, and brought with it in its first year important events for England. On the 2nd of August, the Red King, haunted it is said by forebodings, and terrified by

A.D. 1100.

---

[1] *Silvâ Torpi*—"Thorpe wood."
Thorpe wood, of which nothing now remains, must have covered a large extent of ground in former days. We are told that on a hill in this wood Herbert built the Priory and Church of St. Leonard, which are described as having stood on the south side of the road up Gas Hill, opposite to Kett's Castle. (The site of Kett's Castle is on the heights to the north, as, after crossing Bishop's Bridge, you mount Gas Hill.) But the wood must have stretched away far to the north-east of this point; for the chapel of St. William, the boy martyr, who was crucified by the Jews in the reign of King Stephen, also stood in Thorpe wood. Now the site of this chapel, (clearly traceable at the present day, and of which there is a still current tradition that no heath or gorse will grow there,) is well known to have been on Mousehold Heath, about a mile north-east of Pockthorpe. The wood probably spread over all the heights which overhang the city on the east. It was only a moiety of the wood of Thorpe which Herbert gave to his monastery; and the wood therefore, about which he now writes, must be understood to be this moiety.

[Blomefield's Norwich, (London, 1806,) Part I. p. 27, and Part II. pp. 425, 426, 556.]

[m] *non ligna, sed denarios*—"not logs of wood, but pence."
The word *denarius*, properly an adjective meaning "containing ten," denoted originally a silver coin of the Romans, which contained at first ten, but afterwards eighteen, *asses*. Of the Anglo-Saxon *denarii*, Ducange tells us that four made a *solidus* under the Saxons, but five under the Normans (Ducange, *sub voce*).

predictions, of his end, rode out into the New Forest, and being separated from his attendants, received a mortal wound from an arrow which glanced from a tree. His body, carried in a cart to Winchester, was hastily laid in the Cathedral, but without the usual obsequies, the performance of which it was thought his impiety and impenitence had precluded. Our prelate, who had long ere this renounced the iniquities of his early career, must have felt a certain awe in hearing of the sudden removal of the man, with whom he had once entered into a corrupt and odious contract, most discreditable to himself as a Christian bishop, but whose conduct to him, since his practical repudiation of that contract, had not been upon the whole ungenerous. Later in the same year (Nov. 18, 1100) Herbert lost by death his Consecrator, Thomas I. of York, the only consecrator whose name has come down to us,—so that now both the men who had joined in raising him to the Episcopal dignity were gone; and we may suppose that the occasion would suggest to so good a man the reviewing of the painful circumstances under which he had obtained that dignity, and the deepening of his penitence by that review.

Meanwhile the Metropolitan of Canterbury had returned to the kingdom. Henry, the younger brother of the late King, had seized by violence the castle and royal treasure at Winchester, and had caused himself to be crowned at Westminster by Maurice, Bishop of London. Conscious of being an usurper (for the crown belonged by every right to his elder brother Robert) he sought to make up for the badness of his title by ingratiating himself with the clergy and people. He published a charter of liberties, a copy of which was deposited in every monastery, solemnly promised to put in force the laws of Edward the Confessor, recalled Anselm, and pledged himself to abide by the counsels which he should give him. At the same time he made certain instalments of a real reformation of manners at court; he expelled those young men of fashion[n], whose luxury and debauchery had given ground for the most horrible scandals, committed Ralph the Firebrand, the pander to the late King's cupidity (and who, in reward for his infamous services, had received from him the Bishopric of Durham), to the Tower, broke off his own vices, and married, at the solicitation of his bishops, but still with an eye to policy (for she was a niece of Edgar Atheling the Saxon), Matilda, the daughter of Malcolm, King of Scots. Anselm, now re-instated in his functions, solemnized the marriage, and crowned the Queen in Westminster Abbey, on the 11th of November, 1100.

Archbishop Anselm recalled.

Morals of the court reformed.

Coronation of Queen Matilda, Nov. 11, 1100.

[n] The "effeminati," or fashionable young men of the day, received that appellation from their manner of dressing, which approached to that of women. They wore long trains to their robes, shoes with peaks twisted to imitate the horn of a ram or coils of a serpent, hair parted in front and falling in ringlets down the back, which was sometimes lengthened by additions of false hair. (See Lingard, vol. ii. p. 154, n. 6.) Unnatural crimes were frequent among these dissolute votaries of fashion. Further on will be found a painful letter of Herbert's, which attests the frequency of these awful vices, and records the severity of the discipline by which he sought to suppress them.

But the good understanding between the King and Archbishop was destined to be very short-lived. The old investiture controversy, which had made an irreparable breach between William and Anselm, broke out afresh more virulently than ever. The King, under whom (according to the feudal system) all estates in the kingdom, and all the endowments of the Church, were held, offered to Anselm investiture in the temporalities of the see of Canterbury. Now Anselm had actually received investiture in the temporalities of the Abbey of Bec from the Conqueror, and in those of the see of Canterbury from William Rufus; and it was reasonable, therefore, to expect that he would not decline a similar grant at the hand of their successor. But in his exile the Archbishop had visited Rome, and, amid Roman surroundings and influences, had studied the question of investitures afresh. It now presented itself to him in a wholly different light. He was informed of a synod held at Rome in the year 1075, which forbade ecclesiastics to receive investiture from the hands of emperor, king, or any lay person. And he resolved to abide by this sentence of the Roman Church, which he conceived to be the mother and mistress of all Churches. Hence he curtly declined to accept investiture at Henry's hands, and thereby created no small amount of surprise and indignation among the barons (who perceived that his refusal, if imitated, would be the virtual overthrow of the feudal system), as also among the bishops, who had not drunk so deeply as himself of Romanist and anti-national influences. After many vain attempts to bring Anselm round to his views, the King at length consented to an envoy's going to Rome, to endeavour to come to an understanding with the Pope on the subject. The envoy selected was William of Warelwast, an eminent diplomatist, afterwards (as we shall see) consecrated to the see of Exeter. It was agreed meanwhile that till the result of Warelwast's mission was known, Anselm should enjoy all the property, and exercise all the rights, of his see. While the matter was pending, an entire good understanding between Anselm and Henry seems to have been resumed. The Archbishop did the King signal service when his brother, Duke Robert of Normandy, invaded the kingdom in 1101. He preached to the barons on the obligation under which their oaths had laid them, "recalled from the camp of Robert some of the deserters, confirmed the wavering loyalty of others, and threatened the invaders with the sentence of excommunication°."

[Sidenotes: William of Warelwast sent to Rome, to obtain some settlement of the investiture question. Good service done by Anselm to the King in A.D. 1101.]

Meanwhile Herbert's great church at Norwich was advancing towards completion, or towards such a completion as he designed to give it. It was consecrated on the 24th of September, in the year 1101, and dedicated in the Name of the Holy and Undivided Trinity. The Charter of the Church, which we here give *in extenso*, was sealed at the same time, It is touching to ob-

[Sidenote: Sept. 24, A.D. 1101. Consecration of Norwich Cathedral.]

° Lingard, vol. ii. p. 159.

serve how the penitence of our Bishop for the errors of his past life comes out in the beginning of this document; a circumstance quite in harmony with some of his letters, which show that his shameful fall was never effaced from his memory.

The Charter[p] of the Foundation.

The Charter of the foundation of the Cathedral.

"In the Name of the Father, and of the Son, and of the Holy Ghost. Amen. I, Herbert the Bishop, conscious of my own weakness and sinfulness [*impuritatis*], lay bare my life and conversation before God, the just and merciful Judge, disclosing and confessing to Him my sins of ignorance, and where I have had knowledge [of the right], my painful deviations from it, before Whose eyes all things are naked and open, Whose word pierceth to the dividing asunder of soul and spirit, and is an observer of all hearts. To Him, I say, I acknowledge the evils of my heart, Who to me hath done nothing but good, encouraging myself in the abundance of the compassions of my God, who might and ought to be discouraged for the multitude of my shameful iniquities; but to have any distrust of the Holy Spirit is impious, whereas to trust in Him is Christian and Catholic. For in Him[q], from whom the spiritual comeliness of the whole Church is derived and maintained, all offences are forgiven to the soul who acknowledges and repents of them. Just as they are therefore, and lest God Himself should judge them, I condemn my sins, and confess that they have to be remitted before the tribunal of the justice and mercy of Christ. I re-

---

[p] The copy of the Charter which we follow is that found in the *Registrum Primum* among the archives of Norwich Cathedral.

[q] A theologian of the Reformed Church would probably have said that *in Christ* (rather than in the Third Person of the Blessed Trinity) all offences are forgiven, &c. But as it is the Holy Spirit who brings us into union with Christ by faith, and as justification by Christ is uniformly accompanied by the santification of the Spirit, Herbert's expression is at least justifiable.

pent; but God demandeth the fruits of penitence; what fruits wilt thou bring forth, O tree, which art dried up, and fit only to be cut down and cast into the fire? with what tears wilt thou wash away thine uncleannesses? What wilt thou render unto thy God for all that He hath done unto thee? Oh would that thou mightest drink the cup of thy salvation, and by the shedding of thy own blood reconcile thy most gracious Creator to thy frailty! This if thou couldst, thou oughtest to render; but because thou canst not do this, thou oughtest in no wise to be slack [in doing what thou canst]. Therefore for the redemption of my soul, and for the absolution of all my sins, I am the first who have built at Norwich a church in the honour and in the Name of the Holy and Undivided Trinity, and have constituted and consecrated it the head and mother church of all the churches of Norfolk and Suffolk.

"Under the instructions, therefore, and grants accorded to me by King William and King Henry his brother, and with the advice of Anselm Archbishop of Canterbury, and of all the bishops and nobles of the whole kingdom of England, I have established [*ordinavi*] in the same church monks[r] by the authority aforesaid, there to continue for ever, and never to be cast out thence by any of my successors; before God and before the heavenly Jerusalem this I ordain, this I ratify, that the monks whom I have established shall continue and be constant in the service and offices of the Church which I have prescribed, and in the manner I have pre-

---

[r] Blomefield tell us (Hist. of Norwich, part ii. p. 556) that "Herbert appointed his monks in the room of secular priests, which had always hitherto attended the bishops as their chapter." It seems to have been the fashion of the day to throw contempt upon the secular canons, who had been attached from the earliest times to cathedral churches, and to substitute for them regulars, that is, monks. Ugutio, and other mediæval writers quoted by Ducange, speaks of the absurd incongruousness of the title, secular canons. A canon, they say, means a man who lives by rule, or a regular; whereas a secular priest is one who does not live by rule. To speak therefore of a secular canon, is to speak, according to them, of an irregular regular, as if one should speak of a white black.

scribed, not to be driven out by any force, not to be
altered by any counsels, not to be ejected at any time.
Let no one, who looks to give an account before God
Himself concerning the house of God, venture at his
peril to alter the appointment of his predecessor. God
forbid that one man should incur an anathema by vio-
lating an arrangement, from establishing of which another comes to be gathered into life eternal. Let all
things, therefore, which up to the present time were, and
were called, the property of the bishops, henceforth be,
and be called, the property of the Church of the Holy
Trinity, both lands and men, both customs and all other
revenues,—let all belong to God and His Church, while
the use and enjoyment thereof belong to us and our
successors. Out of this property I make a division, and
for the works and the other needs of the Church (that
is to say, for the food and clothing of the monks) I do
assign such things as are hereunder written. The offerings which are made in the church, and likewise the
fees upon burials, belong entirely to the monks. The
fairs held by grant of King William in the week of Pentecost, I make over to the brethren, with the tithes of
my manors (those only excepted which I had given to
my chaplains), Lakenham, with all things which pertain
to the same township (*villam*), except the land of
Osbern the archdeacon of Ameringhale (Arminghall),
likewise the mediety of the wood of Thorpe, on the
understanding however that it be not lawful for any
monk to sell or give anything from thence without
licence[1] from the bishop, but that the wood should be
in the custody of the servants of the bishop and the
servants of the monks, for the needs of the bishop and
his monks. The privilege of hunting game in the wood
and warren of the aforesaid townships is in the keeping
and guardianship of the bishop. Hyndringham [I also
make over], just as I had it in my own demesne; and
Hyndolveston likewise. At Norwich, the mill-precinct,

[1] See his touchiness on the subject of Thorpe wood in Letter VIII.,
p. 141.

both land and meadow, which anciently belonged to the bishoprick. Of the Thorpe meadows a mediety, as well on this side the river as on the other. At Helegeia (Hilgay) the bishop's residence which is there, and the marsh and the eels which belong to it. At Martham in Flegge[1], whatsoever property was in my demesne.

---

[1] Flegg is a district on the sea-board of Norfolk formed by the rivers Bure and Thirne (the latter being also called the Hundred Stream or North River). It was originally an irregular-shaped island; but now by the retirement of the sea forms part of the mainland. Almost all[*] the parishes in the Diocese of Norwich, the names of which end in *by*, are found in Flegg. We find there Ash*by*, O*by*, Billock*by*, Clippes*by*, Fil*by*, Hems*by*, Herring*by*, Maut*by*, Ormes*by*, Scrat*by*, Rolles*by*, Stokes*by*, and Thrig*by*.

Mr. Isaac Taylor, in his most able and interesting work, "Words and Places," thus speaks of Flegg (which he connects with the Norse word *flegg*, or Danish *vlak*, flat), (pp. 165, 166);

"In the extreme south-eastern corner of Norfolk there is a dense Danish settlement, occupying the Hundreds of East and West FLEGG, a space some eight miles by seven, well protected on every side by the sea, and the estuaries of the Bure and the Yare. In this small district eleven names out of twelve are unmistakably Norse, compounded mostly of some common Danish personal name, and the suffix *by*.

"The word *byr* or *by* originally meant a dwelling, or a single farm, and hence it afterwards came to denote a village. In Iceland, at the present day, the ordinary name given to a farmstead is *boer*, and in Scotland a cow-stall is still called a *byre*. We find this word as a suffix in the village-names of Denmark, and of all countries colonized by the Danes. In Normandy we find it in the form *bue* or *bœuf*, and in England it is usually contracted into *by*. In the Danish district of England—between Watling Street and the river Tees—the suffix *by* frequently takes the place of the Anglo-Saxon *-ham* or *-ton*. . . . About one-fourth of the village-names in Lincolnshire present the characteristic Danish suffix *by*, while the total amount of Danish names in this county amounts to about 300—more than are found in all the rest of Southumbrian England." (pp. 157, 158, 167.)

It should be added that Mr. J. W. Robberds in his "Geological and Historical Observation of the Eastern Vallies of Norfolk" (Norwich, 1826), connects the termination *by* with the word *bight*, pronounces it to be of Anglo-Saxon rather than Danish origin, and makes out that it means a sinuous indentation of water, in short, a *bay*. With great ingenuity he seeks to show that the places in Norfolk and Suffolk, the names of which end in *by*, stood formerly upon one of these sinuous indentations, and that

---

[*] There are seventeen such parishes in the diocese, thirteen of which are in Flegg. The deanery of Flegg contains twenty-four parishes, more than half of which therefore have names ending in *by*.

Hemesby (Hemsby), and whatever belongs to the domain of the same township. The church of S. Nicholas at Jernemuda (Yarmouth), with all things which belong to the same. The church of S. Leonard, which I built from its first foundation, on a certain rising ground [*colliculo*] in the wood of Thorpe. Catton, with all things belonging to the said township. Newton, which Godfrey the sewer, and Nigreda his wife, and their son Radulphus made a grant of to me, the said Radulphus receiving ten pounds from the estate for the confirmation and perpetuity of the grant so made. Whatever Herbert Ros possessed in Plumstede (Plumstead) and Becham (W. Beckham?). The church of Hoxene (Hoxne), with the chapel of Saint Edmund in the same township, where the said martyr was slain. The church of Lynnie (Lynn), and all my salt-works at Geywode (Gaywood) (excepting those which belonged to the farm on the same manor), I grant, as unmolested and as exempt from all customs of the aforesaid manor, as they were ever held by myself, or Arfastus, or Willelmus, as part of our domain. I have ceded to them also my mill which I ordered to be built in Geywode marshes, and the church of Elmham[u] with all its appurtenances. The church of Langham, which belonged to Alanus, and its tithes. All the possessions aforesaid I have given to God and the Church for the food and clothing of my monks, and for the supply of other necessaries to them, so absolutely that none of my successors shall have the power of changing or diminishing them, but that they shall be kept for ever for the uses of the monks. And lest this diminution of the episcopal domain should be grudged by any of my successors, I have made restitution as follows. At Norwich I have recouped the [episcopal] establishment by an endowment of twenty pounds from the demesne of Thorpe, which I have retained in my own hands. In Suffolk [I have en-

traces of marine or inland waters are to be found near them. See the map at the beginning of his volume.

[u] Probably North Elmham in Norfolk.

dowed it] with Elmham, which I bought of William of Neueris: [also] with Ekles (Eccles), which I redeemed from King Henry at the cost of sixty pounds: [and I have also granted to the see] the manor of Colkirk. These grants and ordinances King Henry and Queen Matilda confirmed, and signed with their cross [1]."

This Charter appears to have been in the first instance provisionally confirmed "sine magnâ sollempnitate, . . . ne forte morte preventus (*sic*) predicti monachi super bonis ecclesie Norwicensis ab ipso et ceteris fidelibus collatis, et ab eodem

---

[1] In Maitland's "Dark Ages" (Lond. 1845) will be found a most interesting answer to a general charge brought by Robertson, the historian, against kings and eminent persons in the Middle Ages, who, on account of their ignorance, affixed the sign of the cross to documents which they wished to confirm. Maitland shews that Robertson argues from an insufficient induction, three or four instances only being known of charters *avowedly* signed with a cross because the signer was unable to write. Maitland shows that a king's not signing his name is no evidence at all that he could not have done so; and then gives from Mabillon four reasons why charters might be signed by proxy; i. the inability to write, upon which Robertson had commented; ii. inability arising from blindness, disease, or old age; iii. an affectation of dignity, through which many high official persons chose that their names should be written by the notary; and then iv. "what is most to our purpose, a custom growing out of this, and extending so far as that by the eleventh century it had become almost universal. In imitation of their superiors, almost all persons—all at least who could pretend to any kind of distinction or title—preferred having their names written by the notary (who could say of them what it might have seemed ostentatious to say of themselves), and then adding, or sometimes omitting to add, their mark—that is, the sign of the cross made with their own hands. . . . Robertson says that it was usual '*for persons who could not write* to make the sign of the cross in confirmation of a charter.' No doubt; but it was also usual for those who *could* write. The sign of the cross was, in fact, '*the* confirmation and *the* signature;' and the subscriber, in thus making the sign of his holy religion, was considered as taking an oath. He was, in fact, said *manu jurare;* and, for greater solemnity, the cross was sometimes made with the consecrated wine. The subscriber's adding his name was no essential part of the confirmation, but simply a declaration and notification that the person, whose name was there written, was he who had thus bound himself by his *signature*. If he was unable, or if he did not choose, to do the writing for himself, it was done for him by the notary."

pro dote provisis, securitate carerent" (lest by the Founder's sudden death the monks should be excluded from the benefits, which he had designed to confer upon them). In this provisional form it was signed only by the King and Queen, Waldric the Chancellor, Roger Bigot, Eudo the Seneschal, Robert Malet, Nigel Master of the Horse, and William the Butler. Afterwards in full Parliament the Charter was renewed with all becoming solemnity, and signed by the following besides the King and Queen;

"I Anselm, Abp. of Canterbury, have subscribed +
I Gerard, Abp. of York, have subscribed +
I Gundulf, Bp. of Rochester, have subscribed +
I Maurice, Bp. of London, have subscribed +
I Robert, Bp. of Lincoln, have subscribed +
I Sampson, Bp. of Worcester, have subscribed +
I John, Bp. of Bath, have subscribed +
I Osbern, Bp. of Exeter, have subscribed +
I Rodbert, Bp. of Chester, have subscribed +
I Radulf, Bp. of Chichester, have subscribed +
I John, Bp. of Tusculum, Legate of the Pope, have subscribed +
I Henry, Earl of Warwick, have subscribed +
I Simon, Earl of Northampton, have subscribed +
I William, Earl of Warrenne, have subscribed +
I Roger Bigot, have subscribed +
I Eudo, the Seneschal, have subscribed +
I Hamo, the Seneschal, have subscribed +
I Robert Malet, have subscribed +
I Nigel, the Master of the Horse, have subscribed +
I Alan, son of Flaaldus, have subscribed +
I William Malet, have subscribed +
I William, the Butler, have subscribed +
I Gislebert, Abbot of Westminster, have subscribed +
I Serlo, Abbot of Gloucester, have subscribed +

I Henry, Abbot of Battle, have subscribed +
I Stephen, Abbot of York, have subscribed +
I Eldewyn, Abbot of Ramsay, have subscribed +
I Richard, Abbot of St. Alban's, have subscribed +
I Richard, Abbot of Ely, have subscribed +
I Roger, the Chancellor, have subscribed +
I Herbert, Chamberlain of the King, have subscribed +
I Everard, the Chaplain, have subscribed +
I Roger, the Chaplain, have subscribed +

"This gift was made in the year of the Incarnation of our Lord, 1101, in the month of September, under an ordinance of the blessed Pope Gregory, at Windsor, during the reign of our Lord Jesus Christ, who is of consubstantial and co-eternal equality, honour, and glory with the Father, in the unity of the Holy Spirit, for ever and ever. Amen."

We observe that the King and Queen were witnesses to this Charter. The signing and sealing of it were perhaps the occasion on which Herbert's acquaintance with them began, — an acquaintance which ripened, as we shall see, into a warm and confidential friendship, attested on one side by marks of royal favour, and by his becoming Clerk of the Queen's Closet; and on the other, by such expressions as these, in a letter to one of his most intimate friends[y]; "*After Henry the King*, nothing that this life has to offer is more precious to me than your affection."

The year 1102 was signalized by an event A.D. 1102. which all good Churchmen wished for, the holding of a Synod, at which Anselm presided. It was the Synod held "in St. Peter's Church, in the west end of London," on Michaelmas Day,

[y] Letter xlv. "To John." (Ed. Anstruther, p. 83.)

A.D. 1102. 1102. Several abuses had accumulated in the Church, which had to be rectified by some conciliar decision. A Synod was a great event in those days—what good Churchmen had longed for for some time, but could not succeed in obtaining. William Rufus had refused to Anselm the power of convening a Synod, fearing that it might give the Church too much of independence and authority. But there was a growing demand for it, arising from the necessity of putting down the irregularities which were so widely prevalent, and of practically showing that the Church of England was able to reform its own abuses without the supervision of a legate sent from Rome. Henry therefore acquiesced in Anselm's holding this Synod; and we cannot suppose that any of the Bishops, unless disqualified by illness, were absent from it. Its first act was to depose six Abbots on account of simony, a proceeding which would again bring to our Bishop's memory his own former entanglement in this sin, and would lead him to see in the censure passed upon these erring brethren the sentence which he had himself deserved. "We gather," says Dean Hook, "from the enactments of this council that the immorality of the Anglo-Normans equalled that of their brethren on the continent, and that it was horrible and indescribable." The letter of Herbert, which we now present, contains sad evidences of the existence of such immorality in his days, and shows us that the most hideous forms of vice crossed his path in his eastern diocese. "The whole land," Anselm had said to William, in asking for a Synod, "unless judgment and discipline be exercised in earnest, will soon be a *Sodom.*"

LETTER VI.

To Norman the Ostiary[z].

"Herbert to Norman the Ostiary.

"I hear that there are some who are shocked at my impetuosity, who find fault with the severity of the penalties I inflict,—nay, who even disparage God's sentences of judgment, alleging the most grievous offences to be trifling, and judging that to be a venial sin which God utterly abhors. Let these come forth from their hiding-places, let them set themselves in array, bring forth their arms, enter openly into the encounter, withstand the enemy, and throw their javelins, instead of sharpening their tongues; so that, if they fear to go further, they may at all events learn to keep silence, to bridle their tongues, and to yield to the force of truth; for our weapons wage no war with men, but only with sins, nor do they prepare captivity for the conquered, but on the contrary give liberty to those who are rising again [after their falls]. Observe, dear brother, the point to which my endeavours are directed, and the discipline with which I wish you to be furnished in your ministry. We carry on our warfare under a Captain whom all things serve, the severity of whose discipline overawes both earth and hell, whose court is neither decayed by time, nor defaced by uncleanness. We serve Him, therefore, who is everywhere; and we serve Him there, where there is nothing unclean. In His palace sparkling gems and shining metals, which shed a light infinitely brighter than that of the sun, expose the hearts of the inhabitants, betray their secrets, reward holy

[sidenote: Herbert excuses himself for the severity of his discipline, by the enormity of the crimes which he sought to repress thereby.]

---

[z] See a note on the word "Ostiary," p. 83.

intentions, reprove disgraceful ones. Nothing is cloaked or shut where that light shineth, which lighteth every man that cometh into this world, whose brightness is such that it pierceth even to the dividing asunder of soul and spirit. There is that eternal altar, to which you, my friend, are desirous of ascending, and whereat you are panting to wait,—the altar in the participation of which you seek to be associated. Raise up thine eyes to the excellency of the altar, and then cast them down again upon the infirmity of thy flesh. On this altar Christ is sacrificed; on this altar the Body and Blood of Christ are made, to wit, the true Bread which cometh down from heaven and giveth life unto the world. Give heed unto the Gospel, and fashion thyself by the truth thereof; 'If thou bring,' saith He, 'thy gift to the altar, and there rememberest that thy brother hath ought against thee, leave thy gift before the altar, and go to be reconciled unto thy brother, and then shalt thou come and offer thy gift.' Thou durst not, then, offer thy gift without first appeasing thy neighbour; and wilt thou dare to offer it, while God is wroth with thee? Go we, my brother, go we, and with contrition of heart and bitter tears let us seek the reconciling grace of God, and thus offer with cleansed hands immortal gifts at an immortal board. Hold we before our eyes both the doctrine of the Apostle and the history of the Gospel; for thus cries the Apostle; 'He who eateth and drinketh unworthily, eateth and drinketh judgment unto himself, not discerning the Lord's Body.' And the Gospel saith; 'Judas, after he had received the sop, went out straightway, and betrayed his Master'— not knowing Him, however, to be God. But let us, who not only know Him to be God, but are feasted upon His Body, fear the severity of that judgment; for its severity is to be dreaded, and His judgments are a great deep. For there have been, my brother, there have been, almost from the foundation of the world even to the Advent of our Saviour, foul times in which God was not known, and when unclean spirits were worshipped; the temples of unclean spirits demanded unclean victims, which could not be presented save by unclean priests. In their temples they were wont to celebrate with solemn worship the thefts of Mercury and the adulteries of Jove, while in their theatres they represented [these same things] with all the buffoonery of the stage. These were those foul and abominable sacrifices whereon unclean devils fed, and whereby unhappy souls were beguiled and fashioned with cunning despitefulness unto an imitation of the deities whom they worshipped. The Saviour came and overthrew the fanes of profaneness, drave out the devils, bound them when He had driven them out, and with unspeakable triumph restored His fellow-heirs unto the Eternal City. Jupiter burns, condemned to the vengeance of eternal fire; Venus burns, herself too (no less than her votaries) bound with fiery chains; and shall he, who hath renounced the world and hath become a follower of Christ, wail for Adonis and worship Ganymede? Woe—even the woe of shameful contempt and of the burning brimstone—be unto them, who strive to rekindle those embers of the overthrown cities, which were quenched by holy Baptism. Let not the destruction of those Arabian cities, which the ancients called Pentapolis, slip out of our memory; let us look on their flaming ruin, and dread to follow their example. In these, as Pompeius relates^a (not to

See Deut. xxxii. 17, and 1 Cor x. 20.

See St. Matt. xii. 29.

See Ezek. viii. 14, V.

---

^a "as Pompeius relates." Trogus Pompeius, an author of Gaulish extraction, who flourished about B.C. 20. He wrote the history of the rise and fall of the Macedonian monarchy, but embraced under his design so many digressions, that his work came to be regarded as an Universal History. The *Historiæ Philippicæ* of Justin profess to be entirely derived from the history of Trogus. The passage of Pompeius referred to by Herbert is probably to be found in Orosius, an admirer and friend of St. Augustine (A.D. 413), who, by the instigation of that Father, compiled from Justin and other sources certain Annals (*adversus Paganos*), the object of which was to show, that as monstrous crimes and calamities had existed long before Christianity, the wickedness and misery consequent upon the sack of Rome by the Goths could not be reasonably charged on the wrath of the heathen gods, whose worship had been supplanted by Christianity.

We subjoin a translation of the passage in Orosius. It is true that this

mention our own Moses), there was bred of great variety of fruits plenty, of plenty luxury, and of luxury was bred that abominable form of lust, which God visited with such sweeping destruction, that He delivered up to everlasting burnings not the people only, but also the cities and the lands which the people had inhabited, warning future ages beforehand, that they should not imitate the vices of those whom they remembered to have been chastised with so [horrible] a punishment. And [here] observe a subtle mystery[b], that vengeance for the incest of the lewd sisters with their father was deferred at the time when the aforesaid cities were overthrown with a destruction, whereof was never the like, that you might understand every sin to be less grievous than that sin, for which those workshops of the aforenamed vile deeds (for I cannot call them cities) were

See Ezek. xvi. 49.

See Gen. xix. 5, 31, &c., "Ebrietas decepit quem Sodoma non decepit." (Origen.)

particular item of history is not ascribed by Orosius to Pompeius; but he does often refer to Pompeius, and Herbert may have been quoting from memory;

"In the confines of Arabia and Palestine there are said to have been five cities, Sodom, Gomorra, Adama, Seboim, and Segor. Of these, Segor was a little city, the others were large and wealthy, as possessing a fertile soil and having the river Jordan flowing through the champaign country. To this whole district, which made a bad use of its blessings, the abundance of all things was a cause of mischief. For, from abundance sprang up luxury, and from luxury foul lusts, so that men with men worked that which was unseemly, and rushed headlong [into the act of sin] without regard to either place or condition of life or age. Wherefore God being angry rained upon this land fire and brimstone, and after burning it up consigned to perdition all that country with its peoples and cities, making it a monument of His judgment to future ages. So that although still there is the bare outline of a country there, yet it is found to be a country of ashes, and a sea now covers the midst of the valley which formerly the Jordan watered. And by things so small in themselves, as it is supposed, the blaze of Divine wrath was kindled, that on account of the abuse of their blessings by making them nourish their lusts, the very soil on which these cities stood, first burned with fire and afterwards submerged with water, wears to the look of all the mark of having been eternally withered by the curse of God."

The edition of Orosius which we are using is that of Cologne, 1542. References to Pompeius will be found on the following pages, 33, 37, 182, 457, and 481.

[b] "a subtle mystery"—*subtile sacramentum.* See the note on the meanings of the word *Sacramentum* in the Sermons, p. 21, x. IV.

burned up. Verily the primæval world, though its crimes could no longer be borne, was not so much overflowed as washed, and rose from the flood cleansed of those primæval stains in a laver, which was the figure of our own Baptism. Well, after those primæval sins and (if I may call them so) those primæval punishments, the fruitful earth appeared; it was clad with herbs; it was painted with flowers; it was again variegated with its trees, and stocked with animals of all kinds. But in those haunts of evil fame, as the crime had been execrable, so was the punishment beyond compare, and proceeded to such a length that the earth appeareth not there, but only an infernal lake, deadly brimstone, full of mischief to every living thing, and a hellish stench[c] [thence arising], an evil which hath not its like upon the earth. Hence let the prudent mind gather the great danger which must arise from reviving in holy Churches the abominations which our Saviour destroyed in profane temples. The fanes have been overthrown[d], the idols

See 1 Pet. iii. 21.

---

[c] "a hellish stench"—*tartareus fœtor*. The idea of the odour emanating from the Dead Sea is probably a confusion between profane and sacred literature. Herbert was thinking of the Lake Avernus, and of the pestiferous vapours arising from it, which were said to be so strong that no living thing could approach its banks, and birds were suffocated as they flew across it. This circumstance, and the frowning woods which environed it, gave rise to the fable that it was the mouth of the pit of hell, or the infernal regions.

> " Spelunca alta fuit, vastoque immanis hiatu,
> Scrupea, tuta lacu nigro nemorumque tenebris :
> Quam super haud ullæ poterant impune volucres
> Tendere iter pennis : talis sese halitus atris
> Faucibus effundens supera ad convexa ferebat :
> Unde locum Graii dixerunt nomine Aornon."
> (Virg. Æn. 6. 237—242.)

[d] Almost reminding one of the magnificent stanzas in Milton's Hymn on Christ's Nativity;

> " The oracles are dumb,
> No voice or hideous hum
>   Runs through the arched roof in words deceiving.
> Apollo from his shrine
> Can no more divine,
>   With hollow shriek the steep of Delphos leaving.

have been broken in pieces; the unclean worship of devils has come to nought; that foul and loathsome fornication in which the Gentiles indulged has been cut away, and *the Lord abideth for ever.* The Apostle saith of gluttonous people that their god is their belly; why should we not also say of the followers of lust that their god is lust? Sensual gratification is blinded by its own impurity. In the house of God we cannot serve two masters. A lover of God despises lust; a follower of lust knoweth not God. The Virgin's Son casteth out from His Church lustful and unnatural monsters, nor leaves them, so long as they live, the grace of Christian communion. And that most strict judge and ever-present observer [of our ways], who proceeded forth from a Father without a mother, and from a mother without a father (the virginity of His mother being kept untainted),—He is with us, and is inseparably united with the action of his faithful ones; for thus, when about to ascend to His Father, doth He comfort the sadness of His friends in soothing accents; *I will be with you,* saith He, *always, even to the end of the world."*

<small>Ps. ix. 8, V.
See Rom. xvi. 18, and Phil. iii. 19.
See St. Matt. vi. 24; St. Luke xvi. 13.
See St. Matt. xviii. 18.
From St. Matt. xxviii. 20.</small>

Most of the other acts of the Synod were

> No nightly trance, or breathed spell
> Inspires the pale-eyed priest from the prophetic cell.
> * * * * * *
> " He [Osiris] feels from Judah's land
>   The dreaded Infant's hand,
>   The rays of Bethlehem blind his dusky eyen;
>   Nor all the gods beside
>   Longer dare abide,
>   Not Typhon huge ending in snaky twine:
>   Our Babe to show His Godhead true,
>   Can in His swaddling-bands control the damned crew.
>
> " So when the Sun in bed,
>   Curtained with cloudy red,
>   Pillows his chin upon an orient wave,
>   The flocking shadows pale
>   Troop to the infernal jail,
>   Each fettered ghost slips to his several grave."

directed to such trifling matters as the apparel of the clergy, and sundry other ceremonial restrictions; but there was one which ran thus, and which we name, because it gives us an opportunity of introducing a letter of Herbert's on the subject of marriage. "They who are related within the seventh degree," says the Council, "must not be coupled in marriage." Here is Herbert's reply to an application made to him to sanction the marriage of a woman whose husband was yet living, but possibly separated from her by mutual consent. The mere application to him for such a sanction (made too by an ecclesiastic) seems to show that a lax view was taken in those days of the obligations and restrictions of the marriage vow.

LETTER III.

To William the Chaplain [e].

"Herbert to William the Chaplain.

"As to the question of your sister's marriage, I can make you no other answer than that which you heard from my own mouth when you were with me; which is that, while her husband is alive, she cannot in conformity with the Gospel, and the use prescribed by the Sacred Canons, wed another man. I beseech you, therefore, by your sense of duty, that you regard in this thing not the will of a woman, but the customs of the holy Church whereof you are a minister; since in

Herbert refuses to sanction the marriage of William's sister, while her husband is alive.

---

[e] The word *Capellanus*, according to its etymology, means a *choir-man*, —one engaged in the *capella* or choir. Probably here it may have been a chantry-priest, whose duty it was to say Mass over or near a tomb for the soul of some one departed, and to celebrate the anniversary of his death, called an *obit*. Or the *Capellanus* may have been merely an assistant in the offices of the Church, who served at one of the side altars.

any matter of this kind my judgment must go along with, and cannot be divorced from, the law of Christ my [God]."

After the example of Solomon, who first reared the house of the Lord, and, when it was completed, proceeded to build his own house¹, our Herbert, having brought his choir and transept into such a state of completion, that Divine Service could be celebrated there with the highest solemnity, and on great occasions with magnificence, turned his attention to an episcopal palace. This, we are told, he placed on the north of the Cathedral, designing to shut it off altogether from the monastery, the site of which lay on the south. It was a point of policy to keep his monks secluded as much as possible from secular affairs, and from the hum and distraction of business. He himself, charged with the administration of a large diocese, could not be without constant interruptions, and intercourse with men of all descriptions. He desired therefore to keep the monastery altogether clear of the episcopal quarters. The beautiful ruin in the grounds of the

---

¹ "After the building of the Temple, which, as we have before said, was finished in seven years, the king laid the foundation of his palace, which he did not finish under thirteen years, for he was not equally zealous in the building of his palace as he had been about the Temple; for as to that, though it was a great work, and required wonderful and surprising application, yet God, for whom it was made, so far co-operated therewith, that it was finished in the fore-mentioned number of years; but the palace, which was a building much inferior in dignity to the Temple, both because its materials had not been so long beforehand gotten ready, nor had been so zealously prepared, and because this was only a habitation for kings, and not for God, it was longer in finishing." (Josephus, Ant., viii. ch. 5. sect. 1.)

present palace is of a date long subsequent to Herbert; but that part of the palace, which, till quite recently, joined the Cathedral, is undoubtedly part of the original structure; and thus the site of the episcopal residence, and its position relatively to the Close (or monastic precinct) seem to have remained unaltered since the days of the founder.

But the stately edifices which Herbert raised at Norwich did not altogether draw off his interest from Thetford, the older city of his see. "He instituted Cluniac monks at Thetford," says William of Malmesbury, the nearly contemporary chronicler; and Bartholomew Cotton, at the close of the succeeding century, echoes the words. The account of the matter given by the Centuriators of Magdeburg is perhaps a little more exact. After mentioning the transfer of the see from Thetford to Norwich, they add; "But the convent at Thetford" (the convent probably in connexion with the Cathedral, over which Herbert, as Bishop, would have full control) "he granted as a residence to the Cluniac monks, on account of" (in recognition of) "the communion which that Order had with his." But we are not to think of Herbert as having had the chief hand in the foundation of Thetford Abbey, which did not take place till A.D. 1107, three years after. This was the doing of Roger Bigot, Earl of Norfolk, acting, as he expressly tells us in the charter of the Abbey, under the advice of Herbert the Bishop. This powerful noble was smitten with compunction for the sins of his past life,

A.D. 1104.

and was on the point of endeavouring to expiate them by a pilgrimage to Jerusalem. His steward, however, induced him to resort to the less hazardous, if more expensive, expedient of founding a monastery at home. And accordingly he availed himself of the opportunity of a royal visit to Thetford in 1107 to induce Henry I. to lay the foundation-stone of his new abbey. It became to the nobility of East Anglia what St. Denis was to the French kings, their place of interment, and covered the ashes of the Earls and Dukes of Norfolk, the Bigots, the Mowbrays, and the Howards. And it gave an early and dismal omen of the object to which it was to be devoted; for Earl Roger, the founder, is said to have died on the eighth day after the laying of the first stone. We are not told where he was interred; but it is quite probable that, his own abbey being only in its very earliest stage of construction, it may have been arranged to lay him, at all events temporarily, in the choir of the new Cathedral at Norwich. We have forestalled by three years the course of events, in giving these particulars at the point of Herbert's history at which we have now arrived; but it seemed to us convenient not to break the narrative of the foundation of Thetford Abbey. It would appear that Herbert, in the year 1104, scattered the seeds of a Cluniac foundation at Thetford (of which one Malgod was the first prior) by placing Cluniacs in the Cathedral monastery. Earl Roger two or three years later took up Herbert's design, and (as his vast wealth A.D. 1104. enabled him to do) made a great foundation of Cluniacs in Thetford, richly endowed and thoroughly organized by monks sent thither from Clugni itself.

And here it may interest the reader to have some particulars respecting the Cluniacs. They were a branch of the great Benedictine Order, which had sprung up in the preceding century, and propagated itself with extraordinary rapidity throughout Europe. At first the Cluniacs obtained a great reputation for piety and virtue; but prosperity and great wealth soon operated, as in other monastic communities, to produce laxity and general moral decadence. At the very close of the eleventh century (in 1098), when the Cluniacs were declining, another Benedictine congregation (the Cistercians) arose to revive the decaying strictness[g] of the Benedictine rule; and it is well known how in 1127, some years after our Prelate's death, that most eminent of Cistercians, St. Bernard, directed a literary attack against the Cluniacs on account of their laxity[h].

---

[g] "As mercers, when their old stuffes begin to tire in sale, refresh them with new names to make them more vendible; so when the Benedictines waxed stale in the world, the same Order was set forth in a new edition, corrected and amended, under the names, first, of Cluniacks,—these were Benedictines sifted through a finer search, with some additionals invented and imposed upon them by Odo, Abbot of Clugni, in Burgundy, who lived A.D. 913. . . . Secondly, Cistercians, so called from one Robert living in Cistercium, in Burgundy aforesaid; he the second time refined the drossie Benedictines." (Fuller, as quoted by Maitland in "The Dark Ages," p. 357, No. 5.) The Cistercian Order was founded by Robert in the year A.D. 1098.

[h] The points objected by the Cistercians to the Cluniacs were these, and such as these; (1) that they admitted novices without a year of probation,

But the prestige of their wealth[1], their numbers, and the gorgeous ceremonial in their churches, seems to have fascinated Earl Roger[k], and possibly

during which there might be a trial of their spirits (1 John iv. 1); (2) that they used leather garments and skins; (3) that monks sent on journeys were allowed to wear breeches; (4) that their beds were too warmly covered; (5) that more than two dressed dishes were allowed at the chief meal; (6) that apostates from the monastic profession were received back at Clugni even after the third offence; (7) that the prescribed fasts were evaded; (8) that manual labour was eschewed; (9) that the Abbot and community no longer washed the feet, or poured water on the hands of, strangers, or did reverence to Christ in them; (10) that the Abbot kept no inventory of goods belonging to the monastery; (11) that the Abbot did not take his meals with the guests and strangers; (12) that the younger brethren did not ask a blessing of the elder when they met them; (13) that the porter did not answer "Thanks be to God," or give a blessing, when he heard a knock at the gate; (14) that monks of other monasteries were received at Clugni without the recommendation of the Abbots from whom they came; (15) that the Cluniacs recognised no Bishop; (16) that they held parish churches, first-fruits, and tithes, all which things pertained to the *secular* clergy alone; (17) that they held secular possessions, like secular persons, towns, villages, peasants, servants, tolls, taxes, &c.—All these points, the Cistercians insisted, were contrary to the *letter* of the Benedictine Rule. And the Cluniacs retorted that the Cistercians were Pharisees, priding themselves on minute observances, and omitting that humility which was the true *spirit* of the Rule. (See Maitland's "Dark Ages," pp. 373—378.)

[1] Peter the Venerable, raised to the Abbacy of Clugni two years after Herbert's death (in A.D. 1122), while describing the monastery as almost without revenue, when he entered upon the government of it, yet in giving an account of the invasion of it by his predecessor Pontius (who had resigned his charge), tells us that "he" (Pontius) "seized golden crosses, golden censers, golden boards (of books), golden candlesticks, and all the other vessels, many in number and of great weight. He also took the most holy chalices, and did not spare the gold and silver reliquaries and shrines, containing the bones of many saints and martyrs. *These and the like he melted down into a vast sum of money.*"—We are also told that while the Cistercians had none but iron candlesticks in their churches, there hung from the roof of the church at Clugni a fine chandelier of brass, gold, and silver. (Maitland's "Dark Ages," pp. 347, 348, 358.) These particulars illustrate well William of Malmesbury's statement, that the monks of Clugni were "splendidissimæ religionis in Deo,"—in their relations to God, their religion took the form of outward magnificence.

[k] There is an interesting notice of the foundation of Thetford Priory or Abbey in the twelfth chapter of Martin's "History of Thetford," (Lond. 1779). He tells us that Roger Bigot had formed a design of atoning for

our Herbert, and it was ruled that the monks of the abbey of Thetford should be Cluniacs.

We subjoin here the letters addressed by Herbert to his Thetford monks, whether his own Cluniacs, or some other order which existed there before his foundation.

his sins by a pilgrimage to Jerusalem, but that he was persuaded by his steward to apply the money which would have been spent in this pilgrimage to the erection of a monastery. Hereupon he communicated with Hugh, Abbot of Clugni, and Lanzo, Abbot of Lewes, the earliest Cluniac foundation in this country. Lanzo, by Hugh's permission, sent him twelve monks to start his enterprise, who took possession of the church of St. Mary, formerly the cathedral of East Anglia. Malgod, as stated above, p. 164, was the first Prior. Stephen, a monk of Clugni, succeeded him, and removed the monastery to a more commodious place on the brink of the river, Herbert himself cutting the first sod. One rather wonders at Herbert's alacrity in the whole matter, inasmuch as it was arranged that the monastery should be subject to no law but that of the Abbot of Clugni, and therefore would be exempt from the jurisdiction of Norwich. As an acknowledgment of this dependence, Thetford Abbey was to pay a silver mark to the Abbot of Clugni. In the midst of the work of the new foundation, Roger died at a place called Ercsa (query, Earsham?), ten miles from Norwich. Herbert immediately sent for the body to Norwich against the remonstrances of Roger's wife and of his monks, who came to intercede with Herbert for the restoration of it, in order that it might be buried in the cemetery of the Thetford monastery, according to the expressed wish of the deceased. Herbert, it is said, turned a deaf ear to all their entreaties, and put himself into a passion with their importunity. The Prior then brought an action against him; but, Herbert having made oath that Roger had given himself and his family to the church of Norwich, he was obliged to renounce his claim to the possession of the body, and Roger was buried in Norwich Cathedral. Most of these particulars are taken from the history of Thetford Priory, by Geoffry de Rocherio, who became Prior in 1369. The MS. of his History is to be found in the Library of Corpus Christi College, at Cambridge. We think that in the facts above recorded there is evidence of Herbert's having somewhat resented the erection in his diocese of an independent monastery. He could not help what Roger had done, but he was determined that the greatest noble in his diocese should be claimed by the Cathedral church, and not be allowed to lie in an exempt jurisdiction.

LETTER II.

To the Brethren of Thetford.

Herbert declines to consecrate the atrium *of the new church at Thetford without a previous reference to the king.*

"Herbert to the Brethren of Thetford.

"Willingly, Sirs, would I, for my part, comply with your injunction to consecrate the churchyard[1] of your new church. But my friends do not approve of my doing this without the knowledge and consent of the king, lest, after the new churchyard has received consecration, there should arise some dispute between us about the customary dues arising from the churchyard of the old church. For if even a slight disturbance of this kind got wind, the king would not unreasonably be angry with me for my rashness and want of foresight in precipitately disturbing an arrangement which he himself had made. Wait then patiently, I pray you, until I shall speak with the king or his justiciaries[m], since

---

[1] "Atrii vestræ novæ Ecclesiæ." The *atrium* of a church was, in the first instance, an open space in front of it, surrounded by a colonnade, and in the centre of which there was often a fountain. St. Ambrose's church at Milan, and St. Clement's at Rome, both of them very ancient churches, still retain the *atrium*. Criminals could find sanctuary in an *atrium* as well as in the church itself. It was customary to use the atrium as a cemetery, and hence the word comes to signify, as here, the burying-ground annexed to a church,—a churchyard. The dues mentioned further on were probably either fees upon burials, which accrued to the Bishop, or a stated payment made into his exchequer, as an acknowledgment that the ground held its sacred character from him. Bishop Herbert is not the last divine, who has apprehended some diminution of his income from the opening of a new cemetery.

[m] The King's Justiciaries were the great officers of State, who sat in the King's Court, and were presided over by the Grand or Chief Justiciary. It was the Conqueror who "constituted the office of CHIEF JUSTICIAR. His plan was to have a grand central tribunal for the whole realm, which should not only be a court of appeal, but in which all causes of importance should originate and be finally decided. This was afterwards called CURIA REGIS, and sometimes AULA REGIS, because it assembled in the hall of the King's palace. The great officers of State, the Constable, the Mareschal, the Seneschal, the Chamberlain, and the Treasurer, were the judges, and over them presided the Grand Justiciar. 'Next to the King himself, he was chief in power and authority, and when the King was beyond seas (which frequently happened) he governed the realm like a viceroy.' He was at all times the guardian of the public peace as Coroner-General, and he likewise had a control over the finances of the kingdom. In rank he

otherwise I could not venture to perform the consecration which you demand. Or else, if, when the privileges of the old church are transferred to the new, you will restore to me absolutely and explicitly, without any quibble, the ancient episcopal dues, then without further apprehension or hesitation I would comply with your request."

LETTER VII.
To Stephen[n] the Prior.

"Herbert to Stephen the Prior.

"Certain pieces of business have arisen, by which I am obliged to bring on at an earlier period the consecration of your churchyard: for were I again to defer it, I fear you might impute my doing so more to inclination than necessity. On Sunday [next], then, according to your wish, let the consecration both of your chapel and churchyard be performed; and cause public notice to be given of this in the market towns of your neighbourhood during the four days which will elapse between this time and that."

Herbert fixes a day with the Prior for the consecration of the atrium, and desires notice to be given of it.

had the precedence of all the nobility, and his power was greater than that of all other magistrates." (Campbell's "Lives of the Chief Justices of England." London, Murray, 1849, vol. i. pp. 2, 3.)

The Grand Justiciar was denuded of his military and political functions, the AULA REGIS was abolished as a court of justice, and the whole judicial system of the country was remodelled by Edward I. Lord Campbell shews how the Aula Regis contained the germs of, and in Edward the First's time resolved itself into, the Court of King's Bench (or supreme criminal court), the Court of Common Pleas (for civil suits), the Court of Exchequer (originally for fiscal matters affecting the Crown), and the Court of Chancery (to do justice to the subject, where no remedy was provided by the common law). See ch. ii. pp. 70, 71, of the volume of his "Lives of the Chief Justices," recently quoted.

[n] Stephen, second Prior of Thetford, is described as "a man of great learning and piety, descended from noble parents, an excellent scholar, who had taken upon him the habit of a monk in Burgundy, before Hugh, Abbot of Clugni." He had so attached to himself his fraternity in Burgundy by his preaching and prudent behaviour, that they shed many tears in tearing themselves away from him when he was going to Thetford. His first act there seems to have been the removal of the monastery to a quieter and more rural position, as he found it too closely surrounded by the houses of the townspeople. (Martin's "History of Thetford," chap. xii. pp. 114, 115.)

LETTER XXXV.

To the Brethren of Thetford.

"Herbert the Bishop to R. the Viscount [o] and to all manner of persons in God's diocese [p] and his own in Norfolk and Suffolk, greeting.

Gal. vi. 2. Herbert excommunicates with awful anathemas those who had killed a deer in his park at Homersfield.

"If indeed we be obliged by the precept of the truth to bear one another's burdens, and to mourn for one another's maltreatment, then ought ye more especially to resent affronts offered to him who is your head, and to humble yourselves from the bottom of your hearts on account of his troubles. Great are those bonds of charity by which you and I are knit together, and as generally useful to mankind as they are closely linked by God's own appointment and dispensation. For the same law [of indissoluble union] which, in respect of the body, God ordained between the bridegroom and the bride, Christ in a spiritual sense promulgated between the bishop [q] and his flock,—nay, even a higher law, inasmuch as the former was framed in reference to a carnal, the latter in reference to a spiritual union. All which I bring before your minds, in order that ye may form a just estimate on the one hand of the labours of mine office, in which day by day I do you service, offering for you the body and blood of Christ, and on the other hand of the loving obedience, wherewith ye ought

[o] See note w, on p. 24.

[p] "to all manner of persons in God's diocese and his own"—*Cunctis parochianis Dei et suis.* The word *parochia* had not in mediæval times the limited signification to which it is now confined. It originally signified a diocese, that is, the territory within the jurisdiction of a bishop. The diocese or province was the larger territory within the jurisdiction of a primate or metropolitan. Bingham tells us that down to the fourth century the word παροικία signified a diocese, but that about that time the word diocese began to be used in the same sense. ("Antiquities of Christian Church," bk. ix. chap. ii. sec. 1, 2.)

[q] Hence the arms of a bishop are empaled with those of his see. "Such as are preferred to the honour of pastoral jurisdiction are said to be knit in nuptial bands and care for the cathedral churches whereof they are superintendents. Therefore their paternal coat is marshalled on the left side of the escutcheon, giving the pre-eminence of the right side to the arms of their see." Hence the arms of the wife of a Protestant bishop are excluded from his coat. (Clark's "Introduction to Heraldry," p. 64.)

to meet me in the exercise of this office. Thus much
have I prefaced [on the subject of our mutual relations
and duties], as I find it necessary to raise the hue-and-
cry among you about certain evil-minded men, who in
the past week broke into my park at Homersfield[r] in
the night, and killed the only deer I had there, and
having thrown away his head with his feet and intes-
tines, committed an abominable theft by carrying off
the carcase. Wherefore I entreat and implore the lord
Viscount, and all God's faithful Christians in the counties aforesaid, that, if they should hear anything of
the matter, or have an inkling on the subject, they
would inform me, and with praiseworthy zeal give up
my concealed foes. Meanwhile I excommunicate those
who have broken into my park and killed my deer with
that anathema, wherewith God in His anger smiteth the
souls of the wicked. I interdict them from entrance
into the church, from partaking of the body and blood
of Christ, and from fellowship in the whole circle of
Christian offices. May the curse and the excommunication rest upon them in their homes; in the ways and
in the fields, in the woods and in the waters, and in all
places wheresoever they shall be found! May the flesh

[r] "The name of this village, as written in the Domesday Book, is Hum-
bresfelda, which signifies the land of Humber; whence it would appear
that some Danish rover, sailing up the broad channel of the Waveney, had
seized on this bold promontory, and established himself in the demesne of
the Saxon bishop, by compromise or the strong arm." [Mr. Isaac Taylor
tells us that the termination *field* is both Norse and Anglo-Saxon. As
a Norse termination it denotes a hill-side; as an Anglo-Saxon termination
it means a forest-clearing: both words, he says, are from the same root,
which is in fact the word to fall. The Danish field or feld is a place
where the ground is on the fall; the Anglo-Saxon field or feld is where
the trees have been felled. The word *fold* is of the same origin, a fold
being a stall constructed of felled trees for the protection of cattle or
sheep. ("Words and Places," p. 163, n. 3, and p. 121.)] Homersfield was
in early times closely connected with the see of the East Angles. William,
Bishop of Thetford, Herbert's predecessor, held a manor there, which
Bishop Almar had held in Saxon times, and the manor and advowson
of Homersfield remained with the bishops of the diocese till the reign of
Henry VIII., when they passed to the Norths, as parcel of the manor
of South Elmham. These particulars are taken from Suckling's "History
of Suffolk" (London, 1846), vol. i. pp. 212, 213.

of those who have devoured my stag rot, as the flesh of Herod rotted^s, who shed the blood of Innocents in order to come to Christ; may they have their portion with Judas the traitor, with Ananias and Sapphira, with Dathan and Abiram. Let them have the Anathema^t

See 1 Cor. xvi. 22.

^s "as the flesh of Herod rotted." It was on his death-bed that Herod must have ordered the massacre of the Holy Innocents. He went out of life "breathing threatenings and slaughter;" for one of his last orders was that the men who had pulled down the golden eagle which he had set up over the gates of the Temple should be burnt alive (Josephus, Wars, bk. i. c. 33, 44), and only five days before his own death he gave an order for the execution of his son Antipater. The description given by Josephus of his disease is frightful; exulceration of the entrails, inflammation of the abdomen, and a putrefaction of the privy member, which produced worms, being mentioned among the features of it. (Ant., bk. xvii. c. 6, § 5; and Wars, bk. i. c. 33, § 5.) Herbert could not have imprecated upon any one a more terrible end.

^t The words are taken, of course, from 1 Cor. xvi. 22; and it must be confessed that the slightness of the sin on which Herbert pronounces this censure contrasts painfully with the gravity of the offence to which the Apostle annexes it; "If any man love not the Lord Jesus Christ, let him be anathema maran-atha." There were three grades of excommunication among the Jews, of which *anathema maran-atha* was the gravest. The first was *a casting out of the synagogue* (St. John ix. 22); the second, *a delivering unto Satan* (1 Cor. v. 5); the third "is called in the New Testament by the Syriac name *Maranatha*, 1 Cor. xvi. 22, that is, *the Lord cometh*. *Maran* signifieth *the Lord*," (the longer form of "Mar," the Chaldee word for "Lord," which is the title given to ecclesiastical dignitaries in the Syrian Church) "and *Atha*, *cometh*; and this they say was instituted by Enoch. Jude v. 14."

"There can be little doubt that the whole phrase is introduced and preserved in the original language, in order to give greater force to the previous *anathema*; as in like manner the Syriac 'Abba' is preserved in Rom. viii. 15; Gal. iv. 6."

"A pause is to be made after 'Anathema.' *Let him be accursed* (Acts xxiii. 14; Rom. ix. 3; Gal. i. 8, 9; 1 Cor. xii. 3): not however by *man*. For, *the Lord* (*maran*) *cometh* (*atha*) to execute judgment upon him. Cp. Jude 14, 15."

[See Godwyn's Moses and Aaron (London, 1655), pp. 181—183; Dean Stanley's Epistles to the Corinthians; and Bp. Wordsworth's Greek Testament, with notes, *in loc.*]

Speaking of the force of excommunications in Becket's time, *à propos* of that prelate's hurling anathemas from the pulpit of the Church at Vezelay, Dean Hook says; "Excommunications had become so frequent and common as to have lost a considerable portion of the power, with which they at one time invested ecclesiastical authority. For offences personal to themselves, for withholding their property, or *even for treating their animals*

Maran-atha, unless they shall come to a better mind, and make me some reparation. Amen. Amen. Amen. This excommunication I pronounce, well-beloved brethren, not because a single deer is of any great importance to me, but because I am desirous that the evil-doers should repent, and come to confession, and afterwards receive meet correction for so gross a robbery. Those who are privy to the theft, or consenting parties in it, or who contrive the escape of the guilty, shall be laid under the same anathema. To all such let not our words seem a light matter, since what we bind is bound also in the judgment of God, and what we loose is loosed by Him; inasmuch as to Peter, the first of bishops, the Truth thus spake; 'Whatsoever thou shalt bind on earth, shall be bound in heaven; and whatsoever thou shalt loose on earth shall be loosed in heaven.'" St. Matt. xvi. 19.

LETTER XXXVII.

TO HIS BRETHREN AND SONS AT THETFORD.

"Herbert the Bishop to his Brethren and Sons at Thetford.

"Know ye that I have restored to Bond, the dean[u], his schools at Thetford as completely and advantage- Herbert confirms Dean Bond's possession of, and authority over, the schools at Thetford.

with cruelty, ecclesiastics were accustomed to fulminate their excommunications; and what issued from the interested passions of one class of men, the passions of another class were interested in despising."—("Lives of the Archbishops of Canterbury," vol. ii. pp. 449, 450.)

We consider it important to observe the commonness at that time of excommunications for slight offences, showing, as it does, that this anathema of Herbert's was rather the fault of the age than of the man.

[u] We suppose that Bond must have been the earliest Dean of Thetford. Mr. Leigh Hunt, in his "Capital of the Ancient Kingdom of East Anglia" (Lond. 1870), says as follows respecting this dignitary; "To conciliate the people for the removal of the see to Norwich, Blomefield is of opinion that the deanery of Thetford was endowed with peculiar privileges and enlarged jurisdiction. Thetford was always in the archdeaconry of Norwich; but, before the dissolution, acknowledged no archidiaconal jurisdiction; for the deanery of Thetford contained all the city, the two Snarehills, and Santon Downham living, together with the sole, peculiar jurisdiction over all the churches, monasteries, and inhabitants (except the abbey and nunnery, which were exempted from it); and yet the abbey, although it did not acknowledge itself subject to the dean's power, claimed

ously as he ever held them; and I give orders that no other schools shall be held there but his, or such as he has promised should be held."

LETTER XXXVI.

TO ATHSELINUS THE PRESBYTER.

Herbert warns Athselinus, the provost (or mayor) of Thetford, not to throw off his clerical character, or be ashamed of his

"Herbert the Bishop to Athselinus the Presbyter [x], greeting.

"I should much wish to talk to you, and to restrain your impetuosity; for rumour ascribes to you a conduct exemption for some places where they were concerned, from all other spiritual courts, other than that of this dean. The first dean, of whom we have any record, was Ranulf, who lived in the time of William Turbus, third bishop of Norwich; and the last was John Kevelon (made dean in 1422); but the deanery existed in Thetford till the year 1540." Martin, in his "History of the Town of Thetford" (Lond. 1779), p. 37, mentions a striking instance of the ecclesiastical power wielded by the deans of Thetford. The case occurred in the 25th of Henry VII. It was an immemorial custom that all ecclesiastical causes arising within the town of Thetford should be determined before the dean, and that none of the same town should be drawn in plea into any other court Christian for ecclesiastical causes, except before the same dean; and if any were so drawn in suit before any other ecclesiastical judge, that such parties should be presented before the mayor of Thetford and fined six and eightpence. An inhabitant of Thetford being sued in the consistory court of the bishop of Norwich for an ecclesiastical cause arising within the town of Thetford, this was an infringement of the privileges of the dean's court, who thereupon caused the offender to be presented before the mayor of Thetford and fined six and eightpence. Nix, then bishop of Norwich, cited the mayor to appear before him, and enjoined him, under pain of excommunication, to annul the presentment. Hereupon a writ of *præmunire* was issued against the bishop, and being non-suited, he was put out of the king's protection, his person imprisoned, and all his property forfeited to the crown, in the year A.D. 1534. What makes the incident still more memorable is the circumstance that with the forfeiture accruing to the crown from Nix's *præmunire* the splendid windows of King's College Chapel, at Cambridge, were purchased. It appears, however, that this straining of the dean's prerogative issued in rending it asunder; for soon afterwards Bishop Nix, upon his submission, was reinstated, and the jurisdiction which the deans of Thetford had hitherto exercised, was transferred to the bishops of Norwich.

[x] "To Athselinus the Presbyter." Athselinus is described in the latter part of the letter as *præpositus apud Tedford*, provost at Thetford. There were many different kinds of *præpositi*, whose offices are described at great length by Ducange, *sub voc.* Here the internal evidence of the letter shows that the *præpositus* in question was (*qua præpositus*) a secular not an ecclesiastical dignitary, a man in very high position under the crown (for

so harsh as would be unbecoming even in a respectable layman. You are ashamed [it would seem] to wear the tonsure[y], and to sing mass[z]; but whosoever shall be how else could he be compared to Joseph and Daniel?), and one who had the power of annoying persons by legal summonses (*placita*) to attend his court. Probably, therefore, he would be one of the *præpositi regii*, whose functions are described in Ducange's Glossary, *sub voc.*, as being next to that of the king's justiciary in the administration of justice, and to whom cases of theft and murder, &c., were referred from inferior tribunals. Had he been a layman, Herbert would have had no control over him, and perhaps might have been molested personally by his summonses and litigious propensities. But he was a clergyman (*presbyter* and *sacerdos Dei*), the analogue of many clergymen of our own time, who greatly prefer magisterial to ministerial functions, and shine more on the bench at quarter sessions than in the pulpit; and Herbert therefore, as his spiritual chief, had a claim upon him which he here enforces. When the diocesan came to Thetford, he would summon around him the chief ecclesiastics of the place, among whom would appear both the dean and the provost, the former of whom had been vexed by certain secular proceedings which the latter had instituted. Herbert pledges himself to hear their differences, as the ecclesiastical superior of both (*canonice*), and to do his best to bring them to such terms as clergymen ought to be on with one another.—The English word *provost*, together with the school-boy word *præpostor* (which has been made famous by Eton), derives its origin from the Latin *præpositus*. In Scotland the mayors of cities or royal burghs are called *Provosts;* and probably we cannot better accommodate to our own times the relation of Athselinus and Bond, than by imagining a mayor in orders, who should be always vexing the dean of his cathedral church by summonses to attend the common council on matters connected with capitular property or the administration of the Close.—It is to be remarked about the word *provost*, that its application ranges from very high to very low officials. The Grand Provost of France had jurisdiction over all the officers of the royal household, while the Provost of the king's stables is the officer who holds his stirrup when he mounts.

See the word "præpositus" used of an inferior judge, subordinate to the *Ballivus*, on p. 25, note x.

[y] "to wear the tonsure"—*coronam*. The word *corona* (or *tonsure*) indicates the entire clerical dignity and function, of which the tonsure was the chief external mark. Thus St. Augustine (Epist. 147, to Proculianus), "Per coronam nostram adjurant vestri" (Your people adjure us by our clerical office). Bingham shows (Ant., bk. vi. c. 4, sect. 16, 17) that the true ancient tonsure of the clergy was not a shaving of the crown, but merely a clipping of the hair close round the head, as if with a bowl, in order to obviate the luxurious appearance of long locks. Hence it was, he thinks, that the clergy were called *coronati*, because their hair was so cut as to look like a cap or crown. But it is possible that the appellation may merely signify *distinguished*, *dignified*, since *corona* is sometimes used figuratively, and means *honour*, *dignity*.

[z] "to sing mass"—*missam psallere*. The history of the word *psallo* is

orders, not to vex the Church at Thetford with suits and summonses, and to maintain peace with the dean.

See St. Mark viii. 38, and St. Luke ix. 26.

ashamed of Christ and His words, of him shall Christ also be ashamed before His Father which is in heaven. Joseph and Daniel, the one in Egypt, the other in Babylon, held the reins of government; yet neither of them [on this account] dropped the [profession of the] true religion. Do you also administer secular affairs in such a manner that the dignity of the presbyter's office receive no stain in you. I as a bishop charge you as a presbyter that you allow God and our church at Thetford to have its customary dues, which it had in the times of my predecessors, without challenging [a] [or calling them in question], and without the molestation of temporal suits [b]. Learn to love Bond, my dean, and

not without interest. Originally, and according to its etymology (ψάω, ψαύω, to *touch*), it designated exclusively the playing on stringed instruments. (The Greek ψάλλω is used as much of the twanging of the bow-string, as of that of the harp-string). Hence it came to mean, *singing to the sound of the lyre*. And in later (though probably not in classical) Latin, *the singing without any instrument at all*.

[a] "without challenging them"—*sine calumpniâ*. *Calumnia* in mediæval Latin seems to lose its original meaning of a *false* charge. It is a law term, meaning a claim which any one sets up for himself or against another, and which he seeks to establish by legal process. It is probable that our word *challenge* (Fr. *calenge*) is a derivative from *calumnia*. The origin of the word in classical Latin is said to be *calvor*, a verb meaning to *deceive, practise upon*; showing that the idea of *falsity* was an original element in the meaning. And though we cannot say that in such uses of the word as that before us there is any direct implication of the "challenging" being groundless, still there are odious associations which linger round the word, and of which it can never altogether rid itself. A perfectly fair and reasonable claim, made temperately, and not from a litigious spirit, would hardly be called *calumnia*.

[b] "without the molestation of temporal suits"—*sine secularium inquietatione placitorum*. From the old classical word "Placet," signifying the resolution of a deliberative assembly ("Placuit senatui," *it was resolved by the senate*), sprang the mediæval word "Placitum," which represented an essential element of the feudal system. The "Placitum" was the rudiment of the Parliaments of later days,—the great council of all orders of the realm, lay and clerical, held under the king for deliberation upon affairs of state, and adjudication in civil and criminal causes. These councils went down to the very extremities of the feudal system, each lord summoning his vassals periodically [*] for deliberative, judicial, and fiscal purposes, and for the providing the sinews of war, where war was to be made. The

[*] Part of the oath of fealty was, that the vassal would attend his lord either at his *placita* or in war.

be at peace with him, and do not molest him with any suits, until I shall come to Thetford and hear your

Church followed suit in this matter; and bishops and abbots held their *placita* or courts periodically, to hear grievances, settle differences, impose taxes, &c. (Monks, by the way, and probably all ecclesiastics, appear to have been forbidden to attend *secularia placita*,—a circumstance which throws light upon Herbert's bidding the Provost let the Church of Thetford enjoy its dues *sine secularium inquietatione placitorum*, i.e. without summonsing the monks and ecclesiastics to appear in his secular court.) The customary seasons for holding the more solemn *placita* seem to have been after Christmas, after Easter, and after the Feast of St. John Baptist; the place for holding them was (strictly and originally) in the open air, in plains, in streets, under trees, in front of churches or of camps (though local exceptions seem to have been made to this publicity in cases of very inclement weather); from the day before Quinquagesima Sunday to the day after Low Sunday they could not be held, and every Sunday in the year was by a statute of Charlemagne a *dies non* for them. By another statute of the same prince, the judges presiding at *placita* were to do so *fasting*, that their judgment might be clear and calm.

The vexations connected with an institution which made the vassal come to some distance at an expense of time and money, sometimes only to hear what burdens the feudal lord thought fit to impose upon him, can easily be imagined. The vassal of those days was as much harassed with *placita*, as the youth of modern times is with competitive examinations; a summons seemed to lie in wait for him at every turn in life, entailing always a tax upon his time, and almost always one upon his pocket. The *Roman de Rou*, quoted in Ducange *sub voce*, puts this piteous plaint into the mouth of the vassal on the subject; (we present it to the reader all the more willingly, because it makes mention of those characters whom Herbert thought so objectionable, and whom indeed he seems to have regarded almost as demons incarnate (see Letter XXX. p. 25), provosts and bedells);

    "Toute jour sont lor bestes prises,
    Pour ayes[1] et pour servises,
    Tant y a plaintes et querelles,
    Et coustumes viex et nouvelles,
    Ne peuvent une hore avoir pez.
    Toute jour sont, dient[2], as plez[3],
    Plaiz de forez, plaiz de monnoies,
    Plaiz de porprise[4], plaiz de voies,
    Plaiz de gaaing[5], plaiz de graveries[6],
    Plaiz de mellées[7], plaiz d'ayes,
    Plaiz de blet[8], plaiz de moutes[9],
    Plaiz de defautes[10], plaiz de toutes,

---

[1] succours. [2] dient = on dit. [3] as plez = aux plaiz, at the courts. [4] suits about enclosures. [5] about revenues. [6] about enforced service. [7] about quarrels and fraças. [8] about corn. [9] about fees for the use of the seigneur's mill. [10] about failure in attendance at courts, &c.

causes canonically, and establish a friendly feeling and a sincere concord between you. My son, if you will be persuaded by me, you will so exercise your office of provost at Thetford that you shall not cease to be one of God's priests."

A.D. 1105. The political events of the year 1105 were of considerable importance, and some notice of them is necessary, in order to explain the insertion here of two of Herbert's letters. Robert Courthose, the Conqueror's eldest son, whose throne Henry had usurped, and from whom he had extorted the surrender of his annuity of three thousand marks (covenanted to him at the pacification of 1101), by keeping him in captivity and requiring a ransom, at length finally turned to bay, allying himself with Robert Belesme, Earl of Shrewsbury, the most powerful of Henry's

<small>Robert Courthose, the king's elder brother, allies himself with the Earl of Shrewsbury,</small>

> Tant y a provos et bedeaux,
> Et tant baillis viex et nouveaux,
> Ne paons avoir paix une hore," &c. &c.

It is easy to see that, vexatious as certain incidents of the *placita* were, they acted as the cementing bond of the feudal system, and preserved it from disintegration. Such is the fundamental meaning of the word we are undertaking to expound. Its derivative meanings are numerous. Thus it came to signify (1) the royal letters which announced the resolutions arrived at in a *placitum*; (2) the payment made for exemption from attendance at *placita;* (3) the fine which accrued to the lord on the death of a vassal and the tenure's changing hands; (4) any exaction or necessary payment; (5) a statute or decree; (6) the sentence of a judge; and (7) *a suit for the determination of rights thought to be questionable*, attendance at which was enforced by official summonses from bedells and apparitors. This is doubtless the sense which the word bears in Herbert's letter to Athselinus. It had a host of meanings in connexion with litigation and judicature; and those who know how harassing such processes are now, even under the present equitable administration of the laws, will not wonder that the word should have grated upon the ear of any one who was any how implicated in feudal dependence, and that in such a person's mind *placitum* and *inquietatio* (suits and molestations) should have been nearly equivalent terms. The word *placitum* is still preserved in our word *plea*. The court of *communia placita* is the Court of Common Pleas.

barons, who, in addition to vast possessions in this country, held thirty-four castles in Normandy. Henry invaded Normandy, and was eventually successful. In a pitched battle, fought under the walls of Tinchebray, a fortress to which Henry was laying siege, and which Robert sought to relieve, the former was completely victorious; and the unfortunate Robert, Edgar Atheling, and four hundred knights were taken prisoners of war. This sealed the fate of Robert, who was doomed by his brother to perpetual confinement, and whose sight is said to have been destroyed by the application to his eyes of a red-hot copper basin. He lingered in captivity for twenty-eight years, and then died at Cardiff Castle. It may have been when Henry was absent on this Norman expedition that the following letters were written; the first commissioning a youth, who was leaving the country, to plead the bishop's cause with the king; the second, addressed to the king himself, and containing an expression of gratitude for some favour conferred by him upon the bishop,—some post, perhaps, like that of the sewership, which he had held under William Rufus. Mr. Spurdens supposes that the Chancellorship [c] was bestowed upon Herbert; and if so, the letter may have reference to this.

A.D. 1106. but is defeated under the walls of Tinchebray, taken prisoner with Edgar Atheling, blinded, and thrown into captivity.

[c] Lord Campbell reckons him up as one of several Chancellors of Henry I., "respecting whom little is known." ("Lives of the Chancellors," vol. i. p. 54.)

LETTER L.

TO GISLEBERT.

"Herbert to Gislebert.

<small>To a youth who had sent him fruit Herbert gives a playful hint that he might have sent him more;

See Gal. iv. 3.
See Rev. xix. 4.
See St. John xxi. 11.
See Rev. vii. 4, 14; and xiv. 1.</small>

"We are of one heart and one soul. You have sent me five pears and five quinces [d], a great gift doubtless if only they come under some sacred number. But, as you know, a single five signifies the bodily senses, and a double five represents the decalogue of the Jews, who themselves, too, were in bondage to the rudiments of the world. Whence you may easily see, if it so pleases you, that there is no manner of perfection in your quinary numbers; you ought at least to have sent me thirteen, that being the number of the Saviour and His Apostles; or four and twenty, as those elders in the Revelation are so many; or an hundred and fifty-three, in reference to the draught of fishes in the Gospel; or, best of all, 144,000, in reference to the innumerable company of the martyrs [e]. With such a quantity of fruit

---

[d] "five quinces"—*quinque cotana*. The classical form of this word is *cottana*, a small dry fig imported into Rome with the plum from Syria ("advectus Romam quo pruna et cottana vento," Juv. Sat. iii. 85). Martial gives us the further information that the *cottana* had a twisted cone, and that certain fine ones, of which he speaks, wanted only size to be figs:—

"... hæc tibi, quæ tortâ venerunt cottana metâ,
Si majora forent cottana, ficus erant."

The *cottana* of mediæval Latin, and therefore Gislebert's, were nothing more nor less than *quinces*, a word which is derived from the Cretan city Cydonia, in the district of which the quince was indigenous, and was thence exported to other countries. The Latin for a quince is *Cydonium malum*. The intermediary form between the Latin *Cydonium* and the English *quince* is the French *coing*.

[e] The hundred and forty-four thousand, who appear in the sealing vision of Rev. vii., and there represent the elect of the temporal Israel, and the other similar number in chap. xiv., who perhaps represent a special election out of the *Christian* Church, are not called in so many words *martyrs*; but it is said of the former body that they came out of the "great tribulation," which, no doubt, in many cases would involve martyrdom. In the sixth chapter moreover, "the souls of *those that were slain for the word of God and for the testimony which they held,*" are seen to be clothed with

as this, your offering would indeed have gone up as a sacrifice of sweet savour, and the horn of your friend, who sends you this letter of thanks, would have teemed with abundance. Howsoever, your tribute is estimated by me in reference not to the quantity of the thing given, but to the affection of the giver, who in this instance gave as much as he could muster; for in the giving and receiving of gifts it is not the quantity of the gift, but the quality of the spirit in which it is offered, which is the real fruit to be gathered.—You shall go on your way then, and cross the seas in safety, absolved by the authority which my office gives me from all the sins of which you have made confession, and from which you shall purpose to abstain in future. You shall be mindful of us, and shall plead our cause with the King of the English, and I will be mindful of thee, and plead thy cause with the King of the Heavens, prevailing with Him by the daily sacrifice of the Host[1], that He, the almighty and merciful One, may restore thee to thy country and to mine eyes, O youth, who art dearer to me than any earthly source of delight."

[margin: and then dismisses him on his voyage across the channel with his absolution, and instructions to plead Herbert's cause with the King.]

white robes, and with precisely the same emblem the hundred and forty-four thousand are invested, see chap. vii. 9, 14; so that Herbert, quoting from memory, might easily mix up the two in his mind.

[1] "prevailing with Him by the daily sacrifice of the Host"—*quotidianis exorans holocaustis.* The hosts, or consecrated wafers, were called *holocausta*. We find in Ducange, *sub voc.*, a curious mediæval rubrical direction to this effect, "Let so many holocausts be offered upon the altar as shall suffice the people. But should any of them remain till the following day, let them not be reserved save for the viaticum of the dying, or on account of the virtue which they have in preserving the church, lest any adverse influence should prevail to injure it." We apprehend, however, that the term *holocausta*, as applied to the consecrated wafer, is of rare occurrence. One would look for it in highly-wrought and figurative language rather than in rubrics.

LETTER XI.

To Henry the King.

"To his Lord and King Henry, Herbert, his priest of Norwich, sendeth greeting.

Herbert warmly thanks the King for conferring upon him some great favour at a time when Henry's thoughts were engrossed by war and affairs of state, and promises to requite it with his prayers.

I render thanks to your munificence, most excellent king, and father of your country. I render thanks, I say, and thanks as many as were the joys of my heart, when it was comforted by the receiving of your gift. Royal indeed the gift was, and worthy of so great a giver, and [in itself] altogether contenting to my desire; but it acquired an ampler grace, and was welcomed with a livelier pleasure, from the fact that your Highness had been mindful of my lowly self in another quarter of the world, amidst military turmoils and equipments of war, and amidst the cares and anxieties which beset the affairs of princes. What, then, shall I render again to you for this favour? I am yours, and all that I have is yours; and of the things which are yours I am bound continually to do you service, even though your royal favour had not shined on me with a new and additional gift. And hence I have nothing to requite these great benefits withal, which is not thine; since all that I have has been collected by your favour, and is preserved to me by your protection. What therefore is wanting in my circumstances, let my vows supply, and let my continual prayer for thee stand [g] in stead of the offering, which the state of my resources puts out of the question. Therefore before the Sacrament of the Lord's Body and Blood, which is daily offered, I implore the mercy of our Redeemer and Saviour with tears and unceasing supplications, that He who hath sent forth into your heart this [welcome] remembrance of me, would bestow upon you, in return

---

[g] "let my continual prayer stand in stead of the offering," &c.—*repræsentet quod facultatum impossibilitas negat.* So Pliny (lib. 28, c. 10); "Butyrum per se prodest contra venena; nam si oleum non sit, vicem ejus *repræsentat.*" (Butter is good as an antidote to poisons; for, if it is not oil, it at least supplies its place).

for the favour you have conferred, a worthy recompense.
And may the King of kings who, in the secret counsel
of human redemption, suffered Himself with unspeakable patience to be crowned with thorns by men and
for men,—may that same King, after many long and
happy years, crown your soul, when it is absolved from
the frailties of an earthly conversation, with the diadem
of incorruption, in the glory of the saints triumphant, in the court of the heavenly elders ʰ, in the lofty throne, in the everlasting delight, in the full sight of His Presence, in the general shining forth of the saints, among His Constantines, and Theodosiuses ⁱ, and Gratians ʲ, and all other emperors and nobles who have been

See Rev. iv. 4.

ʰ "the court of the heavenly elders"—*in cælestium curiâ senatorum*. We suppose Herbert must refer to the vision of the four and twenty elders in the Revelation; who however are not called *senatores* in the Vulgate, but *seniores*. The former word occurs only in Daniel vi. 7 (of "the counsellors" who consulted together with "the presidents of the kingdom, the governors, the princes, and the captains," to establish the new statute on the subject of prayer), and in Prov. xxxi. 23, "Her husband is known in the gates, when he sitteth among the *elders* of the land."

ⁱ Theodosius the Great, Emperor of the East, A.D. 378—395, proclaimed Emperor of the East by Gratian, who felt himself unable to sustain the burden of empire. He was a man of military genius, as he showed in his victories over the Goths, but of savage and uncontrollable temper, as was shown by his infamous conduct on the occasion of a riot which broke out at Thessalonica, and in which the imperial officer was murdered. Theodosius, after inviting the people of Thessalonica to the circus to see the games, sent in upon them an army of barbarians with orders to massacre the whole of them. On his repairing to the basilica at Milan to perform his devotions, Ambrose met him on the steps and required that he should do penance for his sin. He complied, and was for eight months suspended from communion. He seems to have been a firm Catholic and a fierce opponent of Arians and all heretics. "In his reign the formal destruction of Paganism took place, and we still possess a large number of the laws of Theodosius prohibiting the exercise of the Pagan religion under severe penalties." The account of his penance and humiliation will be found at length in Ambrose's *de Obitu Theodosii Oratio*. This is one of Ambrose's eulogies upon him in a letter which he addresses to him, "Verily the Lord is propitious to the Roman empire, inasmuch as He has appointed over it such a prince and father of princes, whose valour and power, although raised to such a height of earthly greatness, yet rests upon such lowliness of mind, that while he excels emperors in valour, he equally excels priests in humility."

ʲ Gratian, A.D. 359—383, a Roman emperor, highly appreciated by

sound in the faith; and in the last day may He renew your flesh and clothe it with the glory of the resurrection, and the robe of immortality."

Ambrose, and sure therefore to be in the good graces of the Benedictines, with whom Ambrose was a prime authority. He was educated by the poet Ausonius, who seems to have given him a taste for poetry, and so flattered his efforts in that line as to call him a Roman Homer. He appears to have been amiable and well disposed, as well as a man of cultivated understanding, but greatly wanting in that strength of character which his position demanded. He nourished a great reverence for ecclesiastics, refused to put on the insignia of Pontifex Maximus on the plea that a Christian could not wear them, prohibited heathen worship at Rome, and showed a tendency to tolerate no worship but that of the Church, though this was a principle that he found impossible to carry out consistently. The greatest of pleasures according to him was the somewhat frivolous one of hitting the bull's-eye at an archery match. A competitor for the empire of stronger character soon appeared in the person of Maximus, who defeated Gratian near Paris, and sent an envoy in pursuit of him to Lyons, who assassinated him. The treatise of Ambrose, *De Fide*, is dedicated to him; and we think that our Herbert, who has been greatly censured as fulsome in his panegyrics of royalty, may shelter himself under the example given him by the great saint of the Benedictines. For thus the treatise opens: "The queen of the south came to hear the wisdom of Solomon, as we read in the book of Kings. Hiram the king, too, sent to Solomon to make his acquaintance. Thou, also, holy Emperor Gratian, after the model set thee by these ancient stories, hast expressed a wish to hear my profession of faith. But I am not Solomon, so that thou mightest admire my wisdom, nor art thou the king of one nation, but the emperor of all the world, who hast thought it good that the faith should be expressed in a treatise, not that thou mightest learn, but that thou mightest approve it. For why shouldest thou learn, august Emperor, that which from thy very cradle thou hast ever cherished with pious affection? 'Before I formed thee in the belly I knew thee,' saith the prophet, 'and before thou camest forth from the womb I sanctified thee.' Sanctification, therefore, is not handed down but infused; and therefore, keep the divine gifts entrusted to thee; for what no one hath taught thee, God, as its author, hath poured into thy mind."

Ambrose's treatise on the Holy Ghost is also addressed to Gratian, and contains passages in a similar strain, attributing Gratian's conduct about the Basilica, which he had first sequestered and then restored, to the special operation of grace, &c. &c. (*De Spiritu Sancto*, lib. i. cap. 1.) Ambrose, in a letter addressed to him (tom. ii. col. 809, 11), speaks of him as having purged the Churches of Christ from all sacrilegious stain; and in the *Consolatio de obitu Valentiniani* (tom. ii. col. 1193, 74), as faithful in the Lord, devout, meek, of a pure heart, and eminently chaste. Gratian in his turn addresses Ambrose as "parent," and, when near his end, and surrounded by dangers (so Ambrose said), called pite-

And now we must say a word of the building A.D. 1106. of the Norwich Monastery, the beginning of which work Harpsfeld assigns to the year 1106. A glance at Mr. Harrod's interesting work ("Gleanings amongst the Castles and Convents of Norfolk," Norwich, 1857) will show its general plan, a plan which it has in common with several other conventual establishments in the county,— possibly with all Benedictine foundations. On the southern and sunny side of the church, nestling as it were under its wing, was the cloister, from the centre of the eastern side of which jutted out, parallel with the choir, the chapter-house. Immediately adjoining the chapter-house on the south, and flanking together with it the eastern wall of the cloister, was the dormitory. The refectory flanked the southern side of the cloister, and the stranger's hall the western. As to the cloister, "the fair and spacious cloister" which Herbert built is not that which now remains[k]. Fair and spacious, indeed, the present cloister is, —possibly, with the exception of Gloucester, the fairest and most spacious in England,—but it belongs to the Decorated period of architecture,

---

ously upon the bishop (who was far away) for sympathy and counsel. (*De ob. Valent.* 79.)

[k] Mr. Harrod says; "Whether the Norman cloister was of stone or wood, is now unknown. The present cloister is in no part earlier than the close of the thirteenth century. There is not a vestige of the Norman one remaining; one thing alone is certain,—it was nothing more than a covered walk round the enclosure, as the remains of a range of interlaced arches extending the whole west side, and the arcade on the north side of the refectory, and the remains of the Norman triforium on the south wall of the nave and on the west wall of the south transept, clearly show." —("Castles and Convents," p. 304.)

and is due to the piety and munificence of succeeding prelates. The original Norman cloister was destroyed by the great fire in 1272. Indeed, whether any vestige of Herbert's monastic buildings remains may be doubted. The beautiful columns in the Close, and the room used as the kitchen of the present deanery, which has two fine Early English windows, are both of an architectural date subsequent to his time. The monastery was built to accommodate upwards of sixty monks. It was of that celebrated Benedictine Order which, in the ninth century, absorbed and extinguished every other in Western Christendom. This order was founded by Benedict of Nursia at Monte Cassino, in the year 529. One distinguishing feature of it was, that it allowed no alteration or relaxation of the original rule. The order was first planted in England by Augustine, first Archbishop of Canterbury (A.D. 600), and rapidly overran the island, as it did all the rest of Europe. We present the reader with the following short account of the Benedictine rule.

<small>Short summary of the Benedictine rule.</small> "According to the rules of Benedict, the monks were to rise at 2 A.M. in winter, (and in summer at such hours as the abbot might direct,) repair to the place of worship for vigils, and then spend the remainder of the night in committing Psalms to memory, private meditation, and reading. At sunrise, they assembled for matins; then spent four hours in labour; then two hours in reading; then dined, and read in private till half past 2 P.M., when they met again for worship; and afterwards laboured till their vespers. In their vigils and matins, so many Psalms were appointed to be chanted each day, as might complete the Psalter every week.

Besides their social worship, seven hours each day were devoted to labour, two at least to private study, one to private meditation, and the rest to meals, sleep, and refreshment. The labour was agriculture, gardening, and various mechanical trades; and each one was put to such labour as his superior thought fit; for they all renounced wholly every species of personal liberty. They ate twice a-day at a common table; first, about noon, and then, at evening. Both the quantity and the quality of their food were limited. To each was allowed one pound of bread per day, and a small quantity of wine. On the public table no meat was allowed, but always two kinds of porridge. To the sick, flesh was allowed. While at table all conversation was prohibited; and some one read aloud the whole time. They all served as cooks and waiters, by turns of a week each. Their clothing was coarse and simple, and regulated at the discretion of the abbot. Each was provided with two suits, a knife, a needle, and all other necessaries. They slept in common dormitories of ten or twenty, in separate beds, without undressing, and had a light burning, and an inspector sleeping, in each dormitory. They were allowed no conversation after they retired; nor at any time were they permitted to jest, or to talk for mere amusement. No one could receive a present of any kind, not even from a parent; nor have any correspondence with persons without the monastery, except by its passing under the inspection of the abbot. A porter always sat at the gate, which was kept locked day and night; and no stranger was admitted without leave from the abbot, and no monk could go out unless he had permission from the same source.

"The school for the children of the neighbourhood was kept without the walls. The whole establishment was under an abbot, whose power was despotic. His under officers were a prior or deputy, a steward, a superintendent of the sick and the hospital, an attendant on visitors, a porter, &c., with the necessary assistants, and a number of deans, or inspectors over tens, who attended the monks at all times. The abbot was elected by the common suffrage of the brotherhood; and when inaugurated, he appointed and removed his under officers at pleasure. On great emergencies he summoned the whole brotherhood to meet in council; and on more common occasions, only the seniors; but in either case, after hearing what each brother was pleased to say, the decision rested wholly with himself. For admission to the society, a probation of twelve months was required; during which the applicant was fed and clothed, and employed in the meaner offices of the monks, and closely watched. At the end of his probation, if approved, he took solemn and irrevocable vows of perfect chastity, absolute poverty, and implicit obedience to his superiors in everything. If he had property, he must give it all away, either to his friends, or the poor, or the monastery; and never after must possess the least particle of private property, nor claim any personal rights or liberties. For lighter offences, reprimand was to be administered by some under-officer. For greater offences, after two admonitions, a person was debarred his privileges, not allowed to read in his turn, or to sit at table, or enjoy his modicum of comforts. If still refractory, he was expelled the monastery; yet might be restored on repentance."

An insight will be given into the moral and spiritual character of the rule by a citation from its fourth chapter, as given by Maitland in his "Dark Ages" (pp. 169, 170). It contains a series of resolutions to be made by the brethren,—certain memoranda for daily conduct, which must be borne in mind in order to holy living;

Extract from the fourth chapter of the Benedictine rule, showing

"1. In the first place, to love the Lord God with the whole heart, whole soul, whole strength; 2. Then his neighbour as himself; 3. Then not to kill; 4. Then not to commit adultery; 5. Not to steal; 6. Not to covet; 7. Not to bear false witness; 8. To honour all men;

9. And what any one would not have done to him, let him not do to another; 10. To deny himself, that he may follow Christ; 11. To chasten the body; 12. To renounce luxuries; 13. To love fasting; 14. To relieve the poor; 15. To clothe the naked; 16. To visit the sick; 17. To bury the dead; 18. To help in tribulation; 19. To console the afflicted; 20. To disengage himself from worldly affairs; 21. To set the love of Christ before all other things; 22. Not to give way to anger; 23. Not to bear any grudge; 24. Not to harbour deceit in the heart; 25. Not to make false peace; 26. Not to forsake charity; 27. Not to swear, lest haply he perjure himself; 28. To utter truth from his heart and his mouth; 29. Not to return evil for evil; 30. Not to do injuries, and to bear them patiently; 31. To love his enemies; 32. Not to curse again those who curse him, but rather to bless them; 33. To endure persecutions for righteousness' sake; 34. Not to be proud; 35. Not given to wine; 36. Not gluttonous; 37. Not addicted to sleep; 38. Not sluggish; 39. Not given to murmur; 40. Not a slanderer; 41. To commit his hope to God; 42. When he sees anything good in himself, to attribute it to God, and not to himself; 43. But let him always know that which is evil in his own doing, and impute it to himself; 44. To fear the day of judgment; 45. To dread hell; 46. To desire eternal life, with all spiritual longing; 47. To have the expectation of death every day before his eyes; 48. To watch over his actions at all times; 49. To know certainly that, in all places the eye of God is upon him; 50. Those evil thoughts which come into his heart immediately to dash to pieces on Christ; 51. And to make them known to his spiritual senior; 52. To keep his lips from evil and wicked discourse; 53. Not to be fond of much talking; 54. Not to speak vain words, or such as provoke laughter; 55. Not to love much or violent laughter; 56. To give willing attention to the sacred readings; 57. To pray frequently; 58. Every day to confess his past sins to God, in prayer, with tears and groaning; and from

its moral and spiritual character.

thenceforward to reform as to those sins; 59. Not to fulfil the desires of the flesh; to hate self-will; 60. In all things to obey the commands of the abbot, even though he himself (which God forbid) should do otherwise; remembering our Lord's command, 'What they say, do; but what they do, do ye not;' 61. Not to desire to be called a saint before he is one, but first to be one, that he may be truly called one; 62. Every day to fulfil the commands of God in action; 63. To love chastity; 64. To hate nobody; 65. To have no jealousy, to indulge no envy; 66. Not to love contention; 67. To avoid self-conceit; 68. To reverence seniors; 69. To love juniors; 70. To pray for enemies, in the love of Christ; 71. After a disagreement, to be reconciled before the going down of the sun; 72. And never to despair of the mercy of God."

We here introduce a letter in which a reference is made to a part of the Benedictine rule. The rule instilled humility as the fundamental grace of the Christian character, and laid down certain grades of proficiency in that grace, which are thus given us by St. Bernard;

The twelve grades of humility as given by St. Bernard out of the Benedictine rule. " But we must not omit to notice after what manner the grades of humility are arranged in the Rule of St. Benedict. He says, then, that to the first grade of humility pertaineth fear; to the second, the not loving our own will; to the third, obedience; to the fourth, patient perseverance in obedience; to the fifth, the disclosure of our thoughts to our [ghostly] father; to the sixth, the putting up with every kind of slight and strait, and the judging ourselves, in all that is enjoined upon us, unworthy to be so employed; to the seventh, the not only declaring with the tongue, but also believing in the heart, that one is lower and more worthless than all besides; to the eighth, the doing nothing except in pursuance of the common rule of the monastery and the example of superiors; to the ninth, the placing on the tongue the restraint of silence till a question is put to us; to the tenth, the not being ready to laugh; to the eleventh, when any one speaks, that he should do so mildly, modestly, and seriously, and that his words be few and reasonable; to the twelfth, that a man should not only be humble in heart, but by suitable tokens, by the meanness of his garb, and the openness of his countenance, should shew his humility, as an example to those who look on the outward appearance[1]."

Here is another exposition (also from the pen of St. Bernard) of the twelve grades of humility. Speaking of the Blessed Virgin, he says;

"This is the ladder of Jacob, who, when he lay down his head on the stone, was privileged to see the angels ascending and descending. This ladder hath twelve stairs between the two sides. The right side is, contempt of self stretching upwards into the love of God; the left, contempt of the world stretching upwards into the love of the kingdom. Its steps of ascent are the twelve grades of humility. The first grade is hatred of sin; the second, avoiding omissions of duty; the third is the fear of giving offence; the fourth, the being in all these things under the control of the Creator; the fifth, the obeying our betters; the sixth, compliance with the humours of our equals; the seventh, accommodating ourselves to the will of inferiors; the eighth, to be under one's own control; the ninth, perpetual meditation on our end; the tenth, always to be apprehensive about our own works; the eleventh, humbly to confess our thoughts; the twelfth, to be guided in all things by the hand, nod, will of the Lord. By these steps the angels ascend and exalt men [to heaven]; thus are the steps of ascent arranged in their hearts, as they gently make progress

The grades of humility compared by Bernard to the steps of Jacob's ladder.

[1] S. Bernard, Tractatus de statu virtutum, sec. 14, Opp., tom. ii. p. 554, col. 1, B.

and rise step by step; and thus do they come at length to the bright mansions in the Father's house [m]."

There is a reference to these twelve grades of humility in the following letter to Felix;

LETTER XXIII.

To Felix.

Herbert excuses himself for slackness in his correspondence with Felix, because only the self-indulgent monks need his letters; but Felix is a model of humility and every other grace, and is felicitated on the prospect of the glorious end of his conversation.

" Herbert to Felix.

" I have listened, Felix, to your complaint with a sympathy equal to the simplicity with which you advance it. You complain that I never write to you; but my writings are directed against those only who neglect their rule. My writings are directed against gluttons and drunkards, against the votaries of lust, the covetous, the wrathful, the melancholy, the apathetic [n], the vainglorious, and the proud; against those are my writings directed, who walk contrary to the truth, and with stiff neck shamelessly resist the commands of God. But to thee wherefore should I write, who art versed both in the old and new learning, and continually and laboriously performest the things which the doctors both of the old [o] and new learning prescribe to be done? Shall I discourse with thee of faith? But thou believest in the Father, and the Son,

---

[m] S. Bernard de B. M. V., Sermo (sec. 4), tom. ii. p. 705, col. 2, B, C.

[n] "the apathetic"—*acidiosis*. See a full note on the subject of *accidia*, p. 37.

[o] "the old and new learning"—*veterum et novarum doctrinarum doctores*. As the only attainments of Felix which Herbert specifies are in sacred lore, we presume that by the old and new learning he means the Old and New Testament, although it is possible that by the doctors of the old learning he may mean teachers of moral truth among the heathen, such as Plato, Aristotle, and Seneca. In Maitland's "Dark Ages," p. 447, will be found a letter from Peter, Abbot of Clugni, to one of his monks, in which, though recognising the vanity of profane learning, he yet commends his correspondent for his acquaintance with it. "If I wanted to investigate any of the deep things of holy Scripture, I always found you most ready and prepared. If I wanted to look out anything in profane literature (for the sake of that which is sacred), I found you prompt and shrewd."

and the Holy Ghost, one and yet a threefold God, one in the sameness of their substance, three in the distinctness of their Persons. Shall I exhort you to a holy conversation? Nay, but there resteth upon thee the spirit of love, joy, peace, longsuffering [p], goodness, kindness, gentleness, modesty, continence, chastity. Shall I persuade you to a holy life? But you are assiduous in your attendance upon all the ecclesiastical offices, that is to say, matins, prime, tierce, sext, nones, vespers, and compline [q]. You exercise yourself diligently in the Scriptures, and as for the study you bestow on works of piety, it never ceases or is intermitted. You sit in the cloister, and while you bridle your tongue [r], you restrain even your fingers from useless signs. What, therefore, shall I write to you? You have ascended those twelve steps of true humility, and are now singing the Song of degrees [s] in anticipation of coming in thy

Gal. v. 22, 23.

See Ps. xxxix. 1.

---

[p] Herbert in quoting this text, Gal. v. 22 and 23, has omitted the graces of *longanimitas* and *fides*, and transposed *benignitas* and *bonitas*.

[q] *Complines, completoriis. Compline*, the latest service of the mediæval Church, so called from its filling up and completing the round of offices, is said to have been instituted by St. Benedict in the sixth century. The sixteenth chapter of Benedict's Rule rests the seven offices on the practice of the Psalmist, "Seven times a day I have given praise to Thee." The forty-second chapter of the Rule strictly enjoins silence after Compline.

[r] "while you bridle your tongue." The practice of Felix was founded on the sixth chapter of the Rule of Benedict, which begins thus; "Let us act in conformity with that saying of the prophet: *I said I will take heed to my ways, that I sin not with my tongue: I have set a guard to my mouth ; I was dumb and was humbled, and kept silence from good things.* If then, according to the Prophet, we ought, for the sake of silence, sometimes to refrain from speaking good words, with how much more caution should we not avoid speaking evil words, lest we incur both the guilt and penalty of sin? The maintenance of silence being, then, a matter of so great moment, let even the perfect brethren be rarely permitted to speak, though it should be for the purpose of mutual edification: for it is written ; *In the multitude of words there shall not want sin;* and again, *Death and life are in the power of the tongue.*"

Ps. xxxix. 1, 2.

[s] "The Song of degrees." Herbert applies the term "Song of degrees," which appears in the title of the fifteen Psalms immediately succeeding the cxix[th], to the grades of humility (unfortunately only twelve), which are given in the seventh chapter of the Benedictine Rule. It is no doubt an interesting application of these Psalms to see in them the various stages of

virginity to that place where the Lamb (the great Lamb which taketh away the sins of the world) singeth amidst His undefiled ones a song which none [1] save an undefiled

Ps. cxx. 5. the spiritual life, from the first discontent of the soul with the world ("woe is me, that I sojourn in Mesech, that I dwell in the tents of Kedar") up to the arrival of the disciple in the heavenly sanctuary, where he is met and greeted by those who stand in the house of the Lord, and exhorted to lift up his hands in the sanctuary and bless the Lord. (Ps. cxxxiv. 1, 2.) And it is a noble thought that the humbler a man becomes, so much higher he mounts in the spiritual life,—that in the kingdom of God humility is exaltation. This and other beautiful thoughts are to be found in Augustine's *Enarratio in Psalmum* cxix. (Opp., tom. iv. p. 1364 B.), in which he takes occasion, from the words of the first Song of degrees ("Deliver my soul, O Lord, from lying lips"), to observe that the first resolution of the Christian to rise in the spiritual life calls forth the calumnies of the world, which he must scorn at the outset and press onward. St. James and St. John, he says, wished to climb to the highest places in Christ's kingdom without previous humiliation, but Christ taught them that they must drink of the brook of suffering in the way, before they could thus lift up their heads.

What the title, *Songs of degrees* (ᾠδαὶ τῶν ἀναβαθμῶν, *Cantica graduum*), really means, expositors are not agreed. Some think the fifteen Psalms are so called from an ascending scale in their metrical structure ; others, from their having been sung on the fifteen steps of the Temple leading from the court of the men to the court of the women ; others suppose that these Psalms were composed for, and sung during, the going up from the Babylonish captivity; while others (among whom is the Rev. J. J. S. Perowne) think that these Psalms are pilgrim hymns sung at the various stages of the pilgrimage to Jerusalem at the time of the three great festivals. "They are all pervaded by the same quiet, graceful, tender beauty, the charm of which was so felt by a Spanish commentator, that he does not hesitate to say that this collection is to the rest of the Psalms what Paradise was to the rest of the world at its first creation." (Perowne, Psalms, vol. ii. p. 310, Introd. to Ps. cxx.)

[1] "a song which none save an undefiled one singeth." The twenty-sixth chapter of St. Bernard's *Vitis mystica seu Tractatus de Passione Domini* is devoted to the consideration of this song, which is to be sung by the virgins. The old songs were such as Lucifer sung when he fell, songs of pride, of detraction, of doubt, of lying, of excuse for sin. But the new song is the song of love, which St. Mary copied in her *Magnificat*. It is a song which breathes humility, for love is not puffed up. The lowly spirit of Mary exulted in her Saviour; therefore God highly exalted her. The haughty spirit of Lucifer exulted in himself; therefore he was cast down from heaven and doomed to eternal misery. Bede makes the new

Isa. liv. 1, song to be, *Rejoice thou barren that bearest not;* and, *I will give to the* and Gal. *eunuchs a place and a name in my house, and within my walls, better than* iv. 27. *of sons and of daughters ;*—thus making it a *Canticum virginum* in the Is. lvi. 4, 5. literal sense of the words.

one singeth, and those who follow the Lamb whither-soever He goeth. When thou hast arrived there, thou shalt no more remember the earthly delights which thou didst forsake for heavenly treasures; thou shalt no more remember thy father or thy mother, nor those other tender ties of thine, which thou hast renounced for Christ's sake; no more shalt thou remember the invisible foes over whom thou hast gloriously triumphed. But there thou shalt have an everlasting possession, to wit, instead of earth, heaven; instead of a father of thy flesh, God; instead of temporal pleasure, the eternal blessedness, whereof the Holy Ghost in the Psalms singeth; 'Oh how great is the multitude of thy sweetness, O Lord, which thou hast hidden for them that fear thee! Which thou hast wrought for them that hope in thee, in the sight of the sons of men.' Do therefore, my well-beloved son, what thou doest; work still what thou workest; let not thy hands, let not thy feet have respite. Persevere in the strife for mastery on which thou hast entered, since no man shall be crowned save he who striveth lawfully. The Saviour hath risen from the dead; hath ascended into heaven; is now preparing for us mansions; and will return again, to take our very selves unto His own self amidst those joys which none shall take from us, which neither eye hath seen, nor ear hath heard, nor have entered into the heart of man. These things hath the Saviour prepared for thee and thy companions, who are washed in the blood of the Lamb, and have not defiled your garments with fleshly conversation. With that blessedness, Felix, thou shalt be blessed, not in name only, but in deed [u]."

Rev. xiv. 3, 4.
See St. Matt. xix. 21, and St. Luke xii. 33.
See St. Matt. x. 37.
See Heb. xii. 9.
Ps. xxx. 20, Vulg.
2 Tim. ii. 5.
St. John xiv. 2, 3.
Is. lxiv. 4.
1 Cor. ii. 9.
See Rev. iii. 4, and xiv. 4.

Here is a second letter to Felix. If this is the same monk, and not another of the same name, we

---

[u] "Eâ felicitate, Felix, eris felix et re et nomine." A play upon the name, which it is impossible to reproduce. If we remember rightly, Dr. Donaldson connects the French adjective "feu" (the late) with the Latin "felix" (passed into the state of the blessed). Bescherelle derives it from *functus vitâ*.

must suppose in him a lamentable falling off from
the promise given in his youth. "His goodness
was as the morning cloud, and as the early dew
it passed away."

Hos. vi. 4.

LETTER XLIII.

"Herbert to Felix.

Herbert reproves Felix for a falling off in the character of his studies, and for becoming copyist general for the house.

"Herbert the father to Felix the son. You had made an excellent beginning; and you used to occupy your youth with studies of a noble sort. You were wont to write out Augustine, to sustain thyself with the bread of so great a doctor, and to gladden thy heart with the wine of the divine Scriptures[x], proposing by the contemplation [of them] to fashion thyself after the image of thy Saviour. But now, dismissing such studies as these, you have come down to grammar[y], desiring to be

---

[x] "the divine Scriptures,"—not necessarily what we mean by the Bible. Such phrases as "sacri libri," "scriptura sacra," "divina scriptura," were used by mediæval writers to designate "religious books" in general. (See Maitland's "Dark Ages," p. 87, note 3.) The words "inebriabaris vino divinarum scripturarum" might be illustrated by many passages of mediæval writers. We give the following parallel from Alcuin, in which he describes a school which he had founded in connexion with the convent of St. Martin at Tours; "I, your Flaccus, in accordance with your admonitions and wishes, endeavour to administer to some in the house of St. Martin, the honey of the Holy Scriptures; others I would fain *intoxicate with the pure wine* of ancient wisdom; others I begin to nourish with the fruits of grammatical subtleties: many I seek to enlighten by the order of the stars." (Alcuin, i. ep. 38, p. 52, as quoted in Dr. Lorenz's "Life of Alcuin," Lond. 1837, p. 54.)

[y] "you have come down to grammar"—*ad grammaticam descendisti.* The word *grammatica* has in mediæval writers a far more extensive signification than our word *grammar.* "The *ars grammatica*," says Mr. Maitland, "might be more properly translated classical, or, what is the same thing, profane literature: the *grammaticus* was, as his name imported, a man of letters—those letters, however, to borrow the words of Augustine, 'non quas *primi magistri*, sed quas docent qui *grammatici* vocantur.'" Augustine's words, however, show that *grammatica* had a narrow as well as an extensive signification, and was used sometimes for the rudiments of classical literature (i.e. Latin grammar) as well as for the

instructed (which is right enough) in grammatical rules ; a praiseworthy pursuit, if you had persevered in your purpose, but instead of that you have allowed yourself to become the scribbler of all the nonsense of our house, and the trifles penned by every simpleton find their way to thee, as into the sink of the immodesties of the whole ship. It is you who compose the martyrologies, the hymn-books, the little breviaries[1], the secret communications of all members of the monastery. Your abilities, the ripening of which we looked forward to with hope, have so much declined, that you do nothing in our house save what had better not be done. Listen to the advice of your father, and take up again your former studies. Either write out your Augustine, or learn your grammar, since he who aims at pleasing everybody pleases nobody. Love Christ, and confirm thyself in His truth, and avoid, as you would serpents, those who endeavour to tear you away from Him."

literature itself. "In the schools which are supposed to have borrowed light from Lanfranc and Anselm, a keen perception of the beauties of the Latin language, as well as a knowledge of its idiom, was imparted. After the first grammatical instruction out of Donatus and Priscian, the pupils were led forward to the poets, orators, and historians of Rome ; the precepts of Cicero and Quintilian were studied, and sometimes observed with affectation." (Hallam's "Literature of Europe," vol. i. p. 70.) Herbert calls Felix's change of study a coming down, because it was a change from sacred to secular literature.

[1] "It is you who write the *martyrologia, psalteria, breviariola*," &c. And why should he not? we are apt to ask. Was not the copying and illuminating of books, specially of devotional books, great part of a monk's duty? Hallam says of the three great orders which sprung from the Benedictine stock (the Clugniacs, the Carthusians, and the Cistercians), that "the monks of these foundations exercised themselves in copying manuscripts ; the arts of calligraphy, and, not long afterwards, of illumination, became their pride ; a more cursive handwriting and a more convenient system of abbreviations were introduced ; and thus from the twelfth century we find a great increase of manuscripts, though transcribed mechanically as a monastic duty, and often with much incorrectness." ("Lit. of Europe," vol. i. p. 69.) Felix, whatever else he may have written, was usefully employed when he copied psalters and breviaries ; but he had given promise of a higher flight, for he had been in his youth a contemplative student of theology ; and this mere mechanical occupation, which perhaps Felix found more lucrative than study on his own account, was a disappointment of the promise he had given,—a great "coming down" indeed. The passage is a very remarkable one.

And here a third, which Mr. Anstruther supposes to be addressed to the same person;

LETTER XLVI.

"Herbert to F.

<small>Herbert, thinking that monks have no business with money, pays F. for his psalter in tablets and ink.</small>

"Herbert to F. You bid me return you your psalter [a], or the sum agreed upon as its equivalent. I, however, do not return the psalter, but the sum agreed upon, three shillings' worth [b], that is, of tablets [c] and ink [d]. I would have paid you in coin, but that monks have no business [e]

[a] "your psalter"—*tuum psalterium.* By a psalter is meant not merely a collection of the Psalms, but such a collection as is arranged for the services of the church. "The Roman Psalter, for instance, does not follow the course of the Psalms as in Scripture; they are arranged for the different services, in the several accompaniments, as antiphons, &c. In our psalter, the notice of the divisions for the days of the months, and the pointing in the middle of each verse, are a part of the *psalter* though not of the Psalms; and some part of the Psalms unfit for recitation is omitted, as the titles, the words *Selah*, *Higgaion*, &c., and the Hallelujahs with which many Psalms begin or end, or both." (Hook's "Church Dictionary," *sub voc. Psalter*.)

[b] For the origin of the word *solidus* see p. 102, footnote s. We translate *solidi*, shillings, with no better authority than that the *s* in £. *s. d.* is, we believe, the initial of the word *solidus*.

[c] "tres videlicet solidos in *ligno* et atramento." The word *lignum* is used even in the classics (by synecdoche) for tablets made of wood. (See Letter LIV. p. 7, in which Herbert speaks of box-wood tablets having been given to his brother by Richard the Archdeacon.) Thus Juvenal, Sat. xvi. vv. 40, 41—

"Debitor aut sumptos pergit non reddere nummos,
Vana supervacui dicens chirographa ligni."

(The debtor does not return the money which he had borrowed, alleging that the note of hand on the useless tablet is to be considered of no account.) We find that the same synecdoche crept into the mediæval Latin; for one of the meanings given by Ducange to *lignum*, is wooden tablets on which a will is engrossed. See Ducange, *sub voce.*

[d] The word here used for ink is the more classical *atramentum*. In another letter subsequently introduced Herbert uses the more mediæval word *encaustum*, from which the French *encre*, the Italian *inchiostro*, and the English *ink*, are derived.

[e] "non est monachorum habere argentum." Chapter xxxiii. of the Benedictine Rule prescribes that "the abbot shall take special care to root the sin of proprietorship out of the monastery. Hence it shall be unlawful for any of the brethren to give, take, or appropriate anything whatever, either a book, a tablet, a pen, or anything at all without the sanction of

with money, and that a father has no business to hold out a scorpion to a son who asks for a fish [f]."

We may here say a word upon the office of Prior in Norman monasteries. Mr. Church gives this account of it:

"Under the abbot, and next to him in office and honour" (under the bishop, where, as at Norwich, there was no abbot), "was the prior, who was the working hand and head in the interior administration of the house. The servants were specially under his control; he was to 'hold the chapter' for the judgment of their behaviour, and for the infliction of necessary punishment. And the police of the house was under his special charge; he was to observe behaviour in choir and in the cloister, and at stated times of day and night—by night with a dark lantern (*absconsa*)—he was to go round the house, the crypt and aisles of the minster, the cloister, the chapter-house, the infirmary, and the dormitory, to see that there was no idling or foolish gossip. At night he was to take care that all was well lighted in the house. In this work of going his rounds, he was assisted by officers specially appointed for the purpose (*circumitores, quos alio nomine circas vocant*), elected from the more discreet of the brethren, men who would act without favour or malice, who from time to time were to pass through the monastery, observing everything, but never speaking till they made their report in the chapter [g]."

the abbot. For by their profession they have renounced all right, even to their own bodies and their own wills. But they will apply to the abbot for whatever they may want, and keep nothing in their possession, except what he has either given them or permitted them. All things shall be common to them, as it is written, neither shall any one call anything his own, or claim it as such."

[f] Herbert, quoting from memory, has mixed up two scriptural clauses together. Our Lord's words as given by St. Luke (xi. 11, 12) being, "If he ask a fish, will he for a fish give him a serpent? Or if he shall ask an egg, will he offer him a scorpion?"

[g] Pp. 63, 64.

The first prior of Herbert's monastery was Ingulfus. We have already presented the reader with letters addressed to him (pp. 135—140), exhorting him and his monks to make strenuous progress with their buildings. We now introduce one, in which the bishop censures him and his colleagues for the slackness of their discipline, and another addressed to the monks in general (but containing a special charge to the prior), which shews how solicitously this good pastor yearned over his flock in some temporary absence from them.

LETTER LII.

"Herbert the Bishop, to Ingulf the Prior, and the other Officers [b] of the Church of Norwich, greeting.

In connexion with thefts which had frequently occurred in their

"In proportion to the value which I set upon your credit and advantage, is the displeasure which I feel in hearing of what is scandalous and disgraceful to you, nor has my mind any peace so long as your order [i] is in

---

[b] *cæteris Norwicensis Ecclesiæ Procuratoribus. Procurator Ecclesiæ* is defined by Ducange to be one who has the goods of the Church under his administration and guardianship. A statute of the Church of Utrecht forbids the priests and procurators of churches to pawn the chalice and sacred vessels. The particular officers of a Benedictine monastery, called "procurators of the church," would probably be the secretary or sacrist, who had charge of the ornaments, the bells, and the sacred vessels; the chamberlain, who was charged with everything relating to the dress of the brethren, and the good order of their rooms; the cellarer, whose business it was to look after the housekeeping; the hostellar, who was to provide everything necessary for the strangers' lodgings; the almoner, whose business it was to seek out and relieve the poor and the sick; and the infirmarer, who looked after the sick in hospital, with his own separate cook and kitchen for their needs. (See Church's "Life of Anselm," pp. 65, 66.)

[i] "your order"—*vestræ religionis habitus*. The monastic habit or dress was so characteristic of monks, that in mediæval Latin *habitus* by itself

disrepute. Look you, I am informed that nothing is safe in your house, but that the holy Church is polluted by acts of theft proceeding from its own members. You lose books, cups [k], covers [l], in short, everything except what is of no service to those who rob you. I did not know that ye had a Judas lying hid among you; but as Judas fell from theft to the lower deep of the betrayal, and after the betrayal became his own universally-execrated murderer, so within a few days shall that enemy of your household stuff be condemned with a well-deserved anathema, and made over to the severe judgment of God; for as corruption is in the body and yet not of the body, so that thief is among you, and yet not of you. But it is too clear, that in the community in general a great deal of neglect and indolence hides its head; witness the gossiping of clerks; witness the intimacies with serving brothers; witness the young ones [m] which certain of our dignitaries [n], both within our

Herbert reproves the Prior and other officers for slackness of discipline.

See Letter XVI., p. 105, note w.

sometimes stands for monks and nuns of the various orders. See Ducange, *sub voc.*

[k] "cups"—*sciphos*. This word denoted (i.) a cup or goblet of the usual kind, from which monks had a custom of drinking in a manner peculiar to themselves, holding it with both hands on either side, and not by the rim. (See the metrical direction given in Ducange, "Si sciphum capias, utraque manu capiatur; Et per utrumque latus, non per ripam teneatur.") (ii.) The bowl of a candlestick. (See Exod. xxv. 31, Vulg.) (iii.) One of the communion vessels, into which the wine used at the mass was refunded from the chalice. (iv.) A vase used for containing relics.

[l] "covers"—*coöpertoria*. By *coöpertoria* is meant either common coverlets of beds, or more probably articles of sacred furniture, such as altarcloths, palls, and corporals, or else perhaps ornamental metal tops or covers for ecclesiastical vessels. Mr. Maitland makes mention of very costly caskets for the book of the Gospels, made of gold inlaid with gems, to which the name of *coöpertoria librorum* was given ("Dark Ages," p. 212, and n. 7); but we hardly think that at that earliest period of its existence the Norwich monastery could have been possessed of these, otherwise they would have been a glorious temptation to conventual pilferers.

[m] "young ones"—*pullos*. He probably means the young children, which some of the monks had left behind them in the world, when they assumed the monastic habit. Others had brought their children into the monastery, to receive education there among the *Infantes*. These last were no doubt provided for by the house; but their fathers might now and then pilfer and sell things, and give them the proceeds.

[n] "certain of our dignitaries"—*quidam domini nostri*. Ducange tells

precinct and without, are rearing by means of their daily depredations. In heaven there was a Satan; in Paradise a serpent; in the ark a Ham; amongst the apostles a Judas; amongst the deacons a Nicholas°. So among you there have crept in unawares certain men, demoniacs rather than monks ᵖ, to spy out your liberty, and to waste and consume [the substance of] your monastery. Ye most negligent and lukewarm shepherds, wherefore have ye thrown open the fold of Christ to fell wolves? Certainly Christ, by His own death, had redeemed His own sheep, and ye now expose them to be torn in pieces by the teeth of wild beasts. God is not mocked, as a man may be; think not to allege to Him in your defence any vain excuses, for He imputes to your indolence and carelessness whatever hath been wrongfully and despitefully done in His house. Mine eyes ye may indeed escape; but the care and anxiety with which ye watch over your charges cannot lie hid from God, the Judge of your consciences. Much more might I say in this indignant strain; but to a soul which is apt to receive correction it sufficeth to be reminded of what has hitherto been neglected. Let this letter, addressed to all of you in common, be recited and exhibited in chapter before all of you."

margin notes: See Gal. ii. 4. — See Gal. vi. 7.

---

us that the canons of a church were sometimes called *domini*, its lords. The nearest rendering of the idea in our own language seems to be "dignitaries." In German, a canon is still called *Domherr*.

° "Nicholas." Referring to the catalogue of the seven deacons in Acts vi. 5, Bishop Wordsworth remarks that "Nicolaus, who holds the last place in the catalogue, is charged with heresy and licentiousness by Irenæus, Tertullian, Hilary, Jerome, and others, and identified by them with the leader of the Nicolaitans." Herbert would naturally take his view of the character of Nicolaus from these early Fathers.

ᵖ "demoniacs rather than monks"—*non monachi sed demoniaci*. Observe the play upon words, which, strange to say, the English expresses nearly as well as the Latin.

LETTER LVII.

"Herbert to the Brethren of the Church of Norwich, greeting.

"It has been my custom hitherto, when departing from you in the body, still to remain with you in spirit and by my words; so that those who have one heart and one soul might not be divided by removal from place to place. But as a bad practice ought to be abolished, so does a good custom require to be kept up. I write to you, then, that ye should all speak the same thing*; and that there be no divisions among you. Be ye perfect in faith, in truth, in charity, in obedience, in humility, in chastity, in simplicity, in patience, in poverty, and in other duties of this kind; whereby, though estranged from temporal, ye are received into eternal palaces. Behold I speak in the sight of God, not as your Master, but as your servant for God's sake; hold fast your rule, rear up your buildings, be constant in church, absent from none of the services, silent in the cloister, or in any other office within your precinct ꝗ. Where all are, there let each be, and where each is, there let all be; let all things be done in common, and let no room be left for solitary action. God is light, and in Him is no darkness at all; he who followeth the truth cometh to the light, and is made a child of light, according to that word of the New Testament ʳ; Ye are all children of the light, not the

Marginalia: Herbert, going to court, expresses his anxiety for the spiritual wellbeing of the convent in his absence, and his apprehension lest some root of bitterness should spring up among them. He exhorts them to walk worthy of their vocation. See 2 Cor. iv. 5. 1 John i. 5. St. John iii. 21. 1 Thess. v. 5.

---

* 1 Cor. i. 10.

ꝗ "or any other office within your precinct"—*aliisve regularibus officinis.* The *regulares officinæ* were the various parts of the establishment in which the rule was observed. They would embrace the refectory, dormitory, infirmary, scriptorium, guest-hall, kitchen, cellar, &c.

Ducange quotes a passage from the letters of Peter of Clugni, in which the phrase *officinæ regulares* occurs; "Wherever the brethren meet one another, the younger requests benediction from the prior, by saying, *Benedicite,* in case he should be outside the places where the rule is kept (*regularia loca*), and by humbly bending himself, but uttering nothing orally, if the meeting takes place within the offices of the precinct (*intra officinas regulares*)."

ʳ "that word of the New Testament"—*juxta illud Evangelii.* We

children of darkness. Would God, my sons, that either your spirit were in mine or mine in yours; then would ye see evidently with what throes I travail for your salvation, anxious with a father's apprehensions, and apprehensive with a father's anxiety, lest among you also Satan should venture upon [some malicious enterprise]. What can be purer than heaven? but yet even among His angels God found perverseness. What can be more blessed than Paradise? but even in Paradise Adam transgressed the command of God. The ark was of small compass; but yet even there Ham preserved the arts of magic and idolatry¹. Among the Jews God was

<small>Job iv. 18.</small>

<small>Gen. iii. 6.</small>

---

have adopted the translation "New Testament," by way of covering the slip of memory which Herbert makes in ascribing to the Gospels a passage of St. Paul's Epistles.

¹ "even there Ham preserved the arts of magic and idolatry"—*sed et ibi Cham magicæ et idololatriæ conservavit artes.* We subjoin passages from Bp. Patrick and from Bochartus, the first of which traces up post-diluvian idolatry to Ham, while the second indicates the singular method adopted by him, before he went into the ark, for the preservation of magic.

"Ham is generally thought to have been an impious man: and some take him to have been the first inventor of idols after the flood; nay, of magic, which he learned of the wicked Cainites before the flood. Thus Gaspar Schottus, lib. i. de Magia, cap. 3. *prolegom.;* where he endeavours to shew that Ham was the same with him whom the Persians call Zoroaster." (Patrick on Gen. ix. 22.)

"They say that Ham is the same as Zoroaster the magician, the first author of which opinion is the Pseudo-Clemens, who in the 4th Book of his Researches (*Recognitiones*) tells us that magic was handed down to men before the flood by those angels who manifested such a propensity for the daughters of men; that Misraim, the founder of the Egyptians, had learned it from his father Ham, and that Ham was on that account called by his posterity, who were admirers of this art, Zoroaster, or living star, and was taken for a god. Cassian, following this account in the 21st chapter of his 8th Sacred Dialogue (*Collationes*), says, 'So far as ancient traditions tell, Ham the son of Noah, who was imbued with those superstitions and profane and sacrilegious arts, knowing that he could not openly introduce a book transmitting them to future ages into the ark, which he was about to enter in company with his righteous father and holy brethren, engraved those wicked and profane inventions on plates of divers metals such as could not be eaten away by the flood of waters, and on the hardest stones which he could find. After the cessation of the deluge, he sought them out with the same eager study with which he had concealed them, and thus transmitted to posterity a very seed-plot of sacrilege and perpetual iniquity!' Whence the opinion gained ground that

crucified[t]; and the creature, whom from the foundation of the world God had nourished and brought up, most persistently persecutes God through the whole world. The world reeks with the blood of martyrs, and the whole Church, in all quarters, groans under the continual persecutions of apostates. No place is inaccessible to Satan. Satan has been loosed for a thousand years, a furnace of trial for us, if so be we be not burnt up in it as straw, but purified as gold. The profession of a monk is a most excellent thing; but the profession of a monk is not the sad-coloured robe, but humility and obedience, chastity, and a following in our Saviour's footsteps. The Truth crieth aloud; 'He who forsaketh all that he hath, he is My disciple.' Whereunto Peter replies; 'Behold, we have left all and followed Thee: what shall we have therefore?' 'As for you,' saith the Truth, 'who have left all and have followed Me, ye shall sit upon twelve thrones, judging the twelve tribes of Israel; and all who have left house, or father, or mother, or servant[u], or brethren, or sisters, or lands for My name's sake,

See Rev. xx. 7.
See 1 Cor. iii. 12, &c.

See St. Luke xiv. 33.
St. Matt. xix. 27.
St. Matt. xix. 28, 29.

Ham was a magician, and with magic incantation so bewitched and bound his father as he lay exposed in his sleep, that thenceforth he felt no propensity for women. He is said to have written magical books, some of which were burnt by Ninus, while the rest remain. For even to this day there exists an impious treatise which contains the rudiments and practice of the art of necromancy, under the title of the writing of Ham, son of Noah."

[t] "among the Jews God was crucified," &c.—*apud Judæos crucifixus est Deus*, &c. Herbert's argument is that the most privileged places and societies are not exempt from the intrusion of evil. Satan among the angels of heaven, Adam in Paradise, Ham in the ark, are exemplifications of this truth; and a still more striking instance of it is to be found in the fact that in the very bosom of the chosen nation, He who is God was put to a cruel and shameful death. The thoughts of the writer seem then to fly off to Isaiah i. 2; "Hear, O heavens, and give ear, O earth: for the Lord hath spoken, I have *nourished and brought up* children, and they have rebelled against Me." Wicked men, the seed of the wicked one, though owing their existence and every blessing to God, have consistently and from the beginning of time, persecuted God in His children. The persecution began with the murder of Abel, reached its climax in the crucifixion of Christ, and will proceed until the final triumph of Christ puts away all evil for ever.

[u] It is observable that Herbert should have inserted the word "servant,"

shall receive an hundredfold, and shall inherit eternal life.' See, my sons, the purpose and the terms on which ye entered into covenant with God. God is the searcher of our hearts; He pierceth to our inmost parts, and reacheth even to the dividing asunder of our carnal and spiritual thoughts. No middle course is left for monks; for either the monk will have nothing and will have God, or if he have something he will lose God. Strait is the way; but it is by these steps that we mount up to God. Prior, I am going to the court; the house of God I commend to thee, and thee I commend to God. Get together materials for the future work, and especially stones, bearing in mind that you will cheer up your (spiritual) father in all his trials, if you do not neglect my injunction. Dignitaries[x], sit ye in your cloister and study to be quiet, occupying yourselves with God alone, and taking good heed that no base, or idle, or slanderous word defile your tongues. Render thanks that ye are not compelled to serve God in any other than the pleasant occupation of studying sacred writings[y]. Youths, submit humbly to the correction of your schoolmaster, and when absent from me, prepare suitable answers to the examination which I shall hold when I am with you again. Finally, to our whole convent may there be grace, peace, and perseverance in the truth, from God our Father and the Lord Jesus Christ, in the Holy Ghost, for ever and ever. Amen."

See Heb. iv. 12.

1 Thess. iv. 11.

Here is the fragment of another letter to

which is not found in the text, and omitted the word "wife," which is found there; more especially as some of his monks would in all probability have actually left their wives to enter upon the religious life. Possibly, when he introduced the word *servant*, he had in his mind the text, "they left their father Zebedee in the ship with the *hired servants* and went after Him." St. Mark i. 20.

[x] On the term "Domini," as applied to the canons of a Church, see above, on the foregoing Letter (LII.), p. 201, note n.

[y] "studying sacred writings"—*in deliciis scripturarum*. In mediæval Latin the word *scriptura* itself, without the epithets *divina*, *sacra*, &c., sometimes means sacred writings,—not exclusively the Holy Scriptures, but theological and religious works in general. See p. 196, note x.

a monk (apparently one in authority), in which (as elsewhere) the bishop defends himself from the charge of being an over-strict Church disciplinarian.

LETTER XLVIII.

"JACOB is said to have had multitudes of herds and flocks of all sorts of cattle, when he returned out of Mesopotamia in Syria, to Isaac his father into the land of promise. To the pressing invitation of Esau his brother, who wished him to go with him, he replied; 'Brother, thou knowest that I have with me tender children, and women, and sheep with young*; if I should cause them to toil in marching more than they can endure, I know that in one day all of them will die.' Even so I, brother, do not lay upon you a burden which your shoulders cannot bear, nor do I seek reputation [as a director] from the asceticism and the skilfulness of my prescriptions; your salvation is my only object. I shut out all vices and occasions of sin, and for the rest, I insist upon nothing else than that you shall be bound by the strict ᶻ observance of your rule. You are free to talk in your cloister, but [only] at the stated and customary hours. You are free also to talk in your parlours ᵃ, but it should be respecting things con-

Herbert defends his discipline as not being inconsiderate or excessive, but insists upon conventual silence, except at stated times and in stated places.

* See Gen. xxxiii. 13.

ᶻ "solius vestræ *regulæ religioni* vos *religare* contendo." A play upon words, which cannot be reproduced in the translation.

ᵃ "in your parlours"—*in auditoriis vestris*. The *auditorium* of a monastery (*spræc-hus*, Anglo-Sax.; *parloir*, Fr.) was the room where persons who paid visits to members of the monastic body were permitted to converse with them. Fosbroke ("British Monachism," vol. ii. p. 171) tells us that of these apartments there were usually two, one for the monks, another for the visitors; that the *minuti* (see note y, p. 107) had an indulgence of going to the locutory of the visitors to converse immediately after refection and grace, from compline to curfew. Mr. Harrod is of opinion that the great locutory of Norwich Cathedral was the Norman chamber, at the north-west angle of the cloister, formerly the kitchen and larder of a canon's house, but now converted to the more appropriate use of a school-room for the choristers. (Fosbroke tells us that the western side

ducive to the honour and usefulness of your church, or such things as your necessities demand. Moreover, let all disparaging talk and all backbiting and murmuring be far from the mouth and heart of a monk, both in the parlour and the strangers' hall [b], and in every place whither the brethren resort [c];—the Apostle pronounces slanderers and backbiters to be hateful unto God [d].

Rom. i. 30.

of cloisters was usually appropriated to the school.) "Norman and Early English features are much intermixed in this apartment; some noble Norman arches span part of the space, whilst the western portion has Early English vaulting, and the west window is a noble Early English one." (Harrod's Gleanings, pp. 314 and 267.) It appears from Ducange that in Clugniac and Cistercian houses, the word *auditorium* had another meaning, being applied to the lecture-room or apartment where instruction was given. See more on the word *auditorium* above, p. 105, note w.

[b] "in the strangers' hall"—*in atrio*. We hazard the rendering *strangers' hall*, though not being altogether sure that these apartments, which flanked the western side of the cloister in a Benedictine monastery, were called *atria*. Of the strangers' hall which flanked the western side of the cloister of Norwich Mr. Harrod says, "the door leading into it is in the next bay but one to the lavatories. The only portion of the west wall of this magnificent hall stands in a garden" (which once belonged to a canonical residence), "and consists of a fine Early English doorway, with a fragment of an Early English window to the north of it."

[c] "whither the brethren resort"—*in omni suæ consistentiæ loco*. Such is the true reading of the Brussels MS. We do not profess to understand the word. Our translation is only a guess as to what may be its meaning.

[d] "to be hateful unto God"—*Deo odibiles*. The passage referred to by Herbert is Romans i. 29, 30, "susurrones, detractores, Deo odibiles," translated in the Rhemish version, "whisperers, detracters, hateful to God." Our authorized version represents God as the person *hated* not the person *hating;* "whisperers, backbiters, haters of God." The Greek is ψιθυριστὰς, καταλάλους, θεοστυγεῖς. Dean Alford informs us that the Rhemish translation is correct, and our own incorrect. Θεοστυγὴς is never found in an active sense, *hater of God*, but always in a passive, *hated by God* (cf. Eur. Troad. 1205, ἡ θεοστυγὴς Ἑλένη); and such is apparently the sense here. The order of crimes enumerated would be broken, and one of a totally different kind inserted between καταλάλους and ὑβριστὰς, if θεοστ. is to signify *haters of God.* But on the other supposition,—if any crime was known more than another as *hated by the gods*, it was that of *delatores*, abandoned persons who circumvented and ruined others by a system of malignant espionage and false information. And the crime was one which the readers of this part of Roman history know to have been the pest of the state. See Tacitus, Ann., vi. 7, where he calls the *delatores* "principi quidem grati, at *Deo exosi*." So Prof. Jowett, who says; "The use of

Judge then how great an evil it must be for one who is a monk to indulge in a vice which God hath in utter abhorrence. Whence it followeth, Neither do you mur- See 1 Cor. mur, as some of them murmured, and perished by the x. 9, 10. serpents[e]. Let your conversation, therefore, be after the manner and custom of cloistered men, in the parlours, where such talk is authorised, but, as I said before, only respecting things conducive to your honour and usefulness. Most assuredly I never prescribed anything else."

And here another fragment, addressed to one of the youths under instruction in the monastery, in which also he defends himself from the suspicion of harshness and partiality, to which it appears his correspondent thought him to be obnoxious.

the word in classical Greek, as well as of the analogous word $\beta\rho o\tau o\sigma\tau\upsilon\gamma\eta s$, requires the passive sense, *hated of God*. To this it is objected, that it is unmeaning to single out a particular class as hateful to God, because all sinners are so. With the view of avoiding this difficulty it has been proposed to render the word actively after the analogy of $\theta\epsilon o\mu\iota\sigma\eta s$, in Arist., Aves, 1555." The Professor however prefers the passive meaning, remarking, in words which we think would have been better withheld; "here, either the active or passive sense is deficient in point, yet a fair meaning may be given to the passive usage. $\Theta\epsilon o\sigma\tau\upsilon\gamma\eta s$ does not signify hateful to God in the same degree that all sinners may be said to be so, but more than this,—'reprobate,' 'marked with the seal of the Divine wrath,' in a special sense and pre-eminently above other men 'hated of God.'" This concurs well with Herbert's argument. Alas! how doctors differ! Bishop Wordsworth tells us that "the sense *haters of God* seems most consistent with the context. The Apostle is describing here the *sins* of the heathen and not their *punishment;* and it was competent for him to pronounce that they were *haters of God* (for this was seen from their own words and works), but it was not for him to declare that they were hated by God. Perhaps therefore the *active* sense is preferable."

[e] "perished by the serpents"—*a serpentibus perierunt.* Our Herbert is *not* always accurate when he quotes from memory, *pace tanti viri.* 1 Cor. x. 10 does not follow upon Rom. i. 30, nor are the murmurers said to have perished by the serpents, but by the destroyer. The words in the Rhemish translation are; "neither let us tempt Christ: as some of them tempted, and perished by the serpents. Neither do you murmur: as some of them murmured, and were destroyed by the destroyer."

The letter shows his insight into the character of those with whom he had to do, and also his preference of moral over intellectual proficiency.

LETTER XLII[1].

HERBERT OF NORWICH.

Herbert defends himself against the charge, brought against him by a young student, of having kept him back in his studies, and justifies his own motives in the good which he had done.

"You complain of me, and virtually charge me with bearing you a grudge, because I do not allow you to read, nor to be present at the studies of our young people. But the fact is, I neither grudge you the acquisition of knowledge, nor forbid you to be present at the lections aforesaid. I am not changed towards you, nor have I become estranged from you; such as I have been hitherto, such I continue to be, except that in proportion to your advancement in devotion, my affection will gather round you in greater force daily. Read therefore and learn as much as you like, and wherever you like, and do not make a fault of mine out of what is really your fault. I can divine why you are out of humour, and whence it is that your vexation has arisen. You see that your school-fellows are placed on a level with you; and you cannot brook the having as equals those over whose heads you cannot rise. Do not be apprehensive; you will not be surpassed, if only you will comport yourselves charitably among your brethren, and love them in all humbleness of mind. You allege that some show themselves ungrateful for my instruc-

See 1 Cor. iv. 3.

tion; but I am not looking for the day of man's judg-

---

[1] In Mr. Anstruther's edition of Herbert's Letters (from which we are translating) there are two derangements of the numeration. The Brussels MS. however, not Mr. Anstruther, is responsible for these derangements. The first derangement is, that Epistle XXXVI. comes *between* Epistle XXXIV. and Epistle XXXV. The second is, that two consecutive Epistles (of which the present one stands first) are numbered XLII., Epistle XLIV. not being found at all. The present Epistle is really the forty-second. When we come to that which follows it, we must call it XLII. *bis*.

ment[g]. From God alone I expect a recompence for all the good I may have done in Norwich."

The year 1106 was memorable in Herbert's life, not only on account of the commencement of his monastery, but also because he was that year called upon to assist and preach on occasion of a great ceremonial held at Ely,—the second translation of the body of St. Etheldreda. The first removal of this saint's body had been made by her sister, Queen Sexburga, sixteen years after Etheldred's death, as related in the succeeding extract. The second was made by Abbot Richard, after he had completed the new church, which had been commenced by his predecessor. The abbot had been thrust out of his abbacy by Henry I., chiefly on account of his appearing at court with too much state[h], and affecting, as an

A.D. 1106.

Abbot Richard of Ely,

after deposition by the king,

---

[g] The reference in this phraseology of Herbert's is no doubt to 1 Cor. iv. 3.

Greek.	Vulgate.	Rhemish.
ἐμοὶ δὲ εἰς ἐλάχιστόν ἐστιν ἵνα ὑφ' ὑμῶν ἀνακριθῶ, ἢ ὑπὸ ἀνθρωπίνης ἡμέρας· ἀλλ' οὐδὲ ἐμαυτὸν ἀνακρίνω.	Mihi autem pro minimo est, ut à vobis judicer, aut ab *humano die;* sed neque meipsum judico.	But to me it is a very small thing to be judged by you, or by *man's day:* but neither do I judge my own self.

The Commentators tell us that the use of the word *day* for *judgment* is to be explained by the Latin phrase "diem dicere" = to cite to trial (to *subpœna* to appear before a court) on a stated day. In the Apostle's use of the term there is however a higher reference to "the day of the Lord," when the great final judgment will be held. Bengel's terse remark on the phrase "man's day" is, "Every day on this side of the day of the Lord is man's day."

[h] Perhaps to some of our readers, who are versed in such lore, may here suggest itself the quaint old ballad descriptive of King John's calling the abbot of Canterbury to account for keeping too sumptuous an establishment:—

" And I'll tell you a story, a story so merry
Concerning the abbot of Canterbury ;

A.D. 1106. ecclesiastic, an independence of the civil power. Under these circumstances he resorted to Rome, the refuge in those days of all ecclesiastics who felt themselves aggrieved by crowned heads.

and re-instatement by the Pope, Nor was his appeal in vain. Pascal II. re-instated him in his dignity, and he returned to Ely in triumph, reconciled himself to the king, and devoted himself to the completion of the new church of his abbey. Having finished this work,

determines to translate the body of St. Etheldreda from the old into the new church. he determined to translate, with all due formalities, from the old church to the new the body of the patron saint. We give an account of the ceremony from the *Liber Eliensis*, which brings out two points respecting our prelate,—one, that he was deeply interested in the Church movements of his own time; the other, that he was eminent as a preacher.

"*Of the Second Translation of the holy virgin's body, which the Abbot aforesaid made.*

"The Abbot Richard, then, desiring with the utmost desire, and deliberating, in his own good time, to transfer the most sacred body of this most sacred virgin from the old church to the new, from a church inconsiderable to one larger, and fairer; remembering that

> How for his housekeeping and high renown,
> They rode post for him to fair London town.
>
> " An hundred men, the king did hear say,
> The abbot kept in his house every day;
> And fifty gold chains, without any doubt,
> In velvet coats waited the abbot about.
>
> " 'How now, father abbot, I hear it of thee,
> Thou keepest a far better house than me;
> And for thy housekeeping and high renown
> I fear thou workest treason against my crown,'" &c.

Joseph also, with a view to greater reverence, had transferred the body of his father from Egypt into the land of Canaan; lest so bright a lamp and candle should lie hid under a bushel, and that it might, by being placed upon a candlestick in the presence of witnesses, and amid a concourse of the people, be known and shine forth before all, he appointed a day, to wit, the sixteenth of the Kalends of October, on which her first translation also might be solemnized, as if it were one with the second. Being a man, then, of a great and liberal soul, in order that he might give the weight of solemn authority, and specially of pontifical authority, to this solemnity, he in the first place invited Anselm, the metropolitan of Canterbury, a man most venerable and devout, with that reverence which was due both to his office and to his character, praying him that, in fulfilment of the duty of his high position, he would condescend to grace the ceremony with his presence, attended by such of his suffragans as he might deem most devout; and invited also very many others of pontifical dignity and rank, as well as abbots, and devout monks, and other ecclesiastical persons, who might justly be put on a level with (that I may not say preferred to) the chiefest bishops, if not in dignity, yet at least in desert. The nobles and chief men of the kingdom were also invited by him to approach to so joyous a festivity, and to rejoice with them that rejoiced. But certain of the persons invited being hindered from attending by public or private affairs and ties, other some, who were ordained by Divine Providence to take part, and were apt and especially needful for the furtherance of so great a design, came together most devoutly [on the appointed day]. Among whom were that renowned man, Herbert Bishop of Norwich, Adelwyn of Ramsey, Richard Abbot of St. Alban's, Gunter of Thorne, Wydo Abbot of Pershore, Nicholas Archdeacon of Lincoln, Gaufrid Treasurer of Winchester, and numberless other men of great probity and authority. When, then, the procession had been marshalled in an orderly way, they approach reve-

A.D. 1106.

Anselm invited to the ceremony.

Herbert attends.

A.D. 1106. rently to the tomb of the holy and venerable virgin Etheldreda, which was of Parian marble, purest white, as became her virgin purity. In this tomb, which formerly had been prepared for her by the ministry of angels, and offered by the Divine Grace to those who were seeking [for her a resting-place], her blessed sister, Queen Sexburga, after she had been sixteen years buried, had laid her with cries of admiration and loud-sounding praise, which rose to heaven, her corpse having been found perfectly whole and firm, the body and the raiment being alike milk-white, and unspotted. It redounded to her greater glory on the present occasion, that no one presumed to open her tomb, no one to inspect her corpse. For formerly, when the pagans invaded this place, one of them, bent on incurring a judgment, drove a hole in the sarcophagus, and was immediately deprived of his eyes and his life; afterwards a rash presbyter, being the head of the convent, drove a cleft stick into that hole, and succeeded in extracting a part of her robe by twisting it up into a wrinkle: with still madder presumption he cut off that portion of the robe, when suddenly the hand of the saint, who was lying within, twitched back the robe into the sarcophagus with wakeful indignation. To a further length did this experimentalist proceed, thrusting into the hole a candle fixed to the end of a stick. The candle, falling down upon her sacred body, burnt itself out, yet did no harm to anything within. But the presumptuous man, with all his house, perished. Since, however, in the account of her miracles, these things are related more at large, let us return to our present narrative.—At length, with the utmost devotion, they take up the virgin's most holy body, and carry it out of the old church from the place whither the blessed Sexburga had transferred and laid it, where also the venerable father Ethelwold (when restoring and renovating the decayed church) had left her as he found her, never experimented upon, never removed, never beheld [since those former attempts], her sepulchre not lying hid under the earth, but rising above it;

and from that spot they now carry her into the church
with hymns and praises. And thus was the royal lady
Etheldreda translated into the new temple, experimented upon and beheld by none; and amidst the worthy praises of those who sang psalms in her honour, was
placed in a chamber prepared for her behind the high
altar. And at length when, in the course of the solemnity, a sermon was addressed to the people concerning it (as was becoming), and the venerable Bishop
Herbert, a most eloquent man, [discoursing] of the
life and death and miracles of the blessed virgin, and
the wonderful incorruptibility of her sacred body, exhorted the multitude to show forth the utmost joy
and gladness, on account of those things that were
done in the tabernacles of the just. Such was the
heavenly grace which was diffused among them, that
you could hardly see a single person in so large an
assembly who would (or, indeed, could) refrain from
tears. But of the many wonders which occurred at that
translation, this only do we report for the eternal honour
of the most holy virgin and queen Etheldreda, a wonder, which numberless of the faithful who still survive,
and our fathers who were present and saw it, have related to us, whose report, joined with the authority of their
lives and integrity of their manners, hath given us such
assurance thereof, that no one need entertain any doubt
of the fact. For then were repeated those ancient portents,
which are said to have occurred[1] at the finding of the body

A.D. 1106.

Herbert's sermon at the translation of St. Etheldreda, and its effects.

---

[1] The feast of the invention of St. Stephen, or the discovery of his relics, is celebrated by the Roman Church on the third of August. He is said to have been buried at Caphargamala (a word meaning *burrow of Gamaliel*), twenty miles from Jerusalem, where was a church served by a venerable priest of the name of Lucian. To this Lucian, on Friday the third of December, A.D. 415, Gamaliel, St. Paul's preceptor, appeared, and revealed to him that St. Stephen, Nicodemus, and Gamaliel himself, had been buried at Caphargamala; and that Lucian must go to Jerusalem and bid the bishop come and open their tombs. The apparition having been thrice repeated, Lucian obeyed Gamaliel's injunction; and eventually Bishop John of Jerusalem, with Bishop Eutonius of Sebaste, and Bishop Eleutherius of Jericho, assembled at the spot indicated. "Upon the opening of St. Stephen's coffin the earth shook, and there came out of the coffin

of the blessed martyr Stephen. For there were thunders, and tempests, and such flashes of lightning, that almost all the windows of the church were dashed in with frightful blows, and frequent fires ran along on the pavement in the presence of the bodies of the saints : and marvellous it was that the fire travelled without producing its customary effects, and seemed to change its quality among pieces of wood, and straw, and other dry materials, so that whatever of this sort fell, or had fallen, into the church did no harm. Which great miracle, wrought by the saint, fell out in such a manner (according to the opinion of sundry persons), that, while she showed by these terrors of the sky that so public a handling of her sarcophagus was displeasing to her, she might yet hurt no one in her wrath ; and that thus every one might be convinced that the signs of heaven were obedient to her nod.

"Few were there present whose secret thought did not suggest to them that these signs, the horror of which they on the one hand dreaded to look upon, on the other rejoiced to escape from unscathed, portended something great. Anselm himself, the archbishop, who was in Kent, far removed from the scene, when he saw the heaven shaken with such crashes of thunder, said, 'I feel

such an agreeable odour that no one remembered to have ever smelt anything like it. There was a vast multitude of people assembled together in that place, among whom were many persons afflicted with divers distempers, of whom seventy-three recovered their health upon the spot." A small portion of the martyr's remains was left at Caphargamala ; "the rest were carried in the coffin with singing of psalms and hymns to the church of Sion at Jerusalem. At the time of this translation there fell a great deal of rain, which refreshed the country after a long drought. The translation was performed on the twenty-sixth of December, the discovery of the relics having taken place on the third of August. The history of the discovery and of the translation, written by Lucian himself, and translated into Latin by the priest Avitus, a friend of St. Jerome's, is published by the Benedictine Monks in the Appendix to the seventh volume of St. Augustine's works." That father, in his work *De Civitate Dei*, makes mention of five persons raised from the dead in his own times by the relics of St. Stephen, "mentioning their names, families, and all the circumstances of the facts." (Butler's "Lives of the Saints," August 3rd.)

sure that our brother Richard, the Abbot of Ely, has A.D. 1106.
translated his holy virgins to-day, and has handled
them irreverently; and I doubt not that this stress of
hard weather is a sign of some dismal augury.' Nor
was he mistaken in his opinion; for few, indeed, of
those who were then present, and had seen St. Withburga
face to face, lived out the whole year. Wherefore, dear
brethren, you who, not upon a single occasion only,
but perpetually, keep up righteously and devoutly the
memory of so holy a virgin, in the very sight and presence of her sacred body, must address prayers and
instant supplications unto Him, Who for the thirsty
people made water well forth in abundance from the
rock beneath the stroke of Moses' rod, that through your
intercessions He would condescend to water both us and
you with the precious dews of His grace; to whom be
praise, and honour, and glory, for ever and ever [k]."

"How [Abbot Richard] found other saints, and in what manner he translated them.

"When the virgin Etheldreda, as abbess (*primiceria* [l]),
had in this manner been decorously laid over against
the high altar, Richard, the shepherd of this great flock,
took counsel with the elders [thereof], that on that same
day whereon, under the abbacy of St. Sexburga, the
first translation of the blessed virgin Etheldred had
been made, a translation should also be made of all

---

[k] Liber Eliensis, [Londini, 1848], pp. 289—292.

[l] *Primicerius* was a name given to various officers and dignitaries under the later Roman empire, and signifies generally the person who holds the first rank in anything. The alleged derivation is from *cera*, "wax," the name of the *primicerius* standing first on the waxen tablet which contained a list of persons of rank. (But query?) Singularly enough the word occasionally meant the *second* in a department, the *primicerius sacri cubiculi* under the Roman empire being the *second* lord of the bed-chamber, the first being called *præpositus*. St. Augustine calls St. Stephen *primicerius martyrum*, and St. Bernard calls the Virgin *primiceria virginitatis*. In a nunnery *primiceria* is simply the superior, whether abbess or prioress. These particulars are taken from Ducange, and Smith's "Dictionary of Greek and Roman Antiquities."

A.D. 1106. the holy women resting there. And accordingly they opened the sepulchres of the mother and daughter, which St. Ethelwold had sealed up with lead on either side, to wit, of the holy Queen Sexburga, and of the renowned Ermenilda, whose praises are so highly celebrated throughout the Church. Their corpses they found to have decayed after the common lot of humanity, and to have paid to the earth, which bare them, the debt which they owed her. For as regards the body of the blessed Sexburga, he found it wrapped in silks and fair white linen, the bones by themselves, and the dust by itself, and each of these [both bones and dust] in a case of its own made of wood, and contained in a stone monument, just as the blessed Ethelwold had left it. Her they solemnly replaced, at the feet of St. Etheldreda, [looking] towards the east.

"But the remains of the most holy Ermenilda he [Abbot Richard] found, as the blessed Ethelwold had laid them, on the bare floor of the sepulchre without any covering. These he collected in a snow-white cloth, wrapping up the dust separately, and replacing all in the original coffin, which he then laid, with equal care, on the south, at the right hand of St. Etheldreda, and sealed up again with lead both coffins. Now these holy women were translated, with every befitting solemnity, in the year of our Lord's Incarnation 1106, on the same day of the year on which formerly the blessed Etheldreda had been translated; so that those who had one faith, one Christ, and one charity, might with one and the same solemn rite be interred [m]."

"Four years before the translation of the holy virgins (related above), they had removed from its place the famous sepulchre of the blessed virgin Withburga, and had placed it in another part of the church. The enlargement of the church which was then proceeding made that removal necessary, for when the building reached that point it could not stop there; and when in going down some steps the monument was ruptured,

[m] Liber Eliensis, [Londini, 1848], pp. 292, 293.

the heedless workmen proving unfit for such a work as A.D. 1106, this, the lower slab on which the eminent virgin rested was broken, and then appeared a great fissure in the tomb; but I think this was not done without the overruling of God's Providence, but [was allowed] in order that the Lord's power might shew the merits of the holy virgin, and might repair the fracture of the tomb by a new species of miracle; for they removed in like manner [and in safety] the blessed Queen Ermenilda, the progress of the works in the church inviting them to this great enterprise. . . . .

"Now Richard, the aforesaid ruler of the monastery of Ely, had prepared a new sepulchre for the illustrious Withburga, of the exact measure of the old sarcophagus, which had now for some years been broken, in order that the pure virgin, laid in that new sepulchre, might there find a pure harbour [for her remains]. But the Providence of God frustrated his design by a new miracle never heard of hitherto. For as the new tomb, which was destined to receive the sacred body, stood ready [for its reception], when a measuring-rule was applied to it of the same dimension as the former sarcophagus, it proved to be just one foot shorter. And whoever tried to repeat the measurement of both sepulchres, arrived at the same result, the new one always proving a foot shorter than the old. All present were stricken with wonder and amazement, and knew not what to do, seeing that their intention, in reference to the coffin which they had prepared, was precluded by the larger stature of the virgin's body. Meanwhile, when the cover of the old mausoleum, which gaped with the fissure, was removed, still greater miracles terrified those who were present. For the virgin's corpse, which was thought after so many ages to be now at length consumed (although there was a rumour, grounded upon former experience, which maintained its present incorruptibility), appeared whole and sound in all its limbs and raiment, just as it had been originally placed there. For the wooden shell, in which the corpse

A.D. 1106. had been brought to Ely, was preserved without injury, only the iron nails which fastened it being eaten away. Meanwhile some supposed that the dust of the body, not having been stirred, presented only an outward show of firmness without the reality; but on its being touched, its solidity, which had endured for so many years, was made manifest. For a certain elder from the sheepfold of the Apostles at Westminster, Warner by name, who with many others had come together [to witness this solemnity], approached [the corpse] with a marvellous audacity of faith, and touched the limbs of the virgin in every part of her person, on her feet, on her hands, on her arms, reverently lifted her flexible joints, and crying out at the wonderful works of God, drew many of the most notable persons to that spectacle. But no one scrutinized with irreverent gaze the graces of her person, shrouded as they were in snow-white raiment. Fair for the Lord, [and for Him only,] was her face, animated with the breath of life, the rose still sitting on her cheeks, her breasts were full and perfect as in the spring-tide of her age, her chaste limbs were fresh and supple as with the beauty of Paradise. Thereupon came that most learned man, the aforesaid Herbert, Bishop of Thetford, looked upon her with awe, and blessed the Lord who is glorious in His saints. And many other persons of high character were present and stood by, whom we have named above. They saw with their eyes these wonderful works of God. We report their testimony, as an evidence of the faith; let not those, who are privileged [only] to hear, disdain our recital. But at length that renowned Bishop Herbert expounded to a dense throng of people these marvels and new sources of joy, and kindles in all of them the desire of praising God, and offering thanks to Him. Nay, so powerfully did grace operate, shed abroad like dew from heaven, that rivers of tears flowed from the eyes of all [for very joy],—a thing which might seem incredible to those who did not witness it. But when, in the midst of these joyous emotions, all felt

Herbert inspects the body of St. Withburga,

and addresses the people on the prodigy, of which he had been an eye-witness.

some perplexity as to what they should do, because the A.D. 1106. old tomb from its fracture seemed derogatory to the virgin's dignity, but the new one, shortened as it had been by the Divine power, had ceased to be desirable; at length our gracious patroness resolved these doubts, and shewed by a glorious miracle that she was unwilling to be dislodged from her former resting-place. For that fissure, which might easily have been penetrated by a knife or a reed, was all of a sudden so perfectly repaired, that no trace of any fracture thenceforth appeared therein. And thus the scruples of all were satisfied; for they understood by this evident sign that the virgin was unwilling to be removed from her former resting-place. They placed therefore the lid over her, and having carefully closed the sarcophagus, transport her with glad triumph to her blessed sister from the old monastery to the new one, and there lay her, with much acceptability, looking eastward, at her side. Now on the subject of the incorruptibility of the holy virgin Withburga, it is rehearsed on this wise in the English Chronicles, that in the year of our Lord 798, the body of the saint was found incorrupt after it had rested fifty-five years in Dereham. Two hundred and two years being added to the above 798, make up exactly a thousand years. And another hundred and six years, following thereupon, make up together [with the fifty-five, and two hundred and two] three hundred[a] and fifty-four years, from the falling asleep of the blessed Withburga, to that day of our own time, on which she was shown publicly with her body still incorrupt. In like manner, as hath been said, they lovingly associated [with Etheldreda and Withburga] her blessed sister Sexburga and her holy daughter Ermenilda, the worthy with the

---

[a] We cannot account for this reckoning. We make the number 363.

Withburga died	. . .	A.D. 743
Found incorrupt at Dereham		A.D. 798
Translated to Ely	. .	A.D. 974
Transported into the new church	. . . .	A.D. 1106

The difference therefore between 1106 and 743 (=363) will represent the years which elapsed between her death and final transportation.

A.D. 1106. worthy; all of whom, resting side by side, both singly and conjointly, implore with acceptance special blessings for those who call upon them."

In the succeeding Chapter of the *Liber Eliensis*, the four saints thus translated by Abbot Richard, —Etheldreda, Sexburga, Ermenilda, and Withburga°,—are compared to the four winged living

---

° The reader may possibly be puzzled as to the relation borne to each other by these sainted ladies. Annas, king of the East Angles, had four daughters, i. Sexburga, ii. Ethelburga, iii. Etheldreda or Audry, iv. Withburga. (i.) Sexburga married Ercombert, king of Kent, and had by him Ermenilda, who was married to Wulpher, king of Mercia. Sexburga founded a nunnery in the isle of Sheppey, of which she became abbess after her husband's death; but being attracted by the superior fame of Etheldreda's monastery at Ely, she migrated thither; and in 679, after Etheldreda's death, was chosen abbess of Ely. (ii.) Ethelburga died a virgin and a nun in France. (iii.) Etheldreda, the most renowned of the four, married the prince of the Girvii (people who inhabited Rutland, Northamptonshire, Huntingdonshire, and part of Lincolnshire), who survived the marriage only three years and then died, leaving her the isle of Ely for a dowry. She took the somewhat extraordinary step of marrying Egfrid, king of Northumberland, though she would not live with him as his wife, treating him in this respect as she had treated the prince of the Girvii. After Egfrid's death she took the veil, and lived in obedience to St. Ebba, at Coldingham, beyond Bury. In 672 she returned to the isle of Ely, where she founded a double monastery on her own estate, and governed it herself. She ate only once a day; wore nothing but woollen clothes; never returned to bed after matins, which were sung at midnight; and rejoiced in a painful red swelling on her neck, which she regarded as a chastisement for wearing necklaces. On June 23, 679, she breathed her last, and was buried in a wooden coffin, for which afterwards her sister Withburga substituted a stone one. Her story, "written and engraven in stones," may be seen in the sculptures under the lantern of Ely Cathedral. (iv.) Withburga, the youngest of the four sisters, appears never to have been married. She lived on the royal estates, first at Holkham, and then at Dereham, at which latter place she died, March 17, 743. In 974 her body was removed to Ely, where her sisters, Sexburga and Etheldreda, and her niece Ermenilda, had already been laid. The result of the examination in 1106 was, as we see from the above extract, that Sexburga and Ermenilda were found skeletons, Etheldreda entire, and Withburga, not only entire, but fresh and flexible. Alban Butler tells us that in the part of Dereham churchyard, where Withburga was first buried, a spring of clear water gushed forth, which is called to this day St. Withberge's well, and is paved, covered, and enclosed.

creatures of Ezekiel and St. John, to the four rivers which watered Paradise, to the four Maries who attended on and anointed Christ, &c.; and we are told that Abbot Richard, moved by the sight of her incorruptibility, felt a special devotion towards Withburga, and would have made her a silver coffin had he lived long enough; but his time was much occupied in endeavouring to frustrate the attempts of the Bishop of Lincoln to establish episcopal jurisdiction over the monastery of Ely. He stood in high favour with the king, and was one of his chief privy-councillors.

The Abbot Richard, who had so large a share in the transactions above recorded, is very probably the same man who appears in Herbert's correspondence as Abbot Richard, and who (if this be so) was a fair-weather friend, looking coldly on him in the hour of adversity, and writing him a flattering letter when his reputation was at its zenith, as will by-and-by appear. *Abbot Richard of Ely possibly the same man as the 'Ricardus Abbas' of Herbert's letters.*

In the year 1107, we find Herbert engaged, with the Primates of Canterbury and York, and with the Bishops of Durham, Lichfield, Bath, Chichester, and Lincoln, in consecrating five bishops at Canterbury, to fill the vacant sees of Winchester, Sarum, Exeter, Hereford, and Llandaff. William of Warelwast, who had now returned from his mission to Rome (see p. 145), was on this occasion consecrated Bishop of Exeter. Roger, who was appointed to the see of Sarum, became a favourite at court, and rose to great eminence as a royal justiciary. *A.D. 1107. Herbert assists in consecrating five bishops at Canterbury.*

This prelate made so distinguished a figure in this and the succeeding reign, and Herbert seems to have entertained such awe of him as one who had, in fact, gathered up all the power of the kingdom into his own hand, that a brief sketch of his career will not be felt to be out of place here. He owed his rise to the circumstance of Henry I., before he came to the throne, having casually entered into a little church near Caen, in which, as parish priest, Roger was saying mass. The office was gone through with such extraordinary rapidity as to gratify a soldier's love of brief devotions; and the prince, pleased to find himself so soon out of church, bade Roger follow his camp. He was somewhat illiterate; but the king finding him pliant and clever, gave him the great seal, and made him Chancellor. Having taken the king's side against Anselm, he was preferred (on the occasion before us) to the bishopric of Salisbury. Thence he rose after an interval of some years to the dignity of Chief Justiciary, which, in fact, was the office of prime minister; and during the king's absence in Normandy, he governed England as regent. It was he who ruled, in the interests of Matilda, Henry's daughter, that the crown, like a private inheritance, should descend to the daughter and heiress of the person last seized. And yet afterwards, notwithstanding this decision, he announced, on the death of Henry, the new constitutional doctrine, "that only males could mount the throne," in pursuance of which he urged the Archbishop of Canterbury to anoint and crown Stephen. Basking awhile in the sunshine of Stephen's favour, he built a huge castle at Devizes, where he maintained the state and independence of a sovereign, but he soon quarrelled with his new friend, who sent a strong force to besiege him in his castle, and induced him to surrender by threatening to hang up before the walls his illegitimate son, to whom he was strongly attached. Soon after this he died of a quartan ague, Dec. 4, 1149, more than twenty years after our Herbert had closed his career. He had some points of affinity with Wolsey, having known by experience how precarious a pinnacle is the favour of princes, and by how slight an accident he who stands upon it may be hurled to the ground and dashed to pieces. He indulged largely that love of magnificence, which often took possession of mediæval ecclesiastics, at a time (how long gone by!) when devotion was thought to consist very much in crowning the ministers of God with all manner of endowments, distinctions, and prerogatives. Malmesbury tells us that Henry denied him nothing; gave him estates, churches, prebends, abbeys, and committed the whole kingdom to his fidelity; and that, in a word, he had the entire administration of justice and finance in his hands. As for Stephen, he would say of Roger, "By the birth of God, I would give him half England, if he asked for it. Till the time be ripe, he shall tire of asking before I tire of giving." These particulars, which are drawn from Lord Campbell's "Lives of the Chancellors" (vol. i. pp.

50—54), throw great light upon the manner in which Herbert speaks of and addresses Roger; and we cannot but think that the letters now to be presented to the reader have considerable historic interest, as showing how Roger had, at that time, monopolized all the power of the realm. Another indication of the same fact will be found in a letter (hereafter to be given) from Herbert to the Queen, in which he desires his compliments to the Bishop of Salisbury, and deprecates the insinuations against himself which enemies have instilled into that prelate's ear. Calumnies of this kind are again referred to, and their utter groundlessness declared, in the first of the following letters.

LETTER XXI.

To Roger the Bishop.

"To Roger the Bishop, Herbert, his Presbyter of Norwich, sendeth greeting.

Herbert vindicates himself

"When the lord, Radulph de Belfage[p], first visited me and gave me your greeting, my heart bounded with as

---

[p] "Radulph de Belfage"—*Radulphum de Bellofago.* This is probably the same name as Beaufeu, or Beaufoy. And probably Ralph de Beaufeu was more or less connected with William de Beaufeu, Herbert's immediate predecessor in the see of Thetford. Mr. Walter Rye, in his genealogical account of the family of Rye, thinks he has discovered that Bishop William de Beaufeu (or Beaufoy) married Agnes of Todeni. By her he had a son named Richard de Beaufeu, who was placed in the Norwich Monastery A.D. 1096 (that is, at its first foundation), and became second Archdeacon of Norwich (Osbert having been the first) in A.D. 1107. This was doubtless "Richard the Archdeacon" of Herbert's Letter LIV., who had given Herbert's brother some box-wood tablets, (See p. 7). Bishop William de Beaufeu being dead, Agnes his widow married Hubert de Rye, castellan of Norwich Castle, a Crusader, and a great benefactor of Norwich Cathedral. This lady it was who granted the Church of Aldeby with the tithes of that place to the cathedral.

The name has numerous forms, Galsagus, Belfagus, de Bellofago, Beaufo, Beaufeu, Beaufoy, Bewfewe, Bella-Fago,—even Velson.

much joy as if a salutation had been brought down
to me from heaven by an angel of God. But when,
after the greeting, the same man recounted the calumny
against us [which had been poured into your ears], I
shuddered exceedingly, and my face being clouded with
tears, as my mind was with grief, I felt quite ignorant
what answer I should make to this charge. I have,
however, narrowly questioned my thought, my will, my
speech, my action, if in any respect they have erred.
They reply that they have erred in no respect; they
reply that by no manner of means could they have
poured back the poison of wormwood into that breast,
from which I have hitherto drawn, in my every necessity,
the milk and honey of counsel and of aid. Wherefore,
O man of God, I have not sinned against thee by any
motion of the mind or the body; and I will maintain
mine innocence in every place, appealing to the truth
as my witness, and to the purity of my conscience. My
ears, it is true, I have not been able to prevent from
hearing certain things, which would have been worthy
of reproof, if the language which preceded them had
been followed up by acting upon it. These things, however, I reserved for the present (communicating my
secret to no one), but intending to recount them to you
alone, when I shall find a time and place opportune for
so doing. Send back to me, I entreat you, with all
speed, Walter my archdeacon[q], for he is so essential to

from a calumny against him, which had reached Roger's ears, and which he promises to explain further when they meet. He also entreats Richard to send back Walter the Archdeacon, whom he finds indispensable for his coming synod. He himself is unable to move from a complaint of the leg.

---

[q] We think that some credit is due to us for having unearthed from these Letters of Herbert a new Archdeacon of our Diocese, though whether of Norwich, Norfolk, or Suffolk, we cannot say. There was an Archdeacon of Herbert's, who bore the name of Walter;—this is sufficiently clear. But Blomefield knows nothing of this dignitary. The only Archdeacons of Norwich in Herbert's time which he enumerates are, (1) *Osbert*, A.D. 1101; (2) *Richard de Bella-fago*, son of Bp. William Beaufeu of Thetford, of whom we have spoken in the previous note, A.D. 1107; and (3) *Eborard*, A.D. 1115, afterwards Bishop. The only Archdeacon of Norfolk given by Blomefield as contemporaneous with Herbert is Adam, one of his chaplains. The only Archdeacon of Suffolk of that day whom he mentions is Alured, A.D. 1103. The assigned date of the next Archdeacon of Norfolk after Adam being 1147, and that of the next Archdeacon of Suffolk after Alured being a man who lived down to 1175, it seems that the names of one or

me in the synod which I purpose holding in the second week after Easter[r], that without his presence I feel myself quite unable to fix the day of the synod. For I am afflicted with such a troublesome complaint of the leg and shin-bone that I am unable to move at all, except when carried by the hands of my brethren."

more Archdeacons must have been omitted from both lists. In one of these vacant places we may insert Archdeacon Walter, a dignitary of such importance in his day that the synodical action of the Diocese could not be carried on without him.

[r] "Which I purpose holding in the second week after Easter."— Mr. Anstruther deserves the thanks of every student of mediæval literature for having been the first to print and publish Herbert's letters, and thus make them accessible to those who could not accomplish a pilgrimage to the Burgundian Library at Brussels. We duly appreciate his labours, and desire to acknowledge our obligations to him; yet we cannot resist a quiet chuckle over the way in which he has cut the Gordian knot of a difficulty, which in the original the passage before us presents. The MS. runs thus: "in sinodo quam habiturus sum ad Misericordia Domini plena est terra." Mr. Anstruther, unable to extract any sense from this, omits the Scriptural text altogether in his edition, substituting for it a row of dots, as if there were a *lacuna*, and then in a foot-note coolly informs his readers that "the name of the place" (at which the synod was to be held) "is wanting in the manuscript." Doubtless it is. The text ("the earth is full of the mercy of the Lord") is a note of time, not of place. In those days, Ecclesiastical seasons were denoted by the beginning of the Introits, Anthems, &c., appropriated to them. A trace of the practice still lingers among us in the words "O Sapientia," to denote the 16th of December, because on that day was sung the first of a series of seven Antiphons to the Magnificat, beginning "O Sapientia." And we have heard the last Sunday of the Ecclesiastical Year vulgarly called "*Stir up* Sunday," from the commencement of the Collect, and (curiously enough) the Second Sunday after Easter (from the double lesson about Balaam, prescribed by the Old Lectionary) "Balaam and Balak Sunday." Herbert proposes to hold his Synod at *Misericordiâ Domini*,—this text forming the Introit in the Roman Missal for the aforesaid Second Sunday after Easter. We find from Ducange that Episcopal Synods for disciplinary purposes were usually held in the middle of May and November. The middle of May, in a year when Easter fell late, might coincide with the Second Sunday after Easter.

LETTER XXVI.
To Roger of Salisbury.

"To Roger, his Pastor of Salisbury, Herbert, his sheep of Norwich, sendeth greeting.

"Although during the whole period of your administration my infirmities have demanded care, yet at this crisis more especially, when I am fettered with the bonds of ill-health, and a more severe adversity frowns upon me, I urgently implore your fatherly goodness, that as you have hitherto given me your support, you would allow no engagements of business to make you despise me now that I am cast down. I cry to you as a father, I cry to you as a pastor, and with such cries as wounded hearts alone send forth. Let the cries of my trouble penetrate, I beseech you, your affectionate paternal heart. The sheepfold has been broken into[*], and I am exposed to the teeth of cruel beasts, and unless you graciously come to my aid and protect me, I am put forth to be torn in pieces by the enemies who rush upon me. I leave it to your compassion to consider what answer you shall give to the pleadings of your sheep. I leave altogether in your hands the counsels which should be taken in my troubles. My lands are assessed at fifty pounds[t] for arbitrary levies,

[Herbert, being in weak health, and in great trouble about certain exactions and assessments, implores Roger to maintain the exemptions of the manor of Thorpe from all fiscal burdens, which had been granted by Royal Charter.]

---

[*] "the sheepfold has been broken into"—*confractis caulis*.
Herbert has borrowed this word *caula* (said to be etymologically connected with *cavus*, qu. *cavile*) from one of Virgil's most spirited similes, in which he compares Turnus when the Trojans would not give him battle, but hugged their camp, to a wolf baulked of his prey by the security of the sheepfold:—

> " Ac veluti pleno lupus insidiatus ovili,
> Quum fremit ad caulas, ventos perpessus et imbres,
> Nocte super media ; tuti sub matribus agni
> Balatum exercent ; ille asper et improbus ira
> Sævit in absentes ; collecta fatigat edendi
> Ex longo rabies, et siccæ sanguine fauces."
> Virg. Æn. ix. 59—64.

[t] "fifty pounds for arbitrary levies"—*quinquaginta libræ pro placitis*.
See a full note on *placita*, p. 176, b. The meaning of the word in the present instance will be found on p. 178 (iv)—any exaction, decreed by a *placitum*, of men, money, or both.

though my men on those lands have committed no offence, either in deed or in making answer to the demand. Also sixty pounds are demanded of me for soldiers, which I find a great difficulty in furnishing, inasmuch as in past years my resources have undergone a very serious diminution. But the most grievous thing of all is, that my neighbours are endeavouring to drag Thorpe into an assessment [u] for customs, which our lord the king presented to us for the building of his church, to be as free from rates and customs as it was when in his own hand, and as his other manors are; and you have often seen the charter [x] containing the

[u] "to drag Thorpe into an assessment for customs"—*contrahere Thorpum in consuetudinem*. Any customary due, whether of money or service, the origin of which was not known, nor by whom it was originally imposed, was called *consuetudo*. The word occurs in an exemption granted by the Frank kings to the town of Nevers, a fragment of which is quoted by Ducange *sub voce*. It is much the same sort of exemption as Herbert here claims for Thorpe: "All *customs* whatsoever, which we and our predecessors had, or were wont to have, in the town of Nevers, and specifically the service done to us in our military expeditions, whether on foot or horseback" (*chevaucheiam nostram et exercitum nostrum*), "we have made the burghers aforesaid, and do hereby make them, altogether and for ever free of," (*eisdem burgensibus quittavimus in perpetuum penitus et quittamus*).

[x] The original charter, by which the manor of Thorpe was granted to Herbert, cannot now be traced; a copy of it (printed in Dugdale's *Monasticon*, vol. iv. p. 16, No. 5, ed. Caley and Ellis, London, 1823) is to be found in the British Museum, (Add. MSS. 5846, pp. 386, 7,) to which this note is added, "Autogr. penes Math. Howard, generosum, dominum manerii Thorp juxta Norwicum, 1728." It appears that part of the manor—enough for the building of the Cathedral—was originally obtained from William Rufus. Henry I. confirmed Rufus's grant, and added to it the rest of the manor.

We have carefully collated the printed copy of the charter given in Dugdale, as above, with the MS. copy in our own Treasury. The variations are so slight as to be unworthy of notice, with this exception, that the printed copy has "ecclesia *sancta civitatis* de Nordovico," whereas the MS. (which in this case is evidently right) has "ecclesia *sanctæ Trinitatis* de *Norwyco*." Moreover in the MS. the initial formula, "In nomine Patris et Filii et Spiritus Sancti. Amen," has been erased, we cannot say why, and a *lacuna* left in the place of it. We present our readers with a translation:—

"The Son of God, the Lover and Redeemer of men, so loved the holy Church that He redeemed her with His blood, and sealed her with His Spirit, and satiated her with the nourishment of His flesh. He purged her

grant to this effect, and the repeated writs [y] on the same subject. Here I take my stand; here I make

of errors and sins, and clad her with the purple of innocence, and with the ornaments of all graces: He enriched her moreover with gifts and invisible treasures, and investing her with the consecrated robe of immortality, joined her in wedlock unto Himself, dowered her with spiritual and eternal wealth, and decorated her with the heavenly crown which fadeth not away. Happy is the bride affianced to such a husband in an union in which modesty is ever green, and yet fertility is granted, in which the house is filled with children, and yet virginity maintained inviolate. The Holy Ghost, in admiration of the beauty of this queen, crieth aloud, 'Who is she that cometh forth as the morning rising, fair as the moon, bright as the sun, terrible as an army set in array?' And the prophet saith, 'The queen stood on thy right hand in gilded clothing; surrounded with variety.' And a little afterwards: 'After her shall virgins be brought to the king: her neighbours shall be brought to Thee.' Rightly therefore doth the whole world meet and conspire to pay homage to so great a dignity, and all human loftiness is humbled before her; the kings and potentates of all the earth exult in doing homage to her, and in a happy exchange buy of her things eternal with things temporal, heavenly blessings with those of earth. Lavishly do the kings of earth bestow their temporal goods on the holy Church, and after the example of the King of kings, who enlightens her by His grace within, prepare for her external necessaries. Which thing I, Henry the King, son of William the King, laying to heart, am bent myself also on doing service to my holy mother the Church, and have honoured her with a portion of the substance which I received by hereditary right from my predecessors. Therefore in the church of the Holy Trinity of Norwich have I given unto God, and to Herbert the Bishop and his successors, and to the monks who in the said church serve God, and shall hereafter serve Him there, my manor of Thorpe with all its appurtenances, with my sac and soc [*], and all my customary rents and payments, as freely as either I or my father ever held the same in our own hands at the time when we held it most securely. And this I have done in my own soul's behalf, and in behalf of the soul of my father and mother, and of William the King, my brother, and of all my predecessors and successors, in the presence of Queen Matilda, daughter of the King of Scotland, and of the illustrious men of all England, ecclesiastics and seculars, whose names are underwrit: and that my donation may continue to perpetuity, I have confirmed

---

[*] The Saxon word *sac*, from which comes the German word *sache* and the English word *sake*, meant contention, discord, a suit at law, a meaning still retained in the German phrase *eines Sache führen*, "to plead one's cause." As a legal term, it signifies the privilege enjoyed by the lord of a manor of holding courts for his tenants, trying causes, and imposing fines. *Soc*, or *soke*, is connected with the Latin *sequor* and the English *seek*. It, too, signifies the right of holding a court in a certain district, though it is sometimes applied to the district in which the court is held. The surrender of *sac* and *soc* to any one receiving a grant of land, was virtually giving him all manorial rights over the district.

my moan; here I entreat you with passionate entreaties, and with all the urgency of which I am capable, that you would not allow your church to forfeit that freedom from burdens, which hitherto by the king's favour and your advice she hath enjoyed inviolate. Give charge, I pray you, that Thorpe may be undisturbed, as it has been in times past, or at least grant a truce until our lord the king come hither; or, at all events, if it cannot be arranged otherwise, grant a considerable delay, during which I may send to our lord the king, and throw myself upon his compassion. In making these concessions and following them up, I have full confidence that by the Lord's fatherly kindness our lady the queen will help you. Surely, you will not find her difficult to move, since of her own compassion she has acted to me a mother's

---

it with the sign of the holy cross, and have ratified it with the seal of my royal dignity."

The date of this deed of gift is then assigned September 3, 1101. The names appended to the Charter are, of the royal family, Henry, Matilda, and Robert, Duke of Normandy; of the prelates, Anselm of Canterbury, Gerard of York, and nine suffragans, John Bishop of Tusculum, legate of the Pope, and Tiberius, chamberlain of Pope Paschal. After the above follow the words "At Windsor. May God who worketh all things in the saints, and to whom kings offer gifts beginning at Jerusalem, confirm this deed of gift." Then come the names of nine earls, of Eudo and Hamo the Seneschals, William the Butler, and six personages whose offices are not indicated. Then the names of the abbots of Westminster, Gloucester, Battle, York, Ramsey, Chertsey, St. Alban's, and Ely (the renowned Abbot Richard, of whom so much has been said above), Roger the Chancellor, (at that time not risen to the height of power which he had attained when Herbert addressed to him the letter before us), seven Chaplains, Herbert the royal Chamberlain, Peter Walonensis, and William of Warelwast.

⁷ "the repeated writs on the same subject"—*iterata brevia*. The word *breve* seems exactly equivalent to our word *writ*. In the case before us, these repeated *brevia* probably took the form of royal precepts against the levying of any assessments, whether of men or of money, on Thorpe. Ducange tells us that it is a moot point whether the Latin writers ever used the neuter gender of *brevis* without a substantive, and that Gruter proposes in certain passages, where *breve* seems to stand as a substantive, to read *brevem*, agreeing with *libellum*, understood. We suppose that this remark will hold only of classical Latin, early or late; for the instances in medieval Latin of *breve* used as a substantive are legion.

part, and has the advantage on every occasion of the advice which you can give her. I live, therefore, if you will but give these orders, and with continual tears I implore the mercy of Jesus our Saviour that you may be disposed to give them. A certain brother of ours is about to petition you for mercy to his brother, who is in gaol. Let me entreat you to listen to his earnest prayer with the same compassion with which you desire that your own prayers should be listened to by God."

The year 1107, the events of which we are at present chronicling, was one full of interest and activity for Herbert. This was the year, it will be remembered, in which Roger Bigot, Earl of Norfolk, died on the feast of the Nativity of the Blessed Virgin (Sept. 8), eight days after he had founded and endowed the Abbey of Thetford, and decreed its exemption from all jurisdiction save that of the Abbot of Clugni. This exemption no doubt was unpalatable to Herbert, though he was obliged so far to humour the greatest of East Anglian nobles as to present himself at the laying of the foundation-stone, and to witness the foundation charter. But Roger being dead, the good bishop, released from the restraint of his influence, not unnaturally perhaps showed a little temper. As already related by anticipation (in p. 166, note k), he ordered the Earl's body to Norwich, for interment in the Cathedral, contrary to the desire expressed by the deceased a little before his death, which was to the effect that he should lie in the Abbey of Thetford; refused the most urgent entreaties of the widow and of the Prior of Thetford (made, we are told,

A.D. 1107.

Death of Roger Bigot.

Dispute of Herbert with the Prior of Thetford with reference to Roger's burial.

A.D. 1107. on bended knees) to restore the corpse; alleged on oath, when an action for its recovery was brought against him by the Prior, that Roger had given himself and his family to the church of Norwich; and succeeded in procuring the interment to be made in some part of Norwich Cathedral. (It has often been supposed that the square aperture immediately under the relics of the Norman bishop's throne was in fact a window giving light to the vault in which Earl Roger was laid; but in recent explorations of that part of the church no traces whatever of a vault have been discovered.)

Part of the Cathedral in which the burial took place, unknown.

But the year, as we have said, was full of activity for Herbert, as well as of interest. It must have been, we think (and we desire to speak very undogmatically on such obscure points as the dates of mediæval chronology), in this year, or thereabouts, that our bishop was employed on a most important and difficult embassy. William of Warelwast had returned from the mission (on which Anselm had employed him) to the court of Rome, the object of which was to come to some understanding with the sovereign pontiff on the subject of lay-investitures. The mission had been a failure. The pope temporised. He earnestly desired to keep well with the king, while at the same time he could not yield the point of lay-investiture which the king sought to carry. Warelwast was charged with a civil letter from Pascal to Henry, which, though couched in friendly phrases, meant nothing, while at the same time

Failure of Warelwast's embassy to the papal court.

he was instructed to forbid the archbishop to submit to the investiture. Then the quarrel broke out afresh. The king threatened that no man should remain in his kingdom who would not do homage to him as suzerain. Anselm defied him, refused the homage, and yet remained in the kingdom.

The bishops, who, almost to a man, took the king's side in this quarrel, suggested a second embassy to Rome. And it shews their confidence in our Herbert that he, with the Bishop of Chester, and Gerard[1], Archbishop of York, was

A.D. 1107.

Herbert with other ecclesiastics appointed to represent the king on the second embassy.

[1] Dean Hook (Archbishops of Cant., ii. 248) tells us that the embassy consisted of the Bishops of Norwich and *Lichfield*, with the Archbishop elect of York. (By the Archbishop elect we suppose that he must mean Thomas II., who was appointed to the archbishopric in the succeeding year.) We know not what is his authority for this statement, and being ignorant of it, prefer to take Eadmer's account of the embassy, who says distinctly that it consisted of Girardus (*de Herefordensi nuper factus archiepiscopus Eboracensis*), Herbertus Theodfordensis, and *Robertus Cestrensis*. As to Dean Hook's mentioning the Bishop of Lichfield, whereas Eadmer says that it was Robert of Chester, this seeming discrepancy admits of an easy reconciliation. Earl Hugh, surnamed the Wolf, having restored the monastic church of Chester, and filled it with monks in the year 1094, Peter, Bishop of Lichfield, transferred thither his Cathedral from Lichfield. But Robert of Limesey, Peter's successor, left Chester, and fixed the see at Coventry, which soon after however was brought back to Lichfield again. Chester was not made a regular Cathedral church till Henry VIII. converted the monastery into a Cathedral. Godwin tells us that the bishops of Coventry were commonly called bishops of Chester, down to the erection of the see of Coventry; and therefore this Robert may have continued to take his title from Chester, though his see was not there, but at Lichfield. Herbert's being called bishop of Thetford so long after he had removed his see to Norwich [*], as the reader may have observed is the case also in one of the extracts given above (p. 220) from the *Liber Eliensis*, is similarly to be explained from the fact that the East Anglian see, having been for some time located at Thetford, did not drop that name for some time after in popular parlance. The East Anglian bishop was still bishop of Thetford, though in formal and legal documents he would be called Norwicensis.

[*] In Eadmer's notice of the consecration of Samson to Worcester and Gerard to Hereford, Herbert (who was one of the consecrators) is strangely called *Robertus Tydfordensis seu Norwicensis*. (Hist. Nov., p. 45.)

A.D. 1107. selected to represent the king upon an embassy so delicate and difficult. Two monks, Baldwin of Bec and Alexander of Canterbury, were deputed by Anselm to act as *his* representatives. The king's envoys were directed to address more decided language to the pope, warning him that Peter-pence would be withdrawn, communion with Rome broken off, and the archbishop banished, unless he rescinded the decree of the synod of 1076, and consented, in this instance, to lay-investiture. But this embassy was no more successful than Warelwast's mission had been. The pope was still evasive and shifty. He wrote a letter to Anselm, commending his zeal for the papal cause; and another to the king, which Henry suppressed; while to the latter he also sent a verbal message by the bishops, assuring him that if he would only be careful to appoint devout prelates, the court of Rome would never interfere with his appointments. This two-faced answer left the parties as much at issue as it found them. The king's party quoted the verbal message, as meaning that he might compel Anselm to receive investiture without any interference on Pascal's part. The archbishop's letter, in which Anselm was thanked for his steadfast maintenance of papal claims, of course encouraged him to maintain them more stoutly than ever. Much must the ambassadors (our bishop among them) have been harassed by inquiries as to the exact terms of a message, which it was part of Pascal's policy not to put in black and white.

The course taken by the pope still evasive.

It will relieve and gratify the reader to have A.D. 1107. the result of this embassy of the three bishops and two monks, given in Dean Church's vigorous and lively narrative; and we therefore subjoin his account, only adding that as Dean Church takes Anselm's part very warmly in his disputes with the king, he naturally looks with little favour upon those who, like our bishop, rather took the side of royalty.

"A curious transaction followed. On the return of the envoys, an assembly of the great men was summoned in London, and Anselm was again required by messengers from the king to submit to the 'usages.' But the Pope's letter to the king was not made public. Anselm showed to every one who chose to see it the letter which he had himself received, and asked that the letter to the king should be made known. But Henry refused; he put aside the Pope's reply as irrelevant, and, throwing himself on his own rights, required unconditional submission. Meanwhile the Pope's letter to the king got abroad. Then occurred a scene, which is like nothing so much as some of the passages in Napoleon's negotiations through the bishops of his party with Pius VII. The Archbishop of York and his brethren, the Bishops of Chester and Thetford, announced what they declared on the faith of bishops to be the real result of their embassy. The Pope, they said, in a private interview, had charged them with a verbal message to the king, that so long as he acted as a good king and appointed religious prelates, the Pope would not enforce the decrees against investiture. And the reason, they said, why he could not give this privilege in writing was lest, if it became public, other princes might use it to the prejudice of the Roman see. They also, equally on their faith and honour as bishops, conveyed, in the Pope's name, his commands to Anselm to

Dean Church's account of the proceedings on the return of the envoys.

A.D. 1107. give them full credit and follow their counsel. If he refused, the king might act as he pleased on the Pope's authority, in spite of Anselm, and might, if Anselm still insisted on the Pope's letter, banish him from the kingdom. This strange story took every one by surprise, and called forth immediate remonstrance from Anselm's representatives. They had heard nothing of the message, which was utterly inconsistent with everything which had passed in public between them and the Pope. When the bishops insisted that the Pope's language was one thing in public, and another to themselves in a private interview, Baldwin indignantly charged them with breaking their canonical oaths and making the apostolic see infamous. But they held to their story, and there was a strong division of opinion and hot altercation in the excited assembly. When one side insisted on the authority of the actual document, sealed with the Pope's signet, the rejoinder was fierce and insolent. The word of these bishops ought to weigh more than parchments—'sheepskins with a lump of lead at the bottom,' backed by the testimony of 'paltry monks, who, when they renounced the world, lost all weight as evidence in secular business.' 'But this is no secular business,' said Baldwin. 'We know you,' was the reply, 'to be a man of sense and vigour; but difference of rank itself requires us to set more by the testimony of an archbishop and two bishops than by yours.' 'But what of the testimony of the letters?' he asked. He was answered with a sneer; 'When we refuse to receive the testimony of monks against bishops, how could we receive that of sheepskins?' 'Woe! woe!' burst forth from the shocked and excited monks, 'are not the Gospels written on sheepskins*?'"

Hitherto we have spoken of our bishop's conduct on this embassy in his public capacity. But Eadmer informs us that he, as well as the arch-

* P. 260, &c.

bishop of York, had private affairs of their own A.D. 1107. at Rome, and went thither on their account no less than on the king's. The archbishop wanted to secure the *pall*, without which he could not enter on his functions [b] as a metropolitan. Herbert wished to gain from the pope an acknowledgment of his episcopal rights over the abbey of St. Edmund's Bury. Ever since the foundation of that abbey the abbots had been engaged in an internecine war of independence against the bishops of the East Anglian See. In the reign of the Conqueror it seemed as if they had carried their point. Abbot Baldwin had gone to Rome, and obtained from the wearer of the tiara (Alexander II., 1061—1073) the exemption of St. Edmund's Abbey from all episcopal control, saving always the obedience due to the metropolitical see of Canterbury. Lanfranc, says Eadmer, took offence at this step of Abbot Baldwin's (upon

Private ends which Herbert had to serve at Rome.

---

[b] The pall, as a privilege in the exclusive gift of the pope, plays a very important part in the history of the struggles between the Norman kings and the papacy. It is a part of the pontifical dress worn only by the pope, archbishops, and patriarchs. An heraldic representation of it may be seen in the arms of the sees of Canterbury, Armagh, and Dublin. It is a woollen band worn over the shoulders and crossed in front, with one end hanging down over the breast, and thus exhibiting, when worn, the form of a Y. It is made of the wool of white sheep, which are yearly offered and blessed in St. Agnes' church on St. Agnes' day. The pope wears it on every occasion of his officiating; but archbishops and patriarchs can only wear it in their own churches on solemn occasions. Before an archbishop has received it from Rome, and paid for it, he cannot exercise an archiepiscopal function, such as holding a provincial visitation, or summoning a provincial council. It was decreed in the Lateran Council, A.D. 1215, under Innocent III., to be a symbol of the plenitude of apostolic power, and not capable of transmission from one archbishop to another;—each new archbishop must receive his pall from the pope afresh. This council, however, did nothing but reduce to a system of definite rules usages respecting the pall which had been growing up long previously.

A.D. 1107. which he had not been consulted), and at first showed his displeasure by disallowing altogether the papal exemption, and refusing to acknowledge the privilege of St. Edmund's. Towards the end of his life, however, he thought better of his opposition to the abbey. By the entreaties of his friends he was induced to append his signature to an instrument, securing the independence of St. Edmund's Abbey, which was formally executed by the king and many of his nobles and prelates. This, one would have thought, might have sufficed to set the question at once and for ever at rest. But the East Anglian bishops were always seeking, notwithstanding this decision, to bring under their control this splendid monastery, an opulent little city of itself[e], the abbot of which was a prince, whose estates and retainers made him more than the equal of the proudest baron in the realm. The monkish chroniclers belonging to such a foundation would love to trick out

Jurisdiction over St. Edmund's Abbey eagerly coveted by the East Anglian bishops.

---

[e] Leland, quoted by Alban Butler, says of the Abbey of St. Edmund's, in the town of St. Edmundsbury; "The sun hath not seen either a city more finely seated, or a goodlier abbey, whether a man consider the revenues and endowments, or the largeness and the incomparable magnificence thereof. A man who saw the abbey would say, verily, it was a city; so many gates there are in it, and some of brass; so many towers, and a most stately church, upon which attend three other churches, also standing gloriously in the same churchyard, all of passing fine and curious workmanship."

"The monastery of St. Edmundsbury," observes Mr. Yates, "has been generally supposed to have exceeded in magnificent buildings, splendid decorations, important privileges, valuable immunities, and ample endowments, all other ecclesiastic and monastic establishments in England, Glastonbury alone excepted."

The Psalter from which St. Edmund learned the Psalms by heart (having retired for that purpose to his royal tower of Hunstanton) was preserved in this abbey until the dissolution of monasteries.

with marvels any and every failure to reduce their *A.D. 1107.*
house to a state of dependence on any suffragan
bishop. And we confess that, to our ears, the whole
narrative of Herbert's failure has a fabulous sound.
Doubtless it may have a foundation of truth. Our *Probable*
bishop may have been unduly elated by the smooth *reasons for Herbert's*
and prosperous course which things had taken *attempt upon the*
with him lately. His cathedral was finished and *liberties of St. Ed-*
consecrated; its charter was sealed; the king and *mund's Abbey.*
queen had shewn him marks of favour, which he,
no doubt, appreciated at their full value. "His
heart was lifted up," and he thought he would endeavour to revive an old claim of jurisdiction over
the most famous of East Anglian abbeys, which,
if it could be established, would leave him and
his successors absolutely without an ecclesiastical
rival in that part of the kingdom. The proposal
made by the bishops that he should go on an embassy to the pope, and represent the king's interests at Rome, seemed marvellously to favour his
design. As one of Henry's representatives he
would have great weight with the pope. A prelate entrusted with so grave an embassy was not
one whom Pascal could afford to offend; and his
knowledge of the world taught him that a sum
of money carried with him, and judiciously distributed at the papal court, might materially further his views; though we confess to feeling both
surprise and regret that the repentance manifested
by him for his former simoniacal proceedings did
not keep him back from an offence of a somewhat
similar nature. But if indeed he contemplated

A.D. 1107. bribery, he was made to smart for it. Eadmer says that he travelled fast, and left his companions behind, and had reached Burgundy, and had come into the province of Lyons, when he and his retinue fell into the hands of Count Guido and were made prisoners. The charge made against him was, that he was bound on an errand injurious to Anselm, his spiritual chief and metropolitan. This Herbert denied, and with reason; for the going on an embassy to lay before the pope the king's view of the question pending between him and the primate, could not be said to be injurious to the latter. But his most solemn denial went for nothing; and he was required, as a condition of his release, to swear upon the relics of the saints that he would not wittingly do anything at Rome at all derogatory to the honour, or contrary to the wishes, of Anselm. Having made this oath, he was set at liberty, but told that he must ransom his retainers, if he wished them to accompany him. Thus was extorted from him the sum of money (about forty marks, it is said,) which he had brought from England for the purpose of facilitating his access to the pope; and he rejoined his brethren on their embassy a stripped and humbled man. One of the chroniclers adds, that on Herbert's return to England a council was held by Anselm, at which the question of jurisdiction over St. Edmund's was discussed and examined, and that on the abbot's producing evidence of the former decree of exemption in the Conqueror's time, under the primacy of Lan-

He falls into the hands of Count Guido, and is imprisoned;

but released on paying down, as the ransom of his retainers, the sum which he had brought from England, wherewith to purchase the jurisdiction over St. Edmund's. Anselm holds a council, at which the independence of

franc, it was decreed *nem. con.* that the abbey was to hold its privilege against all occupants of the East Anglian see. And thenceforth "the aforesaid Herbert dared not, while he lived, so much as to wag his tongue against the Church of St. Edmund; and so he utterly failed in his unrighteous cause through the merits of the blessed Edmund^d."

<small>St. Edmund's is finally decreed.</small>

And if so crushing a disappointment and calamity fell upon Herbert at this time, we may perhaps suppose the following letters to contain, the one a figurative description of his condition on his return to his country, the other an expostulation with a fair-weather friend (probably Abbot Richard of Ely), who, in that hour of adversity, had turned his back on our bishop.

<small>Herbert's frantic expression of disappointment.</small>

LETTER XII.

HERBERT TO NORMAN THE OSTIARY.

"Unmindful of the accidents which befall man, like an improvident pilot, I have been thrown ashore on a foreign and barbarous realm. I trusted in the soft breeze, and the calm sea deceived and made me venturesome. I was ignorant of the quicksands, and took no precautions against the rocks which lay hid [in my course]; pirates were [in those seas], but I knew not of them; and my hold being broken, the water^e entered, and swamped my frail bark. I have not escaped Charybdis, no nor yet Scylla; I have been swallowed by

<small>Herbert, in an hysterical fit of anguish over some disaster which he describes figuratively as a shipwreck, admits at length that he was himself in fault, and turns his grief into repentance.</small>

^d The account of Herbert's misadventure, from which these words are taken, is given in a cartulary of the Abbey of St. Edmund, an extract from which is found in a MS. book belonging to the deanery of Norwich, in the handwriting of Dean Prideaux.

^e *fractâ sentinâ latex ingrediens.* The poetical word for water, which is here used, may serve in some measure to corroborate our hypothesis, that this is a figurative description of Herbert's calamity.

them, but not as yet vomited forth from them. The softness of the breeze and the pleasantness of the sea are changed. I am driven by frightful blasts of the south-west wind, and running before the gale through the swelling waves, and doomed to be dashed against Palinurus¹, I look forth upon my death which is now imminent. Here is grief, here is wailing, here that last and most to be deprecated of all ills, despair! Ah me! from what shores have I been [cruelly] torn asunder, and into what a ruinous shipwreck have I unhappily been entrapped. The one pursuit of my youth and of my old age has been frustrated. The wealth which I had amassed by watching, by exposure to cold, and to sweltering heat, I have all lost by one shipwreck. Through the breaking up of my ship I have lost my [goodly] raiment, my pearls, and all the precious wares with which I proposed to trade; the sea has the wealth which I amassed; and my barbarian enemy is in possession of the costly spoils which I have gathered together. Oh wretched lot incident to human life! Oh the shocking vicissitudes to which human affairs are subject! Once I shone in [all the pride and circumstance of] wealth, and was filled to the full with every possible luxury; lo!

---

¹ "doomed to be dashed against Palinurus"—*Palinuro illidendus*. Herbert is fond of displaying his classical knowledge. He has not forgotten his Virgil. Palinurus was a promontory on the coast of Lucania, subject to sudden and violent storms, and having an ill name among the Romans, from two great naval disasters in their history of which it had been the scene. Whole fleets had been wrecked there. It took its name from Palinurus, a mythical character, the pilot of the ship of Æneas, who fell into the sea at that spot, and was washed ashore and buried there. Thus naval disaster was associated with the mythology as well as the history of the spot. According to Virgil's poem, Palinurus afterwards met Æneas when he descended into the infernal regions, and requested him to scatter earth upon his body. Æneas consoled him with the somewhat shadowy comfort that expiatory rites should be performed to his manes, a mound erected, and games instituted in his honour. See Æn., v. 833, vi. 337. Our good bishop, half-frantic with despair, becomes a little slipshod in his writing. It does not seem to strike him that his being swallowed up by Charybdis is hardly compatible with his running aground on Palinurus.

now I sit here a poor shipwrecked mariner, cast out upon the seaweed of a foreign strand, and behold the swords of the barbarians hanging over my neck. And in good sooth, the more excellent and pleasant were the things I have lost, so much the heavier and more dismal is the grief which overwhelms me; my day is turned into dark night, and the night, by my wakefulness, turned into day. All hope of revisiting my country has died away; and I, an outcast on a foreign soil, find life and death indifferent to me. I had conceived, I had brought forth, I had given suck [to my offspring] with nourishment more genial than that which is drawn from mothers' breasts. Like a nurse I was [fondly] embracing the cradle, as I sat on the dunghill, and drawing forth the milk from my very vitals; I was giving sustenance enough to my crying babe. Yes, in good truth, I was turning my meat into flesh, my flesh into blood, my blood into food, preparing, as I have said, from my own vitals, nourishment sufficient for my own progeny. But whence have I a right to complain? Shall I vow vengeance on the winds? But it was I who, in my imprudence, committed a small and heavily-laden bark to blasts of which I had made no trial. I ought to have discerned what weather it was likely to be; I ought to have marked the changefulness of the clouds. Navigation [doubtless] is in itself dangerous, but most especially if it be conducted by an incautious pilot. Incautious man, why do you lay the blame on the risks of foreign travel? Why do you condemn the elements, and not rather reprove your own conscience, you who weakly deplore with such bitterness the treasures which you had not the manly discretion to keep safe? The sun has arisen upon the secret places of your conscience, and in your own soul within you have found the [true] source of tears, which once you fancied to be in external circumstances. Away with all laying of the blame on external things; let there be on my part no further condemnation of the sea, none of Scylla or

Charybdis. Dear Jesus, Thou hadst entrusted unto me Thy Sacraments, Thou hadst revealed unto me Thy secrets, I was guardian of the living waters, which purge away the sullage of the soul; I distributed the ministrations of Thy Spirit; I made Thy Body and Blood. Great were these privileges, and my sinful soul was all unworthy of them. Thou hast laid the foundation of Thy Church; Thou hast set up her walls; Thou hast compacted the roof thereof from above; from Thee have flowed to me all blessings, while from my own careless want of forethought my present troubles have sprung. But now, my soul, restraining thy digressions, return to thy tears, and delight thyself in thy [penitential] anguish. Let the pang, wherewith Christ pricketh [the heart], abide in thee; let those tears flow on, wherewith the Holy Spirit waters [the barren and dry land of the soul]; the cry of the heart pierceth the sky, and devout weeping unbars the gates of the divine mercy. David and Peter both of them sinned; both of them did penance; both blotted out their sin with their tears; and thus it came to pass that David sitteth on [the throne of] his kingdom, and Peter in the chair of the apostolic senate. Verily He was a gentle Master who before [Peter's] denial [of Him] had said, 'Whatsoever thou shalt bind on earth shall be bound in heaven,' and after the denial said further to the same Apostle; 'Peter, feed My sheep;' so as to shew Peter that he had not lost, through his timid denial, the grace which he had before won through his bold confession of the truth. These things, beloved brother, have I touched upon to thee in brief sum, that you may understand both the severe discipline which [g] is to be used with

See St. Matt. xix. 28.

St. Matt. xvi. 19, V.

From St. John xxi. 17.

[g] We think it clear that Norman the Ostiary must have held some position, which made it incumbent upon him to exercise ecclesiastical discipline. This is apparent not only from the passage before us, but also from Letter VI. p. 155 et seqq., in which Herbert says to him; "Observe, dear brother, the point to which my endeavours are directed, *and the discipline with which I wish you to be furnished in your ministry;*"—indeed, the letter begins with a vindication of Herbert's own ecclesiastical censures, as being not unduly severe. We learn from it also, that Norman, at the time of its

offenders, and the compassionate gentleness to be applied to penitents. For the more mad in cruelty Paul was in his unconverted state, so much the more fervent was he after his conversion, and so much the more abundantly did our holy religion profit by him. After which example every good man rises up from his falls all the more bravely, in proportion as he feels himself to have wandered more weakly from the truth. And hence it is written; Even unto Babylon shalt thou pass over, and there shalt thou be delivered. A marvellous thing! In Jerusalem she is taken captive, and in the captivity of Babylon she is set free. But this is the high privilege of him only, who even in the confusion [of face] incurred by sin is not unmindful of the true God [h]." ... *Collated.*

From Micah iv. 10. The Prophet is speaking of the daughter of Zion.

being addressed to him, was aspiring to the priesthood. Perhaps, when he received the letter now before us, he may have been an ordained priest, and may be still called Ostiary, possibly from having once served in that capacity (cp. the appellations Simon the leper, Matthew the publican), or from the circumstance of his retaining still the office of porter in the monastery. Some of these porters must have been ordained, else how could they ever have been raised to the dignity of abbot, as we are told they occasionally were; (see p. 83, note x.)?

[h] We subjoin a sentence at the end of this letter which, as it stands in the Brussels MS., is, we think, untranslateable. It runs thus: "Et alia manu scripta tibi et tuis familiaribus rescripta perscriptis exigo." The only solution we can suggest is that the words "alia manu" were originally a marginal remark of the scribe, which by negligence has found its way into the text, and which means that in the MS. which he was transcribing the final sentence was written in a different hand. If this be so, and if we were suffered to eliminate the word "perscriptis," we might suppose the meaning to be, "I expect an answer to the letters which I have addressed to you and to your friends." The last word of the letter is "Contuli," for the meaning of which see p. 13, note h.

A good deal of Herbert's character transpires in this somewhat hysterical letter. First of all, there is that exceeding sensitiveness of soul which takes trouble so much to heart, and which we have noticed in previous letters. Then, again, there is the great redeeming trait of his character,— the way in which this sensitiveness helped forward and deepened his personal repentance, flowed in the channel which grace had carved out for it, and was thus preserved from being the mere frantic self-laceration of the natural man.

LETTER X.

To Richard the Abbot.

"Herbert to Richard the Abbot.

<small>Herbert remonstrates with Abbot Richard for having turned his back on him in adversity, and begs to be recognised as a friend once more, now that brighter days shine on him.</small>

"The great waves of difficulty, which during the present year have tossed and battered my weak little bark, cannot I think have escaped your Paternity, who have sate securely on the shore and looked forth upon my toil in rowing and my cruel shipwreck. Several misfortunes have combined against me; but those disturb my mind most bitterly, which steal from me the reciprocal affection of those on whom my love is set[1]. A grievous hardship it is, and more intolerable than the waves themselves, that with the change of my affairs the friendship [of my friends] has also undergone a change. I am become an alien to my mother's children, and am banished from the eyes of my friends, to whom, while I was safe and my own master, I was acceptable as a sweet-smelling perfume. Such is the way of the human heart; such the fickleness with which men's minds are swayed hither and thither. The only point in our fortunes to which any respect is paid is our prosperity; when that takes its departure, everything else flies away; the only man who is loved is he who has something; when he is deprived of his resources, men know him no more; so altogether true is that verse of the poet's;

---

[1] *quæ meo amori meorum amatorum redamorem subripiunt.* Herbert has coined the substantive *redamor* (reciprocal affection), very much as he found Cicero coining the verb *redamo* in his treatise *De amicitia.* "Quid enim tam absurdum, quam delectari multis inanibus rebus, ut gloria, ædificio, vestitu; animo autem virtute prædito, qui vel amare, vel ut ita dicam, redamare possit, non admodum delectari?" The *ut ita dicam,* as Forcellinus remarks, shows that Cicero did not altogether approve of the word *redamo,* or at all events, that it was but little used in his time. Our Herbert evidently likes alliteration and the repetition of cognate words, as we saw just now in that enigmatical sentence at the close of the last letter, "scripta tibi et tuis familiaribus rescripta perscriptis exigo."

"Friends shall flow in, an ample shoal,
With Fortune's flowing tide;
But when the angry sky doth scowl,
Thou shalt alone abide [j]."

Long could I declaim [against the unkindness of my friends]; many are the reproaches which I could vent [k]; but I will restrain my pen, and hold in my tongue, though sharpened for reproof, lest I should seem to be making an onslaught on you, and to be finding fault with your neglect of me,—you who in the present year have not even seen your friend (that is to say, your own bowels), nor have greeted him in your letters, nor have consoled him with the living accents of your voice [l]. Yet

See Philemon 12.

---

[j] From Ovid's *Tristia*, i. 8. 5, 6, "Cum fueris" being substituted for "Donec eris."

[k] *digna eructuarem convitia.* The word is *eructo* (to throw up or vomit forth), but Herbert spells it *eructuo*, which is the case also in the immediately preceding letter, where we had *deliciarum omnium eructuabam abundantiam.* This may be a slight incidental proof that the two letters were written about the same time, which indeed is apparent from their argument, Herbert's calamity being spoken of in both of them as a shipwreck.

[l] If the abbot to whom this letter was addressed was, as we have supposed, Abbot Richard of Ely, in whose new abbey church Herbert had preached so touching a sermon at the translation of Etheldreda, on the incorruptibility of her person, that all the audience burst into tears of joy, and first among whose guests on that notable occasion is enumerated "vir laudabilis, Herbertus Norwicensis episcopus," we think our bishop had reason to complain of the abbot's turning his back upon him in adversity. This Abbot Richard was, according to the *Liber Eliensis*, of royal extraction on both sides. He received his education at Bec, became a proficient in philosophy as well as theology, and was advanced by King Henry to the abbacy of Ely. The Bishop of Lincoln claimed the right of giving him benediction upon his appointment, but he resisted the claim, and unlike other abbots received no episcopal benediction at all. But, like the abbot of Canterbury in the old ballad, the king found Richard too powerful and magnificent for a subject. He appeared at court with too stately a retinue; and the collateral members of his family, the Richards and Giffards, gathered round him there in a little galaxy of nobility which might well make the proudest sovereign somewhat afraid of him. He was no reed shaken by the wind, says his monastic biographer, that he should waver beneath the breath of princes. Accordingly, the king, upon some trivial pretext, deposed him, and thus suspended for a time the work of building the new abbey church upon which his predecessor had entered.

he had entered with you, and you mutually with him, into so close a covenant, that this union of hearts ought never to have been sundered, or even disturbed, by adversities. But now, when more propitious gales are blowing, and the course of our affairs has taken a turn for the better, take courage again, however reluctantly, acknowledge once more the friend who still loves you, and burying the past in oblivion, let your affection for me revive, and transform yourself once again into the friend who formerly lay in my bosom, even as I lay

He forthwith went to Rome to appeal against this judgment, and was reinstated by Pope Pascal in the dignity of which Henry had deprived him. He entertained a special devotion for St. Withburga, and, according to the monastic chronicler, found his account therein when his last moments approached. After confessing and receiving the viaticum, Withburga appeared to him, and he bade the brethren retire from him; "for," said he, "my lady Withburga comes; lo! she stands by me, do ye not see her? O lady, have mercy upon me," and so he passed away. Richard's never having received benediction is regarded by the monastic chronicler as a kind of omen that the abbey would be converted into an episcopal see, and that the offices of bishop and abbot would be united in one person. This change was made after Richard's death, Hervè le Breton, his successor, being made first bishop of Ely, and a slice of the enormous diocese of Lincoln being assigned to him. The abbot-bishop, however, still continued to sit in the right-hand stall at the entrance of the choir, where he had sat when simple abbot. And this arrangement continues at the present day, the bishop of Ely occupying that stall, which in other cathedrals is occupied by the Dean. Richard ruled the abbey from 1100 to 1107, so that if our chronology is at all correct, he must have died shortly after this letter reached him. His great zeal for the regulars as against the seculars, a zeal which in Herbert's judgment led him to depreciate the latter, comes out in another letter addressed by Herbert to him, which we shall present in a different connexion. It is however quite possible that this Richard of Ely may not be the abbot whom Herbert here addresses. In the account of the translation of Etheldreda, already extracted from the *Liber Eliensis*, we find that there was a Richard, abbot of St. Alban's, who was present at the translation; and the Rev. S. Griffith, Rector of Sandridge, near St. Alban's, has sent us an extract, (found in his baptismal register,) from Newcourt's *Repertorium Ecclesiasticum*, published in 1708, to this effect; "The church at Sandridge (which was consecrated and dedicated to St. Leonard by Herbert, Bishop of Norwich, under the denomination of a chapel) was of old, it seems, appropriated to the same monastery" (of St. Alban's), "and a vicarage endowed." This is evidence of a connexion between Herbert and St. Alban's, which it is hard to account for, but which shows that Richard, Abbot of St. Alban's, might have been his correspondent.

wholly in his. Send me your Josephus [m], which you have so often excused yourself from sending on the ground of the binding having come undone [n]. But now, as the book has been put to rights and bound, you have no longer any room to make up an excuse. Lend me the Epistles of Augustine and the Epistles of Jerome, either

[m] Our bishop was, for one of his time, a man of very considerable attainments. The reader may here refer to Letter V. p. 64, where he requests the Abbot of Fécamp to get Suetonius transcribed for him. Josephus, we imagine, was a book less generally known among mediæval divines of his time, than any of the regular classics. So very rare were the instances of learned men in the Western Empire knowing Greek (see Hallam's "Middle Ages," vol. ii. p. 522), that we must suppose Herbert to have read Josephus in a Latin translation. Indeed, the first printed edition of Josephus, which seems to have contained only a portion of the Antiquities, was a Latin translation without notice of the place or date of publication.

On the *commercium librorum* system of exchanging loans of books, which went on among learned men in the Middle Ages, see Maitland's "Dark Ages," p. 441, and note F, p. 502, where many instances of it are given. Among others, an amusing one in which Abbot Peter of Clugni asked the Prior of Chartreuse to lend him the volume of Augustine which contained the letters to and from St. Jerome, because a great part of his copy, while lying in one of the cells, had been accidentally eaten by a bear. The classical books for which we find applications in note F, referred to above, are Persius, Horace, Statius, Juvenal, and the *Liber Invectivarum Tullii Ciceronis in Sallustium*.

[n] *Correcto et ligato*. Mr. Maitland gives much curious information on the binding of mediæval books. He tells us that books, especially those used in the church service, were often "bound in, or covered with, plates of gold, silver, or carved ivory, adorned with gems, and even enriched with relics;" that "a certain Elector of Bavaria offered a whole town for a single MS., but that the monks, wisely considering that he could, and suspecting that he would, retake the town whenever he pleased, declined the exchange;" that Charlemagne, in 790, gave a right of hunting to the abbot and monks of Sithiu, that they might use the deer-skins for bookbinding. It may be added, that several monasteries had rules for the loan of their books. Thus, at Croyland, the smaller unbound volumes and the larger bound ones were distinctly forbidden to be lent to any far distant schools, without the leave of the abbot, and a distinct understanding as to the time at which they should be returned. "As to lending lesser books, however, such as Psalters, copies of Donatus, Cato, and the like poetical (?) works, and the singing lesson-books, to children and the relations of the monks, we strictly forbid the cantor, or any one who shall act as librarian, under pain of disobedience, to allow them to be lent for a longer space of time than one day, without leave of the Prior."—("Dark Ages," pp. 68, 204, 215, 266.)

one or both; I earnestly entreat you to do this; but yet more urgently still do I ask you to lend me one of the lectionaries, which, with your usual diligence, you have recently compiled.

"To demand these books from you I send Gregory, who is both your son and your serving brother, who will also communicate to you certain matters on which I have been silent in my letters, and will bring me back your answer."

<small>A.D. 1108.</small>

<small>Thomas II. appointed to the Archiepiscopal see of York.</small>

The next year, 1108, was marked by the death of Gerard, Archbishop of York, on the 21st of May. Thomas, the son (so says Bale; but Stubbs, the monastic chronicler, says more decorously, the nephew) of the elder Thomas, Gerard's predecessor, was appointed to succeed to the archiepiscopal see, but was not consecrated till the June of 1109. In the year which intervened between his appointment and his consecration, he appears as archbishop-designate on two important occasions, the latter of which associates him closely with our prelate. First, it appears that he

<small>While only archbishop-designate he joins Anselm in holding a synod.</small>

joined with Anselm in holding a synod at London, which doubtless was attended by the suffragans of both provinces (Herbert among them), the enactments of which were designed to make more stringent than heretofore the restraints of clerical celibacy. Dean Hook thus summarizes them (Vol. II. p. 264) :—

"They" (the clergy) "were forbidden to have in their houses any women, except near relations. Those who had married since the council of 1102 were to discard their wives, so entirely as not to be with them or to meet them, knowingly, even in a friend's house; if they had occasion to speak with them on business, it was to be in the presence of two witnesses; those who determined to remain with their wives were to be deprived of their benefices and put out of the choir, being first declared impious: archdeacons were to make oath that they would not take money to connive at the transgression of this statute: those who chose to leave their wives, who were styled adulterous concubines, were to undergo a penance at the bishop's discretion for forty days; during which time they might have vicars to officiate for them in their respective churches."

And now the course of events leads us to speak of another contest for ecclesiastical independence within the Church of England itself. The delay of Thomas's consecration to the archbishopric of York may be explained by the difference which arose between himself and Anselm,—a difference which, unhappily, the latter did not live to see composed. Instigated thereto by the monks of Canterbury, who were jealous of the prerogatives of their cathedral as the mother church of the whole realm, Anselm summoned Thomas to Canterbury for consecration, and required from him a profession of obedience to himself and his successors. Thomas consulted the king, who at first (probably from a feeling against Anselm) seemed favourably disposed to his claims of independence, and forbade him to make the required profession. In this complication of claims and interests, Herbert seems to have thought that he could be useful as a peacemaker. For this office we can quite conceive (from the tone of several of his letters, and from Cotton's description of his

A.D. 1108.

Anselm requires from Thomas a profession of obedience to the see of Canterbury, which Thomas, by the king's advice, declines.

A.D. 1108.

Herbert's qualifications for negotiating between the parties.

outer and inner man) that he was well qualified. His attractive looks and demeanour, his placid and radiant countenance, his discretion, integrity, modesty, and great tenderness of heart, would make him a suitable envoy of peace between prelates, each of whom insisted stoutly on his own claims. He had acquired an intimacy with Thomas from their recent employment on a common mission, and would be more acceptable to that prelate than any other suffragan of the southern province. So Anselm not unwisely fixed on him as his medium of communication with Thomas, and commissioned him to offer terms of accommodation. The Archbishop of Canterbury would dispense with the profession of obedience, if Thomas would only acknowledge him and his successors as Primates of the whole realm. Thomas, thinking doubtless that, in the king's then state of feeling towards Anselm, he might count upon royal support, demurred even to this compromise. And then Anselm would seem to have retracted his offer, and to have demanded the usual profession of obedience to the see of Canterbury in the following stern letter, given us by Eadmer (*Hist. Nov.*, lib. iv.) :—

"ANSELM, A SERVANT OF THE CHURCH OF CANTERBURY, TO THOMAS, ARCHBISHOP ELECT OF YORK.

Anselm, on his terms of accommodation being re-

"Unto thee, Thomas, in the sight of the Almighty God, do I Anselm, Archbishop of Canterbury, and Primate of all Britain, speak. Speaking on the part of God Himself, I interdict thee from the sacerdotal office, which thou didst receive in my diocese[o], and by my order, at the hands of my suffragan, and I enjoin thee that thou presume not to introduce thyself in any wise into any pastoral charge, until thou ceasest from that rebellion, which thou hast begun against the Church of Canterbury, and dost make that profession of subjection to it which thy predecessors,—Thomas, to wit, and Archbishop Gerard,—according to the ancient custom of their predecessors, did make. But if thou dost elect rather to persevere in what thou hast begun than to desist from it, I interdict all the bishops of the whole of Britain, on pain of a perpetual anathema, from any of them laying hands on thee to promote thee to the episcopate, or, if thou shalt be so promoted by aliens [to this Church and realm], from receiving thee as a bishop, or to any act of Christian communion. Thee also, Thomas, on pain of the same anathema, I interdict on the part of God from ever receiving consecration[p] to the bishopric of York, unless

rejected, interdicts Thomas from the exercise of the priesthood, and forbids any other English bishop to give him consecration.

---

[o] *in Parochiâ meâ.* The words *parish* and *diocese* have exchanged meanings, the first having in primitive times denoted the territory under the jurisdiction of a bishop, and the second the cure of a presbyter. *Parochia* (which, coming from the Greek παροικία, should rightly be spelt *parœcia*) meant (1) the company of Jews sojourning in a heathen city; (2) a company of Christianized Jews so sojourning, or even of Christianized Gentiles, whose faith and worship would be as strange to the heathen, in whose midst they dwelt, as that of the Jews themselves; (3) as Christianity spread, and Christians became more numerous, it came to mean "the towns or villages near a city, which, together with the city, was the bishop's παροικία, or, as we now call it, his *diocese.*" *Parœcia* was the only word denoting a diocese in the three first centuries (*diœcesis* not making its appearance before the fourth); and for ages afterwards (as we see by the letter before us), though also used to denote much more limited jurisdictions, it clung to the meaning it had originally borne. (See Bingham, *Ant.*, Book IX. chapter ii.). The word is specially interesting, as being one of the evidences furnished by language that Judaism was the cradle of Christianity.

[p] *ut nunquam benedictionem Episcopatûs Eboracensis suscipias. Benedictio* is the word specially appropriated to the consecration of an abbot, which was performed by the bishop of the diocese. It is often, however, used (as here) of the consecration of a *bishop*. Thus Dagobert, (King of France (A D. 628—638), the first monarch interred at St. Denis), writing to Archbishop Sulpitius requests "ut ad eum (*Desiderium*) *benedicendum* properare

thou first makest that profession [of obedience] to the Church of Canterbury which thy predecessors Thomas and Gerard made. If however thou shalt altogether resign the bishopric of York, I allow thee to exercise the sacerdotal office which thou hast already received."

A.D. 1108. A copy of this letter, sealed with his own seal, he sent to every bishop in England, enjoining them by the obedience which they owed to the Church of Canterbury, to bear themselves to Thomas according to the terms of it. The next event which Eadmer records of him is his death at Canterbury in the sixteenth year of his episcopate, and the seventy-sixth of his age. In July, 1108, he had a seizure which prevented him from giving to the king his benediction before his departure for Normandy, and necessitated his conveyance home to Canterbury. There he lingered in feeble health till the Friday of *A.D. 1109.* Passion Week, 1109, when he was confined to his bed. But though the outer man was perishing, his subtle mind was still at work, and he expressed himself to the effect that he only wished to live in order that he might solve a certain question, which long had occupied him, about the origin of the soul. His last conscious act, for which he roused himself by a strong effort, was to give his blessing to king and country, by making from his bed the sign of the cross. Thenceforth he sank into a stupor, till at the

Death of Anselm.

debeatis, et litteras ad comprovinciales fratres vestros dirigatis, ut et illi adesse debeant, ut canonice et juxta Apostolicam institutionem sub nostri præsentia in sancta Paschali solemnitate Pontificali *benedictione* debeat confirmari." (Du Cange, *s.v.* Benedictio.)

hour of Matins on the Wednesday in Holy Week, A.D. 1109. April 21, 1109, he ceased to breathe. The next day, Maundy Thursday, he was interred in his cathedral.

At the Whitsuntide following the death of the primate, the king, not sorry possibly to be relieved of Anselm's presence, held his Court with unusual splendour at London. And when the days of festivity and rejoicing were finished, he called the attention of his bishops and barons to the question of the consecration of Thomas to the Archbishopric of York, which was still pending. Anselm's death, we can easily believe, had given to his opinion a weight and authority with all persons, which it might not have had, if he had been still alive. The bright parts of his character (and they were many) now began to stand out in relief; it was felt by his partisans chiefly, by all more or less, that the realm had lost in him a prelate almost unmatched in the subtlety of his mind, and the deep devotion of his heart; and special deference was held to be due to his dying wishes. The letter in which he had definitely refused consecration to Thomas unless he would make a profession of obedience to the see of Canterbury, was read before King Henry and his assembled court, and was probably felt by those who caused it to be read as decisive on the question to which it referred. Then Robert, Count of Mellent, a bitter foe of Anselm's, on the purport of the letter being explained to him, rose up in a whirlwind of wrath, and demanded

A.D. 1109. to know which of the bishops dared to adopt that letter, and take it under his patronage, without the assent and express command of "our Lord the King." This insolent query would seem to have set up the back of the bishops, and they acted for a time (our Herbert among them) in a spirit of independence, and suitably to their dignity. They saw plainly that the count aimed at bringing them into disfavour with the king; and they withdrew for a while, to deliberate with one another as to the best means of meeting his tactics. They came to a resolution, which we must presume they announced, of rather submitting to be despoiled of everything than receding from the ground their late chief had taken up, and disobeying his express precept. The bishops mentioned as forming this spirited resolve are, besides our Prelate, Richard of London, William of Winchester, Robert of Lincoln, Roger of Salisbury, Ralph of Rochester, Reinhard of Hereford, Robert of Chester, John of Bath, Ralph of Chichester, and William of Exeter (Warelwast). But alas! even mitred heads are not proof against human frailty. Somehow (we are not told how) the king's wishes seem to have prevailed over the resolution of his bishops. Possibly the compromise which had been already tendered to Thomas through Herbert, but refused, may have been under altered circumstances accepted. The elect of York may have consented to acknowledge Canterbury's primacy of all England, without an actual profession of obedience to Canterbury. Neither he nor the king might feel the same reluctance to admit a right in the abstract as to recognise the inherence of that right in a living and somewhat obnoxious champion. Thomas was consecrated at St. Paul's by the Bishop of London, June 27, 1109, our Herbert and four other bishops assisting.

A.D. 1109.

After Anselm's death the see of Canterbury remained vacant (as it had done at the last avoidance) for a considerable time. From April 21, 1109, to April 26, 1114, rather more than five years, no primate of all England sate upon the archiepiscopal throne. Dean Hook (Archbishops, vol. ii. p. 284) gives this account of the delay in the appointment. "King Henry, always specious, asserted that he was following his father's example, and that he only delayed the appointment from his anxiety to find a person duly qualified to discharge the duties of an office so important." From the first of the following letters, which is addressed to Herbert by Abbot Richard (of Ely?), whom we have already made acquaintance with, it may be gathered that our founder had been thought of and talked of as Anselm's successor in the primatial see. Herbert's answer is deeply interesting, as showing that he entertained a sympathy with the secular clergy, not in unison with the views of the high monastic party. We are told that, during the avoidance of the see of Canterbury, these parties were in collision as to the proper person

A.D. 1109. to fill the vacant throne. The monks of Canterbury desired a monk. "The bishops on the contrary, after their experience of Anselm, were fully persuaded that the times required a man of the world to preside over a distracted Church, and they were determined only to accept a *secular*^q." Herbert would have been a suitable compromise, for he had been Abbot of Ramsey, as a bishop had had no small experience of secular affairs, and evidently enjoyed a considerable share of court favour. But there was another candidate, Ralph of Escures, who, while equally suitable as a compromise, had the additional claim and advantage of having ably administered the affairs of the arch-diocese during the five years of the vacancy. As Bishop of Rochester, he had been regarded even in Anselm's lifetime as coadjutor of the primate. And perhaps our Herbert, being now probably about sixty years of age, was feeling the infirmities incidental to the decline of life more acutely than was consistent with his undertaking so onerous a charge. We have seen in a letter of his introduced on a former occasion, but written probably about this time, that he accounted himself old at sixty (Letter I. p. 85), and that he was sensible of the burden of advancing age. At all events, to whatever causes the preference of Ralph over Herbert may have been due, the lot fell upon Ralph, and he was numbered with the primates of all England, being enthroned at Canterbury May 17, 1114.

Difference of opinion between the regulars and the bishops as to the necessary qualifications of an Archbishop of Canterbury.

Ralph de l'Escures translated from Rochester to Canterbury.

q Hook's "Archbishops," vol. ii. p. 286.

Here are the letters. Abbot Richard's is stilty and pompous in a high degree, and fulsome withal, as if he really thought that Herbert was likely to be raised to the highest ecclesiastical position in the Church of England; and if he is the *Ricardus Abbas* to whom Letter X. is addressed (p. 248), (of which there can be little or no doubt, since there, as in the answer to him here, Herbert asks for the loan of an Augustine and a lectionary, and mentions the monk Gregory as a messenger going between the parties,) we can quite understand the tone of our bishop's reply, in which he throws cold water upon the view taken by the Abbot of the prerogatives of the monastic order, and gives this dignitary a quiet snub. It was a courteous way of saying; "You remember that in adversity you turned your back upon me; now, when you think I may be raised to the Primacy, you fawn upon me for your own ends, and flatter me by asking me to write a book in the interest of the monks. I by no means jump at such a proposal." The tenth Letter should by all means be read previously to, and together with, the sixtieth.

LETTER LIX.

RICHARD THE ABBOT TO HERBERT.

"Richard the Abbot to Herbert the Bishop, his well-beloved father.

"The enemy of the human race, who bears a grudge against all religion, as he envied man the obtaining of eternal life, from the time when God created him, so

Abbot Richard complains to Herbert of the

<small>canons who, under the instigation of the devil, disparaged the monks and their way of life, and exhorts him to write a short treatise in vindication of monasticism.</small> on earth also, through [the instrumentality of] his disciples and followers, the same [malignant being] in no wise desists from wreaking his old hatred upon the later offspring [of the stock of Adam]. Nay, being utterly opposed to peace and charity, and prompted by that same envy wherewith he contrived the ejection of the first man from the pleasantness and glory of Paradise, he throws into holy Church schisms and dissensions, and [thereby] molests orthodox fathers who are passing their life in tranquil contemplation, lest they should rejoice in the blessedness of the heavenly kingdom, from which the audacious enemy, through his execrable presumption, had been driven into exile. For [these schisms and dissensions] rear their heads, as it were, for conflict with our warfare ʳ; but I speak with a feeling of security under your protection. Some men of perverse mind, with all the wild lawlessness of canons ˢ, and raving at and bearing a grudge to monastic devotion, are inflamed into arrogance and pride ᵗ

ʳ "for conflict with our warfare"—*in conflictum nostræ militiæ*. It is observable how monasticism had absorbed into itself not only all the ideas of the clerical office, as Herbert complains in the letter following this, but also all the ideas of the Christian profession. This profession is constantly represented in Scripture as a warfare, and the persons making it at Baptism are spoken of as soldiers of Christ. But in the view of Abbot Richard and his cotemporaries, the monk was the only soldier of Christ, the cowl Christ's uniform, and the way of life in convents the true warfare under the Captain of our salvation.

ˢ "with all the wild lawlessness of canons"—*canonicæ feritatis*. The Abbot sneers not only at secular canons, who, as living abroad in the world, would be sure to incur his heavy censure, but also at the regular canons, of whom Dean Hook tells us (Church Dictionary, s. v. *Canon*), "they were a less strict sort of religious than the monks, but lived together under one roof, had a common dormitory and refectory, and were obliged to observe the statutes of their order." The chief rule for regular canons is that of St. Augustine. The Augustinians are supposed to have come into England about the beginning of the twelfth century, and possessed two mitred abbeys, Waltham and Cirencester. Monks were always shaven and shorn, but regular canons wore beards, and caps on their heads. It surely is an unworthy and barbarous sneer of Abbot Richard to indicate their way of life by such a word as *feritas*.

ᵗ "inflamed into arrogance and pride"—*typum*. See on the word *typus* or *typus*, the Sermons, p. 96, note d.

(enkindled, as it were, by the fires of malice), and bring to bear all the incitements of mischievous talk to stigmatize and weaken the communities of monks, and disturb by the storm-clouds[u] of their boasting the serenity of our secret contemplation. For they assert, but with an empty verbosity, that there be worthier steps [to heaven] than the monastery, and that the habit characteristic of our way of life does little or no good to any one who renounces the world; a position which it is clear must be entirely false, because when the penalty of death[x] is speedily advancing towards them, priests and laymen, and even kings and persons belonging to any order of the community, under the pressure of necessity, become monks, not priests nor canons[y]. Their opinion, therefore, is rather to be execrated than accounted worth a straw, who despise and deride that life which our Redeemer in His mercy made known in the world[z], that men might make experiment of it,

---

[u] "disturb by the storm-clouds"—*nubilo obtundunt*. The stilted Latin of the Abbot is "suarum jactationum nubilo contemplationis nostræ serenitatem obtundunt." *Obtundere nubilo* is a decided confusion of metaphor, which we do not wish to reproduce in the translation. The word *obtundo*, however, gives a forcible representation of the teasing annoyance which the Abbot underwent from the attacks directed against monasticism by the lawless canons and others.

[x] "penalty of death"—*irruente mortis districtione*. The word *districtio*, according to its etymology, means a pulling or stretching asunder, and hence molestation, or distraction. From the notion of molestation it passes into that of severity, a rigid observance of discipline. The next step is that of judgment, with all its collateral ideas, such as censure, sentence, fines, penalty. The pressure put upon a debtor by seizing his furniture in payment of his debts, is still called in our language a distress, and the act is called distraining,—the English representatives these of the Latin *distringo*.

[y] "not priests nor canons"—*non sacerdotes nec canonici*. It is observable how the Abbot looks down upon canons as well as priests, and what a distinction he draws between monks and canons. Yet the Black Canons of St. Augustine were popularly called monks, as the Dominicans and Franciscans were called Friars.

[z] "our Redeemer in His mercy made known in the world"—*in mundo Redemptor noster misericorditer intimavit*. How the Redeemer first made the monastic life known in the world, and how He Himself was the first to exemplify it, we must leave the good Abbot to explain. Probably he

follow it, and animated by zeal for love might explore it profoundly,—a life, too, which many fathers of an admirable sanctity have commended as full of sacred mysteries. [I said that our Redeemer was the first to make it known; but] He was also the first who, as a Master, taught His faithful ones by His own conversation this way of innocence. Moreover, we have endured the injurious attacks which these perverse men have made upon us without losing our meekness, according to what is written, 'God is faithful, who will not suffer you to be tempted above that which you are able: but will make also with temptation issue, that you may be able to bear it.' But since we have lost our powerful patron, Anselm[a], the guardian and defender of his servants, respecting whom, although we deplore his severance from temporal life upon earth, yet we have received this consolation that, although he has made his exodus from the flesh, he is seated at the spiritual banquet in heaven,—[since, I say, we have sustained this loss,] the only city of refuge that remains to us is the grace of God. You, however, are a mighty comfort against our fears of those who hate us, and a shield against the blows of those who strike at us. In no wise are we over fearful of the assaults of the hosts [arrayed against us], when we lay to heart that which

1 Cor. x. 13. (Rheims).

would have referred to the counsel given to the rich young man to sell all that he had, give to the poor, and follow Christ, and to the fact that our blessed Lord called the twelve Apostles into a close little brotherhood, separate from the world, of which He Himself was the centre. Doubtless he would dexterously have omitted all reference to certain women, of whom St. Luke speaks as following our Lord in one of His pilgrimages, and ministering unto Him of their substance (St. Luke viii. 1—3).

[a] "our powerful patron, Anselm"—*patronum nostrum, Anselinum*. Without supposing Abbot Richard to refer to any particular occasion on which Anselm had thrown his shield over the monasteries, we can quite understand that his deep attachment to Bec, over which he had presided as Abbot, and his speculative and devotional turn of mind, which inclined him to retirement, would enlist all his sympathies in favour of the cloister. It was with tears, and every expression of reluctance, that he was torn away from the monastery to be placed on the archiepiscopal throne of Canterbury.

is said, 'Whatsoever you shall ask in My Name, it shall be done for you.' Therefore I, the fellow-servant and friend of your paternity, and all those in all England who mourn with me the loss of Anselm, and fight the good fight of faith in the monastic habit, under God, the King of kings, earnestly beg you of your charity, that you would condescend to administer to the Lord's sheep, who are thirsting in the desert, a draught out of the cup of devotion, drawn from that celestial fountain wherewith you are, above other prelates, inebriated, according as the Holy Spirit hath given you to pour out words of grace. Let thy muse sound forth some fresh melody, draw up for us some dissertation which may do us good service, and supply what is at present a need of all the faithful, so that cloistered men, pressed hard by their adversaries, may take courage again, and that their enemies, being confuted, may be put to utter confusion,—a work which may make it clear to all, what, and how much, and for whom, the life of the cloister avails. Do this, we pray you, and in order to do it effectively, rest for a while from business for God's sake. We are scattered in divers parts, yet are perfectly united in mind in making this petition. Seated at a board [of sacred literature], we do not need a full inundation of the heavenly stream, but only implore some drops of it, sweet as nectar. Let our holy mother the Church be cheered and raised in spirit, so that she who has sustained a bereavement by the departure of our father Anselm to heaven, strengthened by the support of Herbert the bishop, and fortified by his protection, may show a vigour equal to that which she has manifested hitherto; and that, in like manner as Anselm is enrolled among the citizens above, so in the heavenly rest, at all events, if not in the pontifical chair, Herbert may succeed Anselm."

See St. John xiv. 13.

LETTER LX.

TO RICHARD THE ABBOT.

"Herbert the Bishop to Richard the Abbot, greeting.

Herbert replies to Richard that monks and clergy are on a level as to dignity, and equally to be respected, if their lives are equally good.

"You, who, in your excellence, so strenuously defend, above the other abbots in England, the devotion of the monastic order, instruct me, in my humility, to undertake the defence of that devotion against the clergy, by whose unjust and insatiable gnawing, monasticism is assailed. But far be it, most discreet father, both from your instructions and from my compliance with them, to undertake anything against the clergy, who are ministers of the holy Altar, who with chaste hands make the Lord's Body and Blood, and by whose vigilance God's sheepfold is watched over, and the sheep of Christ fed with the sweet pasturage of His doctrine. Exalted is the prerogative attached to this dignity; but it has in these days been wholly transferred to the monks. Look at the various offices of the Church, and gather from your survey of them the sort of victory which you may anticipate in your battle; popes[b], primates, archbishops, bishops, presbyters, deacons, subdeacons, and the other inferior offices of the Church, have been all reduced to a single province of the monastic order. It would be absurd for us to condemn what we ourselves are; a monk is the very same thing as a clerk; for if a

---

[b] "popes"—*apostolici*. In the earliest times of the Church, all bishops were called *apostolici*, as representing and being successors of the apostles; but in later days, the word *apostolicus*, like the word *papa*, which also in the first instance applied to all bishops, came to denote the pope exclusively, and this is the meaning which it almost uniformly bears in mediæval authors. The verbs, *apostolico* and *apostolo*, mean to hold the office of pope.

monk[c], [according to the etymology of the word,] signifies a unit, and a clerk signifies a lot[d], the end for which both monk and clerk exist is the worship of the

[c] "for if a monk.... signifies a unit, and the clerk signifies a lot"—*si monachus monadem et clericus significat sortem*. Herbert here derives *monachus*, (μοναχός) from *monas*, a unit, agreeably to an epigram from the Anthology, which is given in Ducange, *sub voce*,

Εἰ μοναχοί, τί τοσοίδε; τοσοίδε δὲ, πῶς πάλι μοῦνοι;
Ὢ πληθὺς μοναχῶν ψευσαμένη μονάδα.

(If they be monks, why so many of them? but being so many, how is it again that they are called solitaries? O crowd of monks, which belies the name of being single!)

It is remarkable that although by the name monk is meant a solitary, the first kind of monks, according to St. Benedict, and those whom he pronounces to be most formidable to the powers of hell, are cœnobites, or those who live in community, under rule and an abbot. The other three kinds of monks which he mentions in the first chapter of his rule, are anchorites, or hermits, who have exchanged the cloister for the desert; and Sarabites, whom he describes as a most wicked class, observing no other law than the gratification of their vicious appetites. [The Fathers and mediæval writers often fall foul of this class of monks. The derivation of their name is a great crux, nor is it quite clear what their way of life was, except that from a passage in Cassian, quoted by Ducange, which traces up their spiritual descent to Ananias and Sapphira, and from the distich, which he also quotes:—

"Plus his si quæris, jam Sarabaïta vocaris,
Conductor cupidus, mangoque non monachus."

(If thou seekest more worldly goods than these, thy just title is a Sarabite, a covetous contractor and dealer, not a monk), one would suppose that these "cursed children" had "a heart exercised with covetous practices."] The fourth kind of monks are the Gyrovagues, who played the same trick of old among the convents as tramps and beggars are now found to play among the nightly refuges of London, spending two or three nights in each, and going the round of all. See Herbert's censure of a Gyrovague, pp. 138, 139, and note h.

[d] The word clergy is derived from κλῆρος, 'a lot,' probably because it was said of the Jewish clergy, that is, of the Priests and Levites, "they shall have no inheritance among their brethren: the Lord is their inheritance, as he hath said unto them." (Deut. xviii. 2; Numb. xviii. 20). But as the Lord was the priest's portion, so we find the people to be the Lord's portion, according to that other passage of Deuteronomy (xxxii. 9), "The Lord's portion is his people, Jacob is the lot of his inheritance." Hence the flock is called God's heritage by St. Peter (1 Pet. v. 3), "Neither as being lords over God's heritage, but being ensamples to the flock." And on the other hand, the ministry is also called a lot in Acts i. 25, "that he may take part in this ministry and apostleship" (literally, the *lot* of this ministry and apostleship, τὸν κλῆρον τῆς διακονίας).

one God ᵉ. Due honour therefore is not to be withheld from good clerks on account of the vices of criminous ones; as neither, on the other hand, are bad monks to be honoured on account of the devotion of good monks. Let a just award be made to the merits of either order. Let reverence, then, be shown to the clerical order both among laymen and among monks, since both clerk and monk are on a level with one another in point of dignity, unless this natural equality is disturbed by dissimilarity of life and conduct. Send me the books, as you promised me, the Augustine and the Lectionary ᶠ, by your servant and monk, Gregory. Content yourself with simply bidding me to do what you wish, assured that my friendship for you is so perfect, that I confide in the perfection of yours for me without laboured professions of it ᵍ. Farewell!"

Before bidding final adieu to Abbot Richard, whom we have supposed to be the Abbot of Ely bearing that name, we ought to say that our attention has been called by the Rev. John Griffith, (Vicar of Sandridge, St. Alban's,) to a passage in the "Gesta Abbatium Monasterii

---

ᵉ "the end for which both monk and clerk exist is the worship of the one God"—*utriusque finis in unius Dei consistit theosebia.* Mr. Anstruther has written *theosophia* for *theosebia*,—why, we know not, for the MS. clearly has the latter. The word *theosebia*, which is a Greek word Latinised, occurs once in the Greek Testament, where our translators have rendered it, 'godliness' (1 Tim. ii. 10); and its cognate adjective, θεοσεβής, is found in the blind man's apology for Christ (John ix. 31), where it is rendered 'a worshipper of God.'

ᶠ "Lectionary"—*lectionarium.* A lectionary was a book which contained the lections or readings appointed to be used in the Church Service. The compilation of it was attributed to St. Jerome. The word, however, had a narrower application to the book containing the Epistles, technically so called, which were read in the service of the Mass. It was the Epistoler's book.

ᵍ The Latin of this sentence is, "Nude impera, sed perfectio amicitiæ nostræ de vestræ amicitiæ perfectione confidit." We can make nothing of this sentence but what we have given above. Perhaps the text may be corrupt.

Sancti Albani," (p. 147), from which we gather that Herbert was on friendly terms with Abbot Richard *of St. Alban's*. Among other instances of the independence of the Abbots of St. Alban's of the Bishop of the Diocese (Lincoln), occurs the following;

"Herbert, Bishop of Norwich, dedicated the church of Redburn, Richard the presbyter being witness thereof. And the same bishop dedicated also the church of Niweham (Newnham), Thurkill and Sahrith being witnesses thereof. The same dedicated also the chapel of Sandrugge (Sandridge), Richard, Radulphus, and Alexander, the presbyters, being witnesses thereof. And the same dedicated the chapel of St. Andrew the Apostle, and also the church of Northona" (Norton, near Baldock, in Broadwater Hundred), "and also the chapel of St. Mary Magdalen, ... and moreover, Herbert, Bishop of Norwich, held a general ordination at Langley, at the time when Abbot Richard proposed to found a cell of monks in that place." _(marginal: Herbert consecrates churches and ordains out of his own diocese.)

Richard, Mr. Griffith kindly informs us, was fifteenth Abbot of St. Alban's, and his abbacy as nearly as possible coincided with the period of Herbert's episcopate, lasting from 1097 to 1119. "In his time the cell of Wymondham, *cum omnibus ad eandem pertinentibus*, was given to St. Alban's," (another evidence this of Herbert's interest in St. Alban's, and of the connexion of his diocese with it,—circumstances traceable possibly, Mr. Griffith thinks, "to the neighbourhood of Herbert's earlier abbey life to St. Alban's"). Our informant adds that, in consecrating and ordaining in the diocese of Lincoln, our bishop did no more than the Bishops of Rochester, Durham, Limerick, and Ely had done. We take it that he not only had precedents for his action, but acted regularly, and in conformity with the common law of the Church. The Abbot of St. Alban's was doubtless ordinary of it and its peculiars. And the ordinary (though not a bishop, but some other prelate) might give leave to any bishop to exercise episcopal rights and functions within his peculiars, *if those peculiars were extra-diocesan*, and was the only person who could give such leave. (See Van Espen, *Jus Ecclesiasticum Universum*, Part I. Tit. xvi. *De Curâ Episcopali*, cap. v. sec. 8.) Herbert's position in consecrating and ordaining within the liberties of St. Alban's would be an analogous to the position of one of our own bishops called in by the head of a peculiar (when peculiars existed) to administer Confirmation to the children in the peculiar. He would come as a friend, to perform episcopal rites for a dignitary of his acquaintance not in episcopal orders.

During the five years' vacancy of the metropolitical see, a frightful plague devastated Norwich. Alexander Neville's notice of it is very brief. He describes it as occurring during Herbert's episcopate, visiting almost every house in the city, and carrying off hundreds of people. It took place, he says, in 1112.

A.D. 1112. Plague at Norwich.

A.D. 1115. On the 27th of June, 1115, Herbert would have an opportunity of seeing and congratulating

the new Primate, who had been translated in A.D. 1115.
the spring of the preceding year from Rochester
to Canterbury. For we then find him assisting
Ralph in the consecration of Theulf to the see
of Worcester, the Bishops of London, Bath, Chichester, Ely, and Sarum also joining in the imposition of hands. Later in the same year (Dec.
26) he is again called up to Canterbury with
the bishops of Winchester, Chichester, and St. *The last bishops whom Herbert joins in consecrating.*
David's to join the Archbishop in setting apart
Geoffrey de Clive (for Hereford) and Ernulf
(for Rochester) to the episcopal office. These,
it would appear from Mr. Stubbs's most valuable record of "the Episcopal Succession in England," were the last bishops he joined in consecrating. Life was now on the wane with him, though
he had one more enterprise to undertake for his
Church and country, before he was brought face
to face with the realities of another world.

We here introduce his letter to Ralph, from
which it appears that he had induced the Primate
to promise that he would pay him a visit at
Norwich. Although in the address there is a
very deferential acknowledgment of the new
Archbishop's rank and position, the letter itself
is that of an equal, and one who had been an
old friend. Are we right in imagining in it
the very slightest shade of annoyance, because
his old friend, Ralph of Rochester, had been
put over his head?

LETTER XXXVIII.

To Radulfus.

"To Radulfus[h], the greatest of priests, Herbert, the least of presbyters, sendeth greeting.

<small>Herbert begs Ralph to fulfil his promise of visiting him at Norwich.</small> "You often threaten to pay us a visit; but hitherto, with your customary forgetfulness, you have weakly allowed your threats to prove futile. Now therefore at length make good your speeches, and fulfil your promise. Visit your brethren at Norwich; and as in the past year you [not unnaturally] kept aloof from the labours in which we were engaged, so in the present, somewhere about the coming equinox, come and wish us joy of our delightful repose. Let one of your servants announce to us your coming at least eight days beforehand, that I may place myself somewhere on the road so as to meet and receive you worthily."

And here is a letter from Ralph to him sent <small>A.D. 1115.</small> some time in the year 1115, the occasion of which seems to have been as follows. The church of Edwardston, in Suffolk, had been given by King Henry (as appears from a charter dated Woodstock, and addressed to Herbert, "and the viscounts [see note w, on p. 24] of Suffolk and Essex, and all his barons, both French and English, of both of those shires") to the monastery

---

[h] "To Radulfus, the greatest of priests, Herbert, the least of presbyters" —*Radulfo maximo sacerdoti, Herbertus, minimus presbyter.* The reader's attention should be called to the evidence furnished by this address that in Herbert's estimation *sacerdos* was a more honourable term than *presbyter*. Words change their value as times go on, and some, like coins, are depreciated. One would think that no word expressive of the ministerial office could convey a higher idea than that which St. Peter gives to himself (1 Pet. v. 1), "The elders which are among you I exhort, who am also an elder." It appears that in a general sense, bishops, priests, and deacons were all called *sacerdotes*, but the name was considered distinctively applicable to the second order of the ministry.

of St. Mary at Abingdon. Thereupon Ralph addressed to Herbert the following letter, commending to his kind offices certain Abingdon monks:—

> "To the venerable lord and his brother Herbert, by God's grace, bishop of Norwich, brother Ralph, an unworthy minister of the Church of Canterbury, sends greeting, and friendly regards, and sincere prayers to the utmost of his power.

"Forasmuch as we are well aware that the piety and devotion of Faritius, the Lord Abbot of Abingdon, and of all the congregation entrusted to him by God, have not escaped your discernment, there can be no need that I should signify it to your reverence. On behalf of these, therefore, we are minded to request you in the kindness of your charity, that for God's sake, whose they are, and for our sake, who are devoted to you, and for their own sakes too, who profess to be your friends and sons, you would receive with fatherly kindness certain brethren of the Church into a certain church [recently] granted to them as an endowment by a certain person in your diocese, and would afford them friendly counsel and help, as you may be able and see your way to do. In doing which, may Almighty God long preserve you safe, right reverend father, and keep you mindful of us."

We are much indebted to Mr. Parker, our learned publisher, for calling our attention to this letter, which is found in the Chronicle of the Monastery of Abingdon, vol. ii. p. 62, Rolls' Series, 1858. The royal charter, confirming to Abingdon Monastery the grant of the church of Edwardston, will be found in Appendix C,

The old dispute between the Archbishops of

Canterbury and York as to supremacy, and independence of one another, was in Ralph's primacy renewed in a more aggravated form than ever. On the death of Thomas II., Archbishop of York, which took place Feb. 24, 1114, Thurstan, a man of valour, piety, and munificent almsgiving, but bent, as a point of honour, on maintaining every privilege attaching to his position, was appointed to the vacant archbishopric. Ralph however declined to consecrate him, unless he took the usual oath of canonical obedience to the see of Canterbury; and was supported in this proceeding by the king, who, now that he had a primate of Canterbury more in accordance with his own views than Anselm, was willing to abet him in all his just claims. Thurstan hereupon renounced his appointment to the see; but soon (possibly owing to the remonstrances of his friends) regretted and retracted his resignation. He applied to the king, who had gone to Normandy, to re-appoint him; and when he could make no way in this quarter, sent his legates to Rome, to lay the matter before the pope. The Pope (Pascal II.) took upon himself to decide the question between the two metropolitans; but Ralph and Henry would not recede from the settlement of the matter which they themselves had made. Thurstan must submit to take the oath of canonical obedience to Ralph and his successors, or he could not receive consecration. This was one of the matters which Herbert's last journey to Rome was intended to settle.

A.D. 1114.

Thurstan declines to take the oath of canonical obedience to Ralph.

A.D. 1116.

The reasons of Herbert's last visit to Rome.

But there was another. The pall being deemed A.D. 1116. necessary for the exercise of metropolitan authority, Ralph had (with permission of the king) applied for it, when he had been appointed metropolitan. And Pascal, though he received very ungraciously the legates sent by Ralph and the king, was persuaded by Anselm (a nephew of the late archbishop, resident in Italy) to entrust him with the pall, that he might convey it to Canterbury. The pall was gratefully accepted by the archbishop; but at the same time it was intimated to Anselm that he himself could not be received in England in the character of papal legate without invitation from the king. The sending into a country of papal legates, armed with full ecclesiastical powers, and commissioned to supersede and suspend for the time being all exercise of the episcopal authority, was part of the encroaching policy by which the popes sought to bring national Churches into dependence upon themselves. The bishops of a country had only to show an independent spirit; and they were at once overruled and superseded by a nuncio. But at the period we write of, both king and primate were resolved to resist this tyrannical usurpation. Anselm was sent a second time to England in 1116, in the character of papal nuncio. The king was absent in Normandy; but the Privy Council, under the regency of the queen, very properly decided that to receive in England a papal legate uninvited would be an infraction of the common law. Anselm therefore

The legate not allowed to land without an invitation from the king.

A.D. 1116. was prohibited from landing; and it was resolved that the archbishop, attended by two of the most eminent prelates of the day, Herbert Bishop of Norwich, and Hugh Abbot of Chertsey, should proceed to Rome, to set at rest for ever, by an explanation with the pope, the question of the independence of the English Church. They found Henry at Rouen, and brought him readily to concur with the decision of his Privy Council, and with their projected expedition. Their further progress was stopped for a month by the archbishop's serious illness, an ulcer in the face, which caused his whole head to swell up. But when he was convalescent, they set forward in great state and with a large retinue, Ralph sparing no expense to make his dignity as Archbishop of Canterbury appreciated in the foreign Churches through whose territory he passed. But another stoppage awaited them when they reached Placentia. We give the account of it in the words of Eadmer, who, as one of Ralph's retinue, accompanied the expedition :—

Deputation to the Pope on the subject of the independence of the English Church.

"When we arrived at Placentia, the Bishop of Norwich (Herbert by name), who had left England with us to go to Rome, was seized with so grievous a sickness, that in the progress of his disorder he lay ten successive days without taking food or uttering a word. On which account we spent four weeks in that place, in suspense as to what God would do with the bishop. But when we perceived of a certainty that he was recovering his strength, our father (the archbishop), by Herbert's request and advice, recommenced his journey. The bishop, who was as yet too weak to bear the exertion of travelling, remained at Placentia, designing, either there to wait till the Primate returned, or, if he should tarry long at Rome, intending, when he felt himself strong enough, to precede him on his return. So after some days we succeeded in reaching Rome, and he Normandy, as the Lord enabled us."

But the journey was altogether an ill-starred one. Ralph and Hugh failed in their great object, which was a personal interview with the Pope. The Roman Church was distracted by factions; and the Pope, driven out of Rome, had been obliged to flee to Beneventum. The archbishop communicated with him by letter, and received a general and evasive answer, to the effect that all the privileges of the Church of Canterbury should be maintained, not stating however what those privileges were. The archbishop and his retinue, after staying a time in Italy, but finding a personal interview with the pope precluded by the disturbed state of the country, rejoined the king in Normandy. Thence the Bishop of Norwich, and the Abbot of Chertsey, somewhere in 1117, betook themselves again to their country and their respective flocks.

This was the last act of Herbert's public life. He had been twice chosen as an ambassador from England to Rome, commissioned to treat upon that great question of the day, the independence of foreign control, which had always been claimed by the English Church. That neither embassy had any satisfactory result was attributable to the evasive policy of the pope, which defeated every attempt at a definite conclusion. But the fact of Herbert's being chosen shows conclusively that he was one of the foremost prelates of the realm, one to whom weight attached from a general persuasion, not only of his piety, but of his judgment and tact in the administration of affairs, and of his address in conciliating opponents. Such a prelate as Cotton describes him to have been, would have been naturally selected for missions of a difficult and delicate character, in which the rival claims of national independence and ecclesiastical supremacy were to be adjusted.

"A man imbued with every sort of learning, secular as well as religious, of incomparable eloquence, handsome in his person, and of bright countenance, so that the generality of those who knew him not might guess he was a bishop from only looking at him. For the beauty of his mind shone forth in his countenance, and the serenity of his character controlled and communicated itself to the very movements of his body. Sound in faith, and animated by [Christian] hope, he ordered with wisdom, confirmed with truth, tempered with meekness, and flavoured with charity all that he did, and all that he said; and ever set mercy (a grace in which he specially abounded) before judgment, so that he himself might in the end obtain mercy as his meed."

Here, at the close of our narrative, we insert those letters of Herbert which we have not been able to assign to any particular occasion or period of his life. The first is one of special interest, as showing both the yearning which he (in common with many good men of his day) experienced for the ascetic or purely contemplative life, and also his keen perception of the snare which such a life might prove to one who abandoned himself to it.

LETTER LVI.
To Wido the Anchorite[1].

"Herbert the Bishop to Wido the Anchorite, greeting.

Herbert congratulates Wido on his way of life, warns him against the snares of it, and asks his prayers. Phil. iii. 20. 1 Cor. xiii. 1.

"It is superfluous for you to seek, my well-beloved son, correspondence with us by means of letters, since thy conversation is in heaven, and as thou speakest with the tongues of angels, thou hast small need of the comfort which man can give. For thee prayer is the one law, and the one flower of skilful and glowing eloquence.

"Thou reclinest in the company of the Prophets and Apostles, and thy soul is refreshed and gladdened by the meat and drink of heavenly doctrine. Nor are modern authors who serve up the heavenly banquet wanting to thee; thou hast an abundance of them, proportioned to the ardour of thy zeal for study and thy diligence in reading. Wherefore then askest thou again for our bran, thou who revellest in an abundance of such flour of wheat. That preacher's discourse is not

---

[1] "Wido the Anchorite." The word Anchorite, ἀναχωρητής, comes from ἀναχωρέω, 'to retire, to withdraw.' Hermits were those who withdrew from the world. St. Jerome tells us that Paul the Hermit was the originator of this way of life, St. Anthony its illustrator, and St. John the Baptist its head and priest. We have already seen (p. 267, n. 3) that St. Benedict in his Rule describes anchorites as one class of monks. Many years ago a grating was found in the south wall of the procession-path of Norwich Cathedral, which was supposed to be part of an anchorite's cell, through which he could gain a view of the high altar. This curious relic was presented by the Dean and Chapter to the Norwich Museum. It may be added, that one of Herbert's great works in Norwich was the Church and Hospital of St. Paul, which were dedicated to Paul the Apostle and Paul the Hermit conjointly. The Church was completed by Herbert's successor, Everard, and consecrated by Theobald, Archbishop of Canterbury.—The first hermit had, according to the legend, a grave meet for an anchorite,—scratched in the ground for him by two lions.

pure who is defiled by the filthiness of his lusts, and whom the stings of worldly affairs are continually pricking and galling. Whence, my well-beloved son, call me no more Naomi, but call me Mara, for I have been enslaved to many sins, and am exposed to the punishment of many, my crimes having well deserved what I am called on to endure. But seeing that it is the taller cedars which are struck by the most awful thunderbolts, I beseech thee with all modesty and humility to look carefully to it that thou guardest the treasures of thy purity and simplicity from the fell assaults of arrogance, envy, wrath, sadness, and vainglory; for the deeper is the hell from which those enemies issue forth, so much the more are they to be dreaded by thee and other great warriors of the heavenly army. It is true that all enemies are to be feared; but those more especially which are wont to be engendered by the loftiness of a man's virtues and the glory of his triumphs. I would say more; but my parchment runs short, and at the bidding of my colleagues[k], I am forced to return to the workshop of carnal affairs. And as I have been prostrated by another hand than yours, lend me, a sinner, the hand of your prayers to lift me up."

[Ruth i. 20.]

The following are addressed to William Turbo, who was Herbert's next successor but one in the see of Norwich, being consecrated in 1146, on the deposition of Bishop Everard, his *immediate* successor. The future of this man was sufficiently remarkable to warrant a few words about him in this place. It is quite possible,

---

[k] "colleagues"—*complicibus*. A somewhat unusual word in this sense. The word is used for a confederate in crime (accomplice), for persons who side with a prince in war (partisans), and also for the devotees or worshippers of a particular saint. Here it would be used more or less in this latter sense, and would indicate some of the monks of the Cathedral monastery, whom Herbert recognised as his brethren.

(as we have already conjectured in the Ancient Roof Sculptures of Norwich Cathedral, p. 140,) that he may simply be the boy William, to whom, in conjunction with Otho, Herbert writes so many letters, grown into a man. There are many forms of his surname (de Turibus, Turbes, de Turbe, Turbe, Turbus, Turbervile, Turba, de Turba), and in using the form Turbo (that is, *hurricane*), we suspect Herbert may have designed a punning allusion to the impetuosity of his character. It is evident from the tone of the following letters, that Herbert was really attached to him. He became Prior of the Cathedral monastery; in after days, as Bishop of Norwich, he, at the bidding of Becket, publicly excommunicated Hugh Bigod from the pulpit of the Cathedral, and walking thence to the altar, laid his pastoral-staff thereon, and made this redoubtable challenge; " Let him that dares seize either the lands, goods, or possessions of my church." From this and the circumstance that, when the Norman Lady-Chapel of the Cathedral was burnt down, he vowed that he would not stir from within twelve *leucas* of the Cathedral, until the ravages were repaired, and seating himself in person at the entrance, begged alms of all the faithful who entered, we should judge that he was a man of strong character, and one who had his hurricane-fits of temper, whether for good or evil. On his death he was laid by the left side of Herbert, in the Presbytery before the high altar.

LETTER XLII. (*bis.*)

To William Turbo.

"Herbert to William Turbo.

Herbert remonstrates with Turbo for communicating to him the secrets of his conscience through a third person.

"Good grounds have I for being angry with you, and well deserved is the wrath with which I reprove the strange course you have adopted, in choosing to reveal to my ears the secret of your heart with another's lips rather than your own. But this was not the bond of friendship with which formerly your soul and mine were cemented together. Write to me then with the ink[1] of your heart and with the pen of your own tongue, guided by your own hands; tell me all you have a mind to say, and the motions by which your heart is disquieted. The disease must be disclosed to the physician, and the conscience to the priest; on these terms only can health be gotten from the physician, and ghostly counsel from the priest."

LETTER XLI.

To William Turbo.

"Herbert to William Turbo.

Herbert, hearing of Turbo's penitence, absolves him, and gives to him and

"I receive the tidings of your penitence for your excesses with a joy proportioned to the bitterness with which you lament them; for as he who despises little things shall fall by little and little, so he who abhors the smallest sins will in no wise dare to rise to graver

---

[1] "ink"—*incaustum*. The word here used for ink is *incaustum*, the other form of which is *encaustum*. (See note d, p. 198.) The writing-department of a monastery was a place of great importance, and fenced with several precautions. One of the statutes of the monastic house at Sempringham, in Lincolnshire, in which William Turbo, when he became bishop, showed a lively interest, ran as follows: "Let no one enter the warming room except the precentor to smooth his writing tablet and to warm his ink, and the writers for the purpose of drying their parchment." The *scriptoria*, or writing-cells, were sometimes built round the calefactory, because satisfactory writing required three things, warm ink, warm parchment, and warm fingers. See Maitland's Dark Ages, p. 406.

ones. Since then your penitence and confession justly warrant such a sentence, may you be absolved before the judgment-seat of Christ from all anathema and from all your sins, by virtue of that authority whereby it was said unto the prince of the Apostles; one of his fellow-students a rule for mastering difficult study.
Ecclus. xix. 1.
St. Matt. xvi. 19. (Rheims.)

"'Whatsoever thou shalt bind upon earth, it shall be bound also in heaven; and whatsoever thou shalt loose on earth, it shall be loosed in heaven.'

"So much for that subject. But as to your reading[m], I feel annoyed, in my anxiety about you, on account of its desultoriness. [You remember] I had given instructions that by running cursorily over difficult ground in the first instance, ye should get a taste of the laborious discipline which ye have undertaken, and afterwards, going over it again, should linger more attentively over the study of the difficulty. With your customary sluggishness ye evade, in your shuffling way, obedience to my salutary precept; I might fairly wax wroth, but I am a father who joyfully puts up with blemishes in his children, and who cannot neglect the charge of his offspring, inasmuch as he embraces them with sincere affection. Read therefore logic in pursuance[n] of my plan for you, intending to resume it frequently with deeper study, if your carelessness does not stand in the way of the fulfilment of your intention. Write frequently to me in prose[o]; and in what ye write attend carefully to the propriety of your phrases and periods."

[m] "your reading"—*vestræ lectionis*; whereas in the former part of the letter the singular had been employed, *Tuorum pœnitentiam excessuum, &c.* No doubt this is because, as regards studies and reading, the letter is addressed to another pupil as well as William Turbo, probably Otho, to whom, in conjunction with William, several letters have been addressed.

[n] The words in Anstruther's printed edition are, "*idus* ordinationem meam;" but the initial letters of *idus* are in the MS. contracted, and we doubt not that the word intended is *secundus*, written by mistake for *secundum*.

[o] We find from other letters that Otho and Wilhelm were accustomed to write to Herbert in verse, and on one occasion had demanded from him a versified answer, which he declines to give. (See p. 27, and Letter XXXII. p. 29.)

Probably, Letter XLII. (p. 210), (coming, as it does, between Letter XLI. and Letter XLII. *bis*, and speaking of the studies of Herbert's correspondent,) was also meant for Turbo, though it is without an address. The reader will do well to refer to it.

We have seen in other Letters how sensitive Herbert was to any coldness in those whom he regarded with affection,—how poignantly, for example, he felt Abbot Richard's turning his back upon him in the hour of adversity. Here is another instance of the same feature of character:—

LETTER XXXIII.

To Robert, his brother and son.

"Herbert the Bishop to Robert, his brother and son [p].

<small>Herbert remonstrates with Robert upon his fickleness to an old and attached friend, and promises to requite his friendship, if he will be more steady for the future.</small>
"Mindful of the old intimacy and affection which subsisted between us, I bring against you a well-merited accusation of being unmindful of the same, and find you guilty of this fault on clear evidence, inasmuch as you never send me a word of greeting by the mouth of a new comer, nor comfort me by the appearance of a letter. I know indeed that this was of old your custom, ingrained in your character, to take delight in new friendships, and to become forgetful of the old. And this fashion might be endured in the fickleness of boyhood and youth; but as you are now passing into the more staid and settled age of a young man, do recall to mind your former friends, and gather them up again

---

[p] He probably calls Robert his *son*, as having been educated under his superintendence, and being now under his pastoral care, and his *brother*, as having been admitted into the monastery. He cannot be addressing his real brother, because he had only one, whose name began with G. See p. 7, Letter LIV.

into your heart, and into that inner chamber of your heart, in which you were wont in old times to cherish them beyond all delights and gratifications. Thereupon I will become to you once again such a friend as I sometime was to you, prompt in every emergency to give you counsel or aid, as often as your need or your will may dictate. You need suffer no pressure of circumstances; you need dread the hostility of none. My resources are abundantly sufficient both for my wants and your own; and you shall partake of them with as much ease as you can possibly desire. We have an abundant supply of all things, except wine; wine you shall find here, but in moderate quantity; of everything else there is as much as you can need."

The following attests his kindness of heart. It shows him interceding with another bishop for an erring presbyter. Perhaps the bishop in question was Richard de Beames, who in 1108 was consecrated by Anselm (the year before his own death) to the see of London. Anselm was then unwell; and the consecration was performed at his country seat, Pagham, a peculiar of the archbishop. The reader will not fail to notice a slight touch of caustic humour at the close of this letter. The Scriptural examples of the success of persistence, which Herbert adduces, go no further than repeated application. But Herbert thinks it well to remind Richard that Hunfrid has a decided "determination of words to the tongue," and is apt to stick to people, and talk them to death, "non missura cutem nisi plena cruoris hirudo," a leech who will not let them go till he has sucked out of them what he wants.

LETTER XXXI.

To Richard the Bishop.

"Herbert the Bishop to Richard the Bishop.

Herbert, admitting that Bp. Richard has reason to complain of Hunfrid's conduct, urges many passages of Scripture, and finally Richard's own comfort, as reasons why he should be forgiven. See Eph. iv. 26, and Rom. xii. 17. St. Matt. vi. 12. St. Matt. xviii. 22. St. Luke xxiii. 34. St. John x. 15.

"In taking up my pen to intercede with thee, most gracious father, for the presbyter Hunfrid, I am doubtful what sort of exordium to devise, since on the one hand the nature of the cause entrusted to me is not altogether clear, while on the other the affronts of which you have to complain are patent. But I speak to a bishop, whose anger cannot endure after the going down of the sun, and who is not wont to render to any man evil for evil. We pray daily for our own sins and those of the people; 'And forgive us our debts, as we also forgive our debtors.' Unto the prince of the Apostles, when he asked whether he should forgive one who sinned against him unto seven times, the Truth replied; 'I say not unto thee, Until seven times: but, Until seventy times seven.' Such was the law which the Truth promulgated to His followers, and which He at the very point of death confirmed by a memorable example, when He thus pleaded in excuse for His murderers; 'Father, forgive them; for they know not what they do.' So thou also, most gracious father, to whose office it appertaineth to lay down thy life for the sheep committed to thy charge, canst not surely deny pardon to any one who repents and confesses his faults. He who prosecutes with implacable resentment his revenge

St. Matt. v. 39.
for affronts offered to him, surely is not offering the other cheek to him who smites him on the right. The

St. Luke xviii. 4, 5.
wicked judge in the Gospel, who feared not God neither regarded man, conquered at length by importunity, did justice to the widow, lest by her continual coming she

St. Luke xi. 5—9.
should weary him[q]; and the drowsy friend in the middle

---

[q] "lest by her continual coming she should weary him"—*ne iterum veniens suggillaret* (MS. Bruxell.) *eum*. *Suggillo*, or *sugillo*, is a very rare word (indeed, an ἅπαξ λεγόμενον in the Vulgate, used in no other passage); and Jerome's employment of it here shows his fidelity to the

of the night, rose up on account of the persistence of him who knocked at the door, and gave him as many loaves as he had need for. So do thou also, a prelate of the Church of Christ, if not out of a regard to mercy, yet on account of this presbyter's persistence, rise and restore him to thy favour, freeing thy soul thereby from the infliction of his great talkativeness."

The next shows how he was occasionally mixed up with the domestic affairs of those under his charge. It was perhaps written on some episcopal tour he was making, which brought him into the neighbourhood of the family of two of his monks.

LETTER XXVII.

To Godwin and William.

"Herbert to Godwin and William.

"Take comfort, and obliterate from your hearts all trace of rancour and of sorrow. Your father is safe and sound, and has his every wish gratified. In obedience to the messages you sent me, I bade him (not without some apprehension) come to me, and bade W. send him; but as peace is now finally concluded between them, your father answered me that he was not minded to return home just at present, lest either he himself should be branded with fickleness and incon-

[margin: Herbert assures them that their father, who has been recently reconciled with their uncle, has good reasons for staying away from home, and has all he wants where he is.]

original, where the word ὑπωπιάζω is used. Ὑπωπιάζω is a pugilistic term, signifying to bruise one's antagonist in the face, give him a black eye; and if *sugillo* is derived from *sub* and *cilium*, the eyelid, (which query), no more exact representative of the Greek word could be found. Anyhow, *sugillo* means to give a black eye. We have in Pliny the words, "oculi ex ictu suffusi cruore et sugillati" (eyes suffused with blood, and bruised from a blow). The only other place of the Greek Testament in which ὑπωπιάζω occurs, is where St. Paul, comparing the good fight of faith to a pugilistic encounter, says, "I keep under my body, and bring into subjection;" literally, "I bruise my body, and reduce it to a condition of slavery." (See 1 Cor. ix. 27.)

stancy of purpose, or should be censured for making his brother unpopular, or throwing temptation in his way.

"It was therefore by his own will that he went thither, and by his own special request that he stays, being in want of nothing, but on the other hand abundantly supplied with the necessaries of daily life. So let your lamentation and my letter end here."

The following seems to be addressed to a novice, who had proposed to take the monastic vow, but was wavering and drawing back, through dread of the hardship, monotony, and ennui of such a life. Those who have seen Gustave Doré's picture of "The Novice," will be able to understand poor Odo's reluctance. Herbert's tone to him is, "If any man draw back, my soul hath no pleasure in him."

LETTER XIII.
To Odo.

"Herbert to Odo.

Herbert implores Odo not to draw back from the

"[1] While writing this letter, I have dipped my pen not into my ink-horn [2], but into my heart. I instruct thee from the warm affection of my own bosom, desiring to

---

[1] We can make literally nothing of the words with which this letter begins. They are, "Conflectere, dilectissime fili, tuæ visitationis consolationem quam dum scriberem, non cornu sed in corde calamum intinxi," &c. Chancellor Benson suggests, "conforter consolatione," for "conflectere consolationem;" but even so, we cannot construe the words in with what succeeds.

[2] "ink-horn"—*cornu*. Horace uses this word (Sat. II. ii. 61) for an oil-cruet. In mediæval Latin it signified an ink-horn. Ducange gives an interesting extract from one of the Carthusian statutes, giving a list of their writing apparatus, viz. quill-pens, chalk, two pumice-stones, two ink-horns (*cornua duo*), one knife, two scrapers, or razors, to scrape the parchment, a pricking instrument, an awl, lead, a metal ruler, a wooden ruler, tablets, a metallic pen. The wood used in the Vulgate for a writer's ink-horn (Ezekiel ix. 2) is *atramentarium*.

see thee received into the bosom of the Church of Norwich. Arms must be prepared for your early training in [the spiritual] warfare, equipped with which you may go on your way and succeed in avoiding the hidden snares of your enemies; your breast has to be protected by the breastplate, your head by the helmet, lest that old serpent instil the poison of his malice into your thoughts, lest your firmness of purpose should be wrecked by some rock of mistrust. My son, the religious life [on which you are about to enter] is a warfare; and under the eye of God, and with the angels as spectators, we have to fight in the theatre of this world[t] with beasts, who are all the more fell [and dangerous] because they are invisible. Snatch up then the shield of obedience[u], gird thyself with the sword of patience, brandish the spear of a prudent foresight, but take heed that the banner of our Lord's cross be attached

monastic life, but to take up the cross, that he may win the crown, resisting by a strong will all temptations to softness. See Eph. vi. 14, 17, & 1 Thess. v. 8. Rev. xii. 9, and xx. 2. See 2 Tim. ii. 3. See 1 Cor. iv. 9. See 1 Cor. xv. 32.

---

[t] "in the theatre of this world"—*in circo hujus mundi*. *Circus* is not a word found in the Vulgate; it belongs to classical antiquity. The original circus was the arena, in which races and pugilistic contests were exhibited by Tarquinius Priscus, to commemorate a victory over the Latins. It was of an oval, not a circular form, or rather in the form of a long church nave, with an apsidal termination.

[u] "the shield of obedience"—*clypeum obedientiæ*. It is perhaps to be regretted that Herbert makes the Christian shield obedience (and that, we presume, monastic obedience, obedience to the *regula*,) and not faith, which is the Apostle's image, (Eph. vi. 16); but it is to be remembered that the Apostle himself is not altogether consistent in this imagery, since he speaks of the breastplate of righteousness to the Ephesians, and to the Thessalonians (1 Thess. v. 8) of the breastplate of faith and love. It may also be questioned whether Herbert had the passage of St. Paul in his mind, inasmuch as he uses the word *clypeus* for shield, whereas the word used in the Vulgate translation of Eph. vi. 16 is *scutum fidei*. *Scutum* and *clypeus* differ materially, the former denoting the oblong shield, made of wood covered with leather, which protected the whole person, while the *clypeus* was a round brazen shield, which merely sheltered the breast and upper part of the body, and was much more easily wielded.—We cannot help thinking also that Herbert would have done better to represent patience and prudence as parts of the defensive armour. What he means by the spear of a prudent foresight, but having the banner of the cross attached to it, is doubtless that the young man should look well before him previously to becoming a professed monk, but at the same time should not allow any indisposition to take up the cross to stand in his way.

thereto and never severed from it. Mount the chariot of fortitude, and under the guidance of Truth, press towards the prize[x] which is set [before you]. Thou art enlisted in the army of that victorious Captain, whose immortal kingdom maketh mortal kingdoms to dwindle, setting bounds to each of them, and undermining the perishable glories of each by its own authority and jurisdiction [y]. Having come forth out of the world,

See Phil. iii. 14, and 1 Cor. ix. 24.

---

[x] "the prize"—*bravium*. The word used by Herbert is *bravium*, the Latinized form of the Greek βραβεῖον. This signifies a prize in the games, and is derived from the word βραβεύς, the judge, or arbiter, who assigns such prizes. The word occurs twice in those well-known passages of St. Paul's Epistles, "one receiveth the prize," and "I press towards the mark for the prize." (1 Cor. ix. 24, and Phil. iii. 14.)

[y] Judging from this passage, which breathes entirely the spirit of Hildebrand, we are inclined to think that Herbert must have deeply imbibed the doctrines which Gregory VII. seems to have considered it his mission to set forth and propagate. Chancellor Massingberd says (Engl. Reformation, p. 33); "Seeing that the world cannot be governed, while two rival authorities are at strife with each other, he (Hildebrand) was not content with asserting the independent power of the Church, but maintained its supremacy, as one to which all temporal sovereignties were subject; he claimed the right not only of investing bishops and abbots with the spirituals, but also with the temporals attaching to their offices. This, in fact, amounted to a claim to give away a third part of all the property in the country." "Hildebrand's purpose," says Dean Hook, "was to elevate the Church above the State, and to make the civil authorities subordinate to the ecclesiastical. So long as the right of investiture remained in the State, this was impossible." (Abps. of Cant., vol. II. ch. iii. pp. 240, 241.) The imperious spirit of Gregory VII., which no doubt was veiled even to himself under the pretext of zeal for the Church's honour, was exhibited in full strength when he made the Emperor Henry IV. stand three days fasting, with naked feet in the snow, before he would admit him to his presence,—a story which, though probably exaggerated, must still have been founded in fact. Anselm, we know, abetted all the claims which Gregory set up for the papacy; and Herbert here, albeit of the king's party rather than Anselm's, speaks the language of Anselm. See what is said (p. 6) as to the date of Herbert's birth. It is true that Herbert only insinuates, and does not express openly, the supremacy of the Pope over temporal kingdoms, but this is evidently what he meant; the *spiritual* kingdom of Christ could not in any sense be said to set bounds to mortal kingdoms, or make them dwindle. While we are on this subject, we cannot refrain from subjoining the following striking passage from the first of Canon Mozley's recently published University Sermons, on the text "My kingdom is not of this world."

"This is a text which has, as it were, looked at the Church ever since the Church was founded. It is like an eye fixed upon her, from which

are you seeking peace in the camp of the Church? [In a certain sense] 'much peace,' saith the Holy Spirit, 'have they that love thy name, O Lord¹.' But are you seeking [a carnal] peace? Nay, you entered the lists, to do battle against invisible spirits, malignant, as I have said, in proportion to their invisibility, and all the more practised in this warfare as their enmity began when sin did, and will continue unto the end of the world. Will that veteran undying foe, who in the pride of his heart aspired to an equality with the Creator Himself, and who in envy of their happiness, drove out the first inhabitants of Paradise, the forefathers of the human race, and afterwards, by his wiles, exposed their posterity to the sudden and severe visitation of the flood², inflicted upon them for the excess of their un-

From Ps. cxviii. (Vulg.), 165.

See Eph. vi. 12.

---

she cannot escape; she has in times past thought she has escaped from it, she has acted according to her own will, and taken her own way in claiming earthly sovereignty, in wielding the arms of this world, and converting herself into a kingdom of force; but that eye has been upon her; go where she will, and in whatever divergent paths, and circuits of those paths,—that eye has been upon her. It was upon her when St. Augustine, contrary to his first and natural convictions, which he confesses he did violence to, called in the imperial arms to suppress the Donatists; it was upon her when Gregory VII. in her behalf claimed the monarchy of the world, and exercised the rights of such a monarchy; it was upon her, and more sternly, when by simple carnage she suppressed the Reformation in Italy, Spain, and France; it was upon her when she sat in the judicial halls of the Inquisition; upon her very tribunal, while her eye was fixed upon the subjects of her power, that eye was looking upon her; it was upon her afterwards when she kept up prohibitions, penalties, imprisonments, and the like, in behalf of her own faith; and it is looking upon her now—now, when the circuit of her worldly power seems to be accomplished, when the whole cycle is over; and when, after ages of earthly supremacy, from which she has lately step by step descended, the order of things has all but rolled back again upon its hinges, and the Church stands face to face again with Christ in the judgment-hall, saying, 'My kingdom is not of this world.'"

¹ "thy name, O Lord"—*nomen tuum, Domine*. Herbert here is quoting from memory. It is the *law* of the Lord, not His *name*, which is the object loved. The Vulgate has, "Pax multa diligentibus legem tuam, et non est illis scandalum:" the Douay, "Much peace have they that love thy law, and to them there is no stumbling-block."

² There are certain words with which this sentence is cumbered (here marked in italics) to which we can give no meaning, and therefore content

cleanness—will that foe spare, think you, a raw recruit like yourself? My son, the city of God is a pilgrim in this world, and from righteous Abel unto the last of the elect no man is crowned, except he have striven lawfully. Before the Law and under the Law our forefathers battled and endured much hardness, greeting from afar the presence of their Saviour, and by the virtues which decorated them prefiguring Him who should come in the fulness of the time.

<small>See 1 Pet. ii. 11.
See St. Matt. xxiii. 35.
From 2 Tim. ii. 5.
See Heb. xi. 13.
Gal. iv. 4.</small>

"The Captain [of our salvation], so long waited for, came at length to his labouring forces, made a charge upon the bands of the enemy, slew them, subdued them, humbled them, demolished them, and dooming to eternal disgrace the first murderer and father of sin, bound and cast him into everlasting burnings. Satan burns, condemned to the prison of hell, and shall the soul which Christ hath set free consent to the promptings of Satan? It is only the flagging camp-followers [b] of our army whom Satan harasses, and the wrath, which he dares not vent upon those who manfully fight him, he puts forth in stripping the faint-hearted of their spoil. That great and truly matchless wrestler, St. Paul, well knew how emasculated the strength of our enemy is, whose overthrow he thus taunts in the accents of victory, being secure of his own triumph over him: 'I have fought a good fight,' saith he, 'I have finished my course, I have kept the faith. As to the rest, there is

<small>See John viii. 44.
See Rev. xx. 2, 10.

2 Tim. iv. 7, 8, V.</small>

---

ourselves with simply transcribing the whole clause; "eorumque sobolem *novæ peregrinationis exilio errabundam* Divinæ severitatis inopinato cataclismo obscenitatis intemperantia fraudulenter opposuit." Is there possibly some confusion between the narrative of the tower of Babel and that of the flood, and is Herbert thinking of the scattering abroad of the human family " upon the face of all the earth," when he speaks of the posterity of Adam and Eve as " wandering into exile with a new journeying " (hitherto unheard of)?

[b] "camp-followers"—*lixas*. *Lixa* means properly a victualler in a camp, who cooked what was needed. It is connected with *lix*, an old Latin word (as some say) for boiling water, though *lix* (*licis*), a word actually used by Pliny, and meaning *ashes*, answers nearly as well for a derivation. *Elixus*, which means seethed or sodden, is probably connected with the same word.

laid up for me a crown of justice, which the Lord the just judge will render to me in that day.' And elsewhere [he saith], 'To me, to live is Christ: and to die is gain.' Phil. i. 21, V.

"The ungodly tell you their idle tales, but [heed them not]; leaning on the cross of thy Lord's Passion, 'thou shalt walk upon the asp and the basilisk: and thou shalt trample under foot the lion and dragon;' Ps. xc. 13, 7, V. 'a thousand shall fall at thy side, and ten thousand at thy right hand: but it shall not come nigh thee.' You dread a weariness of the life which is temporal; but the recompence of the life which is eternal is held forth to thine expectations. You shrink from poverty; but Christ calleth the poor blessed. You praise good cheer; but 'Meats for the belly, and the belly for the meats: but God shall destroy both it and them.' You See Luke vi. 20. 1 Cor. vi. 13, V. dwell in memory upon the lusts which once were so agreeable to you; but the stern virtue of the Apostle replies in these terms to the charms of your [enervating] pleasures; 'He that soweth in his flesh, of the flesh also shall reap corruption. But he that soweth in the spirit, of the spirit shall reap life everlasting.' Gal. vi. 8, V.

"This is a heavy yoke, but the fear of [eternal] death and the yearning for [eternal] life enables men to bear it easily. Art thou not equal to the endurance of what youths and maidens can endure? The Virgin Agnes[c]

---

[c] "The Virgin Agnes"—*Anna virgo*. The name, as given in the MS. of the Letters, is "Anna virgo." The allusion however must be to St. Agnes. Neale says (Lit. Gall. p. 60) that the genitive case of this saint's name often takes the form of *Agnæ*. This would point to *Agna* as one of the nominative forms, and *Agna*, by a slip of the pen, might easily be written *Anna*.

"St. Agnes" (whose festival appears among the black-letter days of the Church of England, and is kept on Jan. 21) "left a name behind her, which was very much cherished by the early Church. She was a young Roman lady of patrician birth, who was sought—not, probably, in honourable marriage—by the son of a Prefect of the city, A.D. 304. Her refusal to accede to his desires brought upon her the full force of the brutal heathenism which characterised the age of martyrdoms. Before the Prefect she made an open confession that she was a Christian, making the sign of the Cross instead of offering incense to Vesta, as she was required

despised the dignity of the Roman prefecture, and became the spouse of Christ; thy kinsmen and countrymen of rank betake themselves in crowds to the religious habit; and wilt thou still gloat over the uncleanness of thy former conversation? Away with your entreaties; let me hear no more of your begging off. Listen, my son; thou canst not here rejoice with the world, and afterwards reign with Christ. He is rich enough, who, associated with Christ in poverty, shall by

See 2 Tim. ii. 12.

to do for the renunciation of Christianity. The holy maiden was then vilely disrobed and tortured on the rack; and after vain endeavours to bring about her apostasy, was at last beheaded. The circumstances of her death made a great impression upon the Christian world, for St. Jerome says that the tongues and pens of all nations were employed in praising her constancy; and her memory has ever since his time been greatly venerated. It was recorded that while her parents were praying at her tomb (probably in the Catacombs) she appeared to them in vision, and spoke words of comfort to them respecting her rest and peace with her Saviour. St. Augustine speaks touchingly of her name: 'Blessed is the holy Agnes, whose passion we this day celebrate; for the maiden was indeed what she was called; for in Latin Agnes signifies a *lamb*, and in Greek it means *pure*.'" (Blunt's "Annotated Book of Common Prayer," Rivingtons, 1866, vol. i. p. 39.) She is represented in Christian Art with a lamb standing by her side, and a sword or a palm-branch in her hand. Two lambs are annually offered at the altar of the Basilica of St. Agnes outside the walls of Rome, the fleeces of which are used in making the palls which the Pope sends to Archbishops, as the symbol of their investiture with metropolitical jurisdiction. A long letter attributed to St. Ambrose, and found at the end of the Benedictine edition of his works, gives the story of St. Agnes with a minuteness of detail which is evidently imaginary. The Prefect's son is said to have fallen in love with her as she was coming from school (she was only thirteen at the time of her martyrdom), and to have offered her the richest presents and ornaments to induce her to marry him. Agnes refused, saying that she had received more precious ornaments from the Spouse to whom she had already plighted her troth. The youth fell ill with his passion; and his father the Prefect (one Symphronius) applied to her parents to give her in marriage to his son. On Agnes's still making the same refusal, and on the same ground, the Prefect told her that he had the fasces carried before him as Prætor, and wondered that another suitor for her hand could be considered more worthy than a man of his son's rank. A parasite having informed the Prefect that the Spouse to whom Agnes had plighted her faith was Christ, with whom she was connected by certain magical arts, she was formally arraigned, tortured, and eventually executed. ("Cùmque pater diceret in fascibus se constitutum præturam agere, et idcirco quemvis etiam illustrem virum minimè sibi

his sad-coloured robe [d], and coarse bread, and constant attendance in the narrow cloister, earn the presence of God and the free expanse of heaven. Hear thou where and when and what recompence Christ promiseth to His faithful followers [e]; 'In the regeneration,' saith He, 'when the Son of man shall sit on the seat of His majesty, you also shall sit on twelve seats, judging the twelve tribes of Israel;' and 'Every one who shall forsake house, or lands, or father, or mother, or wife, or

Matt. xix. 28, v.

From Matt. xix. 29.

debere præferri; cæpit tamen vehementissimè inquirere quis esset sponsus, sancta cujus Agnes potestate gloriaretur. Tunc exstitit quidam ex parasitis ejus, qui diceret hanc Christianam esse ab infantiâ, et magicis artibus ita occupatam, ut dicat Christum sponsum suum esse." *Ambrosii Opp. Ed. Ben. Parisiis*, 1690, tom. ii. pp. 479, 480, &c. &c.)

[d] "sad-coloured robe"—*pulla tunica*. *Pullus*, derived from the Greek πελλός, means darkish gray, dun; Ducange gives as an equivalent the word *fuscus*. Singularly enough *pullus* means also white (but apparently the white of a natural production, not artificially produced); and in this sense is derived from *purus*, dim. *purulus*. As Herbert is addressing a young man who thought of making his profession in the Cathedral Monastery of Norwich, and as this was a Benedictine house, it may be presumed that *at this period* the Benedictine habit was dark or sad-coloured. The Rev. I. Gregory Smith in Dr. William Smith's "Dictionary of Christian Antiquities" (*Art.* Benedictine Rule and Order) tells us; "About dress, as if foreseeing the varying requirements of various climes," [Benedict] "leaves a discretionary power to the abbat, affirming merely the unvarying principle that it is to be cheap and homely (c. 55); and that there are to be two dresses, the 'scapulare,' or sort of cape, for field-work, and the 'cucullus,' or hood, for study and prayer, (cf. Fleury, *Hist. Ecc.* xxxii. 16). The colour of the tunic or toga, being left undetermined by the founder, has varied at different times: till the eighth century it was usually white (Mab. *Ann.* iii.)." In Lanfranc's rule for the English Benedictines nothing seems to be said on the colour of the costume, the rule for the reception of novices being merely that they shall be divested of all secular garments, and invested with the regular things of the monastery (*rebus monasterii regularibus*), with the exception of the cowl, a collar being sewn to the tunic (præter cucullum, capitio assuto tunicæ). At the close of the ceremony of reception, the abbot is to bless the cowl, and divesting the youth of the sheep-skins in which he appeared, with the words, "May the Lord put off thee the old man," he is to invest him with the cowl, saying, "May the Lord put on thee the new man." (cap. xvii.)

[e] "faithful followers"—*asseclis*. In classical writers the word *assecla* seems to be used in a contemptuous sense, equal to "a hanger-on." In mediæval Latin it is often equivalent to client.

children for my name's sake, shall receive an hundredfold, and shall inherit eternal life.' Break loose, brother, from these trammels, and the whole toil and difficulty of thy undertaking dwindles to nothing."

The next Letter is to Hugh the Prior (possibly of Thetford); and in three short lines despatches business and expresses affection.

LETTER IV.
HERBERT TO HUGH.

"Herbert to Hugh the Prior.

A short affectionate letter, asking for ink and parchment.

"Send me some ink[f] and one or two skins of parchment[g]. I would have written more; but it is enough for one who loves to say to the object of his love that he cannot do without him."

[f] "some ink"—*encaustum*. This word is originally an adjective, formed from the Greek, and signifying *burnt in*. It denoted a kind of painting practised by the ancients, in which the crayon was dipped in wax of various colours. *Encausto pingere* is to practise this art, paint in encaustic or enamel. *Encaustum* afterwards came to signify an ink for the purpose of writing; and the "sacred *encaustum*" of Justinian's Code was an ink which the Roman Emperors used for imperial subscriptions. It was of the imperial colour, reddish purple, and was made of the purple dye, prepared in some way by the application of fire. (So that in this use of the word, the notion of burning which there is in the etymology, is still retained.) This word is the origin of the French *encre*, and the Italian *inchiostro*. The classical word for ink used by Pliny and Cicero is *atramentum*, literally anything that serves to dye black. (See note d, p. 198, and note l, p. 282.

[g] "parchment"—*pargomentum*. This form of the Low Latin word for parchment is interesting as being, perhaps, the nearest approximation to our English parchment. Curiously enough the form is not found in Ducange, the forms there given being, i. pergamena, ii. pergamenum, iii. pergamentum, iv. pergamerium, v. pargamenum, and vi. parquamenum. The original form was doubtless pergamena, sc. charta, = paper of Pergamus. The usual story is that Eumenes II., king of Pergamus, invented parchment about 190 B.C., when founding his celebrated library at Pergamus on the model of the Alexandrian library. Our English word parchment comes, not direct from the Latin, but through the Norman French, *parchemin*, the *t* finding its way into the word from the tendency of the tongue to make the *t* sound after a final *n*, as in *hound*, where only the letters *hun* are of the root.

And now we hasten to the termination of our Bishop's career. The year 1118 witnessed A.D. 1118. the death of Pascal II. of Tuscany, and the accession to the papal throne of Gelasius II. of Gaëta. His reign was but short. He was succeeded in the course of the next year by Callixtus II. of Burgundy, who very soon after his accession struck a heavy blow at the cause in which Herbert felt such an interest, the independence of the English Church, by presuming to consecrate Thurstan Archbishop of York without communicating with the king and Archbishop of Canterbury, and therefore without making that profession of obedience to the see of Canterbury which both king and archbishop had decided to be a necessary condition of this consecration. This act of defiance to the Crown and Church of England was done at Rheims, where Callixtus had convened a synod.

But another death occurred this year, which must have been more trying to Herbert than that of the Roman bishop, with whom probably he had only once had an interview ten years ago. On May day, 1118, died Queen Matilda, whose virtues were so venerated by the people, that she went under the name of "Molde the good." The king in the preceding year had gone to Normandy, drawn thither by a revolt which the partisans of William his nephew (now eleven years of age) had raised. His spouse being in declining health, he had returned to console her with his company at the Christmas of 1117. Prince

A.D. 1118. William, her son (afterwards lost in the White Ship at the Catteraze), had gone to Normandy with his father, but did not return, like his father, to spend the Christmas in England. Henry's stay with his queen was very brief; and he soon hurried back again to the scene of war. She never saw him again. She was a devout and cultivated woman, whose pursuits were those of piety and charity, while poetry and minstrelsy formed her recreations. We are told that for the last twelve years of her life she resided at the palace of Westminster. There probably Herbert, who · admired greatly the purity and devoutness of her character, often visited her. The following letter, together with the devotional piece, which he composed for her use, both seem to indicate that he acted as her spiritual counsellor. The tone of the epistle is adulatory, no doubt; but perhaps not more so than that of the preface to a certain Book, which speaks of Queen Elizabeth as "that bright occidental star."

LETTER XXV.

To the Queen Matildis.

"To his sovereign lady, and to the common mother of all England, Matildis the Queen, Herbert her priest of Norwich, sendeth greeting.

Herbert expresses his ardent desire to see the queen, compares her to the

"As the sucking child longeth for the breast, or the thirsty soul for water, or the wearied for rest, or the exile for his country, so longeth my soul for the refreshment of thy presence. Thy name is as ointment poured forth, and the lovers of truth in our country, attracted by its sweet savour, run after it with an insatiable desire. Esther, the eastern queen [h], who took more delight in piety than in royal pomp, filled the earthly Jerusalem with garments and precious stones, with ointments and spices, the excellence of which Solomon so much admired that there was no more spirit in him. So thou also, most blessed queen, hast enriched our western coast with such a wealth of faith and graces, of virtues [i] and beneficent actions, that we have

Queen of Sheba, eulogises her devotion to the Virgin Mary, and deprecates misrepresentations which had been made of him to Roger of Salisbury.

[h] "Esther, the eastern queen." Our Herbert resembles Homer in more than one point. First, there are several places which contest the honour of his birth. Secondly, *aliquando bonus dormitat*. Here he appears to confuse Esther with the Queen of Sheba (to whom, by the way, the unpoetical name of *Bilkees* is given by the Arabs, Bilkees being the oldest name of a Queen of Sheba on record); he makes Solomon to have "no more spirit in" him, from his admiration of the Queen's presents, instead of the Queen to "have no more spirit in her" on witnessing the display of Solomon's wisdom; and finally, he represents the "vestes" in the same episode of Israel's history as part of *her* munificence, instead of (as the Scriptures represent them) part of *his* state,—"the apparel of his ministers."

See Cant. i. 3. See 1 Kings x. 5, and 2 Chron. ix. 1, 4.

[i] However exaggerated this strain of eulogy may be thought, Queen Matilda really seems to have been an excellent and devout person. She went by the name of "Molde the Good," and the extract which we now give from Miss Strickland's "Queens of England" (vol. i. pp. 133, 134, etc.), shows that she was renowned, as Herbert says, for "*actus*" (works of usefulness), no less than for devotional and ascetic exercises. "Matilda fully verified the primitive title bestowed by the Saxons on their queens, Hlafdige, or the 'giver of bread.' Her charities were of a most extensive character, and her tender compassion for the sufferings of the sick poor carried her almost beyond the bounds of reason, to say nothing of the restraints imposed on royalty. She imitated the example of her mother, St. Margaret, Queen of Scotland, both in the strictness of her devotional exercises, and in her personal attentions to those who were labouring under bodily afflictions. She went barefoot every day in Lent to Westminster Abbey, clad in a garment of hair-cloth; and she would wash and kiss the feet of the poorest people, for which, according to Robert of Gloucester, she was once reproved." After mentioning the incident of her brother, Alexander the Fierce, finding her in one of her English palaces, engaged in washing the feet of some aged mendicants, and declining with a smile to assist her, as she intreated him to do for the benefit of his soul, Miss Strickland continues thus; "But to do Matilda justice, her good works in general bore a character of more extensive usefulness; so much so, that we can feel the benefit of them to this day in the ancient bridge which she built over the Lea. Once being, with her train on horseback, in danger of perishing while fording the river Lea at

none beside thee to whom we are minded to cling with a similar love. The odour of thy devotion hath reached to the end of the earth; and in the regions round about thy genuine innocence and modesty is well known. 'The queen,' saith the prophet, 'stood on the right hand' of God, 'in gilded clothing, surrounded with variety.' And thou, too, standest by that Queen, to whom none but queens do service; queens who are so much the happier, by how much the more devout is the homage which they pay her. By the side of this Queen, I say, thou standest, and dost service with insatiable longing to her sons Christ and John, whose power of recompensing you is as great, as is your desire of receiving blessings from them. The Queen, whom thou servest, hath power to do all things, because she bare Him, Who is the most powerful of all, to wit, Christ her Son, the Bridegroom of your soul, Who is fairer than the children of men. I have said but little, while I desire to say much; but I feared to seem as if I were adding an additional burthen to the affairs of the kingdom, which you administer with such praiseworthy solicitude. I aspire to high things; but the accustomed benefits conferred on me by your munificence embolden me to presume so far. I pray your highness to salute my Lord the Bishop of Salisbury[k] from me,

Ps. xliv. 10, Douay.

Ps. xliv. 3, V.

Oldford, during a high flood, in gratitude for her preservation *she built the first arched bridge ever known in England*, a little higher up the stream, called by the Saxons Bowbridge, still to be seen at Stratford-le-Bow." In addition to this, she founded the Hospital of St. Giles's-in-the-Fields, directed her attention to making new roads and repairing the ancient highways, and generally facilitating communications between different parts of the country,—one great condition this of civilization. "These public benefits, which Matilda the Good conferred upon the people, were in all probability the fruits of her regency during the absence of her royal husband in Normandy." It was doubtless during some such period of absence that the present letter was addressed to her; for she is spoken of lower down as "burdened with the affairs of the kingdom, and administering them with praiseworthy solicitude."

[k] "my Lord the Bishop of Salisbury." This was Roger de-la-Poer, one of the most powerful magnates of the realm. He began his career (as the humorous Sydney Smith tells us that "all rose-and-shovel men"—

and to beg him not, in disdain of my poverty, to find an occasion of becoming cool to me, and not to trust

"Charles James" included—have begun theirs) as a poor curate at Caen, where he so delighted king Henry by getting through the morning service rapidly, as to elicit from him an oath in a loud voice that he had at length met with a priest fit for a soldier. It seems that he compressed both matins and mass into half-an-hour. Such merit could not be passed over; and Roger climbed from a royal chaplaincy to a bishopric, and enjoyed in that position more than episcopal (or even archiepiscopal) power. Henry finding him pliant (for he seems to have had that easy good-nature which often compounds for higher qualities) made him first Chancellor and afterwards Chief Justiciary,—then a much higher office than that of Chancellor, the holder of which was prime minister, as well as (under the king) supreme judge. "The king," says William of Malmesbury, "denied Roger nothing, giving him estates, churches, prebends, and abbeys, and committing the kingdom to his fidelity. He decided causes, had the charge of the treasury, and regulated the expenditure of the kingdom. Such were his occupations when the king was in England; such, without an associate or inspector, when the king resided in Normandy. And not only the king, but the nobility—even those who were secretly stung with envy by his good fortune, and more especially the inferior ministers and the debtors of the king—gave him almost whatever he could fancy. Did he desire to add to his domain any contiguous possession, he would soon lay hold of it by entreaty, or purchase, or force. He erected splendid mansions of unrivalled magnificence on all his estates; and his cathedral he dignified to the utmost with matchless buildings and ornaments." Royal favour however is a precarious tenure; and Roger, for some offence, of which we do not know the nature, was dismissed from the office of Chief Justiciary two years before Henry's death. The worst part of his history is to follow. Though, while Henry was alive, he had solemnly pronounced his daughter, Matilda, to be heiress to the crown, and had led the way in swearing fealty to her, he allowed himself to be bribed by Stephen to assert that "males only could mount the throne of England," and to support Stephen's usurpation accordingly. In this world he had his reward; for Stephen was even more profuse in his bounty to him than Henry had been. "By the birth of God," said the usurper, "I would give him half England, if he asked for it. Till the time be ripe, he shall tire of asking before I tire of giving." He was made lord treasurer, and allowed under royal licence to build a castle at Devizes, where he lived in almost regal state. But before long he quarrelled with Stephen, as he had done with Henry, refusing to attend a council, to which he was summoned at Oxford. Stephen sent a strong force to Devizes to lay siege to his castle; but Roger was prepared for the assault, and showed a disposition to fight. The king however had a shaft in his quiver, which was to bring down this proud churchman. He had got possession of an illegitimate son of Roger's, whom he threatened to hang before the walls of the castle, unless it were at once surrendered. The threat had the desired effect, and Roger

his enemies in regard to his friends. But as regards my illness, about which your excellence condescends to enquire, our brother and son, Stannard, who conveys to you this letter, will give you all particulars."

The following prayer for the use of the queen, occurring among the Letters, and numbered as Letter XVIII., has beauty as a literary and rhetorical effusion, much of which is necessarily lost by presenting it in an English dress, and we have no doubt that a sincerely devout feeling (though lamentably alloyed with the superstitions of the age) dictated it to him and welcomed it in her; but we must be allowed to express our hope and belief that, if in her last hours he visited the queen, he pointed her to some surer ground of hope and comfort than the intercession of one of God's holiest saints. The piece has great historical interest, from the witness which it bears to the deep corruption of faith and worship which had eaten like a gangrene into the Church of that period. Here alas! is that overlaying of Holy Scripture with legends and fables of man's invention, that indelicate and almost prurient recognition of virginity as the queen of Christian

---

made his submission, and was spared out of respect to the sacredness of his office. He died not long after of a quartan ague in the December of 1139. He cannot have been at any time of his life a man of principle; but we think it important, for the credit of our author, to remark that the worst parts of his character did not show themselves till long after Herbert's death. He must have had that art of ingratiating himself with others, which, of course, like other talents, might be used for good, but as a fact is often found united with the most unprincipled conduct. The particulars given above are for the most part (including the extract from Malmesbury) drawn from Lord Campbell's "Lives of the Chancellors," (London, 1845,) vol. i. chap. 2, pp. 50—54.

virtues, taking precedence of them all in the favour of God and the veneration of man, and that reposing of confidence in the intercession and patronage of Saints, and particularly of the Blessed Virgin, which constitute the virus of the Roman system, and which in this country three centuries later ensured its downfall. We can only allege in Herbert's defence, what we think some of the foot-notes will show, that men far more eminent in the Church than he, both for their gifts and their undoubted Christian character, held and taught exactly similar views. The vices are those of the theology of the day, to which we cannot expect him to rise superior; and it should be remembered, in forming a general estimate of his religious character, that these errors are balanced by very many passages both of his Letters and Sermons, which indicate in the writer a simple and uncorrupted piety. It is the last piece of Herbert's with which we shall garnish this memoir.

LETTER XVIII.

A Prayer for the Queen, which Herbert the Bishop made.

"John, thou friend of Christ, whom Christ loved with a peculiar love, at whose marriage He turned the water into wine, that He might withdraw thee, who wast ordained to preach unto the world the Word made flesh, from that same marriage[1], lest thou shouldst be   St. John ii. 9.
St. John i. 14.

---

[1] "that He might withdraw thee ... from that same marriage"—*ut te ex iisdem abstraheret nuptiis.* Archbishop Trench ("Notes on the Miracles,"

defiled by touching another carnally; John, I say, thou
lover of Christ, who at the *last* supper of our Saviour
with His disciples, and at the *first* supper wherein the

London, 1846, p. 96, note) says, "A late tradition makes St. John not
merely an eye-witness, but to have been himself the bridegroom at this
marriage, who, seeing the miracle that Jesus did, forsook the bride, and
followed Him. The author of the Prologue to St. John, attributed to
St. Jerome, relates 'Joannem nubere volentem a nuptiis per Dominum
fuisse vocatum,' though without more close allusion to this miracle. The
Mahometans have received this tradition that John was the bridegroom
from the Christians." We have been unable to find the passage of Jerome
referred to by the Archbishop. The reader who is curious in the matter
may find the traditions on the subject in the Apostolicæ Historiæ of
Fabricius, liber v., Codex Apocryphus, tom. ii. These histories profess
to give every legend which at various times may have been fabricated respecting the doctrine, miracles, lives, epistles, and other supposed writings
of the Apostles. The fifth book treats of St. John. It represents him as
making a long prayer to our Lord before lying down in his grave, to this
effect; "Unto Thee, O Lord, do I pray, who hast granted unto Thy
servant to be pure from intercourse with woman, and who when in my
youth I was hastening unto marriage, didst say to me, Thou art necessary
unto me, John; I need thy help. But when through the ardour of youth
it appeared to me that I could not keep Thy commandment, and distrusting
my ability to preserve my chastity, inclined my mind a second time to
marriage, Thou, good Lord that Thou wast, by bringing on me sickness
of body, didst severely chastise me, and gavest me not over to death.
When a third time I meditated marriage, Thou recalledst me from it by
a slighter impediment" (this is supposed to have been an unusually stormy
night, on which the wedding was to have been celebrated); "Thou, Lord,
didst deign to say to me upon the sea, John, hadst thou not been Mine,
I would have permitted thee to marry." A full note is appended to this
narrative by Fabricius, in which he too, like the Archbishop, refers to
a preface to St. John's Gospel, which passed under the name of Jerome.
He tells us also that the bride's name is variously given as a certain
Anachita, or as Mary Magdalen, and says that similar stories are found
in Rupertus Tuitiensis, Ludolph of Saxony, Pelbartus of Temesvar, and
others of later date. None of the above authors is earlier than the twelfth
century; and Haymo, who is also referred to by Fabricius, lived in the
ninth. Baronius (Annal. Eccles., A.D. 31, sect. xxx.), after mentioning
the legend, states that it is entirely fictitious and of quite late origin, since
no mention at all is made of it in the early Fathers. "If," he says, "the
ancients had been acquainted with such a story, Jovinian the heresiarch,
who so pertinaciously denied that St. John the Apostle and Evangelist was
unmarried, would have given Jerome no trouble at all." So far were
the Fathers from having any idea of such a story, that they rather set
forth the miracle in Cana as a solemn sanction given by our Lord to
the marriage rite.

Lord's Body and Blood were sacrificed and partaken of [m], didst lean upon the bosom of our Saviour Himself, St. John and there didst rest, that from the hidden fountain of xiii. 23. His bosom thou mightest drink in that which thou mightest preach to all nations (to wit, the true light which lighteth every man that cometh into the world), St. John fastening thine eyes, after the manner of an eagle [n], i. 9. upon that sun, whereunto never man had yet lifted up his mind; John, who at the cross of Christ and under the cross of Christ, wast made the brother of Christ, and the son of Christ's mother, when He said to His mother concerning thee, 'Behold thy son;' and St. John to thee in like manner concerning the mother which xix. 26, 27. was granted thee, 'Behold thy mother;' John, who when cast into the boiling oil [o], didst not burn, the re-

[m] "sacrificed and partaken of"—*immolationis et participationis*. The reader will not fail to observe the distinction here brought out by Herbert between the sacrificial and sacramental aspects of the Holy Communion. Unhappily these two aspects have been kept asunder in practice as well as in theory; and hundreds now attend the mass who do not communicate, thus acting in direct contravention of the Lord's command, who instituted the Supper to be received, saying, as it has been well remarked, "Take, eat, this is my body," not "This is my body, take, eat." (See Rev. W. Scudamore's "Notitia Eucharistica," Part I. chap. xiv. sec. ii. London, Oxford, and Cambridge, 1876.)

[n] "fastening thine eyes, after the manner of an eagle"—*more aquilæ, tuos oculos infigens*. Hugo de S. Victore in his first book, *De bestiis et aliis rebus*, cap. lvi. tells us that the eagle (*aquila*) derives its name from its keenness of sight, *de acumine oculorum*, and that the hen-bird hangs her young upon her claws, and holds them up against the sun's orb, and if she observes any of them, through weakness of the eye, declining to look steadily at the sun, throws them away as degenerate. He quotes a passage from St. Gregory, which gives the twofold symbol of the eagle in Scripture, according to which the word sometimes denotes the powers of darkness or the powers of this world (this sense corresponding to the rapacity of the eagle), sometimes the subtil intelligence of the saints, or even the incarnate Lord Himself, who passed quickly through our lower atmosphere, and soon sought again His native heaven. St. John, being the great mystic and contemplative among the Apostles, and soaring in the opening of his gospel to the Pre-existence and Deity of Christ, is supposed to be symbolized by the fourth living creature in Ezekiel i., inasmuch as, by flying aloft in contemplation, he deserted the earth, and penetrated with an eyesight of subtil intelligence into the inner mysteries of the Word.

[o] Herbert very probably obtained this well-known legend from Jerome,

freshing coolness of thy virginity obtaining for thee this honour that thou feltest not that fiery heat;—but to what end am I thy handmaid, who am not able to utter worthily thy praises, prolonging my prayer? Rev. i. 9. John, then, who, when driven into banishment, didst live among the angels [p], and, when brought back unto the chief city of thy bishopric, didst raise the dead [q],

who in his commentary on St. Matthew (chap. xxi. "Ye shall drink indeed of my cup," &c.) says, "If we read the ecclesiastical histories, in which it is related that John, for the testimony which he bore to Christ, was thrown into a vat of boiling oil, and came forth thence a [victorious] wrestler to receive Christ's crown, and was immediately banished to the Isle of Patmos, we shall see that the spirit of martyrdom was not wanting to him, and that he actually drank the cup of confession, which cup the three youths in the furnace of fire drank, although the persecutor did not shed their blood. (S. Hierom. tom. iv. part i. col. 92, ed. Bened.) We fail to find the legend of the boiling oil in Eusebius. The earliest author in whom we have met with it is Tertullian (circ. 200 A.D.) In his *De præscriptione hæreticorum*, a treatise giving rules for Catholics in dealing with heretics, it is ruled that all disputes on matters of faith or practice must be decided by the judgment of some church planted by an apostle. "Go to the church next to you," says Tertullian, "and seek its judgment. Is Achaia near you? You have Corinth to go to. If you are not far from Macedonia, you have Philippi, you have the Thessalonians. If you are able to go into Asia, you have Ephesus. But if Italy is adjacent to you, you have Rome, where to us also there is an authority ready at hand. How happy is that church unto which the Apostles poured forth, together with their blood, the whole doctrine of Christ, where St. Peter was made like unto his Lord in His passion, where St. Paul was crowned with the same form of martyrdom which St. John the Baptist underwent, where the Apostle John, after being plunged in boiling oil and suffering nothing, was banished into an island." Possibly the attributing this marvellous effect to the refreshing coolness of St. John's virginity, is a flourish with which Herbert has decorated the narrative.

[p] "didst live among the angels"—*inter angelos vivebas*. Probably this is an allusion to the number of angels whom St. John sees or holds intercourse with in the Revelation, see chap. xiv. 6, 8, 9, 15, 17, 18, and chap. xv. 6, chap. xvi. 1, 3, 4, 8, 10, 12, 17, chap. xvii. 1, chap. xviii. 1, chap. xxii. 8, 16.

[q] "didst raise the dead"—*mortuos resuscitabas*. Eusebius tells us (lib. v. c. 16), on the authority of Apollonius, that St. John at Ephesus raised to life again, by the divine power of God, one that was dead. This Apollonius is a Christian writer, supposed to have been Bishop of Ephesus about 192 A.D. He wrote against the Montanists, and Tertullian in reply wrote against him. Those who are curious as to miracles of resuscitation wrought by St. John, should consult the *Apostolicæ Historiæ*

didst drink poison and feltest no harm[r], didst turn stones into jewels and boards into gold[s], and didst [St. Mark xvi. 18.]

in the Codex Apocryphus of Fabricius, where several such stories are given. One of them seems to be framed on the model of the miracle wrought by our Lord on the widow of Nain's son; the son of a widowed mother is being carried out of the city attended by a large crowd of mourners, who throw themselves at the Apostle's feet, and beg that he would raise the youth (Stacteus) to life. He prostrates himself, weeps and prays intensely for a long time; then, after ordering the corpse to be divested of its cerements, he makes him an address, in which he says, that though, allured by carnal love, he had lost his soul (Stacteus had been married only thirty days before), yet in consideration of his ignorance of God and Christ, he (St. John) has poured forth prayers and tears for his resuscitation, in order that he might go and warn Atticus and Eugenius, two lapsed disciples of the Apostle, what glory they had lost, and what penalty they had incurred. Stacteus rises up from his bier, adores the Apostle, and says to the reprobate disciples, "I saw your angels weeping, and Satan's angels rejoicing in your discomfiture."

[r] "didst drink poison and feltest no harm"—*virus bibebas et non curabas.* This story also will be found at great length in the *Apostolicæ Historiæ* (chap. xx. *et sequent.*). When St. John had made all the idols in the temple of Diana crumble into dust with his word, and twelve thousand Gentiles were converted by that spectacle, he was challenged by the idol priest Aristodemus to drink poison. St. John, relying upon his Master's promise (Mark xvi. 18), said that the poison could not hurt him. Aristodemus went to the proconsul, and procuring from him two criminals under sentence of death, gave them deadly poison to drink in presence of the Apostle, in order to shake his resolution when he should see them fall down dead. St. John however took the poison-cup, made the sign of the Cross over it, and prayed to Him in whose Name the serpent resteth, the dragon taketh flight, the viper is silent, and the restless toad becomes torpid, the scorpion is destroyed, the regulus (a species of serpent) is overcome, and the venomous spider worketh no mischief, to neutralise the poison,—and then drank it off. The people waited three hours to see what would happen, and then as John exhibited a more cheerful countenance than ever, and gave no symptoms of trembling or becoming pale, began to cry aloud, "There is one true God, whom John worshippeth." The authority for this legend seems to be Isidorus Hispalensis, who flourished at the beginning of the seventh century, or rather an unknown writer *De morte sanctorum,* whose treatise is found among Isidore's works. Mr. Plumptre, in Smith's "Dictionary of the Bible," *art.* John the Apostle, says, "The memory of this deliverance is preserved in the symbolic cup, with a serpent issuing from it, which appears in the mediæval representations of the Evangelist. Is it possible that the symbol originated in Mark x. 39 ('Ye shall indeed drink of the cup that I drink of'), and that the legend grew out of the symbol?"

[s] "didst turn stones into jewels, and boards into gold—*lapides in gemmas, ligna in aurum convertibas.* The story is told in the *Apostolicæ Historiæ* of Fabricius, lib. v. c. 15. Two eminent citizens of Ephesus, con-

change these same things back again into their own nature; John, unto whom, when waxen old in the truth, that almighty Captain of our Salvation, under whom thou hadst so gloriously fought the good fight, appeared most graciously before thine end¹, together

vinced by the miracles, and moved by the exhortations of the Apostle, had followed the counsel given by our Lord to the rich young man, had sold all their goods and distributed to the poor, and followed St. John in his peregrinations about the country. But when they arrived in the city of Pergamus, they saw certain persons who had previously been their servants, clothed in silk garments, and going about the streets in great state and pomp. Hereupon an arrow from the devil's quiver winged its way to their hearts, and they began to regret the sacrifice they had made, and to wish their property back again. St. John told them they might recover it all, if they would bring him bundles of straight rods, each of them separately swathed. When they had done this, the Apostle invoking the name of Christ, turned the rods into gold; and then ordered small stones to be brought from the beach. When this latter order was executed, he again invoked the name of the Lord, and turned the stones into jewels. An appeal being made to the goldsmiths and jewellers of the neighbourhood, who were allowed to test the materials thus miraculously produced, they said that gold so pure, and gems so precious, they had never seen. Then St. John bade them redeem their earthly property with these jewels and this gold, for they had lost all their interest in heavenly property. He bade them in an ironical strain buy silk garments, that for a time they might bloom as the fading rose. He cited to them *in extenso* the parable of Dives and Lazarus, reminded them of the miraculous powers with which they themselves had been endowed, of healing the sick, casting out devils, &c., and warned them that these powers had ceased by reason of the preference they gave to earthly over heavenly wealth. Then he read them a lecture on the vanity of superfluous possessions, whether in the way of meat, drink, or raiment, and of the precariousness of worldly wealth, the possessors of which, as they brought nothing into the world, so they can carry nothing out of it. He closed with telling them that they should endure everlasting punishment. And so ends the story. This legend also seems to be drawn from the unknown writer *De vita et obitu Sanctorum*, whose work is bound up with those of Isidore of Seville. Isidore became Bishop of Seville in 600 A.D., about five hundred years before Herbert's time. He was a man with a voracious appetite for learning, and has left numerous works behind him, the chief of which is an encyclopædia of arts and sciences, treating of all subjects of human knowledge, from God and the angels down to etymology, domestic utensils, book-binding, and writing materials. The work *De vita et obitu*, &c., (attributed to him, but as Fabricius thinks falsely,) contains short biographical notices of sixty-five Old Testament saints, from Adam to the Maccabees, and twenty-two New Testament saints, from Zacharias to Titus.

¹ "before thine end"—*ante tuum finem*. This legend too is found in

with hosts of angels and the reverend company of the Apostles, and said unto thee, 'Come my beloved one, to banquet at my supper with thy brethren, whose fellowship thou hast longed for with deep-drawn sighs;' John, who having been comforted with such exceeding great consolation, didst approach the holy altar [of thy Church] arrayed in thy chasuble and priestly ornaments, didst there salute thy people, didst fortify thy own last moments with the unfailing viaticum, which thou hadst made with thine own hands, and then didst enter in safety into the place of thy burial, which had been dug for thee beforehand, and there composing thyself to rest in a strange and solemn manner of burial, didst restore thy soul and body unto Christ thy lover, as free from the pain of death as thou hadst lived pure from the plague-spot of the flesh [u] ; John, then, who art such and

the Codex Apocryphus: " When St. John was ninety-seven years of age, the Lord Jesus Christ with His disciples appeared unto him and said, Come unto Me, for it is high-time for thee to sit down at My banquet with thy brethren. Hereupon, when the Apostle had risen up, the same Lord added, Thou shalt come to Me on Sunday next, the day of My resurrection, five days hence." The legend goes on to say, that on the following Sunday an immense multitude assembled at the church, and joined in the celebration of the mysteries from the earliest dawn. St. John makes them a short address, which passes into a prayer, and when he had finished it, breaks and blesses bread, looking up to heaven, and bequeaths his portion of the holy loaf to the people, while he retains theirs. Then begin the arrangements for digging his grave, according to the subsequent part of the legend, which will be found in the next note.

[u] "plague-spot of the flesh"—*contagione carnis*. After breaking and preserving a portion of the bread, as was stated in the former note, St. John ordered two coffins with iron tools to be brought, and dismissing the multitude, went with a few of his disciples to a sepulchre, where he ordered the young men to dig a deep grave, and preached while they were kneeling. The grave being dug, he took off his outer garment and laid it in the grave, and appeared in a single linen vestment. He then spread out his hands towards heaven, commending to Christ the disciples who had followed him, and asking the Lord to receive him, that he might be with his brethren. The bystanders responding *Amen*, so brilliant a light shone forth from the Apostle's countenance, that no one could bear to look at him by the space of one hour. Then having given them the *Pax vobiscum*, and bade them Adieu, he laid himself down in the grave, and ordered them to cover him in, and straightway he gave up the ghost. The narrative, which professes to be from a spectator, says that some of those present rejoiced,

so great as I have said before, yea rather as I have wished to say, but the matter of thy praises, being so

others wept. Forthwith manna issued from the sepulchre, which natural production the place to this day produces. Augustine and others record another particular of the same legend, that this manna comes from the heaving and bubbling of the earth over the Apostle's grave, which is an effect of his still-continued breathing; for as he was buried while sleeping, consequently his bosom still heaves and agitates the earth above him. With a candour and a discretion truly Herodotean, the great Latin father adds, "Let those decide the truth of the matter who know the place; for myself, I can truly say that I have heard the report from those whose authority is of weight," (*non a levibus hominibus*). Augustini Opp. (ed. Bened.) vol. iii. col. 820 v. in Johan. Evang. chap. xxi. tract. 124.

The work from which the above extracts are made, and which is given by Fabricius in his *Codex Apocryphus*, is called the Apocryphal Acts of the Apostles, or a history of the Apostolic Conflict, ascribed to Abdias, said to have been the first bishop of Babylon, and divided into ten books, the first treating of St. Peter, and the last of St. Philip. The work was originally written in Latin about A.D. 910. Herbert therefore may have seen it, as it was published a good century and a half before his time. A few particulars, not given in this and the preceding notes, which Herbert mentions, are

i. St. John's fortifying his last moments with the unfailing viaticum. This perhaps is Herbert's addition to the story as told by Abdias, an addition suggested to him by what is said of the Apostle's reserving for himself a portion of the Eucharist.

ii. His arraying himself in his mitre and priestly ornaments. The word for "arrayed in thy chasuble," is *infulatus*, whereupon we commend to our readers the following remark of the Rev. Wharton Marriott, in his *Vestiarium Christianum*, London, 1868, p. 132, note 267, (he is commenting on a passage from Hugo de Sancto Victore on sacerdotal vestments): "This is one of the few early instances of the use of the word *infula* to designate one of the Christian vestments. It here means not a covering for the head, (which would be in accordance with the classical use of the word), but a chasuble." Hugo describes the *infula*, or chasuble, as put on last, over the other vestments, and being more excellent than the rest. It symbolizes love, of which the Apostle speaks, "Yet shew I unto you a more excellent way." We cannot but think that Hugo might have more appositely quoted Col. iii. 14, "Above ('Επὶ πᾶσι τούτοις) all these things put on charity, which is the bond of perfectness." Polycrates, quoted by Eusebius, lib. iii. c. xxxi., tells us that St. John wore upon his brow a plate of gold (πέταλον, *lamina*) with the sacred Name inscribed upon it, such as was worn by the Jewish High Priest, and called the crown of the mitre.

Polycrates is included in Jerome's *Catalogus Scriptorum Ecclesiasticorum* (also called *Liber de viris illustribus*), being the forty-fifth writer there enumerated. The extract from his writings, in which the notice occurs of St. John's *aurea lamina*, is to be found in the Synodical Epistle which he

weighty, hath choked the endeavours of the speaker, I beseech thee, look upon thy handmaid, listen to the devotion of a weary and heavy-laden mind, heal my sickness, hold forth to me the long-expected healing. Behold my groans, behold my sighs, behold my lamentations, and comfort the heart of thine afflicted handmaiden. Thou indeed art a virgin, and a son of the Virgin[1], but then He thy Master was a virgin also.

addressed to Victor, Bishop of Rome, in which he rests his own time of keeping Easter on the authority of St. John and the ancients. Polycrates was Bishop of Ephesus, and is naturally proud of Ephesus and of the Asiatic Churches generally. He tells us that St. Philip and two of his virgin daughters sleep at Hierapolis, St. John and another daughter of St. Philip's at Ephesus, St. Polycarp at Smyrna. (See S. Hieron. (ed. Bened.) tom. iv. part 2, col. 114.) In an earlier article of the same work, containing a notice of St. John himself, No. ix. in the Catalogue, he speaks of two sepulchres of St. John at Ephesus, which he calls *duæ memoriæ*, though he says that one of these is usually assigned to John the Presbyter, the other to the Apostle.

[1] "Thou indeed art a virgin, and a son of the Virgin"—*Virgo quidem es et Virginis filius.* In Jerome's first book against Jovinian (ed. Bened.), tom. iv. part 2, col. 169, where he is speaking of the sublime way in which St. John commences his Gospel, as compared with the other Evangelists, he says, "Virginity hath expounded what marriage did not attain to know; and that I may embrace much in few words, and set forth the singular privilege enjoyed by John and in John by virginity, the virgin mother was commended to the virgin disciple by the virgin Lord;" and again, in his letter to the virgin Principia (Epist. xcvi. tom. iv. part 2, col. 780), he speaks of St. John as a virgin son receiving a virgin mother as the legacy of a virgin Lord. Ambrose, in his *De Trinitate Tractatus*, traces in like manner with Jerome St. John's superior spiritual sagacity to his virginity. He is speaking of St. John's recognising our Lord in the morning light on the shore of the lake of Galilee, whereupon he says, "Truly it was becoming and every way suitable that virginity should first recognise the virgin body." It is questionable however whether the work is Ambrose's. Ambros. Opp. (ed. Bened.) tom. ii. Appendix, col. 340 E. In a fine passage of Anselm's Meditations, (Med. xv. p. 231, col. 2 C, D,) he says, "Who is that, I pray thee, that is leaning upon His breast, and reclining his head on His bosom? Happy is he, whosoever he be. Oh, now I see! John is his name. O John! what sweetness, what grace, what suavity, what light and devotion didst thou drink in from that fountain! there truly are hidden all the treasures of wisdom and knowledge. There is the fount of mercy, there the domicile of fatherly affection, there the honey-comb of eternal sweetness. Whence came all those privileges to thee, O John? Art thou loftier than Peter, holier than Andrew, or at least more acceptable to God than the other Apostles? This is a special privilege of thy virginity, because as a virgin thou wast elected by the

He who received the sinner Mary and submitted His head to her anointing, who presented His feet to be washed by her tears, who refused not her kisses, who cherished the repentant sinner, and answered the thoughts of the murmuring Pharisee, 'Many sins are forgiven her, because she hath loved much;'—He had done no sin. John, have compassion on this thy handmaid bowing down with her face towards the earth and throwing herself at thy feet; despise her not, as she lies, for whom thy lover, Christ, laid down His life. By thy intercessions I pray that I may be reconciled unto Christ, who hath honoured thee with the peculiar favour of His love. Before all other Saints have I chosen thee alone; yea, I have chosen as mine advocate him whom I hear to have been beloved before all others. Obtain thou pardon for my negligences, and lighten thou with thy visitation the burden of my soul, which hath well-nigh cast away hope. And oh! in lightening these my cares, thou blessed John, see that thou have on thy side as thy companions all thy friends, whom by my naughty life I have procured to be mine enemies. Plead, yea, plead the cause of thy mourning handmaid, John, in the most gracious ears of the eternal Judge, who will have mercy rather than judgment, and chooseth rather our resurrection unto newness of life, than to exercise His wrath in the way of punishment. He who solemnly charged thee and thy partners that ye should pray even for those at whose hands ye were suffering persecution, will not be able to deny to thy request the forgiveness of my sins. O blessed John, may I attain, may I attain at length through thy merits to reconciliation! May I gaze upon the holy calm of God's countenance, may I embrace the fruition of God; may I come unto the king-

Lord, and more beloved than the rest on that ground. Now, therefore, O virgin, whosoever thou art, draw nearer to the Saviour, and delay not to claim for thyself some portion of this sweetness. But if thou art not able to walk in this more excellent way, leave the breast of John, where he inebriates himself with the wine of gladness in contemplating the Lord's

dom, may I come unto the palace, may I come unto the supper, with the delights of which the blessed angels and all the elect, their fellow-citizens, are refreshed, and, everlastingly gazing thereupon, are satiated with the inexpressible sweetness and the sweet inexpressiveness of the divine nature[y]. Grant, O blessed John, that I, being gathered into that eternal city, may hear the song which both thou singest and those virgins also sing with thee, who follow the Lamb whithersoever Rev.xiv.4. He goeth. Finally, O most blessed John, that the cry both of my heart and of my prayer may be at length brought to an end, commend and give thine handmaid, to be preserved for evermore, unto the protection of thy lady and mother the Virgin Mary, who both mercifully adopted thee, and also was the mother by nature of Christ, her Son, our Lord, who with the Father and the Holy Ghost liveth and reigneth, God for ever and ever[z]. Amen."

divinity; run thou to the breasts of His humanity, and there suck the milk which may be the nourishment of thy soul."

Augustine, *de bono conjugali*, (Opp. tom. vi. col. 335 B,) speaks with much greater moderation of the merits of celibacy. The gist of his remarks is that there may be continence in a man's habit of mind, although being wedded, he is not continent in deed, just as there may be as much of the virtue of Christian patience in other saints, whose trial is lifelong, as in a martyr, whose trial is compressed into an hour. John was equal in patience to Peter, though he was not, like Peter, actually a martyr; and Abraham, who begat children, may have been equally continent with John, who was never married. "The celibacy of the one, and the marriage of the other did Christ service, according to the difference of times and circumstances upon which each of them fell."

[y] "of the divine nature" — *divinæ substantiæ*. The word used by Herbert to express the divine nature is *substantia*, which here means the complex of the divine attributes. We cite an apposite passage from the Rev. J. H. Blunt's "Dictionary of Doctrinal and Historical Theology," *Art.*, Substance. "Of the Divine Substance it can only be stated that God is the Divine attributes, and these attributes are God. 'Absit ut spiritus secundum substantiam dicatur Deus, et bonus secundum qualitatem; sed utrumque secundum substantiam,' [Aug. de Trin., xv. 5]. His substance is a simple multiplicity of attributes, as His attributes are the manifold unity of His substance [Ibid. vi. 4]. 'Quicquid attribuitur Deo est ejus essentia; et propter hoc, sapientia et virtus idem sunt in Deo, quia ambo sunt in Divina essentia,' [Aquin. *Summa*, I. XL. 1.]"

[z] The reader should observe the formula with which Herbert closes his

The venerable bishop himself did not long survive his sovereign lady. The following her to her grave (whether the abbey of Westminster, or of Reading, or the cathedral of St. Paul was her final resting-place) is his last recorded act. On the 22nd of July, 1119, he himself expired, in the twenty-ninth year of his episcopate, and (if we have rightly conjectured the date of his birth) hard upon the threescore years and ten, which are the appointed limit of human life. His monks were plunged into the deepest grief by the loss of one who was not only their bishop, but their founder. Cotton, who joined the Benedictine community at Norwich in the latter half of the succeeding century, thus bewails his memory;—

Marginalia: A.D. 1119. Death of Bishop Herbert.

"O happy society of Religious, had it only been allowed for a longer time to enjoy such a pastor's superintendence! O woeful, O wretched condition of human existence, that those things which we devoutly wish to continue with us longest, the soonest fade away! O day deserving to be bewailed with every fountain of tears [which was ever shed], deserving of being doomed to eternal darkness, which deprived the world of the presence of so great a man!"

Marginalia: Bartholomew Cotton's lamentation, in looking back at the event. See Job iii. 4, 5.

prayer, though addressed, we regret to say, to St. John throughout. On this formula we extract a passage from the Rev. J. H. Blunt's "Annotated Book of Common Prayer," (4to. Lond. 1866), p. 70. "The last member of Collects has always been constructed with great care, and according to rules which were put into the form of memorial verses, at a period when it was the custom to write the collect in a short form, and only to indicate the ending by 'per,' 'qui vivis,' 'per eundem,' or whatever else was its first word or words. One of these aids to memory is as follows :—

"'*Per Dominum* dicas si Patrem presbyter oras.
 Si Christum memores *per eundem* dicere debes.
 Si loqueris Christo *qui vivis* scire memento ;
 Qui *tecum*, si sit collectæ finis in Ipsum ;
 Si memores flamen, *ejusdem* dic prope finem.'"

Herbert has adopted the third of these terminations, only changing the verb from the second to the third person.

He goes on to say that the bishop was interred in his cathedral church "with many tokens of grief from all his comprovincial bishops," most of whom (it may be presumed) attended his funeral, in token of the esteem and confidence with which they regarded him, as a light of their Church, which was now, in the good Providence of God, quenched for ever. He was laid before the high altar in a sarcophagus, "worthy," says Cotton, "of being the burial-place of so great a man." The monkish epitaph on the sarcophagus, as given by Weever ("Funeral Monuments," London, 1631, p. 787, &c.) runs thus:—

"Inclytus Herbertus jacet hic, ut pistica [a] nardus,
    Virtutum redolens floribus et meritis.
A quo fundatus locus est hic, edificatus
    Ingenti studio, nec modico precio.

[a] *pistica nardus*—"pure" (or genuine) "spikenard." The word *pistica* is the Latin form of the word πιστική, which is used by St. Mark (xiv. 3), where our translators have not attempted to render it in the text except by the *spike* in *spikenard*, but in the margin have suggested the words "pure" or "liquid" as its equivalent, and again by St. John (xii. 3), where there is no marginal rendering. In St. Mark's Gospel the Vulgate rendering of the word is *spicatus;* in St. John's (as here) *pisticus*. It is observable that in both these places the Vulgate uses the substantive *nardum*, not *nardus*, which (as Herbert's monkish panegyrist has represented it) is *feminine*. The Rheims version has "*right* spikenard" in the passage of St. John, and in that of St. Mark represents the πιστική (as our own version does) merely by the *spike* in *spikenard*. This *spike*, however, being from the Latin *spica* (because the blossom of the nard-plant is shaped like an ear of corn), cannot possibly give the sense of πιστικός. That word may, if from πίνω, mean *potable, liquid;* or, if from πίστις, *genuine, unadulterated*, which is the preferable sense. We learn from Bede that there were many sorts of nard, and "all less pungent than the Indian nard, which is the costliest." Hence the word πιστικός in the Gospels probably means that the nard used in anointing our Lord was unadulterated, and of the best sort. The saying that the memory of a good man yields a fragrant odour is a just, and not an uncommon, comparison. Compare the well-known couplet;

    "Only the actions of the just
      Smell sweet and blossom in the dust."

Vir fuit hic magnus probitate, suävis ut agnus,
  Vitâ conspicuus, dogmate precipuus.
Sobrius, et castus, prudens, et Episcopus almus,
  Pollens concilio, clarus et officio.
Quem .... [b] vndecimas Iulio promente Kalendas,
  Abstulit vltima sors, et rapuit cita mors.
Pro quo, qui transis, supplex orare memor sis
  Vt sit ei saties [c] alma Dei facies."

Of this not very favourable specimen of monkish versification, we present to the reader the following translation;—

"Here lieth renowned Herbert, the blossoms and merits of whose virtues yield a sweet savour, as of pure spikenard, and by whom this temple was founded, and builded [afterwards] with great zeal, and at no moderate cost. A great man was he, of sterling integrity, yet gentle as a lamb, alike exemplary in his life and eminent in his teaching, a bishop sober-minded and chaste, wise, and a foster-father [to his flock], able as a councillor, and celebrated for his fulfilment of the duties of his office. But alas! when the eleventh day of the Kalends of July appeared, death swiftly snatched him away, and the destiny which awaits all at last took him from us. Thou, who passest by, be mindful to offer

---

[b] It is difficult to see what word would meet the exigencies of the metre and sense but *tamen*, which we would suggest.

[c] We believe the allusion to be to that exquisite verse of Psalm xvii. 15, "As for me, I will behold thy face in righteousness: I shall be satisfied, when I awake, with thy likeness." "Ego autem in justitia apparebo conspectui Tuo; *satiabor*, cum apparuerit gloria Tua." *Vulgate* (xvi. 15); "But as for me, I will appear before thy sight in justice: I shall be satisfied when thy glory shall appear." *Douay* (xvi. 15). Our Prayerbook Version ("When I awake up after thy likeness, I shall be satisfied with it") distorts the sense. It is not the image *within us*, but the shining in *from without* of God's image (which is Christ), that will satisfy us at the Resurrection morning, the same image which the disciples beheld on the mount of Transfiguration. The Hebrew word *Temunah* occurs again in Numb. xii. 8, where it is said of Moses, "The *similitude* of the Lord shall he behold." (See Dr. Kay on Psalm xvii. 15.)

supplications and prayers for him, that [when he waketh up] he may be satisfied with the light of God's gracious countenance."

The reader will observe that there is a *lacuna* in this epitaph, probably from there being a word in it, which Weever was unable to decipher, though how it came to pass that the slab had suffered such an erasure in a single word only, we are unable to offer a conjecture. As far as we know, Weever is the first author who mentions the above epitaph, and as he died about the year 1632, nearly a century after the Reformation, we presume that the monument, the inscription on which had evidently a monastic origin, must have survived that great crisis in the religious history of the country. We are left to suppose that it continued down to the time of the Rebellion, when it was probably razed by the Puritans, and its contents scattered to the winds[d]. In the margin of this epitaph, as it is

[d] The frightful desecration done by the Puritans in Norwich Cathedral is thus chronicled by Bishop Hall in his *Hard Measure* (Works, Oxford, 1837, vol. i. lv.) :—

"There was not that care and moderation used in reforming the cathedral church bordering upon my palace. It is no other than tragical to relate the carriage of that furious sacrilege, whereof our eyes and ears were the sad witnesses, under the authority and presence of Linsey, Toftes the sheriff, and Greenwood. Lord, what work was here! what clattering of glasses! what beating down of walls! *what tearing up of monuments!* what pulling down of seats! what wresting out of iron and brass from the windows and graves! what defacing of arms! what demolishing of curious stone-work, that had not any representation in the world, but only of the cost of the founder, and the skill of the mason! what tooting and piping upon the destroyed organ-pipes! and what a hideous triumph on the market-day before all the country; when, in a kind of sacrilegious and profane procession, all the organ-pipes, vestments, both copes and surplices, together with the leaden cross which had been newly sawn down from over the green-yard pulpit, and the service-books and singing-books that could be had, were carried to the fire in the public market-place;

found in Weever, are the words, "Ex vet. MSS. in bib. Cot." Desirous of ascertaining as nearly as possible the age of the epitaph, we asked the assistance of Mr. Edward A. Bond, Superintendent of the MSS. department in the British Museum. He has favoured us with the following letter, which he kindly allows us to print :—

"*British Museum,*
7 *July,* 1876.

"The folio Catalogue of the Cottonian MSS. published in 1802 gives no guide to the Epitaph, but in the earlier Catalogue of 1696, one of the volumes, Tiberius, B. xiii., is stated to contain, amongst other things, 'Epitaphia, sive versus conscripti in loculos quorundam virorum magnorum Angliæ.' The MS. suffered in the fire of 1732, and the Epitaphs which were at the end are now wanting. It is probable that the verses on Bp. Herbert were in this collection, for the MS. was of the thirteenth century. There is a considerable collection of old Epitaphs by Camden in one of the Cotton volumes, but that on the Bishop is not amongst them. I have little doubt that Weever copied from Tiberius, B. xiii., now, as far as the Epitaphs are concerned, irrecoverably gone.

"EDWARD A. BOND."

The MS., then, from which in all probability Weever copied this epitaph, was of the thirteenth century,—the century succeeding that in which Herbert died. The epitaph itself may have been, probably was, composed earlier. William de

a lewd wretch walking before the train, in his cope trailing in the dirt, with a service-book in his hand, imitating in an impious scorn the tune, and usurping the words of the litany used formerly in the church."

We may be tolerably sure that among the first "monuments" "torn up" would be that of the Founder, which doubtless was an object of special veneration.

Turbe, the third bishop of Norwich in succession to Herbert, had been, as we have seen, a disciple and correspondent of his; and whatever Eborard, his immediate successor, whose episcopate was full of troubles, may have done, we can hardly think that De Turbe (who held the see from 1146 to 1174) would have allowed his old bishop and preceptor to go without some commemoration by way of inscription on his sarcophagus. The question is interesting, as throwing some light upon a moot point respecting the origin of the verses called Leonine, that is, Latin hexameters and pentameters, which rhyme at the middle and the end. The invention has been ascribed to Pope Leo II. (681—683), an hymnologist and reformer of the Gregorian chant; to a poet of the name of Leon in the reign of Louis VII. of France, which would fall just in the middle of the twelfth century, (Louis joined the crusades in 1146); and to a celebrated canon of Notre Dame of Paris, named Leonius[e], of a later date. Du-

[e] Here is an article from a French Biographical Dictionary, which questions Leonius's authorship of Leonine verses, and asserts they may be met with some six centuries earlier.

"LEONIUS. Poëte Latin moderne, vivait vers le milieu du douzième siècle. Les critiques l'ont diversement supposé chanoine de S. Victor, de S. Benoît, et de Notre-Dame de Paris. M. Ginguené s'efforce d'établir que Leonius ne fut jamais chanoine régulier de S. Victor, mais qu'il fut successivement chanoine séculier de S. Benoît et de Notre-Dame. Ses poëmes n'ont pas été imprimés. Le principal est une traduction de l'ancien Testament en vers latins. Le volume 97 du fonds de S. Victor nous offre le recueil le plus complet de ses œuvres. Suivant la mode de son temps, Leonius a composé quelques vers rimés; mais rien ne prouve qu'il ait jamais fait usage de la rime *léonine*. On l'a donc mal à propos considéré comme l'inventeur de ce rhythme. *On a des vers léonins du sixième et même du cinquième siècle.*"

It must be remembered that rhyming verses are quoted by Cicero (Tusc. Disp.) from Ennius, the father of Roman poetry (B.C. 239—169); and the rhymes can hardly have been unintentional. "Rhyme being already well-

cange says that Leonine verses existed long before this Leonius (whose exact date, however, he does not give); but that he possibly may have developed them by the addition of a second rhyming syllable. Second rhyming syllables, however, are found, no less than single ones, in the above epitaph; for we have

   A quo fundatus locus est hic, edificatus,
as well as
   Ingenti studio, nec modico precio.

And the *probabilities* certainly are that the epitaph was not later than 1174, when De Turbe died. We may, perhaps, suppose that the French poet in the reign of Louis VII. first set the fashion of Leonines, and that either De Turbe himself, or one of the Norwich monks under his inspiration, was bitten with the fashion, and composed these verses in the infancy of the art. —But it is right to say that there is, in favour of its having had a later origin, the circumstance that Bartholomew Cotton, who died shortly after 1298, does not mention the epitaph. It is not very easy to account for his omission, if we suppose it to have existed in his time.

known in the Latin language, many circumstances naturally occasioned its more extensive use. As the language degenerated in purity, as the tone of literature was debased, false ornaments, antithesis, puns and rhyme, became more usual in prose writers, particularly the ecclesiastics. Cyprian, Sidonius Apollinaris, Cassiodorus, and Augustine, abound with them. As the genuine spirit of poetry evaporated, poets gradually substituted other contrivances to maintain their distinguishing character." (Sir Alexander Croke's Essay on Latin rhyming verse.) Sir Alexander, who thoroughly investigated the subject, derives the word *leonine* "from Leonius, or Leoninus, a canon of the order of St. Benedict at Paris, and a monk of St. Victor's at Marseilles, who lived about the year 1135." (Essay, Oxford, 1828.)

The next notice we find of Herbert's tomb is by the celebrated Sir Thomas Browne, author of "Religio medici," in his treatise called "Repertorium;" or, "The antiquities of the Cathedral Church of Norwich, A.D. 1680." (Sir Thomas was born in 1605, and died in 1682, the year after the admission of Humphrey Prideaux to a prebend of Norwich). It runs thus :—

"In the Choir towards the high Altar, and below the Ascents, there is an old Tomb, which hath been generally said to have been the Monument of Bishop WILLIAM HERBERT" (see p. 1 of this Memoir, *n.* a), "Founder of the Church, and commonly known by the name of the Founder's Tomb. This was above an Ell high; but when the Pulpit, in the late confusion, was placed at the Pillar where Bishop *Overall's* Monument now is, and the Aldermen's Seats were at the East End, and the Mayor's Seat in the middle of the High Altar, the height of the Tomb being a Hindrance unto the People, it was taken down to such a Lowness as it now remains in."

It should be observed that Sir Thomas says nothing of any inscription; and we may presume therefore that none existed in his time, the monastic epitaph having been erased (to use his own term) "in the late confusion." But the Founder was not to remain without some record in his own Cathedral of his great and good deeds. In the year 1681, on the fifteenth of August, Humphrey Prideaux, a clergyman of great attainments and unusually strong character, was, on the presentation of Lord Chancellor Finch, then Earl of Nottingham, admitted to a prebendal stall in the church of Norwich. It appears that he threw his usual energy with very little delay into the antiquities of the Cathedral, for among his recently-published letters to John Ellis, edited by Mr. Edward Maunde Thompson (Camden Soc., 1875, pp. 121, 122), we find the following. The foot-notes are by Mr. Thompson.

"*Norwich*, Dec. 26. [1681].

"... Ransackeing our treasury I find several old manuscripts, from which I have gathered a very particular account of the foundation and history of our church. Herbert de Lozinga[f], first Bp. of Norwich, was our founder; he was born in pago Oxamiensi in Normandy, was prior of Fischamps in that country, and was after, by William Rufus, made abbot of Ramsey, and then Bp. of Thedford, from wch place he translated ye episcopal sea to this city and built ye cathedral here, and was after a long while Chancellor of England under Henry ye First. That I would desire you to inform me is, when he was first chancellor, and when he ceased so to be; of which you will find an account in Dugdale's Origines Jurisdiciales, at the end of which is a catalogue of all ye chancellors since ye Conquest; and if you have any bookes of French geography I would gladly be informed what kind of place this Oxam might be which gave birth to him, and likewise ye same of Fischamps in which he was prior. In our manuscripts I find ye name writ differently; one hath it Fiscanum Monasterium, another Fiscamum, and a third Fischamps, ye French name. Pray let me receive your information herein as soone as you can. Y^e defect of bookes in this place makes me trouble you, for I have occasion to be informd herein; for ye truth is, our founders monument being defaced in the late wars,

---

[f] Herbert Losinga, born at Exmes (or Hiemes) in Normandy; Prior of Fécamp; made Abbat of Ramsay by William II. in 1087, and Bishop of Thetford in 1091. He removed the see to Norwich in 1094. Died 1119. He was never Chancellor. Prideaux completed the restoration of his tomb in 1682.

I am again restoreing it, and would gladly be informed in those particulars in order to the contriveing of a new inscription. Our mayor, since his goeing to London to appear at ye Councill, hath an estate of 700^l per annum fallen to him, his elder brothers family being extinct in (a) child which dyed last week."

"*Norwich, Jan.* 2^d. 1681(2).

"I doe most heartyly thanke you for ye favour of yours, and ye account you are pleased to give me concerneing Oxam. If there be any such place near Feschamps, y^t is ye place where our founder was born; for he was prior of Feschamps, and in our registers of great antiquity, is said to be born in pago Oxamiensi, which some mistakeing have given occasion to Alexander Nevel [g], and afterwards to Bp. Goodwin [h] in his History of Bps., to publish to the world y^t he was born in Oxford. I hope by this you are secured of a faculty place; if soe, I wish you much joy of it, and advise you to thinke of takeing your D^{rs} degree in laws as soon as you can, next Act if I may be harkned to. . . ."

From the perusal of these two letters, coupled with the fact that Prideaux in his epitaph upon Herbert distinctly declares him to have held the office of Chancellor, one would naturally suppose that the Dean's correspondent had consulted Dugdale's "Origines Juridiciales [i]," and found the name of our Herbert in the "Chronologie of the Lord Chancellors and Keepers of the Great

---

[g] Alexander Nevile, in his "Norwicus," printed at the end of "De Furoribus Norfolciensium Ketto duce," 1575.

[h] Francis Godwin, Bishop of Hereford, "De Præsulibus Angliæ," 1616.

[i] "Originales Juridiciales; or, Historical Memorials of the English Laws, Courts of Justice, &c., &c. . . . . Also a Chronologie of the Lord Chancellors and Keepers of the Great Seal, &c., &c. By Sir William Dugdale, Kt. now *Garter*, Principal King of Arms. London: 1680."—Dugdale was born in 1605, and died in 1686.

Seal" appended to that work. This however could not have been the case. Under the reign of Henry I. Sir William Dugdale mentions only five Chancellors (one of whom held the post twice, once before and once after his consecration as bishop); 1. "*Will. Giffard* (Episc. *Wint.*)," 2. "*Rogerus* (postea factus Episc. Sarum)," 3. "*Galfridus* cogn. *Ruffus* (postea Episc. Dunelm.)," 4. "*Randulphus*," and 5. "*Gauf.* Episc. Dunelmensis." Dugdale took this list from Selden's "Brief Discourse[j]," which he himself had edited in 1672, when *Norroy* King of Arms. Selden gives references; for Giffard, *Text. Roff. cap.* 6; for Roger, *W. Malm. f.* 91. *a. l.* 2; for Geffrey Ruffus, *H. Hunt. f.* 220 *b.* 10; for Randulph, *H. Hunt. f.* 218 *b. n.* 40; for Geffrey (when Bishop), *Regist. Eccl. Elien. in Bibl. Cotton. f.* 29 *a*,—which references in his "Origines" Dugdale omits. But this is all the difference between the two.—Philipot on the other hand, in his "Catalogue of the Chancellors[k]," enumerates a Herbert among those of the reign of Henry I., but expresses a doubt whether he is to be identified[l]

[j] "A Brief Discourse touching the Office of Lord Chancellor of England. Written by the learned *John Selden* of the *Inner Temple*, Esq[re], and Dedicated by him to Sir *Francis Bacon*, Knight, then *Lord Keeper* of the *Great Seal* of ENGLAND. By WILLIAM DUGDALE, Esquire, NORROY King of Arms. LONDON, 1672.—A true CATALOGUE of the *Lord Chancellors* and *Keepers of the Great Seal* of England, from the *Norman Conquest*, untill this present Year 1671."—Selden was born in 1584, and died in 1654.

[k] "The Catalogue of the Chancellors of England, the Lord Keepers of the Great Seale: and the Lord Treasurers of England. With a Collection of divers that have beene Masters of the Rolles. By J. P[hilipot], Summerset Herald. Printed at LONDON by *Tho. Cotes*, and are to be sold by *Andrew Crooke* in Paul's Church-yard, 1636."—Philipot died prematurely, Nov. 12, 1645.

[l] Philipot got his doubts from Holinshed, who (under the reign of

with Herbert de Losinga. This is his list under Henry the First's reign. "*Waldricus*, Chancellor to Henry the first, in *Anno dom.* 1103, being *Anno* 3 of his raigne." 2. "*William Gifford*, aforesaid was againe Chancellor." 3. "*Herbertus*, Chancellor in *Anno* 4 *Henry* the first, in *Anno dom.* 1104 as appeareth by an annonymall pamphlet in written hand, of whom I am not yet resolved, whether this were *Herbertus Losinga*, Bishop of Norwich, or noe." 4. "*Roger*, Bishop of Salisbury . . . . was Chancellor to King *Henry* the first, in *Anno dom.* 1101 being the first year of King *Henry* the first." This catalogue of Philipot's was compiled from earlier ones, as appears from the following extract from Wood's "Athenæ Oxonienses" (Bliss ed. vol. ii. col. 108, London, 1815) under the head THYNNE. Among Thynne's works is enumerated "A Catalogue of the Lord Chancellors of England.—MS.—From which, as also from the endeavours made this way by Robert Glover, sometimes Somerset herald, and of Tho. Talbot, formerly clerk of the records in the Tower of London, John Philpot, Som. herald, did frame his *Catalogue of the Chanc. of England*, &c. Lond. 1636. qu."

"Queene Elizabeth," *An. Dom.* 1579. *An. Reg.* 21) gives a list of the Chancellors. Among them (p. 1273, 2d col.) occurs the following;

"Herbertus chancellor in the fourth yeare of Henrie the first, in the yeare of our saluation one thousand one hundred and foure (as appeareth by an anonymall pamphlet in written hand) of whome I am not yet resolued whether this were Herbertus Losinga bishop of Norwich or no."

Blomefield, in his history of Norwich, refers to this passage of Holinshed as bearing out his own statement (made without any qualification);

"After the death of *William Rufus*, he" [Losinga] "was in great Favour with his Successor *Henry* the *Ist.* whose *Chancellor* he was in 1103." (But Holinshed makes it out to have been 1104, as above.)

Sir Henry Spelman's Glossary[m] also makes Herbert to have been Chancellor in the year 1104 A.D.

So that here we have two authorities (Spelman and Philipot) in favour of Herbert's Chancellorship, against two which exclude him from that dignity (Selden and Dugdale), Dugdale's testimony, however, resolving itself evidently into that of Selden.

Philipot's list, we are told by Anthony à Wood, was partly "framed" from the researches of Talbot, "*who was clerk of the records in the Tower of London;*" and the latest and most eminent authority on this subject, Sir Thomas Duffus Hardy, who searched all those records with a view to his "Catalogue of the Lord Chancellors" (London, 1843), inserts Herbert among them (between Godfrey and Geoffrey Rufus) with this note; "(Cart. Antiq. Turr. Lond. Y. 31). Supposed by Philpot to be HERBERT Bishop of Norwich. The year 1104 is assigned for his Chancellorship by Spelman and Philpot. His name does not occur in Dugdale's list."

Sir Thomas, with great kindness and courtesy, has consulted for us (Feb. 21, 1877) the charter from the Tower referred to in his Catalogue as "Y. 31," but fails to make out the name of Herbert there at present. "Y. 31" is a grant to

[m] "Glossarium Archaiologicum, Continens Latino-Barbara, Peregrina, Obsoleta, et novatæ significationis vocabula; quæ post labefactatas à Gothis, Vandalisque res Europæas, in Ecclesiasticis Profanisque Scriptoribus occurrunt."—The Glossary is not a mere glossary, but embodies numerous notices of ancient customs and institutions. Spelman was born in 1562 and died in 1641.

Roger, son of Richard, of the manor of Chaveley with all its appurtenances. There has been an abrasion on the edge of the parchment, which may account for the disappearance of the name; and we fancy that the letters *rt* followed by *C.* [Herbe]rt[o] C (for *Cancellario*), are still on the abraded part. If this be not the case, Sir Thomas says the "Y. 31" must be a wrong reference. We do not think it a matter of very great moment. Certain it is that in the year 1843 Sir Thomas Hardy (probably more conversant with our ancient records than any other man in the kingdom) *satisfied himself that in one of the Tower Charters he had found the name of Herbertus Cancellarius as an attesting party, and that Lord Langdale from the same records came to the very same conclusion.* This of itself is quite enough to shew that Mr. Maunde Thompson is much too positive in his assertion, "Herbert was never Chancellor," as is also Mr. Foss ("Judges of England," London, 1848—1864), although the latter assigns reasons for his opinion, which it is right to give in his own words. " HERBERT, the only authority for the mention of whose name in 1104 Thynne acknowledges to be 'an annonymall pamphlet in written hand.' The absence, however, of any other testimony, and the fact that Waldric was Chancellor at the time named, will be sufficient to exclude him." It is not, however, Thynne, but Philipot "framing" a list from Thynne and others, *one of whom had access to the records in the Tower,* who mentions the "annonymall pamphlet;" nor is Thynne (as reproduced and represented by Philipot) "the *only* authority" for the mention of Herbert's name as Chancellor; for (as mentioned above) Spelman is another. And Sir Thomas Hardy has actually seen the name of Herbert as Chancellor appended to one of the charters in the Tower. Nor was so painstaking and thorough an investigator of historical questions as Dean Prideaux likely to be satisfied that Herbert was Chancellor without what seemed to him sufficient evidence of the fact. He was the last man to write Herbert down in an epitaph as having held the office of Chancellor, unless he had obtained some palpable evidence of his being so. Upon the whole, then, while we admit that some doubt rests upon the fact, (for Holinshed's and Philipot's question as to the identification of the Chancellor of the name of Herbert with our prelate raises an ugly surmise in connexion with the subject), we think the evidence inclines in this direction rather than the other, and have adopted this view in the present memoir. It may be added that Lord Campbell (Lives of the Chancellors, vol. i. p. 54) mentions Herbert as one of the five ecclesiastics who succeeded Roger of Sarum in the Chancellorship, but whom his superior splendour threw into obscurity.

It is not said in the last of the letters just quoted what suggestion Prideaux's correspondent made to him as to the modern name of the Pagus Oxamiensis. But from Baudrand's "Geographia," we gather that it must have been Hiesmes, which is described as a town in Normandy, situated on a hill, four leagues from Seez on the north, eight from Aigle on the west (in the direction of Argentan), nine from Falaise (also on the west), and sixteen from Caen on the quarter in which the sun rises in winter. Baudrand adds that the district in the neighbourhood took its name of *Oximensis pagus* from this town [n].

The result of Prideaux's ransacking the treasury seems to have been a resolution on the part of the Dean and Chapter to erect a suitable monument to the Founder, bearing a suitable inscription. As he speaks of "restoreing" the monument, it seems probable that he raised it to its original height, from which it had been taken down "in the late confusion," and that the "Lowness," to which it had been then reduced, no longer characterised it after its restoration. It was guarded, according to Blomefield, with an iron palisade, and exhibited on the sides and ends the arms of the See with those of the Dean and Prebendaries. The epitaph which Prebendary Prideaux "contrived," and of which a translation will be found in the note, runs as follows; (we give an exact transcript, reproducing even the false punctuation of the stone-mason):—

MEMORIÆ SACRUM
HERBERTI DE LOZINGA hujus Ecclesiæ
Episcopi et Fundatoris. Qui Oximi in Nor=

[n] OXIMUM, *Hiesmes*, oppidum est Normanniæ, in Gallia, in colle, 4. leucis à Sagio in Septentrionem, 8. ab Aquila in occasum, Argentanum versus, 9. à Falesia etiam in occasum, et 16. a Cadomo in ortum hybernum, hinc dictus fuit Oximensis pagus tractus in viciniis. (M. A. Baudrand Parisini Geographia; Parisiis: M DC LXXXI.)

mannia natus in Fiscanensi Monasterio
se pietati et bonis literis devovit, qua=
rum merito ejusdem Prior evasit.   Deinde
a Guillielmo Rufo in Consiliarium assumptus
Cum eo A°. Dñi. MLXXXVII° (defuncto
Guillielmo Conquestore) in Angliam trajecit,
eiq; in capessendo Regno consiliis valde : ad=fuit.
Eodem Anno fit Ramesiæ Abbas, et trienn¹o post
hujus Diœceseos Episcopus.   Sub Henrico 1mo Summi
Cancellarij officio et duabus ad Papam Legationib=
us optime fungebatur : Sub utroq; Rege sapientissimi
Consiliarij in Republica munus exequebatur ; necnon
sanctissimi Episcopi in Ecclesia ; præc^{ip}ue in Diœcesi suâ ;
cui. semper : intentus, quas favore Regum obtinuit : ope^s
hic inter proprium Gregem in promovenda pietate
expendit. Ptochodochia enim et Cœnobia in multis
locis per Norfolciam et Suffolciam fundavit ;
Ecclesias item Linnæ, Iarnemuthæ, Elmhamiæ, ali=
=asq; plures extruxit.   Sed maximum laudis monu=
=mentum est hæc Cathedralis nostra ; Cujus prima
fundamenta posuit A°. Dñi MXCVI°.   Deinde auto=
=ritate Regia & Papali instructus in eam Cathedra^m
suam Episcopalem Theodfordo transtulit.   Cœno=
=bium etiam adjecit et cum amplis reditibus di=
=tasset Sexaginta Monachis Benedictinis ad divin^a
in Ecclesia sua celebranda replevit.   Quos postea
Henricus VIII^{us}. A° Regni xxx^{mo}. in Decanum et
Capitulum transmutavit.   Tandem cum hunc Episco=
patum xxix annos tenuisset, xi° Kal: Aug. A° Dñi
MCXIX° vita quam optim^e egerat defunctus : exu=
=vias carnis suæ in spem felicis Resurrectionis
        ·   hic reposuit
Hoc Monumentum nuperæ Rebellionis rabie
dirutum restituerunt Decanus et Capitulum hujus
      Ecclesiæ A°. Dñi MDCLXXXII°. °

° "Sacred to the memory of Herbert de Losinga, Bishop and Founder of this Church, who was born at Oximum in Normandy, and devoted himself to piety and sound learning in the monastery of Fécamp, where by his deserts he ultimately reached the dignity of Prior. Afterwards, being

We have searched in vain the *Chapter Orders* of 1682, with the view of finding that for the erection of the above monument. But among the disbursements in the *Audit Book* for 1683 is the following entry;

"To M^r. Brigstock his Bill for the Founders new Tomb £30. 00s. 0d."

This would have been in those days a considerable proportion of one year's rents of Chapter Property. The capitular body at that time consisted of the Dean, Dr. John Sharpe, (afterwards Dean of Canterbury, in succession to Tillotson, and subsequently Archbishop of York) and six prebendaries, Joseph Loveland, Nathaniel

called to be a councillor of William Rufus, he passed over with him into England, A.D. 1087, at the death of William the Conqueror, and rendered him powerful help by his counsels in the administration of the realm. In the same year he became Abbot of Ramsey, and three years afterwards Bishop of this Diocese. Under Henry I. he most efficiently discharged the office of Lord Chancellor, and on two occasions of ambassador to the Pope. Under both kings he performed the duties of a most wise Councillor in the State, and of a most holy Bishop in the Church, more particularly in his own Diocese; of which ever mindful, he expended the wealth, which by the favour of the kings he obtained, in promoting piety here among his own flock. For he founded throughout Norfolk and Suffolk houses for the reception of the poor, and monasteries in many places. He also built churches at Lynn, Yarmouth, Elmham, and many others besides. But the greatest monument to his praise is this our Cathedral; of which he laid the first foundations, A.D. 1096. Afterwards, fortified with the authority of the King and the Pope, he transferred into it from Thetford his episcopal chair. He also added a monastery, and after endowing it with ample revenues, he filled it with sixty Benedictine monks for the celebration of Divine service in his Church. These in after times Henry VIII. changed to a Dean and Chapter. At length, after he had held this bishopric twenty-nine years, on the eleventh of the Kalends of August, A.D. 1119, having finished the life which he had so nobly led, he divested himself of the raiment of the flesh, and laid it down here for the hope of a happy resurrection. This monument, demolished in the madness of the late Rebellion, the Dean and Chapter of this Cathedral have restored, A.D. 1682."

Hodges, Humphrey Prideaux, William Smith, William Hawkins, and Richard Kidder, (Kidder will be remembered as having been consecrated Bishop of Bath and Wells in the room of Ken, who declined to take the oaths to William and Mary. He was killed in his bed at Wells by the fall of a stack of chimneys in 1703).

The arms of Dean Sharpe and these six prebendaries were removed when the tomb was taken down, and some of them may still be seen on the gate-posts of a canonical house built in 1862. For the monument, we regret to say, *was* taken down. The late Dean Pellew, with the view of making more room for the accommodation of a congregation in the presbytery, caused it to be removed. The slab however which covered it, and on which is inscribed Prebendary Prideaux's epitaph, is still preserved, being let into the floor of the presbytery. That this slab represents the exact spot on which the original sarcophagus stood, may be inferred from the hole in the roof of the presbytery which appears above, and which was used doubtless for the suspension of a lamp before the high altar, a little in advance of the sepulchre.

Herbert left behind him, in addition to the cathedral, five other churches; one, St. Leonard's, on the other side of the river (occupying a site above that of the present church of Thorpe hamlet), another "in the court of the bishop" (corresponding to the present palace chapel), a third at Elmham, a fourth at Lynn, and a fifth at Yarmouth. The two last still remain to attest the magnificence of his architectural designs.

His literary remains, according to Bale, were;

1. Eighteen Sermons (wrongly called eighteen, from mistaking anecdotes annexed to some of them for separate sermons).
2. A treatise on the length of the ages.
3. A treatise on the end of the world.
4. A book of monastic Constitutions.
5. Letters to different persons.
6. A letter addressed to Anselm against bad priests.

The Sermons and Letters are in this work presented to the reader. The other treatises have been lost. Mr. Anstruther, in the preface to his edition of the Letters, mentions two other works of Herbert, about which we can gain no information. His words are;

"There exist in the catalogue of the MSS. in the abbey of Cambron two writings under the name of Herbert, 'Herbertus de septem Sacramentis,' 'de situ terræ Jerosolymitanæ.'"

The catalogue in question is to be found in "Ant. Sanderi Bibliotheca, Belgica Manuscripta, 4to. Insulis 1641." Mr. Anstruther's references will be found in vol. i. p. 357 of this work, in the "Index librorum manuscriptorum Bibliothecæ amplissimi Cœnobii Camberonensis." Mr. R. L. Bensly, however, who has very kindly obtained for us this information about the catalogue, sees no reason at present for identifying this Herbert with the Bishop of Norwich, and tells us that "a work *de Sacramentis*, by Herbert d'Auxerre, is found in some catalogues of MSS."

The memory of Herbert's death was kept up in his Cathedral church by a solemn service on the anniversary. We give a translation of this service from the Norwich *Ordinale*, which is now among the treasures of the Parker Collection, in the library of C. C. C., Cambridge. The original, which was furnished to us by the kindness of Mr. Henry Bradshaw, will be found in Appendix B.

From the Norwich Ordinale,

[A MS. of the xiv[th] century, formerly belonging to Norwich Cathedral, and now MS. 465 in the Parker Collection at Corpus Christi College, Cambridge.]

Between the orders for the feast 'S. Marie Magdalene, in capis' (July 22), and the feast 'S. Apollinaris [p], Martyris,' (July 23), are the following chapters:—

Of the light round the tomb [q] *of the Lord Herbert the Bishop on his anniversary.*

On the vigil of S. Mary Magdalene immediately after Chapter [r], let a pall be spread on the yonder side of

[p] *S. Apollinaris.* Perhaps the good monks, who were adroit at finding significance in times and seasons, &c., may have thought it an appropriate coincidence that Herbert died on St. Mary Magdalene's day, and on the eve of the Festival of St. Apollinaris, he having been eminent as a penitent for the offences of his youth, and also being the first bishop of a city then rising into eminence as the capital of East Anglia. St. Apollinaris is said to have been made by St. Peter first bishop of Ravenna, which from the year 404 became the residence of the emperors and the seat of Roman government, and continued to be the capital of Italy under the Gothic kings, and subsequently under the exarchs, who ruled Italy in the name of the Eastern emperors.

[q] "Round the tomb," *circa tumbam.* The word *tumba*, from the Greek τύμβος, bears curious testimony to the old heathen fashion of cremation instead of burial, inasmuch as its root is τύφω, 'to raise a smoke.' The parallel word in Latin is *bustum*, connected with *uro, comburo.*

[r] In Benedictine houses a Chapter was held every morning, after the

the tomb of the Lord Herbert the Bishop, and let two wax tapers be lighted, to wit, one at the head and the other at the feet. And they shall burn all that day and night, and on the day of S. Mary Magdalene until after Chapter. And then let four wax tapers be lighted, which shall burn all that day and night and on the morrow, until after the high Mass which shall be celebrated for Herbert the Bishop. And the wax tapers shall be renewed as often as it shall be necessary. And Mass having been sung and finished, two out of the four wax tapers shall be removed; and the other two shall remain burning in the same place until after Compline. Then let them be extinguished, and the tomb uncovered.

✠ *The anniversary of the Lord Herbert the Bishop. In copes.*

On the anniversary of the Lord Herbert the Bishop the service shall be ordered on this manner. Let his obit* be read on the vigil of S. Mary Magdalene after

prayers of the third hour and the morning Mass. A little bell then rang, on hearing which all the monks in choir were to rise and stand towards the east (as if in secret devotion), and on its cessation all of them, in the order of their standing, were to pass into the Chapter-house, with the Prior at their head. (See Lanfranci Statuta pro Ord. Sti. Benedicti, cap. xviii., and Dean Church's "St. Anselm," p. 60.)

* The original meaning of the word "obit" (*obitus*) is death. Hence it comes to mean the anniversary of a death; and hence the psalms and prayers with which such an anniversary is observed. Here, of course, it is used in the last of these three meanings. "To make an obit" is to observe the anniversary with psalms, masses, &c. :—

"I have the *obit* of my lady dere
Made in the chirche of love full solempnely
And for hir sowle the service and the prayere
In thought waylying" (wailing) "have songe hit hevyly."
&c., &c., &c.

The above words are the beginning of the translation (made perhaps at the end of the fifteenth century,) of a poem by Charles, Duke of Orleans, upon the death of Isabella of Valois, virgin-widow of Richard II. of England :—

"J'ay fait l'obseque de Madame
Dedens le moustier amoureux,
Et le service, pour son ame
A chanté penser doloreux," &c.

the table [t] of ecclesiastical functions for that day ; and his soul shall be absolved [u]. And these prayers shall be said by the Prior in choir after Chapter.
Deus qui inter apostolicos [x].

[t] *Post tabulam quæ erit de illa.* The *tabula* (*tabula officialis*) was the list of ecclesiastical functionaries for the week, which was drawn up by the Precentor, and exhibited on a board in the Chapter-house. This list was usually read out in Chapter before the commemoration of the dead (or *obit*) was made.

[u] *Et absolvetur anima ejus.* The meaning seems to be, that the founder's soul shall have the benefit of the "obit" which has just been read. The form of precatory absolution found in the Office for the Dead in the Missal of Sarum, is as follows :—

Deus, cui proprium est misereri semper et parcere, propitiare animæ famuli tui, et omnia peccata ejus dimitte, ut mortis vinculis absolutus transire mereatur ad vitam. Per Dominum.

O God, whose property is ever to have mercy and to spare, be merciful unto the soul of thy servant, and remit all his sins, that he being loosed from the chains of death, may be counted worthy to pass unto life. Through the Lord.

Here is another form, taken from the *Commendatio animarum*, an Office performed in the house of the deceased immediately after death. (This Office is printed by Maskell in his "Monumenta Ritualia Eccl. Anglicanæ" (vol. i. 104), amongst the "Occasional Offices selected from the Manual and Pontifical of the Church of Sarum.")

Absolve, quæsumus, Domine, animam famuli tui N. et animas omnium fidelium defunctorum ab omni vinculo delictorum, ut in resurrectionis gloria, inter sanctos et electos tuos resuscitati respirent. Per Christum.

Absolve, we beseech thee, O Lord, the soul of thy servant N. and the souls of all the faithful deceased from every bond of sin, so that, in the glory of the resurrection, they being raised may live again among thine holy and elect ones. Through Christ.

[x] *Deus, qui inter Apostolicos.* This Collect is to be found in the daily Masses for the Dead ("Missæ quotidianæ Defunctorum). The Introit is, "Requiem æternam dona eis, Domine : et lux perpetua luceat eis," with the two first verses of Ps. lxiv. Vulgate ; for the Epistle is read our Burial Office anthem, "I heard a voice from heaven saying," &c., and St. John vi. 51—55 is the Gospel. Here is the Collect, with an English translation. It is headed *Pro defunctis Episcopis seu Sacerdotibus oratio.*

Deus, qui inter Apostolicos sacerdotes, famulos tuos Pontificali fecisti dignitate censeri, præsta, quæsumus, ut quorum vicem ad horam gerebant in terris, eorum perpetuo consortio lætentur in cœlis. Per.

O God, who among apostolic priests hast made choice of thy servants to be counted worthy of the pontifical dignity, grant, we beseech thee, that they may enjoy for ever in heaven communion with those, whose place they held for a time on earth. Through.

(Prayer for Bishops, from the *Orationes pro Defunctis*, in the Sarum Missal.)

Deus venie ʸ.
Fidelium ᶻ.
On the day of S. Mary Magdalene shall be read the table of ecclesiastical functions for the anniversary of the Lord Herbert the Bishop, after the table which pertains to that day, to wit, the Placebo and the Dirige ᵃ. And after Chapter these prayers shall be said.

> ʸ Deus, veniæ largitor et humanæ salutis auctor, quæsumus clementiam tuam, ut nostrarum congregationum fratres et sorores, qui ex hoc sæculo transierunt, intercedente beata Maria semper Virgine et beato Michaele archangelo cum omnibus sanctis, ad perpetuæ beatitudinis consortium pervenire concedas. Per Dominum.

O God, the bountiful giver of pardon, and the author of man's salvation, we beseech thee of thy clemency to grant unto the brethren and sisters of our communities who have passed out of this life, that by the intercession of the blessed Mary, ever Virgin, and the blessed Michael the Archangel, together with that of all the Saints, they may attain to a fellowship with them in perpetual blessedness. Through the Lord.

(Prayer for members of brotherhoods and sisterhoods, from the *Orationes pro Defunctis*, in the Sarum Missal.)

> ᶻ Fidelium, Deus, omnium conditor et redemptor, animabus omnium fidelium defunctorum remissionem cunctorum tribue peccatorum ; ut indulgentiam quam semper optaverunt, piis supplicationibus consequantur. Qui.

O God, the Creator and Redeemer of all the faithful, grant unto the souls of all the faithful departed remission of all their sins, that the mercy which they always wished for they may obtain by devout supplications. Who.

(Prayer for all the faithful departed, from the *Orationes pro Defunctis*, in the Missal of Sarum.)

ᵃ The Placebo and the Dirige. "The mediæval services" (for the Dead) "included the *Commendation*, between the death and the burial, the *Burial* itself, the *Mass for the Dead* (*Missa pro Defunctis*, called also *Requiem*), and the *Office for the Dead*, together with *Trentals* (thirty masses said on as many days), and *Anniversary Commemorations*." "The *Office for the Dead* (called also *Vigiliæ mortuorum*, or the "Dirge,") consisted of two parts ; the Vespers, or *Placebo*, so called from the antiphon with which the service commenced,—' Placebo Domino in regione vivorum,' (Brev. Sar. Psalt. fol. lxii.) ; and the Matins, also called '*Dirige*,' from its first antiphon,—' Dirige Domine Deus meus in conspectu tuo viam meam,' (*Ibid.* fol. lxiii.)" [Procter on the Book of Common Prayer, Cambr., 1855, p. 394, n. 7.] The words "Placebo Domino in regione vivorum," are professedly taken from Psalm cxiv. 9, (Vulg.), where they stand in connexion with the beautiful context, "Return unto thy rest, O my soul ; for the LORD hath dealt bountifully with thee ; for thou hast

Deus qui inter apostolicos. [See note x, p. 336.]
Deus indulgentiarum [b].
Deus venie. [See note y, p. 337.]
Fidelium. [See note z, p. 337.]

Which same prayers shall be said also at the Placebo and the Dirige. On the same day after None, when the time shall have arrived, all the bells shall be rung at the Dirige. After the first Psalm in the Placebo, the Sacrist shall make request for the Prior and two seniors to bring in the incense.

❧ At the Dirige in the first Nocturn the Sacrist at the first *lesson* (?) shall make request for two [of the brethren] to bring in the incense; and a like order shall be observed at the second and third Nocturn. And at Lauds, after the third Psalm, he shall make [a similar] request for the Prior and two brothers with him. Let the brethren whose names are in the table of functions read the lessons at the step above the Analogium [c], which last is to be covered with a pall. Let

---

delivered my soul from death, mine eyes from tears, and my feet from falling." The words are, according to the Vulgate arrangement of the Psalms, at the end of the 114th Psalm; according to our own arrangement, they are found in the heart of the 116th. The LXX and Vulgate give the force rather than the literal meaning of the Hebrew in the word Placebo. The true rendering is not "I will please the Lord," but "I will walk before the Lord."

[b] Deus, indulgentiarum Domine, da animæ famuli tui, cujus anniversarium depositionis diem commemoramus, refrigerii sedem, quietis beatitudinem, luminis claritatem. Per Dominum.

Lord God of mercies, grant unto the soul of thy servant, the anniversary of whose decease we are commemorating, the abode of refreshment, the blessedness of rest, the brightness of light. Through the Lord.

This is the Collect for the general anniversary of the dead (in anniversario defunctorum), the Introit being "Requiem eternam dona eis, Domine: et lux perpetua luceat eis," together with the two first verses of Psalm lxiv. (Vulgate); a Lesson from Maccabees, bk. ii. ch. xii. v. 43, being read for the Epistle, and St. John vi. v. 37—41 forming the Gospel. If we believed (as we do not) that the Apocryphal Books might be applied to establish doctrine, the remarkable passage substituted for the Epistle would go far towards justifying prayers for the dead.

[c] *Ad gradum super analogium.* The *analogium* was a desk or pulpit used for the reading of Lessons, Epistles, and Gospels. Sometimes the

every respond be sung with special solemnity by two
of the brethren ; the third by four, the sixth by five, the
ninth by the Precentor and six others ; and when the
verses are finished, let the respond be sung by all. And
let each verse be sung by two, as well at the Placebo
as at the Nocturns and at the Lauds.

¶ On the morrow let all sit in the Cloister singing
the Psalter.

¶ After Tierce all shall go into the Dormitory, and
in returning shall wash their hands and pass into the
Choir ; and after prayer let them go to vest themselves
again. But let only the Prior, vested in his cope, go to
the altar with his chaplain. Meanwhile let the Cantor
begin the respond in Choir.

Subvenite [d].

Let two brethren, on request being made to them,
sing

Vers. Suscipiat te [e], etc.

Afterwards let the Prior at the Altar say,

Or. Tibi Domine commendamus [f], and

word is applied to the moveable desk shifted about, with the various
movements of the priest, at the altar.

[d] *Subvenite.* This is the initial word of a respond in the Office for the
Commendation of the soul of the Departed, the first of the four services
connected with the dead which were used in the mediæval Church. (See
above, p. 337, note a.) This *Commendatio animarum* was directed to be
said, without musical accompaniment, in the chamber of the deceased, or in
the hall of his house, and near the body. The respond, which is directed
to be said immediately after the patient has breathed his last, is :—

Subvenite, Sancti Dei, occurrite, Angeli Domini, Suscipientes animam ejus, Offerentes eam in conspectu altissimi.	Succour him, ye saints of God, meet him, ye angels of the Lord, receiving his soul, and offering it up in the sight of the Most High.

[e] *Suscipiat te.* This is the beginning of an Antiphon in the *Commendatio animarum* :—

Suscipiat te Christus qui vocavit te ; et in sinum Abrahæ Angeli deducant te.	May Christ, who hath called thee, receive thee ; and may the Angels conduct thee to the bosom of Abraham.

[f] This is a Collect in the *Commendatio animarum* :—

Tibi, Domine, commendamus animam filii tui, *N.*, ut defunctus sæculo tibi vivat ; et quæ per	To thee, O Lord, we commend the soul of thy son, *N.*, that he being dead to the world may live

Misericordiam [g].
Then let the officiating minister for the week begin in the choir

fragilitatem humanæ conversationis peccata commisit, tu venia misericordissimæ pietatis absterge. Per Christum Dominum nostrum.

unto thee; and those sins which he has committed through the frailty which besets human life, do thou wipe away by thy pardon in thy most merciful fatherly love. Through Christ our Lord.

[g] This also is a Prayer from the *Commendatio*:—

Misericordiam tuam, Domine, Sancte Pater, omnipotens æterne Deus, pietatis affectu rogare pro aliis cogimur, qui pro nostris supplicare peccatis nequaquam sufficimus: tamen de tua confisi gratuita pietate et inolita benignitate clementiam tuam deposcimus, ut animam famuli tui N. ad te revertentem cum pietate suscipias. Adsit ei Angelus testamenti tui Michael, et per manus sanctorum angelorum tuorum in sinu Abrahæ patriarchæ tui eam collocare digneris: quatenus liberata de principibus tenebrarum et de locis pœnarum, nullis jam primævæ nativitatis vel ignorantiæ aut propriæ iniquitatis seu fragilitatis confundatur erroribus, sed potius agnoscatur a tuis, et sanctæ beatitudinis requie perfruatur, atque cum magni judicii dies advenerit, inter sanctos et electos tuos aggregata, gloria manifestæ contemplationis tuæ perpetuo satietur. Per Christum.

O Lord, holy Father, Almighty and Everlasting God, we who in no wise suffice to offer prayer for our own sins, are driven by natural affection to make suit for others. Yet trusting in thy free and unmerited fatherly love, and in thy loving-kindness which hath been ever of old, we humbly implore thee of thy clemency, that thou wouldst receive with fatherly love the soul of thy servant N. which now returns unto thee. May Michael, the Angel of thy Covenant, be present with it; and vouchsafe to place it by the hands of thy holy angels in the bosom of thy patriarch Abraham; that being set free from the powers of darkness and from the realm of punishment, it may not be put to confusion by its [past] errors, whether they be due to its birth in sin and ignorance, or to its own iniquity or frailty, but rather may be welcomed by thy [saints] and may enjoy the repose of holy blessedness, and, when the day of the great judgment shall come, may be gathered unto the flock of thy holy and elect people, and may be for ever satisfied with the contemplation of thy glory. Through Christ.

The reason why Michael's presence and assistance rather than that of any other angel is sued for in this prayer is, that he "is the type and leader of the strife of the angels, in God's name and His strength, against the power of Satan," (Dr. Barry, in Smith's "Dictionary of the Bible"); but

Ant. Suscipiat. [See note e, p. 339.]
Ps. In exitu [h].
Or. Omnipotens sempiterne Deus [i].
Afterwards the officiating minister for the week [sings]
Ant. Chorus angelorum [k].

why Michael should be called "Angelus testamenti tui," "the Angel or Messenger of God's Covenant" (see Mal. iii. 1), *unless it be intended to identify him with the Angel-Jehovah, or, in other words, with our Lord*, it is not so easy to say. Malachi's "messenger of the covenant" can be none other than our Lord.

A certain amount of unreality in these prayers from the *Commendatio Animarum*, as used on the *anniversary* of a death, years after it had taken place, and not merely said while the spirit was returning to God who gave it, cannot fail to strike one. Here for example the soul of Herbert, centuries after he had passed away, would be spoken of as "returning to God." There is a strong dramatic element in the mediæval Offices, which is the true account of this unreality. The commemorators of the dead placed themselves mentally in the position of those who had just sustained the loss of him; they acted his death over again, and adopted the sentiments and phraseologies to which it had given rise, when it actually occurred. We shall have a still more striking instance of this presently in the prayer "Diri vulneris."

[h] *In exitu.* These are the initial words of Psalm cxiii. (Vulg.), which according to our version is cxiv., "When Israel came out of Egypt." It was one of the three Psalms appointed by the Ritual of the Church of Sarum to be sung while the body of the deceased was borne to the grave.

[i] *Omnipotens sempiterne Deus.* These are the initial words of one of the Collects directed to be used by the Ritual of Sarum in committing the body of the deceased person to the grave. It ran thus:—

Omnipotens sempiterne Deus, cui nunquam sine spe misericordiæ supplicatur; propitiare animabus famulorum tuorum, ut qui de hac vita in tui nominis confessione decesserunt, sanctorum tuorum numero facias aggregari. Per Dominum.	Almighty and everlasting God, to whom prayer is never made without hope of mercy, be favourable to the souls of thy servants, so that those who have departed out of this life in the confession of thy name may be gathered by thee unto the flock of thy saints. Through the Lord.

[k] *Chorus angelorum.* The reference probably is to words which form one of two sentences formerly sung while carrying the body to the grave. It ran as follows:

Chorus Angelorum te suscipiat et cum Lazaro quondam paupere æternam habeas requiem.	May the choir of the Angels take thee up, and with Lazarus, once the beggar, mayest thou have eternal rest.

In the *Commendatio animarum* the clause "et in sinu Abraham te col-

Ps. Dilexi, down to
Ad Dominum cum tribularer[1].
Or. Diri vulneris [m], etc.
Let two brethren, on being requested, say the 'Requiescant in pace.'
Then let the Prior return to the sacristy and lay aside his cope, and put on a chasuble for the celebration of the Mass. The servants of the Church, and the Subdeacon and Deacon vested in chasubles, shall precede him. Then let the Precentor begin in the Choir,

---

locet" ("and place thee in Abraham's bosom") is inserted between *suscipiat* and *et*.

[1] The Psalms here referred to are, according to the Vulgate arrangement, cxiv. down to cxix. inclusive; according to our own arrangement, cxvi. to cxx. inclusive.

[m] *Diri vulneris.* These also are the first words of a prayer in the *Commendatio animarum*, directed to be said immediately after the Antiphon "Chorus angelorum :"—

| Diri vulneris novitate percussi et quodammodo cordibus sauciati, misericordiam tuam, mundi Redemptor, flebilibus vocibus imploramus, ut cari nostri N. animam ad tuam clementiam (qui fons es pietatis) revertentem blande leniterque suscipias : et si quas illa ex carnali commercio contraxit maculas, tu Deus solita bonitate clementer deleas, pie indulgeas, oblivioni in perpetuum tradas, atque hanc laudem tibi cum cœteris reddituram, et ad corpus proprium quandoque reversuram, sanctorum tuorum cœtibus aggregari præcipias. Qui cum Deo Patre, et Spiritu Sancto vivis. | Recently stricken with a grievous blow, and wounded (as it were) in our hearts, we implore thy mercy, Redeemer of the world, with wailing voices, [beseeching thee] who art the fountain of fatherly compassion, that thou wouldst lovingly and gently receive the soul of our dear N., returning to thy clemency; and if it have contracted any defilements from its conversation in the flesh, do thou, O God, with thy accustomed goodness graciously blot them out, lovingly condone them, and consign them to forgetfulness for ever, and command it to be gathered into the assemblies of thy saints, hereafter with many others to render praise to thee [for this thy mercy], and to return at a future time unto its own body. Who livest with God the Father and the Holy Spirit. |

It is evident that this Prayer suggested our own "Commendatory Prayer for a sick person at the point of departure," in which it is perhaps to be regretted that there is not, as there is here, any reference to the re-union of the soul with the body.

Offm. Requiem eternam [n].
Or. Deus qui inter apostolicos. [See note x, p. 336.]
Deus indulgentiarum. [See note b, p. 338.]
Both these Collects being said under one concluding, "through our Lord," and
Deus venie [see note y, p. 337], and
Fidelium [see note z, p. 337].
Epist. Nolumus vos [o].
Resp. Si ambulem [p].
Tractus. De necessitatibus [q], etc.

[n] *Requiem æternam.* These are the initial words of the Introit used at the Mass for the Anniversary of the Dead in the mediæval Church of England. It is here designated as *Officium*, that being the word employed in the Missal of Sarum to express what the Roman Liturgy terms *Introitus*, and the Ambrosian *Ingressa.* The words of this particular *Officium* are—

| Requiem æternam dona eis, Domine : et lux perpetua luceat eis. | Grant unto them everlasting rest, O Lord, and may perpetual light shine upon them. |

[o] *Epist. Nolumus nos.* This is the Epistle for the Mass on the day of the obit, that is, on the anniversary of the death of the person commemorated. It forms the consolation administered by St. Paul to his Thessalonian converts when suffering by bereavement. The Gospel which belongs to it is from St. John xi., and records our Blessed Lord's conversation with Martha before the resurrection of Lazarus. The Epistle has a special interest for English Churchmen, as being that appointed by King Edward the Sixth's first Prayer-book for the celebration of the Holy Communion when there is a burial of the dead, the greater part of the Collect for that occasion being still retained (under the title of "the Collect") as the last prayer in our Burial Office.

[p] *Si ambulem.* The passage referred to is from Ps. xxii. (xxiii. 4).

| Si ambulem in medio umbræ mortis, non timebo mala : quoniam tu mecum es, Domine. V. Virga tua et baculus tuus : ipsa me consolata sunt. | If I walk in the midst of the shadow of death, I will not fear evils, since Thou art with me, O Lord. V. Thy rod and Thy staff they comforted me. |

This is the Gradual appointed by the Sarum Missal to be sung at the Office of the Dead whenever the body is present, and in all Masses for Bishops even when the body is absent. [The reason for the latter direction being probably, that in the rod and staff was seen a reference to the pastoral-staff. The Gradual was a Respond immediately after the Epistle, so called from its being sung on the step of the Choir (ad gradum chori.)]

[q] This doubtless is the passage from Ps. xxiv. (xxv. 17). "De necessitatibus meis erue me. Vide humilitatem meam et laborem meum, et

⁋ On the same day before vespers shall be sung the Dirige and the Placebo [see note a, p. 337], as for a Prior. Or. Deus qui inter apostolicos [see note x, p. 336], and Inclina ʳ.

Omnipotens sempiterne Deus [see note i, p. 341], and as follows in order.

⁋ If this day shall fall on a Sunday, on the preceding day the Dirige and the Placebo shall be sung in the manner directed above. After Chapter and the washing of hands, let the ministers resume their vestments for the Mass of the day. Then let Tierce be sung. Afterwards let the Mass of the Sunday be sung at the high altar, as it usually is on Sundays in the Chapter.

dimitte universa delicta mea;" according to our authorised Version, "O bring thou me out of my distresses. Look upon mine affliction and my pain; and forgive all my sins." Was this Tract chosen for Herbert's anniversary in reference to the afflictions and distresses which his sins brought upon him, and to the humbleness of mind with which he underwent them? Certain it is that the Tract appointed in the Sarum Missal to be said at Masses for deceased Bishops is not *De necessitatibus*, but that other exquisite passage of the Psalms, Ps. xli. (xlii.) 1—3, in which the Psalmist expresses the longing of his soul after God, *as the hart panteth after the water-brooks*.

The Tract was a series of verses with repetitions, substituted in penitential seasons for the *Alleluia* with its verse, which immediately precedes the Gospel at other times of the year. Hugo de S. Victore tells us that the Tractus, being of a lugubrious character, represents the tears of the Saints, and that it derives its name *Tractus* from the verb *traho*, because the sighs and groans of the Saints, which it is designed to express, are drawn from the depth of their bosom. Probably however the Tractus is only the Latin word for what in the Greek Ritual is called εἰρμός.

ʳ *Inclina.* This is the beginning of the Collect appointed by the Missal of Sarum to be said at Trentals, (thirty masses said on as many different days after the burial, and with more particular solemnity on the third, seventh, and thirtieth days) :—

Inclina, Domine, aurem tuam ad preces nostras, quibus misericordiam tuam supplices deprecamur; ut animas famulorum famularumque tuarum, quas de hoc sæculo migrare jussisti, in pacis ac lucis regione constituas, et sanctorum tuorum jubeas esse consortes. Per Dominum.	Incline thine ear, O Lord, to our prayers, in which we humbly sue for Thy mercy, that Thou wouldst place in the realm of peace and light the souls of Thy servants and handmaidens, whom Thou hast bidden to depart out of this life, and wouldst bid them to be fellow-heirs with Thy saints. Through the Lord.

But after Mass let the water be sanctified and sprinkled. Then let the Prior in his cope proceed with his chaplain to the altar, the Cantor beginning

Subvenite, with the versicle,
Suscipiat [see note e, p. 339],

and let the Commendation be sung as above [see note d, p. 339], and when it is finished let two say,

Vers. Requiescant.

And while the Prior is returning into the Choir, all shall put on their copes, and let a procession be made with due solemnity round the choir-aisle, the relics going first as is the manner in Chapter. The Prior shall say the suffrages and the Collects in the Church. After the procession let the prayer "Via sanctorum^s" be said by the priest of the week. Then let the Precentor and others lead off the

Off^m. Requiem æternam. [See note n, p. 343.]

We will close this Memoir with an extract from Weever's "Funeral Monuments," which shews the very high estimation in which Herbert's memory was held by the monks of his foundation. "The Monkes of Norwich made great meanes and sute to hauve this Herbert a canonized Saint, but such impediments were alwaies in the way that it could not be obtained." While we doubt not that many men, far inferior to Herbert in moral and spiritual endowments, have had the honour of canonization paid to their memory,— we think that, even putting aside the question of the propriety of formal acts of canonization on the part of the Church, Herbert was scarcely

---

^s We are sorry to be obliged to inform our readers that, after a most diligent search, we have been unable to meet with the prayer beginning, *Via Sanctorum*.

a fit subject for it. We have seen reason to think, not only that he was amiable and manifested great suavity of manners and great kindness of heart, but also that he was endowed with sensibility both of feeling and of conscience, and was animated with a genuine love to God and his neighbour, however much taint his piety may have taken from the errors and superstitions of his time. There is a geniality as well as a humour about his letters, which makes them, we think, more attractive than they would have been, if they had been more historically useful, and had shewn more absorption of the writer's mind in the political and ecclesiastical movements of his day. Had it been permitted him to form domestic ties, we can readily imagine that he would have been the most loveable of husbands and fathers, while his high cultivation and his affability would have made him acceptable in any intellectual circle. If he accepted the erroneous views of religion current in his age, that is only what may be said of many Fathers of the Church, whose writings, notwithstanding, have done eminent service to religion, and are looked upon as repositories of Christian wisdom; if he spoke in terms of adulation to the great men of the earth, his flatteries may be abundantly paralleled with, however little they may be justified by, the language used on similar occasions by modern as well as ancient divines; and we take our leave of him with the feeling that he has a true title to the veneration and affection of posterity, not only as one in advance of his times in respect of intellectual gifts and attainments, but also as a good pastor, who tended gently and faithfully the sheep of Christ, and as a character intensely human, if in his sins and foibles, so also in his sympathies and affections.

APPENDIX A.

Page 4.

Letters from Archdeacon Hopper on the name LOSINGA.

LETTER I.

"LOES Hundred is in East Suffolk; Framlingham and Woodbridge are places in it. The adjoining Hundred is that of Plomesgate, of which the chief town is Orford,—one of the places which claim to have been the birth-place of Herbert de Losinga.

"The title of the Hundred, Loes, is peculiar, not being taken from any parish within its limits, nor from the features of the locality, as in the cases of Flegg, Depwade, &c., but probably from the name of some hero or founder of a sept, perhaps the Saxon Loid, from whence *Leeds* (Loidis) and the *Lothians*. From him, I presume, came the clan or family of the *Leasings*, whom Isaac Taylor mentions among the Teutonic settlers in England, and who have left traces of their name at Lessingham, Norfolk; Lossingham, Kent; and Lozinghem, France.

"Now if Herbert was born at Orford (there is strong evidence that he was a Suffolk man),—may we not have here the clue to his appellation, de Losinga, i.e. de Losingâ terrâ?

"He certainly had *family* property at Wykes, near Ipswich, some six miles from the border of Loes Hundred. Blomefield speaks of his father as Robert *de Losing*, a name which could not have come to him from the subsequent character of his son.

"Your idea of *Lothingland*, now the Hundred between Yarmouth and Lowestoft, being a cognate word, is, I have no doubt, well founded. The lake and the land may have both taken their name from the Lo-things or Leasings, the sons of Loid; and my derivation of Lowestoft (formerly Loystoft) would fall to pieces: the origin would plainly be Loids-toft.

"Believe me,
"Yours very truly,
"A. M. HOPPER."

LETTER II.

. . . .

"When I was in town last week, I went to the British Museum, in the hope of finding something about the Hundred of *Loes* in a History of Suffolk.

"There is, however, only one County History of Suffolk, that of Suckling, and it does not contain Loes Hundred.

"In Domesday Book it is called *Hundreda de Losa*. I have no doubt that the name is a remnant of the old appellation of the *March* or frontier, which often extended to a considerable distance, and was subdivided into tithings and hundreds; and that it derives its origin from the old mythic hero Loð, or Loth.

"Holinshed in his Chronicle makes *Loth* the King of the Picts, and contemporary with King Arthur. He was more probably a Norse chieftain.

"Kemble, in his 'Saxons in England,' speaking of the origin of the names of the Marks or Marches, says: 'Even where a few adventurers, one only, bearing a celebrated name, took possession of a new home, comrades were glad to gather around him under his appellation. I have reason to believe all the local denominations of the early settlements to have thus arisen, and to have been thus perpetuated.'

"Amongst the patronymic names of clans thus forming settlements, he mentions the *Lodingas* and *Locingas*, who have left traces of their footsteps at Loddington, Kent; Locking, Somerset; Lossingham, ·Kent; and Lozinghem on the French coast of Artois and Picardy.

To these I would add *Loðine*, *Loidis*, the district about *Leeds*, and the *Lothians*.

"In *Suffolk*, the settlements of the clan are clearly marked, not only in *Loes*, but also at *Lowestoft* (in Domesday Book, *Lothu-wis-toft*, 'the enclosure of the water of Loth,' now Lake Lothing), and the Hundred of Lothingland, which in Domesday Book is called the half Hundred of *Ludingalanda*, as if the original Hundred had extended much further. I imagine that Losa, and Locinga or Losinga, are abbreviations formed from the genitive of Loð, Loðesa, Loðes-ing. At any rate, the root is the same.

"Bale, himself a Suffolk man, says that Herbert de Losinga was born in *Suffolk*, '*in pago Oxunensi in Sudvolgiâ natus.*' Pitts fixes his birthplace at Orford; Mr. Spurdens in his Memoir (Norfolk Archæology, iii. 140) at Hoxne,—both places situate in hundreds adjoining to Loes.

"Here then, I argue, is to be found the origin of Herbert's appellation, *de Losinga*. It is not a sobriquet from 'his losing tongue,' but a family name derived from the locality in which his family had lived, or possessed property,—the Losings-land. Herbert certainly possessed *patrimonial* property at Wykes, near Ipswich, and at Syleham, near Hoxne, both of them in hundreds adjoining the present Hundred of Loes, the one on the south, the other on the north of it.

"I mentioned also the fact of Herbert's father, *Robert de Losing*, bearing the same surname (it could not have been derived from the after-characteristics of the son), as a strong argument in confirmation of my conjecture. Blomfield, who calls the father by this name, does not, however, produce his authority for doing so. But, oddly enough, I was looking over Sir H. Ellis's Introduction to Domesday Book, when at vol. i. p. 434, I found recorded in the list of the ancient Bishops of Hereford, 'Robert de Losing, consecrated Bishop of Hereford Dec. 29, 1079, died 26 June, 1095.' Quære, was not this *Herbert's father?* We know that he was an abbot, and the dates would agree. At any rate, here we have *two* persons bearing the same surname, which therefore could not have been invented to stigmatize the younger in date.

"I am quite ashamed of the length to which these jottings have run, and I only venture to send them to you now, as somewhat amplifying and supporting my former surmises. If they are of any use in solving the vexed riddle of the name, I shall be very glad; if not, please put them in the fire.

"Believe me,
"Yours most truly,
"A. M. HOPPER."

APPENDIX B.

Page 334.

Original of Herbert's Anniversary Service in the Norwich *Ordinale* (MS. 465 in the Parker Collection in the library of C.C.C., Cambridge).

De lumine circa tumbam dompni Herberti episcopi in anniuersario suo.

In vigilia sancte Marie Magdalene post capitulum statim extendatur pallium ultra tumbam dompni Herberti episcopi· et accendantur duo cerei, scilicet vnus ad capud et alius ad pedes· et ardebunt tota die illa et nocte· et in die Sancte Marie Magdalene vsque post capitulum· et tunc accendantur quattuor cerei et ardebunt tota illa die et nocte et in crastino vsque post magnam missam· que celebrabitur pro Herberto episcopo· et renouabuntur cerei quandocunque necesse fuerit· et missa percantata? duo ex quattuor cereis deponentur· et alii duo remanebunt ardentes ibidem vsque post completorium· et tunc extinguantur et tumba discooperiatur.

✠ *Anniuersarium dompni Herberti episcopi? In capis.*
In anniuersario dompni Herberti episcopi hoc modo

Appendix.

ordinabitur seruicium. Legatur eius obitus in vigilia sancte Marie Magdalene post tabulam que erit de illa. et absoluetur eius anima. Et dicentur iste orationes in choro post capitulum a Priore.

Deus qui inter apostolicos.
Deus venie.
Fidelium.

In die sancte Marie Magdalene legetur tabula de anniuersario dompni Herberti episcopi post tabulam ad illum diem pertinentem scilicet 'Placebo' et 'Dirige.' Et post capitulum dicentur iste·orationes.

Deus qui inter apostolicos.
Deus indulgentiarum.
Deus venie.
Fidelium.

Eedem vero dicantur ad 'Placebo' et 'Dirige.'

Eodem die post Nonam cum tempus fuerit pulsabuntur omnia signa ad 'Dirige.' Post primum psalmum de 'Placebo'? rogabit sacrista Priorem et duos seniores ad incensum deferendum.

¶ Ad 'Dirige' vero in primo Nocturno ad primam (? lectionem *erased*) rogabit sacrista duos ad incensum deferendum. Similiter in secundo et tertio Nocturno. Et in laudibus post tercium psalmum rogabit Priorem et duos alios cum eo. Lectiones vero legant fratres qui sunt in tabula ad gradum super analogium et quod cooperiatur pallio. Singula responsoria honorifice a duobus cantentur. tercium vero a quattuor. sextum a quinque. nonum vero a precentore et sex aliis· et finitis versibus cantetur responsorium ab omnibus. Singuli etiam versus a duobus cantentur tam ad 'Placebo' quam ad Nocturna et ad laudes.

¶ In crastino? sedeant omnes in claustro cantantes Psalterium.

¶ Post terciam ibunt omnes in dormitorium et reuertentes lauent manus et uenient in chorum· et facta oratione? eant reuestitum. Prior vero in capa cum capellano suo tantum eat ad altare. Interim incipiat cantor responsorium in choro.

Subuenite.
Duo rogati cantent
Vers. Suscipiat te. etc.
Postea Prior ad altare dicat.
Or. Tibi Domine commendamus· et
Misericordiam.
Tunc ebdomadarius in choro incipiat
Ant. Suscipiat.
Ps. In exitu.
Or. Omnipotens sempiterne Deus.
Deinde ebdomadarius.
Ant. Chorus angel'.
Ps. Dilexi.   usque
Ad dominum cum tribularer.
Or. Diri vulneris, etc.
'Requiescant in pace' dicant duo rogati: Tunc reuertatur Prior in vestiarium et deponat capam et induat casulam missam celebraturus. Quem precedent seruitores ecclesie et subdiaconus et diaconus induti casulis. Cantor in choro incipiat.
Off^m. Requiem eternam.
Or. Deus qui inter apostolicos.
  Deus indulgentiarum
sub uno 'Per dominum'· et
  Deus venie· et
  Fidelium.
Epist. Nolumus vos.
Resp. Si ambulem.
Tractus. De necessitatibus. etc.

⁋ Eodem die ante vesperas cantabitur 'Dirige' et 'Placebo' sicut pro Priore.
Or. Deus qui inter apostolicos· et
  Inclina.
  Omnipotens sempiterne deus·
et cetera in ordine.

⁋ Si in dominica contigerit? in precedenti die cantabitur 'Placebo' et 'Dirige'· ut supra notatur. Post capitulum et lotionem manuum? reuestiant se ministri ad missam de die. Deinde cantetur tercia. Postea cantetur missa de dominica ad maius altare sicut mos est in dominicis diebus in capitulo. Post missam vero sanctificetur aqua et aspergatur. Deinde procedat Prior in capa cum capellano suo ad altare cantore incipiente

Subuenite·   cum versu
Suscipiat.

et cantetur commendatio ut supra· et cum finita fuerit? dicant duo

Vers. Requiescant.

Et reuertente Priore in choro? sument omnes capas et fiat processio honorifice circa choream precedentibus reliquiis ut mos est in capitulo. Prior dicet preces et orationes in ecclesia. Post processionem dicatur oratio 'Via sanctorum' ab ebdomadario sacerdote. Deinde imponat cantor cum aliis.

Off^m. Requiem eternam· etc.

APPENDIX C.

(p. 273.)

A Translation of the Royal Charter confirming to Abingdon Monastery the grant of the Church of Edwardston.

HENRY, King of the English, to Herbert, Bishop of Norwich, and to the Viscounts of Suffolk and Essex, and to all his barons, French and English, of both those shires [a], greeting.

> [a] "of both those shires"—*de utráque scirá*, i.e. both of Suffolk and Essex. It is observable that the royal letter is *not* [addressed to the viscounts and barons of *Norfolk*, probably because the church of Edwardston, which was granted away to the convent of Abingdon by these letters, was in Suffolk. Norfolk viscounts and barons would have no temptation to advance claims to it, since it was remote from their district. The divisions of our country into shires, hundreds, and tithings, are aseribed to King Alfred. The word *shire* means originally "a section." It comes

Know ye that I grant unto God, and unto Saint Mary in the church of Abingdon, and unto Faritius the abbot thereof, and unto all his successors, and unto the monks of the same place, that endowment [b] which Hubert of Montchensy gave to the church aforesaid, to wit, the church of Edwardston [c], with its lands and tithes, and all things of right appertaining unto him [there], and moreover two acres [d] of land near the church, and two parts of the tithe of all things at Staureton [e] and Standstede [f], and the tithe of the produce of the mills and coppices (and, wheresoever his hogs shall have been pastured, there the abbot's own hogs shall be exempt from payment for pasture [g]); except

from the Anglo-Saxon verb *scyran*, "to divide." But what would the modern inhabitants of Suffolk and Essex say to these counties being called *shires?* At all events, the Norfolk people count the "people of the *sheers*" (as they contemptuously call the inhabitants of counties to which, in popular parlance, the word *shire* is annexed) as altogether an inferior caste.

[b] "that endowment"—*eleemosynam illam*. Norman law recognised four species of tenure. Property might be held *per homagium* or *hominium* (on certain terms of service done to a feudal lord); or *per divisionem* (property devised by will to heirs-at-law); or *per eleemosynam* (endowment of churches or religious houses, &c.); or *per vadium* (land held in pawn, by having a mortgage upon it). [See Ducange's Glossary.]

[c] Edwardston is a small parish in Suffolk, six miles west of Hadleigh. At present it is in the diocese of Ely.

[d] "two acres of land"—*duas acras terræ*. *Acra* is the Latinized form of the Saxon *æcer*, Germ. Acfer, "a field." "The size of the acre varied considerably in England." The Chronicle of Battle Abbey makes the perch to be 16 ft. in length, and the acre to be 40 perches in length and 4 in breadth. (Stevenson's Latin Glossary to the Abingdon Chronicle.)

[e] We can offer no conjecture as to this place.

[f] Is this Stanstead-Mountfitchet, a parish in Essex, eighteen miles northwest of Chelmsford? in which case one understands the letter being addressed to the viscounts and barons of Essex. (In this case might the *Mons* in *Hubertus de Monte Canesi* have some connection with Mountfitchet?) Or is it Stanstede near Lavenham, in Suffolk?

[g] The Latin is, *et ubicunque porci sui fuerint in pasnagio erunt dominici porci abbatis sine pasnagio*. *Pasnagium* (connected with *pascor*, *pastio*) has two nearly-allied significations. Sometimes it signifies the pasture of hogs on acorns or beechmast; and this is its sense in the first clause, "wheresoever his [Hubert's] hogs shall be in pasture;" more commonly, the price paid to the lord of the soil for such pasture (one hog in every ten, or as the case might be); and this is the sense in the latter clause,

Standstede park ʰ, and a tithe of the produce of the turfs of Staureton, and whatsoever for the love of God he hath willed to accrue to the property aforesaid.

Witnesses hereof are Ranulfus the Chancellor, Grimaldus the physician, &c., &c. at Woodstock.

The charter of the above grant was drawn in the year from our Lord's Incarnation 1115.

APPENDIX D.

SOURCES OF THE HISTORY OF HERBERT DE LOSINGA, ARRANGED IN CHRONOLOGICAL ORDER.

I.—ANGLO-SAXON CHRONICLE.

[The work of many successive hands, embracing the whole period from Cæsar's invasion to the middle of the twelfth century. There is no means of knowing the exact date at which the following extract was written.]

1094. This year, at Christmas, King William held his Court at Gloucester; and there came messengers to him out of Normandy, from his brother Robert, and they said that his brother renounced all peace and compact if the king would not perform all that they had stipulated in the treaty; moreover, they called him perjured and faithless unless he would perform the conditions, or would go to the place where the treaty had been concluded and sworn to, and there clear himself. Then at Candlemas the king went to Hastings, and whilst he waited there for a fair wind, he caused the monastery on the field of battle to be consecrated;

"there the abbot's hogs shall pay nothing for pasturage." *Dominicus* means that which is a man's own property, which he does not hold as a tenant or occupier. Ducange gives an extract from a charter of Ed. III.: *Et quod idem Abbas et Canonici haberent porcos suos proprios, sive dominicos, tempore pannagii* (at the time of collecting the pasture-tax) *liberos et quietos.* Hence the word *domain*.

ʰ "Standstede park"—*haiam de Standstede.*

Haia or *haga* is the Anglo-Saxon *hæg*, Germ. *hage*, French *haie*, English *hedge*. Hence it comes to mean an enclosure surrounded by a hedge, a park.

Herbert deprived of his staff by William Rufus.

and HE TOOK THE STAFF FROM HERBERT LOSANGE, BISHOP OF THETFORD. After this, in the middle of Lent, he went over sea to Normandy.

II. FLORENCE OF WORCESTER.

[Next after the ecclesiastical history of Beda and the Saxon Chronicle, the principal source of early English history is the chronicle, grafted on that of Marianus Scotus, by Florence, a monk of Worcester. Marianus's was a *general* chronicle from the creation to his own time. Florence inserted into this a chronicle of English affairs. His work is called *Chronicon ex Chronicis*. It commences with the arrival of Hengst and Horsa (A.D. 450), and goes down to the year A.D. 1117. A.D. 1119 is the date generally given of Florence's death, but Walter of Coventry states that it took place in 1118. Thus it will be observed that Florence's death and that of Herbert de Losinga occurred about the same time. What Florence says therefore of our bishop is a contemporary record; and on this account, as well as because Florence displays considerable ability in his Chronicle, and bestowed much labour upon it, his testimony is of the highest importance.]

The name of Losinga —Herbert's former preferments— his father.

A.D. 1094. Arfasto prius Willelmi comitis, post Willelmi regis capellano, processu vero temporis Theodfordensi episcopo, jam de medio facto, ejusque successore Willelmo, Hereberhtus, qui cognominabatur Losinga, quod ei ars adulationis nuper egerat, ex primore Fescamni et ex abbate Ramesiæ empto præsulatu, Theodfordensis ecclesiæ factus est episcopus, patre suo Roberto ejusdem cognominis in abbatiam Wintoniæ intruso. Veruntamen erroneum impetum juventutis

His penitence, and journey to Rome.

abolevit penitentia; Romam profectus severioribus annis, ubi loci simoniacum baculum et annulum deponens, indulgentia clementissimæ sedis iterum recipere meruit. Domum vero reversus, sedem episcopa-

Transference of his see.

lem transportavit ad insignem mercimoniis et populorum frequentia vicum, nomine Nordwic, ibique monachorum congregationem instituit. Rex Willelmus Hæstingam adiit, ibidemque ecclesiam de Bello dedicari fecit, et post Normanniam petiit; ad fratris colloquium sub statuta pace venit, sed inpacatus ab eo recessit[1].

[1] In the best extant MS. of Florence,—that found in the library of C.C.C., Oxford,—this paragraph stands as we have given it. But this

It will be observed that this, the earliest notice in any detail of Herbert's proceedings, and a notice from a contemporary, pronounces on several moot points; (1) that Herfast was Bishop of *Thetford;* (2) that William intervened between Herfast and Herbert; (3) that the surname *Losinga* was given him from his adroitness in adulation; (4) that nevertheless his father Robert had the same surname; (5) that he rose to be *prior* of Fécamp; and (6), that some considerable time elapsed between his simoniacal purchase of the bishopric and his act of penitence, for the one is called " erroneus impetus *juventutis*," while he is said to have gone to Rome to lay down his staff "*severioribus annis.*"

Three other notices of Herbert (but merely incidental) occur in Florence's "Chronicle from Chronicles;" (1) his attendance at the council of Westminster held by Anselm in 1102, on which occasion he is called

part of the MS. is palimpsest, i.e. written upon an erasure. The erased paragraph, for which the above was substituted, was probably that given in the first printed edition, 1592, in which inferior MSS., now in the possession of Trinity College, Dublin, are followed. In this first printed edition the paragraph stands thus :—" Comes Normannorum Rotbertus, fratri suo regi Willelmo juniori per legatos mandavit, pacem quam inter se firmaverant non esse diutius servaturum : insuper illum vocavit perjurum et perfidum, nisi conventionem inter illos, in Normannia factam, esset ei persoluturus. Ob hanc causam rex, circa cal. Februarii, Heastingam adiit, et dum ibi moraretur ecclesiam de Bello dedicari fecit. [ª Hoc anno venerabilis Herbertus, Theotfordensis episcopus, a Roma cum benedictione apostolica rediit : et a Willelmo rege impetravit ut sedes episcopalis in Norwicensi ecclesia firmaretur, ubi ipse, Christi juvante gratia, pulcherrimam congregationem monachorum, ad honorem sanctæ Trinitatis, adunavit.ª] Dein media quadragesimæ rex Normanniam petiit : ad fratris colloquium sub pace statuta venit, sed impacatus ab eo recessit." This paragraph seems to be merely an insertion of what is found in the Saxon Chronicle, and which is given in the preceding Article. William Rufus' sanction of the transfer of the see.

ª *Hoc anno . . . adunavit.* The Lambeth MS. of Florence, which is the second best extant, after the words *dedicari fecit,* inserts as follows :—
" Ubi etiam Herebertum, Theotfordensem episcopum, pastorali baculo privavit. Latenter enim Urbanum papam adire, et ab eo pro episcopatu quem sibi, et abbatiam quam patri suo Rotberto ab ipso rege Willelmo mille libris emerat, absolutionem quærere voluit." Reason of Herbert's deprivation of the pastoral staff.

"Herebertus *Northwicensis* ;" (2) his assisting Anselm (Aug. 11, 1107) in consecrating five bishops at Canterbury; and (3) his death in A.D. 1119, a year marked also by the death of Pope Gelasius (Gelasius II., John of Gaëta, a Benedictine monk of Monte Cassino), and of Gosfrid, Bishop of Hereford. The Pope died on the 29th Jan. ; the Bishop of Hereford on the 3rd Feb. ; Herbert on the 22nd July.

III.—EADMER.

[Eadmer was a Benedictine of Canterbury,—spiritual director, friend, disciple, and biographer of St. Anselm, Archbishop of Canterbury. In 1120 (the year after Herbert's death) he was appointed Archbishop of St. Andrew's, at the desire of Alexander I. of Scotland, but threw up the appointment, because he would not be consecrated by any other than the Archbishop of Canterbury, who, Alexander maintained, had no authority in Scotland. His great work is called, *Historia Novorum, sive sui sæculi libri sex*, from 959 to 1122. Wharton thinks that he died in 1124. —Thus he, too, was a contemporary of Herbert, and his testimony is of the highest value.]

In 1096, the third year of Anselm's pontificate, Eadmer notices Herbert as assisting the Primate in the consecration of Gerard to Hereford, and of Samson to Worcester; for Herbert it must have been, though, perhaps by a mistake, Eadmer calls him *Robertus Tydfordensis seu Norwicensis* (p. 45, ed. Lut. Par. 1721).

Of Herbert's second visit to Rome (in 1107), Eadmer is the first writer who gives us the full details. We therefore transcribe him *in extenso* (ed. Lut. Par. 1721, p. 60) :—

Non multum temporis fluxerat, et ecce cum Pater, suarum securus injuriarum, Ecclesiæ damnis non nihil metueret, literæ sibi amicabiles a rege transmissæ deferuntur, in quibus, primo salutationis alloquio cum perfectæ pacis oblatione soluto, rogatur venire ad Regem gesti negotii sententiam alio consilio moderari volentem. Auditurus itaque, (ne forte Deus sua gratia cor ejus tetigerit), quo mandatur Wintoniam vadit, ubi episcopis terræque principibus sub uno coactis, communi assensu apud Anselmum actum est, quatenus sub aliis induciis alii nuncii, prioribus excellentiores, ex utraque parte Romam mitterentur, Romano Pontifici viva voce exposituri illum aut a sententia necessario discessurum, aut Anselmo cum suis extra Angliam pulso, totius regni subjectionem et commodum, quod inde singulis annis habere solebat, perditurum. Ab Archiepiscopo igitur missi sunt monachi duo, præfatus scilicet Baldwinus Beccensis, et Alexander Cantuariensis, non quidem ut eorum instinctu Romanus Pontifex rigorem justitiæ causa Anselmi ullo modo exiret, sed partim ut curialibus minis testimonium, cui Papa incunctanter crederet, ferrent; partim ut de negotio certam apostolicæ sedis sententiam Anselmo referrent. Ad ipsum vero negotium conficiendum directi a rege sunt tres episcopi, Girardus videlicet de Herefordensi nuper factus Archiepiscopus Eboracensis, Herbertus Theodfordensis, Robertus Cestrensis. Sed horum episcoporum duos sua quoque causa Romam agebat, Girardum scilicet adeptio pallii, et Herbertum intentio recuperandi ablatam ecclesiæ suæ curam Christianitatis super abbatiam sancti Eadmundi. Ante paucos siquidem annos Baldwinus, ipsius cœnobii abbas, Romam adierat, et apud Alexandrum Papam privilegium ipsi abbatiæ adquisierat, per quod eam a subjectione omnium episcoporum (salvâ Primatis obedientiâ), liberam effecerat. Quod factum Lanfrancus Archiep. moleste accipiens, ipsum privilegium abstulit; nec illud ei nisi circa finem vitæ suæ, multorum precibus motus, reddere voluit. Præfatus ergo episcopus, (Episcopatum Theodfordensem seu Norwicensem, in cujus parrochiâ eadem Abbatia esse scitur, suo jure non jure privatum esse ægre ferens, ut diximus,) Romam ire, et, si forte posset, in antiquam dignitatem ecclesiam, cui præsidebat, restituere, adminiculante æquitate cogitabat. Hic itaque Herbertus [k], cum, relictis sociis, Burgundiam

Herbert's mission to Rome on the subject of investitures.

His private motive in going.

The privilege of St. Edmund's Abbey.

---

[k] We print here another account of Herbert's misadventure, extracted from a Cartulary of the Abbey of St. Edmund's. The extract is in a MS. book belonging to the Deanery of Norwich, in the handwriting of Dean Prideaux.

Herbert seized and detained by Guy.

cum suis venisset, et partes Lugdunensis provinciæ impiger attigisset, comprehensus a quodam Guidone viro præpotente ac fero est, et quod de Angliâ episcopus esset, quodque pro damno Domini sui Anselmi, Cantuariorum Archiepiscopi, Romam iret, ab eodem calumniatus. Negat ille; nec ei creditur. Instat negando et dejerando, sed nequicquam. Tandem, prolatis sanctorum reliquiis, super eas jurare cogitur, et

Fol. 39 and 40. De ultione factâ in Herbertum Episcopum Thetfordensem versus Romam iter facientem, cupidine dominandi super Abbatiam Sti. Edmundi.

Circà annum 1101 (secundum Marianum) Herbertus Episcopus tunc Thetfordensis versùs Romam iter arripuit, iniquâ cupidine dominandi super Abbatiam Sti. Edmundi. Eadem quippe Abbatia, ex quo primùm fundata fuit, semper à subjectione omnis Episcopi libera fuit, libertatem ipsam quasi à beati Martyris Edmundi jure trahens, qui loco, in quo jam sita est ipsa Abbatia, regali quondam potentiâ præsidens, speciali quâdam eum locum, inibi corporaliter dum viveret degens, libertate donaverat; quam libertatem Reges et Romani Pontifices Sto. Edmundo annuerunt, roboraverunt, et inconvulsam manere constituerunt. Hic itaque Herbertus Episcopus, cum partes Lugduni attigisset, comprehensus est a quodam Guidone, viro præpotente et fero, cui 4 marcas invitus reliquit, quas contrà Ecclesiam Sti. Edmundi, Angliam egrediens, disposuerat expendisse. Hinc rediens domum sedem Episcopalem transtulit de Thetfordiâ ad Norwicum, et intra breve posteà, anno videlicet proximo sequenti, et *anno Regis Henrici Primi* 3°, *proposuit calumniam satis facundè de subjectione Ecclesiæ Sti. Edmundi, multisque de causis justam ac necessariam ibi fore suam prælationem. Sed causa diligenter ventilata calumniam ipsius irritam esse debere comprobavit ac decrevit universa Synodus*, ab Anselmo Archiepiscopo Cantuariensi Londoniæ celebrata, *quia Episcopi quamplures et Abbates necnon Duces Regni considentes affirmaverunt se interfuisse causis Arfasti Episcopi* Elmhamensis *et Baldwini Abbatis* Sti. Edmundi, *ipsumque Arfastum à causâ cecidisse, Abbatem vero Baldwinum per legitimos testes comprobâsse se ac suam Abbatiam per 53 annos liberam ac quietam ac sine calumniâ fuisse ab omnibus antecessoribus ipsius Arfasti. Demonstrâsse quoque testati sunt prædictum Abbatem monasterium suum dedicatum ab Agelnotho Archiepiscopo Dorobernensi, seque posteà Abbatem consecratum fuisse à metropolitano ejusdem sedis; antecessorum etiam ipsius alterum ab Episcopo Londinensi, alterum à Præsule Wintoniensi, ordinatos; monachos quoque sui Monasterii à quibuslibet Episcopis ad diversos ordines promotos sine contradictione Thetfordensis sive Elmhamensis Episcopi eleganti testimonio comprobâsse. Discussâ tandem causâ, calumniâque præfati Herberti honestis rationibus refutatâ per decretum universalis consilii, ne mutire quidem ausus est deinceps contrà Ecclesiam Sti. Edmundi quoad vixerat*, et sic in causâ suâ minùs justâ meritis Sti. Edmundi planè defecit. Hæc Marianus Scotus.

Appendix. 363

asseverare se nullâ omnino ratione Romæ scienter quid Forced to acturum, quod aut honori aut voluntati Patris An- swear that he intend-selmi videri posset obnoxium. Post quæ, ut pace ac ed no harm to Anselm. securitate viri comitatus viæ reddi mereretur, ferme quadraginta, sicut fertur, marcas argenti (non gratâ ei Robbed largitate) reliquit, quas suo negotio super ecclesiam of forty marks. sancti Edmundi Romæ adminiculaturas, Angliam egrediens, mage putavit.

On the extract from the Cartulary several observations arise.

(1.) For the *forty* marks of Eadmer, which Herbert took with him to assist him in procuring jurisdiction over the Abbey, the Cartulary says *four* marks.

(2.) The Cartulary, belonging to St. Edmund's Abbey, would naturally make the most of a story against one who had invaded the prerogatives of the Abbey.

(3.) The Cartulary represents Herbert as transferring his see from Thetford to Norwich after his misadventure, apparently making a confusion between his first journey to Rome, which had for its object the laying down his pastoral staff at the feet of the pope, and the later one, the object of which was to procure jurisdiction over the Abbey. The date of the first journey would be 1095 or 1096; that of the second, eleven or twelve years later, in 1107. Anyhow, A.D. 1101 cannot have been the date of a journey, on his return from which Herbert removed the see to Norwich. For the see must have been removed *before* Norwich Cathedral was built, and this cathedral is well known to have been founded in 1096. The foundation charter was *sealed* in A.D. 1101.

(4.) The Cartulary refers to Marianus as its authority. The Chronicle of Marianus proper (*Chronicon universale à creatione mundi*) only carries the history down to A.D. 1083. It was, however, continued to A.D. 1200 by Dodechin, Abbot of St. Disibod, in the diocese of Treves. This work of Marianus's continuator must be what is referred to in the Cartulary. And the whole passage of the Cartulary which is printed in italics is found *verbatim* in Marianus's continuator. But it will be observed that this passage does not include the account of Herbert's misadventure, his falling into Guy's hands and losing his four marks. This story may exist in Marianus, but we have not found it there. The italicised passage will be found in MS. Bodl. of Marianus, pp. 406, 407, in the note at the foot of the pages. The Bodleian MS. seems to have belonged to the Abbey of St. Edmund; for we find at the top of the first page the words, " Liber sčī Eadmundi regis et m."—the rest is cut off.

Eadmer also mentions that Herbert (with six others) assisted Anselm in consecrating Roger of Salisbury and four other bishops, in the Aug. of 1107 (p. 77); that he was one of eleven bishops who, after Anselm's death, stoutly maintained the right of the Primate of Canterbury to exact a profession of canonical obedience from him of York, determining among themselves "rather to be despoiled of all they had, than not to obey the injunctions Anselm had given them in regard of that difference" (p. 82); that he eventually assisted Richard of London in consecrating Thomas II. Archbishop of York, June 27, 1109 (p. 83); that he assisted Archbishop Ralph (A.D. 1115) in consecrating Geoffrey to Hereford and Ernulf to Rochester (p. 90); after which (p. 91) he gives this account of Herbert's setting out for Rome with Archbishop Ralph, and being stopped by serious illness :—

Herbert falls ill, when on a journey to Rome with Radulfus, on the question of the Legatine power in England.

Cum itaque Placentiam pervenissemus, Episcopus Norwicensis (Herbertus nomine) qui nobiscum Romam iturus Angliam exierat, validâ infirmitate correptus est, ita ut ingravescente languore, decem continuis diebus sine cibo et voce mutus jaceret. Quamobrem quatuor hebdomadas ibi exegimus, suspensi quid de episcopo faceret Deus. Ubi vero illum convalescere certo advertimus, ad petitionem et consilium ejus Pater noster cœpto sese itineri reddidit : ipse, debilitate nimiâ fessus, ibi remansit, Archiepiscopum aut illic præstolaturus, aut convalescens (si moram faceret) redeundo præcessurus. Nos itaque Romam, ille Normanniam, prout Dominus posse dedit, póst nonnullas dies usque pervenimus. *His return from Placentia into Normandy.*

IV.—ORDERICUS VITALIS.

[Born 1075 at Atcham, near Shrewsbury, of which latter place his father was a priest—removed, when only ten years old, to Ouche, a convent in Normandy—took the name of Vitalis from the circumstance of his receiving the tonsure on St. Vitalis' day, in the year 1086—ordained priest 1107—visited England and consulted the records of Croyland Abbey and Worcester. His "Ecclesiastical History" is a chronicle from the birth of Christ down to the year 1141. He is supposed to have died about 1143.]

Under date 1087—1100 Orderic describes Flambard's profligate administration of ecclesiastical revenues under William Rufus, how the king's ministers went the round of the convents, seized the revenues, and allowing but the narrowest pittance for the subsistence of the monks, threw the remainder into the royal exchequer; how the ecclesiastical preferments vacated by such men as Osmund of Salisbury and Remigius of Lincoln, were filled unscrupulously with unworthy court favourites, in whom the king might find not piety, but a servile compliance with his own wishes. Among these court favourites, thus unworthily preferred, he enumerates Herbert, qualifying his censure, however, by observation that some of them, when the burden of Church government was laid upon their shoulders, turned out well. In making this qualification, we apprehend that he adverts principally to Herbert; and we give the passage, which is a striking one, *in extenso :—*

Guillelmus quoque de Guarel-Guest episcopium habuit Exoniense, Johannes Medicus Badense, Radulfus cognomento Luffa Cicestrense, et Rannulfus Flambardus Dunelmense, Herbertus vero Losengia Tetfordense. Sic utique capellani regis et amici præsulatus Angliæ adepti sunt, et nonnulli ex ipsis præposituras ad opprimendos inopes, sibique augendas opes nihil- *Herbert, one of many Court favourites, corruptly preferred.*

How some corrupt appointments turned out well.

ominus tenuerunt. Alii vero pro suscepto ecclesiastici regiminis onere divinitus perterriti sunt, sibique commissis intus et exterius salubriter prodesse studuerunt, vitasque suas secundum beneplacitam voluntatem Dei laudabiliter correxerunt. Homines enim multa faciunt culpabiliter pro explenda sua voluntate, nil appetentes nisi libitum suum in perpetrata pravitate; quæ sapiens Arbiter omnium ad multorum commoditatem sua bene disponit ineffabili pietate. Plerumque leves et indocti eliguntur ad regimen Ecclesiæ tenendum, non pro sanctitate vitæ, vel ecclesiasticorum eruditione dogmatum, liberaliumve peritia litterarum, sed nobilium pro gratia parentum, et potentum favore amicorum. Quibus ita promotis clemens Deus parcit ac miseretur, eisque postmodum supernæ ubertas gratiæ infunditur, et cœlestis sophiæ per eos luce Dei domus illuminatur, et utilibus studiis plures salvantur.

V.—WILLIAM OF MALMESBURY.

[A Benedictine monk, Precentor and Librarian of the Abbey of Malmesbury in Wiltshire. He flourished in the year 1130, and died about 1143. He wrote five Books on the Acts of the English Kings, from the first coming of the Saxons to the 28th year of Henry I., and four Books on the Acts of the English Bishops, from the arrival of Augustine, Archbishop of Canterbury, to his own times. The following passage is from the latter of these works (*De gestis Pontificum Anglorum*), as given in Sir Henry Savile's *Rerum Anglicarum Scriptores post Bedam*, Francofurt, 1601. Lib. 2, p. 238.]

As later writers do little else than reproduce Malmesbury, we give his account *in extenso*. The parts of it enclosed in square brackets, and having F. W. in the margin, are, it will be seen, borrowed almost *verbatim* from Florence of Worcester :—

Herfast, cons. to Elmham 1070.

Post Ethelmerum fuit Helmanensis Episcopus Herfastus, sicut invenitur in concilij textu, quod sexto anno Willielmi regis pro primatu duorum Metropolitanorum factum est. Qui ne nihil fecisse videretur, ut sunt Normanni famæ in futurum studiosissimi, episcopatum de

Helmaham transtulit ad Thethfordum. Parcæ (ut ai- Herfast
unt) mentis homo, nonnullâ ex parte literis eruditus: the see to
quique ante adventum Lanfranci in Normanniam pro- Thetford,
babilis in eis scientiæ æstimatus sit. Sed eo apud 1075.
Beccum monachato, cum ubique scholares inflatis buc-
cis dialecticam ructarent, Herfastus jam Willielmi Co- Herfast
mitis (postea regis) capellanus, ad famosum gymnasium ridicule by
magnâ sociorum et equorum pompâ peruenit. Tum Lanfranc.
Lanfrancus ex primâ colloquutione intelligens quàm
propè nihil sciret, Abecedarium ipsi expediendum apposuit, ferociam hominis Italicâ facetiâ illudens. Quo
is irritatus per Comitem effecit, ut Lanfrancus Becco Herfast
Normanniâque omni summoveretur. Sed intercedente Lanfranc's
Dei gratiâ animus Willielmi pacatus est, alterque re- banish-
tentus, satagente maximè Willielmo filio Osberni. Max- Nor-
imaque fuit recuperandæ gratiæ occasio, quòd cum Lan- mandy.
francus ad curiam commeatum petiturus venisset, equus queror re-
eius fortè claudicans Comiti cachinnum excussit[1]. conciled to
Lanfranc.
[Post hunc diebus Willielmi minoris emit episcopa- Herbert
tum Tetfordensem HEREBERTUS cognomento LOSINGA, cons. by
quod ei ars adulationis impegerat, ex Priori Fiscanij, 1091.
et ex Abbate Rameseiæ factus episcopus, patre suo F. W.
Roberto eiusdem cognominis in Abbatiam Wintoniæ
intruso.] Fuit ergo vir ille magnus in Angliâ symoniæ Herbert
fomes, etiam Abbatiam Episcopatumque nummis aucu- fautor of
patus, pecuniâ scilicet regiam sollicitudinem inuiscans, simony.
et principum favori promissiones non leves assibilans.
[Veruntamen erroneum impetum iuuentutis aboleuit
pœnitentiâ, Romam profectus seuerioribus annis, ubi F. W.
loci baculum symoniacum et annulum deponens, indulgentiâ clementissimæ sedis iterum recipere meruit;]
quòd Romani sanctius et ordinatius censeant, ut eccle- The Papal
siarum omnium sumptus suis potius serviant marsupijs, tuated by
quam quorumlibet regum usibus militent. mercenary
motives.
[Ita Herebertus domum reuersus sedem episcopalem F. W.
transportauit ad insignem mercimonijs et populorum

---

[1] Here is omitted the episcopate of William de Beaufeu. He was consecrated to Thetford (by Lanfranc) in 1086, and died 1091. See Angl.-Sax. Chron., 1085.

frequentiâ vicum, nomine NORWIC. Ibi monachorum congregationem numero et religione percelebrem instituit], omnia ijs necessaria sumptu mercatus domestico. Providens scilicet successorum querelæ, nullas de Episcopo terras monachis largitus est, ne illi Dei famulos fraudarent victualibus, si quid offendissent, quod suis competeret rebus. Præterea apud Theodfordum monachos Cluniacenses instituit, quòd sint illius cœnobij professores ubique gentium pene dispersi, locupletes in seculo, et splendidissimæ religionis in Deo. Ingenti ergo et numerosâ virtutum gratiâ præteritarum offensarum obumbrauit molem, præcipuè Prognostico[m] antecessoris et suo à malo exterritus, et ad bonum erectus. Herfasti fuit, *Non hunc, sed Barabam:* suum; *Amice, ad quid venisti:* quo audito nec lachrymis, nec his ferè verbis abstinuit: *Malè quidem intravi, confiteor, sed Dei gratiâ operante benè egrediar.* Erat ergo disertitudinis et literarum copiâ, nec minus secularium rerum peritiâ, Romanæ celsitudini suspiciendus. Mutatusque Herebertus fuit (ut Lucanus de Curione dicit) *momentum et mutatio rerum;* sicut tempore Willielmi regis symoniæ causidicus, ita regnante Henrico propulsator invictus. Neque ab alijs fieri voluit, quod à se quondam præsumptum iuuenili fervore indoluit. Præ se (ut ferunt) semper ferens Jeronimi dictum; *Errauimus iuuenes, emendemus senes.* Postremo quis in illius facti laudem digne attexat, quod tam nobile monasterium episcopus non multùm pecuniosus fecerit, in quo nihil frustra desideres vel in ædificiorum specie sublimium, vel in ornamentorum pulchritudine, tum in monachorum religione, et sedulâ ad omnes charitate? Hæc et viuum

---

[m] The *Prognosticon* was a passage of the Gospel, or of some other sacred book, which first presented itself to the eye, after opening the book. This was a species of divination not uncommon in mediæval times, and usually resorted to in the election and consecration of bishops, by way of ascertaining the character of the future prelate. The Prognostic at the consecration of Anselm was; "He called many; and sent his servant.... and they all with one consent began to make excuse." See Rad. de Diceto, in Twysden's "10 Scriptores," Lond. 1652, p. 491, line 52.

spe felici palpabant, et defunctum (si non vana fides pœnitentiæ) super æthera tulerunt.

In Malmesbury's Chronicle of the *Kings* of England (*De gestis Regum*) the account of Herbert is given in identically the same words. It follows the account of the Cistercian order (bk. iv. ch. i.), and is thus introduced;—

(*De gestis Regum*. Lond. 1596. Fol. 72 b.)

His temporibus in Angliâ tres episcopatus ex antiquis sedibus transierc alias; Wellensis in Bathoniam per Johannem, Cestrensis per Robertum in Coventriam, Tedfordensis per Herbertum in Northwich; omnes majori ambitu, quam ut tantorum virorum debuisset interesse studio. Denique, ut primum de postremo dicam, Herbertus, cognomento Losinga, quod ei ars adulationis impegerat, ex abbate Ramesiensi emit episcopatum Tedfordensem, patre quoque suo Roberto ejusdem cognominis in Abbatiam Wintoniæ intruso. * * * *Herbert's removal of his see from ambitious motives.*

The *De gestis Regum*, however, omits all reference to Herfast, and to the *Prognosticon* of him and Herbert; and in speaking of his being the great source of simony in England, adds these verses (we give the whole context);—

Pecunia scilicet regiam sollicitudinem inviscans, et principum favori non leves promissiones assibilans unde quidam egregie tunc temporis versificus ait.

Surgit in Ecclesiâ monstrum, genitore Losingâ,
Symonidum secta, canonum virtute resectâ.
Petre, nimis tardas, nam Symon ad ardua tentat:
Si præsens esses, non Symon ad alta volaret.
Proh dolor! Ecclesiæ nummis venduntur et ære;
Filius est Præsul, pater Abbas, Symon uterque!
Quid non speremus, si nummos possideamus?
Omnia nummus habet, quod vult facit, addit et aufert.
Res nimis injusta, nummis fit Præsul et Abba.

Satirical verses made upon Herbert and his father.

In other respects the accounts are exactly the same.

In fol. 128 of the *De gestis Regum*, is given the account, already cited from Eadmer, of Herbert's mission to Rome, as one of the king's representatives, on the subject of investitures (his second journey thither) ; of his being seized by *prædones* (robbers), and falling into the hands of Guy, the *raptorum magister* (captain of their gang), and of his being made to swear by all the saints that he would not, when at Rome, do anything from which injury might accrue to Anselm. (It should be observed that Malmesbury, like Eadmer, makes the money of which Herbert was robbed forty marks, not four, which is the sum given in the St. Edmund's Cartulary.) This is followed by a spirited account of what took place on the return of the mission to England, with letters (apparently of a different tenour) to the king and to Anselm.

Fol. 129 b records Herbert's assisting Anselm at the consecration of Roger of Salisbury, William of Warelwast, and three other bishops, at Canterbury, already recorded by Florence and Eadmer.

Fol. 131, an account is given of Herbert's third and last journey to Rome, in the train of Abp. Ralph, on the question of the Legatine power. Malmesbury mentions the Archbishop's carbuncle, which caused a month's stoppage, but not Herbert's illness, which obliged him to turn back at Placentia. The words are these ;—

Sed cum ad castellum, quod Feritatem vocant, venisset, fœdissimum ulcus faciem ejus invasit et tumefecit, certum futuræ paralyseos indicium. Carbunculum vocat *Plinius* secundus, peculiare vultus vitium, quod vel cutem ad ossa corrodat, vel, medicorum præventum diligentia, deformem cicatricem relinquat. Multis ergo diebus decubuit. Sed postea valetudine sedata, seu potius morte dilata, Romam pervenit.

Pope Pascal's letter on the prerogatives of the see of Canterbury, which was the result realized by this mission, is given at length by Malmesbury.

VI.—HENRY OF HUNTINGDON.

[Flourished about 1150. He was a canon of Lincoln, and raised to the Archdeaconry of Huntingdon by Alexander, Bishop of Lincoln. He wrote a History of the English in eight Books (*De rebus gestis Regum Angliæ libri octo*, from Julius Cæsar to the death of King Stephen), and a letter to Walter on the Bishops and illustrious men of his own time, which letter Wharton says was written in A.D. 1145, and belongs to the tenth book of the History. It is from this letter that the following passage is an extract—short, but valuable, inasmuch as it is the first notice we have of Herbert's being an author.]

"Norwiciæ sedit Herbertus, *vir benignus* et doctus, cujus extant scripta."

Herbert's writings extant in Henry of Huntingdon's days.

We make another extract from Henry of Huntingdon, to which our attention has been called by Mr. Parker, the learned publisher of this work. It is contained in Capgrave's work, *De Illustribus Henricis* [ed. Hingeston, London, 1858, pp. 176, 177], which was written out of compliment to King Henry VI. The author gives to Henry of Huntingdon a place among the illustrious Henries [a], and quotes from his work entitled *De Summitatibus Rerum*, which by the author's own account was written in the thirty-fifth year of Henry the First's reign. Towards the end of the book, Henry of Huntingdon gives his opinion on the subject of the end of the world thus:—

Ad vos igitur jam loquor, qui in terno millenario circa XXXV. annum, (si contigerit, quod valde desiderat anima mea, vestras ut in manus hoc opusculum prodeat,) precor, ut Dei clementiam inexcogitatam pro me misero exoretis, et sic pro vobis orent, qui et impetrent, qui in quarto vel quinto millenario cum Deo ambulabunt, si generatio mortalium tamdiu protelabitur. Quærit aliquis cur de sequentibus millenariis ita loqueris, cum in nos fines sæculi devenerint et mundi terminum cotidie cernentes expectemus? Ad hæc ego: "Mundi terminus tibi est dies quâ morieris. Christus autem

---

[a] One of his twelve "Illustrious Henries," by the way, is Henry le Spenser, the warlike Bishop of Norwich, who quelled the rebellion of Jack the Litster in 1381, and died 1406.

sæculorum finis est, qui non primam sæculi partem adventui suo elegit, sed ultimam, in qua finirentur lex, et prophetæ, et significantia, veniente Significato." Quia verò de prolixitate temporum nullus nisi Pater omnium novit, quod scripsi secundum estimationem meam est, quam de Herberto, Norwycensi episcopo, viro doctissimo, jamdudum extraxi. Dicebat enim secundum quod æstimo, et ex ratione compensare queo. Multo magis durabit veritas quam figura, lux quam umbra, significata tempore [tempora?] gratiæ quam legis. Quod si figura et umbra, præcedentes et præsignantes Christi gratiam, pene per quinque mille annos extensæ sunt, quanto magis Christi lux et Christi gratia. Æstimationem namque eorum jam frustratam esse vidimus, qui post passionem Domini mille tantum annos sæculum duraturum putaverunt, quia in ultima ætate venerit Christus. Nec Judæorum opinio sequenda est, qui post sex mille annorum, numerum ab initio numerando, in millenario septimo sabbatum suum inchoandum asserunt, et reversionem in terram suam, et totius mundi dominium, affirmans etiam post modicum exinde tempus totius mundi terminationem futuram. Sed potius veritatem, multis temporibus promissam, multo amplius, præstante Domino nostro Ihesu Christo, credimus duraturam.

Herbert's speculations on the end of the world followed by Henry of Huntingdon.

"Hæc est opinio," adds Capgrave, "hujus venerabilis viri de fine mundi. Et si quis alia ejus dicta videre desideraverit, ad librum ejus festinet legendum, quæ de Chronicis compilavit."

VII.—THOMAS ELIENSIS.

[A monk of Ely, who flourished about 1170, and wrote a " History of the Isle of Ely, of the life of St. Ætheldrida, of the abbats and bishops of Ely, and of the translation of Ætheldrida, in three Books." The two former parts of this work were epitomised by a monk of Ely; and the Epitome appears in Wharton's *Anglia Sacra*, London, 1691. Part I., p. 613.]

Translatio Sanctarum Virginum per Ricardum Abbatem facta.

Facta est hæc Translatio Anno Domini MCVI. sub

die Kal. Novembr. xvi. quo quidem die prima ejus Trans- Octobr.
latio, à S. Sexburgâ facta, tanquam una cum novâ cele- Thomas legit.
bratur. Eodemque die facta fuit Translatio Sanctarum
Sexburgæ, Withburgæ, et Ermenildæ condecentissima
ordinatione ; ut omnium esset una solempnitas, quibus
erat una fides, unus spiritus, et una caritas.

De secunda translatione corporis sacræ virginis [Etheldredæ] *quam idem abbas fecit.*

Summo igitur desiderio desiderans abbas Ricardus, et deliberans suo in tempore corpus sacratissimum sacratissimæ virginis, de veteri ecclesiâ in novam, de modicâ in majorem et pulchriorem transferre ; memorans quia et Joseph patris sui corpus, ad majorem reverentiam, de Ægypto in terram Chanaam transtulerat ; ne tam præclara lampas et lucerna sub modio lateret, sed quasi super candelabrum posita, sub præsentiâ testium et frequentiâ populorum, cunctis innotesceret et luceret ; diem statuit, videlicet decimo sexto Kal. Octobris, quo et prima ejus translatio, tamquam una cum novâ celebretur. Vir itaque magni et liberalis animi ad hanc solennitatem solenni et maxime pontificali auctoritate corroborandam, imprimis virum venerabilem et religiosissimum, Anselmum Cantuariensem metropolitanum, eâ quâ debuit et eum decuit reverentiâ invitavit ; ut pro sui debito officii, adjunctis sibi ex suis quos religiosiores arbitraretur quotquot vellet suffraganeis, suam ipse præsentiam dignaretur exhibere ; invitatis etiam quampluribus pontificalis dignitatis et ordinis viris, et abbatibus et religiosis monachis aliisque personis ecclesiasticis, pontificibus summis, etsi non dignitate, tamen meritis non immerito coæquandis, ne dicam præferendis. Invitati ab ipso fuerunt et regni proceres et optimates, ut ad tam jucundam festivitatem accederent, et cum gaudentibus et ipsi gauderent. Quibusdam autem vel privatis vel publicis negotiis vel necessitatibus occupatis, quidam a divinâ providentiâ destinati, et tali ac tantæ rei proficiendæ idonei ac plurimum necessarii, devotissime confluxerunt. Inter quos vir laudabilis, *Herbertus Norwicensis episcopus*, Adelwinus Rameseiensis, Ricardus S. Albani abbas, Gunterus Thorniensis, Wydo Persoriensis abbas, Nicolaus Lincolniensis archidiaconus, Gaufridus Wintoniensis thesaurarius, et alii innumeri magnæ honestatis et auctoritatis viri. Ordinate igitur ordinatâ processione, ad sanctæ ac reverendæ virginis Ætheldrethæ tumulum reverenter accedunt, Pario de marmore candidissimum, uti decebat candorem virgineum. In hoc quondam angelicis obsequiis sibi præparato et divinâ gratiâ quærentibus oblato, beatissima germana ejus regina Sexburga, post sexdecim annos sepulturæ, inventam ipsius solidissimam glebam, toto corpore et vestibus lacteam et intemeratam, cum clamosâ admiratione et laudisonâ in cœlum benedictione, recondidit: unde nunc id illi ad majorem gloriam accrescit quod nemo ipsius tumbam pandere, nemo inspicere præsumpsit. Aliquando enim, paganis irruentibus in hunc locum, pro plagâ foramen intulit unus, qui mox oculis et vitâ est privatus; postea presbyter temerarius, quasi præses monasterii, in illud foramen fissam virgam impingens torquendo in rugam, partem vestis extraxit, majorique vesaniâ abscidit, quam subito intus jacentis manus cum vigili indignatione ad se retraxit. Adhuc tentator affixam virgæ candelam immittere addidit; candela autem decidens super sacrum corpus tota exarsit, et nihil rerum læsit: præsumptor vero cum domo suâ periit. Hæc quoque cum in miraculis ejusdem plenius digesta sint, ad narrationem redeamus.

Tandem cum ingenti devotione sacrosanctum corpus virginis assumunt, ex vetere ecclesiâ exportantes de loco quo eam transtulerat et collocaverat Sexburga beatissima; ubi et pater Ædelwoldus venerandus, postea destructam ecclesiam restaurans et renovans, eam certissime intentatam, irremotam, et inconspectam, non sub terra delitescentem, sed desuper eminentem, sicut invenit, reliquit; unde nunc et in ecclesiam cum laudibus et canticis deferunt. Translata est itaque in novum templum regia domina Ætheldreda intentata et incon-

Appendix. 375

specta ; et condignâ psallentium laude, post autenticum altare parato thalamo collocata. *Habito tandem, ut decebat, ad populum de tantâ, et in tantâ solemnitate sermone, et venerabili episcopo Herberto, viro eloquentissimo, de vitâ et obitu et miraculis beatæ virginis, sacrique corporis admirabili incorruptione, populum exhortante ad summæ jucunditatis et lætitiæ indicium propter ea quæ facta sunt in tabernaculis justorum; raro quempiam cerneres tantâ multitudine, qui gratiâ cœlesti perfusus, a lacrymis se vellet aut valeret cohibere.* Hoc vero solum de pluribus, quæ in translatione contigerunt sacratissimæ virginis reginæ Ætheldredæ, ad æternam referimus memoriam, quod fidelium innumeri adhuc superstites et patres nostri qui viderunt et adfuerunt, narraverunt nobis, quorum relatio et auctoritas vitæ et honestas morum nos instruxit, ut de facto nemo diffidat. Tunc quippe renovantur antiqua miracula, quæ contigisse leguntur in inventione º beati corporis Stephani martyris. Facta sunt enim tonitrua, tempestates, et fulgura talia, ut omnes pæne fenestræ ecclesiæ horridis ictibus frangerentur, et crebri ignes in pavimentum coram sanctis corporibus laberentur: eratque mira-

Herbert preaches in the new cathedral of Ely, on the Life, Miracles, and Death of St. Etheldreda.

The effect of his Sermon.

º "Quæ contigisse leguntur in inventione beati corporis Stephani martyris."

The last resting-place of the Protomartyr is said to have been revealed to Lucian, a priest, on the 3rd Dec., in the year 415. Gamaliel appeared to him in a vision, and directed him to search for St. Stephen's remains at Caphargamala, about twenty miles from Jerusalem, where he should find him lying close by Nicodemus and Abibas (Gamaliel's son). Lucian repaired to Jerusalem, and, after obtaining the sanction of the Bishop John, discovered the place where the remains lay. The coffin was opened in the presence of John, who was accompanied by the Bishops of Sebaste and Jericho. On the opening of the coffin there was an earthquake, and the exhalation of a delicious odour; and when it was closed again, and transported to the church of Sion at Jerusalem, (which was done on the 26th Dec.,) *there fell a great deal of rain, which refreshed the country after a long drought.* This is probably the portent alluded to by Thomas of Ely.

The finding of St. Stephen is celebrated by the Roman Church on the 3rd August.

The finding is also placed on that day in the Sarum, French, Spanish, Scotch, and German Calendars.

bile, ignem labi sine effectu naturæ suæ; suamque, inter ligna et stramina cæterasque arentes materias, mutare qualitatem, ut quidquid hujusmodi in ecclesiam ceciderit innocuum extaret. Hoc siquidem magnum miraculum, sanctâ illâ operante, sic contigit; ut juxta quorundam opinionem cœlesti terrore ostenderet, sibi displicere tam publice se tractari, et tamen in hâc suâ indignatione nullum læderet; ut nullum lateret ad nutum ejus cœli signa famulari.

Rarus ergo fuit ibi, cujus cogitatio magnum aliquid ista non dictaret portendere, quorum horrorem hinc timebat videre, hinc gaudebat evadere. Anselmus quoque archiepiscopus, longe in Cantiâ positus, videns cœlum tanto fragore concuti; "Scio" inquit "fratrem nostrum Ricardum, abbatem Elyensem, hodie sanctas suas transtulisse, et irreverenter tractasse; nec dubito hanc intemperiem dolendi auspicii esse signaculum." Nec eum fefellit sententia; quia rarus eorum, qui tunc aderant et sanctam Withburgam facie ad faciem adspexerant, integrum annum exierunt. Quapropter, fratres carissimi, a vobis, qui non momentaneè sed continuè tantæ virginis memoriam in conspectu præsentiæ sacri corporis, juste et sancte recolitis; et orandum est et attentius exorandum, quatenus per vos suæ et nos et vos dignetur gratiæ rore perfundere, qui populo sitienti aquam de petrâ, Moyse percutiente, in abundantiâ fecit emanare; cui sit laus, honor, et gloria per omnia sæculorum sæcula.

Quod abbas novum mausoleum paravit, sed minus aut plus quantitate formæ corporis Withburgæ habuit, et quod palam sacrum corpus illius ostendit, et in sepulchro veteri divinitùs sanato recondidit.

Præfulgidæ autem Withburgæ, ad certissimam mensuram veteris sarcofagi, quod jamdudum fuerat fractum, memoratus rector Eliensis aulæ Ricardus paraverat novum; quatenus in novo reposita incorrupta virgo incorruptum haberet hospicium; sed superna Providentia id consilii novo et insolito miraculo evacuavit. Nam ut nova tumba quæ sacrum corpus exciperet parata astitit, appositâ prioris mensuræ virgâ, unius pedis quantitate brevior extitit. Quisquis iterare mensionem utrius que temptavit, non amplius invenit; semper nova a veteri prescriptâ brevitate defecit. Hærebant omnes stupore et extasi, videntes suum propositum a parato locello productioris corporis majestate arceri. Interea, cum auferretur operculum hiantis fissurâ mausolei, majora omnes terruere miracula. Virginea quippe gleba, quæ putabatur post tot sæcula jam olim consumpta; quamvis eam ab antiquâ experientiâ clara defenderet fama, tota et membris et vestibus apparuit integra, sicuti primitus erat imposita. Lignea etiam theca, ferreis tantum clavis exesis, cum quâ fuerat in Ely delata, servata est illæsa. Interea quidem putavere quod quasi immotus pulvis exhausti corporis tantum imaginem prætenderet integritatis; sed tactu patuit veritas perdurantis hactenus soliditatis. Nam quidam senior ex apostolico ovili Westmonasterii, Warnerus nomine, ut inter plures convenerat, mirâ fidei audaciâ accessit, virginea membra passim tangit, a vestigiis manibus et brachiis, flexibiles artus reverenter attollit, exclamansque Dei mirabilia plures spectabilium personarum ad videndum attraxit. Verumptamen tectum nivalibus operimentis decorem, nullius irreverentia oculis attigit. Candet Domino rosatis genis facies spiraculo vitæ inspirata; vernant suâ integritate stantia ubera; florent paradisiacâ amœnitate innuba membra. *Venit vir doctissimus præfatus Herbertus, episcopus de Tedfordâ, tremens inspexit, et gloriosum in sanctis suis Dominum benedixit.* Aliique plures honestatis conspicuæ præsentes astitere, quos supra meminimus. Hæc Dei mirabilia oculis conspexere. Sed his ignoscant auditorum fastidia, quæ in argumentum Fidei retulimus testimonia. *Tandem vero memorabilis episcopus Herbertus hæc tam mira tamque nova gaudia condensissimo populo exponit, omnesque in laudem Dei et gratiarum libamina*

The new coffin prepared for St. Withburga found to be too short for her body.

The soundness of her body ascertained by an experiment.

Herbert's inspection of the uncorrupt body of Withburga.

His sermon thereon,

accendit. *Immo vero (quæ absentibus videantur incredibilia) tanta hic de rore cœli invaluit gratia, ut pene per omnes currerent lacrimarum flumina.* Sed cum inter hæc tripudia anxiarentur omnes quid agerent, quia vetus tumba ex fracturâ injuriosa videbatur ad dignitatem virginis, nova vero divinitus contracta desierat esse suffragabilis, tandem pia adjutrix has fluctuationes demisit, et quod a priori requie mutari nollet glorioso miraculo comprobavit. Nam illa fissura, quæ cultello aut calamo ultro penetrabilis erat, ita subito resolidata est ad integrum, ut nec ullum deinceps fracturæ appareret ibi vestigium. Hic etiam omnium conclusa est questio; intellexere enim tam evidenti signo quia virgo nollet transponi ab antiqui monumenti thoro. Imposito ergo operculo, et clauso diligenter sarcofago, lætissimo cum jubilo transferunt eam ad beatam sororem de veteri monasterio in novum, et componunt gratissime contra orientem ad latus suum.—De hujus quippe sacratissimæ virginis Withburgæ integritate, taliter in cronicis Anglicis recitatur, anno Domini septingentesimo nonagesimo octavo, corpus sanctæ Withburgæ sine corruptione inventum est, post annos fere quinquaginta quinque in Dyrham. His septingentis nonaginta octo additis duobus et ducentis, completi sunt mille anni. Quos alii centum et sex subsecuti faciunt insimul trecentos et quinquaginta IIII^{or}. annos a dormitione ipsius beatæ Withburgæ usque ad hunc nostri temporis diem, quo incorrupto ostensa est corpore. Similiter etiam, ut dictum est, beatam germanam Sexbergam et sacratissimam filiam ipsius Ærmenildam, dignas ad condignas amabiliter associant, ubi et pariter et singulæ superna beneficia supplicantibus prærogant.

VIII.—"Annales Ecclesiæ Wintoniensis, authore Monacho Wintoniensi."

[These Annals reach from the year 633 to 1277. They are to be found in Wharton's *Anglia Sacra* (London, 1691). Vol. i., pp. 295, 297, 298.]

Anno 1091. Radulfus Episcopatum Cicestriæ suscepit, et *Herebertus Abbas Ramesiæ Episcopatum*

Nordfolchiâ, et Willelmus Episcopatum Dunelmensem. Ecclesia Croilandiæ combusta est.

There is also in these Annals (under the years 1116 and 1117) a notice of Herbert's third journey to Rome in the train of Abp. Ralph, and of his return with Hugh, Abbot of Chertsey.

IX.—BARTHOLOMEW COTTON.

[Bartholomew Cotton was a monk of the Benedictine monastery of Norwich, which was founded by Herbert in connexion with the cathedral. His work is entitled, *Bartholomæi de Cotton, Monachi Norwicensis, Historia Anglicana; necnon ejusdem Liber de Archiepiscopis et Episcopis Angliæ*. The history extends over a period of 849 years, commencing with A.D. 449, when the Roman Britons—those who had lived with the Romans and learned their language—had been exterminated by civil war, and Vortigern, King of South Britain, harassed by the Picts and Scots, and having appealed in vain to Rome, invited the Saxons to his aid; and concluding with the year 1298, when the Scots under Wallace were crushed by Edward I. in the battle of Falkirk. With this year Cotton's Chronicle of English History breaks off, and we are left to conclude that he did not live to continue it. Assuming then that he died about the close of the thirteenth century, and that he had reached the age assigned by the Psalmist to man, we shall place his birth about A.D. 1228, in the early part of the long, but comparatively uneventful, reign of Henry III. His times were stirring ones, both for the see of Norwich, and for the Church and kingdom of England in general. He lived through the episcopate of Bishop Suffield, in which were built St. Helen's Hospital (an almshouse still of great mark among the charitable institutions of the country), and the Early English Lady-Chapel of the cathedral, the arches giving admission to which are all that now remain to attest its architectural beauties; through that of Roger de Skerning (A.D. 1265-6—A.D. 1277-8), when the quarrel which had so long been brewing between the monks of the Priory and the citizens broke out at Tombland into acts of blood and violence, when the cathedral precinct was turned into a fortress, and underwent the horrors of a siege, and of the cathedral church nothing was left save the stone shell and Bishop Suffield's Lady-Chapel at the eastern extremity. Henry III., apprised of this sacrilege, thought it an occasion worthy of a royal visit for the purpose of trying and punishing the offenders, and accordingly took up his abode at Norwich Castle on Sept. 14, 1272. We must suppose that Cotton, who describes the riot in detail, was one of the few monks who escaped the general massacre. But he had yet more to see and to record in connexion with his church and convent. Bishop William de Middleton succeeded Skerning in 1277-8; and Cotton must have been present when—the ravages done by the fire to the cathedral and conventual buildings having been made good—this prelate was enthroned, and the cathedral re-dedicated with a magnificent ceremonial, in the presence of Edward I. and Queen Eleanor, on the Advent Sunday of 1278. It should be added, that Cotton also nearly lived through the Episcopate of Bishop Walpole (1288—1299), and saw the erection by that prelate of the eastern walk of the present magnificent cloister. He died about the time that Walpole was translated by the Pope to Ely, and John Salmon, whom the monks of Ely had elected as their bishop, was consecrated Bishop of Norwich Nov. 15, 1299.]

Matt. of West. p. 232.

Anno gratiæ MXCI. dominus Herbertus episcopus [p] suscepit episcopatum Theofordensem .... Eodem anno ventus vehemens .... percussit Londoniam xvi. kalendas Novembris [q] .... Eodem anno, Mechis corpus beati Clementis, primi episcopi ab apostolis ordinati, inventum est.....

Matt. of West. p. 233. Establishment of the see of Norwich.

Anno gratiæ MXCIIII. V. Idus Aprilis, episcopatus Theofordensis translatus est Norwycum ab Herberto episcopo [r]..... Hic Herbertus ex abbate Ramesiensi, empto præsulatu, factus est episcopus Theofordensis; sed postmodum pœnitentiâ ductus, Romam profectus est, et symoniacum baculum et annulum papæ resignavit. Verumtamen apostolicæ sedis indulgentiâ propitiante, restitutus est.

Anno gratiæ MXCVI. Norwycensis ecclesia fundata est [s] a Domino Herberto episcopo.... *Eodem anno idus Aprilis Urbanus papa concilium tenuit apud Clarum Montem, iter Jerusalem prædicans* [t]..... Eodem anno perrexit comes [u] Robertus Ierusalem. Et eodem anno fuit interfectio Judæorum apud Rothomagum. Stellæ visæ sunt labi de cœlo. Eodem anno Willelmus rex Normanniam accepit [v].....

[p] M. W. *abbas de Ramissia.*
[q] This date is from Florence of Worcester, ii. p. 29. This and the following sentence are placed in M. W. before the previous one.
[r] M. W. *Losenga.*
[s] M. W., who has *ecclesia S. Trinitatis N.*, puts this under the following year.
[t] Abridged, and the date wrongly given: the Council of Clermont was held in November, 1095. It is given by M. W. under that year.
[u] M. W. *dux.*
[v] M. W. *cepit sibi in tutelam.*

Anno gratiæ MCXIX. Herbertus episcopus Norwy- Death
censis (heu) diem clausit extremmum[x]*. . . . .* Eodem anno of Herbert, first
commissum est bellum nimis cruentum inter reges Bishop of
Francorum et Anglorum, in quo hostes regis Henrici, Norwich.
Willelmus consul Eboraci, comes Flandrensis Balde- France.
winus, capti incarcerantur.

Ed. Luard. London, 1859, p. 389, *et seq.*

Arfastus. Hic transtulit sedem de Elmham apud   26.
Thefordiam, tempore Willelmi regis, ex edicto concilii Arfastus.
ut prius dictum est. Hic fuit antea capellanus Will- A.D. 1070.
elmi regis.

Willelmus de Belfago, vir egregius, prædicto successit;   27.
et apud Thefordiam similiter sedit; et isti duo tantum. A.D. 1086.

Herbertus Willelmo successit, tempore Willelmi juni-   28.
oris, cognomento Losinga. Hic prius fuit prior Fis- Herbert
canni, postea abbas Ramesseye; et pater suus Robertus Losinga,
abbas Wintoniæ. Hic Herbertus *in pago Oxymensi*[y] A.D. 1091.

---

[x] M. P. *obiit N. antistes.* This is placed by M. P. after the account of the French war.

[The M. P. of Mr. Luard's foot-notes is Matthew Paris, and the M. W. Matthew of Westminster. The former was a Benedictine monk of St. Alban's, of great learning and piety, who was commissioned by the Pope to go to Norway, and reform a celebrated monastery there. On his return, he was in high favour with Henry III. He died in 1259. Matthew of Westminster was also a Benedictine monk, who flourished in the year 1377. His work, called "Flowers of Histories," is a Book of Annals from the Creation to the year 1307. In the early part of it he borrows much from Matthew Paris.]

[y] The reading given by Wharton in the *Anglia Sacra* (London, 1691, p. 407, line 5) is OXONIENSI. Wharton's note on the name HERBERTUS may here be given :—

"Sæpiùs Herebertus dictus, ex Priore Fiscamnensi Abbas Ramesiæ
"à Willelmo II. Rege factus, post tres annos Episcopus Thetfordensis
"efficitur. Ipse cœpit ædificare Ecclesiam Norvicensem anno 1096, *in*
"*loco vocato Cowholme.* Cartam Monachis introductis dedit anno 1101,
"mense Septembri. Sic Cartularium de Binham (in Collect. Dodsworth,
"vol. lix. f. 3, in Biblioth., Oxon.). Episcopus Thetfordensis creatus est
"anno 1091, consecratus a Thomâ Eboracensi Archiepiscopo, vacante
"tunc Sede Cant. Anno 1094, 9 April, sedem Episcopalem à Thet-
"fordiâ ad Norwicum transtulit, fide Annalium Bartholomæi. Obit 1119,
"22 Julii. Sic enim Chronicon breve Norwicense (Vitellius, c. 9), Flo-
"rentii Continuator, et Radulphus de Diceto produnt. Malè Hovedenus
"diem 23 Aug., diem 21 Junii Weaverus posuit."

*natus, Fiscanni monachus, post eiusdem loci prioratum
strenue administratum, translatus in Angliam a Rege
Willelmo, qui secundus ex Normannis obtinuit imperium,
Ramesseye abbatis (abbatiæ ?) jure prælatus est. Unde
post exactum triennium ad Orientalium Anglorum episcopatum electus et consecratus est. Erat quippe vir omnium litterarum tam secularium quam divinarum imbutus
scientiâ, facundiâ incomparabili, venustus corpore, jocun-
dus aspectu, ut solo visu plerumque a nescientibus quod
esset episcopus deprehenderetur. Mentis quippe gratia
radiabat in vultu ; et morum tranquillitas corporis officia
suo famulatui subigebat. Fide integer, spe erectus, quicquid agebat, quicquid loquebatur, sapientiâ disponebat,
confirmabat veritate, caritate saporabat, temperabat mo-
destiâ ; et misericordiæ bonum, cujus maxime visceribus
affluebat, superponebat judicio, ut eandem ipse consequi
mereretur. Vir igitur prudentis consilii, vagæ sedis non
ferens injuriam, quæ nunc in vico qui Elmham dicitur
in sacello ligneo, nunc vero apud Thefordense oppidulum
in alienæ possessionis ecclesia, sive in aliis quibuslibet
locis pro singulorum episcoporum libitu habebatur ; multâ
sibi locum Norwyci comparavit pecuniâ, primo a regi-
bus Willielmo secundo et Henrico, deinde ab ipsius loci
civibus ; in quo in Sanctæ Trinitatis nomine incepit et
maiori ex parte perfecit ecclesiam. Congregatisque in
eâ sexaginta et eo amplius monasticæ disciplinæ viris,
ibidem tam sibi quam successoribus suis episcopalem ca-
thedram collocari et in perpetuo conservari a domino Paschali papâ obtinuit. Monachorum quoque paci consulens
et securitati, oblationes ecclesiæ ab omni exactione liberans,
monachorum omnino esse censuit, eorum usibus omni-
modis profuturas. Sed et possessiones discrevit ; quarum
partem non modicam tam a rege Henrico quam a ceteris
fidelibus ipsius regis assensu multo labore et pretio adquisierat, ut liquido constaret quæ monachorum quæque
episcopalibus usibus deservirent. Nec parum in hoc quoque vir sagacis ingenii providit posteritati, quod hinc
monachorum, inde episcopales, seorsum constituit officinas ;
ne popularis frequentia, quâ episcopus carere non potest,*

monasticæ paci inquietudinem generaret: manifestis declarans indiciis, quam studiosus religiosæ traditionis emulator exstiterit. Nec prius destitit, quam constitutionem suam apostolicæ et regiæ auctoritatis privilegiis confirmaret; apostolici anathematis mucrone feriendum obtinens, si quis monachos expellere vel temere vexando fatigare, vel eorum bona auferre, minuere, retinere moliretur. Præterea ut sanctorum patrocinia sibi compararet, alias præclari operis constituit ecclesias; primam in colle, qui episcopali ecclesiæ interjecto flumine imminet; secundam Norwyci in curiâ episcopi; tertiam apud Elmham; quartam Lenniæ; quintam Gernemutæ, id est ad hostium Gerni fluminis; quas omnes perpetuo jure monachorum tradidit dominio. Felix religio[so]rum collectio, si tali ei pastore diutiùs uti licuisset! Dira, O misera mortalium conditio, ea citiùs deperire, quæ nobis diutiùs constare præoptamus! O diem omni lacrimarum fonte plangendam, æternis damnandam tenebris, quæ mundum tanti viri præsentiâ viduavit! *Obiit autem Herbertus episcopus, vir per omnia catholicus, æternam mundo sui nominis suis in operibus memoriam derelinquens; multoque omnium comprovincialium dolore sepultus est in ipsâ episcopali ecclesiâ, quam ipse stabilierat, possessionibusque, libris, et diversi generis ornamentis ditaverat, ante Dominicum altare in sarcophago tanti viri humatione digno. Transiit autem ab incarnatione Domini MCXIX.; pontificatûs autem sui XXIX.; XI. kal. Augusti, sub rege Henrico primo, præsidente Romanæ ecclesiæ domino papâ Gelasio, regnante Domino nostro Jesu Christo, cui cum Patre et Spiritu Sancto honor sit et gloria in sæcula sæculorum. Amen.*

Iste Herbertus apud Thefordiam monachos Cluniacenses instituit. Unde licet quidam Symoniæ culpam ei imponant, quia à rege Willelmo episcopatum per adulationem et pecuniam adquisivit, quia tunc temporis reges sine omni electione pro libitu suo conferebant episcopatus, licet injuste; mihi tamen videtur, quod excusatur per apostolum dicentem, *Redimentes tempus* Eph. v. 16.

quoniam dies mali sunt, et per decretalem qui dicit, quod licitum est clerico jus ecclesiæ suæ de manu laici emere, si aliter haberi non possit. Verumtamen vir prudens in omnibus, tandem sentiens conscientiam suam aliquantulum læsam, Romam profectus, annulum et baculum resignans, et culpam suam confitens, indulgentiam et restitutionem, bonis actibus exigentibus, a domino Papâ meruit.

[We have not thought it worth while to give the various readings of the Oxford MS. (Laud. B. xvi., No. 675), which Mr. Luard exhibits in his foot-notes.]

X.—REGISTRUM PRIMUM.

[A manuscript in the possession of the Dean and Chapter of Norwich, of which the following account is given by H. T. Riley, Esq., in the first Report of the Royal Commission on Historical MSS., pp. 87, 88 :—" This Register was probably made for the Prior's especial use; Henry de Lakenham has been suggested, about A.D. 1306. The first seven leaves contain entries of a later date than the body of the work; such entries being of a miscellaneous nature, and belonging mostly to the reigns of Edward III., Henry IV., and Henry VI. At page 15 the original commencement of the Register begins. It opens with a History of the foundation of the church of the Holy Trinity in Norwich, and the erection there of the episcopal see; the establishment there of a house of monks of St. Benedict; and an account of the royal charters, the various papal confirmations of grants and privileges, and the endowments of benefactors. This History comes down to about A.D. 1300, shortly after which date the bulk of the volume, no doubt, was written."]

The passages of Cotton which are printed in italics in the preceding article, are given *verbatim* in the *Registrum*, fol. 15 a, and therefore are not here repeated. In fol. 23 b occurs the following summary of Herbert's acts, with the notice of his death :—

Idem vero Herbertus episcopus, pluribus privilegiis super statu ecclesie sue et monasterii sui a predicto domino papa impetratis, que ad presens huic opusculo inserere nolumus, ne malivolis secreta monasterii pateant ullo modo. Set qui hiis indiget, thesauriam requirat, et ibidem plura inveniet, que malicie hominum poterunt resistere et jura monasterii confouere. Demum

Appendix.

negociis suis feliciter expeditis a summo pontifice licentia petita et optenta in Angliam ad suam ecclesiam est reversus. Quo cum omni gaudio a suis monachis et toto clero et populo sue dyocesis recepto? aliquanto tempore in ieiuniis, vigiliis, orationibus, ceteris penitentiæ operibus, et in omni sanctitate vitam ducens, tandem viam universæ carnis, per primum parentem nostrum per lapsum ejusdem humano generi inpositam, est ingressus cum summo deo et eterno, ut veraciter credimus, prout ex gestis precedentibus elici poterit sine fine feliciter regnaturus. Obiit autem dictus Herbertus Episcopus vir per omnia catholicus, &c., &c., &c. [as in Cotton above.]

XI.—THOMAS STUBBS (Stobæus).

[A Yorkshireman, who was a Dominican monk, and a Doctor of Divinity. He flourished, A.D. 1360. His death cannot have taken place before 1373. He wrote a "Chronicle of the Archbishops of York," from St. Paulinus to the death of John Thoresby, that is, from the first foundation of the see to the year 1373. This Chronicle is contained in Twysden's "Historiæ Anglicanæ Decem Scriptores," London, 1652.

The following passages (which shew how it was that Herbert was consecrated by Thomas I., Archbishop of York, and inform us that he acted as intermediary between Anselm and Thomas II., Archbishop-elect of York) are extracted from it. P. 1707, L 10, &c.]

Defuncto vero Lanfranco sedes Cantuariensis aliquot vacabat annis. Ex antiquo tamen extitit consuetudo inter duos Angliæ metropolitanos, ut altero defuncto alter in provinciâ defuncti archiepiscopalia faceret, utpote episcopos consecrare, regem coronare, coronato rege Natalis Domini, Paschæ, et Pentecostes majorem missam cantare. Hæc interim fecit Thomas archiepiscopus, nec quisquam episcoporum erat qui hæc in suâ ipsius diocesi præsente archiepiscopo præsumeret. *Ordinavit etiam episcopos, Herveum Norwicensem, Radulphum Cicestrensem, et Herveum Bangornensem.*

DE THOMÂ JUNIORE ARCHIEPISCOPO.

Vicesimo septimo loco septimo die successit in archiepiscopatu Eboracensi Thomas junior regis capellanus, ecclesiæ sancti Johannis Beverlaci præpositus, ac nepos venerandi Thomæ senioris. Cui rex eâdem die vel in proximâ Londoniensem episcopatum daturus, requisitione Hugonis decani Eboracensis mutavit consilium, et Eboracensem ecclesiam ei tradidit. Hunc ad consecrandum Anselmus archiepiscopus monachorum instinctu Cantuariam vocare, et ab eo professionem exigere statuit; super quo Thomas regem consuluit, qui primo benigne respondit, et ne profiteretur prohibuit. *Quo jam morante, venit Herbertus Norwicensis episcopus ad electum Eboracensem, dicens, quod archiepiscopus professionem suam dimitteret, si tantum in Primatem eum recognosceret; sed nec hoc electus voluit concedere, bonam confidentiam habens de rege.*

XII.—HENRY KNIGHTON.

[A canon regular of Leicester, flourished about 1395, wrote a "Chronicon de Eventibus Angliæ libris V. ab anno circiter 950, ad ann. 1395." His works are given by Twysden in his "Historiæ Anglicanæ Scriptores X." London, 1652.]

Circa hæc tempora Herbertus, dictus Losinga, Abbas quondam Remesiæ, set tunc episcopus Tedfordiæ, magna in Angliâ fomes Symoniæ extitit, eo quod sedem suam à rege emerat. Hic tamen postquam erroneum juventutis impetum deflevisset, Romam ivit, unde rediens sedem suam usque Norwicum transtulit, ubi quidem celebre cœnobium fundavit de rebus utique suis, non episcopalibus. Set et apud Tedfordiam monachos Cluniacenses instituit, locupletes quidem in seculo et splendidæ religionis. Sic igitur correctus est Herebertus duplici quidem prognostico, uno videlicet prædecessoris sui Herfasti indicio, quod erat, *Non hunc, set Barabam:* et suo proprio, quod erat, *Amice, ad quid venisti?* Quo audito, lacrimabiliter ait, *Male intravi, fateor, set per Dei gratiam bene egrediar;* unde sæpiùs postmodum illud Petri recoluit, *Erravimus juvenes, emendemus senes.*

Interea rex Willielmus, de Normanniâ rediens, cum

primo magnam aulam Westmonasterii aspexisset, dixit eam debitæ magnitudinis dimidiâ parte carere, quâ de causâ ipsam aulam proposuerat ordinasse pro camerâ. (P. 2370, line 33, &c.)

XIII.—POLYDORUS VERGILIUS (de Castello).

[A native of Urbino in Italy, first a literary rival, and then a friend, of Erasmus, sent into England about 1501 by Pope Alexander VI. to collect Peter-pence—there made successively Rector of Church Langton, Leicestershire, Prebendary of Lincoln, Archdeacon of Wells, and Prebendary of St. Paul's — undertook to write an English History at the request of Henry VII. This history, dedicated to Henry VIII., appeared 1534, printed at Basle. In 1550 his infirmities compelled him to seek his native climate, and he obtained a licence from Edward VI. to hold his preferments in his absence. He died at Urbino, 1555.]

Et *Henricus* qui, quanquam aliquando peccârat, quod dum Remensiensis cœnobii abbas erat, cum omnia venalia cerneret, emisset episcopatum Nordovicensem, sed tamen reliquam ætatem integerrimam vixit, quippe quem adeo pœnituit, ut delictorum eluendorum causâ Romam profectus, sponte se dignitate abdicaverit, traditis indumentis insignibus in manum Urbani secundi pontificis, a quo mox, omnis peccati labe jam deletâ, munus spretum obire jussus est; qui posteà domum reversus, sedem episcopalem ex oppido Thetfordiâ, Nordovicum, hominum conventu et negotiatorum copiâ maximè celebre, invexit: ubi loci collegium monachorum Ordinis divi Benedicti doctrinâ et religione excellentium instituit, *qui ibi dies noctesque Deo hymnos canerent*, quibus omnia ad victum necessaria abundè ex suo suppeditavit, ut ne diceretur imminuisse episcopatûs sui vectigalia: templum vero Thetfordiense Cluniacensibus monachis donavit. (*Anglica Historia*, Basle, 1570, p. 178, line 25.)

XIV.—JOHN LELAND.

[Born early in the 16th century, educated at St. Paul's School (under the famous William Lilly), and at Christ's College, Cambridge; Chaplain, Librarian, and Antiquary Royal (the first and last man who ever held this position) to Henry VIII.,—received a commission under the great seal to search for English Antiquities,—pleaded hard, on the dissolution of the Monasteries, for the preservation of their MS. treasures. He was made Vicar of Haseley in Oxfordshire, Canon of Christ Church, and Prebendary of Sarum. He was insane before his death, (which took place in 1552,) and committed by Edward VI. to the charge of his elder brother.

The following is from his "View of the Mitred Abbeys," at the end of vol. vi. of his Collectanea (London, 1770), p. 227.]

ABBATS OF RAMSEY.

6. AIELSINUS, who governed eight years, and was succeeded, Anno 1087, by

7. HERBERT [1], *who continued Abbat only four years,* and being then made Bishop of Thetford, he translated that See to Norwich, and became the first Bishop thereof. Upon his said promotion he was succeeded, Anno 1091, in the Abbatship by

8. ALDWIN, who was deprived, Anno 1100, for Simony.

XV.—JOHN BALE (Balæus).

[Born at Cove in Suffolk, in 1495—educated in the Carmelite convent at Norwich, but became a vehement Protestant—he was made Bishop of Ossory by Edward VI.; but insisting on being consecrated according to the reformed rite, he found Ireland too hot to hold him, and fled into Holland. During Mary's reign he resided at Basle. He returned to England under Queen Elizabeth, and declining to undertake again the duties of his Irish Diocese, was made Prebendary of Canterbury, and died in possession of that preferment, 1563.

---

[1] It is curious that in a MS. preserved in the British Museum (Vespas. A. xviii. fol. 147, &c.), and referred to by Tanner in his *Notitia Monastica* (Huntingdonshire. 5. RAMSEY), professing to record the "Nomina et gesta Abbatum Rames. ab Ednotho ad Joannem de Sautre," Herbert should be passed over altogether, and Aldwin made the *immediate* successor of Aielsinus. Here is the extract;

"*Eylsinus Abbas.* Iste constituit celebrare conceptionem B.V.M.

"*Eldwynus Abbas.* Iste fecit assissam domûs Ramsey, et degratus (*sic*) fuit injustè a Lanfranco Archiepiscopo, et posteâ recuperavit Abbatiam suam."

The date of this MS. is quite early in the fourteenth century.

How Eldwyn, who succeeded Herbert as Abbat, can have been degraded by *Lanfranc,* when Lanfranc was dead at the time of Herbert's appointment to the Bishopric of Thetford, and Herbert therefore had to be consecrated by the Abp. of York, it is a little hard to understand. (See the excerpt from Stubbs above, pp. 385, 386.;

Appendix. 389

The following is from his "Scriptorum illustrium majoris Brytanniæ Catalogus." Basileæ, 1557.]

Herebertus Losinga, ex pago Oxunensi *in Sudovolgiâ Anglorum comitatu*, natus fertur, patre Roberto, abbate olim Wintoniensi, matre vero ignotâ, *ex monacho monachus*. Vir fuit, ut ejus habet legenda, omnium literarum, tam divinarum quam secularium scientiis imbutus, facundiâ incomparabilis, venustus corpore, jucundus aspectu. Hic, *patre monacho procurante*, primum fuit Fiscanensis prior (inquiunt) in Normanniâ: postea currentibus nummis, abbas Ramesiensis in Angliâ, ac tandem episcopus Thetfordiensis: et idcirco fax simoniæ ab ejus temporis Chronographis appellabatur. Antichristi sui authoritate pestilentem sedem, sine regis notitiâ (nam regem habebat Abadonem) ambitiosè transtulit a Thetfordiâ Nordovicum usque anno Domini 1096, profligatis inde presbyteris cum conjugibus, ac monachis cœlibatûs nomine introductis: ut et illam ecclesiam, magnæ civitatis instar, novam Sodomam atque Ægyptum efficeret, Apoc. xi. Hujus extant, Henrici Huntingdoniensis testimonio, scripta quam plurima: *composuit enim*,

Sermones octodecim, lib. i. Convenistis, dilectissimi fratres.
De prolixitate temporum, lib. i.
De fine mundi, lib. i.
Constitutiones monachorum, lib. i.
Epistolas ad diversos, lib. i.
Ad Anselmum contra sacerdotes, lib. i.

Et alia quædam. Obiit anno a Christi incarnatione 1120, pontificatûs sui 29, et 11 Calendas Augusti, Nordovici in suâ synagogâ sepultus. Alii istum, dum viveret, Barrabam, alii Judam vocabant: ut Malmesburius, Ranulphus [a], et Trevisa referunt.

---

[a] Bale refers to Ranulphus Higden, a Benedictine monk of St. Werberg's monastery in Chester, who died about 1360. His "Polychronicon" was translated by John de Trevisa. The translation appeared, printed by Caxton, in 1482.

Alii adhuc erant in Angliâ his temporibus, prolifici abbates, episcopi, et monachi, præter Hereberti hujus genitorem Robertum. Nam Robertus Bloet, monachus de Evesham, et episcopus Lincolniensis, filium genuerat Simonem, quem fecit ejusdem ecclesiæ decanum. Robertus Peche, episcopus Cestriensis, genuit Ricardum Peche, archidiaconum Coventrensem. Eastanus, monachus Wigorniensis, ex Vulgenâ monachâ genuit S. Wolstanum episcopum ejusdem ecclesiæ. Ethelwoldus, Wintoniensis præsul, Wolstanum Wintoniensem monachum. Oswaldus, Wigorniensis episcopus, Oswaldum Wigorniensem monachum. Thomas, Eboracensis archiepiscopus, Thomam juniorem archiepiscopum. Et alii alios, qui tamen proscripserant nuptias. De Lanfranci et Anselmi fœturis non loquor, qui et mucidum Missæ idolum iniquè erigebant, et sacra ministrorum conjugia damnabant. Hoc penè præterieram, quod in prædicta civitate Nordovicensi, quidam Antichristi satellites, anno Domini 1545, uxorem meam Dorotheam, mulierem fidelissimam, quæ illuc tunc casu venerat, violenter capiebant, in carcerem detrudebant, et ad mortem ignominiosam quærebant: non ob aliud quicquam, quam quod fuisset, contra Pontificum sanctiones diabolicas, mihi in matrimonio Christiano copulata. Sed misericors omnium pater Deus, non absque miraculo, a sanguinolentis eorum manibus eandem liberavit.

De præfato Hereberto, poeta ejus temporis hoc protulit carmen, ut Guil. Malm.

(*Then follow the nine Latin lines, given above under* MALMESBURY, *page* 369.)

There is another incidental notice of Herbert in the latter part of the "Scriptores Illustres" (under the 13th century, Article 17). Bale is speaking of Gotcelinus Bertinianus, a Frenchman by birth, and a famous Latin scholar, who was invited by S. Anselm into England, where he obtained fame by teaching and writing. "Habitavit enim Ramesiæ primum in famigerabili illo cœnobio, *quod à divitiis cognomen acceperat, sub Hereberto Abbate*.... Claruit Gotcelinus a Divini Verbi incarnatione 1110, regnante in ipsâ Angliâ Henrico ejus nominis primo." Gotcelinus afterwards migrated to Canterbury.

XVI.—CENTURIATORS OF MAGDEBOURG.

[Illyricus (Matthias Francowitz) began the history called the Centuries of Magdebourg. He lived 1520—1575. The history was carried down, by other Protestant Divines of Magdebourg, to the year 1298. The work is in 13 vols. folio.]

Under the 11th century of their Eccl. History (Oporinus, Basle, 1567) the Centuriators say:
NORDOVICENSES, SEU *Tedfordenses*. (Sc. Episcopi).

HEREBERTUS.

Heinricus, seu Herebertus, cognomine Losinga (quâ ignominiæ notâ propter adulationem insignis erat) abbas Ramesiensis, largitione adeptus est episcopatum Tedfordensem: eâdemque arte patrem suum *Rotherbertum* monachis Vuintoniæ obtrusit rectorem. Quod factum quidam his versibus notavit:

(*Here are introduced the nine Latin lines cited by* MALMESBURY, *page* 369.)

Ad detergendam verò Simoniæ labem, Romam abijt: et iuvenilis ambitûs et largitionis impiæ pœnitentiam, depositione annuli et baculi pastoralis ostendit. Quæ insignia ei Romanus pontifex Urbanus restituit. Videtur autem Herebertus pecuniæ aucupium Romæ edoctus. Sedem enim episcopalem ex oppidulo Thetfordiâ transtulit Nordovicum, urbem populosam, mercimonijs celebrem, ac omnibus rebus affluentem: ibique monachorum Benedictinorum collegium instituit, cui de suo necessaria comparauit: *fundos verò nullos attribuit, ne videretur liberalis de alieno*. Tedfordiense autem cœnobium monachis Cluniacensibus, propter professionis communionem, incolendum dedit. Malmesburiensis libro quarto, capite trigesimo quarto. Et Polydorus libro decimo.

Under the 12th century (Oporinus, Basle, 1569, page 1586,) there is a notice as follows :—

NORDOVICENSES.

Herebertus Losinga, cujus et superiori seculo meminimus, scripsit quamplurima:
Sermones octodecim, lib. i.
De prolixitate temporum, lib. i.
De fine mundi, lib. i.
Constitutiones monachorum, lib. i.
Epistolas ad diversos, lib. i.
Ad Anselmum contra sacerdotes, lib. i.
Et alia quædam. Obijt anno 1120, cum episcopus fuisset annis 29. Sepultus est Nordovici 11. calend. Augusti. Balæus Centuria 2, capite 62; et Malmesburiensis libro quinto, capite 28.

XVII.—ALEXANDER NEVILLE.

[A native of Kent, born in 1544. Secretary to Archbishops Parker and Grindal, to whom he dedicated his account of the Norfolk insurrection under Kett ("De furoribus Norfolcensium Ketto duce," London, 1575). His "Norvicus," which is to be found in the same volume, is the first printed account of Norwich. He died in 1614.]

Ægelmaro episcopo Gulielmus rex sacellanum suum Arfastum substituit: qui ex consilii sententiâ sedem episcopalem Elmhamo Thetfordiam transtulit. Ubi is solus, ac qui illi surrogatur, Gulielmus Galfagus, consedere.

Proximus ab his *Gulielmus* Herbertus pontificiæ dignitatis gradus conscendit, vir sanè illustris, ac (ut illa ferebant tempora) insigni eruditione præditus.

[Then follows a long and eloquent digression, in which the author thinks it necessary to justify himself for recording the acts of Popish Prelates, and shews that his so doing implies no approval of their superstitions, &c., &c.]   Then he resumes :

Fuit igitur Herebertus iste (de quo anteà diximus) *Oxonii natus*, et Roberti cujusdam de Losinga, Wintoniensis Abbatis, filius, quem Fiscani tum Normanniæ

Monasterio præpositum (Priorem vulgò nuncupant) Gulielmus Rufus in Angliam accivit. Cui cùm in aulâ versaretur assiduus, omnibus in rebus ita se probavit, ut et illum Rex non solùm magnoperè diligeret, sed et *præmiis etiam cumularet amplissimis*. Unde factum est ut infrà triennium tantos nummorum acervos construxerit, ut et sibi pontificatum (dicitur enim sedem suam a Gulielmo Rufo 1900 libris obtinuisse) et patri cœnobium turpissimo mercatu coëmerit. Cujus execrandæ Symoniæ labem ac maculas multi scriptis suis ambitiosissimo præsuli sempiternas asperserunt, et *ejus delicti causâ, eam quam mox dicam templorum extruendorum necessitatem, ad tanti facinoris pœnam, à Papâ Paschali inflictam*, monumentis perscriptum veteribus reliquerunt.

Illud certè constat fuisse eum cæteroqui virum (ut temporibus illis) pereruditum, et haud vulgari doctrinâ excultum. Quò magis miror, quænam ratio ipsum ad hanc tantam turpitudinem impulerit, ut cùm artibus se instruxisset optimis, quæ semper hominibus ad decus et dignitatem præsidio esse consueverunt, nihilominùs tamen aditum sibi ad eam quam animo complexus est amplitudinem, tam immani flagitio muniverit. Enimvero illius inexplebilem (ut ita dicam) pecuniæ sitim, ac insaturabilem ambitionis ingluviem Gulielmus Malmsberius hujuscemodi verbis perstrinxit.

[Then follows the passage from the "De Gestis Regum" of William of Malmesbury, which is given above (p. 369), and then the account of the repentance of Herbert, as given in the same work.] Then follow these reflections:—

Sed enim o verè miseram illorum temporum conditionem, cùm divini numinis ignoratio cuncta densissimis erroribus obsepsisset, cùm homines non vitæ integritas, sed turpitudo summa et indignitas; non pietatis ardor, sed ambitionis flammæ; non sacrarum rerum scientia, sed scelestissimæ libidines, ad ecclesiasticas dignitates eveherent. Quantò nos feliciori fortunâ nati sumus, qui Dei benignitate ex hoc superstitionis veluti orco, ad cœlum et vitam æternam emersimus. Alia siquidem jam nostræ Ecclesiæ species et dignitas, alia Romanæ, alia Christianorum ratio, alia Papistarum, non idem relligionis splendor, impietatisque tenebræ : lux denique longè alia est Evangelii, et lychnorum, quibus illorum tenebricosissima templa collucent. Jam verò illud cujus tandem stupiditatis ac dementiæ fuit, quòd cùm juvenis tam diris se flagitiis dedecorâsset, decursâ jam propè ætate, non ad Christum (unicum æternæ salutis fontem) sed Romam, ad lutulentas impuri pontificis lacunas confugeret. Quâ profectione tantum abest ut illius facinoris dedecus deleverit, ut ad symoniæ potiùs infamiam, meo judicio, perfidiæ quoque scelus adjunxerit.

Utcunque se res habet, domum reversus, extremis pænè ætatis temporibus ita vixisse dicitur, ut tum Regi carus, tum jucundus omnibus esset. Etenim posteà episcopatûs sui munere magnâ cum laude perfunctus, et sibimet ipsi perennem gloriam conflavit, et posteros consimili virtutis ardore flagrantes, exemplo suo non mediocriter ad studia pietatis incendit. Nam cùm Romæ (uti suprà memoravi) beneficio Papæ, eam esset, quam opinionis errore sibi confinxerat, peccatorum impunitatem consecutus, omnesque symoniæ sordes in cœnosissimis Romanæ curiæ puteis abluisset, nihil post reditum in Angliam prius, neque antiquius habuit, quàm ut eam pecuniam, quam juvenis rapinis coacervaverat, senex in sacris ædibus construendis collocaret. Ac primùm non ferens vagæ pro hominum arbitrio sedis molestiam, certum aliquem locum, ac veluti domicilium episcopali dignitati constituere decrevit. Et quoniam eo tempore Norwycus civitas esset Orientalium omnium, et ad aspectum pulcherrima, et ad vitæ necessitates instructissima, idcircò urbs ea maximè præ cæteris opportuna visa est, quæ et pontificii splendoris amplitudinem, et tantæ sedis dignitatem sustineret. Quod cùm cives omnes libentissimis excepissent animis, Regesque Gulielmus, et Henricus primus, Papaque Paschalis (uti temporibus illis fieri consuevit) diplomatibus suis confirmâssent ; omni cogitatione in curam ecclesiastici muneris incumbendum sibi existimavit. Itaque primùm ædem Cathedralem suis impensis exstruendam locavit, areamque pulchram coëmit (*locum quem veteres Cowholme appellârunt*) inibique templum augustissimum et monachorum domus exædificavit. *Cujus fundamenti lapidem primum ipse suis jecisse manibus dicitur, paucisque majusculis litteris lapide incisis, ejus rei memoriam posteris sempiternam tradidisse. Eæ autem erant hujusmodi. Hunc primum hujus templi lapidem Dominus Herbertus posuit : in Nomine Patris, et Filii, et Spiritûs Sancti. Amen.* Dein templum Sanctæ Trinitati dedicavit, locupletissimisque prædiis donavit, adeò ut agrorum fructus quos quotannis perciperent, sexaginta monachis atque ampliùs alendis sufficerent. Tum *libris, omnique sacrâ supellectile instruxit,* brevique effecit, ut nihil nec ad Monachorum usum, nec ad tanti templi splendorem majestatemque deësset.

Hanc tantam publicæ utilitatis curam excepit haud minor domesticæ dignitatis cogitatio. Itaque ex Aquilonari parte ecclesiæ palatium ipse sibi construxit : quod prudens à monachorum cellulis secrevisse dicitur, ne crebro hominum huc et illuc discurrentium tumultu, illorum solitariæ mentes à cælestibus rebus contemplandis abstraherentur.

Quinque insuper fana exstruxit, quorum unum sancto Leonardo consecravit, idque in summo colle, cathedrali ecclesiæ adversum (interjecto flumine) constituit. Alterum Norwyci, Elmhami tertium, quartum Lhynni, quintum ad ostium Gerni fluminis. Ea fana perpetuò Monachorum potestati subjecit, *quosdamque ex eo cœtu ac numero semper esse voluit, qui votis concipiendis alternatim vacantes, Romanos ritus cæremoniasque indies obirent.*

Fertur etiam Thetfordiæ Monachos Cluniacenses instituisse, multaque alia designâsse, quibus plebis imperitæ animi (ut illa fuerunt secula) rudes superstitionum laqueis implicarentur.

HÆC à me eò referuntur, non quòd illa probem ; (quis enim tantam impietatem non aspernetur et oderit?) sed ut nostri homines, horum in Romanis sacris ac ritibus asciscendis sollicitam industriam contemplantes, illorumque exemplis excitati, ad Dei optimi maximi amorem, et veræ pietatis cultum flagrantiùs exardescant. Etenim cùm homines anili superstitione et inexpiabili fraude constrictos, eò divini numinis metus impulerit, ut maximas facultates in res perversas ac impias profundere non dubitârint; quo nos tandem animo esse debemus, qui, dispulsâ erroris nube, cœlestis disciplinæ solem dispicimus? Quapropter quemadmodum hi in templis construendis, et sacrificulorum cœtibus conflandis, nullo neque labori neque sumptui pepercerint; sic nos vicissim miserorum hominum inopiam egestatemque sublevemus, et nuda Christi membra, mærore ac luctu perculsa, mansuetudine ac misericordiâ (ut par est) complectamur.

Hujus pontificis tempore (*Anno Domini* 1112) *pestis magna, omnium ferè civium domus pervagata, multos mortales absumpsit.*

Obiit. a.d. xi. Kal. August 1113. regnante Henrico primo, atque Norwici in ecclesiâ cathedrali ad altare summum sepultus est. (Alexandri Nevylli Angli, Norwicus. *Londini, ex officina Henrici Binnemani. A. S.* 1575. *Pp.* 118—138.)

XVIII.—NICHOLAS HARPSFELD.

[Regius Prof. of Greek in the University of Oxford, in the reign of Henry VIII., having been first a fellow of New College. He was imprisoned in the reign of Elizabeth for denying the Queen's supremacy, and remained in captivity more than twenty years, dying in 1583.

The following extract is from his "Historia Anglicana Ecclesiastica," Douay, 1622, p. 247.]

Flor. anno 1070. Catalogus appellat Arcastum, sed forte vitiose.

Post Ethelmerum Herfastus, sive Arfastus, renuntiatur Episcopus. Is sedem inde Tedfordiam transposuit. Erat Duci Guilielmo in Normanniâ à sacris, nonnullamque doctrinæ, ante Lanfranci aduentum, opinionem sustinebat. Cuius cum ille inscitiam palam coarguisset, adeo est adversus eum irritatus, ut graues contra eum apud Ducem querelas deferret: qua ex occasione maiorem sibi Lanfrancus apud Ducem gratiam, ut diximus, collegit : in cujus demortui locum Guilielmus de Belsago, eidem etiam Regi à sacris, submissus. Post quartum annum sedem ad Herebertum transmisit. Tedfordiæ humatus est, *sed eius postea corpus*, et ipsam adeo sedem *Nordovicum*, quasi ad illustriorem et magis populosum locum, *Herebertus transtulit;* qui à mendaci adulatione, quâ se ad Regis, potentiorum, ad aliorumque non modò sensum, et voluntatem, sed quasi nutum atque vultum turpiter blandiendo conuertebat, Losinga dictus est : et quos huiusmodi adulantis linguæ, quam omnium auribus dabat, blanditijs allicere non potuit, pecuniâ oppugnabat. His artibus ex priori Fiscanensi Abbas primo Ramesiæ, deinde et Episcopus factus est. Sed hanc ille turpitudinem, quâ et ipse, et pater ejus Robertus, cœnobii Vintoniensis Abbas, magnâ apud omnes passim infamiâ laborabant, egregiâ pœnitentiâ præclarisque operibus eluit. Quam illi pœnitentiam prognosticon, quod illi et Herfasto, de quo commemorauimus, forte accidit, potissimum expressit. Herfastus in illud, Non hunc, sed Barrabbam ; Herbertus in istud incidit, Amice, ad quid venisti ? Quorum auditio mirum in modum emollijt, hominisque animum ad lachrymas, pœnitentiamque capiendam confregit. Qui cum illud audisset, illacrymans, Turpiter, inquit, ingressus sum in hanc dignitatem : sed honestius, ut spero, ab eâ discedam. Constat certe Romam, *Henrico regnante*, profectum, et propter huius suæ turpitudinis conscientiam, episcopatui (traditis Romano Pontifici baculo et annulo) nuntium misisse. Mille enim libris Guilielmo Regi datis, et sibi episcopatum, et patri abbatiam comparauit. Cuius delicti expiandi causâ, tentauit furtim Romam ad Urbanum proficisci : sed eum Rufus Rex retinuit, et baculo pastorali spoliauit. Profectus est tamen, ut dixi, posteà ; et restituit illum Pontifex in priorem locum.

Huius peccati causâ, utque Deum sibi magis reconciliaret, celebre Nordovici cœnobium, et ædium, et omnium ornamentorum, et proborum etiam atque doc-

[marginalia:] Herbertus factus Episcopus an. 1091. Transtulit sedem, an. 1094. occœpit structuram cænobii an. 1106. Gul. Mal. de Reg. lib. 4. c. 32 et de Pont.

Joan. 18. Matth. 26.

torum hominum splendore illustre condidit. Neque
ille de Episcopalibus possessionibus quicquam ad usum
monachorum detraxit, ne sedem iniuriâ afficeret, neve
id posteà monachis extorqueretur. Aliunde omnibus
abundè prospexit et consuluit. Nec eloquentia, nec
doctrina, nec ulla rerum gerendarum peritia et pru-
dentia homini defuit: acremque se adversus simoniacos
vindicem ostendit. Peruenit ad decimum nonum annum
Henrici Regis. Atque utinam qui vitiosos et depra-
vatos illius mores imitantur, pœnitentiam et resipis-
centiam illius imitandum sibi etiam proponerent: et
qui vel clam vel palam grauia scelera admittere non
verentur, neque palam cum Hereberto confiteri de
sceleribus erubescerent, eaque pijs operibus redimere
conarentur. *Cuius resipiscentiæ clara apparent docu-
menta in ijs, quæ hodie extant, scripti illius exemplaribus;
quo testatur se cœnobium Nordovici, ut esset princeps
totius diœceseos ecclesia, ex Romanæ sedis authoritate
condidisse. Quòd quidem scriptum Henrici Regis, Episcoporum, et Procerum regni sigillo munitum est, ad annum
incarnati Christi millesimum centesimum primum.* Re-
pleuit dictum Herbertus cœnobium sexaginta monachis,
multaque eius privilegia tam à summo Pontifice, quam
à Rege impetravit. Construxit præter princeps illud
templum et alias ecclesias; primam in colle, qui cathe-

<small>Catal.
Norwic.
Episco-
porum.</small>

drali ecclesiæ interiecto. flumine imminet; secundam
Norwici, in curiâ Episcopi; tertiam apud Elingham;
quartam apud Linne; quintam apud Gorledunum, sive
Gorlestonum, (vulgò Jernemutham appellant,) è regione
ostiorum Garieni fluminis. Obijt anno millesimo cen-
tesimo nono, post viginti novem Pontificatûs annos.
Primus cœnobij præfectus fuit Ingulphus, quem secuti

<small>Ex veteri
quodam
Nordowi-
censis ec-
clesiæ mo-
numento.</small>

sunt Elias, Richardus, Elfricus, Tancredus, Girardus,
Guilielmus, Walsamus, Ranulphus, Guilielmus, Odo,
Simon, Elinghamus, Rogerus Skeringe, Nicolaus Bra-
merton, Guilielmus Brumham, Guilielmus Chirby, Hen-
ricus Lakenham, Robertus Langley, Guilielmus Clapton,
Simon Bohonum, Laurentius Leeke, Nicolaus de Loc,
Alexander Totington, Robertus Brumham, Guilielmus

Worsted, Joannes Heverland, Joannes Mallet, Thomas Bohonum, qui obijt anno millesimo quadringentesimo septuagesimo primo, et hunc Joannes Bonnvelle.

Posvit et Tedfordiæ Cluniacenses monachos Herbertus, qui monasticas regulas exactè id temporis obseruabant.

XIX.—ANTONIO POSSEVINO.

[A learned Jesuit, born at Mantua in 1533.—He was sent by the Superior of the Jesuits on several embassies.—The interest he took in the reconciliation of Henri IV. of France to the holy see offended the Pope, and led to his suspension from public business. He died at Ferrara in 1611.

The following extract is from his "Apparatus Sacer," edited at Cologne, 1608, page 735, tom. i.]

Herebertus Losinga Anglus, et monachus Congreg. Cluniacensis, qui obijt an. 1120, scripsit librum ad Anselmum Episcopum adversus malos sacerdotes. Alterum item, quo *Sermones duodeviginti* continebantur. Alium, De prolixitate temporum. Alium, De fine Mundi. Alium, Constitutionum monachorum. Epistolas ad diversos, libro uno.

XX.—JOHN PITS (PITSÆUS).

[Born in 1560, at Alton in Hants,—educated at Winchester School, and New College, Oxford. Before completing his academical career at Oxford, he went abroad as a voluntary Romish exile, and became a student at Douay, and afterwards at the English College at Rome : he was made dean of Liverdun on the Moselle, where he died in 1616. He has borrowed largely from Bale without sufficient acknowledgment.

The following is from his "Relationes Historicæ de Rebus Anglicis," the fourth part of which ("De Illustribus Angliæ Scriptoribus") was published three years after his death (Thierry and Cramoisy, Paris, 1619).]

DE HEREBERTO LOSINGA.

Herebertus cognomento Losingâ, *nonnullis Cosinga*, A.D. 1120, natione Anglus, patriâ Suffolcensis, patre Roberto in pago Oxunensi procreatus. Successu temporis, Ordinis S. Benedicti Monachus, Congregationis Cluniacensis. Vir omnium virtutum, et bonarum litterarum studiis impensè deditus, mitis, affabilis, corpore venusto, vultu decoro, moribus candidus, vitâ integer. Qui tamen posteà miram passus est mutationem. Nam ambitione honorum, et cupiditate captus divitiarum (omnium enim malorum radix cupiditas) in execrabile Simoniæ crimen incidit. *Primum enim non sine interventu pecuniæ factus est prior Fiscanensis in Normanniâ*, tum Abbas Ramesiensis in Angliâ, et tandem Episcopus Tedfordiensis. De quibus suo loco. Hæc crimina posteà precibus, eleëmosynis, jejuniis, lacrimis, et aliis prolixis operibus pœnitentiæ redemit. De quo Guilhelmus Malmesberiensis libro quarto in Guillielmo secundo sic (inter cætera) scribit; *Præ se semper (ut aiunt) ferens Hieronymi dictum, Erravimus juvenes, emendemus senes.* Henricus Huntingdoniensis eum virum doctum fuisse asserit, et multa scripsisse testatur. Titulos sequentes producunt aliqui.

Ad S. Anselmum contra malos Sacerdotes, Librum unum.

Sermonum octodecim, Librum unum. Convenistis dilectissimi fratres.

De constitutionibus Monachorum, Librum unum.

De fine mundi, Librum unum.

De prolixitate temporum, Librum unum.

Epistolarum ad diversos, Librum unum. Et alia plura.

Animam creatori reddidit anno Gratiæ 1120, et in Ecclesiâ Norwicensi sepultus est, dum in Angliâ regnavit Henricus primus. Vide nostrum quem congessimus de Episcopis Norwicensibus Catalogum.

XXI.—FRANCIS GODWIN.

[Born at Havington, in Northants, in 1561,—educated at Christ Church, Oxford, where his father was dean, and he a student. He invented a quick mode of carrying on correspondence by signals, instead of letters,—he held a prebend of Salisbury, and was sub-dean of Exeter,—accompanied Camden in 1590 on his archæological travels in Wales. His "Catalogue of the Bishops of England" was rewarded by Queen Elizabeth with the bishopric of Llandaff, and when afterwards enlarged and translated into Latin, under the title "De Præsulibus Angliæ," was acknowledged by James the First's raising him to the see of Hereford. He died in 1633.

Appendix. 401

The following passage is from his book "De Præsulibus," (pp. 426, 427).]

Gulielmus Galsagus.

Qui illi subrogatus est Gulielmus Galsagus, ad Thet- (1085.)
fordiam suam exornandam nihil non fecit. De eo Gul. 1, 20.
tamen apud *Malmesburiensem* (*quod miror*) *nulla habetur mentio.*

I.—Herebertus Losinga.

Proximus ab hiis Herebertus, Pontificiæ dignitatis (1091.)
gradus conscendit, *à nonnullis Gulielmus Herbertus ap-* Gul. 2. 4.
pellatus, plurimis vero Herebertus Losinga[b]; quem
Oxoniæ natum[c], et Fiscanensem in Normanniâ Priorem
creatum, Gulielmus secundus Rex in Angliam[d] accivit. Hic cùm in aulâ versaretur, omnibus in rebus
ita se probavit, ut et illum Rex non solùm magnoperè diligeret, sed et præmiis etiam cumularet amplissimis. Unde factum est, ut infra triennium, ingenti
pecuniâ comparatâ, et sibi Pontificatum (dicitur enim
sedem suam à Rege 1900 libris obtinuisse) et patri[e]
Abbatiam Wintoniensem, turpissimo mercatu potuerit
coëmere[f]. Quâ de re sic lusit illorum temporum
poëta;

(*Then follow the nine Latin lines, given above under*
MALMESBURY, *page* 369.)

Ædem cathedralem suis sumptibus construxit, areâ
cöemptâ in loco quem veteres Cowholm appellârunt,
et ornamentis abundè instructam, sacrosanctæ Trinitatis
nomini dicavit, ac Monachis etiam habitacula [seorsim
ab Episcopalibus] ædificavit, primo lapide à se anno salutis 1086[g] posito, cui hæc verba dicuntur incisa;

---

[b] Vel Lusingi propter adulationem; Lusingare enim Italis est adulari. Caius de Antip. Acad. Cant., l. 2, p. 193.
[c] In Pago OXINNENSI in Normanniâ, fortè OXIMENSI. Sic Gyrald. Cambr. vel OXUNENSI. MS. suprad. C. Cant. B. 16.
[d] Ubi factus est Abbas Ramseiæ.
[e] Roberto MS. Lameth.
[f] Malmesb. de Pontif. l. 2, f. 136. M. Par., p. 15. Hoved. f. 226.
[g] A. 1096. Paris.

"Dominus Herbertus posuit primum lapidem, in nomine P. et F., et S. s. Amen."

Sibi tum et successoribus palatium extruxit ab Aquilonari parte Ecclesiæ, quod à Monachorum cellulis ideo dicitur secrevisse, ut hominum huc et illuc discurrentium tumultu, mentes illorum à cælestium rerum contemplatione non abstraherentur. Ecclesias deinde parochiales quinque insuper condidit, quarum unam sancto Lenardo consecravit, idque in summo colle, Ecclesiæ cathedrali (interjecto flumine) adversam; alteram etiam Norwici nescio quam [h]; Elmhami tertiam; quartam Lynnæ; ac quintam denique Yarmuthæ: quas omnes Monachorum potestati subjecit, et ex eo cœtu ut semper essent qui sacra ibidem alternatim obirent, ordinavit. Excessit è vivis vicesimo secundo Julii, 1119[l], et in Ecclesiâ suâ prope summum altare sepultus est.

[The following is from the "Catalogue of the Bishops of England, by Francis Godwin, now Bishop of Llandaff," (Thomas Adams, London, 1615.) It will be seen that there is a material discrepancy between this book, which is in English, and the "Præsulibus," on the subject of Herbert's immediate predecessor. In the "De Præsulibus," Gulielmus Galsagus is represented as immediately preceding, of whom Godwin expresses his surprise that Malmesbury makes no mention. In "the Catalogue," *William Herbert is said to be the same as Galfagus*, and his immediate predecessor is said to be Arfastus. This discrepancy is by no means easy to account for. Is Godwin's "Catalogue" simply a reproduction of the Catalogue of Pits, referred to above under the article PITS—"nostrum quem congessimus de Episcopis Norwicensibus Catalogum?"]

GODWIN. "Catalogue of Bishops." [London: for Thomas Adams. 1615.]

After Arfastus, the first Bishop of Thetford, follows (p. 419):

William Herbert, last of Thetford, and first Bishoppe of Norwich.

William, *surnamed Galfagus*, succeeded him in Thetford, a man very famous for his excellent learning. *He was borne at Orford.* His father was Robertus

---
[h] In curiâ Episcopi. *Barth. Cotton* de Episc. Norw.
[l] *Florent.* et *Dunelm. Hovedenus* verò diem 23 malè assignat. f. 272.

de Losinge, Abbot of Winchester. This *Herbertus* being Prior of the Monastery of Fiscanum in Normandy, came into England at the request of William Rufus, and living in the Court for a time, behaved himself in such sort, that hee was much favoured of the king, and obtained divers great preferments at his hands, whereby it came to passe, that within the space of three yeeres, he had so feathered his nest, as he could buy for his father the Abbacy of Winchester, and for himselfe this Bishopricke, paying to the king for the same, as it is reported, the summe of £1900. For satisfaction of which symony this pennance was enjoined him by Paschalis the Pope, that he should build certaine churches and monasteries, as afterwards he did. Hee translated the see from Thetford to Norwich, and built there the Cathedrall Church at his owne charges, laying the first stone of the foundation with his owne hands, as this elogium declareth, which hee caused to be engraven upon the wall: Hunc primum hujus templi lapidem, dominus Herebertus posuit in nomine Patris et Filij et Spiritus Sancti. Amen. This church he dedicated to the blessed Trinity, endowing it with great landes and possessions, books, and all other necessaries. Having finished it according to his minde, he then determined to build an house for himself (for as yet he had none in Norwich, the see beeing so lately removed from Thetford) and therfore on the north side of the church he founded a stately pallace. Againe, hee built fine churches,—one over against the Cathedrall church, on the other side of the river, called S. Leonard's, another at Norwich also, another at Elmham, a fourth at Linne, and a fifth at Yarmouth. He departed this life, July 22, in the yeere of our Lord 1119. And was buried in his Cathedrall church of Norwich, by the high aultar.

XXII.—JOHN WEEVER.

[A native of Lancaster,—educated at Cambridge,—died about the year 1632,—buried in St. James's, Clerkenwell.
The following is from his "Funeral Monuments" (London, 1631), p. 787, &c.]

NORWICH. S. TRINITIES, THE CATHEDRALL CHURCH.

The foundation of the Bishop's See at Norwich.

"Herebertus dictus Losinga, abbas quondam Rame-
" seie, qui sedem Thedford a Rege Willelmo emerat, in
" Angliâ magnus fuit Simonie fomes. Hic, postquam
" erroneum iuuentutis impetum defleuisset, Romam iuit,
" ac rediens sedem suam usque Norwicum transtulit,
" ubi et celebre fundavit monasterium, de rebus quidem
" proprijs, non Episcopalibus: sed et apud Tedford
" monachos Cluniacenses instituit. Hic sæpiùs dicere
" consueuit; Errauimus iuuenes. Emendemus senes."

Thus much out of an old manuscript of the abbey of Evesham, anciently put into English by the translator of Polychronicon, as followeth :—

Herbert the first Bishop of Norwich.

"Abowte that time, Herbert Losange, that had ben
" som tyme Abbat of Ramsay, and was thenne Byshop
" of Tedford, was a grete noury for Simony, for he had
" boughte the Bysshopryche of the Kynge. But after-
" warde, he was sory, and bywept the unskylfull rest
" of his youth: and toke the waye to Rome, and came
" home agayne, and chaunged and torned his see from
" Tedford to Norwyche. And he founded a solempne
" abbaye with his owne catayle, and not wyth the catayle
" of his Bysshopryche. But at Tedford he ordained
" monkes of Cluny that were ryche in the world, and
" clere of religion to Godward; and had ofte in mynde
" the worde of Jherom, that sayd, We erryd in our
" yougth, amende we us in our age."

His repentance doth also appear by the context of his Charter, beginning thus :—

Cart. Antiq. in Arch. Turris Lond.

"In nomine Patris et Filij et Spiritus sancti. Amen.
" Herbertus Episcopus, infirmitatis et impuritatis

"proprie conscius, ante iustum et clementem Judicem
"Deum, mores et vitam expono meam, ei reuelans iu-
"ventutis mee ignorantias, &c. Igitur pro redemptione
"vite mee, meorumque omnium peccatorum absolu-
"tione, apud Norwicum, in honore et nomine sancte
"et individue Trinitatis, Ecclesiam primum edificaui,
"quam caput et matrem Ecclesiam omnium Ecclesi-
"arum de Northfolke et Suffolke constitui et conse-
"craui. Preceptis igitur et concessionibus Willelmi
"Regis, et Henrici Regis fratris sui, et consilio An-
"selmi Cant. Archiepiscopi, et omnium Episcoporum
"et Primatum totius Regni Anglie, in Ecclesiâ eâdem
"monachos ordinaui," &c.

His donations to this his mother church of Norfolke and Suffolke follow, which are many and great, for he endowed it with as much lands as might sufficiently maintaine threescore monkes, who had their faire and spacious cloisters. But after they were thrust out by King Henry the Eighth, there were substituted for them a deane, sixe prebendaries, and others.

Witnesses to this his Charter, were King Henry the First, and Maud his Queene; eleven bishops, and foure and twenty earles, lords, and abbots: to every name the signe of the crosse.

"Facta est hec donatio anno Domini MC., ordina-
"tione Gregorii Episcopi Rom., apud Wyndressores."

The first stone of this religious structure was laid by Herbert himselfe, in the yeare after Christ's nativitie, One thousand ninetie sixe, with this inscription:

> Dominus Herbertus posuit primum lapidem, in nomine Patris, Filij, et Spiritûs Sancti. Amen.

That is,

> Lord (Bishop) Herbert laid the first ston, in the name of the Father, the Sonne, and Holy Ghost. Amen.

This Bishop was borne at Orford in Suffolke. His father's name was Robert de Losing. Hee was Prior of the monasterie of Fiscane in Normandie, and came backe into England at the request of William Rufus, Godwin de Præsul. Ang.
Malms. de gest. Regum Ang. Lib. 4.

and living in the Court for a time, behaved himselfe in such sort that hee was much favoured of the King, and obtained divers great preferments at his hands, whereby it came to passe that within the space of three yeares hee had so feathered his nest, as hee could buy for his father the abbacy of Winchester, and for himselfe the bishopricke of Thetford, which I have partly touched here, and in another place.

Having finished this pious fabricke according to his minde, hee then determined to build an house for himself (for as yet he had none in Norwich, the see being so lately removed from Thetford), and therefore on the north side of the church he founded a stately palace. And more (such was his repentance for his Simony committed), hee built five churches, one over against the Cathedrall church, on the other side of the river, called S. Leonards, another in this city, also another at Elmham, a fourth at Linne, and a fifth at Yarmouth. Hee was an excellent scholler for those times, and writ many learned treatises, mentioned by Pitsæus, in his booke "De illustribus Anglie Scriptoribus Ætat. duo-"decimâ," where he cals him "vir omnium virtutum, "et bonarum literarum studijs impensè deditus, mitis, "affabilis, corpore venusto, vultu decoro, moribus can-"didus, vitâ integer." (A man earnestly addicted to the studies of all vertues and good learning, milde, affable, comely of personage, gracefull of countenance, blamelesse in his carriage, pure, innocent and sincere in the course of his life.) *The monkes of Norwich made great meanes and sute to hauve this Herbert a canonised saint, but such impediments were alwaies in the way that it could not be obtained.*

He departed this life the two and twentieth of July, in the yeare of grace One thousand one hundred and twenty, and was buried in this church of his owne foundation by the high altar, *to whose memory these verses following were engraven upon his monument:*

Ex. vet. MSS. in bib. Cot.

*Inclytus Herbertus iacet hic, vt pistica nardus,
Virtutum redolens floribus et meritis.*

*A quo fundatus locus est hic, edificatus
Ingenti studio, nec modico precio.
Vir fuit hic magnus probitate, suāvis ut agnus,
Vitâ conspicuus, dogmate precipuus.
Sobrius, et castus, prudens, et Episcopus almus,
Pollens concilio, clarus in officio.
Quem . . . , vndecimas Julio promente Kalendas,
Abstulit vltima sors, et rapuit cita mors.
Pro quo, qui transis, supplex orare memor sis
Vt sit ei saties alma Dei facies.*

XXIII.—THOMAS FULLER.

[Born in 1608,—educated at Queens' College, Cambridge,—became a Fellow of Sidney Sussex, and incumbent of St. Bennet's,—preferred to a prebend of Salisbury, and to the rectory of Broadwinsor in Dorsetshire. He was also lecturer at the Savoy,—ejected from his living by the Parliament,—held the post of chaplain to the King's army, and in that post, while accompanying the troops, collected materials for his "Worthies of England." After the Restoration, he was reinstated in his prebendal stall at Salisbury, and appointed chaplain extraordinary to the King, and would have been raised to the Bench, had not a fever cut short his life prematurely, Aug. 15, 1661. He was a man of extraordinary memory, "who could repeat 500 strange words after twice hearing them."

The following is from his "Worthies of England," (London, 1662,) under the heads Oxfordshire and Suffolk.]

OXFORDSHIRE. Pp. 325, 326.

Herbert Losing was born in Oxford, his father being an abbot, *seeing wives in that age were not forbidden the clergy;* though possibly his father turned Abbot of Winchester in his old age, his son purchasing that preferment for him. But this Herbert bought a better for himself, giving nineteen hundred pounds to King William Rufus for the bishoprick of Thetford [k]. Hence the verse was made—

" Filius est Præsul, pater Abbas, Simon uterque,"

meaning that both of them were guilty of simony, a fashionable sin in the reign of that king, preferring more for their gifts than their endowments.

[k] Godwin's Catalogue of the Bishops of Norwich, p. 481. Ibid., p. 225.

Reader, pardon a digression. I am confident there is one, and but one, sin frequent in the former age, both with clergy and laity, which in our dayes our land is not guilty of, and may find many compurgators of her innocence therein; I mean, the sin of simony; seeing none in our age will give anything for church livings, partly because the persons presented thereunto have no assurance to keep them, partly because of the uncertainty of tithes for their maintenance. But whether this our age hath not added in sacrilege what it wanteth in simony, is above my place to discuss, and more above my power to decide.

To return to our Herbert, whose character hitherto cannot entitle him to any room in our Catalogue of Worthies; but know that afterwards he went to Rome, (no such clean washing as in the water of Tyber,) and thence returned as free from fault as when first born. Thus cleansed from the leprosie of simony, he came back to England, removed his bishoprick from Thetford to Norwich, laid the first stone, and *in effect finished* the fair Cathedral therein, and built five beautiful parish churches. He dyed anno Domini 1119. See more of his character on just occasion, in Suffolk, under the title of prelates.

SUFFOLK. Vol. ii., pp. 329, 330.

Bale, cent. 2, page 271.

Herbert Losing was born in this county, as our antiquary informeth us [1]; "In Pago Oxunensi in Sudovolgiâ, Anglorum Comitatu, natus:" but on the perusing of all the lists of towns in this county, no Oxun appeareth therein, or name neighbouring thereon in sound and syllables [m]. This I conceive the cause why Bishop Godwin so confidently makes this Herbert born Oxoniæ, in Oxford, in which county we have formerly placed his character.

However, seeing Bale was an excellent antiquary,

---

[1] Bale, cent. ii. p. 271.

[m] Dr. Fuller did not recollect the town of Hoxon, otherwise Hoxne, in the Hundred of that name. N.

and being himself a Suffolk man must be presumed knowing in his own county; and conceiving it possible that this Oxun was either an obscure churchless village, or else is this day disfigured under another name; I conceive it just that, as Oxfordshire led the front, Suffolk should bring up the rear of this Herbert's description.

Indeed he may well serve two counties, being so different from himself, and two persons in effect. When young, loose and wild, deeply guilty of the sin of simony. When old, nothing of Herbert was in Herbert, using commonly the words of St. Hierome; Erravimus juvenes, emendemus senes. "When young we went astray, when old we will amend [a]." Now, though some controversie about the place of his birth, all agree in his death, July 22, 1119; and in his burial, in the Cathedral Church of Norwich.

Will. Malmesbury.

APPENDIX E.

Mr. E. M. Beloe on Herbert's Birthplace.

In the "Original Papers published under the direction of the Committee of the Norfolk and Norwich Archæological Society," vol. viii. part iv. [Norwich, 1878], there appears a most learned and interesting disquisition by Mr. Edward Milligen Beloe on Herbert's "cognomen and birthplace." Mr. Beloe has come to a conclusion on these points different from that at which we ourselves had arrived (and which is given on pages 4 and 5 of the "Life and Letters.") After great research and study of the question, he has convinced himself that Exmes in Normandy (as stated by Bartholomew Cotton, and in the epitaph, "Life and Letters," pp. 329, 330) was Herbert's birthplace; and he shews that the "pagus Oxymensis" of

[a] William of Malmesbury.

Cotton, and other writers, was a considerable district of France, reaching from the coast near Dives to Belleme, and embracing portions of the dioceses of Bayeux and Lisieux, as well as the whole diocese of Seez. The surname "Losinga" he takes to be equivalent to "Lotharingian," or "Lorrainer" (man of Lorraine). We cannot conceal from ourselves that there is much in Mr. Beloe's arguments in favour of the view which he expresses, although he does not dispose of (nor indeed notice) the circumstance pointed out by Mr. Spurdens (which leads to a different conclusion), that Herbert's father held manors in Suffolk. Anyhow, we feel sure that our readers will thank us for the following extracts from this very able paper.

"Several writers, from the sixteenth century downwards, have endeavoured to prove an English, and even an East Anglian, origin for Herbert. For his birthplace they have gone, not to the country from which it is clearly recorded that he came, but to the district where he last resided, and where he died. This seems to me an inverted process of reasoning.

"Herbert de Lozinga was not the only bishop in England of that name, nor by many, of his country. The bishop who stands to Hereford in the same relation as Herbert does to Norwich, as the great builder, was Robert Lozing. * * * William of Malmesbury says of him " (Robert Lozing), " under Hereford, *Gest. Pont.*, p. 300: 'Non multo post accepit sedem illam Rotbertus Lotharingus,'—and he built the cathedral on the pattern of Aix. On his tomb in Hereford Cathedral, probably of the thirteenth century, he is inscribed 'Dñs Robertus de Lorraine Epūs Herefordensis obiit A.D. 1095.' * * *

" The name Lozinga is the French form of Lotharingia Latinised in its last syllable, and this form only obeys the well-known laws, by which Latin was worn down and deteriorated into French. We have to apply four of these laws in the present case;—

"1st. The tonic or accented syllable of the Latin form, remains the accented syllable in French; 'the continuance of the accent is a general and absolute law,' and preserves the 'ing' in Lotharingia.

"2nd. 'The atonic syllable, which directly precedes the tonic vowel, always disappears in French,'—which seems to erase the first 'a' in Lotharingia.

"3rd. 'The third characteristic is the loss of the medial consonant, that is, the consonant which stands between two vowels,' as the 'g' in Augustus, 'Août;' 'lachrymæ, larmes.' This disposes of the 'r' between the 'a' and the 'i.'

"4th. 'Atonic suffixes.' All these suffixes disappear in French; 'ia' into 'e,' as 'historia, histoire;' 'Britannia, Bretagne.'

"It follows, therefore, that Lotharingia becomes Lothinge, the 'th' and the 'z' being transposable, and this especially necessary to Norman writers, who could not pronounce the 'th' (see Tedford). Thus we have 'Lozinge,' and in Latin 'Lozinga.'

"The appointment of Lotharingian bishops to English sees during this and the immediate preceding period, and down to the reign of Henry the Third, is an established fact[o]. Mr. Freeman, in his 'History of the Norman Conquest[p],' says that the first was Herrmann of Lotharingia, who in 1045 was appointed to the see of Wilton. Walcher, Bishop of Durham, killed in 1080, was a Lotharingian; and (page 83) Mr. Freeman adds, 'Herrmann was a Lotharingian by birth, Leofric was equally so by education;' and he sees in this an attempt of Godwin and the patriotic party to counterbalance the French influence of Edward.

"This Lorraine, varying in its extent, and reaching from sea to sea, divided by a narrow slip Germany and what is now France, and comprised the most enthusiastically religious people of the Continent; and on the lowering of the culture of the English Church by

---

[o] Stubbs' Const. Hist., vol. i. p. 243.   [p] Vol. ii. pp. 80, 81.

the disorder attendant on the Danish invasion, we were glad of these men, skilled in the ritual and traditions of the Church, as bishops."

APPENDIX F.

REASONS FOR INFERRING THAT THE CHARGES OF SIMONY AND DECEITFULNESS WERE PREFERRED AGAINST HERBERT ON ACCOUNT OF THE ENMITY WHICH HE EXCITED BY ASSISTING ARCHBISHOP ANSELM IN THE REFORMATION OF CLERICAL ABUSES.

THE Rev. J. Gunn, a learned antiquary of Norwich, has favoured us with the following remarks, in vindication of our bishop from the charges of simony and flattery. While we fear that the charge of simony is too well attested to be entirely groundless, we entirely agree with Mr. Gunn that the name "Losinga" is not in any way indicative of moral character.

* * * *

"It appears that such a reformation had been attempted by Anselm's predecessor, who, it is recorded, 'had brought the monks to some good, that before his time followed hunting and hawking, dicing and carding, to the great discredit of their profession.' (Baker's Chronicles, p. 36.) Bloomfield (vol. iii. p. 467, quarto edition) quotes from Dugdale, Bale, and others, to this effect ;—

"'Before Herbert's time the clergy attending the bishop were canons, in whose places he was licensed by Archbishop Anselm to substitute monks, "dispossessynge the prests and their wyves, and placynge the monks in their rooms to make that church a Sodome," saith Bale.... However, it is plain that this very thing made him generally hated by the secular clergy, who took care to remember his faults so much, that, though great suit was made by the monks to have had him canonized and made a saint, such impediments were always in the way that it could not be obtained ᵠ.'

"Bloomfield especially relies upon Herbert's confession in the 'Carta Herberti Episcopi,' as a proof and admission of his simoniacal guilt. But a close examination of that document leads me to the conclusion that there is no ground for such a supposition. It contains nothing more than the ordinary expressions of deep humiliation and acknowledgment of general sinfulness, 'vitam expono meam, revelans juventutis meæ ignorantias, et scientiæ ʳ prevaricationes anxias,' &c.

"There is abundant evidence that he was a favourite with William Rufus, a fact which sufficiently accounts for the preferments he received (even from that avaricious and unscrupulous king), without resorting to the hypothesis of his having advanced large sums for the purchase of those preferments. It is alleged (William of Malmesbury, lib. ii. 151) that he was called Losinga on account of his addiction to falsehood and hypocrisy. It is well ascertained that his father, Robert, bore the name of Losinga, and we know that the Normans handed down their patronymic from father to son.

"The excellence of his life after his promotion to the see has led to the supposition that he became a converted man immediately on his installation; that a sense of the solemnity of the episcopal duties and office influenced him to consecrate to the service of God in building churches the revenues of his see, which he had gained by simony. This appears highly improbable, on the ground that, as 'nemo repente fuit turpissimus,' so the converse also is true. He was no extraordinary sinner, as the Seculars (piqued by his correction of their abuses) represented him; nor, on

---

ᵠ The proposal to have him canonized shews the high esteem he was held in by the monks.—J. G.

ʳ I presume that by *scientiæ prevaricationes*, "wilful prevarications," he means sins of which he was conscious, as opposed to sins committed in ignorance.

the other hand, was he a saint, as he was regarded by the Regulars. Probably there is as little truth in the view taken by one party of his character, as in that taken by the other. I may add, that I am inclined to believe that the charge of simony, flattery, and falsehood was a pure calumny, vented against him in spite by the secular clergy, because he aided Anselm in enforcing the celibacy of the clergy and the reformation of the Church."

APPENDIX G.

A CHARTER OF HERBERT, CONFIRMING THE GRANT OF CRESS-INGHAM, HELD BY GODWIN OF THE FEE OF THE BISHOP, TO THE BENEDICTINE PRIORY OF NORWICH.

IN the *Registrum Quartum* of the Benedictine Priory of Norwich, which is still preserved in the treasury of the Cathedral Church, are copies of nine charters subscribed and confirmed by Herbert. The first of them is as follows. It is of interest enough to have claimed insertion in the text of this work; but, as it has been omitted, we supply it in an Appendix. Possibly the Godwin who makes the grant of his church at Cressingham to the monks of the church of the Holy Trinity at Norwich, may be the same person to whom (with his brother William) Herbert's twenty-seventh Letter (see p. 287) is addressed. If so, it would appear that Herbert knew, and felt an interest in, Godwin's father. Possibly also the G., to whom Letter LV. is addressed (see p. 100), may be this very Godwin, an impulsive but fickle British monk, who, having taken the religious habit (as he here promises he will do on the death of his wife), afterwards became tired of his vows, and, on the plea of ill-health, withdrew from the convent, and plunged once again into secular business. Be he who he may, this is a copy of the instrument by which he makes over his church of Cressingham to the monks of the Cathedral Priory:—

CARTE HERBERTI EPI.

Ego Godwinus diaconus donaui deo in ecclesia sancte Trinitatis apud Norwicum et monachis eiusdem ecclesie Ecclesiam meam de Cressingeham et quicquid ad eam pertinet. Domum suppellectilem terras et annualia et quicquid habeo mobile et immobile apud Cressingham de feudo Episcopi. totum donam (*sic*) monachis sancte Trinitatis apud Norwicum pro anima mea et pro anima uxoris mee Ediue et hoc facio concessione et voluntate domini mei Herberti Episcopi. Promitto in prædictam ecclesiam me accepturum sacre religionis habitum et monachum futurum quando deus animam meam inspiraverit et quando dominus meus Herbertus Episcopus præceperit. defuncta uxore mea Ediua. Deprecatus etiam sum dominum meum Herbertum ut præsentem donacionem confirmet et auctoritate sancte crucis et a stipulatione sui sigilli.

Ego Herbertus Episcopus subscribo et præsentem donacionem mea auctoritate confirmo.

CHARTERS OF HERBERT THE BISHOP.

I, Godwin the Deacon, have presented to God in the church of the Holy Trinity at Norwich, and to the monks of the said church, my church of Cressingham, and whatsoever pertaineth thereto, house, furniture, lands, annual revenue, and whatsoever I have of fee of the Bishop, moveable and immoveable, at Cressingham. The whole of this donation I give to the monks of the Holy Trinity at Norwich, for my soul and that of my wife Ediva; and this I do by permission and at the will of my Lord Herbert the Bishop. I promise that in the church aforesaid I will assume the sacred habit of religion, and become a monk, when God shall have inspired my soul with such a resolution, and when my Lord Herbert the Bishop shall have so enjoined me, after the death of my wife Ediva. I further besought my Lord Herbert that he would confirm the present donation both by the authority of the holy cross, and with the ratification of his seal.

I, Herbert the Bishop, subscribe, and by my authority confirm, the present donation.

The after-history of Cressingham is curious, and will

be found in the recently-published work descriptive of "The Ancient Sculptures in the Roof of Norwich Cathedral," [Henry W. Stacy, Haymarket, Norwich, 1876]. We find from the above charter that the church of Cressingham was part of "the fee of the Bishop," and that it was held under Herbert by Godwin the Deacon. Bishop Eborard, Herbert's immediate successor, being greatly harassed by the wars going on in those days, granted away to two powerful chieftains of the day the towns of Blickling and Cressingham, with the view of securing the rest of the episcopal property. In his later days, when he had retired from the bishopric, he made a penitent confession of this sacrilege to Pope Eugenius, and requested absolution, and that the property might be restored to the Church. ("Ancient Sculptures," p. 79.) In King John's reign, Blickling and Cressingham were formally restored by the king to the see of Norwich, at the petition of Bishop John de Grey ("Sculptures," p. 234); after which the Prior and Convent of Norwich exchanged with the Bishop some property held by them at Lynn, for the manors of Cressingham and Sedgeford. Great Cressingham descended from the Prior and Convent to the Dean and Chapter, who have there a peculiar jurisdiction. ("Sculptures," p. 88, note †.)

APPENDIX H.

RESULTS OF THE COLLATION OF THE MS. OF HERBERT'S LETTERS WITH MR. ANSTRUTHER'S PRINTED TEXT.

THE only manuscript of the Letters of Herbert de Losinga, which is at present known to be extant, is to be found in the library of the Dukes of Burgundy at Brussels. We have been allowed to inspect and collate this manuscript, and now offer to our readers a short description of it. It is a late and indifferent copy of the Letters on paper, made in the seventeenth century, and from the erroneous punctuation, and other indications, it is clearly the work of a scribe who understood Latin, if at all, very imperfectly. It has been partially revised and corrected by another hand, apparently very soon after it was made. It will be seen that the title-page, which here we give *in extenso*, refers to an *autographus codex* then in the possession of the persons, whoever they were, that owned the copy. We have made enquiries for this *autographus codex* at Paris and at the Hague, as well as in several of the great libraries of England, but have been unable to hear anything of it. Here is the title-page of the copy, which is bound up with manuscript histories of six English monasteries (among them Ramsey), stories of Glastonbury (perhaps from Giraldus), and historical fragments respecting the monastery of Durham :—

ω
Ex MS. S. Albani
[Then in another hand]
Habemus etiam autographum codicem
signatum ✠ MS. 73. pag. 108
[Then in another hand]
Epistolæ
Heriberti Losingæ
Prioris Fiscannensis
in Normannia
Abbatis Ramesiensis
in Anglia
primi Nortwicensis Episcopi
qui floruit circa annum
Domini 1100
[Then in another hand]
Obijt 1120 teste Baleo, qui turpissimus
ipse, turpissimum illum depingit.

These Letters were published in the original Latin by Mr. Robert Anstruther (Brussels : A. Vandale ; London : D. Nutt, A.D. 1846), apparently as one of a series of similar works, entitled *Scriptores Monastici*. The same volume contains also the Letters of Osbert de Clara, Prior of Westminster, and of Elmer, Prior of Canterbury. A careful collation of the manuscript with the printed text has brought to light many divergences between the two, which we now proceed to enumerate. In the right-hand column is the reading of the manuscript, in the left that of Mr. Anstruther's printed text. We may notice once for all, before beginning, that in the titles of the letters Mr. Anstruther has indicated the person addressed by *ad* with an accusative case, over and above the title in the MS., which always runs "Herbertus," &c., with a dative case.

	R. A.	*MS.*
p. 2, l. 4.	annotare	adnotare.
,, l. 8.	condemnas	condempnas.
,, l. 18.	mimi	mime } *sic.* minime
p. 3, l. 12.	persuasionibus	persuationibus.
,, l. 16.	hoc	hic.
,, l. 20.	hi	hii.
,, l. 23.	(et)	not in *MS.*
p. 4, l. 2.	loquebatur spiritus sanctus	spiritus sanctus loquebatur.
,, l. 10.	?	a full point.
,, l. 13.	lacesere	lacescere.
,, l. 17.	æque	equa.
p. 5, l. 9.	temeritatis	temeritati.
,, l. 18.	in jussionibus	jussionibus.
p. 6, l. 6.	sancti evangelii	sanctæ ecclesiæ.
,, l. 14.	necessarius	necessarium.
,, l. 17.	abbatti	abbati.
,, l. 19.	commendare	commodare.
p. 7, l. 2.	monachus	monachis.
,, l. 9.	abhorrent	obhorrent.
,, l. 16.	accuant	acuant.
p. 8, l. 1.	venerentur	reverentur.
,, ,,	cujus	hujus.
,, l. 5.	metalla	metella.
,, l. 12.	cum angilis	cui anhelas.
,, l. 13.	participationi	participationem.

R. A.	MS.
p. 9, l. 8. indigne judicium	indigne, judicium.
„ l. 21. In templis.	

In the MS. the words "In templis" are not in this place, but in the next line, after the word "venerabantur."

p. 10, l. 4. expulsit	expulit.
p. 11, l. 6. (sed)	*not in MS.*
„ l. 20. elegationum	a legationum.
„ l. 21. calligat	colligat.
p. 12, l. 17. elocutione	allocutione.
p. 13, l. 5. impuriis	emporiis.
„ l. 20. sedulis	Sedulio.
p. 14, l. 4. compositione sinseparabiliter	compositiones inseparabiliter.
„ l. 5. Expergiscemini	Expergiscimini.
„ l. 14. præparatis	præparetis.
p. 15, l. 4. filius	filiis.
„ l. 12. fuerunt	fuerint.
p. 16, l. 12. mihi. Ad hæc	*no fresh paragraph.*
p. 17, l. 19. idem	isdem.
„ l. 23. iisdem	isdem.
„ l. 24. sane	sanæ.
p. 19, l. 16. mei	meæ.

This plainly shewing what a blunder of the scribe's was the word "servitii" in the MS. for "cervici."

„ l. 21. diem. Concidit, &c.	*no fresh paragraph.*
p. 20, l. 2. sterquillinio	sterquilinio.
„ l. 4. præhebam	præbebam.
„ l. 14. pericula? Quare	*no fresh paragraph.*
„ l. 18. Exhortus	Exortus.
p. 21, l. 10. conciatibus	cruciatibus.
p. 22, l. 4. mansuetudinem Quanto	*no fresh paragraph.*
„ l. 6. ferventiis	ferventius.
p. 23, l. 13. branium	brauium.
p. 26, l. 5. meditaveris	meditaberis.
„ l. 10. acti	arti.
„ l. 11. promereberit	promereberis.
p. 27, l. 6. judicat	indicat.
„ l. 20. "volet" written first, then erased and altered to "cupit."	

Appendix.

R. A.	MS.
p. 28, l. 5. usuriam	usuram.
„ l. 9. usuriam	usuram.
„ l. 14. instaretis	instauretis.
p. 29, l. 2. contenditis	contendite.
„ l. 7. thesauros in cœlo	thesauros sed in cœlo.
p. 31, l. 4. creditoribus	debitoribus.
„ l. 22. corrigere	corrige.
p. 33, l. 4. spirituum contuli	spirituum. Contuli.
„ l. 10. contaminaris	contaminareris.
„ l. 22. es	est.
p. 34, l. 19. tuas insulatus	tuis infulatus.
p. 35, l. 4. es	est.
„ l. 15. confortabat	confovebat.
p. 36, l. 12. intercederitis	intercederetis.
„ l. 22. illæ	illi.
p. 37, l. 18. quem sacrarum	quem in sacrarum.
p. 38, l. 17. sequererve	sequererne.
p. 40, l. 1. Bellafago	Bellofago.
„ l. 11. absinthi	absintii.
p. 41, l. 1. ad	[read] ad misericordia Dei plena est terra.
p. 42, l. 20. in malis	animabus.
p. 44, l. 7. vestræ	vestri.
„ l. 19. acidiosis	accidiosis.
p. 45, l. 9. continuis	continuus.
„ l. 16. vere	veræ.
p. 46, l. 1. tuarum nec	tuarumne.
„ l. 7. canet	canit.
„ l. 17. at	ad.
„ l. 22. ut	et.
p. 47, l. 18. exsequuturi	exsequeturos.
„ l. 21. extrahuntur	extruuntur.
p. 48, l. 2. scribitis	scribite.
„ l. 4. quid scite	quiescite.
„ l. 9. anima	animam.
„ l. 12. Ester quæ	Ester altam quæ.
„ l. 13. fastidio	fastigio.
p. 49, l. 24. dignorata	dignitata.
p. 50, l. 1. The scribe was going to write "Stannardus," and then altered it to "Starnardus."	

Appendix.

R. A.	MS.
p. 50, l. 13. sancius	saucius.
„ l. 18. dilaniandus	dilaniendus.
p. 51, l. 1. responsionem	responsione.
„ l. 3. quos	quas.
„ l. 14. integrum	integram.
„ l. 16. donant	donante, (*Pro* donate?).
„ l. 21. confido. De	confido de.
p. 53, l. 12. quiescentes!	quiescentes.
p. 54, l. 1. quas	quam.
„ l. 17. ore Christus	ore et Christus.
p. 55, l. 1. opima victima et tuis infirmitatibus necessaria	opimam victimam et tuis necessitatibus necessariam
„ l. 2. dignis	dignisve.
„ l. 9. sæviore	sæviora } severiora } (*sic*).
„ l. 11. opere et conscientia	opere et in conscientia.
p. 57, l. 7. serenissime	severissime.
p. 58, l. 17. fragrantiis impletus	fragrantiis totus impletus.
p. 59, l. 8. virginitam	virginitatem.
„ l. 10. vadit	ierit *is in the text*, vadit *is in the margin.*
„ l. 11. solæ	soli.
p. 60, l. 4. coleret	coloret.
„ „ Adsum	Assum.
„ l. 5. nequaquam	quam nequam (*sic*).
„ l. 10. quo	quorum has been written, but altered to quo.
„ l. 17. inferius	infernus.
p. 61, l. 11. lasciviis	lascivis.
„ l. 19. squalidis comorantes	squallidis commorantes.
„ l. 23. multa	multum.
p. 62, l. 5. humeris	numeris.
„ l. 13. bonum	bono.
„ l. 18. solvis (*sic*)	solius.
p. 63, l. 5. senex longevus	senex et longevus.
p. 64, l. 3. Sed dimitte nostris debitoribus debita, et dimitte nobis	The passage runs thus in the MS.:— "Demitte" [this word runs into the

R. A.	MS.
	sewing of the book, and the next line begins with] "tes nostris debitoribus debita. Exaudimur. Arcta (?) conditis, et dimitte nobis."
p. 64, l. 13. tuam	tu.
,, l. 14. confidenti	confitenti.
,, l. 15. negari	negare.
,, l. 20. venerebatur	venerabatur.
,, l. 22. sigillaret	suggillaret.
p. 65, l. 4. animos	amicos.
p. 66, l. 20. fano	favo.
p. 68, l. 10. invenias	invenies.
,, l. 12. cætera	cæteras.
,, l. 17. partitorem	portitorem.
p. 69, l. 11. judicavi	judicavit.
p. 73, l. 13. desinas	desinat.
p. 74, l. 11. quieto	quieti.
p. 75, l. 20. Ex Ovidio deinceps	Ex Ovidio igitur deinceps.
p. 76, l. 11. Epistola xl.	Epistola xl. Herbertus.
,, l. 13. Expergiscemini	Expergiscimini.
,, l. 20. pacentantes	parentantes.
p. 77, l. 2. Egypti	Egyptii.
p. 78, l. 15. meam	meam præceperam.
p. 79, l. 1. [What is to be done with "idus?" the contracted word in the MS. *may be* "secundus," but it would be a short and violent contraction for such a word.]	
p. 79, l. 19. est	sit.
p. 81, l. 4. decebat	decebas.
,, l. 6. es	est.
p. 82, l. 10. spiritualiter	spiritualibus.
p. 83, l. 10. in	is.
p. 84, l. 11. genere	genere / generum } (*sic*).
p. 85, l. 15. habetis	habete.

Appendix.

R. A.	MS.
p. 87, l. 3. constitui	constituo.
„ l. 10. profitetur. Saluta.	profitetur. Certissime non tibi deerunt magistri, nisi tu desinas esse discipulus. Saluta.
p. 89, l. 8. reserebat	referebat.
„ l. 10. victituum	victiturus.
„ l. 16. servat	serviat.
p. 90, l. 1. et	est.
p. 91, l. 11. quotidianis	cotidianis.
„ l. 18. apparuistis	aparuistis.
p. 92, l. 5. publice	publicæ.
„ l. 8. Herbertus W. G. et W. aparibus	H. & W. G. A. W. aparibus.
p. 94, l. 14. totius	totus.
p. 95, l. 2. Herbertus episcopus	H. episcopus.
p. 96, l. 16. Herbertus Norwicensis	H. Norwicensis.
p. 97, l. 1. discatis	dicatis.
„ l. 15. afficitur	efficitur.
p. 99, l. 15. mihi	nisi.
„ l. 16. cogemini	cogimini.
„ l. 18. præsenti	præsentiæ.
p. 100, l. 16. admirarentur	mirarentur.
p. 101, l. 23. sanctitatim	sanctitatem.
p. 102, l. 2. extollent	extollant.
p. 104, l. 15. exitum	exutum.
„ l. 24. deposimus	deposcimus.
p. 105, l. 3. effundere	effundet.
„ l. 18. episcopo	episcopi.
p. 106, l. 3. quæ	quo.
„ l. 5. defendit	defenditis.
„ l. 7. aliquid	aliqua.
„ l. 9. manipulis	manibus.
p. 107, l. 1. fortem	sortem.
„ l. 2. theosophia	theosebia.
„ l. 4. monachi propter	monachi mali propter.
„ l. 6. Veneremur clericatum	Veneremur igitur clericatum.

CHRONOLOGY OF THE LIFE OF HERBERT DE LOSINGA.

A.D.

HERBERT DE LOSINGA born	. *c.* 1050
Alexander II. elected Pope	. 1061
Battle of Hastings	Oct. 14, 1066
Gregory VII. (Hildebrand) elected Pope	. 1073
Domesday Book completed. Victor III. elected Pope	1086
Death of William the Conqueror: William Rufus seizes the crown	. 1087
Herbert sent for to England, and appointed Abbot of Ramsay	. *ib.*
Urban II. elected Pope	. 1088
Archbishop Lanfranc dies	May 24, 1089
Herbert appointed Bishop of Thetford	. 1091
Anselm consecrated Archbishop of Canterbury, Herbert assisting	Dec. 4, 1093
Herbert's first visit to Rome, to seek absolution for his simony	. 1094
Herbert, returned from Rome, removes the see to Norwich	. 1095
First Crusade undertaken	. *ib.*
Norwich Cathedral founded	. 1096
Herbert's father dies	. 1098
Pascal II. appointed Pope. Jerusalem taken by the Crusaders; and Godfrey de Bouillon elected king	1099
William Rufus dies	Aug. 2, 1100
Norwich Cathedral consecrated, and its charter sealed	Sept. 24, 1101
Building of the Cathedral monastery begun	. 1106
Herbert preaches in Ely Cathedral at the translation of St. Etheldreda	Nov. 1, 1106
Roger of Sarum consecrated at Canterbury, Herbert assisting	. 1107
Roger Bigot, Earl of Norfolk, dies, and is brought from Thetford Abbey to be interred in Norwich Cathedral	. *ib.*

Chronology of the Life of Herbert de Losinga. 425

A.D.

Herbert, sent to Rome on the question which arose between the King and Anselm about investitures, is made prisoner on his way by Count Guido, and forced to surrender the money with which he intended to purchase jurisdiction over St. Edmund's Abbey 1107
Archbishop Anselm dies . . April 21, 1109
Plague at Norwich 1112
Ralph, Bishop of Rochester, translated to Canterbury
April 21, 1114
Herbert, with Hugh, Abbot of Chertsey, sets out for Rome in attendance upon Archbishop Ralph, but is turned back at Placentia by serious illness 1116
Herbert returns to England 1117
Gelasius II. elected Pope 1118
Queen Matilda ("Molde the Good") dies . May 1, 1118
Herbert dies . . . . . July 22, 1119

PAGES OF THE LIFE ON WHICH THE DIFFERENT LETTERS OF HERBERT ARE TO BE FOUND.

LETTER	PAGE	LETTER	PAGE
I.	83	XXXII.	29
II.	168	XXXIII.	284
III.	161	XXXIV.	64
IV.	296	XXXV.	170
V.	64	XXXVI.	174
VI.	155	XXXVII.	173
VII.	169	XXXVIII.	272
VIII.	141	XXXIX.	22
IX.	19	XL.	31
X.	248	XLI.	282
XI.	182	XLII.	210
XII.	243	XLII. (bis)*	282
XIII.	288	XLIII.	196
XIV.	131	XLIV.	not* found
XV.	135	XLV.	10
XVI.	105	XLVI.	198
XVII.	135	XLVII.	22
XVIII.	303	XLVIII.	207
XIX.	127	XLIX.	35
XX.	52	L.	180
XXI.	226	LI.	138
XXII.	37	LII.	200
XXIII.	192	LIII.	53
XXIV.	20	LIV.	7
XXV.	298	LV.	100
XXVI.	229	LVI.	279
XXVII.	287	LVII.	203
XXVIII.	43	LVIII.	13
XXIX.	101	LIX.	261
XXX.	24	LX.	266
XXXI.	286		

* See p. 210, note f.

INDEX OF THE PRINCIPAL MATTERS TOUCHED UPON IN THE LIFE AND LETTERS.

ABBOTS, tendency of the mediæval Church to exalt them above the bishops, p. 65, note x; the pope favours their aggrandisement, *ibid.*; not independent of bishops in the primitive Church, *ibid.*

Abdias, first Bishop of Babylon, the Apocryphal Acts of the Apostles ascribed to him, p. 310, note u.

Abingdon, Chronicle of the Monastery of, quoted, p. 273.

Absconsa, p. 199.

Absolution, precatory, form of it in the office for the dead in the Missal of Sarum, p. 336, note u.

Accidia, H.'s mention of this sin, p. 37; what it was, p. 37, note z; proposed monastic remedy for it, p. 39, note z.

Acidiosus, p. 192, and note n.

Adam, Archdeacon of Norfolk, and chaplain to H., p. 227, note q.

Æsop, H.'s reference to, p. 28; his fables Latinized by Phædrus, p. 28, note e.

Agnes, St., the Virgin, her history, p. 293, note c; meaning of her name, p. 294, note c; St. Ambrose's account of her, *ibid.*; representations of her in art, *ibid.*; basilica of, at Rome, two lambs offered there annually, and their fleeces used for palls for archbishops, p. 294, note c.

Album, the chief pontiff's register at Rome, alluded to in a letter to H., p. 14, note k.

Alcuin, his vow when a boy against profane literature, p. 48, note k; a quotation from him, p. 196, note x.

Alexander of Canterbury, sent by Anselm to represent him at Rome, p. 236.

Alford, Dean, his preference of the Rhemish Version of Rom. i. 30 to the Authorized, p. 208, note d.

Alia manu, p. 247, note h.

Alliteration, H.'s liking for, shewn in his letters, p. 248, note i.

Alured, Archdeacon of Suffolk, p. 227, note q.

Ambrose, St., the popularity of his hymns with the Benedictines, p. 16, note n; the penance imposed by him upon Theodosius, p. 183, note i; his fulsome panegyric on Gratian, p. 184, note j; his letter relating the story of St. Agnes, p. 294, note c; on the virginity of St. John: see St. John.

"*Ambrosianum illud*," the probable meaning of this expression, p. 16, note n.

Amphitryon, H.'s allusion to Plautus' comedy of that name, p. 12; argument of the comedy, *ibid.*, note h.

Analogium, what it was, p. 338, note c.

Anathĕma, H.'s use of the word, p. 134; its distinction from *anathēma*, *ibid.*, note b; the former word used by Prudentius, *ibid.*

Anathĕma Maran-atha, the expression explained, p. 172, note t.

Anchorite, cell of, in Norwich Cathedral, p. 279, note i; word whence derived, *ibid.*

Anglo-Saxon Chronicle, one of the authorities for H.'s life, Appendix D. I., p. 357.

Anna Virgo: see St. Agnes.

Annales Ecclesiæ Wintoniensis, one of the authorities for H.'s life, Appendix D. VIII., p. 378.

Annas, King of the East Angles, his four daughters, p. 222, note o.

Anniversary of H.'s death, service for it in the Norwich *Ordinale*, pp. 334, 335; Appendix B., p. 352.

Anselm, St., Dean Church's life of, quotations from, pp. 18, 55, 237, 335, note r.

—— nominated to the archbishopric, p. 73; consecrated by Thomas I. of York, with the assistance of H., p. 82; threatens the Norman courtiers with censures for not clipping their hair and shaving their beards, pp. 92, 93, and note h; urges upon William Rufus the convocation of a synod, p. 93; receives the pallium, June, 1095, p. 126; compromise between him and the King as to the method of receiving it, *ibid.*; quarrel between him and the King on the subject of the contingent furnished by him for the expedition into Wales, *ibid.*; his final parting with William Rufus, p. 127; alteration of his views on the subject of lay investiture, p. 144; declines to accept investiture at Henry's hands, *ibid.*; does good service to the King on occasion of Duke Robert's invasion, p. 145; quarrel with the King breaks out again, p. 235; refuses homage, *ibid.*; is invited to be present at the second translation of St. Etheldreda, p. 213; sends two monks to represent him at Rome, p. 236; confirms the exemption of St. Edmund's Abbey, p. 243; abets the claims of Gregory VII., p. 290, note y; makes fresh enactments to enforce the celibacy of the clergy, p. 252; his differences with Thomas II., Archbishop of York, p. 253; summons Thomas to Canterbury for consecration, *ibid.*; employs H. as mediator, *ibid.*; his letter to Thomas, p. 254; his death, p. 257; his sympathy with monasticism, p. 264, note a; meditation on the virginity of St. John: see St. John.

Anselm, nephew of the Archbishop, is sent as legate to England by Paschal II., but is prohibited from landing, p. 275.

Anstruther, Mr., his edition of H.'s letters, derangement in their numeration, p. 210, note f; quotations from, pp. 228, note r, 283, note n; mentions two works of H. not named by Bale, p. 333; results of the collation of his printed text with the MS. of H.'s Letters, Appendix G, p. 414.

Apares, H.'s use of the word, and its meaning, pp. 53, note o, 131, note y.

Apollinaris, St., his history, p. 334, note p; H. dies on the eve of his festival, p. 334.

Apostolici, term originally applied to all bishops, p. 266, note b.

Apparitor: see *Bedellus*.

Aqualiculus, H.'s use of the term, and its signification, p. 33, and note s.

Archdeacons of Norfolk, Suffolk, and Norwich in H.'s time, p. 227, note q.

Arminghall, p. 148.

Arms (of a bishop), why impaled with those of his see, p. 170, note q.

Assecla, its meaning, p. 295, note e.

Athselinus, Provost of Thetford, in holy orders, pp. 174, 5, note x.

Atramentarium, p. 288, note s.

Atramentum, H.'s use of the word, as well as of *encaustum*, p. 198, and note d; used by Pliny and Cicero to express ink, p. 296, note f.

Atrium, of a church, what it was, p. 168, note l; of a monastery, p. 208, and note b: see Strangers' Hall.

Audit-book, of the Norwich Chapter, for 1683, entry in it for H.'s new tomb, p. 331.

Auditorium, its classical, ecclesiastical, and conventual meanings, p. 105, note w; see also p. 207, note a. See also *locutory*.

Augustine, St., mentions five persons being raised from the dead by St. Stephen's relics, p. 216, note i; *De bono conjugali* quoted, p. 313, note x.

Augustinian canons, possess two mitred abbeys, p. 262, note s.

Avernus, Lake, confounded by H. with the Dead Sea, p. 159, note c; quotation from Virgil descriptive of, *ibid.*

Avitus, his translation of Lucian's account of the discovery of St. Stephen's relics, p. 216, note i.

Baldwin of Bec, sent by Anselm to represent him at Rome, p. 236.
—— Abbot of St. Edmundsbury, obtains from Alexander II. the exemption of his abbey from all episcopal control, except that of the see of Canterbury, p. 239.

Bale, Bishop, his account of H.'s extraction, p. 4; quoted, pp. 71, 252; his abusive language on the subject of the removal of the see, p. 97; one of the authorities for H.'s life, Appendix D. XV., p. 388.

Balnearis: see *Bannearis*.

Bannearis, in Letter XVI., Bishop Chr. Wordsworth's conjecture as to the true reading, p. 108, note z.

Barry, Rev. Dr., quoted, on the functions ascribed to the archangel Michael, p. 340, note g.

Bathing in monasteries, p. 109, note z.

Battle Abbey, its dedication by King William Rufus, p. 91; the Conqueror's offering to it, and the object of its foundation, *ibid.*

Baudrand, mention of Hiesmes in his "Geographia," p. 328; derivation of its name, p. 329.
Baudry, Archbishop of Dol, his description of the beauties of Fécamp, pp. 57, 58, note q; a principal mover in the Crusades, p. 63; his pilgrimage to Fécamp, and intimacy with Abbot Roger, *ibid.*; possibly to be identified with H.'s "Lord Baldwin," p. 65, note u; his admiration of the wheel of fortune in the abbey church of Fécamp, p. 67; and of the organ, p. 68; his justification of instrumental music in churches, *ibid.*
Bavaria, the Elector of, offers a whole town for a MS., p. 251, note n.
Beaufeu, Agnes de, wife of the Bishop of Thetford, H.'s immediate predecessor, pp. 115, 226, note p; marries afterwards Hubert de Rye, pp. 115, 226, note p; her son the second Archdeacon of Norwich, pp. 115, 226, note p; grants the church and tithes of Aldeby to Norwich Cathedral, p. 226, note p.
—— Ralph de, p. 226, note p.
—— Richard de, son of the Bishop of Thetford, second Archdeacon of Norwich, pp. 7, 226, note p.
—— William de, Bishop of Thetford, marries Agnes of Todeni, p. 226, note p; his death in 1091, p. 73; overlooked by William of Malmesbury, *ibid.*
Beckham, p. 150.
Bede, what he makes the song of the undefiled ones to be, p. 194, note t.
Bedellus, office of, and the ground of its unpopularity, p. 25, and note y; etymology of the word, *ibid.*
Belfage, Radulph (or Ralph) de, probably Beaufeu: see Beaufeu.
Belfagus: see Galfagus.
Benedictines, date of the foundation of the order, and of its introduction into England, p. 186; a summary of the Rule, pp. 186—188; it forbade property to monks, p. 139, note i; cited by H., p. 140, and note k; extract from the fourth chapter of the Rule given by Maitland, pp. 188—190; silence strictly enjoined by it, p. 193, note r; their habit sad-coloured in H.'s time, p. 295, note d; Lanfranc's mention of their dress, p. 295, note d; Rev. I. Gregory Smith's remarks on it, *ibid.*; their chapters, when held, p. 334, note r; mention of Anchorites in their Rule, p. 279, note i; they employed themselves as copyists, p. 197, note z.
Benedictines, of Norwich Cathedral priory, reared their children in the monastery, p. 201, and note m.
Benedictio, commonly applied to the consecration of abbots, more rarely to that of bishops, p. 255, note p.
Bengel, his remark on "man's day," p. 211, note g.
Bensly, Mr. R. L., quoted, p. 333.
Benson, Lord Bishop of Truro, his proposed emendation of the text of the Epistles, p. 25, note z, and p. 288, note r.
Bernard, St., quoted, p. 38, note z; attacks the Cluniacs on account of their laxity, p. 165; his description of the song of the undefiled ones, p. 194, note t.
Bigot, Roger, site of his palace purchased by H. for his church, p. 113; founds Thetford Abbey by H.'s advice, p. 163; what induced him to do so, pp. 164 and 167, note k; dies on the eighth day after laying the foundation-stone of Thetford Abbey, pp. 164, 233; motives which induced him to place Cluniac monks at Thetford Abbey, pp. 166, 7; his death at Eresa, p. 167, note k; buried in Norwich Cathedral, p. 234.
Bilkees, name given by the Arabs to the Queen of Sheba, p. 299, note h.
Binding, of mediæval books, p. 251, note n.
Bingham, on the original meaning of the word *Parochia,* p. 255, note o.
Bishops, arms of, why impaled with those of their sees. See Arms.
Bitalassum, H.'s use of the word, and its meaning, p. 40, and note c.
Blomefield, his list of Archdeacons of Norwich, p. 227, note q; states that H. was chancellor, p. 324, note l.
Blunt, Rev. J. H., Annotated Book of Common Prayer, quoted, p. 69, note z; on the last member of the collects, p. 314, note z; Dictionary of Theology, Art. *Substance,* quoted, p. 313, note y.
Bochart, quoted on the subject of Ham, p. 204, note s.
Boëthius, H.'s reference to his Consolation of Philosophy, p. 48; quotation from, p. 49, note l; some particulars of his life, works, and mediæval reputation, p. 50, note l; translation of his work by Alfred the Great, *ibid.*
Bond, Dean of Thetford in H.'s time, pp. 173, 176.

Bond, Mr. Edward A., his letter on H.'s epitaph, p. 318.
Boxwood used for tablets, p. 7, Letter LIV.
Boys, discipline of in Norman convents, p. 137, note g; reasons which justify, and disadvantages of, p. 138, note g.
Bravium, its meaning and derivation, p. 290, note x.
Breve, equivalent to our word "writ," p. 232, note y.
Brigstock, Mr., entry in the Auditbook of his bill for restoring H.'s tomb. See Audit-book.
British character, as exemplified in a British monk, censured by H., p. 100, and note k.
Browne, Sir Thomas, notice of H.'s monument in his *Repertorium*, p. 321.
Brussels, MS. of H.'s Letters at, p. 210, note f; p. 247, note h.
Building, taste for, prevalent in H.'s age, pp. 121, 2.
Bury St. Edmunds, Abbey of, possibly in possession of the old cathedral of Thetford, p. 95, note l; the abbots exempted by the Pope from all episcopal control, save that of the see of Canterbury, p. 239; Lanfranc disallows the exemption, p. 240, but afterwards confirms it, *ibid.*; Anselm confirms it, p. 243; H. wishes to obtain jurisdiction over them, p. 239; East Anglian bishops always seeking to obtain jurisdiction over the abbey, p. 240; the abbey described by Leland, *ibid.*, note c; St. Edmund's Psalter preserved there, *ibid.*
Bustum, connected with *uro*, *comburo*, parallel word to τύφω, p. 334, note q.
Butler, Rev. Alban, his "Lives of the Saints" quoted, p. 216, note i; p. 222, note o; p. 240, note c.
By, termination of names of places found in Flegg and in Lincolnshire, p. 149, note t; different etymologies of it given by Mr. Taylor and Mr. Robberds, *ibid.*

Callixtus II. becomes Pope, p. 297; convenes a synod at Rheims, *ibid.*; consecrates Thurstan Archbishop of York, without communicating with the King or the Archbishop of Canterbury, *ibid.* See Thurstan.
Calumnia, its meaning in the mediæval Latin, p. 176, note a.
Cambron, abbey of, two writings of H.'s mentioned in its Catalogue of MSS. which are not named by Bale, p. 333.
Campbell, Lord, his "Lives of the Chancellors" quoted, pp. 225, 302, note k, p. 328; his "Lives of the Chief Justices" quoted, pp. 168, 9, note m.
Canon, "*utraque duum schola canonis aperitur*," a passage of which the translation is only conjectural, p. 15, note l.
Canonicæ feritatis, referred to by H., p. 262, note s.
Canons, secular, tendency of H.'s time to substitute monks for them, p. 147, note r; secular and regular, p. 262, note s; distinction between canons and monks, pp. 262, note s, 263, note y.
Canterbury, abbot of, old ballad quoted, pp. 211, note h, 249, note l.
Capellanus, derivation and meanings of the word, p. 161, note e.
Caphargamala, St. Stephen, Gamaliel, and Nicodemus buried at, p. 215, note i; opening of St. Stephen's tomb at, *ibid.*; meaning of the name, *ibid.*
Cassian, quoted by Ducange, p. 267, note c.
Categories of Aristotle, referred to by H., p. 35, and note w.
Catton, p. 150.
Caula, the word borrowed by H. from Virgil, p. 229, note s.
Celibacy, St. Augustine on, p. 313, note x; enforced by St. Anselm, p. 252.
Centuriators of Magdebourg : see Magdebourg.
Chancellors, in the reign of Henry I., pp. 324, 5.
Chapter, of Norwich, at the time of the restoration of H.'s tomb, p. 331; their arms still preserved, p. 332.
Chapters in Benedictine houses: see Benedictines.
Charlemagne, gives hunting rights to the abbey of Sithiu, that the deerskins may be used for bookbinding, p. 251, note n.
Charter, of Norwich Cathedral, p. 146 —151; provisionally confirmed in the first instance, p. 151; signatories to it in full parliament, pp. 152, 3; confirmed at Windsor, p. 153.
Chaucer, his description of "accidy" in the Parson's Sermon, pp. 38, 9, note z; his Reve's Tale quoted, p. 106, note x.
Chester, its monastic church restored, p. 235, note z; bishop's seat trans-

THE LIFE AND LETTERS. 431

ferred there from Lichfield, *ibid.*; removed to Coventry, thence back to Lichfield, *ibid.*; made a cathedral church by Henry VIII., *ibid.*

Chester, Earl of: see Hugh.

Children of monks, reared in the Norwich monastery, p. 201, and note m.

Chorus angelorum, p. 341, and note k.

Church, Dean, his description of the uses of a cloister, p. 136, note f; of the prior's office in Benedictine monasteries, p. 199; his account of the results of H.'s embassy to the Pope, pp. 237, 8; quoted on Benedictine chapters, p. 335, note r.

Churches, in Norfolk, built by H., p. 332.

Cibarius panis, H.'s use of, and its meaning, p. 33, and note p.

Circular letters, how headed in the Low Latin, p. 53, note o.

Circular: see *Apares.*

Circumitor, circa, p. 199.

Circus, what it was, p. 289, note i.

Cistercians, a branch of Benedictines who revived the strictness of the rule, p. 165; in which revival they had been preceded by the Cluniacs, *ibid.*, and note g. And see Cluniacs.

Clark's "Introduction to Heraldry" quoted, p. 170, note q.

Clement, St., quotation from his Epistle to St. James, p. 40, note c.

Clergy, derivation of the word, p. 267, note d.

Clerk, its etymology, mediæval meaning, and meaning in the Prayer-Book, p. 52, note m.

Clitellarius, meaning of, p. 128, note s.

Cloister, Dean Church's description of the uses of it, p. 136, note f; of Norwich Cathedral, glazed and provided with mats in 1307, p. 137, note f *.

Cluniac monks, established by H. in the old cathedral at Thetford, p. 163.

Cluniacs, a branch of the Benedictine order, p. 165; their moral decadence at the close of the eleventh century, *ibid.*; the points objected against them by the Cistercians, pp. 165, 6, and note h; their reply, *ibid.*; their wealth and gorgeous ceremonial, p. 166, and note i.

Clypeus, its meaning, p. 289, note u.

Colkirk, p. 151.

Commendatio animarum, p. 336, note u, p. 339, note d.

Commendatory Prayer, our, suggested by the *Diri vulneris,* p. 342, note m.

Commercium librorum: see Loans of books.

Complicibus, sense in which H. uses it, p. 280, note v.

Compline, silence enjoined after it by the Rule of Benedict, p. 193, note q.

Consistentia, in omni suæ consistentiæ loco, an untranslateable passage, p. 208, and note c.

Consuetudo, its meaning, p. 230, note u.

Contuli, its appearance at the end of six of H.'s letters, and probable meaning, p. 13, note i; p. 247, note h.

Conventual buildings at Norwich, original poverty of, p. 101, note r.

Coöpertoria, various meanings of the word, p. 201, note l.

Copyists, Benedictine monks employed as, p. 197, note z.

Cornu, its meaning, p. 288, note s.

Corona, meaning of the term as applied to the clergy, p. 175, note y.

Cotana, the classical and mediæval meanings of the word, p. 180, note d.

Cotton, Bartholomew, referred to, p. 69, note z; his apology for H.'s simony, p. 80; his description of H., p. 278; bewails H.'s memory, p. 314; one of the authorities for H.'s life, Appendix D., IX., p. 379.

Coventry, Bishops of, called Bishops of Chester, p. 235, note z.

Cowholm, meaning of the word, p. 111; its boundaries, *ibid.*; belonged to the manor of Thorpe, *ibid.*

Croke, Sir Alex., on Leonine verses, p. 320, note e.

Cross, the sign of, appended to documents by signatories, p. 151, note x.

Croyland, abbey of, rules about lending books, p. 251, note n.

Crusade, the first, preaching of, the enthusiasm which it kindled in Europe, p. 98; no trace of this enthusiasm found in H.'s writings, p. 99.

Cupa, its meaning and orthography, p. 11, note g.

Cupit, substituted by the scribe of the Brussels MS. for *volet,* p. 132, note z.

Curia, the meanings of the word in classical and mediæval Latin, p. 106, note x.

Customs, exemption from, claimed by H. for Thorpe, pp. 230, 231.

Cutem curare, H.'s use of the phrase, p. 109, note a.

Cutis, its difference from *pellis,* p. 109, note a.

Cydonium malum: see Cotana.

Dagobert, King of France, his letter to Archbishop Sulpitius, p. 255, note p.

Deans of Thetford, their powers and prerogatives, p. 173, note u; success of one of them in litigation against Bishop Nix, p. 174, note u; Ranulf, the first dean of whom we have any record, and John Kevelon, the last, *ibid.*; Bond, the dean in H.'s time, p. 173, note u.
Decretals, the so-called, what they are, p. 80, note u.
Demoniaci,—"*non monachi sed demoniaci,*" p. 202, and note p.
Denarius, its derivation and original meaning, p. 141, and note m; value of the Anglo-Saxon, *ibid.*
De necessitatibus, p. 343, note q.
Deo odibiles, the Rhemish translation of θεοστυγεῖς in Rom. i. 30, preferable to our own, p. 208, note d.
Dereham, St. Withberge's well in the churchyard at, p. 222, note o.
Diem dicere, p. 211, note g.
Dirige, the, what it was, p. 337, note a.
Diri vulneris : see Commendatory Prayer.
Districtio, its etymology and meaning, p. 263, note x.
Divina scriptura : see *Scriptura sacra.*
Domini, in the sense of "dignitaries," pp. 201, and note n, 206, note x.
Donatus, H.'s reference to, p. 20; his Latin grammar, p. 20, note q; the word *donat,* meaning of, *ibid.*
Ducange, quoted or referred to, p. 217, note l, p. 228, note r, p. 230, note u; on *benedictio,* p. 256, note p; his quotation from Cassian on Sarabites, p. 267, note c; his list of the Carthusian writing apparatus, p. 288, note s; on Leonine verses, p. 320.
Dugdale, referred to, pp. 69, note z, 71, note c; at issue with himself on the duration of Robert Losinga's abbacy at Winchester, p. 78, note r; gives a copy of the charter of the grant of Thorpe to Herbert, p. 230, note x; quoted by Prideaux, p. 322; his list of chancellors in the reign of Henry I., p. 324.
Dunwich, the original see of the East Angles, p. 110.

Eadmer, goes with H. to Rome, p. 276; his account of the journey, p. 276; quoted, pp. 235, note z, 239, 242, 254, 256; one of the authorities for H.'s life, Appendix D., III. pp. 360 —365.
Eagle, derivation of the word, p. 305, note n; twofold symbolism of in Scripture, *ibid.*
East Anglian see moved from Elmham to Thetford, in pursuance of an order of the Council of London, 1075, p. 95, note l; motives attributed to H. for its removal to Norwich, *ibid.*
Eborard, Archdeacon and Bishop of Norwich, p. 227, note q.
Eccles, p. 151.
Ecclesiastical seasons : see Introits.
Edmund, St., chapel of, at Hoxne, p. 150.
—— his Psalter preserved in his abbey, p. 240, note c.
Edmundsbury : see Bury St. Edmunds.
Edwardston, church of, given to the monastery at Abingdon, p. 273; charter conferring the grant, p. 273, and Appendix C., p. 355.
Edward the Sixth's Prayer-Book, its Epistle for the Holy Communion at burials : see *Epist. Nolumus nos.*
Effeminati, their costume and their vices, p. 143, note n.
Eliensis, Liber, account of the second translation of St. Etheldreda's body in, pp. 212—222; compares the four saints Abbot Richard translated to the four winged creatures of Ezekiel and St. John, the four rivers of Paradise and the four Maries, pp. 222, 3; quoted, p. 250, note l.
—— Thomas, one of the authorities for H.'s life, Appendix D., VII., pp. 372—378.
Elixus: see *Lixa.*
Ellis, John, Dean Prideaux's letters to, pp. 322, 3.
Elmham, North, divides with Dunwich the see of the East Angles, p. 110; alone the East Anglian see, *ibid.*
Elmham, pp. 150, 1; church built by H., p. 332.
Elogium, meanings of, p. 114, note d.
Ely, church completed at, pp. 211, 12; saints buried at, p. 217; their bodies translated by Abbot Richard, pp. 217—222; comparison of these saints, see under Eliensis, Liber.
Ely Cathedral, sculptures describing St. Etheldreda's history, p. 222, note o; the bishop sits in what is usually the dean's stall, p. 251, note l.
Encaustum, its meaning and derivatives, pp. 198, note d, 282, note h, 296, note f; sacred, of Justinian's Code, p. 296, note f.
Enfeoffment, how purchased by ecclesiastics, p. 77.
Ennius, rhyming verses quoted from him by Cicero, p. 319, note e.
Epist. Nolumus nos, the same appointed in Edward the Sixth's Prayer-Book

THE LIFE AND LETTERS. 433

for the office of Holy Communion at the burial of the dead, p. 343, note o.
Epitaph on H. by the monks, pp. 315—320; by Dean Prideaux, p. 329.
Ermenilda, Queen, her parentage, p. 222, note o; translation of her body, p. 218.
Ernulf, Bishop of Rochester, H. assists in his consecration, p. 271.
Eructo, spelt by H. *eructuo*, p. 249, note k.
Escures, Ralph of: see under Ralph.
Ethelburga, daughter of Annas, King of the East Angles, p. 222, note o.
Etheldreda, St., first removal of her body, p. 211; her second translation, pp. 211—217; her history, p. 222, note o.
Ethelwold, St., seals up the coffins of SS. Sexburga and Ermenilda, p. 218.
Eumenes II., King of Pergamus, invents parchment, p. 296, note g.
Euripus, H.'s use of the word, and its meaning, p. 42, and note f.
Eusebius, quoted, p. 306, note q.
Evangelium, used by H. of a passage in St. Paul's Epistles, p. 203, and note r.
Everard, Bishop, completes the church of St. Paul at Norwich, p. 279, note i.
Excommunication, frequency, and consequent disregard of it, in H.'s age, pp. 172, 3, note t.
Eylsinus, Abbot of Ramsey, his institution of the Festival of the Conception of the Blessed Virgin Mary there, p. 69, note z.

Fabricius, legends of St. John in the *Apostolicæ Historiæ* of his *Codex Apocryphus*, p. 306, note q, p. 307, notes r, s, pp. 309, 10, notes t, u.
Faleratæ orationes: see *Phaleræ*.
Fécamp, abbey of, founded by Richard the Fearless, p. 55; its relic of the precious Blood, p. 56, &c.; etymology of the name, p. 57, and note q; Archbishop Baudry's encomium of the country round, *ibid.*; the church of, appears too narrow for its length, p. 66; dedicated to the Holy Trinity, like Norwich Cathedral, p. 67; its curious wheel of fortune, *ibid.*; its organ, p. 68.
Felix, St., p. 110.
Felix, H.'s laudatory letter to, p. 192, &c., Letter XXIII.; H.'s letter of censure to, p. 196, &c., Letter XLIII.

Feu (the late), its proposed derivations, p. 195, note u.
Field, a Norse and Anglo-Saxon termination of names of places, and its derivation, p. 171, note r.
Flambard, Ralph, his character as given by Dean Church, p. 76; probably the go-between in H.'s purchase of his bishopric, *ibid.*; committed to the Tower, p. 143.
Flegg, boundaries of the district so called, p. 149, and note t; termination of the names of parishes in, *ibid.*, Appendix A., p. 349.
Fleury, *Hist. Eccl.*, quoted, p. 295, note d.
Florence of Worcester, one of the authorities for H.'s history, Appendix D., II. pp. 358—360.
Foss, Mr., in his "Lives of the Judges," denies that H. was Chancellor, p. 327.
Foster, John, his objection to the study of Homer by Christians, pp. 44, 45, note h.
Foundation-stone of the cathedral, inscription on it, p. 114; question as to the part of the cathedral in which it was located, p. 115, &c.; fruitless search recently made for it, p. 116.
Fulbertus, quotation from one of his Epistles, p. 40, note c.
Fuller, twofold notice of H. in his "Worthies of England," p. 5; one of the authorities for H.'s history, Appendix D., XXIII., pp. 407—409.

Gale's *Scriptores quindecim* referred to, p. 70, note a.
Galfagus, William, erroneously confounded with H. by Bishop Godwin and Mr. Spurdens, p. 1, note a. See also Beaufeu.
Gamaliel, appears in a vision to Lucian, priest of Caphargamala, p. 215, note i; buried at Caphargamala, *ibid.*; his tomb opened, *ibid.*
Gaywood, p. 150.
Gelasius II. becomes Pope, p. 297.
Geoffry: see Rocherio.
Geoffry de Clive, Bishop of Hereford, H. assists in his consecration, p. 271.
Gerard, Archbishop of York, goes with H. on an embassy from Henry I. to the Pope, p. 235, and note z; seeks at the same time to obtain the pall, p. 239; dies, p. 252.
Gislebert, H.'s letter to him, acknowledging a present of fruit, pp. 180, 1, Letter L.
Godfrey de Bouillon elected King of Jerusalem, July 15, 1099, p. 130.

INDEX OF THE PRINCIPAL MATTERS IN

Godwin, Bishop, his discrepancy with himself on H.'s birthplace, p. 4; referred to, p. 72, p. 235, note z, p. 323; one of the authorities for H.'s history, Appendix D., XXI., pp. 400—403.

Godwin and William, H.'s letter to them, re-assuring them about their father's absence, pp. 287, 8, Letter XXVII.

Goldwell, Bishop, his roof of the cathedral presbytery a work of the fifteenth century, p. 120.

Gradual, for the office of the dead in the Sarum Missal, p. 343, note p; meaning of the name, *ibid.*

Grammatica, ars, its narrow and more extended meanings, pp. 196, 7, note y.

Gratian, H.'s allusion to him, p. 183; his education and character, p. 184, note j; defeated by Maximus and assassinated, *ibid.*; Ambrose's fulsome panegyric of him, *ibid.*; the sympathy between him and Ambrose, *ibid.*

Gregory VII., H. deeply imbued with the spirit of, p. 290, note y; Dean Hook's remarks on, *ibid.*; Chancellor Massingberd's remarks on, *ibid.*; Canon Mozley on, pp. 290, 1, note y; his treatment of the Emperor Henry IV., p. 290, note y; see Hildebrand.

Gregory, a monk sent by H. to Abbot Richard for some books, pp. 252, 261, 268.

Griffith, Rev. S., quoted, pp. 250, 268, 269.

Grossetête, Bishop, his disinterested refusal of two palfreys which were offered him, p. 129, note t.

Gunn, Rev. John, his acquittal of H. from the charge of simony, p. 78, note s. See Appendix F., pp. 412—414.

Gymnosophistæ, H.'s use of the word, and its meaning, p. 32, and note o.

Gyrovagues, what they were, p. 138, note h, p. 267, note c.

Habitus, used to signify a monastic order, p. 200, and note i.

Haia or *haga*, p. 357, note h.

Hair, long, of men among the Normans censured and cropped by ecclesiastics, p. 93, note h.

Hall, Bishop, his account of the desecration of Norwich Cathedral by the Puritans, p. 317, note d.

Hallam, quotations from, p. 36, note x.

Ham, his preservation in the ark of magic and idolatry, p. 204, and note s; identified with Zoroaster, p. 204, note s.

Hardy, Sir T. Duffus, inserts H. in his Catalogue of Chancellors, pp. 326—328.

Harpsfeld, Nicholas, one of the authorities for H.'s life, Appendix D., XVIII. pp. 396—399.

Harrod, Mr., his opinion that the nave of Norwich Cathedral is a work of H.'s time, p. 119, note i; his description of the original Norman cloister, p. 185, note k.

Hawkins, Mr. Edward, reference to his work on the silver coins of England, p. 103, note s.

Hawkins, William, Prebendary of Norwich when H.'s tomb was restored, p. 332.

Healths, the ancient fashion of drinking, p. 11, note g.

Hemsby, p. 150.

Henry I., H.'s affection for him, p. 12; crowned at Westminster, p. 142; his method of reconciling people to his usurpation, p. 143; H.'s letter to him, p. 182; recalls Anselm, p. 143; reforms the manners of the court, *ibid.*; marries Matilda, the daughter of Malcolm, *ibid.*; quarrels with Anselm, p. 235; sends H. and two other prelates to the Pope, *ibid.*; ends the dispute about the consecration of Thomas of York, pp. 257—259; goes to Normandy to quell a revolt, p. 297; his return, *ibid.*

Henry of Huntingdon, one of the authorities of H.'s life, Appendix D., VI., pp. 371, 2.

Herbert de Losinga, the various names under which he goes, p. 1, and note a; his birthplace a disputed point, p. 4, Appendix A., pp. 349, 351, Appendix E., p. 409; Godwin's discrepancy with himself on the same subject, p. 4; the exact year of his birth doubtful, p. 5; speaks of himself as an old man at sixty, p. 6; his probable age at the time of the Norman Conquest, *ibid.*; striking incident connected with the question of investitures, about the time of his birth, *ibid.*; his father abbot of Winchester, p. 7; his letter to his only brother, *ibid.*, and p. 284, note p; received his education in Normandy, p. 8; a highly-cultivated man, p. 9; his appreciation of literature, pp. 10, 251, and note m; his letter to a learned layman, p. 10; his affection for Henry I., p. 12; the style of his letters praised by a learned layman, p. 14; vindicated from the charge of unchastity, p. 18; his interest in the boys Otto and Willelm, p. 19; renounces classical for theological studies, pp. 29, 30; the vision that warned him to discontinue classical studies, Letter XXVIII., p. 43; Prior of Fécamp, and authorities for his having filled that post, p. 54, and note p; his early devotional associations, pp. 56, 59; made Abbot of Ramsey, 1088, pp. 63, 69; duration of his abbacy, p. 69, note z; his affection for Fécamp, p. 63; his letters to Roger of Argences, *ibid.*; his desire to copy at Norwich the uses of Fécamp, p. 66; his name omitted in a list of abbots of Ramsey of the fourteenth century, and probable reason why, p. 69, note z; no allusion in his letters to his abbacy of Ramsey, pp. 70, 71; sources of his wealth, pp. 71, 72; sewer to William Rufus, p. 72; reasonableness of his appointment to the East Anglian see, pp. 76, 77; his act of simony, how palliated to his own conscience, pp. 77, 78; reasons for thinking that the charge of simony and deceitfulness was preferred against him on account of his joining with Anselm in the reformation of clerical abuses, Appendix F., pp. 412—414; the sums which he paid for enfeoffment to the East Anglian see, pp. 78, 79, and note t; his consecration by Thomas, Archbishop of York, pp. 80, 81; his ominous prognostic, p. 81; takes part in the consecration of Anselm, p. 82; this his only act as Bishop of Thetford, *ibid.*; proof of his penitence in his first epistle, p. 83; feels the infirmities of age at sixty, pp. 6, 85, 260; his resolve to resign the episcopal office to the Pope, pp. 88, 89; difficulties in the way of his going to the Pope, p. 90; of the two claimants to the papacy chooses Urban, *ibid.*; encounters the King at Hastings, 1094, p. 91; deprived of his pastoral-staff by the King, p. 92; his interview with Pope Urban, and its satisfactory result, p. 94; gains the Pope's sanction for the removal of the see to Norwich, p. 95; his alleged motives for moving the see to Norwich, p. 95, note l; alleged penance enjoined him by the Pope, p. 96; removes the see, with the body of William of Beaufeu, from Thetford to Norwich, April 9, 1094, pp. 96, 110; his authority according to Bale for the removal of the see, p. 97; makes no allusion in his extant writings to the Crusade, p. 99; lands granted him at Norwich for building his church by William II., p. 112; lands granted him by Henry I., p. 113; lays the foundation-stone of the cathedral, p. 114; assists Anselm in consecrating Gerard and Samson, p. 125; death of his father, 1098, p. 127; reference to his domestic loss in his letters, p. 128; evidence of his penitence in the foundation charter of the cathedral, p. 146; his friendship with the king and queen, pp. 153, 232; his refusal to restore Roger Bigot's body to the abbey of Thetford, pp. 167, note k, 233; his oath that Roger had given himself and family to the church at Norwich, *ibid.*, and p. 234; request made to him to consecrate the *atrium* of the new church at Thetford, p. 168; his excommunication of those who had killed his deer, pp. 171, 172; apologised for, p. 172, note t; supposed to have been Chancellor by Mr. Spurdens and Lord Campbell, p. 179, and note c; authorities for and against his being Chancellor, pp. 322—328; defends himself from the charge of being an over-strict disciplinarian, Letter XLVIII., p. 207; his letter to a youth in his monastery, defending himself from the charge of keeping the youth back in his studies, Letter XLII., p. 210; derangement in the numeration of his letters, p. 210, note f; preaches at Ely at the translation of St. Etheldreda's body, pp. 211, 215, 249, note l; inspects the body of St. Withburga, and addresses the people on the prodigy, p. 220; assists in consecrating five bishops, p. 223; his letter to Roger of Sarum defending himself from calumny, and begging that his Archdeacon Walter may be sent back to him, Letter XXI., pp. 226—228; another letter from him to Roger, begging his help in order to obtain the exemption of Thorpe from customs, Letter XXVI., p. 229; is sent on an embassy to the Pope by Henry I., respecting the quarrel with Anselm, pp. 235—242; is accompanied by the Archbishop of York and the Bishop of Chester, pp. 235, 239; is made prisoner by Count Guido on the charge of being on an errand unfavourable to Anselm, and clears himself by oath, p. 242; tries to obtain from the Pope jurisdiction over the abbey of St. Edmundsbury, p. 239; continues to be called Bishop of Thetford, p. 235, note z; his letter to Norman the Ostiary, describing some personal disaster under figure of a shipwreck, admitting himself in fault, and ending in repentance, Letter XII., pp. 243—247; his reference to Virgil, p. 244; his sensitiveness, which helped to deepen his repentance, shewn in Letter XII., pp. 247, note h, 248, 284; his liking for alliteration in his letters, p. 248, note i; his letter to Abbot Richard, reproaching him for neglecting him in adversity, begging for a renewal of friendship, and asking for the loan of some books, Letter X., pp. 248—252; dedicates the church of Sandridge, p. 250, note l; his attainments considerable, p. 251, note m; his request to have Suetonius translated, Letter V., pp. 64, 251, note m; is employed by Anselm to mediate between him and Thomas of York, pp. 253, 254; joins ten other bishops in a resolution to maintain the stand taken by Anselm, but gives way to please the King, p. 258; assists in consecrating Thomas of York, p. 259; is possibly talked of as Anselm's successor, p. 259; a flattering letter from Abbot Richard, and asking him to write a treatise in vindication of monasticism, Letter LIX., pp. 261—265; his letter in answer to Abbot Richard refusing to write, and saying that monks and clergy are on a level as to dignity, &c., and asking again for books, Letter LX., pp. 266—268; consecrates churches out of his own diocese, p. 269; assists in consecrating Theulf to the see of Worcester, and later on, Geoffry de Clive to Hereford, and Ernulf to Rochester, p. 271; his letter to Archbishop Ralph, begging him to fulfil his promise of visiting him at Norwich, Letter XXXVIII., p. 272; letter from Ralph, commending to his kindness some monks of Abingdon, p. 273; his last journey to Rome,—goes with Archbishop Ralph and the Abbot of Chertsey to consult the Pope about the dispute between the sees of Canterbury and York, pp. 274, 276, 277; falls ill at Placentia,

p. 276; fails in seeing the Pope, p. 277; his character described by Cotton, pp. 253, 254, 278; his longing for the ascetic life, and perception of the snare it might prove shewn by his letter to Wido the anchorite, Letter LVI., pp. 279, 280; his letters to William de Turbe, remonstrating with him for communicating the secrets of his conscience through a third person, and absolving him on hearing of his penitence, Letters XLII. (*bis*), and XLI., pp. 282—284; gives him a rule for mastering difficult study, p. 283; his letter to Robert, remonstrating with him for his fickleness, Letter XXXIII., pp. 284, 285; his letter to Richard (de Beames?), Bishop (of London?), to intercede for Hunfrid, an erring presbyter, Letter XXXI., pp. 286, 287; his letter to Godwin and William, reassuring them about their father's absence, Letter XXVII., p. 287; his letter to Odo, entreating him not to draw back from the monastic life, Letter XIII., p. 288; makes the Christian shield to be obedience, p. 289, note u; is imbued with the doctrines of Gregory VII., p. 290, note y; his affectionate letter to Hugh the Prior, asking for ink and parchment, p. 296; probably the spiritual counsellor of Queen Matilda, p. 298; his letter to her, Letter XXV., p. 298; he confuses Esther with the Queen of Sheba, p. 299, and note h; his resemblance to Homer, pp. 4, 299, note h; the prayer he writes for the Queen, pp. 303—313; corruption of the faith shewn in this prayer, p. 302; it is addressed throughout to St. John, p. 314, note z; formula at the close, p. 313, note z; the difference he brings out between the sacrificial and the sacramental aspects of the Holy Communion, p. 305, note m; his last recorded act to follow the Queen to the grave, p. 314; his death, 1119, p. 314; grief of the monks, *ibid.*; Cotton's lament for him, *ibid.*; is interred in his cathedral, p. 315; his monkish epitaph, pp. 315—318; word suggested for the *lacuna* in it, pp. 316, note b, and 317; its date, pp. 319, 320; first mentioned by Weever, p. 317; may have been written by W. de Turbe, pp. 319, 320; it was probably destroyed by the Puritans, p. 317; his tomb, notice of it by Sir Thomas Browne,

THE LIFE AND LETTERS.   437

p. 321 ; restored by Dean Sharpe and six prebendaries, pp. 329, 331, 332; epitaph written by Dean Prideaux, pp. 329, 330; tomb taken down by Dean Pellew, p. 332 ; question of his being Chancellor, different authorities upon it, pp. 322—328 ; the churches built by him, pp. 150, 332, 333 ; his literary remains according to Bale, p. 333 ; none remaining except sermons and letters, *ibid.*; service at Norwich Cathedral in memory of his death, pp. 334—343, Appendix B., 352—355 ; appropriate coincidence possibly found by the monks in the date of the day of his death, p. 334, note p; the high estimation in which he was held by the Norwich monks mentioned by Weever, p. 345 ; general view of him, pp. 345—347 ; the authorities for his history, arranged in chronological order, Appendix D., pp. 357—409.
Herbert d'Auxerre, p. 334.
Herfast, the Conqueror's chaplain, the exposure of his ignorance by Lanfranc, p. 74 ; nominated to the see of Elmham, 1070, p. 75 ; prognostic at his consecration, *ibid.*; his transference of the East Anglian see to Thetford, p. 110.
Hermits: see Anchorites.
Herod the Great, his cruelty, and the horrible disease which cut him off, p. 172, note s.
Hervé le Breton, Abbot of Ely, the first bishop, p. 250, note l.
Hexameter lines, occurrence of a couple in H.'s letters, p. 34, and note v.
Hildebrand, his advice to Leo IX. as to the right method of receiving the papal dignity, p.6. See Gregory VII.
Hilgay, p. 149.
Hindolveston, p. 148.
Hindringham, p. 148.
Hodges, Nathaniel, prebendary of Norwich when H.'s tomb was restored, p. 332.
Holinshed, quoted, p. 93, note h; his list of the Chancellors in the reign of Henry I., pp. 324, 325, note l.
Holocaustum, the Host so called, p. 181, note f.
Holy Communion, its sacrificial and sacramental aspects, distinction between them brought out by H., p. 305, note m.
Homersfield, H.'s park at, p. 171 ; etymology of the name, p. 171, note r ; its early connexion with the see of the East Angles, *ibid.*

Hook, Dean, quoted, p. 235, note z ; his remarks on the decrees of the synod of London upon the celibacy of the clergy, p. 252 ; his account of the delay in appointing a successor to Anselm, pp. 259, 260 ; remarks on regular canons, p. 262, note s ; remarks on the spirit of Gregory VII., p. 290, note y.
Hopper, Archdeacon, reference to his letters, p. 4 ; his letters on the name *Losinga,* Appendix A., pp.349—352.
Horace, meaning of his proverb, "*pyris vesci Calaber jubet hospes,*" p. 136, note d.
Hoxne, p. 150.
Hugh, Abbot of Chertsey, goes to Rome with H., p. 276.
——— Earl of Chester, restores the monastic church of Chester, p. 235, note z.
——— Abbot of Clugni, p. 167, note k.
——— the Prior (of Thetford ?), H.'s letter to him, p. 296, Letter IV.
Hugo de Sto. Victore, on the eagle, p. 305, note n ; on the symbolism of the *infula,* p. 310, note u, ii. ; on the *Tractus,* p. 344, note q.
Humility, twelve grades of, as given by St. Bernard out of the Benedictine Rule, p. 190 ; as attributed to the B.V.M. by St. Bernard, p. 191 ; H.'s reference to, p. 193 ; his connexion of the Songs of degrees with the grades of humility, p. 193, and note s.
Hunfrid, H.'s intercession for, Letter XXXI., p. 286.
Huntingdon, Henry of: see Henry.
Hyde, abbacy of, at Winchester, purchased by H. for his father, p. 78, and note r.
Hyssop, H.'s use of the word, p. 33 ; its different forms of meaning in Scripture, &c., p. 33, note q.

Idolatry, preserved and disseminated by Ham, p. 204, and note s.
Idus, a mistake in Mr. Anstruther's edition for *secundum,* p. 283, note n.
Immorality of Anglo-Normans in H.'s time, p. 154.
Incaustum: see *Encaustum.*
Inclina, p. 344, note r.
Indictaminibus, Meis Indictaminibus pedes quæritis, the translation of these words only conjectural, p. 23, note u.
Inebriation, the mental and spiritual sense in which mediæval writers use the term, p. 196, note x.

In exitu, Psalm cxiv., appointed by the Sarum Ritual to be sung while the body was borne to the grave, p. 341, note h.

Infula, its use, and symbolism, p. 310, note u, ii.

Ing, the Saxon patronymic termination, p. 3.

Ingressa, term for *introit* in the Ambrosian Liturgy, p. 343, note n.

Ingulph, first Prior of Norwich, H.'s letters to him, pp. 131, 135, 138, 200, 203; outlived H., p. 135, note c; his anniversary on the 16th of January, *ibid.*

Ink: see *Encaustum*.

Ink-horn: see *Cornu*.

Instrumental music in churches censured by some priests in the twelfth century, p. 68.

Introits, mentioned as dates for the ecclesiastical seasons to which they are appropriated, p. 228, note r.

Introitus, term in the Roman Liturgy, p. 343, note n.

Investiture, ecclesiastics forbidden to receive, at the hands of a lay person, by the synod of Rome, 1075, p. 144.

Isabella of Valois, poem on her death, p. 335, note s.

Isidore of Seville, his works, p. 308, note s.

Janitor: see *Portarius* and *Ostiary*.

Jerome, St., the vision which moved him to renounce pagan literature, p. 47, note k; his account of St. John being thrown into boiling oil, p. 305, note o; on anchorites, p. 279, note i; quotations from, pp. 310, note u, ii., 311, note x.

Jessopp, Rev. Dr., his solution of the question about the *Romanus mimus*, p. 85, note z.

Joannes Climacus: see John of the Ladder.

John, St., tradition of his being the bridegroom at Cana, and forsaking his bride to follow Christ, p. 304, note l; this tradition accepted by the Mahometans, *ibid.*; mentioned by Fabricius, and other writers, *ibid.*; a late tradition unknown to the Fathers, *ibid.*; Archbishop Trench quoted on this tradition, *ibid.*; legend of his being thrown into boiling oil, pp. 305, 306, note o; his raising the dead to life, pp. 306, 307, note q; his drinking poison without harm,—this legend preserved in the mediæval emblem of the cup with the serpent issuing from it, p. 307, note r; his turning stones into jewels, and boards into gold, pp. 307, 308, note s; his death, and burial at Ephesus, pp. 309, 310, and notes t, u; his virginity, pp. 303, 304, and note l, 311, and note x; St. Ambrose on, p. 311, note x; St. Anselm's meditation on, *ibid.*

John, a learned lay correspondent of H.'s, p. 10, Letter XLV.; his letter to H., p. 13, Letter LVIII.; how consolatory it had been to John under bereavement, p. 14; yields precedence in all points to H., p. 16; asks H.'s prayers for the soul of his deceased mother, *ibid.*; compares their friendship to that of Orestes and Pylades, p. 15, and note m; his knowledge of the classical story probably derived from Ovid, p. 16, note m.

John Dalie, Abbot of Fécamp, 1031—1082, pp. 59, 60; called Little John, p. 60; his prayer on entering the office of abbot, *ibid.*; extract from the preface of a devotional work of his, p. 61; his correspondence with the Conqueror, *ibid.*; probably abbot while H. was prior, p. 62; his death, *ibid.*

John, King, and the Abbot of Canterbury: see Canterbury.

John of the Ladder, his description of accidy, p. 38, note z.

John the Presbyter, sepulchre assigned to him at Ephesus, p. 311, note u, ii.

Josephus, on the building of Solomon's temple and palace, quoted, p. 162, note f; read by H., p. 251, note m; first printed edition in Latin, *ibid.*

Jubilee, H.'s reference to, p. 129; reflections on H.'s proposed restoration of Rodbert's palfrey in the, p. 129, note u.

Justiciaries, their office, p. 168, note m; institution and office of Chief Justiciar, *ibid.*

Justin, derives his history from Trogus, p. 157, note a.

Kay, Dr., on Psalm xvii. 15, p. 316, note c.

Kemble, on the origin of names in the Marches, Appendix A., p. 350.

Kidder, Richard, Prebendary of Norwich when H.'s tomb was restored, p. 332; afterwards Bishop of Bath and Wells, *ibid.*; killed, *ibid.*

THE LIFE AND LETTERS. 439

King's College Chapel, its windows purchased with the forfeited property of Bishop Nix, p. 174, note u.
Knighton, Henry, one of the authorities for Herbert's history, Appendix D., XII., p. 386.

Lady-chapel, of Norwich Cathedral, original one corresponded to the Jesus Chapel and St. Luke's, p. 121; destroyed by fire in 1171, *ibid.*; rectangular one substituted by Bishop Suffield, *ibid.*; destroyed by Dean Gardiner, *ibid.*
Lakenham, p. 148.
Lammas-day, when it falls, and etymology of the word, p. 32, note l.
Lanfranc, his skill in Logic, p. 35, note w; quotation from, on the unsuitability of profane literature for the study of a bishop, p. 44, note g; his exposure of Herfast's ignorance, p. 74; his exile from Normandy, and the revocation of it, pp. 74, 75; disallows the exemption from episcopal control granted by the Pope to the abbey of St. Edmund's, but afterwards confirms it, pp. 239, 240; his death, in 1089, p. 73.
Langham, p. 150.
Lanzo, Abbot of Lewes, p. 167, note k; sends twelve monks to start Roger Bigot's new establishment at Thetford, *ibid.*
Latin verses of boys criticized by H., pp. 27, 28; H. himself has given them up for graver studies, pp. 29, 30.
Learning, revival of in France, early in the eleventh century, p. 8.
Lectionary, what it was, its compilation attributed to St. Jerome, p. 268, note f.
Leland, referred to, p. 69, note z; his description of St. Edmund's Abbey, p. 240, note c; one of the authorities for H.'s history, Appendix D., XIV., pp. 387, 388.
Leo II., Pope, Leonine verses attributed to, p. 319.
Leonard, St., church of, built by H. in Thorpe Wood, p. 150.
Leonine verses, their origin, pp. 319, 320; Sir A. Croke on, p. 320, note e.
Leonius, Canon of Notre Dame, Leonine verses attributed to him, p. 319, and note e; his authorship questioned, p. 319, note e.
L'Estrange, Mr. J., his correction of Blomefield as to the situation of the foundation-stone of the cathedral, pp. 115, 116.

Lewes, the earliest Cluniac foundation in England, p. 167, note k.
Liber Eliensis: see Eliensis.
Lichfield, Peter, Bishop of: see Peter.
Lignum, the word used for "tablets" both by classical and mediæval writers, p. 198, and note c.
Lincy, M. le Roux de, no mention made by him of H.'s priorate in his *Essai sur l'Abbaye de Fécamp*, p. 54, note p; etymology of the name Fécamp given by him, p. 57, note q; his quotation from Archbishop Baudry's encomium of Fécamp, *ibid.*; the ground-plan given by him of the church at Fécamp, p. 66.
Lixa, its meaning and derivation, p. 292, note b; *lix* used by Pliny, *ibid.*
Loans, of books, exchanged in the Middle Ages, p. 251, notes m and n.
Locutory, usually two in monasteries, according to Fosbroke, p. 207, note a; the *minuti* had the indulgence of going there, *ibid.*; where the *locutory* of the Norwich Cathedral monastery formerly stood, *ibid.*; a description of the Norman chamber supposed to have been the *locutory*, p. 208, note a. See also *Auditorium*.
Loes, hundred of, p. 3, Appendix A., pp. 349—351.
Logic, H.'s high estimate of, p. 54.
Losing, Robert de, spoken of by Blomefield as the father of H., Appendix A., pp. 349, 351; Bishop of Hereford (?), p. 2, note b; Appendix A., p. 351.
Losinga, the word connected with Harpsfeld with "glosing," p. 2; reason for doubting the etymology of the word, pp. 2, 3; the same name borne by a contemporary bishop of Hereford, p. 2, note b (see Losing); the authors' view of the true etymology, p. 3, Appendix A., p. 351; Mr. Beloe's view, Appendix E., p. 409.
Losinga, Robert, father of H., Appendix A, p. 349; made abbot of Hyde, p. 78, and note r; died 1098, p. 127; reference to his death in H.'s letters, p. 128.
Lothingland, hundred of, in East Suffolk, p. 3, Appendix A, p. 349.
Loveland, Joseph, prebendary of Norwich when H.'s tomb was restored, p. 331.
Lovelly's Stathe, its situation, p. 112.
Lucian, a priest of Caphargamala, p. 215, note i; his vision, *ibid.*, and p. 375, note o; writes an account of St. Stephen's translation, p. 216, note i.

Lyhart, Bishop, stone roof of the nave and choir proper built by him, p. 120.
Lynn, p. 150; church at, built by H., pp. 332, 333.

Magdebourg, Centuriators of, one of the authorities for H.'s history, Appendix D., XVI., p. 391.
Magic, preserved in the ark, and disseminated after the flood by Ham, p. 204, note s.
Magna Britannia, quoted, pp. 69, note a, 71, notes b, c.
Maitland, Rev. S. R., reference to his "Dark Age View of Profane Learning," p. 45, note h; his story of Alcuin's being threatened by infernal chiropodists, and the effect it had upon him, p. 49, note k; his notice of Abbot Little John, of Fécamp, pp. 60, 61; his extract from the Benedictine Rule, p. 188, &c.; quotation from, on the subject of mediæval signatures, p. 151, note x; his remarks on binding mediæval books, p. 251, note n.
Majusculæ litteræ, the meaning of, p. 114, note d.
Malgod, first Prior of Thetford, pp. 164 and 167, note k.
Malmesbury, William of: see William.
Manuscript, the Brussels, an unintelligible sentence found at the beginning of Letter XL., p. 31, note k.
Mark, values of, at different periods, p. 99, note p.
Marriage of persons related within the seventh degree forbidden by the Council of Westminster, p. 161; clerical, not considered a stigma until late in the eleventh century, p. 18; lax view taken of the restrictions of, in H.'s days, p. 161; H.'s decision upon, in a case referred to him, *ibid.*
Marriott, Rev. Wharton, quoted, p. 310, note u, ii.
Martham, p. 149.
Martin, his "History of Thetford," referred to for an account of the foundation of Thetford Abbey, pp. 166, 167, note k.
Martyrs, H.'s assertion that the 144,000 in Rev. vii. and xiv. are of this character, p. 180, note e.
Mary Magdalen, St., H. dies on the festival of, p. 334, and note p.
Maskell, Mr., quoted, p. 336, note u.
Massingberd, Chancellor, his remarks on the claims of Gregory VII., p. 290, note y.

Matilda, Queen, letter to her from H., Letter XXV., pp. 298—302; H. her spiritual counsellor, p. 298; prayer composed for her by H., Letter XVIII., pp. 303—313; Miss Strickland's account of her, p. 299, note i; her death, p. 297.
Mellent, Robert, Count of: see Robert.
Michael, St., situation of the land of, granted to H. for his church, p. 113; his presence sued for in a prayer from the *Commendatio animarum*, p. 340, note g.
Michel, Dan, quotation from his *Ayenbite of Inwyt*, p. 39, note z.
Millennium, H. represents Satan as loosed *during*, not *after*, p. 205.
Milton, his hymn on the Nativity quoted, pp. 159, 160, note d.
Mimus: see *Romanus mimus*.
Minoro, a non-classical word used by H., p. 34, note t.
Minutio, the monastic blood-letting, reasons of its attractiveness to the monks, pp. 107, 108, note y.
Misericordia Domini, introit mentioned by H. as the date of a synod, p. 228, note r.
Monachus, H.'s derivation of, p. 267, note c.
Monasticism, absorbs into itself all the ideas of the Christian profession, p. 262, note r.
"Monk," meaning of the name, p. 267, note c; different kinds of, *ibid.*
Morrison, Mr., quotation from his Life of St. Bernard, p. 44, note h.
Mosheim, quotations from, p. 35, note w.
Mozley, Canon, on the Church's claim of temporal authority, p. 291, note y.

Nard: see Spikenard.
Nevers, its exemption from customs, granted by the Frank kings, p. 230, note u.
Neville, Alexander, quoted, pp. 114, note d, 270, 323, note g; one of the authorities for H.'s life, Appendix D., XVII., pp. 392—398.
Newnham, church at, dedicated by H., p. 269.
Newton, p. 150.
Nicholas the deacon, H.'s notice of, p. 202; charges brought against him by the Fathers, *ibid.*, note o.
Nicodemus, buried at Caphargamala, p. 215, note i.
Nieveham: see Newnham.
Nix, Bishop, the sculptured stone roof of the transept built by him in the sixteenth century, p. 120; incurs

præmunire for infringing the Dean of Thetford's prerogative, p. 174, note u.
Norman the Ostiary, letters to, I., p. 83; VI., pp. 155—160, XII., pp. 243—247; aspires to priest's orders, pp. 156, 247, note g; probably called Ostiary from having held the post, p. 247, note g.
Normandy, causes of the revival of learning there in the beginning of the eleventh century, p. 8; English boys sent there to be educated, p. 9.
Northona: see Norton.
Norton, church at, dedicated by H., p. 269.
Norwich Cathedral, its uses and customs founded on those of Fécamp, p. 65; the foundation-stone laid, p. 114; parts of the present cathedral due to H., pp. 117, 118; nave as well as choir, according to Mr. Harrod, due to H., p. 119, note i; choir and transept of, had originally wooden roofs, p. 120; its original Lady-chapel destroyed in 1171, p. 121; rectangular one substituted for it, but demolished by Dean Gardiner, *ibid.*; foundations of both Lady-chapels still exist, *ibid.*; slow progress of the building, p. 130; servants of the King as well as of the Bishop spoken of as engaged in it, *ibid.*; H.'s censure of the monks for their slackness in building, p. 131, &c.; consecration and dedication of, Sept. 24, 1101, p. 145; foundation charter of, p. 146; made the mother church of Norfolk and Suffolk, p. 147; desecration in it by the Puritans, p. 317, note d.
Norwich Cathedral Monastery, its plan, p. 185; its original Norman cloister, p. 185, note k; this cloister destroyed in A.D. 1272, p. 186; monastery built for sixty monks, *ibid.*
Norwich, plague at, p. 270; church and hospital dedicated to St. Paul the Apostle and St. Paul the Hermit, built by H., p. 279, note i; completed by Bishop Everard, and consecrated by Archbishop Theobald, p. 279, note i.
Norwich *Ordinale*, service in, in memory of H.'s death, p. 334, Appendix B., p. 352.

Obit, original meaning of, p. 335, note s; to make an, *ibid.*
Obtundo, p. 263, note u.

Odibiles: see *Deo odibiles*.
Odo, St., of Cluny, an anecdote of, p. 44, note h.
Odo, letter to him from H., urging him not to draw back from the monastic life, Letter XIII., p. 288.
Officinæ: see *Regulares*.
Officium, term for introit in the Missal of Sarum, p. 343, note n.
Omnipotens sempiterne Deus, collect from the Ritual of Sarum, p. 341, and note i.
Onager, proverb in which this word occurs, p. 26, note b.
Oraculum divinum, the moral apophthegm to which H. gives this name, p. 87, and note b.
Orationes pro defunctis, pp. 336, 337.
Ordericus Vitalis, his account of H., pp. 63, 108, note y, Appendix D., IV., 365, 366.
Ordinale: see Norwich *Ordinale*.
Ordinary, power of, to allow any bishop to exercise episcopal functions in a peculiar which was extradiocesan, p. 270.
Organ, description of the organ in Fécamp Church, p. 68.
Orleans, Charles, Duke of, his poem on the death of Isabella of Valois, p. 335, note s.
Orosius, compiles his history from Justin, p. 157, note a; probably referred to by H. when he speaks of Pompeius, pp. 157, 158, note a.
Osbern, Abbot, his ingenuity in handicrafts, p. 8, note d.
Osbert, first Archdeacon of Norwich, pp. 226, 227, notes p and q.
Ostiary, ecclesiastical and conventual meanings of the word, p. 83, note x.
Otto and Willelm, letters to, pp. 19, 20, 22, 24, 29, 31, 35, 37, 43, and probably 282.
Ovid, H.'s commendation of his style, p. 23; the *Tristia* of, borrowed from by H. in Letter X., p. 249, note j.
Oxunensis pagus, mentioned by Bale as H.'s birthplace, p. 4.
Oxymensis pagus, supposed to be Exmes or Hiesmes in Normandy, pp. 4, 322, 328, 329, and note n.

Pacentantes, vanis pacentantes manibus: see *Parento*.
Palace, episcopal, of Norwich, built by H., p. 162; why on the north of the cathedral, *ibid.*
Palfrey, H.'s reason for keeping that which Rodbert had lent him, p. 129.

Palinurus, H.'s reference to, p. 39, and note a; whence named, p. 244, note f.
Palls, by whom worn, p. 239, note b; decree of the Lateran Council respecting, *ibid.*; heraldic representation of, *ibid.*
Papa, or Pope, in the first instance applied to all bishops, p. 266, note b.
Parchment, invented by Eumenes II., King of Pergamus, p. 296, note g. See *Pargomentum.*
Parento, H.'s use of the word, and its meaning, p. 32, and note n.
Pargomentum, its original form, p. 296, note g; the nearest approximation to our word "parchment," *ibid.*
Parker, Mr., quoted, p. 273.
Parochia, its original meaning and derivation, pp. 170, note p, 255, note o.
Paschal II., accession to the papal throne, 1099, p. 130; re-instates Abbot Richard of Ely, p. 212; temporises between Henry I. and Anselm, pp. 234, 236; offers the pall to Ralph, Archbishop of Canterbury, p. 275; is obliged to fly to Beneventum, p. 277; dies, p. 297.
Pasnagium, its two significations, p. 356, note g.
Patrick, Bishop, quoted on the subject of Ham, p. 204, note s.
Paul, St., church of, at Norwich: see Norwich.
—— the first hermit, p. 279, note i.
Pellew, Dean, causes H.'s monument to be taken down, p. 332.
Pentapolis, or cities of the plain, H.'s reference to, p. 157.
Pergamena, from Pergamus: see *Pargomentum.*
Perowne, Rev. J. J. S., his description of the Songs of degrees, p. 194, note s.
Peter, St., Festival of his Chains, p. 31, and note l; occasion of its institution, *ibid.*
Peter the Venerable, Abbot of Clugni, 1122, his account of the invasion of the monastery by his predecessor Pontius, p. 166, note i; his commendation of acquaintance with profane learning, p. 192, note o.
Peter, Bishop of Lichfield, transfers his cathedral from Lichfield to Chester, p. 235, note z.
Peterborough Cathedral, a description of its Norman roof, p. 120, note k.

Phaleræ, its meanings and derivative *faleratæ,* p. 86, note a.
Philip, St., and his daughters, buried at Hierapolis, p. 311, note u, ii.
Philipot, J., Somerset Herald, his list of Chancellors, p. 324, and notes j, k, l.
Philosophy, change of its aspect in the middle of the eleventh century, and to whom due, p. 35, note w.
Pisticus, its derivation and meaning, p. 315, note a.
Pits, John, one of the authorities for H.'s life, Appendix D., XX., p. 399.
Placebo, what it was, p. 337, note a.
Placitum, the origin of the word, p. 176, note b; an essential element of the feudal system, *ibid.*; seasons for holding *placita,* p. 177, note b; vexations connected with, *ibid.*; derivative meanings of the word, pp. 178, note b, 229, note t.
Plantis non sidentibus, used by H. of Christ's walking upon the waters, and coincidence of the expression with one in his sermons, p. 41, and note e.
Play upon words, in H.'s letters, pp. 202, note p, 207, note z.
Plumptre, Professor, on the symbolic cup with the serpent issuing from it, in the mediæval representations of St. John, p. 307, note r.
Plumstead, p. 150.
Polycarp, buried in Smyrna, p. 311, note u, ii.
Polycrates, Bishop of Ephesus, his mention of St. John and other saints in his writings, p. 310, note u, ii.
Polydorus Vergilius, one of the authorities for H.'s history, Appendix D., XIII., p. 387.
Pompeius, Trogus, his date, and his universal history, p. 157, note a.
Pontius, Abbot of Clugni, his acts of spoliation, p. 166, note i.
Portarius, the porter of a monastery, p. 83, note x.
Porter, his office in Benedictine monasteries, p. 84, note x.
Possevino, Antonio, one of the authorities for H.'s life, Appendix D., XIX., p. 399.
Præpositus, regius, his office, p. 175, note x; held by Athselinus with the priesthood, *ibid.*
Precatory absolution: see Absolution.
Precious Blood, legend of the, pp. 55, 57, 58; mass of the, pp. 58, 59.
Prideaux, Dean, his MS. book containing extract from the Cartulary of St. Edmund's Abbey, p. 243,

note d; admitted Prebendary of Norwich, p. 321; his account of H.'s life in a letter to John Ellis, pp. 321, 322; restores H.'s monument, pp. 321, 322, 329, 331, 332; his epitaph for H., pp. 329, 330.
Primicerius, its meaning and derivation, p. 217, note l.
Prior, Dean Church's account of the office in Norman monasteries, p. 199.
Procuratores ecclesiæ, what officers so named, p. 200, note h.
Prognostic, meaning of the word, p. 75; at Herfast's consecration, *ibid*.; at H.'s consecration, pp. 81 and 368, note m.
Property, forbidden to monks by the Rule of St. Benedict, pp. 139, note i, and 198, note e; the episcopal, reimbursed by H. for what he had taken from it as an endowment to the monastery, pp. 150, 151.
Proverb, H.'s, about a large stock of honey, pp. 135, 136; its source unknown to the authors, *ibid*., note d.
Provost, or *præpositus*, his office, p. 25, and note x; meanings and uses of the word, p. 175, note x.
Prudentius, quotation from, in which he uses the word "anathēma," p. 134, note b.
Psallo, its original and derived meanings, pp. 175, 176, note z.
Psalm xvii. 15, allusion to it in H.'s epitaph, p. 316, note c; Dr. Kay on, *ibid*.
Psalter, the meaning of the word, p. 198, note a.
Pulla tunica, derivation of *pullus*, p. 295, note d.
Puritans, desecration by the, in Norwich Cathedral, p. 317, and note d.

Quadrivium, H.'s use of the word, and its meaning, p. 36, note x.

Ralph of Escures, Archbishop of Canterbury, p. 260; letter to him from H., p. 272; writes to H. commending to him some Abingdon monks, p. 273; renews the dispute for supremacy with the see of York, pp. 273, 274; refuses to consecrate Thurstan, *ibid*.; goes to Rome with H., p. 276; his illness on the way, *ibid*.
Ralph the Firebrand: see Flambard.
Ramsey, duration of H.'s abbacy at, p. 69, note z; derivation of the name, pp. 69, 70, note a; the monks of, privileged to choose their own abbot, p. 70; device and legend adopted by one of the abbots of, p. 71; called Ramsey the Rich, *ibid*.; the place became poor after the destruction of the abbey, *ibid*., note b; property of the abbey in Norfolk and Suffolk, p. 77, note o.
Redamo, coined by Cicero, p. 248, note i.
Redamor, coined by H., p. 248, note i.
Redburn, church of, dedicated by H., p. 269.
Registrum, its meaning and derivation, p. 84, note y.
Registrum primum, quotation from, as to the part of the cathedral built by H., p. 116, note g; one of the sources for the history of H., Appendix D., X., p. 384.
Regulares officinæ, what it means, p. 203, note q.
Relatione: see *Religione*.
Religione, possible meaning of the word in Letter XVI., with Chancellor Benson's conjecture as to the right reading, p. 105, note v.
Repræsento, its meaning, p. 182, note g.
Requiem æternam, p. 343, note n.
Respondit, meorumque verborum ludo me sanativum fieri tuæ interrogationis desiderio, Respondit, an untranslateable passage as it stands, p. 28, note d.
Rhyming verses, quoted by Cicero from Ennius, p. 319, note e; Sir A. Croke on, p. 320, note e. See Leonine verses.
Richard, Abbot of St. Alban's, is present at St. Etheldreda's translation, p. 250, note l; may have been H.'s correspondent, pp. 250, note l, 269.
Richard the Archdeacon, p. 7, Letter LIV.; the son of William de Beaufeu and Agnes of Todeni, pp. 115, 226, note p.
Richard de Beames, Bishop of London, H. intercedes with him for a priest, Hunfrid, pp. 285—287, Letter XXXI.; is consecrated by Anselm, p. 285.
Richard, Abbot of Ely, completes the church of Ely, pp. 211, 212; is deposed by Henry I., p. 211; is restored by the Pope, p. 212; translates St. Etheldreda's body, p. 212, &c.; translates the bodies of four other saints, pp. 217—222; his history, p. 249, note l; possibly the *Riccardus Abbas* of H.'s letters, pp. 223, 261; his letter to H., asking

him to write a vindication of monasticism, Letter LIX., pp. 261—265; H.'s letters to him, Letter X., p. 248, Letter LX., p. 266.
Richard the Fearless, Duke of Normandy, his foundation of Fécamp Abbey, p. 55.
Robert, H.'s father called Robert Herbert by Mr. Spurdens, p. 1, note a.
Robert, a monk of the cathedral monastery, educated by H., who writes to him as his brother and son, Letter XXXIII., p. 284, and note p.
Robert Belesme: see Robert Courthose.
Robert Courthose, allies himself with Robert Belesme, Earl of Shrewsbury, against Henry I., in 1105, p. 178; defeated at Tinchebray in 1106, p. 179; his captivity and death, *ibid.*
Robert of Limesey, Bishop of Lichfield, often called Bishop of Chester, p. 235, note z; transfers his cathedral from Chester to Coventry, thence to Lichfield, *ibid.*; goes with H. on an embassy to the Pope, *ibid.*
Robert, Count of Mellent, takes part with Thomas of York, and opposes Anselm's letter, pp. 257, 258.
Robertson the historian, his charge of ignorance against eminent persons in the Middle Ages, how answered by Mr. Maitland, p. 151, note x.
Rocherio, Geoffry de, particulars taken from his history of Thetford Priory, p. 167, note k.
Rodbert, Bishop, H.'s commendations of his hospitality, p. 128.
Roger of Argences, succeeds William de Ros as Abbot of Fécamp, p. 63; his intimacy with Archbishop Baudry, p. 63.
Roger of Sarum, obtains Henry the First's favour, pp. 224, 300, 301, note k; his rapid rise, becomes Bishop of Salisbury, *ibid.*; Chancellor and Chief Justiciary, *ibid.*; is dismissed before Henry's death, p. 301, note k; breaks his oath to Matilda, and supports Stephen, pp. 224, 225, 301, note k; quarrels with Stephen, but submits, *ibid.*; dies, pp. 225, 302; H.'s letter to him, asking his help in the matter of the exemption of Thorpe from customs, pp. 229, 230.
Roman de Rou, quotation from, on the grievances to which mediæval vassals were exposed, p. 177, note b.
Romanus mimus, question as to whom H. meant by this expression, p. 85, note z.
Rye, Hubert de, lays the second stone of the cathedral, p. 114; his father, Duke William's ambassador to Edward the Confessor, *ibid.*, note e; castellan of Norwich Castle, p. 115; marries Agnes, widow of William de Beaufeu, Bishop of Thetford, pp. 115, 226, note p.
Rye, Mr. Walter, quoted, pp. 115, note f, 226, note p.

Sac and *soc*, the surrender of, meaning and derivation, p. 231, note *.
Sacerdos, a more honourable term than presbyter, p. 272, note h; chiefly applied to the second order of the ministry, *ibid.*
Sacramentum, used in the sense of a mystery, p. 158, and note b.
Sacrifice, a propitiatory, in the Mass, asserted by H., p. 45, note i.
Sacri libri: see *Scriptura sacra.*
Samson and Roger, H.'s letter to, Letter XX., p. 52.
St. Albans, the abbots of, independent of their diocesan, p. 269.
St. Edmundsbury: see Bury.
Sanctimonia, its classical and mediæval meanings, and its etymology, pp. 103, 104, note t.
Sancto Victore: see Hugo de S. V.
Sandridge, St. Leonard's church at, consecrated by H., p. 250, note l; extract from the baptismal register of, *ibid.*
Santon Downham, in the deanery of Thetford, p. 173, note u.
Sarabites, derivation of the name, p. 267, note c; what they were, *ibid.*; mentioned by H. in his rule, *ibid.*; distich about them, mentioned by Cassian, *ibid.*; their spiritual descent traced to Ananias and Sapphira, *ibid.*
Sarum, Roger of: see Roger.
Sarum, Missal of, form of precatory absolution in, p. 336, note u; prayer for bishops in, p. 336, note x; collects, &c., in, pp. 336, 337, notes x, y, z.
Satan, loosed, according to H., *during* the millennium, p. 205.
Satiabor, its meaning, p. 316, note c.
Saturnalia, H.'s use of the word, p. 32, and note m.
Sciphus, meanings of the word, p. 201, note k.
Scriptoria, p. 282, note l.
Scriptura sacra, divina,—such phrases

used of religious books in general, pp. 196, note x, and 206, note y.
Scudamore, Rev. W., *Notitia Eucharistica*, quoted, p. 305, note m.
Scutum, its meaning, p. 289, note u.
Scylla and Charybdis, H.'s reference to, pp. 39, and note a, 245, 246.
Secular canons: see Canons.
Sedulius, H.'s reference to, p. 19; date and works of, *ibid.*, note p.
See of the East Angles, removal of, from Thetford to Norwich, in conformity with the custom of the time, pp. 122, 123; ascribed to different dates, *ibid.*; reasons which justified it, p. 123; H.'s motives in the transference not necessarily ambitious, pp. 123, 124; synodical decision on the transference of the see from Elmham to Thetford, p. 125.
Sempringham, monastic house at, statutes about writing in, p. 282, note i.
Senatores, the elders in the Revelation so styled by H., p. 183, note h.
Seneschal, meaning of the word, and its distinction from *sewer*, p. 72, note d.
Serpentibus perierunt, Rhemish translation of, p. 209, note e.
Service in Norwich Cathedral, in memory of H.'s death, p. 334.
Services for the dead, pp. 336—340, and notes.
Servius, H.'s reference to, p. 20; his grammatical works, p. 20, note r.
Sewer, meaning and derivation of the word, p. 72, note d.
Sexburga, Queen, her removal of St. Etheldreda's body, p. 211; her history, p. 222, note o; translation of her body, p. 218.
Sharpe, Dr. John, Dean of Norwich when H.'s tomb was restored, p. 331; afterwards Dean of Canterbury and Archbishop of York, *ibid.*
Sheba, Queen of, Arab name for, p. 299, note h.
Shield, Christian, H. makes it obedience, not faith, p. 289, and note u.
Shire, its meaning and derivation, p. 355, note a.
Si ambulem, p. 343, and note p.
Silence, the value set upon it by the Rule of Benedict, p. 193, note r.
Simon Magus, his legendary challenge to St. Peter, p. 79.
Simony, regulations made in English councils against, p. 78, note q; six abbots deposed on account of, *ibid.*, and p. 154; monkish verses on H.'s, with Mr. Parker's translation, pp.

79, 369; charge of, against H., possibly owing to the enmity he excited by attempting to reform ecclesiastical abuses, Appendix F., pp. 412—414.
Sinalimphis, eisdem vestris sinalimphis et barbarissimis infantiliter inhæretis, the translation of these words only conjectural, p. 23, note v.
Six, symbolism of the number, p. 27, and note c.
Smith, Rev. I. Gregory, on Benedictine dress: see Benedictine.
Snarehills, the two, in the deanery of Thetford, p. 173, note u.
Soldat, "soldier," whence derived, p. 103, note s.
Solidus, its meaning, value, and derivatives, p. 102, note s: see also p. 198, and note b.
Songs of degrees, term applied by H. to the grades of humility, p. 193, and note s; the progressive stages of the spiritual life found in them by Augustine, p. 194, note s; different explanations of this title, *ibid.*
Sou, whence derived, p. 103, note s.
Spatha, H.'s use of, its meanings and derivatives, p. 25, note a.
Spelling of names, uncertainty in, p. 22, note t.
Spelman, his mention of H. as Chancellor, in his Glossary, p. 326, and note m.
Spicatus: see *Pisticus*.
Spikenard, its derivation and meaning, p. 315, note a.
Spurdens, Rev. W. T., his view of H. as a surname, p. 1, note a; his conjecture that *pagus Oxunensis* is Hoxne probably correct, p. 5; his identification of William de Beaufeu with H., p. 73, note h.
Stacteus, a youth whom St. John raised from the dead, p. 307, note q.
Stannard, a monk of this name mentioned by H., pp. 64, note s, 302.
Stathe, meaning of the word, p. 112, note c.
Stephen, second Prior of Thetford in succession to Malgod, p. 167, note k; H.'s letter to him, p. 169; his character and acts, p. 169, note n.
Stephen, St., Feast of the Invention of, p. 215, note i; buried at Caphargamala, *ibid.*, and p. 375, note o; discovery of his relics, *ibid.*; translation to Jerusalem, *ibid.*
Strangers' hall, where situated in a Benedictine monastery, p. 208, note b; remains of, in the Norwich Cathedral monastery, *ibid.*

Strickland, Miss, her account of Queen Matilda, p. 299, note i.
Stubbs, Mr., his "Episcopal Succession in England," quoted, p. 271.
Stubbs, Thomas, quoted, p. 252; one of the authorities for the history of H., Appendix D., XI., p. 385.
"Substance," Rev. J. H. Blunt on the word, p. 313, note y.
Substantia, used by H. to express the complex of the divine attributes, p. 313, note y.
Subvenite, from the *Commendatio Animarum*, p. 339, note d.
Suckling, his "History of Suffolk" referred to, p. 171, note r, 350.
Suetonius, H.'s desire for a copy of his works, p. 64 and 251, note m.
Sugillo, meaning of, p. 286, note q.
Suscipiat te, from the *Commendatio Animarum*, p. 339, note e.
Synalœpha, H.'s use, of the word, and its meaning, p. 23, and note v.
Synod of London, held by Lanfranc, 1075, its decree about the removal of sees, p. 95, and note l; held by Anselm and Thomas, Archbishop designate of York, 1108,—its decrees enforcing clerical celibacy, p. 252.
Synod at Westminster Abbey in 1102, pp. 153, 154; demanded by the accumulation of abuses, p. 154; deposes six abbots, *ibid.*; its enactments give an insight into the immorality of the times, *ibid.*; forbids marriage of those related within the seventh degree, p. 161.
Synods, episcopal, when held, p. 228, note r.

Tabula officialis, what it was, p. 336, note t.
Tabulæ dictales, corresponded to our slates, p. 8; manufactured by Abbot Osbern of St. Evroul, p. 8, note d.
Tamen, word suggested to fill the *lacuna* in H.'s monkish epitaph, p. 316, note b.
Taylor, Rev. Isaac, an extract from his "Words and Places" on the subject of Saxon immigrations, p. 3; on the terminations *field*, *feld*, p. 171, note r.
Temunah, p. 316, note c.
Tenure, four kinds of, recognised in the Norman law, p. 356, note b.
Tertullian, quoted, p. 306, note o.
Texts of Holy Scripture, misquoted or altered by H., pp. 205, 206, and note u.

Thefts in Norwich monastery, H.'s censure of, p. 201.
Theobald, Archbishop of Canterbury, consecrates St. Paul's Church at Norwich, p. 279, note i.
Theodosius the Great, H.'s allusion to him, p. 183; a notice of the chief incidents of his life, p. 183, note i.
Theosebia, its meaning, p. 268, note e.
Θεοστυγὴς, an active sense erroneously given to this adjective in the Authorized Version of Rom. i. 30, p. 208, note d.
Thetford, transference of the East Anglian see from Elmham to, p. 110; establishment there by H. of Cluniac monks, p. 163.
Thetford Abbey, the mausoleum of the East Anglian aristocracy, p. 164; monks of Lewes sent there by Lanzo, at Roger Bigot's request, p. 167, note k; dependent on the Abbot of Clugni, pp. 167, note k, 233; monks of, H.'s letters to, p. 168, &c., Letters II., VII., XXXV., XXXVII.
Thetford, deanery of, its institution, privileges, and jurisdiction, pp. 173, 174, note u; Bishop Nix incurs a *præmunire* for infringing the dean of Thetford's prerogative, p. 174, note u.
Theulf, Bishop of Worcester, H. assists in his consecration, p. 271.
Thirty, symbolism of the number, p. 27, and note c.
Thomas I., Archbishop of York, H.'s consecrator, p. 80; death of, p. 142.
Thomas II., Archbishop of York, holds a synod in London with Anselm, p. 252; will not recognise the authority of the see of Canterbury, and is therefore refused consecration by Anselm, pp. 253, 254; Anselm's letter to him, pp. 254—256; compromises the matter after Anselm's death, and is consecrated, pp. 258, 259; dies, p. 274.
Thomas Eliensis, one of the authorities for the history of H., Appendix D., VII., pp. 372—378.
Thompson, Mr. E. Maunde, his notes on Prideaux's letters to John Ellis, quoted, pp. 322, 323.
Thorpe, the manor granted to H. by William II. confirmed by Henry I., and by him made over to his monastery, pp. 113, 230, note x; its exemption from customs, H.'s letter respecting, pp. 229, 230, and note u, Letter XXVI.; the charter

THE LIFE AND LETTERS. 447

conferring it, p. 230, note x; translation of the charter, pp. 230—232, note x; names appended to it, p. 232, note x.
Thorpe Wood, its extent in H.'s time, p. 141, and note l; dedicated to the Holy Trinity, p. 141; mediety of, given by H. to his convent, p. 148.
Thurstan, Archbishop of York, refuses the oath of obedience to Canterbury, and is therefore not consecrated, p. 274; renounces the appointment, but retracts his resignation, and appeals to Paschal II., *ibid.* ; is consecrated at Rheims by Callixtus II., p. 297.
Thynne, quoted by Philipot, his mention of H. as Chancellor, p. 328.
Tipus or *typus*, p. 262, note t.
Topics of Aristotle, H.'s reference to them, p. 35 and note w.
Tract, or *tractus*, what it was, and its derivation, p. 344, note q.
Trench, Archbishop, on the Miracles, quoted, p. 303, note l; on the tradition of St. John being the bridegroom at Cana, p. 304, note l.
Trentals, p. 344, note r.
Trivium, H.'s use of the word, and its meaning, p. 36, and note x.
Tumba, its derivation and meaning, p. 334, note q.
Turbo, William, Bishop of Norwich, various forms of his surname, p. 281; its meaning, *ibid.* ; H.'s letters to him, Letters XLII. (*bis*), XLI., &c., pp. 282—284; Prior of the cathedral monastery, p. 281; excommunicates Hugh Bigod, *ibid.* ; begs alms for the repairs of the cathedral, *ibid.* ; buried in the cathedral, *ibid.* ; probably the author of H.'s monkish epitaph, p. 319.

Urban II., death of, 1099, p. 130.

Van Espen, his *Jus Ecclesiasticum Universum*, quoted, p. 270.
Via Sanctorum, p. 345, note s.
Vicini, quorum tanta est copia quo vicini nostri, an untranslateable passage as it stands, with the conjectural emendations of Bishop Wordsworth and Chancellor Benson, p. 25, note z.
Virgil, his description of Lake Avernus, quoted, p. 159, note c.
Virginity, the high value attached to it in H.'s letters, p. 104; various interpretations of the passage, in Rev. xiv. 1—4, touching on virginity, pp. 104, 105, note u; of St. John, p. 311, and note x.
Viscounts, appointment and functions of the officers so called, p. 24, note w.

Walter, an archdeacon of H.'s diocese, p. 227, note q.
Weever, his statement as to H.'s birthplace, p. 4; gives H.'s epitaph, p. 315; mentions the high estimation in which the Norwich monks held H., p. 345; one of the authorities for H.'s history, Appendix D., XXII., pp. 404—407.
Wido, the anchorite, H.'s letter to him, Letter LVI., p. 279.
William, St., of Norwich, site of his altar in the cathedral, pp. 116—118; account of his martyrdom from Capgrave's *Nova Legenda*, p. 117, note h; his chapel on Mousehold Heath, *ibid.*
William, son of Henry I., lost in the White Ship at the Catteraze, p. 298.
William of Malmesbury, one of the authorities for H.'s history, Appendix D., V., pp. 366—370.
William de Ros, succeeds Abbot John at Fécamp, 1082, p. 62; his character and surname of the " Maiden," *ibid.* ; the daily dole of Fécamp instituted by him, *ibid.*
William Rufus, occasion of his journey to Hastings in 1094, p. 91; his dedication of St. Martin's Church at Battle, p. 91; deprives H. of his pastoral office, p. 92; translation of the East Anglian see to Norwich effected during his absence in Normandy, p. 97; his saying as to Westminster Hall fulfilled, p. 122; death and burial of, p. 142.
William de Turbe : see Turbo.
William of Warelwast, sent by Henry I. and Anselm to Rome upon the investiture question, pp. 145, 223, 234; failure of the mission, p. 234; consecrated Bishop of Exeter, p. 223.
Willis, Professor, grounds of his opinion that the nave of Norwich Cathedral is later than the choir, p. 119, note i.
Wine and Milk, H.'s allegorising of these terms in Isaiah lv. 1, p. 10, note e.
Withburga, St., translation of her

body, p. 218, &c.; different dates of her translation, p. 221, note n; her history, p. 222, note o; well named after her at Dereham, p. 222, note o.

Wood, Anthony a, quoted, p. 326.

Wordsworth, Bishop Chr., his proposed emendation of the text of the epistles, p. 25, note z; his interpretation of a proverb in H.'s epistle, p. 26, note b; his interpretation of θεοστυγὴς, p. 209, note d.

Writing in monasteries, statutes respecting, p. 282, note i.

Wymondham, the cell of, given to St. Alban's Abbey, p. 269.

Yarmouth, p. 150; parish church of, a fruit of H.'s alleged penitence, pp. 96, 331, note o, 333.

Yates, Mr., his remarks on St. Edmund's Abbey, p. 240, note c.

Zoroaster, identified with Ham, p. 204, note s.

PASSAGES OF HOLY SCRIPTURE AND OF THE APOCRYPHA QUOTED OR REFERRED TO IN THE "LIFE AND LETTERS OF HERBERT DE LOSINGA."

⁎ n., *subjoined to the number of a page, indicates that the reference is to be sought, not in the text, but in the notes. In some cases the references to Scripture, though really made in the work, have not been indicated in the margin. The references in this Index are to the Authorised English Translation, not to the Vulgate.*

GENESIS.
i. 16, 17, p. 87.
iii. 6, p. 204.
ix. 22, p. 204, n. s.
xviii. 4, 5, 8, 10, p. 127.
xix. 2, 3, 16, p. 128 ; 5, 31, p. 158.
xxxi. 40, p. 27.
xxxiii. 13, p. 207.
xli. 42, 43, p. 176.
xlix. 4, p. 42, n. f.

EXODUS.
ii. 3, 10, p. 30.
iii. 2, p. 30.
vii. 19, &c., p. 30.
xii. 22, p. 33, n. q ; 37, p. 70, n. a.
xv. 19, p. 30.
xvi. 15, p. 30.
xvii. 6, p. 217.
xx. p. 30.
xxv. 31, p. 201, n. k.
xxxiii. 11, p. 87.
xxxix. 32, p. 30.

LEVITICUS.
xiv. 4, p. 33, n. q.
xxv. 13, p. 129, n. u.

NUMBERS.
xii. 8, p. 316, n. c.
xvi. 27, 33, p. 172.
xviii. 20, p. 267, n. d.
xix. 6, p. 33, n. q.

DEUTERONOMY.
xviii. 2, p. 267, n. d.
xxxii. 9, p. 267, n. d ; 17, p. 157.

RUTH.
i. 20, p. 280.

1 SAMUEL.
iii. 12, 13, 18, p. 42.
xvi. 16, 23, p. 68.

2 SAMUEL.
xiii. 15, p. 42, n. f.

1 KINGS.
iv. 33, p. 33, n. q.
vii. 1, p. 162.
x. 1, p. 62 ; 5, p. 299.

2 KINGS.
v. 14, p. 133 ; 27, p. 134.

2 CHRONICLES.
ix. 1, 4, p. 299.

NEHEMIAH.
iv. 17, p. 134.

JOB.
iii. 4, 5, p. 314.
iv. 18, p. 204.

PSALMS.
ix. 7, p. 160.
xii. 1, p. 49, n. k.
xvii. 15, p. 316, n. c.

xxiii. 4, p. 343, n. p.
xxv. 17, 18, p. 343, n. q.
xxxi. 19, p. 195.
xxxiii. 5, p. 228, n. r.
xxxvi. 6, p. 156.
xxxix. 1, p. 193 ; 1, 2, p. 193, n. r.
xlii. 1—3, p. 344, n. q.
xlv. 2, p. 300 ; 9, pp. 231, n., 300.
li. 7, p. 33, n. q.
lvii. 8, p. 18, n. n.
lxv. 1, 2, pp. 336, n. x, 338, n. b.
lxix. 8, p. 248.
lxxiii. 28, p. 140.
lxxxiv. 10, p. 83, n. x.
xci. 7, p. 26 ; 13, 7, p. 293.
xcvi. 6, p. 104, n. t.
civ. 25, p. 40, and n. b.
cxi. 10, p. 132.
cxii. 1, p. 132.
cxiv. p. 341, n. h.
cxvi.—cxx., p. 342, n. l.
cxvi. 7, p. 337, n. a.
cxix. 165, p. 291.
cxx. (title), p. 193, and n. s ; 5, pp. 27, 194, n. s.
cxxxiv. 1, 2, p. 194, n. s.

PROVERBS.
x. 19, p. 193, n. r.
xviii. 21, p. 193, n. r.
xxxi. 23, p. 183, n. h.

ECCLESIASTES.
xi. 9, p. 42.

CANTICLES.
i. 3, p. 299.
vi. 10, p. 231, n. x.

ISAIAH.
l. 2, p. 205, n. t.
liv. 1, p. 194, n. t.
lv. 1, p. 11, n. e.
lvi. 4, 5, p. 194, n. t.
lxiv. 4, p. 195.
lxvi. 2, p. 87.

JEREMIAH.
xiii. 23, p. 100.

EZEKIEL.
i. p. 305, n. n.
viii. 14, p. 157.
ix. 2, p. 288, n. s.
xvi. 49, p. 158.

DANIEL.
ii. 48, p. 176.
vi. 2, 8, 10, p. 176 ; 7, p. 183, n. h.

HOSEA.
vi. 4, p. 196.

MICAH.
iv. 10, p. 247.

MALACHI.
iii. 1, p. 341, n. g.

WISDOM.
i. 5, p. 87.
iv. 9, p. 42.

ECCLESIASTICUS.
xix. 1, p. 283.

SUSANNA.
45, 55, 59, 61, 64, p. 42.

2 MACCABEES.
xii. 43, p. 338, n. b.

ST. MATTHEW.
ii. 16, p. 172 ; 20, p. 104, n. u.
iii. 8. 10, p. 147.
v. 3, p. 13 ; 23, 24, p. 156 ; 39, p. 286 ; 44, p. 312.
vi. 12, p. 286 ; 20, p. 133 ; 24, p. 160.
x. 37, p. 195.
xi. 29, 30, p. 41.
xii. 29, p. 157.
xiv. 25, 26, p. 41.
xvi. 19, pp. 173, 246, 283 ; 24, p. 86.
xviii. 18, p. 160 ; 22, p. 286.
xix. 21, pp. 195, 264, n. z ; 27, p. 205 ; 28, pp. 246, 295 ; 28, 29, p. 205 ; 29, p. 133, n. a, 295.
xx. 23, p. 306, n. o.
xxiii. 3, p. 190 ; 35, p. 292.
xxv. 21, p. 135 ; 27, p. 132.
xxvi. 24, p. 172 ; 26, p. 305, n. m ; 50, p. 81.
xxvii. 4, p. 89 ; 29, p. 183.
xxviii. 20, p. 160.

ST. MARK.
i. 20, p. 206, n. u.
iii. 13, 14, p. 264, n. z.
viii. 38, p. 176.
x. 12, p. 161 ; 29, p. 133, and n. a ; 39, p. 307, n. r.

xiv. 3, p. 312.
xvi. 18, &c., p. 307, and n. r.

ST. LUKE.

iii. 14, p. 102, n. s ; 23, p. 27, n. c.
v. 32, p. 86.
vi. 20, pp. 13, 293 ; 45, p. 28.
vii. 38, p. 312 ; 47, *ib.*
viii. 1—3, p. 264, n. z.
ix. 26, p. 176.
x. 39, 40, p. 61.
xi. 5—9, p. 286 ; 11, 12, p. 199, and n. f.
xii. 33, p. 195.
xiv. 16—18, p. 368, n. m ; 33, p. 205.
xvi. 13, p. 160.
xviii. 4, 5, p. 286.
xix. 17, p. 135.
xxi. 5, p. 134.
xxiii. 34, p. 286.
xxiv. 29—31, p. 128.

ST. JOHN.

i. 9, pp. 156, 305 ; 14, p. 303 ; 29, p. 45.
ii. 9, p. 303.
iii. 21, p. 203.
vi. 33, p. 45, 156 ; 37—41, p. 338, n. b ; 51—55, p. 336.
viii. 44, p. 292.
ix. 22, p. 172, n. t ; 31, p. 268, n. e.
x. 15, p. 286.
xi. 20—27, p. 343, n. o.
xii. 3, pp. 103, 315, n. a.
xiii. 23, pp. 87, 305 ; 27, 30, p. 156.
xiv. 2, 3, p. 195 ; 13, p. 265.
xviii. 36, pp. 290, 291, n. y ; 40, p. 76.
xix. 26, 27, p. 305.
xxi. 11, p. 180 ; 17, p. 246.

ACTS.

i. 25, pp. 172, 267, n. d.
v. 3, 4, p. 133 ; 5, 10, p. 172.
x. 34, 35, p. 140, n. k.
xii. p. 31, n. l ; 3, *ib.*
xvii. 28, p. 104, n. u.
xix. 9, p. 106, n. w.
xxiii. 14, p. 172, n. t.
xxv. 23, p. 106, n. w.
xxvii. 41, p. 40, n. c.

ROMANS.

i. 29, 30, p. 208, n. d ; 30, pp. 208, 209, n. e.
ii. 2, 5, 6, p. 133.
vi. 23, p. 103, n. s.
viii. 15, p. 172, n. t ; 18, p. 133.
ix. 3, p. 172, n. t.
xi. 17, p. 34.
xii. 11, p. 38, n. z ; 17, p. 286.
xiii. 8, p. 7.
xvi. 18, p. 160.

1 CORINTHIANS.

i. 10, p. 203.
ii. 9, pp. 42, 195.
iii. 12, &c., p. 205.
iv. 3, pp. 210, 211, n. g ; 5, p. 135 ; 9, p. 289.
v. 5, p. 172, n. t.
vi. 13, p. 293 ; 18, p. 37.
vii. 11, 39, p. 161.
ix. 7, p. 103, n. s ; 24, p. 290, and n. x ; 27, p. 287, n. q.
x. 9, 10, p. 209 ; 10, p. 209, n. e ; 13, p. 264 ; 20, p. 157.
xi. 29, p. 156 ; 81, p. 146.
xii. 3, p. 172, n. t ; 31, p. 310, n. u.
xiii. 1, p. 279.
xv. 32, p. 289.
xvi. 22, p. 172, and n. t.

2 CORINTHIANS.

ii. 16, p. 41.
iv. 5, p. 203 ; 7, p. 31.
x. 4, p. 262, n. r.
xi. 8, p. 103, n. s.

GALATIANS.

i. 8, 9, p. 172, n. t.
ii. 4, p. 202.
iv. 3, p. 180 ; 4, p. 292 ; 6, p. 172, n. t ; 26, pp. 42, 147 ; 27, p. 194, n. t.
v. 22, 23, p. 193, and n. p ; 24, p. 42.
vi. 2, p. 170 ; 7, p. 202 ; 7, 8, p. 41 ; 8, p. 293.

EPHESIANS.

ii. 2, p. 24 ; 19, p. 42.
iv. 26, p. 286.
vi. 9, p. 140, n. k ; 12, pp. 24, 291 ; 14, 17, p. 289 ; 16, p. 289, n. u.

PHILIPPIANS.

i. 21, p. 293.
iii. 14, p. 290, and n. x ; 19, p. 160 ; 20, pp. 87, 279.
iv. 18, p. 181.

COLOSSIANS.
iii. 1, 2, p. 41 ; 14, p. 310, n. u.

1 THESSALONIANS.
iv. 3—5, p. 104, n. t ; 11, p. 206 ; 13, &c., p. 343, n. o.
v. 5, p. 203 ; 8, p. 289, and n. u.

1 TIMOTHY.
i. 18, p. 262, n. r.
ii. 10, p. 268, n. e.
v. 21, p. 138.
vi. 12, p. 262, n. r.

2 TIMOTHY.
ii. 3, pp. 262, n. r, 289 ; 5, pp. 195, 292 ; 12, p. 294 ; 14, p. 86.
iv. 7, pp. 262, n. r, 308 ; 7, 8, p. 292.

PHILEMON.
12, p. 249.

HEBREWS.
ii. 10, p. 308.
iv. 12, pp. 131, 156, 206 ; 12, 13, p. 146 ; 16, p. 278.
xi. 13, p. 292.
xii. 1, p. 135 ; 9, p. 195 ; 12, p. 133 ; 14, p. 104, n. t.

1 PETER.
ii. 11, p. 292.
iii. 21, p. 159.
iv. 14, p. 87.
v. 1, p. 272, n. h ; 3, p. 267, n. d.

2 PETER.
ii. 14, p. 267, n. c.

1 JOHN.
i. 5, p. 203.
iv. 1, p. 166, n.
v. 19, p. 26.

2 JOHN.
12, p. 87.

JUDE.
14, p. 172, n. t ; 14, 15, *ib.*

REVELATION.
i. 9, p. 306.
iii. 4, p. 195 ; 12, p. 147 ; 15, 16, p. 132.
iv. 4, p. 183.
vi. 9, 11, p. 180, n. e.
vii. 4, 14, p. 180 ; 9, 14, p. 181, n. e ; 14, p. 180, n. e.
xii. 9, p. 289.
xiv. 1, p. 180, and n. e ; 1—4, p. 104, n. u ; 3, p. 105 ; 3, 4, p. 195 ; 4, pp. 104, 195, 313 ; 6, 8, 9, 15, 17, 18, p. 306, n. p.
xv. 6, p. 306, n. p.
xvi. 1, 3, 4, 8, 10, 12, 17, p. 306, n. p.
xvii. 1, p. 306, n. p ; 3, p. 104, n. u.
xviii. 1, p. 306, n. p.
xix. 4, p. 180.
xx. 2, p. 289 ; 2, 10, p. 292 ; 7, p. 205.
xxi. 2, 10, p. 147.
xxii. 8, 16, p. 306, n. p.

INDEX OF AUTHORS AND WORKS CITED OR REFERRED TO IN THE LIFE AND LETTERS.

ABDIAS, 310.
Abelard, 35.
Abingdon Monastery, Chronicle of, 273.
Æsop, 28.
Alcuin, 196.
Alford, Dean, 208.
Alfred the Great, 50.
Ambrose, St., 16, 17, 183, 184, 294, 295, 311.
Anglo-Saxon Chronicle, 92, 357, 358, 359, 367.
Annales Ecclesiæ Wintoniensis, 378.
Annales Ord., St. Benedict: see Benedict, St.
Annotated Book of Common Prayer: see Blunt.
Anselm, 311.
Anstruther, Mr. (Editor of Herbert's Letters), 30, 32, 41, 84, 108, 153, 198, 210, 228, 268, 283, 333, 414, 415.
Ant. Sanderi Bibliotheca Belgica MSS., 333.
Apollonius, 306.
Aquinas, Thomas, 313.
Aristophanis Aves, 209.
Aristotle, 35, 42, 209.
Augustine, St., 175, 194, 196, 216, 217, 294, 310, 313, 320.
Ausonius, 184.
Avitus, 216.

Baker's Chronicle, 412.
Bale, Bp., 4, 5, 7, 71, 97, 122, 252, 333, 351, 388—391, 408, 412.
Baronius, Cardinal, 304.
Barry, Rev. Canon, 340.
Baudrand, M. A., 328, 329.
Baudry, Abp., 57, 68.
Bede, 27, 315.
Beloe, Mr. E. M., 409, 410.
Benedict, St. (Annales Ordinis), 44.
Benedictine Rule, 16, 83, 84, 139, 140, 186—193, 198, 267, 279.
Bengel, 211.
Bensly, Mr. R. L., 333.
Benson, Bishop, 25, 105, 288.
Berenger, 35.
Bernard, St., 38, 165, 190—192, 194, 217.

Bescherelle, 195.
Bingham, Rev. Joseph, 83, 170, 175, 255.
Biographical Dictionary, French, 319.
Blomefield, 115, 116, 119, 135, 141, 147, 173, 227, 325, 329, 349, 351, 412, 413.
Blunt, Rev. J. H., 69, 294, 313, 314.
Bochartus, 204.
Boëthius, 48—50.
Bond, Mr. Edward A., 318.
Bopp, 104.
Bosworth, 111.
Brown, Sir Thomas, 321.
Butler, Rev. Alban, 216, 222, 240.

Cæsar, 100.
Cæsarius, Bp. of Arles, 37.
Camden, 318.
Campbell, Lord, 169, 179, 225, 302, 328.
Capgrave, 117, 371, 372.
Cassian, 204, 267.
Cassiodorus, 36, 320.
Centuriators of Magdebourg, 1, 163, 391, 392.
Chaucer, 20, 38, 106.
Church, Dean, 8, 18, 55, 76, 108, 136, 137, 199, 200, 237, 335.
Church Dictionary: see Hook.
Cicero, 33, 128, 197, 248, 296, 319.
Clark's Introduction to Heraldry, 170.
Clement, St., 40.
Codex Apocryphus: see Fabricius.
Cotgrave, 20.
Cotton, Bartholomew, 2, 4, 9, 54, 69, 74, 80, 95, 96, 116, 122, 163, 253, 278, 314, 315, 320, 379—384, 409.
Cottonian MSS., Catalogue of, 318.
Croke, Sir Alexander, 320.
Cyprian, 320.

Dalie, John, 59—61.
Dan, Michel, 39.
Denton, Rev. W., 38.
Dictionary of the Bible, &c.: see Smith, Dr.
Dodechin, Abbot of St. Disibod, 363.
Domesday Book, 171, 350, 351.
Donaldson, Dr., 104, 195.
Donatus, Ælius, 20, 52, 197.

Dryden, 13.
Ducange, 8, 25, 37, 40, 53, 64, 66, 72, 84, 99, 103, 106, 108, 131, 134, 139, 141, 147, 174, 175, 177, 181, 198, 200, 201, 203, 208, 217, 228, 230, 232, 256, 267, 288, 295, 296, 356, 357.
Dugdale, Sir William, 69, 71, 77, 78, 91, 230, 322—324, 326, 412.

Eadmer, 1, 125, 235, 238, 239, 242, 254, 256, 276, 360—365, 370.
Edmund, St., Abbey of, Cartulary of, 243, 361, 363.
Edward the Sixth's First Prayer-Book, 343.
Eliensis, Liber : see Liber.
Eliensis, Thomas, 372—378.
Ellis, Sir Henry, 351.
Elmer, Prior of Canterbury, 415.
Ennius, 319.
Euripidis Orestes, 16.
Eusebius, 306, 310.

Fabricius, 304, 307, 308—310.
Fleury, 295.
Florence of Worcester, 358—360, 366, 367, 370, 380.
Forcellinus, 248.
Fosbrooke, 39, 84, 108, 109, 207.
Foss, Mr. Edward, 327.
Foster, John, 44, 45.
Fountain's Abbey, Chronicle of, 83.
Freeman, Mr. Edward, 411.
Fulbertus, 40.
Fuller, Thomas, 4, 79, 114, 165, 407—409.

Gale (Scriptores Quindecim), 70.
Gaspar Schottus, 204.
Gesta Abbatium Monasterii Sancti Albani, 268, 269.
Gilbert de la Porre, 35.
Giraldus Cambrensis, 4, 414.
Glover, Robert, 325.
Godwin, Bishop, 1, 4, 5, 72, 79, 114, 235, 323, 400—403, 408.
Godwyn, Thomas, B.D., 172.
Gregory, St., 305.
Griffith, Rev. S., 250, 268, 269.
Gruter, 232.
Gunn, Rev. John, 78, 412.

Hale, Archdeacon, 108.
Hall, Bishop, 317.
Hallam, Mr. Henry, 36, 197, 251.
Hardy, Sir Thomas Duffus, 326—328.
Harpsfeld, Nicholas, 2, 79, 96, 185, 396—399.
Harrod, Mr., 111, 116, 119, 185, 207, 208.
Hawkins, Mr. Edward, 103.

Haymo, 304.
Henry of Huntingdon, 371, 372.
Herbert d'Auxerre, 334.
Herodotus, 16.
Hilary, 202.
Hildebert, 35.
Hincmar, 50.
Holinshed, 93, 324, 325, 328, 350.
Hook, Dean, 32, 52, 65, 73, 74, 77, 78, 91, 93, 94, 126, 127, 130, 154, 172, 173, 198, 235, 252, 259, 260, 262, 290.
Hopper, Archdeacon, 4, 349—352.
Horace, 11, 40, 109, 136, 288.
Hospinian de Monachis, 84.
Hunt, Mr. Leigh, 173.

Ingulph, Prior of Croyland, 25.
Irenæus, 202.
Isidore, St., Rule of, 83
Isidore of Seville (Hispalensis), 307, 308.
Iso Magister, 84.

Jebb, Dr., 52.
Jerome, St., 15, 47, 48, 202, 268, 279, 286, 294, 304—306, 310, 311, 409.
Jessopp, Rev. Dr., 85.
Joannes Climacus (John of the Ladder), 38.
Johnson, Dr., 72.
Josephus, 134, 162, 172.
Jowett, Professor, 208.
Justin, 157.
Juvenal, 180, 198.
Juvencus, 52.

Kay, Dr., 316.
Kemble, J., 350.
Knighton, Henry, 78, 386.

Lanfranc, 35, 44, 137, 138, 295, 335.
Langdale, Lord, 327.
Leland, 69, 240, 387, 388.
Leonius, 319, 320.
Leroux de Lincy, M., 54, 57, 66, 67.
L'Estrange, Mr. J., 115.
Liber Eliensis, 212—222, 235, 249, 250.
Lincy : see Leroux.
Lingard, 143, 145.
Livy, 102.
Longlande, 20.
Lorenz, Dr. (Life of Alcuin), 196.
Luard, Rev. H. R., 129, 381, 384.
Lucian, 216.
Ludolph of Saxony, 304.

Mabillon, 49, 151, 295.
Macrobius, 20.
Magdebourg : see Centuriators, &c.
Magna Britannia, 69, 71, 72.
Maitland, Dr., 45, 49, 61, 151, 165, 166, 188, 192, 196, 201, 251, 282.

CITED IN THE LIFE AND LETTERS. 455

Malmesbury, William of, 1, 2, 54, 71, 73, 78, 79, 95, 122, 123, 163, 166, 225, 301, 302, 366—370, 390, 391, 393, 401, 409, 410, 413.
Marianus Scotus, 358, 363, 364.
Marriott, Rev. Wharton, 310.
Martial, 180.
Martin's History of Thetford, 95, 166, 169, 174.
Maskell, Mr., 336.
Massingberd, Rev. Chancellor, 290.
Matthew of Paris, 381.
Matthew of Westminster, 380, 381.
Milton, 72, 159.
Molière, 12.
Morison, Mr. (Life of St. Bernard), 44.
Moses and Aaron : see Godwyn.
Mosheim, 35.
Mozley, Rev. Canon, 290.
Murray, Mr., Handbook of Eastern Cathedrals, 67.

Neale, Rev. Dr., 293.
Neville, Alexander, 1, 2, 79, 114, 270, 323, 392—396.
Newcourt's Repertorium Ecclesiasticum, 250.
Norwich Cathedral, Sacrists' Roll of, 137.
Norwich "Ordinale," 334, 352.

Odo., St., of Cluny, Life of, 44.
Ordericus Vitalis, 8, 18, 25, 108, 137, 365, 366.
Orleans, Charles, Duke of, 335.
Orosius, 157, 158.
Osbert de Clara, 415.
Ovid, 15, 16, 23, 249.

Palgrave, Sir Francis, 55.
Parker, Mr., 79, 273, 371.
Patrick, Bp., 204.
Pecock, Bp., 20.
Pelbartus of Temesvar, 304.
Perowne, Rev. J. J. S., 194.
Peter, the Venerable, Abbot of Clugni, 166, 192, 203, 251.
Phædrus, 28.
Philipot, J., 324—328.
Pictorial History of England, 93.
Pits, John, 4, 351, 399, 400, 402, 406.
Plautus, 12.
Pliny, 30, 32, 182, 287, 292, 296.
Plumptre, Rev. Professor, 307.
Polycrates, 310, 311.
Polydorus Vergilius, 1, 387.
Pompeius, Trogus, 52, 157, 158.
Porphyry, 33.
Possevino, Antonio, 399.
Prideaux, Dean, 243, 322, 323, 328, 329.
Priscian, 197.

Procter on the Book of Common Prayer, 337.
Prudentius, 134.
Pseudo-Clemens, 204.

Quintilian, 197.

Radulphus de Diceto, 131, 368.
Ranulphus Higden, 389.
Register of Ramsey Abbey, 69.
Registrum Primum, 116, 146, 384, 385.
Riley, Mr. H. T., 384.
Robberds, Mr. J. W., 149.
Robertson, Dr. William, 151.
Rocherio, Geoffry de, 167.
Roger of Hoveden, 79.
Roman de Rou, 177.
Roscellinus, 35.
Rudborne, 122.
Rupertus Tuitiensis, 304.
Rye, Mr. Walter, 115, 226.

Salmasius, 131.
Sancto Victore, Hugh de, 305, 310, 344.
Sarum, Missal of, 31, 336, 337, 341, 343, 344.
Savile, Sir Henry, 366.
Schottus Gaspar : see Gaspar.
Scudamore, Rev. W., 305.
Sedulius, 19, 52.
Selden, 324, 326.
Servius, 20.
Shakspere, 67, 107.
Sidonius Apollinaris, 320.
Simeon of Durham, 79.
Smith, Dr. William, 20, 32, 33, 50, 217, 295, 307, 340.
Smith, Rev. I. Gregory, 295.
Smith, Rev. Sydney, 300.
Spelman, Sir Henry, 326, 328.
Spurdens, Rev. W. T., 1, 5, 18, 73, 179, 351.
Stanley, Dean, 50, 172.
Stevenson, 356.
Stewart, Rev. D. J., 108, 109.
Strickland, Miss, 299.
—————— Mr., 120.
Stubbs, Thomas (Stobæus), 1, 252, 385, 386, 388.
—————— Professor, 2, 73—76, 125, 271, 411.
Suckling, 171, 350.

Tacitus, 25, 103, 208.
Talbot, Thomas, 325, 326.
Tanner, Bishop, 388.
Taylor, Mr. Isaac, 3, 149, 171, 349.
Terence, 86.
Tertullian, 34, 202, 306.
Thierry, 101.
Thompson, Mr. E. Maunde, 322, 327.

Thynne, 325, 327, 328.
Tichonius, 105.
Trench, Abp., 17, 303.
Trevisa, John de, 389.
Twysden, 368, 385, 386.

Ugutio, 147.

Valerius Maximus, 85.
Van Espen, 270.
Virgil, 11, 25, 102, 159, 229, 244.

Weever, 4, 114, 315, 317, 318, 345, 404—407.

Wesley, 68.
Wharton, 360, 371, 372, 378, 381.
Wheatly, on "the Book of Common Prayer," 31.
William of Malmesbury: see Malmesbury.
Williams, Rev. Isaac, 105.
Willis, Professor, 119.
Wood, Anthony à, 325, 326.
Wordsworth, Bp. Chr., 25, 26, 104, 108, 172, 202, 209.

Yates, Mr., 240.

Printed by James Parker and Co., Crown Yard, Oxford.

www.ingramcontent.com/pod-product-compliance
Lightning Source LLC
Chambersburg PA
CBHW051846300426
44117CB00006B/282